THE

COMPLETE PROSE WORKS

OF

MARTIN FARQUHAR TUPPER, ESQ.

COMPRISING

THE CROCK OF GOLD, AN AUTHOR'S MIND,
THE TWINS, HEART,
PROBABILITIES, ETC.

REVISED EXPRESSLY FOR THIS EDITION BY W. C. ARMSTRONG.

HARTFORD:
PUBLISHED BY SILAS ANDRUS & SON

1851.

PUBLISHERS' PREFACE.

Mr. Tupper has achieved a popularity for his works, which has rarely been enjoyed by any one at so early a period of life; he being now only between thirty-five and forty years of age. Where all are so intrinsically valuable, it is difficult to determine which particular work has contributed most to his rapid and enviable advancement; yet, were an award indispensable, we should feel constrained to make it in favour of his '*Proverbial Philosophy.*' It is one of those unique productions which commends itself to all classes of readers, and from the perusal of which *all* cannot but derive substantial means of improvement. Familiar truths are so cogently treated therein, as to leave an indellible impression upon the mind, which could not, perhaps, have been so thoroughly made in any other manner; and the "thoughts and arguments" may be perused and rëperused with an advantage but few other writings are capable of yielding.

The rapid and extensive sale of several editions, issued in other places—some of them of rather an indifferent character, as regards mechanical execution—and the increasing demand still manifested for them, has induced the present publishers to collect the entire works of Mr. Tupper, and to stereotype them in a style worthy of their excellence. Each work has been thoroughly revised, and the errors which disfigure some other editions have been carefully corrected—an advantage readily appreciable by those who discriminate in their selections for the library or the centre-table.

CONTENTS.

THE CROCK OF GOLD.

THE TWINS.

HEART.

AN AUTHOR'S MIND.

PROBABILITIES.

THE

CROCK OF GOLD;

A RURAL NOVEL.

BY

MARTIN FARQUHAR TUPPER, ESQ., M. A.,

AUTHOR OF

"PROVERBIAL PHILOSOPHY."

HARTFORD:
SILAS ANDRUS AND SON.

1851.

THE CROCK OF GOLD.

CHAPTER I.

THE LABOURER; AND HIS DAWNING DISCONTENT.

ROGER ACTON woke at five. It was a raw March morning, still dark, and bitterly cold, while at gusty intervals the rain beat in against the crazy cottage-window. Nevertheless, from his poor pallet he must up and rouse himself, for it will be open weather by sunrise, and his work lies two miles off; Master Jennings is not the man to show him favour if he be late, and Roger cannot afford to lose an hour: so he shook off the luxury of sleep, and rose again to toil with weary effort.

"Honest Roger," as the neighbours called him, was a fair specimen of a class which has been Britain's boast for ages, and may be still again, in measure, but at present that glory appears to be departing: a class much neglected, much enduring; thoroughly English—just, industrious, and patient; true to the altar, and loyal to the throne; though haply shaken somewhat now from both those noble faiths—warped in their principles, and blunted in their feelings, by lying doctrines and harsh economies; a class—I hate the cold cant term—a race of honourable men, full of cares, pains, privations—but of pleasures next to none; whose life at its most prosperous estate is labour, and in death we count him happy who did not die a pauper. Through them, serfs of the soil, the earth yields indeed her increase, but it is for others; from the fields of plenty they glean a scanty pittance, and fill the barns to bursting, while their children cry for bread. Not that Roger for his part often wanted work; he was the best hand in the parish, and had earned of his employers long ago the name of Steady Acton; but the fair wages for a fair day's labour were quite another thing, and the times went very hard for him and his. A man himself may starve, while his industry makes others fat: and a liberal landlord all the winter through may keep his labourers in work, while a crafty, overbearing bailiff mulcts them in their wages.

For the outward man, Acton stood about five feet ten, a gaunt, spare, and sinewy figure, slightly bent; his head sprinkled with gray; his face marked with those rigid lines, which tell, if not of positive famine, at least of too much toil on far too little food; in his eye, patience and good temper; in his carriage, a mixture of the sturdy bearing, necessary to the habitual exercise of great muscular strength, together with that gait of humility—almost humiliation—which is the seal of oppression upon poverty. He might be about forty, or from that to fifty, for hunger, toil, and weather had used him the roughest; while, for all beside, the patched and well-worn smock, the heavily-clouted high-laced boots, a dingy worsted neck-tie, and an old felt hat, complete the picture of externals.

But, for the matter of character within, Roger is quite another man. If his rank in this world is the lowest, many potentates may envy him his state elsewhere. His heart is as soft, as his hand is horny; with the wandering gipsy or the tramping beggar, thrust aside, perhaps deservedly, as impudent impostors from the rich man's gate, has he often-times shared his noon-day morsel: upright and sincere himself, he thinks as well of others: he scarcely ever heard the Gospels read in church, specially about Eastertide, but the tears would trickle down his weather-beaten face: he loves children—his neighbour's little ones as well as his own: he will serve any one for goodness' sake without reward or thanks, and is kind to the poor dumb cattle: he takes quite a pride in his little rod or two of garden, and is early and late at it, both before and after the daily sum of labour: he picks up a bit of knowledge here and there, and somehow has contrived to amass a fund of information for which few would give him credit from his common looks; and he joins to that stock of facts a natural shrewdness to use his knowledge wisely. Though with little of what is called sentiment, or poetry, or fancy in his mind (for harsh was the teaching of his childhood, and meagre the occasions of self-culture ever since), the beauty of creation is by no means lost upon him, and he notices at times its wisdom too. With a fixed habit of manly piety ever on his lips and ever in his heart, he recognises Providence in all things, just, and wise, and good. More than so; simply as a little child who endures the school-hour for the prospect of his play-time, Roger Acton bears up with noble meekness against present suffering, knowing that his work and trials and troubles are only for a little while, but his rest and his reward remain a long hereafter. He never questioned this; he knew right well Who had earned it for him; and he lived grateful and obedient, filling up the duties of his humble station. This was his faith, and his works followed it. He believed that God had placed him in his lot, to be a labourer, and till God's earth, and, when his work is done, to be sent on better service in some happier sphere: the where, or the how, did not puzzle him, any more than divers other enigmatical whys and wherefores of his present state; he only knew this, that it would all come right at last: and, barring sin (which he didn't comprehend), somehow all was right at present. What if poverty pinched him? he was a great heir still; what if oppression bruised him? it would soon be over. He trusted to his Pilot, like the landsman in a storm; to his Father, as an infant in the dark. For guilt, he had a Saviour, and he thought of him in penitence; for trouble, a Guardian, and he looked to him in peace; and as for toil, back-breaking toil, there was another Master whom he served with spade, and mattock, and a thankful heart, while he only seemed to be working for the landlord or his bailiff.

Such a man then had been Roger Acton from his youth up till now, or, if sadness must be told, nearly until now; for, to speak truth, his heart at times would fail him, and of late he had been bitter in repinings and complaint. For a day or two, in particular, he had murmured loudly. It was hard, very hard, that an honest, industrious man, as he was, should so scantily pick a living out of this rich earth: after all said, let the parson preach as he will, it's a fine thing to have money, and that his reverence knows right well, or he wouldn't look so closely for his dues. [N. B. Poor Mr. Evans was struggling as well as he could to bring up six children, on a hundred and twenty pounds per annum.] Roger, too, was getting on in years, with a blacker prospect for the future than when he first stood behind a plough-tail. Then there were many wants unsatisfied, which a bit of gold might buy; and his wife teased him to be doing something better. Thus was it come at length to pass, that, although he had endured so many years, he now got discontented at his penury;—what human heart can blame him?—and with murmurings came doubt; with doubt of Providence, desire of lucre; so the sunshine of religion faded from his path;—what mortal mind can wonder?

CHAPTER II.

THE FAMILY; THE HOME; AND MORE REPININGS.

Now, if Malthus and Martineau be verily the pundits that men think them, Roger had twice in his life done a very foolish thing: he had sinned against society, statistics, and common sense, by a two-fold marriage. The wife of his youth (I am afraid he married early) had once been kitchen-maid at the Hall; but the sudden change from living luxuriously in a great house, to the griping poverty of a cotter's hovel, had changed, in three short years, the buxom country girl into an emaciated shadow of her former self, and the sorrowing husband buried her in her second child-bed. The powers of the parish clapped their hands; political economy was glad; prudence chuckled; and a coarse-featured farmer (he meant no ill), who occasionally had given Roger work, heartlessly bade him be thankful that his cares were the fewer and his incumbrance was removed; "Ay, and Heaven take the babies also to itself," the Herodian added. But Acton's heart was broken! scarcely could he lift up his head; and his work, though sturdy as before, was more mechanical, less high-motived: and many a year of dreary widowhood he mourned a loss all the greater, though any thing but bitterer, for the infants so left motherless. To these, now grown into a strapping youth and a bright-eyed graceful girl, had he been the tenderest of nurses, and well supplied the place of her whom they had lost. Neighbours would have helped him gladly—sometimes did; and many was the hinted offer (disinterested enough, too, for in that match penury must have been the settlement, and starvation the dower), of giving them a mother's kindly care; but Roger could not quite so soon forget the dead: so he would carry his darlings with him to his work, and feed them with his own hard hands; the farmers winked at it, and never said a word against the tiny trespassers; their wives and daughters loved the little dears, bringing them milk and possets; and holy angels from on high may have oft-times hovered about this rude nurse, tending his soft innocents a-field, and have wept over the poor widower and his orphans, tears of happy sorrow and benevolent affection. Yea, many a good angel has shed blessings on their heads!

Within the last three years, and sixteen from the date of his first great grief, Roger had again got married. His daughter was growing into early womanhood, and his son gave him trouble at times, and the cottage wanted a ruling hand over it when he was absent, and rheumatism now and then bade him look out for a nurse before old age, and Mary Alder was a notable middle-aged careful sort of soul, and so she became Mary Acton. All went on pretty well, until Mrs. Acton began to have certain little ones of her own; and then the step-mother would break out (a contingency poor Roger hadn't thought of), separate interests crept in, and her own children fared before the others; so it came to pass that, however truly there was a ruling hand at home, and however well the rheumatism got nursed (for Mary was a good wife in the main), the grown-up son and daughter felt themselves a little jostled out. Grace, gentle and submissive, found all her comforts shrunk within the space of her father and her Bible; Thomas, self-willed and open-hearted, sought his pleasure any where but at home, and was like to be taking to wrong courses through domestic bickering: Grace had the dangerous portion, beauty, added to her lowly lot, and attracted more admiration than her father wished, or she could understand; while the frank and bold spirit of Thomas Acton exposed him to the perilous friendship of Ben Burke the poacher, and divers other questionable characters.

Of these elements, then, are our labourer and his family composed; and before Roger Acton goes abroad at earliest streak of dawn, we will take a casual peep within his dwelling. It consists of four bare rubble walls, enclosing a grouted floor, worn unevenly, and here and there in holes, and puddly. There were but two rooms in the tenement, one on the ground, and one over-head; which latter is with no small difficulty got at by scaling a ladder-like stair-case that fronts the cottage-door. This upper chamber, the common dormitory, for all but Thomas, who sleeps down stairs, has a thin partition at one end of it, to screen off the humble truckle-bed where Grace Acton forgets by night the troubles of the day; and the remainder of the little apartment, sordid enough, and overhung with the rough thatch, black with cobweb, serves for the father and mother with their recent nursery. Each room has its shattery casement, to let in through linchened panes, the doubtful light of summer, and the much more indubitable wind, and rain, and frost of wintry nights. A few articles of crockery and some burnished tins decorate the shelves of the lower apartment; which used to be much tidier before the children came, and trimmer still when Grace was sole manager: in a doorless cupboard are apparent sundry coarse edibles, as the half of a huge unshapely home-made loaf, some white country cheese, a mass of lumpy pudding, and so forth; beside it, on the window-sill, is better bread, a well-thumbed Bible, some tracts, and a few odd volumes picked up cheap at fairs; an old musket (occasionally Ben's companion, sometimes Tom's) is hooked to the rafters near a double rope of onions; divers gaudy little prints, tempting spoil of pedlars, in honour of George Barnwell, the Prodigal Son, the Sailor's Return, and the Death of Nelson, decorate the walls, and an illuminated Christmas carol is pasted over the mantel-piece: which, among other chattels and possessions, conspicuously bears its own burden of Albert and Victoria —two plaster heads, resplendently coloured, highly varnished, looking with arched eye-brows of astonishment on their uninviting palace, and royally contrasting with the sombre hue of poverty on all things else. The pictures had belonged to Mary, no small portion of her virgin wealth; and as for the statuary, those two busts had cost loyal Roger far more in comparison than any corporation has given to P. R. A., for majesty and consortship in full. There is, moreover, in the room, by way of household furniture, a ricketty, triangular, and tri-legged table, a bench, two old chairs with rush-bottoms, and a yard or two of matting that the sexton gave when the chancel was new laid. I don't know that there is any thing else to mention, unless it be a gaunt lurcher belonging to Ben Burke, and with all a dog's resemblance to his master, who lies stretched before the hearth where the peaty embers never quite die out, but smoulder away to a heap of white ashes; over these is hanging a black boiler, the cook of the family; and beside them, on a substratum of dry heather, and wrapped about with an old blanket, nearly companioned by his friend, the dog, snores Thomas Acton, still fast asleep, after his usual extemporaneous fashion.

As to the up-stairs apartment, it contained little or nothing but its living inmates, their bedsteads and tattered coverlids, and had an air of even more penury and discomfort than the room below; so that, what with squalling children, a scolding wife, and empty stomach, and that cold and wet March morning, it is little wonder maybe (though no small blame), that Roger Acton had not enough of religion or philosophy to rise and thank his Maker for the blessings of existence.

He had just been dreaming of great good luck. Poor people often do so; just as Ugolino dreamt of imperial feasts, and Bruce, in his delirious thirst on the Sahara, could not banish from his mind the cool fountains of Shiraz, and the luxurious waters of old Nile. Roger had unfortunately dreamt of having found a crock of gold—I dare say he will tell us his dream anon—and just as he was counting out his treasure, that blessed beautiful heap of shining money—cruel habit roused him up before the dawn, and his wealth faded from his fancy. So he awoke at five, anything but cheerfully.

It was Grace's habit, good girl, to read to her father in the morning a few verses from the volume she best loved: she always woke betimes when she heard him getting up, and he could hear her easily from her little flock-bed behind the lath partition; and many a time had her dear religious tongue, uttering the words of peace, soothed her father's mind, and strengthened him to meet the day's affliction; many times it raised his thoughts from the heavy cares of life to the buoyant hopes of immortality. Hitherto, Roger had owed half his meek contentedness to those sweet lessons from a daughter's lips, and knew that he was reaping, as he heard, the harvest of his own paternal care, and heaven-blest instructions. However, upon this dark morning, he was full of other thoughts, murmurings, and doubts, and poverty, and riches. So, when Grace, after her usual affectionate salutations, gently began to read,

"The sufferings of this present time are not worthy to be compared with the glory—"

Her father strangely stopped her on a sudden with—

"Enough, enough, my girl! God wot, the sufferings are grievous, and the glory long a-coming."

Then he heavily went down stairs, and left Grace crying.

CHAPTER III.

THE CONTRAST.

Thus, full of carking care, while he pushed aside the proffered consolation, Roger Acton walked abroad. There was yet but a glimmer of faint light, and the twittering of birds told more assuringly of morning than any cheerful symptom on the sky: however, it had pretty well ceased raining, that was one comfort, and, as Roger, shouldering his spade, and with the day's provision in a handkerchief, trudged out upon his daily duty, those good old thoughts of thankfulness came upon his mind, and he forgot awhile the dream that had unstrung him. Turning for a moment to look upon his hovel, and bless its inmates with a prayer, he half resolved to run back, and hear a few more words, if only not to vex his darling child: but there was now no time to spare; and then, as he gazed upon her desolate abode—so foul a casket for so fair a jewel—his bitter thoughts returned to him again, and he strode away, repining.

Acton's cottage was one of those doubtful domiciles, whose only recommendation it is, that they are picturesque in summer. At present we behold a reeking rotting mass of black thatch in a cheerless swamp; but, as the year wears on, those time-stained walls, though still both damp and mouldy, will be luxuriantly overspread with creeping plants—honey-suckle, woodbine, jessamine, and the everblowing monthly rose. Many was the touring artist it had charmed, and Suffolk-street had seen it often: spectators looked upon the scene as on an old familiar friend, whose face they knew full well, but whose name they had forgotten for the minute. Many were the fair hands that had immortalized its beauties in their albums, and frequent the notes of admiration uttered by attending swains: particularly if there chanced to be taken into the view a feathery elm that now creaked overhead, and dripped on the thatch like the dropping-well at Knaresborough, and (in the near distance) a large pond, or rather lake, upon whose sedgy banks, gay—not now, but soon about to be—with flowering reeds and bright green willows, the pretty cottage stood. In truth, if man were but an hibernating animal, invisible as dormice in the winter, and only to be seen with summer swallows, Acton's cottage at Hurstley might have been a cantle cut from the Elysian-fields. But there are certain other seasons in the year, and human nature cannot long exist on the merely "picturesque in summer."

Some fifty yards, or so, from the hither shore, we discern a roughly wooded ait, Pike Island to wit, a famous place for fish, and the grand rendezvous for woodcocks; which, among other useful and ornamental purposes, serves to screen out the labourer's hovel, at this the narrowest part of the lake, from a view of that fine old mansion on the opposite shore, the seat of Sir John Vincent, a baronet just of age, and the great landlord of the neighbourhood. Toward this mansion, scarcely yet revealed in the clear gray eye of morning, our humble hero, having made the long round of the lake, is now fast trudging; and it may merit a word or two of plain description, to fill up time and scene, till he gets nearer.

A smooth grassy eminence, richly studded with park-like clumps of trees, slopes up from the water's very edge to—Hurstley Hall; yonder goodly, if not grand, Elizabethan structure, full of mullioned windows, carved oak panels, stone-cut coats of arms, pinnacles, and traceries, and lozenges, and drops; and all this glory crowned by a many-gabled, high-peaked roof. A grove of evergreens and American shrubs hides the lower windows from vulgarian gaze—for, in the neighbourly feeling of our ancestors, a public way leads close along the front; while, behind the house, and inaccessible to eyes profane, are drawn terraced gardens, beautifully kept, and blooming with a perpetual succession of the choicest flowers. The woods and shrubberies around, attempted some half a century back to be spoilt by the meddlesome bad taste of Capability Brown, have been somewhat too resolutely robbed of the formal avenues, clipped hedges, and other topiarian adjuncts which comport so well with the starch prudery of things Elizabethan; but they are still replete with grotto, fountain, labyrinth, and alcove—a very paradise for the more court-bred rank of sylphs, and the gentler elves of Queen Titania.

However, we have less to do with the gardens than, probably, the elves have; and as Roger now, just at breaking day, is approaching the windows somewhat too curiously for a poor man's manners, it may not be amiss if we bear him company. He had pretty well recovered of his fit of discontent, for morning air and exercise can soon chase gloom away; so he cheerily tramped along, thinking as he went, how that, after all, it is a middling happy world, and how that the raindrops, now that it had cleared up, hung like diamonds on the laurels, when of a sudden, as he turned a corner near the house, there broke upon his ear, at that quiet hour, such a storm of boisterous sounds—voices so loud with oaths and altercation—such a calling, clattering, and quarrelling, as he had never heard the like before. So no wonder that he stepped aside to see it.

The noise proceeded from a ground-floor window, or rather from three windows, lighted up, and hung with draperies of crimson and gold: one of the casements, flaring meretriciously in the modest eye of morn, stood wide open down to the floor, probably to cool a heated atmosphere; and when Roger Acton, with a natural curiosity, went on tiptoe, looked in, and just put aside the curtain for a peep, to know what on earth could be the matter, he saw a vision of waste and wealth, at which he stood like one amazed, for a poor man's mind could never have conceived its equal.

Evidently, he had intruded on the latter end of a long and luxurious revel. Wax-lights, guttering down in gilded chandeliers, poured their mellow radiance round in multiplied profusion—for mirrors made them infinite; crimson and gold were the rich prevailing tints in that wide and warm banqueting-room; gayly-coloured pictures, set in frames that Roger fancied massive gold, hung upon the walls at intervals; a wagon-load of silver was piled upon the sideboard; there blazed in the burnished grate such a fire as poverty might imagine on a frozen winter's night, but never can have thawed its blood beside: fruits, and wines, and costly glass were scattered in prodigal disorder on the board—just now deserted of its noisy guests, who had crowded round a certain green table, where cards and heaps of sovereigns appeared to be mingled in a mass. Roger had never so much as conceived it possible that there could be wealth like this: it was a fairy-land of Mammon in his eyes: he stood gasping like a man enchanted; and in the contemplation of these little hills of gold—in their covetous longing contemplation, he forgot the noisy quarrel he had turned aside to see, and thirsted for that rich store earnestly.

In an instant, as he looked (after the comparative lull that must obviously have succeeded to the clamours he had first heard), the roar and riot broke out worse than ever. There were the stormy revellers, as the rabble rout of Comus and his crew, filling that luxurious room with the sounds of noisy execration and half-drunken strife. Young Sir John, a free and generous fellow, by far the best among them all, has collected about him those whom he thought friends, to celebrate his wished majority; they had now kept it up, night after night, hard upon a week; and, as well became such friends—the gambler, the duellist, the man of pleasure, and the fool of Fashion—they never yet had separated for their day-light beds, without a climax to their orgie, something like the present scene.

Henry Mynton, high in oath, and dashing down his cards, has charged Sir Richard Hunt with cheating (it was *sauter la coupe* or *couper la saut*, or some such mystery of iniquity, I really cannot tell which): Sir Richard, a stout dark man, the patriarch of the party, glossily wigged upon his head, and imperially tufted on his chin, retorts with a pungent sarcasm, calmly and coolly uttered; that hot-headed fool Silliphant, clearly quite intoxicated, backs his cousin Mynton's view of the case by the cogent argument of a dice-box at Sir Richard's head—and at once all is struggle, strife, and uproar. The other guests, young fellows of high fashion, now too much warmed with wine to remember their accustomed Mohican cold-bloodedness—those happy debtors to the prowess of a Stultz, and walking advertisers of Nugee—take eager part with the opposed belligerents: more than one decanter is sent hissing through the air; more than one bloody coxcomb witnesses to the weight of a candlestick and its hurler's clever aim: uplifted chairs are made the weapons of the chivalric combatants; and along with divers other less distinguished victims in the melée, poor Sir John Vincent, rushing into the midst, as a well-intentioned host, to quell the drunken brawl, gets knocked down among them all; the tables are upset, the bright gold runs about the room in all directions—ha! no one heeds it—no one owns it—one little piece rolled right up to the window-sill where Roger still looked on with all his eyes; it is but to put his hand in—the window is open to the floor—nay a finger is enough: greedily, one undecided moment, did he gaze upon the gold; he saw the hideous contrast of his own dim hovel and that radiant chamber—he remembered the pining faces of his babes, and gentle Grace with all her hardships—he thought upon his poverty and well deserts—he looked upon wastefulness of wealth and wantonness of living—these reflections struck him in a moment; no one saw him, no one cared about the gold; that little blessed morsel, that could do him so much good; all was confusion, all was opportunity, and who can wonder that his fingers closed upon the sovereign, and that he picked it up?

CHAPTER IV.

THE LOST THEFT.

Stealthily and quickly "honest Roger" crept away, for his conscience smote him on the instant: he felt he had done wrong; at any rate, the sovereign was not his—and once the thought arose in him to run back, and put it where he found it: but it was now become too precious in his sight, that little bit of gold—and they, the rioters there, could not want it, might not even miss it; and then its righteous uses—it should be well spent, even if ill-got: and thus, so many mitigations crowded in to excuse, if not to applaud the action, that within a little while his warped mind had come to call the theft a god-send.

O Roger, Roger! alas for this false thought of that wrong deed! the poisonous gold has touched thy heart, and left on it a spot of cancer: the asp has bitten thee already, simple soul. This little seed will grow into a huge black pine, that shall darken for a while thy heaven, and dig its evil roots around thy happiness. Put it away, Roger, put it away: covet not unhallowed gold.

But Roger felt far otherwise; and this sudden qualm of conscience once quelled (I will say there seemed much of palliation in the matter), a kind of inebriate feeling of delight filled his mind, and Steady Acton plodded on to the meadow yonder, half a mile a-head, in a species of delirious complacency. Here was luck indeed, filling up the promise of his dreams. His head was full of thoughts, pleasant holiday thoughts, of the many little useful things, the many small indulgences, that bit of gold should buy him. He would change it on the sly, and gradually bring the shillings home as extra pay for extra work; for, however much his wife might glory in the chance, and keep his secret, well he knew that Grace would have a world of things to say about it, and he feared to tell his daughter of the deed. However, she should have a ribbon, so she should, good girl, and the pedlar shouldn't pass the door unbidden; Mary, too, might have a cotton kerchief, and the babes a doll and a rattle, and poor Thomas a shilling to spend as he liked; and so, in happy revery, the kind father distributed his ill-got sovereign.

For a while he held it in his hand, as loth to part from the tangible possession of his treasure; but manual contact could not last all day, and, as he neared his scene of labour—he came late after all, by the by, and lost the quarter-day, but it mattered little now—he began to cogitate a place of safety; and carefully put it in his fob. Poor fellow—he had never had enough to stow so well away before: his pockets had been thought quite trust-worthy enough for any treasures hitherto: never had he used that fob for watch, or note, or gold—and his predecessor in the cast-off garment had probably been quite aware how little that false fob was worthy of the name of savings' bank; it was in the situation of the Irishman's illimitable rope, with the end cut off. So while Roger was brewing up vast schemes of nascent wealth, and prosperous days at last, the filched sovereign, attracted by centripetal gravity, had found a passage downwards, and had straightway rolled into a crevice of mother-earth, long before its "brief lord" had commenced his day's labour. Yes, it had been lost a good hour ere he found it out, for he had fancied that he had felt it there, and often did he feel, but his fancy was a button; and when he made the dread discovery, what a sting of momentary anguish, what a sickening fear, what an eager search! and, as the grim truth became more evident, that, indeed, beyond all remedy, his new-got, ill-got, egg of coming wealth was all clean gone—oh! this was wormwood, this was bitter as gall, and the strong man well-nigh fainted. It was something sad to have done the ill—but misery to have done it all for nothing: the sin was not altogether pleasant to his taste, but it was aloe itself to lose the reward. And when, pale and sick, leaning on his spade, he came to his old strength again, what was the rëaction? Compunction at incipient crime, and gratitude to find its punishment so mercifully speedy, so lenient, so discriminative? I fear that if ever he had these thoughts at all, he chased them wilfully away: his disappointment, far from being softened into patience, was sharpened to a feeling of revenge at fate; and all his hope now was—such another chance, gold, more gold, never mind how; more gold, he burnt for gold, he lusted after gold!

We must leave him for a time to his toil and his reflections, and touch another topic of our theme.

CHAPTER IV.

THE INQUEST.

Just a week before the baronet came of age, and a fortnight from the present time, an awful and mysterious event had happened at the Hall: the old house-keeper, Mrs. Quarles, had been found dead in her bed, under circumstances, to say the very least, of a black and suspicious appearance. The county coroner had got a jury of the neighbours impanelled together; who, after sitting patiently on the inquest, and hearing, as well as seeing, the following evidence, could arrive at no verdict more specific than the obvious fact, that the poor old creature had been "found dead." The great question lay between apoplexy and murder; and the evidence tended to a well-matched conflict of opinions.

First, there lay the body, quietly in bed, tucked in tidily and undisturbed, with no marks of struggling, none whatever—the clothes lay smooth, and the chamber orderly: yet the corpse's face was of a purple hue, the tongue swollen, the eyes starting from their sockets: it might, indeed, possibly have been an apoplectic seizure, which took her in her sleep, and killed her as she lay; *but* that the gripe of clutching fingers had left their livid seals upon the throat, and countenanced the dreadful thought of strangulation!

Secondly, a surgeon (one Mr. Eager, the Union doctor, a very young personage, wrong withal and radical) maintained that this actual strangulation might have been effected by the hands of the deceased herself, in the paroxysm of a rush of blood to the brain; and he fortified his wise position by the instance of a late statesman, who, he averred, cut his throat with a pen-knife, to relieve himself of pressure on the temples: while another surgeon—Stephen Cramp, he was farrier as well, and had been, until lately, time out of mind, the village Æsculapius, who looked with scorn on his pert rival, and opposed him tooth and nail on all occasions—insisted that it was not only physically impossible for poor Mrs. Quarles so to have strangled herself, but more particularly that, if she had done so, she certainly could not have laid herself out so decently afterwards; therefore, that as some one else had kindly done the latter office for her, why not the former too?

Thirdly, Sarah Stack, the still-room maid, deposed, that Mrs. Quarles always locked her door before she went to bed, but that when she (deponent) went to call her as usual on the fatal morning, the door was just ajar; and so she found her dead: while parallel with this, tending to implicate some domestic criminal, was to be placed the equally uncommon fact, that the other door of Mrs. Quarles's room, leading to the lawn, was open too:—be it known that Mrs. Quarles was a stout woman, who could'nt abide to sleep up-stairs, for fear of fire; moreover, that she was a nervous woman, who took extraordinary precautions for her safety, in case of thieves. Thus, unaccountably enough, the murderer, if there was any, was as likely to have come from the outside, as from the in.

Fourthly, the murderer in this way is commonly a thief, and does the deed for mammon-sake; but the new house-keeper, lately installed, made her deposition, that, by inventories duly kept and entered—for her honoured predecessor, rest her soul! had been a pattern of regularity—all Mrs. Quarles's goods and personal chattels were found to be safe and right in her room—some silver spoons among them too—ay, and a silver tea-pot; while, as to other property in the house, with every room full of valuables, nothing whatever was missing from the lists, except, indeed, what was scarce worth mention (unless one must be very exact), sundry crocks and gallipots of honey, not forthcoming; these, however, it appeared probable that Mrs. Quarles had herself consumed in a certain mixture she nightly was accustomed too, of rum, horehound, and other matters sweetened up with honey, for her hoarseness. It seemed therefore clear she was not murdered for her property, nor by any one intending to have robbed the house.

Against this it was contended, and really with some show of reason, that as Mrs. Quarles was thought to have a hoard, always set her face against banks, railway shares, speculations, and investments, and seemed to have left nothing behind her but her clothes and so forth, it was still possible that the murderer who took the life, might have also been the thief to take the money.

Fifthly, Simon Jennings—butler in doors, bailiff out of doors, and general factotum every where to the Vincent interest—for he had managed to monopolize every place worth having, from the agent's book to the cellar-man's key—the said Simon deposed, that on the night in question, he heard the house-dog barking furiously, and went out to quiet him; but found no thieves, nor knew any reason why the dog should have barked so much.

Now, the awkward matter in this deposition (if Mr. Jennings had not been entirely above suspicion—the idea was quite absurd—not to mention that he was nephew to the deceased, a great favourite with her, and a man altogether of the very strictest character), the awkward matters were these: the nearest way out to the dog, indeed the only way but casement windows on that side of the house, was through Mrs. Quarles's room: she had had the dog placed there for her special safety, as she slept on the ground floor; and it was not to be thought that Mr. Jennings could do so incorrect a thing as to pass through her room after bed-time, locked or unlocked—indeed, when the question was delicately hinted to him, he was quite shocked at it—quite shocked. But if he did not go that way, which way did he go? He deposed, indeed, and his testimony was no ways to be doubted, that he went through the front door, and so round; which, under the circumstances, was at once a very brave and a very foolish thing to do; for it is, first, little wisdom to go round two sides of a square to quiet a dog, when one might have easily called to him from the men-servants' window; and secondly, albeit Mr. Jennings was a strict man, an upright man, shrewd withal, and calculating, no one had ever thought him capable of that Roman virtue, courage. Still, he had reluctantly confessed to this one heroic act, and it was a bold one, so let him take the credit of it—mainly because—

Sixthly, Jonathan Floyd, footman, after having heard the dog bark at intervals, surely for more than a couple of hours, thought he might as well turn out of his snug berth for a minute, just to see what ailed the dog, or how many thieves were really breaking in. Well, as he looked, he fancied he saw a boat moving on the lake, but as there was no moon, he might have been mistaken.

By a Juryman. It might be a punt.

By another. He did'nt know how many boats there were on the lake-side: they had a boat-house at the Hall, by the water's edge, and therefore he concluded something in it; really did'nt know; might be a boat, might be a punt, might be both—or neither.

By the Coroner. Could not swear which way it was moving; and, really, if put upon his Bible oath, wouldn't be positive about a boat at all, it was so dark, and he was so sleepy.

Not long afterwards, as the dog got still more violent, he turned his eyes from straining after shadows on the lake, to look at home, and then all at once noticed Mr. Jennings trying to quiet the noisy animal with the usual blandishments of "Good dog, good dog—quiet, Don, quiet—down, good dog—down, Don, down!"

By a Juryman. He would swear to the words.

But Don would not hear of being quiet. After that, knowing all must be right if Mr. Jennings was about, he (deponent) turned in again, went to sleep, and thought no more of it till he heard of Mrs. Quarles's death in the morning. If he may be so bold as to speak his mind, he thinks the house-keeper, being fat, died o' the 'plexy in a nateral way, and that the dog barking so, just as she was a-going off, is proof positive of it. He'd often heard of dogs doing so; they saw the sperit gliding away, and barked at it; his (deponent's) own grandmother—

At this juncture—for the court was getting fidgetty—the coroner cut short the opinions of Jonathan Floyd: and when Mr. Crown, summing up, presented in one focus all this evidence to the misty minds of the assembled jurymen, it puzzled them entirely; they could not see their way, fairly addled, did not know at all what to make of it. On the threshold, there was no proof it was a murder—the Union doctor was loud and staunch on this; and next, there seemed to be no motive for the deed, and no one to suspect of it: so they left the matter open, found her simply "Dead," and troubled their heads no more about the business.

Good Mr. Evans, the vicar, preached her funeral sermon, only as last Sunday, amplifying the idea that she "was cut off in the midst of her days:" and thereby encouraging many of the simpler folks, who knew that Mrs. Quarles had long passed seventy, in the luminous notion that house-keepers in great establishments are privileged, among other undoubted perquisites, to live to a hundred and forty, unless cut off by apoplexy or murder.

Mr. Simon Jennings, as nephew and next of kin, followed the body to its last home in the capacity of chief mourner; to do him justice, he was a real mourner, bewailed her loudly, and had never been the same man since. Moreover, although aforetime not much given to indiscriminate charity, he had now gained no small credit by distributing his aunt's wardrobe among the poorer families at Hurstley. It was really very kind of him, and the more so, as being altogether unexpected: he got great praise for his, did Mr. Jennings; specially, too, because he had gained nothing whatever from his aunt's death, though her heir and probable legatee, and clearly was a disappointed man.

CHAPTER VI.

THE BAILIFF; AND A BITTER TRIAL.

Jennings—Mr. Simon Jennings—for he prided himself much both on the Mr. and the Simon, was an upright man, a very upright man indeed, literally so as well as metaphorically. He was not tall certainly, but what there was of him stood bolt upright. Many fancied that his neck was possessed of some natural infirmity, or rather firmity, of unbendableness, some little-to-be-envied property of being a perpetual stiff-neck; and they were the more countenanced in this theory, from the fact that, within a few days past, Mr. Jennings had contracted an ugly knack of carrying his erect head in the comfortless position of peeping over his left shoulder; not always so, indeed, but often enough to be remarkable; and then he would occasionally start it straight again, eyes right, with a nervous twitch, any thing but pleasant to the marvelling spectator. It was as if he was momentarily expecting to look upon some vague object that affrighted him, and sometimes really did see it. Mr. Jennings had consulted high medical authority (as Hurstley judged), to wit, the Union doctor of last scene, an enterprising practitioner, glib in theory, and bold in practice—and it had been mutually agreed between them that "stomach" was the cause of these unhandsome symptoms; acridity of the gastric juice, consequent indigestion and spasm, and generally a hypochondriacal habit of body. Mr. Jennings must take certain draughts thrice a day, be very careful of his diet, and keep his mind at ease. As to Simon himself, he was, poor man, much to be pitied in this ideal visitation; for, though his looks confessed that he saw, or fancied he saw, a something, he declared himself wholly at a loss to explain what that something was: moreover, contrary to former habits of an ostentatious boldness, he seemed meekly to shrink from observation: and, as he piously acquiesced in the annoyance, would observe that his unpleasant jerking was "a little matter after all, and that, no doubt, the will of Providence."

Independently of these new grimaces, Simon's appearance was little in his favour: not that his small dimensions signified—Cæsar, and Buonaparte, and Wellington, and Nelson, all were little men—not that his dress was other than respectable—black coat and waistcoat, white stiff cravat, gray trowsers somewhat shrunk in longitude, good serviceable shoe-leather (of the shape, if not also of the size, of river barges), and plenty of unbleached cotton stocking about the gnarled region of his ankles. All this was well enough; nature was beholden to that charity of art which hides a multitude of failings; but the face, where native man looks forth in all his unadornment, that it was which so seldom prepossessed the many who had never heard of Jenning's strict character and stern integrity. The face was a sallow face, peaked towards the nose, with head and chin receding; lit withal by small protrusive eyes, so constructed, that the whites all round were generally visible, giving them a strange and staring look; elevated eye-brows; not an inch of whisker, but all shaved sore right up to the large and prominent ear; and lank black hair, not much of it, scantily thatching all smooth. Then his arms, oscillating as he walked (as if the pendulum by which that rigid man was made to go his regular routine), were much too long for symmetry: and altogether, to casual view, Mr. Jennings must acknowledge to a supercilious, yet sneaking air—which charity has ere now been kind enough to think a conscious rectitude towards man, and a soft-going humility with God.

When the bailiff takes his round about the property, as we see him now, he is mounted—to say he rides would convey far too equestrian a notion—he is mounted on a rough-coated, quiet, old, white shooting-pony; the saddle strangely girded on with many bands about the belly, the stirrups astonishingly short, and straps never called upon to diminish that long whity-brown interval between shoe and trowser: Mr. Jennings sits his steed with nose aloft, and a high perch in the general, somewhat loosely, and, had the pony been a Bucephalus rather than a Rozinante, not a little perilously. Simon is jogging hitherwards toward Roger Acton, as he digs the land-drain across this marshy meadow: let us see how it fares now with our poor hero.

Occupation—yes, duteous occupation—has exerted its wholsesome influences, and, thank God! Roger is himself again. He has been very sorry half the day, both for the wicked feelings of the morning, and that still more wicked theft—a bad business altogether, he cannot bear to think of it; the gold was none of his, whosesoever it might be—he ought not to have touched it—vexed he did, but cannot help it now; it is well he lost it too, for ill-got money never came to any good: though, to be sure, if he could only get it honestly, money would make a man of him.

I am not sure of that, Roger, it may be so sometimes; but, in my judgment, money has unmade more men than made them.

"How now, Acton, is not this drain dug yet! You have been about it much too long, sir; I shall fine you for this."

"Please you, Muster Jennings, I've stuck to it pretty tightly too, barring that I make to-day three-quarters, being late: but it's heavy clay, you see, Mr. Simon—wet above and iron-hard below: it shall all be ready by to-morrow, Mr. Simon."

Whether the "Mr. Simon" had its softening influence, or any other considerations lent their soothing aid, we shall see presently; for the bailiff added, in a tone unusually indulgent,

"Well, Roger, see it is done, and well done; and now I have just another word to say to you: his honour is coming round this way, and if he asks you any questions, remember to be sure and tell him this—you have got a comfortable cottage, very comfortable, just repaired, you want for nothing, and are earning twelve shillings a week."

"God help me, Muster Jennings: why my wages are but eight, and my hovel scarcely better than a pig-pound."

"Look you, Acton; tell Sir John what you have told me, and you are a ruined man. Make it twelve to his honour, as others shall do: who knows," he added, half-coaxing, half-soliloquizing, "perhaps his honour may really make it twelve, instead of eight."

"Oh, Muster Jennings! and who gets the odd four?"

"What, man! do you dare to ask me that? Remember, sir, at your peril, that you, and all the rest, *have had* twelve shillings a-week wages whenever you have worked on this estate—not a word!—and that, if you dare speak or even think to the contrary, you never earn a penny here again. But here comes John Vincent, my master, as I, Simon Jennings, am yours: be careful what you say to him."

Sir John Devereux Vincent, after a long minority, had at length shaken off his guardians, and become master of his own doings, and of Hurstley Hall. The property was in pretty decent order, and funds had accumulated vastly: all this notwithstanding a thousand peculations, and the suspicious incident that one of the guardians was a "highly respectable" solicitor. Sir John, like most new brooms, had with the best intentions resolved upon sweeping measures of great good; especially also upon doing a great deal with his own eyes and ears; but, like as aforesaid, he was permitted neither to hear nor see any truths at all. Just now, the usual night's work took him a little off the hooks, and we must make allowances; really, too, he was by far the soberest of all those choice spirits, and drank and played as little as he could; and even, under existing disadvantages, he managed by four o'clock post meridiem to inspect a certain portion of the estate duly every day, under the prudential guidance of his bailiff Jennings. There, that good-looking, tall young fellow on the blood mare just cantering up to us is Sir John; the other two are a couple of the gallant youths now feasting at the Hall: ay, two of the fiercest foes in last night's broil. Those heated little matters are easily got over.

"Hollo, Jennings! what the devil made you give that start? you couldn't look more horrified if ghosts were at your elbow: why, your face is the picture of death; look another way, man, do, or my mare will bolt."

"I beg your pardon, Sir John, but the spasm took me: it is my infirmity; forgive it. This meadow, you perceive, Sir John, requires drainage, and afterwards I propose to dress it with free chalk to sweeten the grass. Next field, you will take notice, the guano—"

"Well, well—Jennings—and that poor fellow there up to his knees in mud, is he pretty tolerably off now?"

"Oh, your honour," said the bailiff, with a knowing look, "I only wish that half the little farmers hereabouts were as well to do as he is: a pretty cottage, Sir John, half an acre of garden, and twelve shillings a-week, is pretty middling for a single man."

"Aha—is it?—well; but the poor devil looks wretched enough too—I will just ask him if he wants any thing now."

"Don't, Sir John, pray don't; pray permit me to advise your honour: these men are always wanting. 'Acton's cottage' is a proverb; and Roger there can want for nothing honestly; nevertheless, as I know your honour's good heart, and wish to make all happy, if you will suffer me to see to it myself—"

"Certainly, Jennings, do, do by all means, and thank you: here, just to make a beginning, as we're all so jolly at the Hall, and that poor fellow's up to his neck in mud, give him this from me to drink my health with."

Acton, who had dutifully held aloof, and kept on digging steadily, was still quite near enough to hear all this; at the magical word "give," he looked up hurriedly, and saw Sir John Vincent toss a piece of gold —yes, on his dying oath, a bright new sovereign—to Simon Jennings. O blessed vision, and gold was to be his at last!

"Come along, Mynton; Hunt, now mind you try and lame that big beast of a raw-boned charger among these gutters, will you? I'm off, Jennings; meet me, do you hear, at the Croft to-mor—"

So the three friends galloped away; and John Vincent really felt more light-hearted and happy than at any time the week past, for having so properly got rid of a welcome bit of gold.

"Roger Acton! come up here, sir, out of that ditch: his honour has been liberal enough to give you a shilling to drink his health with."

"A shilling, Muster Jennings?" said the poor astonished man; "why I'll make oath it was a pound; I saw it myself. Come, Muster Jennings, don't break jokes upon a poor man's back."

"Jokes, Acton? sticks, sir, if you say another word: take John Vincent's shilling."

"Oh, sir!" cried Roger, quite unmanned at this most cruel disappointment; "be merciful—be generous—give me my gold, my own bit of gold! I'll swear his honour gave it for me: blessings on his head! You know he did, Mr. Simon; don't play upon me!"

"Play upon you?—generous—your gold—what is it you mean, man? We'll have no madmen about us, I can tell you; take the shilling, or else—"

"'Rob not the poor, because he is poor, for the Lord shall plead his cause,'" was the solemn answer.

"'Roger Acton!"—the bailiff gave a scared start, as usual, and, recovering himself, looked both white and stern: "you have dared to quote the Bible against me: deeply shall you rue it. Begone, man! your work on this estate is at an end."

CHAPTER VII.

WRONGS AND RUIN.

A VERY miserable man was Roger Acton now, for this last trial was the worst of all. The vapours of his discontent had almost passed away—that bright pernicious dream was being rapidly forgotten—the morning's ill-got coin, "thank the Lord, it was lost as soon as found," and penitence had washed away that blot upon his soul; but here, an honest pound, liberally bestowed by his hereditary landlord—his own bright bit of gold—the only bit but one he ever had (and how different in innocence from that one!)—a seeming sugar-drop of kindness, shed by the rich heavens on his cup of poverty—to have this meanly filched away by a grasping, grinding task-master—oh, was it not a bitter trial? What affliction as to this world's wealth can a man meet worse than this?

"Acton's first impulse was to run to the Hall, and ask to see Sir John:—"Out; won't be back till seven, and then can see nobody; the baronet will be dressing for dinner, and musn't be disturbed." Then he made a vain effort to speak with Mr. Jennings, and plead with him: yes, even on his knees, if must be. Mr. Simon could not be so bad; perhaps it was a long joke after all—the bailiff always had a queer way with him. Or, if indeed the man meant robbery, loudly to threaten him, that all might hear, to bring the house about his ears, and force justice, if he could not fawn it. But both these conflicting expedients were vetoed. Jonathan Floyd, who took in Acton's meek message of "humbly craved leave to speak with Master Jennings," came back with the inexplicable mandate, "Warn Roger Acton from the premises." So, he must needs bide till to-morrow morning, when, come what might, he resolved to see his honour, and set some truths before him.

Acton was not the only man on the estate who knew that he had a landlord, generous, not to say prodigal—a warm-hearted, well-intentioned master, whose mere youth a career of sensuality had not yet hardened, nor a course of dissipation been prolonged enough to distort his feelings from the right. And Acton, moreover, was not the only man who wondered how, with such a landlord (ay, and the guardians before him were always well-spoken gentle-folks, kindly in their manners, and liberal in their looks), wages could be kept so low, and rents so high, and indulgences so few, and penalties so many. There were fines for every thing, and no allowances of hedgebote, or housebote, or any other time-honoured right; the very peat on the common must be paid for, and if a child picked a bit of fagot the father was mulcted in a shilling. Mr. Jennings did all this, and always pleaded his employers' orders; nay, if any grumbled, as men would now and then, he would affect to think it strange that the gentlemen guardians, with the landlord at their head, could be so hard upon the poor: he would not be so, credit him, if he had been born a gentleman; but the bailiff, men, must obey orders, like the rest of you; these are hard times for Hurstley, he would say, and we must all rub over them as best we can. According to Simon, it was as much as his own place was worth to remit one single penny of a fine, or make the least indulgence for calamity; while, as to lowering a cotter's rent, or raising a ditcher's wages, he dared not do it for his life; folks must not blame him, but look to the landlord.

Now, all this, in the long absence of any definite resident master at the Hall, sounded reasonable, if true; and Mr. Jennings punctually paid, however bad the terms; so the poor men bode their time, and looked for better days. And the days long-looked-for now were come; but were they any better? The baronet, indeed, seemed bent upon inquiry, reform, redress; but, as he never went without the right-hand man, his endeavours were always unsuccessful. At first it would appear that the bailiff had gone upon his old plan, shrugging up his shoulders to the men at the master's meanness, while he praised to the landlord the condition of his tenants; but this could not long deceive, so he turned instanter on another tack; he assumed the despot, issuing authoritative edicts, which no one dared to disobey; he made the labourer hide his needs, and intercepted at its source the lord's benevolence; he began to be found out, so the bolder spirits said, in filching with both hands from man and master; and, to the mind of more than one shrewd observer, was playing the unjust steward to admiration.

But stop: let us hear the other side; it is possible we may have been mistaken. Bailiffs are never popular, particularly if they are too honest, and this one is a stern man with a repulsive manner. Who knows whether his advice to Acton may not have been wise and kind, and would not have conduced to a general rise of wages? Who can prove, nay, venture to insinuate, any such systematic roguery against a man hitherto so strict, so punctual, so sanctimonious? Even in the case of Sir John's golden gift, Jennings may be right after all; it is quite possible that Roger was mistaken, and had gilt a piece of silver with his longings; and the upright man might well take umbrage at so vile an imputation as that hot and silly speech; it was foolish, very foolish, to have quoted text against him, and no wonder that the labourer got dismissed for it. Then again to return to wages—who knows? it might be, all things considered, the only way of managing a rise; the bailiff must know his master's mind best, and Acton had been wise to have done as he bade him; perhaps it really was well-meant, and might have got him twelve shillings a-week, instead of eight as hitherto; perhaps Simon was a shrewd man, and arranged it cleverly; perhaps Roger was an honest man, and couldn't but think others so.

Any how, though, all was lost now, and he blamed his own rash tongue, poor fellow, for what he could not help fearing was the ruin of himself and all he loved. With a melancholy heart, he shouldered his spade, and slowly plodded homewards. How long should he have a home? How was he to get bread, to get work, if the bailiff was his enemy? How could he face his wife, and tell her all the foolish past and dreadful future? How could he bear to look on Grace, too beautiful Grace, and torture his heart by fancying her fate? Thomas, too, his own brave boy, whom utter poverty might drive to desperation? And the poor babes, his little playful pets, what on earth would become of them? There was the Union workhouse to be sure, but Acton shuddered at the thought; to be separated from every thing he loved, to give up his little all, and be made both a prisoner and a slave, all for the sake of what?—daily water-gruel, and a pauper's branded livery. Or they might perchance go beyond the seas, if some Prince Edward's Company would help him and his to emigrate; ay, thought he, and run new risks, encounter fresh dangers, lose every thing, get nothing, and all the trouble taken merely to starve three thousand miles from home. No, no; at his time of life, he could not be leaving for ever old friends, old habits, old fields, old home, old neighbourhood—where he had seen the saplings grow up trees, and the quick toppings change into a ten-foot hedge; where the very cattle knew his step, and the clods broke kindly to his ploughshare; and more than all, the dear old church, where his forefathers had worshipped from the Conquest, and the old mounds where they slept, and—and—and—that one precious grave of his dear lost Annie—could he leave it? Oh God, no! he had done no ill, he had committed no crime—why should he prefer the convict's doom, and seek to be transported for life?

A miserable walk home was that, and full of wretched thoughts. Poor Roger Acton, tossed by much trouble, vexed with sore oppression, I wish that you had prayed in your distress; stop, he did pray, and that vehemently; but it was not for help, or guidance, or patience, or consolation—he only prayed for gold.

CHAPTER VIII.

THE COVETOUS DREAM.

Once at home, the sad truth soon was told. Roger's look alone spoke of some calamity, and he had but little heart or hope to keep the matter secret. True, he said not a word about the early morning's sin; why should he? he bad been punished for it, and he had repented; let him be humbled before God, but not confess to man. However, all about the bailiff, and the landlord, and the thieved gift, and the sudden dismissal, the sure ruin, the dismal wayside plans, and fears, and dark alternatives, without one hope in any—these did poor Acton fluently pour forth with broken-hearted eloquence; to these Grace listened sorrowfully, with a face full of gentle trust in God's blessing on the morrow's interview; these Mary, the wife, heard to an end, with—no storm of execration on ill-fortune, no ebullition of unjust rage against a fool of a husband, no vexing sneers, no selfish apprehensions. Far from it; there really was one unlooked-for blessing come already to console poor Roger; and no little compensation for his trouble was the way his wife received the news. He, unlucky man, had expected something little short of a virago's talons, and a beldame's curse; he had experienced on less occasions something of the sort before; but now that real affliction stood upon the hearth, Mary Acton's character rose with the emergency, and she greeted her ruined husband with a kindness towards him, a solemn indignation against those who grind the poor, and a sober courage to confront evil, which he little had imagined.

"Bear up, Roger; here, goodman, take the child, and don't look quite so downcast; come what may, I'll share your cares, and you shall halve my pleasures; we will fight it out together."

Moreover, cross, and fidgetty, and scolding, as Mary had been ever heretofore, to her meek step-daughter Grace, all at once, as if just to disappoint any preconcerted theory, now that actual calamity was come, she turned to be a kind good mother to her. Roger and his daughter could scarcely believe their ears.

"Grace, dear, I know you're a sensible good girl, try and cheer your father." And then the step-dame added,

"There now, just run up, fetch your prayer-book down, and read a little to us all to do us good."—The fair, affectionate girl, unused to the accents of kindness, could not forbear flinging her arms round Mary Acton's neck, and loving her, as Ruth loved Naomi.

Then with a heavenly smile upon her face, and a happy heart within her to keep the smile alight, her gentle voice read these words—it will do us good to read them too:

"Out of the deep have I called unto thee, O Lord: Lord, hear my voice.
O let thine ears consider well the voice of my complaint.
If thou, Lord, wilt be extreme to mark what is done amiss, O Lord, who may abide it?
Because there is mercy with thee; therefore shalt thou be feared.
I look for the Lord, my soul doth wait for him: in his word is my trust.
My soul fleeth unto the Lord, before the morning watch, before the morning watch.
O Israel, trust in the Lord: for with the Lord there is mercy: and with him is plenteous redemption.
And he shall redeem Israel from all his sins."

"Isn't the last word 'troubles,' child? look again; I think it's 'troubles' either there, or leastways in the Bible-psalm."

"No, father, sins, 'from all his sins;' and 'iniquities' in the Bible-version—look, father."

"Well, girl, well; I wish it had been 'troubles;' 'from all his troubles' is a better thought to my mind: God wot, I have plenty on 'em, and a little lot of gold would save us from them all."

"Gold, father? no, my father—God."

"I tell you, child," said Roger, ever vacillating in his strong temptation between habitual religion and the new-caught lust of money, "if only on a sudden I could get gold by hook or by crook, all my cares and all your troubles would be over on the instant."

"Oh, dear father, do not hope so; and do not think of troubles more than sins; there is no deliverance in Mammon; riches profit not in the day of evil, and ill-got wealth tends to worse than poverty."

"Well, any how, I only wish that dream of mine came true."

"Dream, goodman—what dream?" said his wife.

"Why, Poll, I dreamt I was a-working in my garden, hard by the celery trenches in the sedge; and I was moaning at my lot, as well I may: and a sort of angel came to me, only he looked dark and sorrowful, and kindly said, 'What would you have, Roger?' I, nothing fearful in my dream, for all the strangeness of his winged presence, answered boldly, 'Money;' he pointed with his finger, laughed aloud, and vanished away: and, as for me, I thought a minute wonderingly, turned to look where he had pointed, and, O the blessing! found a crock of gold!"

"Hush, father! that dark angel was the devil; he has dropt ill thoughts upon your heart: I would I could see you as you used to be, dear father, till within these two days."

"Whoever he were, if he brought me gold, he would bring me blessing. There's meat and drink, and warmth and shelter, in the yellow gold—ay, and rest from labour, child, and a power of rare good gifts."

"If God had made them good, and the gold were honest gains, still, father, even so, you forget righteousness, and happiness, and wisdom. Money gives us none of these, but it might take them all away: dear father, let your loving Grace ask you, have you been better, happier, wiser, even from the wishing it so much?"

"Daughter, daughter, I tell you plainly, he that gives me gold, gives me all things: I wish I found the crock the de— the angel, I mean, brought me."

"O father," murmured Grace, "do not breathe the wicked wish; even if you found it without any evil angel's help, would the gold be rightfully your own?"

"Tush, girl!" said her mother; "get the gold, feed the children, and then to think about the right."

"Ay, Grace, first drive away the toils and troubles of this life," added Roger, "and then one may try with a free mind to discover the comforts of religion."

Poor Grace only looked up mournfully, and answered nothing.

CHAPTER IX.

THE POACHER.

A SUDDEN knock at the door here startled the whole party, and Mary Acton, bustling up, drew the bolt to let in—first, a lurcher, one Rover to wit, our gaunt ember-loving friend of Chapter II.; secondly, Thomas Acton, full flush, who carried the old musket on his shoulder, and seemed to have something else under his smock; and thirdly, Ben Burke, a personage of no small consequence to us, and who therefore deserves some specific introduction.

Big Ben, otherwise Black Burke, according to the friendship or the enmity of those who named him, was a huge, rough, loud, good-humoured, dare-devil sort of an individual, who lived upon what he considered common rights. His dress was of the mongrel character, a well-imagined cross between a ploughman's and a sailor's; the bottle-green frock of the former, pattern-stitched about the neck as ingeniously as if a tribe of Wisconsin squaws had tailored it—and mighty fishing boots, vast as any French postillion's, acting as a triton's tail to symbolize the latter: a red cotton handkerchief (dirty-red of course, as all things else were dirty, for cleanliness had little part in Ben), occupied just now the more native region of a halter; and a rusty fur cap crowned the poacher; I repeat it—crowned the poacher; for in his own estimation, and that of many others too, Ben was, if not quite an emperor, at least an Agamemnon, a king of men, a natural human monarch; in truth, he felt as much pride in the title Burke the Poacher (and with as great justice too, for aught I know), as Ali-Hamet-Ghee-the-Thug eastwards, or William-of-Normandy-the-Conqueror westwards, may be thought respectively to have cherished, on the score of their murderous and thievish surnames.

There was no small good, after all, in poor Ben; and a mountain of allowance must be flung into the scales to counterbalance his deficiencies. However coarse, and even profane, in his talk (I hope the gentle reader will excuse me alike for eliding a few elegant extracts from his common conversation, and also for reminding him characteristically, now and then, that Ben's language is not entirely Addisonian), however rough of tongue and dissonant in voice, Ben's heart will be found much about in the right place; nay, I verily believe it has more of natural justice, human kindness, and right sympathies in it, than are to be found in many of those hard and hollow cones that beat beneath the twenty-guinea waistcoats of a Burghardt or a Buckmaster. Ay, give me the fluttering inhabitant of Ben Burke's cowskin vest; it is worth a thousand of those stuffed and artificial denizens, whose usual nest is figured satin and cut velvet.

Ben stole—true—he did not deny it; but he stole naught but what he fancied was wrongfully withheld him: and, if he took from the rich, who scarcely knew he robbed them, he shared his savoury booty with the poor, and fed them by his daring. Like Robin Hood of old, he avenged himself on wanton wealth, and frequently redressed by it the wrongs of penury. Not that I intend to break a lance for either of them, nor to go any lengths in excusing; slight extenuation is the limit for prudent advocacy in these cases. Robin Hood and Benjamin Burke were both of them thieves; bold men—bad men, if any will insist upon the bad; they sinned against law, and order, and Providence; they dug rudely at the roots of social institutions; they spoke and acted in a dangerous fashion about rights of men and community of things. But set aside the statutes of Foresting and Venery, disfranchise pheasants, let it be a cogent thing that poverty and riches approach the golden mean somewhat less unequally, and we shall not find much of criminality, either in Ben or Robin.

For a general idea, then, of our poaching friend:—he is a gigantic, black-whiskered, humorous, ruddy mortal, full of strange oaths, which we really must not print, and bearded like the pard, and he tumbles in amongst our humble family party, with—

"Bless your honest heart, Roger! what makes you look so sodden? I'm a lord, if your eyes a'n't as red as a hedge-hog's; and all the rest o' you, too; why, you seem to be pretty well merry as mutes. Ha! I see what it is," added Ben, pouring forth a benediction on their frugal supper; "it's that precious belly-ache porridge that's a-giving you all the 'flensy. Tip it down the sink, dame, will you now? and trust to me for better. Your Tom here, Roger, 's a lad o' mettle, that he is; ay, and that old iron o' yours as true as a compass; and the pheasants would come to it, all the same as if they'd been loadstoned. Here, dame, pluck the fowl, will you: drop 'em, Tom."—And Thomas Acton flung upon the table a couple of fine cock-pheasants.

Roger, Mary, and Grace, who were well accustomed to Ben Burke's eloquent tirades, heard the end of this one with anxiety and silence; for

Tom had never done the like before. Grace was first to expostulate, but was at once cut short by an oath from her brother, whose evident state of high excitement could not brook the semblance of reproof. Mary Acton's marketing glance was abstractedly fixed upon the actual *corpus delicti;* each fine plump bird, full-plumaged, young-spurred; yes, they were still warm, and would eat tender, so she mechanically began to pluck them; while, as for poor downcast Roger, he remembered, with a conscience-sting that almost made him start, his stolen bit of money in the morning—so, how could he condemn? He only looked pityingly on Thomas, and sighed from the bottom of his heart.

"Why, what 's the matter now?" roared Ben; "one 'ud think we was bailiffs come to raise the rent, 'stead of son Tom and friendly Ben; hang it, mun, we aint here to cheat you out o' summut—no, not out o' peace o' mind neither; so, if you don't like luck, burn the fowls, or bury 'em, and let brave Tom risk limbo for nothing."

"Oh, Ben!" murmured Grace, "why will you lead him astray? Oh, brother! brother! what have you done?" she said, sorrowfully.

"Miss Grace,"—her beauty always awed the poacher, and his rugged Caliban spirit bowed in reverence before her Ariel soul—"I wish I was as good as you, but can 't be: don 't condemn us, Grace; leastways, first hear me, and then say where 's the harm or sin on it. Twelve hundred head o' game—I heard John Gorse, the keeper, tell it at the Jerry—twelve hundred head were shot at t' other day 's battew: Sir John—no blame to him for it—killed a couple o' hundred to his own gun: and though they sent away a coachful, and gave to all who asked, and feasted themselves chuckfull, and fed the cats, and all, still a mound, like a haycock, o' them fine fat fowl, rotted in a mass, and were flung upon the dungpit. Now, Miss Grace, that ere salt pea-porridge a'n't nice, a'n't wholesome; and, bless your pretty mouth, it ought to feed more sweetly. Look at Acton, isn't he half-starved. Is Tom, brave boy, full o' the fat o' the land? Who made fowl, I should like to know, and us to eat 'em? And where 's the harm or sin in bringing down a bird? No, Miss, them ere beaks, dammem (beg humble pardon, Miss, indeed I won't again) them ere justices, as they call themselves, makes hard laws to hedge about their own pleasures; and if the poor man starves, he starves; but if he stays his hunger with the free, wild birds of heaven, they prison him and punish him, and call him poacher."

"Ben, those who make the laws, do so under God's permission; and they who break man's law, break His law."

"Nonsense, child,"—suddenly said Roger; hold your silly tongue. Do you mean to tell us, God's law and man's law are the same thing! No, Grace, I can't stomach that; God makes right, and man makes might—riches go one way, and poor men's wrong's another. Money, money's the great law-maker, and a full purse frees him that has it, while it turns the jailor's key on the wretch that has it not: one of those wretches is the hopeless Roger Acton. Well, well," he added, after a despondent sigh, "say no more about it all; that's right, good-wife—why, they do look plump. And if I can't stomach Grace's text-talk there, I'm sure I can the birds; for I know what keeps crying cupboard lustily."

It was a faint effort to be gay, and it only showed his gloom the denser. Truly, he has quite enough to make him sad; but this is an unhealthy sadness: the mists of mammon-worship, rising up, meet in the mid æther of his mind, these lowering clouds of discontent: and the seeming calamity, that should be but a trial to his faith, looks too likely to wreck it.

So, then, the embers were raked up, the trivet stuck a-top, the savoury broil made ready; and (all but Grace, who would not taste a morsel, but went up straight to bed) never had the Actons yet sate down before so rich a supper.

CHAPTER X.

BEN BURKE'S STRANGE ADVENTURE.

"Take a pull, Roger, and pass the flask," was the cordial prescription of Ben Burke, intended to cure a dead silence, generated equally of eager appetites and self-accusing consciences; so saying, he produced a quart wicker-bottle, which enshrined, according to his testimony, "summut short, the right stuff, stinging strong, that had never seen the face of a wishy-washy 'ciseman." But Roger touched it sparingly, for the vaunted nectar positively burnt his swallow: till Ben, pulling at it heartily himself, by way of giving moral precept the full benefit of a good example, taught Roger not to be afraid of it, and so the flask was drained.

Under such communicative influence, Acton's tale of sorrows and oppressions, we may readily believe, was soon made known; and as readily, that it moved Ben's indignant and gigantic sympathies to an extent of imprecation on the eyes, timbers, and psychological existence of Mr. Jennings, very little edifying. One thing, however, made amends for the license of his tongue; the evident sincerity and warmth with which his coarse but kindly nature proffered instant aid, both offensive and defensive.

"It's a black and burning shame, Honest Roger, and right shall have his own, somehow, while Big Ben has a heart in the old place, and a hand to help his friend." And the poacher having dealt his own broad breast a blow that would have knocked a tailor down, stretched out to Acton the huge hand that had inflicted it.

"More than that, Roger—hark to this, man!" and, as he slapped his breeches pocket, there was the chink as of a mine of money shaken to its foundations: "hark to this, man! and more than hark, have! Here, good wife, hold your apron!" And he flung into her lap a handful of silver.

Roger gave a sudden shout of wonder, joy, and avarice: and then as instantaneously turning very pale, he slowly muttered, "Hush, Ben! is it bloody money?" and almost shrieked as he added, "and my poor boy Tom, too, with you! God-a-mercy, mun! how came ye by it?"

"Honestly, neighbour, leastways, middling honest: don't damp a good fellow's heart, when he means to serve you."

"Tell me only that my boy is innocent!—and the money—yes, yes, I'll keep the money;" for his wife seemed to be pushing it from her at the thought.

"I innocent, father! I never know'd till this minute that Ben had any blunt at all—did I, Ben?—and I only brought him and Rover here to sup, because I thought it neighbourly and kind-like."

Poor Tom had till now been very silent: some how the pheasants lay heavy on his stomach.

"Is it true, Ben, is it true? the lad isn't a thief, the lad isn't a murderer? Oh, God! Burke, tell me the truth!

"Blockhead!" was the courteous reply, "what, not believe your own son? Why, neighbour Acton, look at the boy: would that frank-faced, open-hearted fellow do worse, think you, than Black Burke? And would I, bad as I be, turn the bloody villain to take a man's life? No, neighbour; Ben kills game, not keepers: he sets his wire for a hare, but wouldn't go to pick a dead man's pocket. All that's wrong in me, mun, the game-laws put there; but I'm neither burglar, murderer, highwayman—no, nor a mean, sneaking thief; however the quality may think so, and even wish to drive me to it. Neither, being as I be no rogue, could I bear to live a fool; but I should be one, neighbour, and dub myself one too, if I didn't stoop to pick up money that a madman flings away."

"Madman? pick up money? tell us how it was, Ben," interposed female curiosity.

"Well, neighbours, listen: I was a-setting my night-lines round Pike Island yonder, more nor a fortnight back; it was a dark night and a mizzling, or morning rather, 'twixt three and four; by the same token, I'd caught a power of eels. All at once, while I was fixing a trimmer, a punt came quietly up: as for me, Roger, you know I always wades it through the muddy shallow: well, I listens, and a chap creeps ashore—a mad chap, with never a tile to his head, nor a sole to his feet—and when I sings out to ax him his business, the lunatic sprung at me like a tiger: I didn't wish to hurt a little weak wretch like him, specially being past all sense, poor nat'ral! so I shook him off at once, and held him straight out in this here wice." [Ben's grasp could have cracked any cocoa-nut.] "He trembled like a wicked thing; and when I peered close into his face, blow me but I thought I'd hooked a white devil—no one ever see such a face: it was horrible too look at. 'What are you arter, mun?' says I; 'burying a dead babby?' says I. 'Give us hold here—I'm bless'd if I don't see though what you've got buckled up there.' With that, the little white fool—it's sartin he was mad—all on a sudden flings at my head a precious hard bundle, gives a horrid howl, jumps into the punt, and off again, afore I could wink twice. My head a'n't a soft un, I suppose; but when a lunatic chap hurls at it with all his might a barrow-load of crockery at once, it's little wonder that my right eye flinched a minute, and that my right hand rubbed my right eye; and so he freed himself, and got clear off. Rum start this, thinks I: but any how he's flung away a summut, and means to give it me: what can it be? thinks I. Well, neighbours, if I didn't know the chap was mad afore, I was sartain of it now; what do you think of a grown man—little enough, truly, but out of long coats too—sneaking by night to Pike Island, to count out a little lot of silver, and to guzzle twelve gallipots o' honey? There it was, all hashed up in an old shawl, a slimy mesh like birdlime: no wonder my eye was a leetle blackish, when half-a-dozen earthern crocks were broken against it. I was angered enough, I tell you, to think any man could be such a fool as to bring honey there to eat or to hide—when at once I spied summut red among the mess; and what should it be but a pretty little China house, red-brick-like, with a split in the roof for droppings, and ticketed 'Savings-bank:' the chink o' that bank you hears now: and the bank itself is in the pond, now I've cleaned the till out."

"Wonderful sure! But what did you do with the honey, Ben?—some of the pots wasn't broke," urged notable Mrs. Acton.

"Oh, burn the slimy stuff, I warn't going to put my mouth out o' taste o' bacca, for a whole jawful of tooth-aches: I'll tell you, dame, what I did with them ere crocks, wholes, and parts. There's never a stone on Pike Island, it's too swampy, and I'd forgot to bring my pocketful, as usual. The heaviest fish, look you, always lie among the sedge, hereabouts and thereabouts, and needs stirring, as your Tom knows well; so I chucked the gallipots fur from me, right and left, into the shallows, and thereby druv the pike upon my hooks. A good night's work I made of it too, say nothing of the Savings-bank; forty pound o' pike and twelve of eel warn't bad pickings."

"Dear, it was a pity though to fling away the honey; but what became of the shawl, Ben?" Perhaps Mrs. Acton thought of looking for it.

"Oh, as for that, I was minded to have sunk it, with its mess of sweet-meats and potsherds; but a thought took me, dame, to be 'conomical for once: and I was half sorry too that I'd flung away the jars, for I began to fancy your little uns might ha' liked the stuff; so I dipped the clout like any washerwoman, rinshed, and squeezed, and washed the mess away, and have worn it round my waist ever since; here, dame, I haven't been this way for a while afore to-night; but I meant to ask you if you'd like to have it; may be 'tan't the fashion though."

"Good gracious, Ben! why that's Mrs. Quarles's shawl, I'd swear to it among a hundred; Sarah Stack, at the Hall, once took and wore it, when Mrs. Quarles was ill a-bed, and she and our Thomas walked to church together. Yes—green, edged with red, and—I thought so—a yellow circle in the middle; here's B. Q., for Bridget Quarles, in black cotton at the corner. Lackapity! if they'd heard of all this at the Inquest! I tell you what, Big Ben, it's kindly meant of you, and so thank you heartily, but that shawl would bring us into trouble; so please take it yourself to the Hall, and tell 'em fairly how you came by it."

"I don't know about that Poll Acton; perhaps they might ask me for the Saving-bank, too—eh, Roger!"

"No, no, wife; no, it'll never do to lose the money! let a bygone be a bygone, and don't disturb the old woman in her grave. As to the shawl, if it's like to be a tell-tale, in my mind, this hearth's the safest place for it."

So he flung it on the fire; there was a shrivelling, smouldering, guilty sort of blaze, and the shawl was burnt.

Roger Acton, you are falling quickly as a shooting star; already is your conscience warped to connive, for lucre's sake, at some one's secret crimes. You had better, for the moral of the matter, have burnt your right hand, as Scævola did, than that shawl. Beware! your sin will bring its punishment.

CHAPTER XI.

SLEEP.

Grace, in her humble truckle-bed, lay praying for her father; not about his trouble, though that was much, but for the spots of sin she could discern upon his soul.

Alas! an altered man was Roger Acton; almost since morning light, the leprosy had changed his very nature. The simple-minded Christian, toiling in contentment for his daily bread, cheerful for the passing day, and trustful for the coming morrow, this fair state was well-nigh faded away; while a bitterness of feeling against (in one word) GOD—against unequal partialities in providence, against things as they exist, and this world's inexplicable government—was gnawing at his very heart-strings, and cankering their roots by unbelief. It is a speedy process—throw away faith with its trust for the past, love for the present, hope for the future—and you throw away all that makes sorrow bearable, or joy lovely; the best of us, if God withheld his help, would apostatize like Peter, ere the cock crew thrice; and, at times, that help has wisely been withheld, to check presumptuous thoughts, and teach how true it is that the creature depends on the Creator. Just so we suffer a wilful little child, who is tottering about in leading-strings, to go alone for a minute, and have a gentle fall. And just so Roger here, deserted for a time of those angelic ministrations whose efficiency is proved by godliness and meekness, by patience and content, is harassed in his spirit as by harpies, by selfishness and pride, and fretful doubtings; by a grudging hate of labour, and a fiery lust of gold. Temptation comes to teach a weak man that he was fitted for his station, and his station made for him; that fulfilment of his ignorant desires will only make his case the worse, and that

> Providence alike is wise
> In what he gives and what denies.

Meanwhile, gentle Grace, on her humble truckle-bed, is full of prayers and tears, uneasily listening to the indistinct and noisy talk, and hearing, now and then, some louder oath of Ben's that made her shudder. Yes, she heard, too, the smashing sound, when the poacher flung the money down, and she feared it was a mug or a plate—no slight domestic loss; and she heard her father's strange cry, when he gave that wondering shout of joyous avarice, and she did not know what to fear. Was he ill? or crazed! or worse—fallen into bad excesses? How she prayed for him!

Poor Ben, too, honest-hearted Ben; she thought of him in charity, and pleaded for his good before the Throne of Mercy. Who knows but Heaven heard that saintly virgin prayer? There is love in Heaven yet for poor Ben Bnrke.

And if she prayed for Ben, with what an agony of deep-felt intercession did she plead for Thomas Acton, that own only brother of hers, just a year the younger to endear him all the more, her playmate, care, and charge, her friend and boisterous protector. The many sorrowing hours she had spent for his sake, and the thousand generous actions he had done for hers! Could she forget how the stripling fought for her that day, when rude Joseph Green would help her over the style? Could she but remember how slily he had put aside, for more than half a year, a little heap of copper earnings—weeding-money, and errand-money, and harvest-money—and then bounteously spent it all at once in giving her a Bible on her birth-day? And when, coming across the fields with him after leasing, years ago now, that fierce black bull of Squire Ryle's was rushing down upon us both, how bravely did the noble boy attack him with a stake, as he came up bellowing, and make the dreadful monster turn away! Ah! I looked death in the face then, but for thee, my brother! Remember him, my God, for good!

"Poor father! poor father! Well, I am resolved upon one thing: I'll go, with Heaven's blessing, to the Hall myself, and see Sir John, to-morrow; he shall hear the truth, for"——And so Grace fell asleep.

Roger, when he went to bed, came to similar conclusions. He would speak up boldly, that he would, without fear or favour. Ben's most seasonable bounty, however to be questioned on the point of right, made him feel entirely independent, both of bailiffs and squires, and he had now no anxieties, but rather hopes, about to-morrow. He was as good as they, with money in his pocket; so he'd down to the Hall, and face the baronet himself, and blow his bailiff out o' water: that should be his business by noon. Another odd idea, too, possessed him, and he could not sleep at night for thinking of it: it was a foolish fancy, but the dream might have put it in his head: what if one or other of those honey-jars, so flung here and there among the rushes, were in fact another sort of "Savings-bank"—a crock of gold? It was a thrilling thought—his very dream, too; and the lot of shillings, and the shawl—ay, and the inquest, and the rumours how that Mrs. Quarles had come to her end unfairly, and no hoards found—and—and the honey-pots missing. Ha! at any rate he'd have a search to-morrow. No bugbear now should hinder him; money's money; he'd ask no questions how it got there. His own bit of garden lay the nearest to Pike Island, and who knows but Ben might have slung a crock this way? It wouldn't do to ask him, though—for Burke might look himself, and get the crock—was Roger's last and selfish thought, before he fell asleep.

As to Mrs. Acton, she, poor woman, had her own thoughts, fearful ones, about that shawl, and Ben's mysterious adventure. No cloudy love of mammon had overspread her mind, to hide from it the hideousness of murder; in her eyes, blood was terrible, and not the less so that it covered gold. She remembered at the inquest—be sure she was there among the gossips—the facts, so little taken notice of till now, the keys in the cupboard, where the honey-pots were not, and how Jonathan Floyd had seen something on the lake, and the marks of a man's hand on the throat; and, God forgive her for saying so, but Mr. Jennings was a little, white-faced man. How wrong was it of Roger to have burnt that shawl! how dull of Ben not to have suspected something! but then the good fellow suspects nobody, and, I dare say, now doesn't know my thoughts. But Roger does, more shame for him; or why burn the shawl? Ah! thought she, with all the gossip rampart in her breast, if I could only have taken it to the Hall myself, what a stir I should have caused! Yes, she would have reaped a mighty field of glory by originating such a whirlwind of inquiries and surmises. Even now, so attractive was the mare's nest, she would go to the Hall by morning, and tell Sir John himself all about the burnt shawl, and Pike Island, and the galli——And so she fell fast asleep.

With respect to Ben, Tom, and Rover, a well-matched triad, as any Isis, Horus, and Nepthys, they all flung themselves promiscuously on the hard floor beside the hearth, "basked at the fire their hairy strength," and soon were snoring away beautifully in concert, base, tenor, and treble, like a leash of glee-singers. No thoughts troubled them, either of mammon or murder: so long before the meditative trio up-stairs, they had set a good example, and fallen asleep.

CHAPTER XII.

LOVE.

WITH the earliest peep of day arose sweet Grace, full of cheerful hope, and prayer, and happy resignation. She had a great deal to do that morning; for, innocent girl, she had no notion that it was quite possible to be too early at the Hall; her only fear was being too late. Then there were all the household cares to see to, and the dear babes to dress, and the place to tidy up, and breakfast to get ready, and, any how, she could not be abroad till half-past eight: so, to her dismay, it must be past nine before ever she can see Sir John. Let us follow her a little: for on this important day we shall have to take the adventures of our labourer's family one at a time.

By twenty minutes to nine, Grace had contrived to bustle on her things, give the rest the slip, and be tripping to the Hall. It is nearly two miles off, as we already know; and Grace is such a pretty creature that we can clearly do no better than employ our time thitherward by taking a peep at her.

Sweet Grace Acton, we will not vex thy blushing maiden modesty by elaborate details of form, and face, and feature. Perfect womanhood at fair eighteen: let that fill all the picture up with soft and swelling charms; no wadding, or padding, or jigot, or jupe—but all those graceful undulations are herself: no pearl-powder, no carmine, no borrowed locks, no musk, or ambergris—but all those feeble helps of meretricious art excelled and superseded by their just originals in nature. It will not do to talk, as a romancer may, of velvet cheeks and silken tresses; or invoke, to the aid of our inadequate description, roses, and swans, and peaches, and lilies. Take the simple village beauty as she is. Did you ever look on prettier lips or sweeter eyes—more glossy natural curls upon a whiter neck? And how that little red-riding-hood cloak, and the simple cottage hat tied down upon her cheeks, and the homely russet gown, all too short for modern fashions, and the white, well-turned ankle, and the tidy little leather shoe, and the bunch of snow drops in her tucker, and the neat mittens contrasting darkly with her fair, bare arms—pretty Grace, how well all these become thee! There, trip along, with health upon thy cheek, and hope within thy heart; who can resist so eloquent a pleader? Haste on, haste on: save thy father in his trouble, as thou hast blest him in his sin—this rustic lane is to thee the path of duty—Heaven speed thee on it!

More slowly now, and with more anxious thoughts, more heart-weakness, more misgiving—Grace approacheth the stately mansion: and when she timidly touched the "Servants'" bell, for she felt too lowly for the "Visiters',"—and when she heard how terribly loud it was, how long it rung, and what might be the issue of her—wasn't it ill-considered?—errand—the poor girl almost fainted at the sound.

As she leaned unconsciously for strength against the door, it opened on a sudden, and Jonathan Floyd, in mute amazement, caught her in his arms.

"Why, Grace Acton! what's the matter with you?" Jonathan knew Grace well; they had been at dame's-school together, and in after years attended the same Sunday class at church. There had been some talk among the gossips about Jonathan and Grace, and ere now folks had been kind enough to say they would make a pretty couple. And folks were right, too, as well as kind: for a fine young fellow was Jonathan Floyd, as any duchess's footman; tall, well built, and twenty-five; Antinous in a livery. Well to do, withal, though his wages don't come straight to him; for, independently of his place—and the baronet likes him for his good looks and proper manners—he is Farmer Floyd's only son, on the hill yonder, as thriving a small tenant as any round abouts; and he is proud of his master, of his blue and silver uniform, of old Hurstley, and of all things in general, except himself.

"But what on earth's the matter, Grace?" he was obliged to repeat, for the dear girl's agitation was extreme.

"Jonathan, can I see the baronet?"

"What, at nine in the morning, Grace Acton! Call again at two, and you may find him getting up. He hasn't been three hours a-bed yet, and there 's nobody about but Sarah Stack and me. I wish those Lunnun sparks would but leave the place: they do his honour no good, I 'm thinking."

"Not till two!" was the slow and mournful ejaculation. What a damper to her buoyant hopes: and Providence had seen fit to give her ill-success. Is it so? Prosperity may come in other shapes.

"Why, Grace," suddenly said Floyd, in a very nervous way, "what makes you call upon my master in this tidy trim?"

"To save my father," answered Innocence.

"How? why? Oh don't, Grace, don't! I 'll save him—I will indeed—what is it? Oh, don't, don't!"

For the poor affectionate fellow conjured on the spot the black vision of a father saved by a daughter's degradation.

"Don't, Jonathan?—it 's my duty, and God will bless me in it. That cruel Mr. Jennings has resolved upon our ruin, and I wished to tell Sir John the truth of it."

At this hearing, Jonathan brightened up, and glibly said, "Ah, indeed, Jennings is a trouble to us all: a sad life I 've led of it this year past; and I 've paid him pretty handsomely too, to let me keep the place: while, as for John Page and the grooms, and Mr. Coachman and the helpers, they don't touch much o' their wages on quarter-day, I know."

"Oh, but we—we are ruined! ruined! Father is forbidden now to labour for our bread." And then with many tears she told her tale.

"Stop, Miss Grace," suddenly said Jonathan, for her beauty and eloquence transformed the cottager into a lady in his eyes, and no wonder; "pray, stop a minute, Miss—please to take a seat; I sha'n't be gone an instant."

And the good-hearted fellow, whose eyes had long been very red, broke away at a gallop; but he was back again almost as soon as gone, panting like a post-horse. "Oh, Grace! don't be angry! do forgive me what I am going to do."

"Do, Jonathan?" and the beauty involuntarily started—"I hope it 's nothing wrong," she added, solemnly.

"Whether right or wrong, Grace, take it kindly; you have often bade me read my Bible, and I do so many times both for the sake of it and you; ay, and meet with many pretty sayings in it: forgive me if I act on one—'It is more blessed to give than to receive.'" With that, he thrust into her hand a brass-topped, red-leather purse, stuffed with money. Generous fellow! all the little savings, that had heretofore escaped the prying eye and filching grasp of Simon Jennings. There was some little gold in it, more silver, and a lot of bulky copper.

"Dear Jonathan!" exclaimed Grace, quite thrown off her guard of maidenly reserve, "this is too kind, too good, too much; indeed, indeed it is: I cannot take the purse." And her bright eyes overflowed again.

"Well, girl," said Jonathan, gulping down an apple in his throat, "I—I won't have the money, that's all. Oh, Grace, Grace!" he burst out earnestly, "let me be the blessed means of helping you in trouble—I would die to do it, Grace; indeed I would!"

The dear girl fell upon his neck, and they wept together like two loving little sisters.

"Jonathan"—her duteous spirit was the first to speak—"forgive this weakness of a foolish woman's heart: I will not put away the help which God provides us at your friendly hands: only this, kind brother—let me call you brother—keep the purse; if my father pines for want of work, and the babes at home lack food, pardon my boldness if I take the help you offer. Meanwhile, God in heaven bless you, Jonathan, as He will!"

And she turned to go away.

"Won't you take a keepsake, Grace—one little token? I wish I had any thing here but money to give you for my sake."

"It would even be ungenerous in me to refuse you, brother; one little piece will do."

Jonathan fumbled up something in a crumpled piece of paper, and said sobbingly—"Let it be this new half-crown, Grace: I won't say, keep it always; only when you want to use that and more, I humbly ask you'll please come to me."

Now a more delicate, a more unselfish act, was never done by man: along with the half-crown he had packed up two sovereigns! and thereby not only escaped thanks, concealed his own beneficence, and robbed his purse of half its little store; but actually he was, by doing so, depriving himself for a month, or maybe more, of a visit from Grace Acton. Had it been only half-a-crown, and want had pinched the family (neither Grace nor Jonathan could guess of Ben Burke's bounty, and for all they knew Roger had not enough for the morrow's meals)—had poverty come in like an armed man, and stood upon their threshold a grim sentinel—doubtless she must have run to him within a day or two. How sweet would it have been to have kept her coming day by day, and to a commoner affection how excusable! but still how selfish, how unlike the liberal and honourable feeling that filled the manly heart of Jonathan Floyd! It was a noble act, and worthy of a long parenthesis.

If Grace Acton had looked back as she hurried down the avenue, she would have seen poor Jonathan still watching her with all his eyes till she was out of sight. Perhaps, though, she might have guessed it—there is a sympathy in these things, the true animal magnetism—and I dare say that was the very reason why she did not once turn her head.

CHAPTER XIII.

THE DISCOVERY.

Roger Acton had not slept well; had not slept at all till nearly break of day, except in the feverish fashion of half dream half revery. There were thick-coming fancies all night long about what Ben had said and done: and more than once Roger had thought of the expediency of getting up, to seek without delay the realization of that one idea which now possessed him—a crock of gold. When he put together one thing and another, he considered it almost certain that Ben had flung away among the lot no mere honey-pot, but perhaps indeed a money-pot: Burke hadn't half the cunning of a child; more fool he, and maybe so much the better for me, thought money-bitten, selfish Roger. Thus, in the night's hot imaginations, he resolved to find the spoil; to will, was then to do: to do, was then to conquer. However, Nature's sweet restorer came at last, and, when he woke, the idea had sobered down—last night's fancies were preposterous. So, it was with a heavy heart he got up later than his wont—no work before him, nothing to do till the afternoon, when he might see Sir John, except it be to dig a bit in his little marshy garden. When Grace ran to the Hall, Roger was going forth to dig.

Now, I know quite well that the reader is as fully aware as I am, what is about to happen; but it is impossible to help the matter. If the heading of this chapter tells the truth, a "discovery" of some sort is inevitable. Let us preliminarize a thought or two, if thereby we can hang some shadowy veil of excuse over a too naked mystery. First and foremost, truth is strange, stranger, *et-cetera;* and this *et-cetera,* pregnant as one of Lyttleton's, intends to add the superlative strangest, to the comparative stranger of that seldom-quoted sentiment. To every one of us, in the course of our lives, something quite as extraordinary has befallen more than once. What shall we say of omens, warnings, forebodings? What of the most curious runs of luck; the most whimsical freaks of fortune; the unaccountable things that happen round us daily, and no one marvels at them, till he reads of them in print? Even as Macpherson, ingenious, if not ingenuous, gathered Ossian from the lips of Highland hussifs, and made the world with modern Attila to back it, wonder at the stores that are hived on old wives' tongues; even so might any other literary blacksmith hammer from the ore of common gossip a regular Vulcan's net of superstitious "facts." Never yet was uttered ghost story, that did not breed four others; every one at table is eager to record his, or his aunt's, experience in that line; and the mass of queer coincidences, inexplicable incidents, indubitable seeings, hearings, doings, and sufferings, which you and I have heard of in this popular vein of talk, would amply excuse the wildest fictionist for the most extravagant adventure—the more improbable, the nearer truth. Talk of the devil, said our ancestors—let "&c." save us from the consequence. Think of any thing vehemently, and it is an even chance it happens: be confident, you conquer; be obstinate in willing, and events shall bend humbly to their lord: nay, dream a dream, and if you recollect it in the morning, and it bother you next day, and you cannot get it out of your head for a week, and the matter positively haunt you, ten to one but it finds itself or makes itself fulfilled, some odd day or other. Just so, doubtless, will it prove to be with Roger's dream: I really cannot help the matter.

Again, it is more than likely that the reader is clever, very clever, and that any attempts at concealment would be merely futile. From the first page he has discovered who is the villain, and who the victim: the title alone tells him of the golden hinge on which the story turns: he can look through stone walls, if need be, or mesmerically see, without making use of eyes: no peep-holes for him, as for Pyramus and Thisbe: no initiation requisite for any hidden mysteries; all arcana are revealed to him, every sanctum is a highway. No art of mortal pen can defeat this mischief of acuteness: character is character; oaks grow of acorns, and the plan of a life may be detected in a microscopic speech. The career of Mr. Jennings is as much prëdestined by us to iniquity, from the first intimation that he never makes excuse, as honest

Roger is to trouble and temptation from the weary effort wherewithal he woke. And, even now, pretty Grace and young Sir John, the reader thinks that he can guess at nature's consequence; while, with respect to Roger's going forth to dig this morning, he sees it straight before him, need not ask for the result. Well, if the shrewd reader has the eye of Lieuenhöeck, and can discern, cradled in the small triangular beech-mast, a noble forest-tree, with silvery trunk, branching arms, and dark-green foliage, he deserves to be complimented indeed, for his own keen skill; but, at the same time, Nature will not hurry herself for him, but will quietly educe results which he foreknew—or thought he did—a century ago. And is there not the highest Art in this unveiled simplicity: to lead the reader onwards by a straight road, with the setting sun a-blaze at the end of it, knowing his path, knowing its object, yet still borne on with spirits unexhausted and unflagging foot? Trust me, there is better praise in this, than in dazzling the distracted glance with a perpetual succession of luminous fire-flies, and dragging your fair novel-reader, harried and excited, through the mazes of a thousand incidents.

Thirdly, and lastly, in this prefatorial say, there is to be considered that inevitable defeator of all printed secrets—impatience. Nothing is easier, nothing commoner (most wise people do it, whose fate is, that they must keep up with the race of current publication, and therefore must keep down the still-increasing crowd of authorial creations), nothing is more venial, more laudable, than to read the last chapter first; and so, finding out all mysteries at once, to save one's self a vast deal of unnecessary trouble. And, for mere tale-telling, this may be sufficient. What need to burden memory with imaginary statements, or to weary out one's sympathies on trite fictitious woes?—come to the catastrophe at once: the uncle hanged; the heir righted; the heroine, an orange-flowered bride; and the white-headed grandmother, after all her wrongs, winding up the story with a prudent moral. Now, this may all be very well with histories that merely carry a sting in the tail, whose moral is the warning of the rattlesnake, and whose hot-exciting interest is posted with the scorpion's venom. They are the Dragon of Wantley, with one caudal point—a barbed termination: we, like Moore of Moore Hall, all point, covered with spikes: every where we boast ourselves an ethical hedge-hog, all-over-armed with keen morals—a Rumour painted full of tongues, echoing all around with revealing of secrets. The feelings of our humble hero, altered Roger Acton, are worthy to be studied by the great, to be sifted by the rich; and Grace's simple tongue may teach the sage, for its wisdom cometh from above; and Jonathan, for all his shoulder-knot and smart cockade, is worthy to give lessons to his master: that master, also, is far better than you think him; and poor Burke too, for true humanity's sake: so we get a mint of morals, set aside the story. It is not raw material, but the workmanship, that gives its value to the flowered damask; our grand-dames' sumptuous taffeties and stand-alone brocades are but spun silk—worms' interiors; the fairest statue is intrinsically but a mass of clumsy stone, until, indeed, the sculptor has rough-hewn it, and shaped it, and chiselled it, and finished all the touches with sand-paper. This story of '*The Crock of Gold*' purports to be a Dutch picture, as becometh boors, their huts, their short and simple annals; so that, after its moralities, the mass of minute detail is the only thing that gives it any value.

Now, whilst all of you have been yawning through these egotistic phrases, Roger has been digging in his garden; there he is, pecking away at what once was the celery-bed, but now are fallow trenches; celery, as we all know, is a water-loving plant, doing best in marshy-land, so no wonder the trenches open on the sedge, and the muddy shallow opposite Pike Island puddles up to them. There needs be no suspense, no mystery at all; Roger's dream had clearly sent him thither, for he should not have levelled those trenches yet awhile, it was a little too soon—bad husbandry; and, barring the appearance of a devil, Roger's dream came true. Yes, under the roots of a clump of bullrush, he lifted out with his spade—a pot of Narbonne honey!

When first he spied the pot, his heart was in his mouth—it must be gold, and with tottering knees he raised the precious burden. But, woful disappointment! the word "Honey," with plenty of French and Fortnum on another pasted label, stared him in the face; it was sweet and slimy too about the neck; there was no sort of jingle when he shook the crock; what though it be heavy?—honey's heavy; and it was tied over quite in a common way with pig's bladder, and his clumsy trembling fingers could not undo that knot; and thus, with a miserable sense of cheated poverty, he threw it down beside the path, and would, perhaps, have flung it right away in sheer disgust, but for the reflection that the little ones might like it. Once, indeed, the glorious doubt of maybe gold came back upon his mind, and he lifted up the spade to smash the baffling pot, and so make sure of what it might contain;—make sure, eh? why, you would only lose the honey, whispered domestic economy. So he left the jar to be opened by his wife when he should go in,

CHAPTER XIV.

JONATHAN'S STORE.

And where has Mrs. Acton been all this morning? Off to the Hall, very soon after Grace had got away; and she rung at the side entrance, hard by the kitchen, most fortunately caught Sarah Stack about, and had a good long gossip with her; telling her, open-mouthed, all about Ben Burke having found a shawl of Mrs. Quarles's on the island; and how, it being very rotten, yes, and smelling foul, Ben had been fool enough to burn it; what a pity! how could the shawl have got there? if it only could ha' spoken what it knew! And the bereaved gossips mourned together over secrets undivulged, and their evidence destroyed. As to the crockery, for a miraculous once in life, Mrs. Acton held her tongue about a thing she knew, and said not a syllable concerning it. Roger would be mad to lose the money. Just at parting with her friend, Mary Acton was going out by the wrong door, through the hall, but luckily did no more than turn the handle; or she never could have escaped bouncing in upon the lovers' interview, and thereby occasioning a chaos of confusion. For, be it whispered, the step-dame was not a little jealous of her ready-made daughter's beauty, persisted in calling her a child, and treated her any thing but kindly and sisterly, as her full-formed woman's loveliness might properly have looked for. Only imagine, if the Hecate had but seen Jonathan's lit-up looks, or Grace's down-cast blushes; for it really slipped my observation to record that there were blushes, and probably some cause for them when the keep-sake was given and accepted; only conceive if the step-mother had heard Jonathan's afterward soliloquy, when he was watching pretty Grace as she tripped away—and how much he seemed to think of her eyes and eye-lashes! I am reasonably fearful, had she heard and seen all this—Poll Acton's nails might have possibly drawn blood from the cheeks of Jonathan Floyd. As it was, the little god of love kindly warded from his votaries the coming of so crabbed an antagonist.

Grace has now reached home again, blessing her overruling stars to have escaped notice so entirely both in going and returning; for the mother was hard at washing near the well, having got in half an hour before, and father has not yet left off digging in his garden. So she crept up stairs quietly, put away her Sunday best, and is just dropping on her knees beside her truckle-bed, to speak of all her sorrows to her Heavenly friend, and to thank him for the kindness He had raised her in an earthly one. She then, with no small trepidation, took out of her tucker, just below those withered snow-drops, the crumpled bit of paper that held Jonathan's parting gift. It was surprising how her tucker heaved; she could hardly get at the parcel. She wanted to look at that half-crown; not that she feared it was a bad one, or was curious about coins, or felt any pleasure in possessing such a sum: but there was such a don't-know-what connected with that new half-crown, which made her long to look at it; so she opened the paper—and found its golden fellows! O noble heart! O kind, generous, unselfish—yes, beloved Jonathan! But what is she to do with the sovereigns? Keep them? No, she cannot keep them, however precious in her sight as proofs of deep affection; but she will call as soon as possible, and give them back, and insist upon his taking them, and keeping them too—for her, if no otherwise. And the dear innocent girl was little aware herself how glad she felt of the excuse to call so soon again at Hurstley.

Meantime, for safety, she put the money in her Bible.

What hallowed gold was that? Gained by honest industry, saved by youthful prudence, given liberally and unasked, to those who needed, and could not pay again; with a delicate consideration, an heroic essay at concealment, a voluntary sacrifice of self, of present pleasure, passion, and affection. And there it lies, the little store, hidden up in Grace's Bible. She has prayed over it, thanked over it, interceded over it, for herself, for it, for others. How different, indeed, from ordinary gold, from common sin-bought mammon; how different from that unblest store, which Roger Acton covets; how purified from meannesses, and separate from harms! This is of that money, the scarcest coins of all the world, endued with all good properties in heaven and in earth, whereof it had been written, "The silver is mine, and the gold is mine, saith the Lord of hosts."

Such alone are truly riches—well-earned, well-saved, well-sanctified, well-spent. The wealthiest of European capitalists—the Crœsus of modern civilization—may be but a pauper in that better currency, whereof a sample has been shown in the store of Jonathan Floyd.

CHAPTER XV.

ANOTHER DISCOVERY, AND THE EARNEST OF GOOD THINGS.

"DAME, here's one o' Ben's gallipots he flung away: it's naught but honey, dame—marked so—no crock of gold; don't expect it; no such thing; luck like that isn't for such as me: though, being as it is, the babes may like it, with their dry bread: open it, good-wife: I hope the water mayn't ha' spoilt it."

The notable Mary Acton produced certain scissors, hanging from her pocket by a tape, and cut a knot, which to Roger had been Gordian's.

"Why, it's bran, Acton, not honey; look here, will you." She tilted it up, and, along with a cloud of saw-dust, dropped out a heavy hail-storm of—little bits of leather!

"Hallo? what's that?" said Roger, eagerly: "it's gold, gold, I'll be sworn!" It was so.

Every separate bit of money, whatever kind of coins they were, had been tidily sewn up in a shred of leather; remnants of old gloves of all colours; and the Narbonne jar contained six hundred and eighty-seven of them. These, of course, were hastily picked up from the path whereon they had first fallen, were counted out at home, and the glittering contents of most of those little leather bags ripped up were immediately discovered. Oh dear! oh dear! such a sight! Guineas and half-guineas, sovereigns and half-sovereigns, quite a little hill of bright, clean, prettily-figured gold.

"Hip, hip, hooray!" shouted Roger, in an ecstacy; "Hurrah, hurrah, hurrah!" and in the madness of his joy, he executed an extravagant pas seul; up went his hat, round went his heels, and he capered awkwardly like a lunatic giraffe.

"Here's an end to all our troubles, Poll: we're as good as gentle-folks now; catch me a-calling at the Hall, to bother about Jennings and Sir John: a fig for bailiffs, and baronets, parsons, and prisons, and all," and again he roared Hooray! "I tell you what though, old 'ooman, we must just try the taste of our glorious golden luck, before we do any thing else. Bide a bit, wench, and hide the hoard till I return. I'm off to the Bacchus's Arms, and I'll bring you some stingo in a minute, old gal." So off he ran hot-foot, to get an earnest of the blessing of his crock of gold.

The minute that was promised to produce the stingo, proved to be rather of a lengthened character; it might, indeed, have been a minute, or the fraction of one, in the planet Herschel, whose year is as long as eighty-five of our Terra's, but according to Greenwich calculation, it was nearer like two hours.

The little Tom and Jerry shop, that rejoiced in the classical heraldry of Bacchus's Arms, had been startled from all conventionalities by the unwonted event of the demand, "change for a sovereign?" and when it was made known to the assembled conclave that Roger Acton was the fortunate possessor, that even assumed an appearance positively miraculous.

"Why, honest Roger, how in the world could you ha' come by that?" was the troublesome inquiry of Dick the Tanner.

"Well, Acton, you 're sharper than I took you for, if you can squeeze gold out of bailiff Jennings," added Solomon Snip; and Roger knew no better way of silencing their tongues, than by profusely drenching them in liquor. So he stood treat all round, and was forced to hobanob with each; and when that was gone, he called for more to keep their curiosity employed. Now, all this caused delay; and if Mary had been waiting for the "stingo," she would doubtless have had reasonable cause for anger and impatience: however, she, for her part, was so pleasantly occupied, like Prince Arthur's Queen, in counting out the money, that, to say the truth, both lord and liquor were entirely forgotten.

But another cause that lengthened out the minute, was the embarrassing business of where to find the change. Bacchus's didn't chalk up trust, where hard money was flung upon the counter; but all the accumulated wealth of Bacchus's high-priest, Tom Swipey, and of the seven worshippers now drinking in his honour, could not suffice to make up enough of change: therefore, after two gallons left behind him in libations as aforesaid, and two more bottled up for a drink-offering at home, Roger was contented to be owed seven and fourpence; a debt never likely to be liquidated. Much speculation this afforded to the gossips; and when the treater's back was turned, they touched their foreheads, for the man was clearly crazed, and they winked to each other with a gesture of significance.

Grace, while musing on her new half-crown—it was strange how long she looked at it—had heard with real amazement that uproarious huzzaing! and, just as her father had levanted for the beer, glided down from her closet, and received the wondrous tidings from her step-mother. She heard in silence, if not in sadness: intuitive good sense proclaimed to her that this sudden gush of wealth was a temptation, even if she felt no secret fears on the score of—shall we call it superstition?—that dream, this crock, that dark angel—and this so changed spirit of her once religious father: what could she think? she meekly looked to Heaven to avert all ill.

Mary Acton also was less elated and more alarmed than she cared to confess: not that she, any more than Grace, knew or thought about lords of manors, or physical troubles on the score of finding the crock: but Mrs. Quarles's shawl, and sundry fearful fancies tinged with blood, these worried her exceedingly, and made her look upon the gold with an uneasy feeling, as if it were an unclean thing, a sort of Achan's wedge.

At last, here comes Roger back, somewhat unsteadily I fear, with a stone two-gallon jar of what he was pleased to avouch to be "the down-right stingo." "Hooray, Poll!" (he had not ceased shouting all the way from Bacchus's,) "Hooray—here I be again, a gentle-folk, a lord, a king, Poll: why daughter Grace, what's come to you? I won't have no dull looks about to-day, girl. Isn't this enough to make a poor man merry? No more troubles, no more toil, no more 'humble sarvent,' no more a ragged, plodding ploughman: but a lord, daughter Grace—a great, rich, luxurious lord—isn't this enough to make a man sing out hooray?—Thank the crock of gold for this—Oh, blessed crock!"

"Hush, father, hush! that gold will be no blessing to you; Heaven send it do not bring a curse. It will be a sore temptation, even if the rights of it are not in some one else: we know not whom it may belong to, but at any rate it cannot well be ours."

"Not ours, child? whose in life is it then?"

Mary Acton, made quite meek by a superstitious dread of having money of the murdered, stepped in to Grace's help, whom her father's fierce manner had appalled, with "Roger, it belonged to Mrs. Quarles, I'm morally sure on it—and must now be Simon Jennings's, her heir."

"What?" he almost frantically shrieked, "shall that white hell-hound rob me yet again? No, dame—I'll hang first! the crock I found, the crock I'll keep: the money's mine, whoever did the murder." Then, changing his mad tone into one of reckless inebriate gayety—for he was more than half-seas over even then from the pot-house toastings and excitement—he added, "But come, wenches, down with your mugs, and help me to get through the jar: I never felt so dry in all my life. Here's blessings on the crock, on him as sent it, him as has it, and on all the joy and comfort it's to bring us! Come, drink, drink—we must all drink that—but where's Tom?"

If Roger had been quite himself, he never would have asked so superfluous a question: for Tom was always in one and the same company, albeit never in one and the same place: he and his Pan-like Mentor were continually together, studying wood-craft, water-craft, and all manner of other craft connected with the antique trade of picking and stealing.

' Where 's Tom?"

Grace, glad to have to answer any reasonable question, mildly answered, "Gone away with Ben, father."

Alas! that little word, Ben, gave occasion to reveal a depth in Roger's fall, which few could have expected to behold so soon. To think that the liberal friend, who only last night had frankly shared his all with him, whose honest glowing heart would freely shed its blood for him, that he in recollection should be greeted with a loathing! Ben would come, and claim some portion of his treasure—he would cry halves—or, who knows? might want all—all: and take it by strong arm, or by threat to 'peach against him:—curse that Burke! he hated him.

Oh, Steady Acton! what has made thee drink and swear? Oh, Honest Roger! what has planted guile, and suspicion, and malice in thy heart? Are these the mere first-fruits of coveting and having? Is this the earliest blessing of that luck which many long for—the finding of a crock of gold?

We would not enlarge upon the scene; a painful one at all times, when man forgets his high prerogative, and drowns his reason in the tankard: but, in a Roger Acton's case, lately so wise, temperate, and patient, peculiarly distressing. Its chief features were these. Grace tasted nothing, but mournfully looked on: once only she attempted to expostulate, but was met—not with fierce oaths, nor coarse chidings, nor even with idiotic drivelling—oh no! worse than that she felt: he replied to her with the maudlin drunken promise, "If she 'd only be a good girl, and let him bide, he 'd give her a big Church-bible, bound in solid gold—that 'ud make the book o' some real value, Grace." Poor broken-hearted daughter—she rushed to her closet in a torrent of tears.

As for Mary Acton, she was miraculously meek and dumb; all the scold was quelled within her; the word "blood" was the Petruchio that tamed that shrew; she could see a plenty of those crimson spots, which might

> "The multitudinous seas incarnadine,
> Making the green, one red,"

dancing in the sun-beams, dotted on the cottage walls, sprinkled as unholy water, over that foul crock. Would not the money be a curse to them any how, say nothing of the danger? If things went on as they began, Mary might indeed have cause for fear: actually, she could not a-bear to look upon the crock; she quite dreaded it, as if it had contained a "bottled devil." So there she sat ever so long—silent, thoughtful, and any thing but comfortable.

What became of Roger until next day at noon, neither he nor I can tell: true, his carcase lay upon the floor, and the two-gallon jar was empty. But, for the real man, who could answer to the name of Roger Actor, the sensitive and conscious soul—that was some where galloping away for fifteen hours in the Paradise of fools: the Paradise? no—the Maëlstrom; tossed about giddily and painfully in one whirl of tumultuous drunkenness.

CHAPTER XVI.

HOW THE HOME WAS BLEST THEREBY.

It will surprise no one to be told that, however truly such an excess may have been the first, it was by no means the last exploit of our altered labourer in the same vein of heroism. Bacchus's was quite close, and he needs must call for his change; he had to call often; drank all quits; changed another sovereign, and was owed again; but, trust him, he wasn't going to be cheated out of that: take care of the pence, and the pounds will take care of themselves. But still it was ditto repeated; changing, being owed, grudging, grumbling: at last he found out the famous new plan of owing himself; and as Bacchus's did not see fit to reject such wealthy customers, Roger soon chalked up a yard-long score, and grew so niggardly that they could not get a penny from him.

It is astonishing how immediately wealth brings in, as its companion, meanness: they walk together, and stand together, and kneel together, as the hectoring, prodigal Faulconbridge, the Bastard Plantagenet in *King John*, does with his white-livered, puny brother, Robert. Wherefore, no sooner was Roger blest with gold, than he resolved not to be such a fool as to lose liberally, or to give away one farthing. To give, I say, for extravagant indulgence is another thing; and it was a fine, proud pleasure to feast a lot of fellows at his sole expense. If meanness is brother to wealth, it is at any rate first cousin to extravagance.

When the dowager collects "her dear five hundred friends" to parade before the fresh young heirs her wax-light lovely daughters—when all is glory, gallopade, and Gunter—when Rubini warbles smallest, and Lablanche is heard as thunder on the stairs—speak, tradesmen, ye who best can tell, the closeness that has catered for that feast; tell it out, ye famished milliners, ground down to sixpence on a ball-dress bill; whisper it, ye footmen, with your wages ever due; let Gath, let Askelon re-echo with the truth, that extortion is the parent of extravagance!

Now, that episode should have been in a foot note; but no one takes the trouble to read notes; and with justice too; for if a man has any thing to say, let him put it in his text, as orderly as may be. And, if order be sometimes out of the question, as seems but clearly suitable at present to our hero's manner of life, it is wise to go boldly on, without so prim an usher; to introduce our thoughts as they reveal themselves, ignorant of "their own degrees," not "standing on the order of their coming," but, as a pit crowd on a benefit-night, bustling over one another, helter-skelter, "in most admired disorder." This will well comport with Roger's daily life: for, notwithstanding the frequent interference of an Amazon wife—regardless of poor, dear Grace's gentle voice and melancholy eyes—in spite of a conscience pricking in his breast, with the spines of a horse-chestnut, that evil crock appeared from the beginning to have been found for but one sole purpose—*videlicet*, that of keeping alight in Roger's brain the fire of mad intoxication. Yes, there were sundry other purposes, too, which may as well be told directly.

The utter dislocation of all home comforts occupied the foremost rank. True—in comparison with the homes of affluence and halls of luxury—those comforts may have formerly seemed few and far between; yet still the angel of domestic peace not seldom found a rest within the cottage. Not seldom? always: if sweet-eyed Grace be such an angel, that ever-abiding guest, full of love, duty, piety, and cheerfulness. But now, after long-enduring anguish, vexed in her righteous soul by the shocking sights and sounds of the drunkard and his parasites (for all the idle vagabonds about soon flocked around rich Acton, and were freely welcome to his reckless prodigality), Grace had been forced to steal away, and seek refuge with a neighbour. Here was one blessing the less.

Another wretched change was in the wife. Granted, Mary Acton had not ever been the pink of politeness, the violet of meekness, nor the rose of entire amiability: but if she were a scold, that scolding was well meant; and her irate energies were incessantly directed towards cleanliness, economy, quiet, and other *notabilia* of a busy house-wife. She did her best to keep the hovel tidy, to make the bravest show with their scanty chattels, to administer discreetly the stores of their frugal larder, and to recompense the good-man returning from his hard day's work, with much of rude joy and bustling kindness. But now, after the first stupor of amazement into which the crock and its consequences threw her, Poll Acton grew to be a fury: she raged and stormed, and well she might, at filth and discomfort in her home, at nauseous dregs and noisome fumes, at the orgie still kept up, day by day, and night by night, through the length of that first foul week, which succeeded the fortunate discovery. And not in vain she raged and stormed—and fought too; for she did fight—ay, and conquered: and miserable Roger, now in full possession of those joys which he had longed for at the casement of Hurstley Hall, was glad to betake himself to the bench at Bacchus's, whither he withdrew his ragged regiment. Thus, that crock had spoilt all there was to spoil in the temper and conduct of the wife.

Look also at the pretty prattling babes, twin boys of two years old, whom Roger used to hasten home to see; who had to say their simple prayers; to be kissed, and comforted, and put to bed; to be made happier by a wild flower picked up on his path, than if the gift had been a coral with gold bells: where were they now? neglected, dirty, fretting in a corner, their red eyes full of wonder at father's altered ways, and their quick minds watching, with astonished looks, the progress of domestic discord. How the crock of gold has nipped those early blossoms as a killing frost!

Again, there used to be, till this sad week of wealth and riotous hilarity, that constantly recurring blessing of the morn and evening prayer which Roger read aloud, and Grace's psalm or chapter; and afterwards the frugal meal—too scanty, perhaps, and coarse—but still refreshing, thank the Lord, and seasoned well with health and appetite; and the heart-felt sense of satisfaction that all around was earned by honest labour; and there was content, and hope of better times, and God's good blessing over every thing.

Now, all these pleasures had departed; gold, unhallowed gold, gotten hastily in the beginning, broadcast on the rank strong soil of a heart that coveted it earnestly, had sprung up as a crop of poisonous tares, and choked the patch of wheat; gold, unhallowed gold, light come, light gone, had scared or killed the flock of unfledged loves that used to nestle in the cotter's thatch, as surely as if the cash were stones, flung wantonly by truants at a dove-cot; and forth from the crock, that egg of wo, had been hatched a red-eyed vulture, to tyrannize in this sad home, where but lately the pelican had dwelt, had spread her fostering wing, and poured out the wealth of her affections.

CHAPTER XVII.

CARE.

But other happy consequences soon became apparent. If Acton in his tipsy state was mad, in his intervals of soberness he was thoroughly miserable. And this, not merely on the score of sickness, exhaustion, prostrated spirits, blue-devils, or other the long catalogue of a drunkard's joys; not merely from a raging wife, and a wretched home; not merely from the stings, however sharp, however barbed, of a conscience ill at ease, that would rise up fiercely like a hissing snake, and strike the black apostate to the earth: these all, doubtless, had their pleasant influences, adding to the lucky finder's bliss: but there was another root of misery most unlooked for, and to the poor who dream of gold, entirely paradoxical.

The possession of that crock was the heaviest of cares. Where on earth was he to hide it? how to keep it safely, secretly? What if he were robbed of it in some sly way! O, thought of utter wo! it made the fortunate possessor quiver like an aspen. Or what, if some one or more of those blustering boon companions were to come by night with a bludgeon and a knife, and—and cut his throat, and find the treasure? or, worse still, were to torture him, set him on the fire like a saucepan (he had heard of Turpin having done so with a rich old woman), and make him tell them "where" in his extremity of pains, and give up all, and then—and then murder him at last, outright, and afterwards burn the hovel over his head, babes and all, that none might live to tell the tale? These fears set him on the rack, and furnished one inciting cause to that uninterrupted orgie; he must be either mad or miserable, this lucky finder.

Also, even in his tipsy state, he could not cast off care: he might in his cups reveal the dangerous secret of having found a crock of gold. A secret still it was: Grace, his wife, and himself, were the only souls who knew it. Dear Grace feared to say a word about the business: not in apprehension of the law, for she never thought of that too probable intrusion on the finder: but simply because her unsophisticated piety believed that God, for some wise end, had allowed the Evil One to tempt her father; she, indeed, did not know the epigram,

> The devil now is wiser than of yore:
> He tempts by making rich—not making poor:

but she did not conceive that notion in her mind; she contrasted the wealthy patriarch Job, tried by poverty and pain, but just and patient in adversity—with the poor labourer Acton, tried by luxury and wealth, and proved to be apostate in prosperity: so she held her tongue, and hitherto had been silent on a matter of so much local wonder as her father's sudden wealth, in the midst of urgent curiosity and extraordinary rumours.

Mary was kept quiet as we know, by superstition of a lower grade, the dread of having money of the murdered, a thought she never breathed to any but her husband; and to poor uninitiated Grace (who had not heard a word of Ben's adventure), her answer about Mrs. Quarles and Mr. Jennings in the dawn of the crock's first blessing, had been entirely unintelligible: Mary, then, said never a word, but looked on dreadingly to see the end.

As for Roger himself, he was too much in apprehension of a landlord's claims, and of a task-master's extortions, to breath a syllable about the business. So he hid his crock as best he could—we shall soon hear how and where—took out sovereign after sovereign day by day, and made his flush of instant wealth a mystery, a miracle, a legacy, good luck, any thing, every thing but the truth: and he would turn fiercely round to the frequent questioner with a "What 's that to you?—Nobody's business but mine:" and then would coaxingly add the implied bribe to secresy, in his accustomed invitation—"And now, what'll you take?"—a magical phrase, which could suffice to quell murmurs for the time, and postponed curiosity to appetite. Thus the fact was still unknown, and weighed on Roger's mind as a guilty concealment, an oppressive secret. What if any found it out?

For immediate safety—the evening after his memorable first fifteen hours of joy—he buried the crock deeply in a hole in his garden, filling all up hard with stones and brick-bats; and when he had smoothed it straight and workmanlike, remembered that he surely hadn't kept out enough to last him; so up it had to come again—five more taken out, and the crock was restored to its unquiet grave.

Scarcely had he done this, than it became dark, and he began to fancy some one might have seen him hide it; those low mean tramps (never before had he refused the wretched wayfarers his sympathy) were always sneaking about, and would come and dig it up in the night: so he went out in the dark and the rain, got at it with infinite trouble and a broken pickaxe, and exultingly brought the crock in-doors; where he buried it a third time, more securely, underneath the grouted floor, close beside the fire in the chimney-corner: it was now nearly midnight, and he went to bed.

Hardly had he tumbled in, after pulling on a nightcap of the flagon, than the dread idea overtook him that his treasure might be melted! Was there ever such a fool as he? Well, well, to think he could fling his purse on the fire! What a horrid thought! Metallurgy was a science quite unknown to Roger; he only considered gold as heavy as lead, and therefore probably as fusible: so down he bustled, made another hole, a deeper one too this time, in the floor under the dresser, where, exhausted with his toil and care, he deposited the crock by four in the morning—and so retired once more.

All in vain—nobody ever knew when Black Burke might be returning from his sporting expeditions—and that beast of a lurcher would be sure to be creeping in this morning, and would scratch it up, and his brute of a master would get it all! This fancy was the worst possible: and Roger rose again, quite sick at heart, pale, worn, and trembling with a miser's haggard joys. Where should he hide that crock—the epithet "cursed" crock escaped him this time in his vexed impatience. In the house and in the garden, it was equally unsafe.

Ha! a bright thought indeed: the hollow in the elm-tree, creaking overhead, just above the second arm: so the poor, shivering wretch, almost unclad, swarmed up that slimy elm, and dropped his treasure in the hollow. Confusion! how deep it was: he never thought of that; here was indeed something too much of safety: and then those boys of neighbour Goode's were birds'-nesting continually, specially round the lake this spring. What an idiot he was not to have remembered this! And up he climbed again, thrust in his arm to the shoulder, and managed to rĕpossess himself a fifth time of that blessed crock.

Would that the elm had been hollow to its root, and beneath the root a chasm bottomless, and that Plutus in that Narbonne jar had served as a supper to Pluto in the shades! Better had it been for thee, my Roger.

But he had not hid it yet; so, that night—or rather that cold morning about six, the drenched, half-frozen Fortunatus carried it to bed with him: and a precious warming-pan it made: for nothing would satisfy the finder of its presence but perpetual bodily contact:—accordingly, he placed it in his bosom, and it chilled him to the back-bone.

Yes; that was undoubtedly the safest way; to carry the spoil about with him; so, next noon—how could he get up till noon after such a woful night?—next noon he emptied the jar, and tying up its contents in a handkerchief, proceeded to wear it as a girdle; for an hour he clattered about the premises, making as much jingle as a wagoner's team of bells; laden heavily with gold, like the ἰβέβυστο genius in Herodotus: but he soon found out this would not do at all; for, independently of all concealment at an end, so long as his secret store was rattling as he walked, louder than military spurs or sabre-tackle, he soberly reflected that he might—possibly, possibly, though not probably—get a glass too much again, by some mere accident or other; and then to be robbed of his golden girdle, this cincture of all joy! O, terrible thought! as well [this is my fancy, not Rogers's] deprive Venus of her zone, and see how the beggared Queen of Beauty could exist without her treasury, the Cestus.

CHAPTER XVIII.

INVESTMENT.

Next day, the wealthy Roger had higher aspirations. Why should not he get interest for his money, like lords and gentlefolk? His gold had been lying idle too long; more fool he: it ought to breed money somehow, he knew that; for, like most poor men whose sole experience of investment is connected with the Lombard's golden balls, he took exalted views of usury. Was he to be "hiding up his talent in a napkin—?"

Ah!—he remembered and applied the holy parable, but it smote across his heart like a flash of frost, a chilling recollection of good things past and gone. What had he been doing with his talents—for he once possessed the ten? had he not squandered piety, purity, and patience? where were now his gratitude to God, his benevolence to man? the father's duteous care, the husband's industry and kindness, the labourer's faith, the Christian's hope—who had spent all these?—Till money's love came in, and money-store to feed it, the poor man had been rich: but now, rotten to the core, by lust of gold, the rich is poor indeed.

However, such considerations did not long afflict him—for we know that lookers-on see more than players—and if Roger had encouraged half our wise and sober thoughts, he might have been a better man: but Roger quelled the thoughts, and silenced them; and thoughts are tender intonations, shy little buzzing sounds, soon scared by coarser noise: Roger had no mind to cherish those small fowls; so they flew back again to Heaven's gate, homeless and uncomforted as weeping peri's.

The bank—the county bank—Shark, Breakem, and Company—this was the specious Eldorado, the genuine gold-increaser, the hive where he would store his wealth (as honey left for the bees in winter), and was to have it soon returned fourfold. It was indeed a thought to make the rich man glad, that all his shining heap was just like a sample of seed-corn, and the pocket-full should next year fill a sack. How grudgingly he now began to mourn over past extravagance, five pieces gone within the week! how close and careful he resolved to be in future! how he would scrape and economize to get and save but one more of those sweet little seeds, that yield more gold—more gold! And if Roger had been privileged in youth to have fed upon the wisdom of the Eton Latin grammar, he could have now quoted with some experimental unction the "*Crescit Amor*" line, which every body well knows how to finish. Truly, it was growing with his growth, and rioting in strength above his weakness.

Swollen with this expanding love, he packed up his money in what were, though he knew it not, ***rouleaux***, but to his plebeian eyes looked more like golden sausages: and he would take it to the bank, and they should bow to him, and Sir him, and give him forthwith more than he had brought; and if those summary gains were middling great—say twice as much, to be moderate—he thought he might afford himself a chaise coming back, and return to Hurstley Common like a nabob. Thus, full of wealthy fancies, after one glass more, off set Roger to the county town, with his treasure in a bundle.

Half-way to it, as hospitality has ordained to be the case wherever there be half-ways, occurred a public-house: and really, notwithstanding all our monied neophyte's economical resolutions, his throat was so "uncommon dry," that he needs must stop there to refresh the muscles of his larynx: so, putting down his bundle on the settle, he called for a foaming tankard, and thanking the crock, as his evil wont now was, sat down to drink and think. Here was prosperity indeed, a flood of astonishing good fortune: that he, but a little week agone, a dirty ditcher—so was he pleased to designate his former self—a ragged wretch, little better than a tramp, should be now progressing like a monarch, with a mighty bag of gold to enrich his county town. To enrich, and be thereby the richer; for Roger's notions of finance were so simple, as to run the risk of being called sublimely indistinct: he took it as an axiom that "money bred money," but in what way to draw forth its generative properties, whether or not by some new-fangled manure, he was entirely ignorant; and it clearly was his wisdom to leave all that mystery of money-making solely to the banker. All he cared about was this: to come back richer than he came—and, lo! how rich he was already. Lolling at high noon, on a Wednesday too, in the extremest mode of rustic beauism, with a bag of gold by his side, and a pot of porter in his hand—here was an accumulation of magnificence—all the prepositions pressed into his service. His wildest hopes exceeded, and almost nothing left to wish. Blown up with the pride and importance of the moment, and some little oblivious from the potent porter—he had paid and sallied forth, and marched a mile upon his way, full of golden fancies, a rich luxurious lord as he was—when all on a sudden the hallucination crossed his dull pellucid mind, that he had left the store behind him! O, pungent terror!—O, most exquisite torture! was it clean gone, stolen, lost, lost, lost for ever? Rushing back in an agony of fear, that made the ruddy hostess think him crazed, with his hair on end, and a face as if it had been white-washed, he flew to the tap-room, and—almost fainted for ecstasy of joy when he found it, where he had laid it, on the settle!

Better had you lost it, Roger; better had your ecstasy been sorrow: there is more trouble yet for you, from that bad crock of gold. But if your lesson is not learnt, and you still think otherwise, go on a little while exultingly as now I see you, and hug the treasure to your heart—the treasure that will bring you yet more misery.

And now the town is gained, the bank approached. What! that big barred, guarded place, looking like a mighty mouse-trap? he didn't half like to venture in. At last he pushed the door ajar, and took a peep;

there were muskets over the mantel-piece, ostentatiously ticketed as "Loaded! Beware!" there were leather buckets ranged around the walls: he did not in any degree like it: was he to expose his treasure in this idiot fashion to all the avowed danger of fire and thieves? However, since he had come so far, he would get some interest for his money, that he would—so he'd just make bold to step to the counter and ask a very obsequious bald-headed gentleman, who sired him quite affably,

"How much, Master, will you be pleased to give me for my gold?"

The gentleman looked queerish, as if he did not comprehend the question, and answered, "Oh! certainly, sir—certainly—we do not object to give you our notes for it," at the same time producing an extremely dirty bundle of worn-out bits of paper.

Roger stroked his chin.

"But, Master, my meaning is, not how many o' them brown bits o' paper you'll sell me for my gold here," and he exhibited a greater store than Mr. Breakem had seen at once upon his counter for a year, "but how much more gold you'll send me back with than what I've brought? by way of interest, you know, or some such law: for I don't know much about the Funds, Master."

"Indeed, sir," replied the civil banker, who wished by any means to catch the clodpole's spoil—"you are very obliging; we shall be glad to allow you two-and-a-half per centum per annum for the deposit you are good enough to leave in our keeping."

"Leave in your keeping, Master! no, I didn't say that! by your leave, I'll keep it myself!"

"In that case, sir, I really do not see how I can do business with you."

True enough; and Roger would never have been such a monetary blockhead, had he not been now so generally tipsy; the fumes of beer had mingled with his plan, and all his usual shrewdness had been blunted into folly by greediness of lucre on the one side, and potent liquors on the other. The moment that the banker's parting speech had reached his ear, the absurdity of Roger's scheme was evident even to himself, and with a bare "Good day, Master," he hurriedly took his bundle from the counter, and scuttled out as quick as he could.

His feelings, walking homeward, were any thing but pleasant; the bubble of his ardent hope was burst: he never could have more than the paltry little sum he carried in that bundle: what a miser he would be of it: how mean it now seemed in his eyes—a mere sample-bag of seed, instead of the wide-waving harvest! Ah, well; he would save and scrape—ay, and go back to toil again—do any thing rather than spend.

Got home, the difficulty now recurred, where was he to hide it? The store was a greater care than ever, now those rascally bankers knew of it. He racked his brain to find a hiding-place, and, at length, really hit upon a good one. He concealed the crock, now replenished with its contents, in the thatch just over his bed's head: it was a rescued darling: so he tore a deep hole, and nested it quite snugly.

Perhaps it did not matter much, but the rain leaked in by that hole all night, and fortunate Roger woke in the morning drenched with wet, and racked by rheumatism.

CHAPTER XIX.

CALUMNY.

More blessings issue from the crock; Pandora's box is set wide open, and all the sweet inhabitants come forth. If apprehensions for its safety made the finder full of care, the increased whisperings of the neighbourhood gave him even deeper reason for anxiety. In vain he told lie upon lie about a legacy of some old uncle in the clouds; in vain he stuck to the foolish and transparent falsehood, with a dogged pertinacity that appealed, not to reason, but to blows; in vain he made affirmation weaker by his oath, and oaths quite unconvincing by his cudgel: no one believed him: and the mystery was rendered more inexplicable from his evidently nervous state and uneasy terror of discovery.

He had resolved at the outset, cunningly as he fancied, to change no more than one piece of gold in the same place; though Bacchus's undoubtedly proved the rule by furnishing an exception: and the consequence came to be, that there was not a single shop in the whole county town, nor a farm-house in all the neighbourhood round, where Roger Acton had not called to change a sovereign. True, the silver had seldom been forthcoming; still, he had asked for it; and where in life could he have got the gold? Many was the rude questioner, whose curiosity had been quenched in drink; many the insufferable pryer, whom club-law had been called upon to silence. Meanwhile, Roger steadily kept on, accumulating silver where he could: for his covetous mind delighted in the mere semblance of an increase to his store, and took some untutored numismatic interest in those pretty variations of his idol—money.

But if Roger's heap increased, so did the whispers and suspicions of the country round; they daily grew louder, and more clamorous; and soon the charitable nature of chagrined wonder assumed a shape more heart-rending to the wretched finder of that golden hoard, than any other care, or fear, or sin, that had hitherto torn him. It only was a miracle that the neighbours had not thought of it before; seldom is the world so unsuspicious; but then honest Roger's forty years of character were something—they could scarcely think the man so base; and, above all, gentle Grace was such a favourite with all, was such a pattern of purity, and kindliness, and female conduct, that the tongue would have blistered to its roots, that had uttered scorn of her till now. As things were, though, could any thing be clearer? Was charity herself to blame in putting one and one together? Sir John was rich, was young, gay, and handsome; but Grace was poor—but indisputably beautiful, and probably had once been innocent: some had seen her going to the Hall at strange times and seasons—for in truth, she often did go there; Jonathan and Sarah Stack, of course, were her dearest friends on earth: and so it came to pass, that, through the blessing of the crock, honest Roger was believed to live on the golden wages of his daughter's shame! Oh, coarse and heartless imputation! Oh, bitter price to pay for secresy and wonderful good fortune! In vain the wretched father stormed, and swore, and knocked down more than one foul-spoken fellow that had breathed against dear Grace. None but credited the lie, and many envious wretches actually gloried in the scandal; I grieve to say that women—divers venerable virgins—rejoiced that this pert hussey was at last found out; she was too pretty to be good, too pious to be pure; now at length they were revenged upon her beauty; now they had their triumph over one that was righteous over-much. For other people, they would urge the reasonable question, how else came Roger by the cash? and getting no answer, or worse than none—a prevaricating, mystifying mere put-off—they had hardly an alternative in common exercise of judgment: therefore, "Shame on her," said the neighbours, "and the bitterest shame on him:" and the gaffers and grand-dames shook their heads virtuously.

Yet worse: there was another suggestion, by no means contradictory, though simultaneous: what had become of Tom? ay—that bold young fellow—Thomas Acton, Ben Burke's friend: why was he away so long, hiding out of the country? they wondered.

The suspected Damon and Pythias had gone a county off to certain fens, and were, during this important week, engaged in a long process of ensnaring ducks.

Old Gaffer White had muttered something to Gossip Heartley, which Dick the Tanner overheard, wherein Tom Acton and a gun, and Burke, and burglary, and throats cut, and bags of gold, were conspicuous ingredients: so that Roger Acton's own dear Tom, that eagle-eyed and handsome better image of himself, stood accused, before his quailing father's face, of robbery and murder.

Both—both darlings, dead Annie's little orphaned pets, thus stricken by one stone to infamy! Grace, scouted as a hussey, an outcast, a bad girl, a wanton—blessed angel! Thomas—generous boy—keenly looked for, in his near return, to be seized by rude hands, manacled, and dragged away, and tried on suspicion as a felon—for what? that crock of gold. Yet Roger heard it all, knew it all, writhed at it all, as if scorpions were lashing him; but still he held on grimly, keeping that bad secret. Should he blab it out, and so be poor again, and lose the crock?

That our labourer's changed estate influenced his bodily health, under this accumulated misery and desperate excitement, began to be made manifest to all. The sturdy husbandman was transformed into a tremulous drunkard; the contented cottager, into a querulous hypochondriac; the calm, religious, patient Christian, into a tumultuous blasphemer. Could all this be, and even Roger's iron frame stand up against the battle! No, the strength of Samson has been shorn. The crock has poured a blessing on its finder's very skin, as when the devil covered Job with boils.

CHAPTER XX.

THE BAILIFF'S VISIT.

One day at noon, ere the first week well was over since the fortunate discovery of gold, as Roger lay upon his bed, recovering from an overnight's excess, tossed with fever, vexation, and anxiety, he was at once surprised and frightened by a visit from no less a personage than Mr. Simon Jennings. And this was the occasion of his presence:

Directly the gathering storm of rumours had collected to that focus of all calumny, the destruction of female character and murder charged upon the innocent, Grace Acton had resolved upon her course; secresy could be kept no longer; her duty now appeared to be, to publish the story of her father's lucky find.

Grace, we may observe, had never been bound to silence, but only imposed it on herself from motives of tenderness to one, whom she believed to be taken in the toils of a temptation. She, simple soul, knew nothing of manorial rights, nor wotted she that any could despoil her father of his money; but even if such thoughts had ever crossed her mind, she loathed the gold that had brought so much trouble on them all, and cared not how soon it was got rid of. Her father's health, honour, happiness, were obviously at stake; perhaps, also, her brother's very life: and, as for herself, the martyr of calumny looked piously to heaven, offered up her outraged heart, and resolved to stem this torrent of misfortune. Accordingly, with a noble indignation worthy of her, she had gone straightway to the Hall, to see the baronet, to tell the truth, fling aside a charge which she could scarcely comprehend, and openly vindicate her offended honour. She failed—many imagine happily for her own peace, if Sir John had not been better than his friends—in gaining access to the Lord of Hurstley; but she did see Mr. Jennings, who serenely interposed, and listened to all she came to say—"her father had been unfortunate enough to find a crock of money on the lake side near his garden."

When Jennings heard the tale, he started as if stung by a wasp: and urging Grace to tell it no one else (though the poor girl "must," she said, "for honour's sake"), he took up his hat, and ran off breathlessly to Acton's cottage. Roger was at home, in bed, and sick; there was no escape; and Simon chuckled at the lucky chance. So he crept in, carefully shut the door, put his finger on his lips to hush Roger's note of admiration at so little wished a vision; and then, with one of his accustomed scared and fearful looks behind him, muttered under his breath,

"Man, that gold is mine: I have paid its price to the uttermost; give me the honey-pot."

Roger's first answer was a vulgar oath; but his tipsy courage faded soon away before old habits of subserviency, and he faltered out,

"I—I—Muster Jennings! I've got no pot of gold!"

"Man, you lie! you have got the money! give it me at once—and—" he added in a low, hoarse voice, "we will not say a word about the murder."

"Murder!" echoed the astonished man.

"Ay, murder, Acton:—off! off, I say!" he muttered parenthetically, then wrestled for a minute violently, as with something in the air; and recovering as from a spasm, calmly added,

"Ay, murder for the money."

"I—I!" gasped Roger; "I did no murder, Muster Jennings!"

A new light seemed to break upon the bailiff, and he answered with a tone of fixed determination,

"Acton, you are the murderer of Bridget Quarles."

Roger's jaw dropped, dismay was painted on his features, and certainly he did look guilty enough. But Simon proceeded in a tenderer tone;

"Notwithstanding, give me the gold, Acton, and none shall know a word about the murder. We will keep all quiet, Roger Acton, all nice and quiet, you know;" and he added, coaxingly, "come, Roger, give me up this crock of gold."

"Never!" with a fierce anathema, answered our hero, now himself again: the horrid accusation had entranced him for a while, but this coaxing strain roused up all the man in him: "Never!" and another oath confirmed it.

"Acton, give it up, I say!" was shouted in rejoinder, and Jennings glared over him with his round and staring eyes as he lay faint upon his bed—"Give up the crock, or else—"

"Else what? you whitened villain."

The bailiff flung himself at Roger's neck, and almost shrieked, "I'll serve you as I—"

There was a tremendous struggle; attacked at unawares, for the moment he was nearly mastered; but Acton's tall and wiry frame soon overpowered the excited Jennings, and long before you have read what I have written—he has leaped out of bed—seized—doubled up—and flung the battered bailiff headlong down the narrow stair-case to the bottom. This done, Roger, looking like Don Quixote de la Mancha in his penitential shirt, mounted into bed again, and quietly lay down; wondering, half-sober, at the strange and sudden squall.

CHAPTER XXI.

THE CAPTURE.

He had not long to wonder. Jennings got up instantly, despite of bruises, posted to the Hall, took a search-warrant from Sir John's study, (they were always ready signed, and Jennings filled one up,) and returned with a brace of constables to search the cottage.

Then Roger, as he lay musing, fancied he heard men's voices below, and his wife, who had just come in, talking to them; what could they want? tramps, perhaps: or Ben? he shuddered at the possibility; with Tom too; and he felt ashamed to meet his son. So he turned his face to the wall, and lay musing on—he hadn't been drinking too much over-night—Oh, no! it was sickness, and rheumatics, and care about the crock; Tom should be told that he was very ill, poor father! Just as he had planned this, and resolved to keep his secret from that poaching ruffian Burke, some one came creeping up the stairs, slided in at the door, and said to him in a deep whisper from the further end of the room,

"Acton, give me the gold, and the men shall go away; it is not yet too late; tell me where to find the crock of gold."

An oath was the reply; and, at a sign from Jennings, up came the other two.

"We have searched every where, Mr. Simon Jennings, both cot and garden; ground disturbed in two or three places, but nothing under it; in-doors too, the floor is broken by the hearth and by the dresser, but no signs of any thing there: now, Master Acton, tell us where it is, man, and save us all the trouble."

Roger's newly-learnt vocabulary of oaths was drawn upon again.

"Did you look in the ash-pit?" asked Jennings.

"No, sir."

"Well, while you two search this chamber, I will examine it myself."

Mr. Jennings apparently entertained a wholesome fear of Acton's powers of wrestling.

Up came Simon in a hurry back again, with a lot of little empty leather bags he had raked out, and—the fragment of a shawl! the edges burnt, it was a corner bit, and marked B. Q.

"What do you call this, sir?" asked the exulting bailiff.

7*

"Curse that Burke!"—thought Roger; but he said nothing.

And the two men up stairs had searched, and pried, and hunted every where in vain; the knotty mattress had been ripped up, the chimney scrutinized, the floor examined, the bed-clothes overhauled, and as for the thatch, if it hadn't been for Roger Acton's constant glance upwards at his treasure in the roof, I am sure they never would have found it. But they did at last: there it was, the crock of gold, full proof of robbery and murder!

"Aha!" said Simon, in a complacent triumph, "Mrs. Quarles's identical honey-pot, full of her clean bright gold, and many pieces still encased in those tidy leather bags;" and his round eyes glistened again; but all at once, with a hurried look over his left shoulder, he exclaimed, involuntarily, in a very different tone, "Ha! away, I say!—" Then he snatched the crock up eagerly, and nursed it like a child.

"Come along with us, Master Acton, you're wanted somewhere else; up, man, look alive, will you?"

And Roger dressed himself mechanically. It was no manner of use, not in the least worth while resisting, innocent though he was; his treasure had been found, and taken from him; he had nothing more to live for; his gold was gone—his god; where was the wisdom of fighting for any thing else; let them take him to prison if they would, to the jail, to the gallows, to any-whither, now his gold was gone. So he put on his clothes without a murmur, and went with them as quiet as a lamb.

Never was there a clearer case; the housekeeper's hoard had been found in his possession, with a fragment of her shawl; and Sir John Vincent was very well aware of the mystery attending the old woman's death; besides, he was in a great hurry to be off; for Pointer, and Silliphant, and Lord George Pypp, were to have a hurdle race with him that day, for a heavy bet; so he really had not time to go deep into the matter; and the result of five minutes' talk before the magisterial chairs (Squire Ryle having been summoned to assist) was, that, on the accusation of Simon Jennings, Roger Acton was fully committed to the county jail, to be tried at next assizes, for Bridget Quarles's murder.

Thank God! poor Roger, it has come to this. What other way than this was there to save thee from thy sin—to raise thee from thy fall? Where else, but in a prison, could you get the silent, solitary hours leading you again to wholesome thought and deep repentance? Where else could you escapè the companionship of all those loose and low associates, sottish brawlers, ignorant and sensual unbelievers, vagabond radicals, and other lewd fellows of the baser sort, that had drank themselves drunk at your expense, and sworn to you as captain! The place, the time, the means for penitence are here. The crisis of thy destiny is come.

Honest Roger, Steady Acton, did I not see thy guardian angel—after all his many tears, aggrieved and broken spirit!—did I not see him lift his swollen eyes in gratitude to Heaven, and benevolence to thee, and smile a smile of hopeful joy when that damned crock was found?

Gladly could he thank his Lord, to behold the temptation at an end.

Did I not see the devil slink away from thee abashed, issuing like an adder from thy heart, and then, with a sudden Protean change, driven from thy hovel as a thunder-cloud dispersing, when Simon Jennings seized the jar, hugged it as his household-god—and took it home with him—and counted out the gold—and locked the bloody treasure in his iron-chest?

Fitly did the murderer lock up curses with his spoil.

And when God smote thine idol, dashing Dagon to the ground, and thy heart was sore with disappointment, and tender as a peeled fig—when hope was dead for earth, and conscience dared not look beyond it—ah! Roger, did I judge amiss when I saw, or thought I saw, those eyes full of humble shame, those lips quivering with remorseful sorrow?

We will leave thee in the cold stone cell—with thy well-named angel Grace to comfort thee, and pray with thee, and help thee back to God again, and so repay the debt that a daughter owes her father.

Happy prison! where the air is sweetened by the frankincense of piety, and the pavement gemmed with the flowers of hope, and the ceiling arched with Heaven's bow of mercy, and the walls hung around with the dewy drapery of penitence!

Happy prison! where the talents that were lost are being found again, gathered in humility from this stone floor; where poor-making riches are banished from the postern, and rich-making poverty streameth in as light from the grated window; where care vexeth not now the labourer emptied of his gold, and calumny's black tooth no longer gnaws the heart-strings of the innocent.

Hark! it is the turnkey, coming round to leave the pittance for the day: he is bringing in something in an earthern jar. Speak, Roger Acton, which will you choose, man—a prisoner's mess of pottage—or a crock of gold?

CHAPTER XXII.

THE AUNT AND HER NEPHEW.

WHILE we leave Roger Acton in the jail, waiting for the very near assizes, and wearing every hour away in penitence and prayer, it will be needful to our story that we take a retrospective glance at certain events, of no slight importance.

I must now speak of things, of which there is no human witness; recording words, and deeds, whereof Heaven alone is cognizant, Heaven alone—and Hell! For there are secret matters, which the murdered cannot tell us, and the murderer dare not—let him confess as fully as he will. Therefore, with some omnipresent sense, some invisible ubiquity, I must note down scenes as they occurred, whether mortal eye has witnessed them or not; I must lay bare secret thoughts, unlatch the hidden chambers of the heart, and duly set out, as they successively arose, the idea which tongue had not embodied, the feeling which no action had expressed.

Hitherto, we have pretty well preserved inviolate the three grand unities—time, place, circumstance; and even now we do not sin against the first and chiefest, however we may seem so to sin; for, had it suited my purpose to have begun with the beginning, and to have placed the present revelations foremost, the strictest stickler for the unities would have only had to praise my orthodox adherence to them. As it is, I have chosen, for interest sake, to shuffle my cards a little; and two knaves happen to have turned up together just at this time and place. The time is just three weeks ago—a week before the baronet came of age, and a fortnight antecedent to the finding of the crock; which, as we know, after blessing Roger for a se'nnight, has at last left him in jail. The place is the cozy house-keepers room at Hurstley: and the brace of thorough knaves, to enact then and there as *dramatis personæ*, includes Mistress Bridget Quarles, a fat, sturdy, bluffy, old woman, of a jolly laugh withal, and a noisy tongue—and our esteemed acquaintance Mister Simon Jennings. The aunt, house-keeper, had invited the nephew, butler, to take a dish of tea with her, and rum-punch had now succeeded the souchong.

"Well, Aunt Quarles, is it your meaning to undertake a new master?"

"Don't know, nephy—can't say yet what he 'll be like: if he 'll leave us as we are, won't say wont."

"Ay, as we are, indeed; comfortable quarters, and some little to put by, too: a pretty penny you will have laid up all this while, I 'll be bound: I wager you now it is a good five hundred, aunt—come, done for a shilling."

"Get along, foolish boy; a'n't you o' the tribe o' wisdom too—ha, ha, ha!"

"I will not say," smirked Simon, "that my nest has not a feather."

"It 's easy work for us, Nep; we hunt in couples: you the men, and I the maids—ha, ha!"

"Tush, Aunt Bridget! that speech is not quite gallant, I fear." And the worshipful extortioners giggled jovially.

"But it's true enough for all that, Simon: how d'ye manage it, eh, boy? much like me, I s'pose; wages every quarter from the maids, dues from tradesmen Christmas-tide and Easter, regular as Parson Evans's; pretty little bits tacked on weekly to the bills, beside presents from every body; and so, boy, my poor forty pounds a-year soon mounts up to a hundred."

"Ay, ay, Aunt Bridget—but I get the start of you, though you probably were born a week before-hand: talk of parsons, look at me, a regular grand pluralist monopolist, as any bishop can be; butler in doors, bailiff out of doors, land-steward, house-steward, cellar-man, and paymaster. I am not all this for naught, Aunt Quarles: if so much goes through my fingers, it is but fair that something stick."

"True, Simon—O certainly; but if you come to boasting, my boy, I don't carry this big bunch o' keys for nothing neither. Lord love you! why merely for cribbings in the linen-line for one month, John Draper swapped me that there shawl: none o' my clothes ever cost me a penny, and I a'n't quite as bare as a new-born baby neither. Look at them trunks, bless you!"

"Ay, ay, aunt, I'll be bound the printer of your prayer-book has left out a 'not,' before the 'steal,' eh?—ha! ha!"

"Fie, naughty Simon, fie! them 's not stealings, them 's parquisites. Where 's the good o' living in a great house else? But come, Si, haven't you struck out the 'not,' for yourself, though the printer did his duty, eh, Nep?"

"Not a bit, aunt—not a bit: all sheer honesty and industry. Look at my pretty little truck-shop down the village. Wo betide the labourer that leaves off dealing there! not one that works at Hurstley, but eats my bread and bacon; besides the 'tea, coffee, tobacco, and snuff.'"

"Pretty fairish articles, eh? I never dealt with you, Si: no, Nep, no—you never saw the colour o' my money."

Jennings gave a start, as if a thought had pricked him; but gayly recovering himself, said,

"Oh, as to pretty fairish, I know there is one thing about the bacon good enough; ay, and the bread too—the very best of prices; ha! ha! is not that good? And for the other genuine articles, I don't know that much of the tea comes from China—and the coffee is sold ground, because it is burnt maize—and there's a plenty of wholesome cabbage leaf cut up in the tobacco—while as for snuff, I give them a dry, peppery, choky, sneezy dust, and I dare say that it does its duty."

It was astonishing how innocently the worthy couple laughed together.

"My only trouble, Aunt Quarles, is where to keep my gains—what to do with them. I am quite driven to the strong-box system, interest is so bad; and as to speculations, they are nervous things, and sicken one. I invest in the Great Western one day—a tunnel falls in, so I sell my shares the next, and send the proceeds to Australia; then, looking at the map, I see the island isn't clean chalked out all round, and beginning to fear that the sea will get in where it a'n't made water-tight by the Admiralty, I call the money home again. You see I don't know what to do with gold when I get it. Where do you keep yours now, aunt, I wonder?"

"O, Nep, never mind me; you rattle on so I can't get in never a word. I'll only tell you where I don't keep it. Not at Breakem's bank, for they're brewers, and hosiers, and chandlers, and horse-dealers—ay, and swindlers too, the whole 'company' on 'em; not in mortgages, for I hate the very smell of a lawyer, with all his pounce and parchment; not in Gover'me't 'nuities, for I'm an old 'ooman, boy; and not in the Three per Cents, nor any other per cents, for I've sense enough to know that my highest interest lies in counting out, as my first principle is dropping in." And the fat female laughed herself purple at the venerable joke.

Simon was a courtier, and laughed too, as immoderately as possible.

"Ah! I dare say now you have got a Chubb's patent somewhere full of gold?" he asked somewhat anxiously; "take your punch, aunt, wont you? I do not see you drink."

"Simon, mark me; fools who want to be robbed put their money into an iron chest, that thieves may know exactly where to find it; they might as well ticket it 'cash,' and advertise to Newgate—come and steal. I know a little better than to be such a fool."

"Yes, certainly—I dare say now you keep it in your work-box, or sew it up in your stays, or hide it in the mattress, or in an old tea-pot, maybe." And Jennings eyed her narrowly.

"Nephew, what rhymes to money?"

"Money?—Well I can't say I am a poet—stony, perhaps. At least," added the benevolent individual, "when I have raised a wretch's rent to gain a little more by him, stony is not a bad shield to lift against prayers, and tears, and orphans, and widows, and starvation, and all such nonsense."

"Not bad, neither, Nep: but there's a better rhyme than that."

"You cannot mean honey, aunt? when I guessed stony, I thought you might have some snug little cash cellar under the flags. But honey? are you such a thorough Mrs. Rundle as to pickle and preserve your very guineas, the same as you do strawberries or apricots in syrup?"

"Oh, you clever little fool! how prettily you do talk on: your tongue's as tidy as your cash-book: when you've any money to put by, come to Aunt Bridget for a crock to hide it in: mayn't one use a honey-pot, as Teddy Rourke would say, barring the honey?"

"Ha! and so you hide the hoard up there, aunt, eh? along with the preserves in a honey-pot, do you?"

"We'll see—we'll see, some o' these long days; not that the money's to be yours, Nep—you're rich enough, and don't want it; there's your poor sister Scott with her fourteen children, and Aunt Bridget must give her a lift in life: she was a good niece to me, Simon, and never left my side before she married: maybe she'll have cause to bless the dead."

Jennings hardly spoke a word more; but drained his glass in silence, got up a sudden stomach-ache, and wished his aunt good-night.

CHAPTER XXIII.

SCHEMES.

We must follow Simon Jennings to his room. He felt keenly disappointed. Money was the idol of his heart, as it is of many million others. He had robbed, lied, extorted, tyrannized; he had earned scorn, ill-report, and hatred; nay, he had even diligently gone to work, and lost his own self-love and self-respect in the service of his darling idol. He was at once, for lucre's sake, the mean, cringing fawner, and the pitiless, iron despot; to the rich he could play supple parasite, while the poor man only knew him as an unrelenting persecutor; with the good, and they were chiefly of the fairer, softer sex, he walked in meekness, the spiritual hypocrite; the while, it was his boast to over-reach the worst in low duplicity and crooked dealing. All this he was for gold. When the eye of the world was on him, and intuition warned him of the times, he was ever the serene, the correct, with a smooth tongue and an oily smile; but in the privacy of some poor hovel, where his debtor sued for indulgence, or some victim of his passions (he had more depravities than one) threw her wretched self upon his pity, then could Simon Jennings lash sternness into rage, and heat his brazen heart with the embers of inveterate malice. It was as if the serpent, that voluble, insinuating reptile, which had power to fascinate poor Eve, turned to rend her when she had fallen, erect, with flashing eyes, and bristling crest, with venomed fangs, and hissing. Behold, snake-worshippers of Mexico, the prototype of your grim idol, in Mammon's model slave and specimen disciple!

Such a man was Simon Jennings, a soul given up to gold—exclusively to gold; for although, as we have hinted, and as hereafter may appear, he could sell himself at times to other sins, still these were but as stars in his evil firmament, while covetousness ruled it like the sun; or, if the beauteous stars and blessed sun be an image too hallowed for his wickedness, we may find a fitter in some stagnant pool, where the pestilential vapour over all is Mammonism, and the dull, fat weeds that rot beneath, are pride, craftiness, and lechery. In fact, to speak of passions in a heart such as his, were a palpable misnomer; all was reduced to calculation; his rage was fostered to intimidate, and where the wretch seemed kinder, his kindnesses were aimed at power, as an object, rather than at pleasure—the power to obtain more gold.

For it is a dreadful truth (which I would not dare to utter if such crimes had never been), that a reprobate of the bailiff Jennings's stamp may, by debts, or fines, or kind usurious loans, entrap a beggared creature in his toils; and then lyingly propose remission at the secret sacrifice of honour, in some one, over whom that dastard beggar has control; and having this point gained, the seducer is quite capable of using, for still more extortion, the power which a threatening of exposure gives, when the criminally weak has stooped to sin, on promises of silence and delivery from ruin. I wish there may be no poor yeoman in this broad land, of honourable name withal, he and his progenitors for ages, who can tell the tale of his own base fears, a creditor's exactions, and some dependant victim's degradation: some orphaned niece, some friendless ward, immolated in her earliest youth at the shrine of black-hearted Mammon; I wish there may be no sleek middle-man guilty of the crimes here charged upon Simon Jennings.

This worthy, then, had been introduced at Hurstley by his aunt, Mrs. Quarles, on the occurrence of a death vacancy in the lad-of-all-work department, during the long ungoverned space of young Sir John's minority. As the precious "lad" grew older, and divers in-door potentates died off, the house-keeper had power to push her nephew on to page-ship, footmanship, and divers other similar crafts, even to the final post of butler; while his own endeavours, backed by his aunt's interest, managed to secure for him the rule out of doors no less than in, and the closest possible access to guardians and landlords, to the tenants—and their rent.

Now, the amiable Mrs. Quarles had contrived the elevation of her nephew, and connived at his monopolies, mainly to fit in cleverly with her own worldly weal; for it would never have done to have risked the loss of innumerable perquisites, and other peculations, by the possible advent of an honest butler. But, while the worshipful Simon, to do him only justice, fully answered Mrs. Bridget's purpose, and even added much to her emoluments; still he was no mere derivative scion, but an independent plant, and entertained views of his own. He had his own designs, and laid himself out to entrap his aunt's affections; or rather, for I cannot say he greatly valued these, to secure her good graces, and worm himself within the gilded clauses of her will; she was an old woman, rolling in gold, no doubt had a will; and as for himself, he was younger by five-and-thirty years, so he could afford to wait a little, before trying on her shoes. The petty schemes of thievery and cheating, which he in his Quotem capacities had practised, were to his eyes but as driblets of wealth in comparison with the mighty stream of his old aunt's savings. Not that he had done amiss, trust him! but then he knew the amount of his own hoard to a farthing, while of hers he was entirely ignorant; so, on the principle of '*omne ignotum pro mirifico,*' he pondered on its vastness with indefinite amazement, although probably it might not reach the quarter of his own. For it should in common charity be stated, that, with all her hiding and hiving propensities, Mrs. Quarles, however usually a screw, was by fits and starts an extravagant woman, and besides spending on herself, had occasionally helped her own kith and kin; poor niece Scott, in particular, had unconsciously come in for many pleasant pilferings, and had to thank her good aunt for innumerable filched groceries, and hosieries, and other largesses, which (the latter in especial) really had contributed, with sundry other more self-indulgent expenses, to make no small havoc of the store.

Still, this store was Simon's one main chance, the chief prize in his hope's lottery; and it was with a pang, indeed, that he found all his endeavours to compass its possession had been vain. Was that endless cribbage nothing, and the weary Bible-lessons on a Sunday, and the constant fetchings and carryings, and the forced smiles, sham congratulations, and other hypocritical affections—fearing for his dear aunt's dropsy, and inquiring so much about her bunions—was all this dull servitude to meet with no reward? With none? worse than none! Fool that he was! had he schemed, and plotted, and flattered, and cozened—ay, and given away many pretty little presents, lost decoys, that had cost hard money, all for nothing—less than nothing—to be laughed at and postponed to his Methodist sister Scott? The impudence of deliberately telling him he "didn't want it, and was rich enough!" as if "enough" could ever be good grammar after such a monosyllable as "rich;" and "want it" indeed! of course he wanted it; if not, why had he slaved so many years? want it, indeed! if to hope by day, and to dream by night—if to leave no means untried of delicately showing how he longed for it—if to grow sick with care, and thin with coveting—if this were to want the gold, good sooth, he wanted it. Don't tell him of starving brats, his own very bowels pined for it; don't thrust in his face the necessities of others—the necessity is his; he must have it—he will have it—talk of necessity!

Wait a bit: is there no way of managing some better end to all this? no mode of giving the right turn to that wheel of fortune, round which his cares and calculations have been hovering so long? Is there no conceivable method of possessing that vast hoard?

Bless me! how huge it must be! and Simon turned whiter at the thought: only add up Mother Quarles's income for fifty-five years: she is seventy-five at least, and came here a girl of twenty. Simon's hair stood on end, and his heart went like a mill-clapper, as he mentally figured out the sum.

Is there no possibility of contriving matters so that I may be the architect of my own good luck, and no thanks at all to the old witch there? Dear—what a glorious fancy—let me think a little. Cannot I get at the huge hoard some how?

CHAPTER XXIV.

THE DEVIL'S COUNSEL.

"Steal it," said the Devil.

Simon was all of a twitter; for though he fancied his own heart said it, still his ear-drum rattled, as if somebody had spoken.

Simon—that ear-drum was to put you off your guard: the deaf can hear the devil: he needs no tympanum to commune with the spirit: listen again, Simon; your own thoughts echo every word.

"Steal it: hide in her room; you know she has a shower-bath there, which nobody has used for years, standing in a corner; two or three cloaks in it, nothing else: it locks inside, how lucky! ensconce yourself there, watch the old woman to sleep—what a fat heavy sleeper she is!—quietly take her keys, and steal the store: remember, it is a honey-pot. Nothing's easier—or safer. Who'd suspect you?"

"Splendid! and as good as done," triumphantly exclaimed the nephew, snapping his fingers, and prancing with glee;—"a glorious fancy! bless my lucky star!"

If there be a planet Lucifer, that was Simon's lucky star.

And so, Mrs Quarles the biter is going to be bit, eh? It generally is so in this world's government. You, who brought in your estimable nephew to aid and abet in your own dishonest ways, are, it seems, going to be robbed of all your knavish gains by him. This is taking the wise in their own craftiness, I reckon: and richly you deserve to lose all your ill-got hoard. At the same time, Mrs. Quarles—I will be just—there are worse people in the world than you are: in comparison with your nephew, I consider you a grosser kind of angel; and I really hope no harm may befall your old bones beyond the loss of your money. However, if you are to lose this, it is my wish that poor Mrs. Scott, or some other honest body, may get it, and not Simon; or rather, I should not object that he may get it first, and get hung for getting it, too, before the sister has the hoard.

Our friend, Simon Jennings, could not sleep that night; his reveries and scheming lasted from the rum-punch's final drop, at ten P. M., to circiter two A. M., and then, or thenabouts, the devil hinted "steal it;" and so, not till nearly four, he began to shut his eyes, and dream again, as his usual fashion was, of adding up receipts in five figures, and of counting out old Bridget's hoarded gold.

Next day, notwithstanding nocturnal semi-sleeplessness, he awoke as brisk as a bee, got up in as exhilarated a state as any gas-balloon, and was thought to be either surprisingly in spirits, or spirits surprisingly in him; none knew which, "where each seemed either." That whole day long, he did the awkwardest things, and acted in the most absent manner possible; Jonathan thought Mr. Simon was beside himself; Sarah Stack, foolish thing! said he was in love, and was observed *to look in the glass* several times herself; other people did not know what to think—it was quite a mystery. To recount only a few of his unprecedented exploits on that day of anticipative bliss:

First, he asked the porter how his gout was, and gave him a thimble-full of whiskey from his private store.

Secondly, he paid Widow Soper one whole week's washing in full, without the smallest deduction or per centage.

Thirdly, he ordered of Richard Buckle, commonly called Dick the Tanner, a lot of cart harness, without haggling for price, or even asking it.

And, fourthly, he presented old George White, who was coming round with a subscription paper for a dead pig—actually, he presented old Gaffer White with the sum of two-pence out of his own pocket! never was such careless prodigality.

But the little world of Hurstley did not know what we know. They possessed no clue to the secret happiness wherewithal Simon Jennings hugged himself; they had no inkling of the crock of gold; they thought not he was going to be suddenly so rich; they saw no cause, as we do, why he should feel to be like a great heir on the eve of his majority; they wotted not that Sir John Devereux Vincent, Baronet, had scarcely more agreeable or triumphant feelings when his clock struck twenty-one, than Simon Jennings, butler, as the hour of his hope drew nigh.

If a destiny like this man's can ever have a crisis, the hour of his hope is that; but downward still, into a lower gulf, has been continually his bad career; there is (unless a miracle intervene) no stopping in the slope on which he glides, albeit there may be precipices. He that rushes in his sledge down the artificial ice-hills of St. Petersburgh, skims along not more swiftly than Jennings, from the altitude of infant innocence, had sheered into the depths of full-grown depravity; but even he can fall, and reach, with startling suddenness, a lower deep.

As if that Russian mountain, hewn asunder midway, were fitted flush to a Norwegian cliff, beetling precipitately over the whirlpool; then tilt the sledge with its furred inmate over the slope, let it skim with quicker impetus the smoking ice, let it touch that beetling edge, and, leaping from the tangent, let it dart through the air, let it strike the eddying waters, be sucked hurriedly down that hoarse black throat, wind among the roots of the everlasting hills, and split upon the loadstone of the centre.

Even such a fate, "down, down to hell," will come to Simon Jennings; wrapped in the furs of complacency, seated in the sledge of covetousness, a-down the slippery launch of well-worn evil habit—over the precipice of crime—into the billows of impenitent remorse—to be swallowed by the vortex of Gehenna!

CHAPTER XXV.

THE AMBUSCADE.

NIGHT came, and with it all black thoughts. Not that they were black at once, any more than darkness leaps upon the back of noon, without the intervening cloak of twilight. Oh dear, no! Simon's thoughts accommodated themselves fitly to the time of day. They had been, for him, at early morning, pretty middling white, that is whity-brown; thence they passed, with the passing hour kindly, through the shades of burnt sienna, raw umber, and bistre; until, just as we may notice in the case of marking-ink; that which, five minutes ago, was as water only delicately dirtied, has become a fixed and indelible black.

Simon was resolved upon the spoil, come what might; although his waking sensations of buoyancy, his noon-day cogitations of a calmer kind, and his even-tide determined scheming, had now given way to a nervous and unpleasant trepidation. So he poured spirits down to keep his spirits up. Very early after dark, he had watched his opportunity while Mrs. Quarles was scolding in the kitchen, had slipped shoeless and unperceived, from his pantry into the housekeeper's room, and locked himself securely in the shower bath. Hapless wight! it was very little after six yet, and there he must stand till twelve or so: his foresight had not calculated this, and the devil had already begun to cheat him. But he would go through with it now; no flinching, though his rabbit back is breaking with fatigue, and his knocked knees totter with exhaustion, and his haggard eyes swim dizzily, and his bad heart is failing him for fear.

Yes, fear, and with good reason too for fear; "nothing easier, nothing safer," said his black adviser; how easily for bodily pains, how safely for chances of detection, was he getting at the promised crock of gold!

Mr. Jennings! Mr. Simon! where in the world was Mr. Jennings?" nobody knew; he must have gone out somewhere. Strange, too—and left his hat and great-coat.

Here 's a general for an ambuscade; Oh, Simon, Simon! you have had the whole day to think of it—how is it that both you and your dark friend overlooked in your calculations the certainty of search, and the chance of a discovery? The veriest school-boy, when he hid himself, would hide his hat. I am half afraid that you are in that demented state, which befits the wretch ordained to perish.

But where is Mr. Jennings? that was the continued cry for four agonizing hours of dread and difficulty. Sarah, the still-room maid, was sitting at her work, unluckily in Mrs. Quarles's room; she had come in shortly after Simon's secret entry; there she sat, and he dared not stir. And they looked every where—except in the right place; to do the devil justice, it was a capital hiding-corner that; rooms, closets, passages, cellars, out-houses, gardens, lofts, tenements, and all the "general words," in a voluminous conveyance, were searched and searched in vain; more than one groom expected (hoped is a truer word) to find Mr. Jennings hanging by a halter from the stable-lamp; more than one exhilarated labourer, hastily summoned for the search, was sounding the waters with a rake and rope, in no slight excitement at the thought of fishing up a deceased bailiff.

It was a terrible time for the ensconced one: sometimes he thought of coming out, and treating the affair as a bit of pleasantry: but then the devil had taken off his shoes—as a Glascow captain deals with his cargo of refractory Irishers; how could he explain that? his abominable old aunt was shrewd, and he knew how clearly she would guess at the truth; if he desired to make sure of losing every chance, he could come out now, and reveal himself; but if he nourished still the hope of counting out that crock of gold, he 'll bide where he is, and trust to—to—to fate. The wretch had "Providence" on his blistered tongue.

If, under the circumstances, any thing could be added to Simon's gratification, such pleasing addition was afforded in overhearing, as Lord

Brougham did, the effect which his rumoured death produced on the minds of those who best had known him. It so happened, Sarah was sick, and did not join the universal hunt; accordingly, being the only audience, divers ambassadors came to tell her constantly the same most welcome news, that Jennings had not yet been found.

"Lawk, Sally," said a helper, "what a blessing it'll be, if that mean old thief's dead; I'll go to town, if 'tis so, get a dozen Guy's-day rockets, tie 'em round with crape, and spin 'em over the larches: that'll be funeral fun won't it? and it'll sarve to tell the neighbours of our luck in getting rid on him."

"I doan't like your thought, Tom," said another staider youth: "it's ill-mirth playing leap-frog over tomb-stones, and poor bravery insulting the dead. Besides, I'm thinking the bad man that's taken from us an't a going up'ards, so it's no use lending him a light. I wish we may all lie in a cooler grave than he does, and not have to go quite so deep down'ard."

"Gee up for Lady-day!" exclaimed the emancipated coachman; "why, Sall, I shall touch my whole lump of wages free for the fust time: and I only wish the gals had our luck."

"Here, Sarah," interposed a kind and ruddy stable youth, "as we're all making free with Mr. Simon's own special ale, I've thought to bring you a nogging on't: come, you're not so sick as you can't drink with all the rest on us—The bailiff, and may none on us never see his face no more!"

These, and similar testimonials to the estimation in which Simon's character was held, must have gratified not a little the hearer of his own laudations: now and then, he winced so that Sarah might have heard him move: but her ear was alive to nothing but the news-bringers, and her eyes appeared to be fixed upon the linen she was darning. That Jennings vowed vengeance, and wreaked it afterwards too, on the youths that so had shown their love, was his solitary pleasure in the shower-bath. But his critics were too numerous for him to punish all: they numbered every soul in the house, besides the summoned aiders—only excepting three: Sarah, who really had a head-ache, and made but little answers to the numerous glad envoys; Jonathan Floyd, whose charity did not altogether hate the man, and who really felt alarmed at his absence; and chiefest, Mrs. Quarles, who evinced more affection for her nephew than any thought him worthy of exciting—she wrung her hands, wept, offered rewards, bustled about every where, and kept calling blubberingly for "Simon—poor dear Simon."

At length, that fearful hue and cry began to subside—the hubbub came to be quieter: neighbour-folks went home, and inmates went to bed. Sarah Stack put aside her work, and left the room.

What a relief to that hidden caitiff! his feet, standing on the cold, damp iron so many hours, bare of brogues, were mere ice—only that they ached intolerably: he had not dared to move, to breathe, and was all over in one cramp: he did not bring the brandy-bottle with him, as he once had planned; for calculation whispered—"Don't, your head will be the clearer; you must not muddle your brains;" and so his caution over-reached itself, as usual; his head was in a fog, and his brains in a whirlwind, for lack of other stimulants than fear and pain.

O Simon, how your prudence cheats you! five mortal hours of anguish and anxiety in one unalterable posture, without a single drop of creature-comfort; and all this preconcerted too!

CHAPTER XXVI.

PRELIMINARIES.

At last, just as the nephew was positively fainting from exhaustion, in came his kind old aunt to bed. She talked a good deal to herself, did Mrs. Quarles, and Simon heard her say,

"Poor fellow—poor, dear Simon, he was taken bad last night, and has seemed queerish in the head all day: pray God nothing 's amiss with the boy!"

The boy's heart (he was forty) smote him as he heard: yes, even he was vexed that Aunt Bridget could be so foolishly fond of him. But he would go on now, and not have all his toil for nothing. "I 'm in for it," said he, "and there 's an end."

Ay, Simon, you are, indeed, in for it; the devil has locked you in—but as to the end, we shall see, we shall see.

"I shouldn't wonder now," the good old soul went on to say, "if Simon 's ventured out without his hat to cool a head-ache: his grandfather—peace be with him! died, poor man, in a Lunacy 'Sylum: alack, Si, I wish you mayn't be going the same road. No, no, I hope not—he 's always so prudent-like, and wise, and good; so kind, too, to a poor old fool like me:" and the poor old fool began to cry again.

"Silly boy—but he'll take cold at any rate: Sarah!" (here Mrs. Quarles rung her bell, and the still-maid answered it.) "Sarah Stack, sit up awhile for Mr. Jennings, and when he comes in, send him here to me. Poor boy," she went on soliloquizing, "he shall have a drop or two to comfort his stomach, and keep the chill out."

The poor boy, lying *perdu*, shuddered at the word chill, and really wished his aunt would hold her tongue. But she didn't.

"Maybe now," the affectionate old creature proceeded, "maybe Simon was vexed at what I let drop last night about the money. I know he loves his sister Scott, as I do: but it'll seem hard, too, to leave him nothing. I must make my will some day, I 'spose; but don't half like the job: it's always so nigh death. Yes—yes, dear Si shall have a snug little corner."

The real Simon Pure, in his own snug little corner, writhed again. Mrs. Quarles started at the noise, looked up the chimney, under the bed, tried the doors and windows, and actually went so near the mark as to turn the handle of the shower-bath; "Drat it," said she, "Sarah must ha' took away the key: well, there can't be nothing there but cloaks, that's one comfort."

Last of all, a thought struck her—it must have been a mouse at the preserves. And Mrs. Quarles forthwith opened the important cupboard, where Jennings now well knew the idol of his heart was shrined. Then another thought struck Mrs. Quarles, though probably no unusual one, and she seemed to have mounted on a chair, and to be bringing down some elevated piece of crockery. Simon could see nothing with his eyes, but his ears made up for them: if ever Dr. Elliotson produced clairvoyance in the sisters Okey, the same sharpened apprehensions ministered to the inner man of Simon Jennings through the instrumental magnet of his inordinately covetous desires. Therefore, though his retina bore no picture of the scene, the feelers of his mind went forth, informing him of every thing that happened.

Down came a Narbonne honey-pot—Simon saw that first, and it was as the lamp of Aladdin in his eyes: then the bladder was whipped off, and the crock set open on the table. Jennings, mad as Darius's horse at the sight of the object he so longed for, once thought of rushing from his hiding-place, taking the hoard by a *coup de main*, and running off straightway to America: but—deary me—that'll never do; I mustn't leave my own strong-box behind me, say nothing of hat and shoes: and if I stop for any thing, she'd raise the house.

While this was passing through the immaculate mind of Simon Jennings, Bridget had been cutting up an old glove, and had made one of its fingers into a very tidy little leather sacklet; into this she deposited a bright half sovereign, spoil of the day, being the douceur of a needy brush-maker, who wished to keep custom, and, of course, charged all these vails on the current bill for mops and stable-sponges.

"Ha!" muttered she, "it's your last bill here, Mr. Scrubb, I can tell you; so, you were going to put me off with a crown-piece, were you? and actually that bit of gold might as well have been a drop of blood wrung from you: yes—yes, Mr. Scrubb, I could see that plainly; and so you've done for yourself."

Then, having sewed up the clever little bag, she dropped it into the crock: there was no jingle, all dumby: prudent that, in his aunt—for the dear morsels of gold were worth such tender keeping, and leather would hinder them from wear and tear, set aside the clink being silenced. So, the nephew secretly thanked Bridget for the wrinkle, and thought how pleasant it would be to stuff old gloves with his own yellow store. Ah, yes, he would do that—to-morrow morning.

Meanwhile, the pig-skin is put on again, and the honey-pot stored away: and Simon instinctively stood a tip-toe to peep ideally into that *wealthy corner cupboard. His mind's eye seemed to see more honey-*pots! Mammon help us! can they all be full of gold? why, any one of them would hold a thousand pounds. And Simon scratched the palms of his hands, and licked his lips at the thought of so much honey.

But see, Mrs. Quarles has, in her peculiar fashion, undressed herself: that is to say, she has taken off her outer gown, her cap and wig—and then has *added* to the volume of her under garments, divers night habiliments, flannelled and frilled: while wrappers, manifold as a turbaned Turk's, protect ear-ache, tooth-ache, head-ache, and face-ache, from the elves of the night.

And now, that the bedstead creaks beneath her weight, (as well it may, for Bridget is a burden like Behemoth,) Simon's heart goes thump so loud, that it was a wonder the poor woman never heard it. That heart in its hard pulsations sounded to me like the carpenter hammering on her coffin-lid: I marvel that she did not take it for a death-watch tapping to warn her of her end. But no: Simon held his hand against his heart to keep it quiet: he was so very fearful the pitapating would betray him. Never mind, Simon; don't be afraid; she is fast asleep already; and her snore is to thee as it were the challenge of a trumpeter calling to the conflict.

CHAPTER XXVII.

ROBBERY.

Hush—hush—hush!

Stealthily on tiptoe, with finger on his lips, that fore-doomed man crept out.

"The key is in the cupboard still—ha! how lucky: saves time that, and trouble, and—and—risk! Oh, no—there can be no risk now," and the wretch added, "thank God!"

The devil loves such piety as this.

So Simon quietly turned the key, and set the cupboard open: it was to him a Bluebeard's chamber, a cave of the Forty Thieves, a garden of the Genius in Aladdin, a mysterious secret treasure-house of wealth uncounted and unseen.

What a galaxy of pickle-pots! tier behind tier of undoubted currant-jelly, ranged like the houses in Algiers! vasty jars of gooseberry! delicate little cupping-glasses full of syruped fruits! Yet all these candied joys, which probably enhance a Mrs. Rundle's heaven, were as nothing in the eyes of Simon—sweet trash, for all he cared they might be vulgar treacle. His ken saw nothing but the honey-pots—embarrassing array—a round dozen of them! All alike, all posted in a brown line, like stout Dutch sentinels with their hands in their breeches pockets, and set aloft on that same high-reached shelf. Must he really take them all? impracticable: a positive sack full. What's to be done?—which is he to leave behind? that old witch contrived this identity and multitude for safety's sake. But what if he left the wrong one, and got clear off with the valuable booty of two dozen pounds of honey? Confusion! that'll never do: he must take them all, or none; all, all's the word; and forthwith, as tenderly as possible, the puzzled thief took down eleven pots of honey to his one of gold—all pig-bladdered, all Fortnumed—all slimy at the string; "Confound that cunning old aunt of mine," said Simon, aloud; and took no notice that the snores surceased.

Then did he spread upon the table a certain shawl, and set the crocks in order on it: and it was quite impossible to leave behind that pretty ostentatious "Savings' Bank," which the shrewd hoarder kept as a feint to lure thieves from her hidden gold, by an open exhibition of her silver: unluckily, though, the shillings, not being leathered up nor branned, rattled like a Mandarin toy, as the trembling hand of Jennings deposited the bank beside the crockeries—and, at the well-known sound, I observed (though Simon did not, as he was in a trance of addled triumph) or fancied I observed Mrs. Quarles's head move: but as she said nothing, perhaps I was mistaken. Thus stood Simon at the table, surveying his extraordinary spoils.

And while he looked, the Mercy of God, which never yet hath seen the soul too guilty for salvation, spake to him kindly, and whispered in his ear, "Poor, deluded man—there is yet a moment for escape—flee from this temptation—put all back again—hasten to thy room, to thy prayers, repent, repent: even thou shalt be forgiven, and none but God, who will forgive thee, shall know of this bad crime. Turn now from all thy sins; the gate of bliss is open, if thou wilt but lift the latch."

It was one moment of irresolute delay; on that hinge hung Eternity. The gate swung upon its pivot, that should shut out hell, or heaven!

Simon knit his brow—bit his nails—and answered quite out loud, "What! and after all to lose the crock of gold?"

CHAPTER XXVIII.

MURDER.

He had waked her!

In an instant the angel form of Mercy melted away—and there stood the devil with his arms folded.

"Murder!—fire!—rape!—thieves!—what, Nephew Jennings, is that you, with all my honey pots? Help! help! help!"

"Phew-w-w!" whistled the devil: "I tell you what, Master Simon, you must quiet the old woman, she bellows like a bull, the house 'll be about your ears in a twinkling—she 'll hang you for this!"

Yes—he must quiet her—the game was up; he threatened, he implored, but she would shriek on; she slept alone on the ground-floor, and knew she must roar loudly to be heard above the drawing-rooms; she would not be quieted—she would shrick—and she did. What must he do? she 'll raise the house!—Stop her mouth, stop her mouth, I say, can't you?—No, she 's a powerful, stout, heavy woman, and he cannot hold her: ha! she has bitten his finger to the bone, like a very tigress! look at the blood!

"Why can't you touch her throat; no teeth there, bless you! that's the way the wind comes: bravo! grasp it—tighter! tighter! tighter!"

She struggled, and writhed, and wrestled, and fought—but all was strangling silence; they rolled about the floor together, tumbled on the bed, scuffled round the room, but all in horrid silence; neither uttered a sound, neither had a shoe on—but all was earnest, wicked, death-dealing silence.

Ha! the desperate victim has the best of it; gripe harder, Jennings; she has twisted her fingers in your neckcloth, and you yourself are choking: fool! squeeze the swallow, can't you? try to make your fingers meet in the middle—lower down, lower down, grasp the gullet, not the ears, man—that's right; I told you so: tighter, tighter, tighter! again; ha, ha, ha, bravo! bravo!—tighter, tighter, tighter!

At length the hideous fight was coming to an end—though a hungry constrictor, battling with the huge rhinoceros, and crushing his mailed ribs beneath its folds, could not have been so fierce or fearful; fewer now, and fainter are her struggles; that face is livid blue—the eyes have started out, and goggle horribly; the tongue protrudes, swollen and black. Aha! there is another convulsive effort—how strong she is still! can you hold her, Simon?—can he?—All the fiend possessed him now with savage exultation: can he?—only look! gripe, gripe still, you are conquering, strong man! she is getting weaker, weaker; here is your reward, gold! gold! a mighty store uncounted; one more grasp, and it is all your own—relent now, she hangs you. Come, make short work of it, break her neck—gripe harder—back with her, back with here against the bedstead: keep her down, down I say—she must not rise again. Crack! went a little something in her neck—did you hear it? There's the death-rattle, the last smothery complicated gasp—what, didn't you hear that?

And the devil congratulated Simon on his victory.

CHAPTER XXIX.

THE REWARD.

TILL the wretch had done the deed, he scarcely knew that it was doing. It was a horrid, mad excitement, where the soul had spread its wings upon the whirlwind, and heeded not whither it was hurried. A terrible necessity had seemed to spur him onwards all the while, and one thing so succeeded to another, that he scarce could stop at any but the first. From the moment he had hidden in the shower-bath (but for God's interposing mercy), his doom appeared to have been sealed—robbery, murder, false witness, and—damnation!

Crime is the rushing rapid, which, but for some kind miracle, inevitably carries on through circling eddies, and a foamy swinging tide, to the cataract of death and wo: haste, poor fisherman of Erie, paddle hard back, stem the torrent, cling to the shore, hold on tight by this friendly bough; know you not whither the headlong current drives? hear you not the roar of many waters, the maddening rush as of an ocean disenthralled? feel you not the earth trembling at the thunder—see you not the heaven clouded o'er with spray? Helpless wretch—thy frail canoe has leapt that dizzy water-cliff, Niagara!

But if, in doing that fell deed, madness raged upon the minutes, now that it was done—all still, all calm, all quiet, Terror held the hour-glass of Time. There lay the corpse, motionless, though coiled and cramped in the attitude of struggling agony; and the murderer gazed upon his victim with a horror most intense. Fly! fly!—he dared not stop to think: fly! fly! any whither—as you are—wait for nothing; fly! thou caitiff, for thy life! So he caught up the blood-bought spoils, and was fumbling with shaky fingers at the handle of the garden-door, when the unseen tempter whispered in his ear,

"I say, Simon, did not your aunt die of apoplexy?"

O, kind and wise suggestion! O, lightsome, tranquillizing thought! Thanks! thanks! thanks!—And if the arch fiend had revealed himself in person at the moment, Simon would have worshipped at his feet.

"But," and as he communed with his own black heart, there needed now no devil for his prompter—"if this matter is to be believed, I must contrive a little that it may look likelier. Let me see:—yes, we must lay all tidy, and the old witch shall have died in her sleep; apoplexy! capital indeed; no tell-tales either well, I must set to work."

Can mortal mind conceive that sickening office?—To face the strangled corpse, yet warm; to lift the fearful burden in his arms, and order out the heavily-yielding limbs in the ease of an innocent sleep? To arrange the bed, smooth down the tumbled coverlid, set every thing straight about the room, and erase all tokens of that dread encounter? It needed nerves of iron, a heart all stone, a cool, clear head, a strong arm, a mindful, self-protecting spirit; but all these requisites came to Simon's aid upon the instant; frozen up with fear, his heart-strings worked that puppet-man rigidly as wires; guilt supplied a reckless energy, a wild physical power, which actuates no human frame but one saturate with crime, or madness; and in the midst of those terrific details, the murderer's judgment was so calm and so collected, that nothing was forgotten, nothing unconsidered—unless, indeed, it were that he out-generalled himself by making all too tidy to be natural. Hence, suspicion at the inquest; for the "apoplexy" thought was really such a good one, that, but for so exact a laying out, the fat old corpse might have easily been buried without one surmise of the way she met her end. Again and again, in the history of crimes, it is seen that a "Judas hangs himself;" and albeit, as we know, the murderer has hitherto escaped detection, still his own dark hour shall arrive in its due place.

The dreadful office done, he asked himself again, or maybe took counsel of the devil (for that evil master always cheats his servants), "What shall I do with my reward, this crock—these crocks of gold? It might be easy to hide one of them, but not all; and as to leaving any behind, that I won't do. About opening them to see which is which—"

"I tell you what," said the tempter, as the clock struck three, "whatever you do, make haste; by morning's dawn the house and garden will be searched, no doubt, and the crocks found in your possession. Listen to me—I'm your friend, bless you! remember the apoplexy. Pike Island yonder is an unfrequented place; take the punt, hide all there now, and go at your best leisure to examine afterwards; but whatever you do, make haste, my man."

Then Jennings crept out by the lawn-door, thereby rousing the house-dog; but he skirted the laurels in their shadow, and it was dark and mizzling, so he reached the punt both quickly and easily.

The quiet, and the gloom, and the dropping rain, strangely affected him now, as he plied his punt-pole; once he could have wept in his remorse, and another time he almost shrieked in fear. How lonesome it seemed! how dreadful! and that death-dyed face behind him—ha! woman, away I say! But he neared the island, and, all shoeless as he was, crept up its muddy bank.

"Hallo! nybor, who be you a-poaching on my manor, eh? that bean't good manners, any how."

Ben Burke has told us all the rest.

But, when Burke had got his spoils—when the biter had been bitten—the robber robbed—the murderer stripped of his murdered victim's money—when the bereaved miscreant, sullenly returning in the dark, damp night, tracked again the way he came upon that lonely lake—no one yet has told us, none can rightly tell, the feelings which oppressed that God-forsaken man. He seemed to feel himself even a sponge which, the evil one had bloated with his breath, had soaked it then in blood, had squeezed it dry again, and flung away! He was Satan's broken tool—a weed pulled up by the roots, and tossed upon the fire; alone—alone in all the universe, without countenance or sympathy from God, or man, or devil; he yearned to find, were it but a fiend to back him, but in vain; they held aloof, he could see them vaguely through the gloom—he could hear them mocking him aloud among the patter of the rain-drops—ha! ha! ha—the pilfered fool!

Bitterly did he rue his crime—fearfully he thought upon its near discovery—madly did he beat his miserable breast, to find that he had been baulked of his reward, yet spent his soul to earn it.

Oh—when the house-dog bayed at him returning, how he wished he was that dog! he went to him, speaking kindly to him, for he envied that dog—"Good dog—good dog!"

But more than envy kept him lingering there: the wretched man did it for delay—yes, though morn was breaking on the hills—one more—one more moment of most precious time.

CHAPTER XXX.

SECOND THOUGHTS.

For—again he must go through that room!

No other entrance is open—not a window, not a door: all close as a prison: and only by the way he went, by the same must he return.

He trembled all over, as a palsied man, when he touched the lock: with stiffening hair, and staring eyes, he peeped in at that well-remembered chamber: he entered—and crept close up to the corpse, stealthily and dreadingly—horror! what if she be alive still?

She was.

Not quite dead—not quite dead yet! a gurgling in the bruised throat—a shadowy gleam of light and life in those protruded eyes—an irregular convulsive heaving at the chest: she might recover! what a fearful hope: and, if she did, would hang him—ha! he went nearer; she was muttering something in a moanful way—it was, "Simon did it—Simon did it—Simon did it—Si—Si—Simon did—" he should be found out!

Yet once again, for the last time, the long-suffering Mercy of the Lord stood like Balaam's angel in the way, pleading with that miserable man at the bed-side of her whom he had strangled. And even then, that Guardian Spirit came not with chiding on his tongue, but He uttered words of hope, while his eyes were streaming with sorrow and with pity.

"Most wretched of the sinful sons of men, even now there may be mercy for thee, even now plenteous forgiveness. True, thou must die, and pay the earthly penalty of crimes like thine: but do my righteous bidding, and thy soul shall live. Go to that poor, suffocating creature—cherish the spark of life—bind up the wounds which thou hast rent, pouring in oil and wine: rouse the house—seek assistance—save her life—confess thy sin—repent—and though thou diest for this before the tribunal of thy fellows, God will yet be gracious—he will raise again her whom thou hadst slain—and will cleanse thy blood-stained soul."

Thus in Simon's ear spake that better conscience.

But the reprobate had cast off Faith; he could not pledge the Present for the Future; he shuddered at the sword of Justice, and would not touch the ivory sceptre of Forgiveness. No: he meditated horrid iteration—and again the fiend possessed him! What! not only lose the crock of gold, but all his own bright store? and give up every thing of this world's good for some imaginary other, and meekly confess, and meanly repent—and—and all this to resuscitate that hated old aunt of his, who would hang him, and divorce him from his gold?

No! he must do the deed again—see, she is moving—she will recover! her chest heaves visibly—she breathes—she speaks—she knows me—ha! down—down, I say!

Then, with deliberate and damning resolution—to screen off temporal danger, and count his golden hoards a little longer—that awful criminal touched the throat again: and he turned his head away not to see that horrid face, clutched the swollen gullet with his icy hands, and strangled her once more!

"This time all is safe," said Simon. And having set all smooth as before, he stole up to his own chamber.

CHAPTER XXXI.

MAMMON, AND CONTENTMENT.

Ay, safe enough: and the murderer went to bed. To bed? No. He tumbled about the clothes, to make it seem that he had lain there: but he dared neither lie down, nor shut his eyes. Then, the darkness terrified him: the out-door darkness he could have borne, and Mrs. Quarles's chamber always had a night-lamp burning: but the darkness of his own room, of his own thoughts, pressed him all around, as with a thick, murky, suffocating vapour. So, he stood close by the window, watching the day-break.

As for sleep, never more did wholesome sleep rëvisit that atrocious mind: laudanum, an ever-increasing dose of merciless laudanum, that was the only power which ever seemed to soothe him. For a horrid vision always accompanied him now: go where he might, do what he would, from that black morning to eternity, he went a haunted man—a scared, sleepless, horror-stricken wretch. That livid face with goggling eyes, stuck to him like a shadow; he always felt its presence, and sometimes, also, could perceive it as if bodily peeping over his shoulder, next his cheek; it dogged him by day, and was his incubus by night; and often he would start and wrestle, for the desperate grasp of the dying appeared to be clutching at his throat: so, in his ghostly fears, and bloody conscience, he had girded round his neck a piece of thin sheet-iron in his cravat, which he wore continually as armour against those clammy fingers: no wonder that he held his head so stiff.

O Gold—accursed Mammon! is this the state of those who love thee deepest? is this their joy, who desire thee with all their heart and soul—who serve thee with all their might—who toil for thee—plot for thee—live for thee—dare for thee—die for thee? Hast thou no better bliss to give thy martyrs—no choicer comfort for thy most consistent worshippers, no fairer fate for those, whose waking thoughts, and dreaming hopes, and intricate schemes, and desperate deeds, were only aimed at gold, more gold? God of this world, if such be thy rewards, let me ever escape them! idol of the knave, false deity of the fool, if this be thy blessing on thy votaries—come, curse me, Mammon, curse thou me!

For, "The love of money is the root of all evil." It groweth up a little plant of coveting; presently the leaves get rank, the branches spread, and feed on petty thefts; then in their early season come the blossoms, black designs, plots, involved and undeveloped yet, of foul conspiracies, extortions on the weak, rich robbings of the wealthy, the threatened slander, the rewarded lie, malice, perjury, sacrilege; then speedily cometh on the climax, the consummate flower, dark-red murder: and the fruit bearing in itself the seeds that never die, is righteous, wrathful condemnation.

Dyed with all manner of iniquity, tinged with many colours like the Mohawk in his woods, goeth forth in a morning the covetous soul. His cheek is white with envy, his brow black with jealous rage, his livid lips are full of lust, his thievish hands spotted over with the crimson drops of murder. "The poison of asps is under his lips; and his feet are swift to shed blood: destruction and misery are in his ways; and there is no fear of God before his eyes."

O, ye thousands—the covetous of this world's good—behold at what a fire ye do warm yourselves! dread it: even now, ye have imagined many deaths, whereby your gains may be the greater; ye have caught, in wishful fancy, many a parting sigh; ye have closed, in a heartless revery, many a glazing eye—yea, of those your very nearest, whom your hopes have done to death: and are ye guiltless? God and conscience be your judges!

Even now ye have compassed many frauds, connived at many meannesses, trodden down the good, and set the bad on high—all for gold—hard gold; and are ye the honest—the upright? Speak out manfully your excuse, if you can find one, ye respectables of merchandise, ye traders, bartering all for cash, ye Scribes, ye Pharisees, hypocrites, all honourable men.

Even now, your dreams are full of money-bags; your cares are how to add superfluity to wealth; ye fawn upon the rich, ye scorn the poor, ye pine and toil both night and day for gold, more gold; and are ye happy? Answer me, ye covetous ones.

Yet are there righteous gains, God's blessing upon labour: yet is there rightful hope to get those righteous gains. Who can condemn the poor man's care, though Faith should make his load the lighter? And who will extenuate the rich man's coveting, whose appetite grows with what it feeds on? "Having food and raiment, be therewith content;" that is the golden mean; to that is limited the philosophy of worldliness: the man must live, by labour and its earnings; but having wherewithal for him and his temperately, let him tie the mill-stone of anxiety to the wing of Faith, and speed that burden to his God.

If Wealth come, beware of him, the smooth false friend: there is treachery in his proffered hand, his tongue is eloquent to tempt, lust of many harms is lurking in his eye, he hath a hollow heart; use him cautiously.

If Penury assail, fight against him stoutly, the gaunt grim foe: the curse of Cain is on his brow, toiling vainly; he creepeth with the worm by day, to raven with the wolf by night: diseases battle by his side, and crime followeth his footsteps. Therefore fight against him boldly, and be of a good courage, for there are many with thee; not alone the doled alms, the casual aids dropped from compassion, or wrung out by importunity; these be only temporary helps, and indulgence in them pampers the improvident; but look thou to a better host of strong allies, of resolute defenders; turn again to meet thy duties, needy one: no man ever starved, who even faintly tried to do them. Look to thy God, O sinner! use reason wisely; cherish honour; shrink not from toil, though somewhile unrewarded; preserve frank bearing with thy fellows; and in spite of all thy sins—forgiven; all thy follies—flung away; all the trickeries of this world—scorned; all competitions—disregarded; all suspicions—trodden under foot; thou neediest and raggedest of labourers' labourers—Enough shall be thy portion, ere a week hath passed away.

Well did Agur-the-Wise counsel Ithiel and Ucal his disciples, when he uttered in their ears before his God, this prayerful admonition, "Two things have I required of Thee; deny me them not before I die: remove far from me vanity and lies; give me neither poverty nor riches: feed me with food convenient for me. Lest I be full, and deny Thee, saying, Who is the Lord? or lest I be poor, and steal, and dishonour the name of the Lord my God."

CHAPTER XXXII.

NEXT MORNING.

Day dawned apace; and a glorious cavalcade of flaming clouds heralded the Sun their captain. From far away, round half the wide horizon, their glittering spears advanced. Heaven's highway rang with the trampling of their horse-hoofs, and the dust went up from its jewelled pavement as spray from the bottom of a cataract. Anon, he came, the chieftain of that on-spurring host! his banner blazed upon the sky; his golden crest was seen beneath, nodding with its ruddy plumes; over the south-eastern hills he arose in radiant armour. Fair Nature, waking at her bridegroom's voice, arrived so early from a distant clime, smiled upon him sleepily, gladdening him in beauty with her sweet half-opened eyelids, and kissing him in faithfulness with dew-besprinkled lips.

And he looked forth upon the world from his high chariot, holding back the coursers that must mount the steep of noon: and he heard the morning hymn of thankfulness to Heaven from the mountains, and the valleys, and the islands of the sea; the prayer of man and woman, the praise of lisping tongues, the hum of insect joy upon the air, the sheep-bell tinkling in the distance, the wild bird's carol, and the lowing kine, the mute minstrelsy of rising dews, and that stilly scarce-heard universal melody of wakeful plants and trees, hastening to turn their spring-buds to the light—this was the anthem he, the Lord of Day, now listened to—this was the song his influences had raised to bless the God who made him.

And he saw, from his bright throne of wide derivative glory, Hope flying forth upon her morning missions, visiting the lonesome, comforting the sorrowful, speaking cheerfully to Care, and singing in the ear of Labour: and he watched that ever-welcome friend, flitting with the gleams of light to every home, to every heart; none but gladly let her in; her tapping finger opened the very prison doors; the heavy head of Sloth rejoiced to hear her call; and every common Folly, every common Sin—ay, every common Crime—warmed his unconscious soul before her winning beauty.

Yet, yet was there one, who cursed that angel's coming; and the holy Eye of day wept pityingly to see an awful child of man who dared not look on Hope.

The murderer stood beside his casement, watching that tranquil scene: with bloodshot eyes and haggard stare, he gazed upon the waking world; for one strange minute he forgot, entranced by innocence and beauty; but when the stunning tide of memory, that had ebbed that one strange minute, rolled back its mighty flood upon his mind, the murderer swooned away.

And he came to himself again all too soon; for when he arose, building up his weak, weak limbs, as if he were a column of sand, the cruel giant, Guilt, lifted up his club, and felled the wretch once more.

How long he lay fainting, he knew not then; if any one had vowed it was a century, Simon, as he gradually woke, could not have gainsaid the man; but he only lay four seconds in that white oblivious trance—for Fear, Fear knocked at his heart:—Up, man, up!—you need have all your wits about you now;—see, it is broad day—the house will be roused before you know where you are, and then will be shouted out that awful name—Simon Jennings! Simon Jennings!

CHAPTER XXXIII.

THE ALARM.

He arose, held up on either hand that day as if fighting against Amalek;—despair buttressed him on one side, and secresy shored him on the other: behind that wall of stone his heart had strength to beat.

He arose; and listened at the key-hole anxiously: all silent, quiet, quiet still; the whole house asleep: nothing found out yet. And he bit his nails to the quick, that they bled again: but he never felt the pain.

Hush!—yes, somebody's about: it is Jonathan's step; and hark, he is humming merrily, "Hail, smiling morn, that opes the gates of day?" Wo, wo—what a dismal gulph between Jonathan and me! And he beat his breast miserably. But, Jonathan cannot find it out—he never goes to Mrs. Quarles's room. Oh! this suspense is horrible: haste, haste, some kind soul, to make the dread discovery! And he tore his hair away by handfulls.

"Hark!—somebody else—unlatching shutters; it will be Sarah—ha! she is tapping at the housekeeper's room—yes, yes, and she will make it known, O terrible joy!—A scream! it is Sarah's voice—she has seen her dead, dead, dead;—but is she indeed dead?"

The miscreant quivered with new fears; she might still mutter "Simon did it!"

And now the house is thoroughly astir; running about in all directions; and shouting for help; and many knocking loudly at the murderer's own door—"Mr. Jennings! Mr. Jennings!—quick—get up—come down—quick, quick—your aunt's found dead in her bed!"

What a relief to the trembling wretch!—she *was* dead. He could have blessed the voice that told him his dread secret was so safe. But his parched tongue may never bless again: curses, curses are all its blessings now.

And Jennings came out calmly from his chamber, a white, stern, sanctimonious man, lulling the storm with his wise presence:—"God's will be done," said he; "what can poor weak mortals answer Him?" And he played cleverly the pious elder, the dignified official, the affectionate nephew: "Ah, well, my humble friends, behold what life is: the best of us must come to this; my poor, dear aunt, the late housekeeper, rest her soul—I feared it might be this way some night or other: she was a stout woman, was our dear, deceased Bridget—and, though a good kind soul, lived much on meat and beer: ah well, ah well!" And he concealed his sentimental hypocrisy in a cotton pocket-handkerchief.

"Alas, and well-a-day! that it should have come to this. Apoplexy—you see, apoplexy caught her as she slept: we may as well get her buried at once: it is unfortunately too clear a case for any necessity to open the body; and our young master is coming down on Tuesday, and I could not allow my aunt's corpse to be so disrespectful as to stop till it became offensive. I will go to the vicar myself immediately."

"Begging pardon, Mr. Jennings," urged Jonathan Floyd, "there's a strange mark here about the throat, poor old 'ooman."

"Ay," added Sarah, "and now I come to think of it, Mrs. Quarles's room-door was ajar; and bless me, the lawn-door's not locked neither! Who could have murdered her?"

"Murdered? there's no murder here, silly wench," said Jennings, with a nervous sneer.

"I don't know that, Mr. Simon," gruffly interposed the coachman; "it's a case for a coroner, I'll be bail; so here I goes to bring him: let all bide as it is, fellow-sarvents; murder will out, they say."

And off he set directly—not without a shrewd remark from Mr. Jennings, about letting him escape that way; which seemed all very sage and likely, till the honest man came back within the hour, and a *posse comitatus* at his heels.

We all know the issue of that inquest.

Now, if any one requests to be informed how Jennings came to be looked for as usual in his room, after that unavailing search last night, I reply, this newer, stronger excitement for the minute made the house oblivious of that mystery; and if people further will persist to know, how that mystery of his absence was afterwards explained (though I for my part would gladly have said nothing of the bailiff's own excuse), let it be enough to hint, that Jennings winked with a knowing and gallant expression of face; alluded to his private key, and a secret return at two in the morning from some disreputable society in the neighbourhood; made the men laugh, and the women blush; and, altogether, as he might well have other hats and coats, the delicate affair was not unlikely.

CHAPTER XXXIV.

DOUBTS.

And so, this crock of gold—gained through extortion, by the frauds of every day, the meannesses of every hour—this concrete oppression to the hireling in his wages—this mass of petty pilferings from poverty—this continuous obstruction to the charities of wealth—this cockatrice's egg—this offspring of iniquity—had already been baptized in blood before poor Acton found it, and slain its earthly victim ere it wrecked his faith; already had it been perfected by crime, and destroyed the murderer's soul, before it had endangered the life of slandered innocence.

Is there yet more blessing in the crock? more fearful interest still, to carry on its story to an end? Must another sacrifice bleed before the shrine of Mammon, and another head lie crushed beneath the heel of that monster—his disciple?

Come on with me, and see the end; push further still, there is a labyrinth ahead to attract and to excite; from mind to mind crackles the electric spark: and when the heart thrillingly conceives, its children-thoughts are as arrows from the hand of the giant, flying through that mental world—the hearts of other men. Fervent still from its hot internal source, this fountain gushes up; no sluggish Lethe-stream is here, dull, forgetful, and forgotten; but liker to the burning waves of Phlegethon, mingling at times (though its fire is still unquenched), with the pastoral rills of Tempe, and the River from the Mount of God.

Lower the sail—let it flap idly on the wind—helm a-port—and so to smoother waters: return to common life and humbler thoughts.

It may yet go hard with Roger Acton. Jennings is a man of character, especially the farther from his home; the county round take him for a model of propriety, a sample of the strictest conduct. We know the bad man better; but who dare breathe against the bailiff in his power—against the caitiff in his sleek hypocrisy—that, while he makes a show of both humilities, he fears not God nor man? What shall hinder, that the perjured wretch offer up to the manes of the murdered the life-blood of the false-accused? May he not live yet many years, heaping up gold and crime? And may not sweet Grace Acton—her now repentant father—the kindly Jonathan—his generous master, and if there be any other of the Hurstley folk we love, may they not all meet destruction at his hands, as a handful of corn before the reaper's sickle? I say not that they shall, but that they might. Acton's criminal state of mind, and his hunger after gold—gold any how—have earned some righteous retribution, unless Providence in mercy interpose; and young Sir John, in nowise unblameable himself, with wealth to tempt the spoiler, lives in the spoiler's very den; and as to Jonathan and Grace, this world has many martyrs. If Heaven in its wisdom use the wicked as a sword, Heaven is but just; but if in its vengeance that sword of the wicked is turned against himself, Heaven showeth mercy all unmerited. To a criminal like Jennings, let loose upon the world, without the clog of conscience to retard him, and with the spur of covetousness ever urging on, any thing in crime is possible—is probable: none can sound those depths: and when we raise our eyes on high to the Mighty Moral Governor, and note the clouds of mystery that thunder round his Throne—He may permit, or he may control; who shall reach those heights?

CHAPTER XXXV.

FEARS.

Moreover, innocent of blood, as we know Roger Acton to be, appearances are strongly against him: and in such a deed as secret, midnight murder, which none but God can witness, multiplied appearances justify the world in condemning one who seems so guilty.

The first impression against Roger is a bad one, for all the neighbours know how strangely his character had been changing for the worse of late: he is not like the same man; sullen and insubordinate, he was turned away from work for his bold and free demeanor; as to church, though he had worn that little path these forty years, all at once he seems to have entirely forgotten the way hither.

He lives, nobody knows how—on bright, clean gold, nobody knows whence: his daughter says, indeed, that her father found a crock of gold in his garden—but she needs not have held her tongue so long, and borne so many insults, if that were all the truth; and, mark this! even though she says it, and declares it on her Bible-oath, Acton himself most strenuously denied all such findings—but went about with impudent tales of legacy, luck, nobody knows what; the man prevaricated continually, and got angry when asked about it—cudgelling folks, and swearing like—like any one but old-time "honest Roger."

Only look, too, where he lives: in a lone cottage opposite Pike Island, on the other side of which is Hurstley Hall, the scene of robbery and murder: was not a boat seen that night upon the lake? and was not the lawn-door open? How strangely stupid in the coroner and jury not to have imagined this before! how dull it was of every body round not to have suspected murder rather more strongly, with those finger-marks about the throat, and not to have opened their eyes a little wider, when the murderer's cottage was within five hundred yards of that open lawn-door!

Then again—when Mr. Jennings, in his strict and searching way, accused the culprit, he never saw a man so confused in all his life! and on repeating the charge before those two constables, they all witnessed his guilty consternation: experienced men, too, they were, and never saw a felon if Acton wasn't one; the dogged manner in which he went with them so quietly was quite sufficient; innocent men don't go to jail in that sort of way, as if they well deserved it.

But, strongest of all, if any shadow of a doubt remained, the most fearful proof of Roger's guilt lay in the scrap of shawl—the little leather bags—and the very identical crock of gold! There it was, nestled in the thatch within a yard of his head, as he lay in bed at noon-day guarding it.

One proof, weaker than the weakest of all these banded together, has ere now sufficed to hang the guilty; and many, many fears have I that this multitude of seeming facts, conspiring in a focus against Roger Acton, will be quite enough to overwhelm the innocent. "Nothing lies like a fact," said Dr. Johnson: and statistics prove it, at least as well as circumstantial evidence.

The matter was as clear as day-light, and long before the trial came about, our poor labourer had been hanged outright in the just judgment of Hurstley-cum-Piggesworth.

CHAPTER XXXVI.

PRISON COMFORTS.

Many blessings, more than he had skill to count, had visited poor Acton in his cell. His gentle daughter Grace, sweet minister of good thoughts—she, like a loving angel, had been God's instrument of penitence and peace to him. He had come to himself again, in solitude, by nights, as a man awakened from a feverish dream; and the hallowing ministrations of her company by day had blest reflective solitude with sympathy and counsel.

Good-wife Mary, too, had been his comforting and cheering friend. Immediately the crock of gold had been taken from its ambush in the thatch, it seemed as if the chill which had frozen up her heart had been melted by a sudden thaw. Roger Acton was no longer the selfish prodigal, but the guiltless, persecuted penitent; her care was now to soothe his griefs, not to scold him for excesses; and indignation at the false and bloody charge made him appear a martyr in her eyes. As to his accuser, Jennings, Mary had indeed her own vague fancies and suspicions, but there being no evidence, nor even likelihood to support them, she did not dare to breathe a word; she might herself accuse him falsely. Ben, who alone could have thrown a light upon the matter, had always been comparatively a stranger at Hurstley; he was no native of the place, and had no ties there beyond wire and whip-cord: he would appear in that locality now and then in his eccentric orbit, like a comet, and, soon departing thence, would take away Tom as his tail; but even when there, he was mainly a night-prowler, seldom seen by day, and so little versed in village lore, so rarely mingling with its natives, that neither Jennings nor Burke knew one another by sight. His fame indeed was known, but not his person. At present, he and Tom were still fowling in some distant fens, nobody could tell where; so that Roger's only witness, who might have accounted for the crock and its finding, was as good as dead to him; to make Ben's absence more unusually prolonged, and his reäppearance quite incalculable, he had talked of going with his cargo of wild ducks "either to London or to Liverpool, he didn't rightly know which."

Nevertheless, Mary comforted her husband, and more especially herself, by the hope of his return as a saving witness; though it was always doubtful how far Burke's numerous peccadilloes against property would either find him at large, or authorize the poacher in walking straight before the judges. Still Ben's possible interposition was one source of hope and cheerful expectation. Then the good wife would leave her babes at home, safely in a neighbour's charge, and stay and sit many long hours with poor Roger, taking turns with Grace in talking to him tenderly, making little of home-troubles past, encouraging him to wear a stout heart, and filling him with gratitude for all her kindly care. Thus did she bless, and thus was made a blessing, through the loss and absence of that crock of gold.

For Roger himself, he had repented; bitterly and deeply, as became his headlong fall: no sweet luxuries of grief, no soothing sorrow, no chastened meditative melancholy—such mild penitence as this, he thought, could be but a soberer sort of joy for virgins, saints, and martyrs: no—he, bad man, was unworthy of those melting pleasures, and in sturdy self-revenge he flung them from him, choosing rather to feel overwhelmed with shame, contrition, and reproaches. A humbled man with a broken heart within him—such was our labourer, penitent in prison; and when he contrasted his peaceful, pure, and Christian course those forty years of poverty, with his blasphemous and infidel career for the one bad week of wealth, he had no patience with himself—only felt his fall the greater; and his judgment of his own guilt, with a natural exaggeration, went the length of saying—I am scarcely less guilty before God and man, than if, indeed, my hands were red with murder, and my casual finding had been robbery. He would make no strong appeals to the bar of justice, as an innocent condemned; not he—not he: innocent, indeed? his wicked, wicked courses—(an old man, too—gray-headed, with no young blood in him to excuse, no inexperience to extenuate), these deserved—did he say hanging? it was a harsher syllable—hell: and the contrite sinner gladly would have welcomed all the terrors of the gibbet, in hope to take full vengeance on himself for his wicked thirst for gold and all its bitter consequences.

CHAPTER XXXVII.

GOOD COUNSEL.

But Grace advised him better. "Be humbled as you may before God, my father, but stand up boldly before man: for in his sight, and by his law, you are little short of blameless. I would not, dearest father, speak to you of sins, except for consolation under them; for it ill becomes a child to see the failings of a parent. But when I know at once how innocent you are in one sense, and how not quite guiltless in another, I wish my words may comfort you, if you will hear them, father. Covetousness, not robbery—excess, not murder—these were your only sins; and concealment was not wise, neither was a false report befitting. Money, the idol of millions, was your temptation: its earnest love, your fault; its possession, your misfortune. Forgive me, father, if I speak too freely. Good Mr. Evans, who has been so kind to us for years, (never kinder than since you were in prison,) can speak better than I may, of sins forgiven, and a Friend to raise the fallen: it is not for poor Grace to school her dear and honoured father. If you feel yourself guilty of much evil in the sight of Him before whom the angels bow in meekness—I need not tell you that your sorrow is most wise, and well-becoming. But this must not harm your cause with men: though tired of life, though hopeless in one's self, though bad, and weak, and like to fall again, we are still God's servants upon earth, bound to guard the life he gives us. Neither must you lightly allow the guilt of unrighteous condemnation to fall upon the judge who tries you; nor let your innocent blood cry to God for vengeance on your native land. Manfully confront the false accuser, tell openly the truth, plead your own cause firmly, warmly, wisely:—so, God defend the right!"

And as Grace Acton said these words, in all the fervour of a daughter's love, with a flushed cheek, parted lips, and her right hand raised to Him whom she invoked, she looked like an inspired prophetess, or the fair maid of Orleans leading on to battle.

In an instant afterwards, she humbly added,

"Forgive me any thing I may have said, that seems to chide my father."

"Bless you, bless you, dearest one!" was Roger's sobbing prayer, who had listened to her wisdom breathlessly. "Ah, daughter," then exclaimed the humbled, happy man, "I'll try to do all you ask me, Grace; but it is a hard thing to feel myself so wicked, and to have to speak up boldly like a Christian man."

CHAPTER XXXVIII.

EXPERIENCE.

THEN, with disjointed sentences, suited to the turmoil of his thoughts, half in a soliloquy, half as talking to his daughter, Roger Acton gave his hostile testimony to the worth of wealth.

"Oh, fool, fool that I have been, to set so high a price on gold! To have hungered and thirsted for it—to have coveted earnestly so bad a gift —to have longed for Mammon's friendship, which is enmity with God! What has not money cost me? Happiness:—ay, wasn't it to have given me happiness? and the little that I had (it was much, Grace, not little, very much—too much—God be praised for it!) all, all the happiness I had, gold took away. Look at our dear old home—shattered and scattered, as now I wish that crock had been. Health, too; were it not for gold, and all gold gave, I had been sturdy still, and capable; but my nights maddened with anxieties, my days worried with care, my head feverish with drink, my heart rent by conscience—ah, my girl, my girl, when I thought much of poverty and its hardships, of toil, and hunger, and rheumatics, I little imagined that wealth had heavier cares and pains: I envied them their wanton life of pleasure at the Hall, and little knew how hard it was: well are they called hard-livers who drink, and game, and have nothing to do, except to do wickedness continually. Religion—can it bide with money, child? I never knew my wicked heart, till fortune made me rich; not until then did I guess how base, lying, false, and bad was "honest Roger;" how sensual, coarse, and brutal, was that hypocrite "steady Acton." Money is a devil, child, or pretty near akin. Then I complained of toil, too, didn't I?—Ah, what are all the aches I ever felt—labouring with spade and spud in cold and rain, hungry belike, and faint withal—what are they all at their worst (and the worst was very seldom after all), to the gnawing cares, the hideous fears, the sins—the sins, my girl, that tore your poor old father? Wasn't it to be an end of troubles, too, this precious crock of gold? Wo 's me, I never knew real trouble till I had it! Look at me, and judge; what has made me live like a beast, sin like a heathen, and lie down here like a felon? what has made me curse Ben Burke—kind, hearty, friendly Ben?—and given my poor good boy an ill-report as having stolen and slain? all this crock of gold. But O, my Grace, to think that the crock's curses touched thee, too! didn't it madden me to hear them? Dear, pure, patient child, my darling, injured daughter, here upon my knees I pray, forgive that wrong!" And he fell at her feet beseechingly.

"My father," said the noble girl, lifting up his head, and passionately kissing it; "when they whispered so against me, and Jonathan heard the wicked things men said, I would have borne it all, all in silence, and let them all believe me bad, father, if I could have guessed that by uttering the truth, I should have seen thee here, in a dungeon, treated as a—murderer! How was I to tell that men could be so base, as to charge such crimes upon the innocent, when his only fault, or his misfortune, was to find a crock of gold? Oh! forgive me, too, this wrong, my father!"

And they wept in each other's arms.

CHAPTER XXXIX.

JONATHAN'S TROTH.

Grace had been all but an inmate of the prison, ever since her father had been placed there on suspicion. Early and late, and often in the day, was the duteous daughter at his cell, for the governor and the turnkeys favoured her. Who could resist such beauty and affection, entreating to stay with a father about to stand on trial for his life, and making every effort to be allowed only to pray with him? Thus did Grace spend all the week before those dread assizes.

As to her daily maintenance, ever since that bitter morning when the crock was found, her spiritual fears had obliged her to abstain from touching so much as one penny of that unblest store; and, seeing that honest pride would not let her be supported by grudged and common charity, she had thankfully suffered the wages of her now betrothed

Jonathan to serve as means whereon she lived, and (what cost more than all her humble wants) whereby she could administer many little comforts to her father in his prison. When she was not in the cell, Grace was generally at the Hall, to the scandal of more than one Hurstleyan gossip; but perhaps they did not know how usually kind Sarah Stack was of the company, to welcome her with Jonathan, and play propriety. Sarah was a true friend, one for adversity, and though young herself, and not ill-looking, did not envy Grace her handsome lover; on the contrary, she did all to make them happy, and had gone the friendly length of insisting to find Grace and her family in tea and sugar, while all this lasted. I like that much in Sarah Stack.

However, the remainder of the virtuous world were not so considerate, nor so charitable. Many neighbours shunned the poor girl, as if contaminated by the crimes which Roger had undoubtedly committed: the more elderly unmarried sisterhood, as we have chronicled already, were overjoyed at the precious opportunity:—Here was the pert vixen, whom all the young fellows so shamelessly followed, turned out, after all, a murderer's daughter;—they wished her joy of her eyes, and lips, and curls, and pretty speeches: no good ever came of such naughty ways, that the men liked so."

Nay, even the tipsy crew at Bacchus's affected to treat her name with scorn:—"The girl had made much noise about being called a trull, as if many a better than she wasn't one; and, after all, what was the prudish wench? a sort of she-butcher; they had no patience with her proud looks."

As to farmer Floyd, he made a great stir about his boy being about to marry a felon's daughter; and the affectionate mother, with many elaborate protestations, had "vowed to Master Jonathan, that she would rather lay him out with her own hands, and a penny on each eye, than see a Floyd disgrace himself in that 'ere manner."

And uncles, aunts, and cousins, most disinterestedly exhorted that the obstinate youth be disinherited—"Ay, Mr. Floyd, I wish your son was a high-minded man like his father; but there 's a difference, Mr. Floyd; I wish he had your true blue yeoman's honour, and the spirit that becomes his father's son: if the lad was mine, I 'd cut him off with a shilling, to buy a halter for his drab of a wife. Dang it, Mrs. Floyd, it 'll never do to see so queer a Mrs. Jonathan Junior, a standing in your tidy shoes beside this kitchen dresser."

These estimable counsels were, I grieve to say, of too flattering a nature to displease, and of too lucrative a quality not to be continually repeated; until, really, Jonathan was threatened with beggary and the paternal malediction, if he would persist in his disreputable attachment.

Nevertheless, Jonathan clung to the right like a hero.

"Granting poor Acton is the wretch you think—but I do not believe one word of it—does his crime make his daughter wicked too? No; she is an angel, a pure and blessed creature, far too good for such a one as I. And happy is the man that has gained her love; he should not give her up were she thrice a felon's daughter. My father and mother," Jonathan went on to say, "never found a fault in her till now. Who was more welcome on the hill than pretty Grace? who would oftenest come to nurse some sickly lamb, but gentle Grace? who was wont, from her childhood up, to run home with me so constantly, when school was over, and pleased my kinsfolk so entirely with her nice manners and kind ways? Hadn't he fought for her more than once, and though he came home with bruises on his face, his mother praised him for it?" Then, with a natural divergence from the strict subject-matter of objection, vicarious felony, Jonathan went on to argue about other temporal disadvantages. "Hadn't he heard his father say, that, if she had but money, she was fit to be a countess? and was money, then, the only thing, whereof the having, or the not having, could make her good or bad?—money, the only wealth for soul, and mind, and body? Are affections nothing, are truth and honour nothing, religion nothing, good sense nothing, health nothing, beauty nothing—unless money gild them all? Nonsense!" said Jonathan, indignantly, warmed by his amatory eloquence; "come weal, come wo, Grace and I go down to the grave together; for better, if she can be better—for worse, if she could sin—Grace Acton is my wealth, my treasure, and possession; and let man do his worst, God himself will bless us!"

So, all this knit their loves: she knew, and he felt, that he was going in the road of nobleness and honour; and the fiery ordeal which he had to struggle through, raised that hearty earthly lover more nearly to a level with his heavenly-minded mistress. Through misfortune and mistrust, and evil rumours all around, in spite of opposition from false friends, and the scorn of slanderous foes, he stood by her more constantly, perchance more faithfully, than if the course of true-love had been smoother: he was her escort morning and evening to and from the prison; his strong arm was the dread of babbling fools that spoke a word of disrespect against the Actons; and his brave tongue was now making itself heard, in open vindication of the innocent.

CHAPTER XL.

SUSPICIONS.

Yes—Jonathan Floyd was beginning to speak out boldly certain strange suspicions he had entertained of Jennings. It was a courageous, a rash, a dangerous thing to do: he did not know but what it might have jeoparded his life, say nothing of his livelihood: but Floyd did it.

Ever since that inquest, contrived to be so quickly and so quietly got over, he had noticed Simon's hurried starts, his horrid looks, his altered mien in all he did and said, his new nervous ways at nightfall—John Page to sleep in Mr. Jennings's chamber, and a rush-light perpetually—his shudder whenever he had occasion to call at the housekeeper's room, and his evident shrinking from the frequent phrase "Mrs. Quarles's murder."

Then again, Jonathan would often lie awake at nights, thinking over divers matters connected with his own evidence before the coroner, which he began to see might be of great importance. Jennings said, he had gone out to still the dog by the front door—didn't he?—"How then, Mr. Jennings, did you contrive to push back the top bolt? The Hall chairs had not come then, and you are a little fellow, and you know that nobody in the house could reach, without a lift, that bolt but me. Besides, before Sir John came down, the hinges of that door creaked, like a litter o' kittens screaming, and the lock went so hard for want of use and oil, that I'll be sworn your gouty chalkstone fingers could never have turned it: now, I lay half awake for two hours, and heard no creak, no key turned; but I tell you what I did hear though, and I wish now I had said it at that scanty, hurried inquest; I heard what I now believe were distant screams (but I was so sleepy), and a kind of muffled scuffling ever so long: but I fancied it might be a horse in the stable kicking among the straw in a hunter's loose box. I can guess what it was now—cannot you, Mr. Simon?—I say, butler, you must have gone out to quiet Don—who by the way can't abear the sight of you—through Mrs. Quarles's room: and, for all your threats, I'm not afeard to tell you what I think. First answer me this, Mr. Simon Jennings:—where were you all that night, when we were looking for you?—Oh! you choose to forget, do you? I can help your memory, Mr. Butler; what do you think of the shower-bath in Mother Quarles's room?"

As Jonathan, one day at dinner in the servants' hall, took occasion to direct these queries to the presiding Simon, the man gave such a horrid start, and exclaimed, "Away, I say!" so strangely, that Jonathan could doubt no longer—nor, in fact, any other of the household: Jennings gave them all round a vindictive scowl, left the table, hastened to his own room, and was seen no more that day.

Speculation now seemed at an end, it had ripened into probability;—but what evidence was there to support so grave a charge against this rigid man? Suspicions are not half enough to go upon—especially since Roger Acton seemed to have had the money. Therefore, though the folks at Hurstley, Sir John, his guests, and all the house, could not but think that Mr. Jennings acted very oddly—still, he had always been a strange creature, an unpopular bailiff; nobody understood him. So, Floyd, to his own no small danger, stood alone in accusing the man openly.

CHAPTER XLI.

GRACE'S ALTERNATIVE.

Very shortly after that remarkable speech in the servants' hall, Jonathan found another reason for believing that Mr. Simon Jennings was equal to any imaginable amount of human wickedness. That reason will shortly now appear; but we must first of all dig at its roots somewhat deeper than Jonathan's mental husbandry could manage.

If any trait of character were wanting to complete the desperate infamy of Jennings—(really I sometimes hope that his grandfather's madness had a kind of rëawakening in this accursed man)—it was furnished by a new and shrewd scheme for feeding to the full his lust of gold. The bailiff had more than once, as we have hinted, found means to increase his evil hoard, by having secretly gained power over female innocence and honest reputation: similarly he now devised a deep-laid plot, nothing short of diabolical. His plot was this: and I choose to hurry over such foul treason. Let a touch or two hint its outlines: those who will, may paint up the picture for themselves. Simon looked at Sir John—young, gay, wealthy; he coveted his purse, and fancied that the surest bait to catch that fish was fair Grace Acton: if he could entrap her for his master (to whom he gave full credit for delighting in the plan), he counted surely on magnificent rewards. How then to entrap her? Thus:—he, representing himself as prosecutor of Roger, the accused, held for him, he averred, the keys of life and death: he would set this idea (whether true or not little mattered, if it served his purpose) before an affectionate daughter, who should have it in her power to save her parent, if, and only if, she would yield herself to Jennings: and he well knew that, granting she gave herself secretly to him first, on such a bribe as her father's liberation, he would have no difficulty whatever in selling her second-hand beauty on his own terms to his master. It was a foul scheme, and shall not be enlarged upon: but (as will appear) thus slightly to allude to it was needful to our tale, as well as to the development of character in Mammon's pattern-slave, and to the fullness of his due retribution in this world. I may add, that if any thing could make the plan more heinous—if any shade than blackest can be blacker—this extra turpitude is seen in the true consideration, that the promise to Grace of her father's safety would be entirely futile—as Jennings knew full well; the crown was prosecutor, not he: and circumstantial evidence alone would be sufficient to condemn. Again, it really is nothing but bare justice to remark, with reference to Sir John, that the deep-dyed villain reckoned quite without his host; for however truly the baronet had oft-times been much less a self-denying Scipio than a wanton Alcibiades, still the fine young fellow would have flung Simon pieoemeal to his hounds, if ever he had breathed so atrocious a temptation: the maid was pledged, and Vincent knew it.

Now, it so happened that one evening at dusk, when Grace as usual was obliged to leave the prison, there was no Jonathan in waiting to accompany her all the dreary long way home: this was strange, as his good-hearted master, privately informed of his noble attachment, never refused the man permission, but winked, for the time, at his frequent evening absence. Nevertheless, on this occasion, as would happen now and then, Floyd could not escape from the dining-room; probably because—Mr. Jennings had secretly gone forth to escort the girl himself. Accordingly, instead of loved Jonathan, sidled up to her the loathsome Simon.

Let me not soil these pages by recording, in however guarded phrase, the grossness of this wretch's propositions; it was a long way to Hurstley, and the reptile never ceased tormenting her every step of it, till the village was in sight: twice she ran, and he ran too, keeping up with her, and pouring into her ear a father's cruel fate and his own detestable alternative. She never once spoke to him, but kept on praying in her own pure mind for a just acquittal; not for one moment would she entertain the wicked thought of "doing evil that good might come;" and so, with flushed cheek, tingling ears, the mien of an insulted empress, and the dauntless resolution of a heroine, she hastened on to Hurstley.

Look here! by great good fortune comes Jonathan Floyd to meet her.

"Save me, Jonathan, save me!" and she fainted in his arms.

Now, truth to say, though Sir John knew it, Simon did not, that Grace was Jonathan's beloved and betrothed; and the cause lay simply in this, that Jonathan had frankly told his master of it, when he found the dreadful turn things had taken with poor Roger; but as to Simon, no mortal in the neighbourhood ever communicated with him, further than as urged by fell necessity. Of course, the lovers' meetings were as private as all such matters generally are; and Sarah's aid managed them admirably. Therefore it now came to pass that Simon and Jonathan looked on each other in mutual astonishment, and needs must wait until Grace Acton could explain the "save me." Not but that Jennings seemed much as if he wished to run away; but he did not know how to manage it.

"Dear Jonathan," she whispered feebly, "save me from Simon Jennings."

In an instant, Jonathan's grasp was tightly involved in the bailiff's stiff white neckcloth. And Grace, with much maidenly reserve, told her lover all she dared to utter of that base bartering for her father's life.

"Come straight along with me, you villain, straight to the master!" And the sturdy Jonathan, administering all the remainder of the way (a quarter of a mile of avenue made part of it) innumerable kickings and cuffings, hauled the half-mummied bailiff into the servants' hall.

"Now then, straight before the master! John Page, be so good as to knock at the dining-room door, and ask master very respectfully if his honour will be good enough to suffer me to speak to him."

CHAPTER XLII.

THE DISMISSAL.

It was after dinner. Sir John and his friends had somehow been less jovial than usual; they were absolutely dull enough to be talking politics. So, when the boy of many buttons tapped at the door, and meekly brought in Jonathan's message, recounting also how he had got Mr. Jennings in tow for some inexplicable crime, the strangeness of the affair was a very welcome incident: both host and guests hailed it an adventure.

"By all means, let Jonathan come in."

The trio were just outside; and when the blue and silver footman, hauling in by his unrelinquished throat that scared bailiff, and followed by the blushing village beauty, stood within the room, Sir John and his half-dozen friends greeted the *tableau* with united acclamations.

"I say, Pypp, that's a devilish fine creature," metaphorically remarked the Honorable Lionel Poynter.

"Yaas." Lord George was a long, sallow, slim young man, with a goatish beard, like the Duc d'Aumale's; he affected extreme fashion and infinite *sangfroid.*

"Well, Jonathan, what is it?" asked the baronet.

"Why, in one word, my honoured master, this scoundrel here has been wickedly insulting my own poor dear Grace, by promising to save her father from the gallows if—if—"

"If what, man? speak out," said Mr. Poynter.

"You don't mean to say, Jennings, that you are brute enough to be seducing that poor man Roger's daughter, just as he's going to be tried for his life?" asked Sir John.

Simon uttered nothing in reply; but Grace burst into tears.

"A fair idea that, 'pon my honour," drawled the chivalrous Pypp, proceeding to direct his delicate attentions towards the weeping damsel.

"Simon Jennings," said Sir John, after pausing in vain for his reply, "I have long wished to get rid of you, sir. Silence! I know you, and have been finding out your rascally proceedings these ten days past. I have learnt much, more than you may fancy: and now this crowning villany [what if he had known of the ulterior designs?] gives me fair occasion to say once and for ever, begone!"

Jennings drew himself up with an air of insufferable impudence, and quietly answered,

"John Vincent, I am proud to leave your service. I trust I can afford to live without your help."

There was a general outcry at this speech, and Jonathan collared him again; but the baronet calmly set all straight by saying,

"Perhaps, sir, you may not be aware that your systematic thievings and extortions have amply justified me in detaining your iron chest and other valuables, until I find out how you may have come by them."

This was the *coup de grace* to Jennings, who looked scared and terrified:—what! all gone—all, his own beloved hoard, and that dear-bought crock of gold? Then Sir John added, after one minute of dignified and indignant silence,

"Begone!—Jonathan put him out; and if you will kick him out of the hall-door on your private account, I'll forgive you for it."

With that, the liveried Antinous raised the little monster by the small of the back, drew him struggling from the presence, and lifting him up like a football, inflicted one enormous kick that sent him spinning down the whole flight of fifteen marble stairs. This exploit accomplished to the satisfaction of all parties, Jonathan naturally enough returned to look for Grace; and his master, with a couple of friends who had run to the door to witness the catastrophe, returned immediately before him.

"Lord George Pypp, you will oblige me by leaving the young woman alone;" was Sir John's first angry reproof when he perceived the rustic beauty radiant with indignation at some mean offence.

"The worthy baronet wa-ants her for himself," drawled Pypp.

"Say that again, my lord, and you shall follow Jennings."

Whilst the noble youth was slowly elaborating a proper answer, Jonathan's voice was heard once more: he had long looked very white, kept both hands clenched, and seemed as if, saving his master's presence, he could, and would have vanquished the whole room of them.

"Master, have I your honour's permission to speak?"

"No, Jonathan, I'll speak for you; if, that is to say, Lord George will——"

"Paardon me, Sir John Devereux Vincent, your feyllow—and his master, are not fit company for Lord George Pypp;"—and he leisurely proceeded to withdraw.

"Stop a minute, Pypp, I've just one remark to make," hurriedly exclaimed Mr. Lionel Poynter, "if Sir John will suffer me; Vincent, my good friend, we are wrong—Pypp's wrong, and so am I. First then, let me beg pardon of a very pretty girl, for making her look prettier by blushes; next, as the maid really is engaged to you, my fine fellow, it is not beneath a gentleman to say, I hope that you'll forgive me for too warmly admiring your taste; as for George's imputation, Vincent—"

"I beyg to observe," enunciated the noble scion, "I'm awf, Poynter."

He gradually drew himself away, and the baronet never saw him more.

"For shame, Pypp!" shouted after him the warm-hearted Siliphant; "I tell you what it is, Vincent, you must let me give a toast:—'Grace and her lover!' here, my man, your master allows you to take a glass of wine with us; help your beauty too."

The toast was drank with high applause: and before Jonathan humbly led away his pleased and blushing Grace, he took an opportunity of saying,

"If I may be bold enough to speak, kind gentlemen, I wish to thank you: I oughtn't to be long, for I am nothing but your servant; let it be enough to say my heart is full. And I'm in hopes it wouldn't be very wrong in me, kind gentlemen, to propose;—'My noble master—honour and happiness to him!"

"Bravo! Jonathan, bravo-o-o-o!" there was a clatter of glasses;—and the humble pair of lovers retreated under cover of the toast.

CHAPTER XLIII.

SIMON ALONE.

Jennings gathered himself up, from that Jew-of-Malta tumble down the steps, less damaged by the fall than could have been imagined possible; the fact being that his cat-like nature had stood him in good stead —he had lighted on his feet; and nothing but a mighty dorsal bruise bore witness to the prowess of a Jonathan.

But, if his body was comparatively sound, the inner man was bruised all over: he crept back, and retreated to his room, in as broken and despondent a frame of mind, as any could have wished to bless him wherewithal. However, he still had one thing left to live for: his hoard —that precious hoard within his iron box, and then—the crock of gold.

He took Sir John's threat about detaining, and so forth, as merely future, and calculated on rendering it nugatory, by decamping forthwith, chattels and all; but he little expected to find that the idea had already been acted upon!

On that identical afternoon, when Simon had gone forth to insult Grace Acton with his villanous proposals, Sir John, on returning from a ride, had commanded his own seal to be placed on all Mr. Jennings's effects, and the boxes to be forthwith removed to a place of safety: induced thereto by innumerable proofs from every quarter that the bailiff had been cheating him on a most liberal scale, and plundering his tenants systematically. Therefore, when Jennings hastened to his chamber to console himself for all things by looking at his gold, and counting out a bag or two—it was gone, gone, irrevocably gone! safely stored away for rigid scrutiny in the grated muniment-room of Hurstley. Oh, what a howl the caitiff gave, when he saw that his treasure had been taken! he was a wild bull in a net; a crocodile caught upon the hooks; a hyena at bay. What could he do? which way should he turn? how help himself, or get his gold again? Unluckily—Oh, confusion, confusion!—his account-books were along with all his hoard, those tell-tale legers, wherein he had duly noted down, for his own private and triumphant glance, the curious difference between his lawful and unlawful gains; there, was every overcharge recorded, every matter of extortion systematically ranged, that he might take all the tenants in their turn; there, were filed the receipts of many honest men, whom the guardians and Sir John had long believed to be greatly in arrear; there, was recorded at length the catalogue of dues from tradesmen; there, the list of bribes for the custom of the Hall. It would amply authorize Sir John in appropriating the whole store; and Jennings thought of this with terror. Every thing was now obviously lost, lost! Oh, sickening little word, all lost! all he had ever lived for—all which had made him live the life he did—all which made him fear to die. "Fear to die—ha! who said that? I will not fear to die; yes, there is one escape left, I will hazard the blind leap; this misery shall have an end—this sleepless, haunted, cheated, hated wretch shall live no longer—ha! ha! ha! ha! I'll do it! I'll do it!"

Then did that wretched man strive in vain to kill himself, for his hour was not yet come. His first idea was laudanum—that only mean of any thing like rest to him for many weeks; and pouring out all he had, a little phial, nearly half a wine-glass full, he quickly drank it off: no use—no use; the agitation of his mind was too intense, and the habit of a continually increasing dose had made him proof against the poison; it would not even lull him, but seemed to stretch and rack his nerves, exciting him to deeds of bloody daring. Should he rush out, like a Malay running a muck, with a carving-knife in each hand, and kill right and left:—vengeance! vengeance! on Jonathan Floyd, and John Vincent? No, no; for some of them at last would overcome him, think him mad, and, O terror!—his doom for life, without the means of death, would be solitary confinement. "Stay! with this knife in my hand—means of death—yes, it shall be so." And he hurriedly drew the knife across his throat; no use, nothing done; his cowardly skin shrank away from cutting—he dared not cut again; a little bloody scratch was all.

But the heart, the heart—that should be easier! And the miscreant, not quite a Cato, gave a feeble stab, that made a little puncture. Not yet, Simon Jennings; no, not yet; you shall not cheat the gallows. "Ha! hanging, hanging! why had I not thought of that before?"

He mounted on a chair with a gimlet in his hand, and screwed it tightly into the wainscotting as high as he could reach; then he took a cord from the sacking of his bed, secured it to the gimlet, made a noose, put his head in, kicked the chair away—and swung by his wounded neck; in vain, all in vain; as he struggled in the agonies of self-protecting nature, the handle of the gimlet came away, and he fell heavily to the ground.

"Bless us!" said Sarah to one of the house-maids, as they were arranging their curl-papers to go to bed: "what can that noise be in Mr. Jennings's room? his tall chest of drawers has fallen, I shouldn't wonder: it was always unsafe to my mind. Listen, Jenny, will you?"

Jenny crept out, and, as laudable females sometimes do, listened at Simon's key-hole.

"Lack-a-daisy, Sall, such a groaning and moaning; p'raps he 's a-dying: put on your cap again, and tell Jonathan to go and see."

Sarah did as she was bid, and Jonathan did as he was bid; and there was Mr. Jennings on the floor, blue in the face, with a halter round his neck.

The house was soon informed of the interesting event, and the bailiff was nursed as tenderly as if he had been a sucking babe; fomentations, applications, hot potations: but he soon came to again, without any hope or wish to repeat the dread attempt: he was kept in bed, closely watched, and Stephen Cramp, together with his rival, Eager, remained continually in alternate attendance: until a day or two recovered him as strong as ever. I told you, Simon Jennings, that your time was not yet come.

CHAPTER XLIV.

THE TRIAL.

THE trial now came on, and Roger Acton stood arraigned of robbery and murder. I must hasten over lengthy legal technicalities, which would only serve to swell this volume, without adding one iota to its interest or usefulness. Nothing could be easier, nothing more worth while, as a matter of mere book-making, than to tear a few pages out of some musty record of Criminal Court Practice or other Newgate Calendar-piece of authorship, and wade wearily through the length and breadth of indictments, speeches, examinations, and all the other learned clatter of six hours in the judgment-halls of law. If the reader wishes for all this, let him pore over those unhealthy-looking books, whose exterior is dove-coloured as the kirtle of innocence, but their inwards black as the conscience of guilt; whitened sepulchres, all spotless without; but within them are enshrined the quibbling knavery, the distorted ingenuity, the mystifying learnedness, the warped and warping views of truth, the lying, slandering, bad-excusing, good-condemning principles and practices of those who cater for their custom at the guiltiest felon's cell, and would glory in defending Lucifer himself.

In the case of sheer innocence, indeed, as Roger's was—or in one of much doubt and secresy, where the client denies all guilt, and the counsel sees reason to believe him—let the advocate manfully battle out his cause: but where crime has poured out his confessions in a counsellor's ear—is not this man bought by gold to be a partaker and abettor in his sins, when he strives with all his might to clear the guilty, and not seldom throws the hideous charge on innocence? If the advocate has no wish to entrap his own conscience, nor to damage the tissue of his honour, let him reject the client criminal who confesses, and only plead for those from whom he has had no assurance of their guilt; or, better far, whose innocence he heartily believes in.

Such an advocate was Mr. Grantly, a barrister of talents and experience, who, from motives of the purest benevolence, did all that in him lay for Roger Acton. In one thing, however, and that of no small import, the kindly cautious man of law had contrived to do more harm than good: for, after having secretly made every effort, but in vain, to find Ben Burke as a witness—and after having heard that the aforesaid Ben was a notorious poacher, and only intimate at Hurstley with Acton and his family—he strongly recommended Roger to say nothing about the man or his adventure, as the acknowledgment of such an intimacy would only damage his cause: all that need appear was, that he found the crock in his garden, never mind how he "thought" it got there: poachers are not much in the habit of flinging away pots of gold, and no jury would believe but that the ill-reputed personage in question was an accomplice in the murder, and had shared the spoil with his friend Roger Acton. All this was very shrewd, and well meant; but was not so wise, for all that, as simple truth would have been: nevertheless, Roger acquiesced in it, for a better reason than Mr. Grantly's—namely, this: his feelings toward poor Ben had undergone an amiable revulsion, and, well aware how the whole neigbourhood were prejudiced against him for his freebooting propensities, he feared to get his good rough friend into trouble if he mentioned his nocturnal fishing at Pike island; especially when he considered that little red Savings' Bank, which, though innocent as to the getting, was questionable as to the rights of spending, and that, really, if he involved the professed poacher in this mysterious affair, he might put his liberty or life into very serious jeopardy. On this account, then, which Grace could not entirely find fault with (though she liked nothing that savoured of concealment), Roger Acton agreed to abide by Mr. Grantly's advice; and thus he never alluded to his connexion with the poacher.

Enlightened as we are, and intimate with all the hidden secrets of the story, we may be astonished to hear that, notwithstanding all Mr. Grantly's ingenuity, and all the siftings of cross-questioners, the case was clear as light against poor Acton. No *alibi*, he lived upon the spot. No witnesses to character; for Roger's late excesses had wiped away all former good report: kind Mr. Evans himself, with tears in his eyes, acknowledged sadly that Acton had once been a regular church-goer, a frequent communicant: but had fallen off of late, poor fellow! And then, in spite of protestations to the contrary, behold! the *corpus delicti*—that unlucky crock of gold, actually in the man's possession, and the fragment of shawl—was not that sufficient?

Jonathan Floyd in open court had been base enough to accuse Mr. Jennings of the murder. Mr. Jennings indeed! a strict man of high character, lately dismissed, after twenty years' service, in the most arbitrary manner by young Sir John, who had taken a great liking to the

Actons. People could guess why, when they looked on Grace: and Grace, too, was sufficient reason to account for Jonathan's wicked suspicions; of course, it was the lover's interest to throw the charge on other people. As to Mr. Jennings himself, just recovered from a fit of illness, it was astonishing how liberally and indulgently he prayed the court to show the prisoner mercy: his white and placid face looked quite benevolently at him—and this respectable person was a murderer, eh, Mr. Jonathan?

So, when the judge summed up, and clearly could neither find nor make a loop-hole for the prisoner, the matter seemed accomplished; all knew what the verdict must be—poor Roger Acton had not the shadow of a chance.

CHAPTER XLV.

ROGER'S DEFENCE.

THEN, while the jury were consulting—they would not leave the box, it seemed so clear—Roger broke the death-like silence; and he said:

"Judge, I crave your worship's leave to speak: and hearken to me, countrymen. Many evil things have I done in my time, both against God and my neighbour: I am ashamed, as well I may be, when I think on 'em: I have sworn, and drunk, and lied; I have murmured loudly—coveted wickedly—ay, and once I stole. It was a little theft, I lost it on the spot, and never stole again: pray God, I never may. Nevertheless, countrymen, and sinful though I be in the sight of Him who made us, according to man's judgment and man's innocency, I had lived among you all blameless, until I found that crock of gold. I did find it, countrymen, as God is my witness, and, therefore, though a sinner, I appeal to Him: He knoweth that I found it in the sedge that skirts my garden, at the end of my own celery trench. I did wickedly and foolishly to hide my find, worse to deny it, and worst of all to spend it in the low lewd way I did. But of robbery I am guiltless as you are. And as to this black charge of murder, till Simon Jennings spoke the word, I never knew it had been done. Folk of Hurstley, friends and neighbours, you all know Roger Acton—the old-time honest Roger of these forty years, before the devil made him mad by giving him much gold—did he ever maliciously do harm to man or woman, to child or poor dumb brute?—No, countrymen, I am no murderer. That the seemings are against me, I wot well; they may excuse your judgment in condemning me to death—and I and the good gentleman there who took my part (Heaven bless you, sir!) cannot go against the facts: but they speak falsely, and I truly; Roger Acton is an innocent man: may God defend the right!"

"Amen!" earnestly whispered a tremulous female voice, "and God will save you, father."

The court was still as death, except for sobbing; the jury were doubting and confounded; in vain Mr. Jennings, looking at the foreman, shook his head and stroked his chin in an incredulous and knowing manner; clearly they must retire, not at all agreed; and the judge himself, that masqued man in flowing wig and ermine, but still warmed by human sympathies, struck a tear from his wrinkled cheek; and all seemed to be involuntarily waiting (for the jury, though unable to decide, had not yet left their box), to see whether any sudden miracle would happen to save a man whom evidence made so guilty, and yet he bore upon his open brow the genuine signature of Innocence.

"Silence, there, silence! you can't get in; there's no room for'ards!" But a couple of javelin-men at the door were knocked down right and left, and through the dense and suffocating crowd, a black-whiskered fellow, elbowing his way against their faces, spite of all obstruction, struggled to the front behind the bar. Then, breathless with gigantic exertion (it was like a mammoth treading down the cedars), he roared out,

"Judge, swear me, I'm a witness; huzza! it's not too late."

And the irreverent gentleman tossed a fur cap right up to the skylight.

CHAPTER XLVI.

THE WITNESS.

Mr. Grantly brightened up at once, Grace looked happily to Heaven, and Roger Acton shouted out,

"Thank God! thank God!—there's Ben Burke!"

Yes, he had heard miles away of his friend's danger about an old sh[illegible] [illegible] a honey-pot full of gold, and he had made all speed, with Tom in his train, to come and bear witness to the innocence of Roger. The sensation in court, as may be well conceived, was thrilling; but a vociferous crier, and the deep anxiety to hear this sturdy witness, soon reduced all again to silence.

Then did they swear Benjamin Burke, who, to the scandal of his cause, would insist upon stating his profession to be "poacher;" and at first, poor simple fellow, seemed to have a notion that a sworn witness meant one who swore continually; but he was soon convinced otherwise, and his whole demeanour gradually became as polite and deferent as his coarse nature would allow. And Ben told his adventure on Pike island, as we have heard him tell it, pretty much in the same words, for the judge and Mr. Grantly let him take his own courses; and then he added (with a characteristic expletive, which we may as well omit, seeing it occasioned a cry of "order" in the court), "There, if that there white-livered little villain warn't the chap that brought the crocks, my name an't Ben Burke."

"Good Heavens! Mr. Jennings, what's the matter?" said a briefless one, starting up: this was Mr. Sharp, a personage on former occasions distinguished highly as a thieves' advocate, but now, unfortunately, out of work. "Loosen his cravat, some one there; the gentleman is in fits."

"Oh, Aunt—Aunt Quarles, don't throttle me; I'll tell all—all; let go, let go!" and the wretched man slowly recovered, as Ben Burke said,

"Ay, my lord, ask him yourself, the little wretch can tell you all about it."

"I submit, my lurd," interposed the briefless one, "that this respectable gentleman is taken ill, and that his presence may now be dispensed with, as a witness in the cause."

"No, sir, no;" deliberately answered Jennings; "I must stay: the time I find is come; I have not slept for weeks; I am exhausted utterly; I have lost my gold; I am haunted by her ghost; I can go no where but that face follows me—I can do nothing but her fingers clutch my throat. It is time to end this misery. In hope to lay her spirit, I would have offered up a victim: but—but she will not have him. Mine was the hand that—"

"Pardon me," upstarted Mr. Sharp, "this poor gentleman is a monomaniac; pray, my lurd, let him be removed while the trial is proceeding."

"You horse-hair hypocrite, you!" roared Ben, "would you hang the innocent, and save the guilty?"

Would he? would Mr. Philip Sharp? Ay, that he would; and glad of such a famous opportunity. What! would not Newgate rejoice, and Horsemonger be glad? Would not his bag be filled with briefs from the community of burglars, and his purse be rich in gold subscribed by the brotherhood of thieves? Great at once would be his name among the purlieus of iniquity: and every rogue in London would retain but Philip Sharp. Would he? ask him again.

But Jennings quietly proceeded like a speaking statue.

"I am not mad, most noble—" [the Bible-read villain was from habit quoting Paul]—"my lord, I mean. My hand did the deed: I throttled her" (here he gave a scared look over his shoulder): "yes—I did it once and again: I took the crock of gold. You may hang me now, Aunt Quarles."

"My lurd, my lurd, this is a most irregular proceeding," urged Mr. Sharp; "on the part of the prisoner—I, I crave pardon—on behalf of this most respectable and deluded gentleman, Mr. Simon Jennings, I contend that no one may criminate himself in this way, without the shadow of evidence to support such suicidal testimony. Really, my lurd—"

"Oh, sir, but my father may go free?" earnestly asked Grace. But Ben Burke's voice—I had almost written woice—overwhelmed them all:

"Let me speak, judge, an't it please your honour, and take you notice, Master Horsehair. You wan't ewidence, do you, beyond the man's confession: here, I'll give it you. Look at this here wice:" and he stretched forth his well-known huge and horny hand:

"When I caught that dridful little reptil by the arm, he wriggled like a sniggled eel, so I was forced you see, to grasp him something tighter, and could feel his little arm-bones crack like any chicken's: now then, if his left elbow an't black and blue, though it's a month a-gone and more, I'll eat it. Strip him and see."

No need to struggle with the man, or tear his coat off. Jennings appeared only too glad to find that there was other evidence than his own foul tongue, and that he might be hung at last without sacking-rope or gimlet; so, he quietly bared his arm, and the elbow looked all manner of colours—a mass of old bruises.

CHAPTER XLVII.

MR. SHARP'S ADVOCACY.

THE whole court trembled with excitement: it was deep, still silence; and the judge said,

"Prisoner at the bar, there is now no evidence against you: gentlemen of the jury, of course you will acquit him."

The foreman: "All agreed, my lord, not guilty."

"Roger Acton," said the judge, "to God alone you owe this marvellous, almost miraculous, interposition: you have had many wrongs innocently to endure, and I trust that the right feelings of society will requite you for them in this world, as, if you serve Him, God will in the next. You are honourably acquitted, and may leave this bar."

In vain the crier shouted, in vain the javelin-men helped the crier, the court was in a tumult of joy; Grace sprang to her father's neck, and Sir John Vincent, who had been in attendance sitting near the judge all the trial through, came down to him, and shook his hand warmly.

Roger's eyes ran over, and he could only utter,

"Thank God! thank God! He does better for me than I deserved." But the court was hushed at last: the jury rĕsworn; certain legal forms and technicalities speedily attended to, as counts of indictment, and so forth: and the judge then quietly said,

"Simon Jennings, stand at that bar."

He stood there like an image.

"My lurd, I claim to be prisoner's counsel."

"Mr. Sharp—the prisoner shall have proper assistance by all means; but I do not see how it will help your case, if you cannot get your client to plead not guilty."

While Mr. Philip Sharp converses earnestly with the criminal in confidential whispers, I will entertain the sagacious reader with a few admirable lines I have just cut out of a newspaper: they are headed

"SUPPRESSION OF TRUTH AND EXCLUSION OF EVIDENCE.

"Lawyers abhor any short cut to the truth. The pursuit is the thing for their pleasure and profit, and all their rules are framed for making the most of it.

"Crime is to them precisely what the fox is to the sportsman: and the object is not to pounce on it, and capture it at once, but to have a good run for it, and to exhibit skill and address in the chase. Whether the culprit or the fox escape or not, is a matter of indifference, the run being the main thing.

"The punishment of crime is as foreign to the object of lawyers, as the extirpation of the fox is to that of sportsmen. The sportsman, because he hunts the fox, sees in the summary destruction of the fox by the hand of a clown, an offence foul, strange, and unnatural, little short of murder. The lawyer treats crime in the same way: his business is the chase of it; but, that it may exist for the chase, he lays down rules protecting it against surprises and capture by any methods but those of the forensic field.

"One good turn deserves another, and as the lawyer owes his business to crime, he naturally makes it his business to favour and spare it as much as possible. To seize and destroy it wherever it can be got at, seems to him as barbarous as shooting a bird sitting, or a hare in her form, does to the sportsman. The phrase, to give *law*, for the allowance of a start, or any chance of escape, expresses the methods of lawyers in the pursuit of crime, and has doubtless been derived from their practice.

"Confession is the thing most hateful to law, for this stops its sport at the outset. It is the surrender of the fox to the hounds. 'We don't want your stinking body,' says the lawyer; 'we want the run after the scent. Away with you, be off; retract your admission, take the benefit of telling a lie, give us employment, and let us take our chance of hunting out, in our roundabout ways, the truth, which we will not take when it lies before us.'"

As I perceive that Mr. Sharp has not yet made much impression upon the desponding prisoner, suffer me to recommend to your notice another sensible leader: the abuse which it would combat calls loudly for amendment. There is plenty of time to spare, for some preliminaries of trial have yet to be arranged, and the judge has just stepped out to get a sandwich, and every body stands at ease; moreover, gentle reader, the paragraphs following are well worthy of your attention. Let us name them,

"MORBID SYMPATHIES.

"We have often thought that the tenderness shown by our law to presumed criminals is as injurious as it is inconsistent and excessive. A miserable beggar, a petty rioter, the wretch who steals a loaf to satisfy the gnawings of his hunger, is roughly seized, closely examined, and severely punished; meanwhile, the plain common sense of our mobs, if not of our magistracy, has pitied the offender, and perhaps acquitted him. But let some apparent murderer be caught, almost in the flagrant deed of his atrocity; let him, to the best of all human belief, have killed, disembowelled, and dismembered; let him have united the coolness of consummate craft to the boldest daring of iniquity, and straightway (though the generous crowd may hoot and hunt the wretch with yelling execration) he finds in law and lawyers, refuge, defenders, and apologists. Tenderly and considerately is he cautioned on no account to criminate himself: he is exhorted, even by judges, to withdraw the honest and truthful plea of 'guilty,' now the only amends which such a one can make to the outraged laws of God and man: he is defended, even to the desperate length of malignant accusation of the innocent, by learned men, whose aim it is to pervert justice and screen the guilty! he is lodged and tended with more circumstances of outward comfort and consideration than he probably has ever experienced in all his life before; and if, notwithstanding the ingenuity of his advocates, and the merciful glosses of his judge, a simple-minded British jury capitally convict him, and he is handed over to the executioner, he still finds pious gentlemen ready to weep over him in his cell, and titled dames to send him white camellias, to wear upon his heart when he is hanging.*

"Now what is the necessary consequence of this, but a mighty, a fearfully influential premium on crime? And what is its radical cause, but the absurd indulgence wherewith our law greets the favoured, *because* the atrocious criminal? Upon what principle of propriety, or of natural justice, should a seeming murderer not be—we will not say sternly, but even kindly—catechised, and for his very soul's sake counselled to confess his guilt? Why should the *morale* of evidence be so thoroughly lost sight of, and a malefactor, who is ready to acknowledge crime, or unable, when questioned, to conceal it, on no account be listened to, lest he may do his precious life irreparable harm? It is not agonized repentance, or incidental disclosure, that makes the culprit his own executioner, but his crime that has preceded; it is not the weak, avowing tongue, but the bold and bloody hand.

* It has been stated as a fact, that a certain Lady L—— S——, in her last interview with a young man, condemned to death for the brutal murder of his sweetheart, presented him with a white camellia, as a token of eternal peace, which the gallant gentleman actually wore at the gallows in his button-hole.

"We are unwilling to allude specifically to the name of any recent malefactor in connexion with these plain remarks; for, in the absence alike of hindered voluntary confession and of incomplete legal evidence, we would not prejudge, that is, prejudice a case. But we do desire to exclaim against any further exhibition of that morbid tenderness wherewith all persons are sure to be treated, if only they are accused of enormities more than usually disgusting; and we specially protest against that foolish, however ancient, rule in our criminal law, which discourages and rejects the slenderest approach to a confession, while it has sacrificed many an innocent victim to the uncertainty of evidence, supported by nothing more safe than outward circumstantials."

At length, and after much gesticulation and protestation, Mr. Sharp has succeeded; he had apparently innoculated the miserable man with hopes; for the miscreant now said firmly, "I plead not guilty."

The briefless one looked happy—nay, triumphant: Jennings was a wealthy man, all knew; and, any how, he should bag a bouncing fee. How far such money was likely to do him any good, he never stopped to ask. "Money is money," said Philip Sharp and the Emperor Vespasian.

We need not trouble ourselves to print Mr. Sharp's very flashy, flippant speech. Suffice it to say, that, not content with asserting vehemently on his conscience as a Christian, on his honour as a man, that Simon Jennings was an innocent, maligned, persecuted individual; labouring, perhaps, under mono-mania, but pure and gentle as the babe new-born—not satisfied with traducing honest Ben Burke as a most suspicious witness, probably a murderer—ay, *the* murderer himself, a mere riotous ruffian [Ben here chucked his cap at him, and thereby countenanced the charge], a mere scoundrel, not to say scamp, whom no one should believe upon his oath; he again, with all the semblance of sincerity, accused, however vainly, Roger Acton: and lastly, to the disgust and astonishment of the whole court, added, with all acted appearances of fervent zeal for justice, "And I charge his pious daughter, too, that far too pretty piece of goods, Grace Acton, with being accessory to this atrocious crime after the fact!"

There was a storm of shames and hisses; but the judge allayed it, quietly saying,

"Mr. Sharp, be so good as to confine your attention to your client; he appears to be quite worthy of you."

Then Mr. Sharp, like the firm just man immortalized by Flaccus, stood stout against the visage of the judge, sneered at the wrath of citizens commanding things unjust, turned to Ben Burke minaciously, calling him "*Dux inquieti turbidus Adriæ*" [as Burke had heard this quotation, he thought it was about the "ducks" he had been decoying], and altogether seemed not about to be put down, though the huge globe crack about his ears. After this, he calmly worded on, seeming to regard the judge's stinging observation with the same sort of indifference as the lion would a dew-drop on his mane; and having poured out all manner of voluminous bombast, he gradually ran down, and came to a conclusion; then, jumping up refreshed, like the bounding of a tennis-ball, he proceeded to call witnesses; and, judging from what happened at the inquest, as well as because he wished to overwhelm a suspected and suspecting witness, he pounced, somewhat infelicitously, on Jonathan Floyd.

"So, my fine young fellow, you are a footman, eh, at Hurstley?"

"Yes, sir, an' it please you—or rather, an' it please my master."

"You remember what happened on the night of the late Mrs. Quarles's decease?"

"Oh, many things happened; Mr. Jennings was lost, he wasn't to be found, he was hid somewhere, nobody saw him till next morning."

"Stop, sirrah! not quite so quick, if you please; you are on your oath, be careful what you say. I have it in evidence, sirrah, before the coroner;" and he looked triumphantly about him at this clencher to all Jonathan's testimony; "that you saw him yourself that night speaking to the dog; what do you mean by swearing that nobody saw him till next morning?"

"Well, mister, I mean this; whether or no poor old Mrs. Quarles saw her affectionate nephew that night before the clock struck twelve, there's none alive to tell; but no one else did—for Sarah and I sat up for him till past midnight. He was hidden away somewhere, snug enough; and as I verily believe, in the poor old 'ooman's own—"

"Silence, silence! sir, I say; we want none of your impertinent guesses here, if you please: to the point, sirrah, to the point; you swore before the coroner, that you had seen Mr. Jennings, in his courage and his kindness, quieting the dog that very night, and now—"

"Oh," interrupted Jonathan in his turn, "for the matter of that, when I saw him with the dog, it was hard upon five in the morning. And here, gentlemen," added Floyd, with a promiscuous and comprehensive bow all round, "if I may speak my mind about the business—"

"Go down, sir!" said Mr. Sharp, who began to be afraid of truths.

"Pardon me, this may be of importance," remarked Roger Acton's friend; "say what you have to say, young man."

"Well, then, gentlemen and my lord, I mean to say thus much Jennings there, the prisoner (and I'm glad to see him standing at the bar), swore at the inquest that he went to quiet Don, going round through the front door; now, none could get through that door without my hearing of him; and certainly a little puny Simon like him could never do so without I came to help him; for the lock was stiff with rust, and the bolt out of his reach."

"Stop, young man; my respected client, Mr. Jennings, got upon a chair."

"Indeed, sir? then he must ha' created the chair for that special purpose: there wasn't one in the hall then; no, nor for two days after, when they came down bran-new from Dowbiggins in London, with the rest o' the added furnitur' just before my honoured master."

This was conclusive, certainly; and Floyd proceeded.

"Now, gentlemen and my lord, if Jennings did not go that way, nor the kitchen-way neither—for he always was too proud for scullery-door and kitchen—and if he did not give himself the trouble to unfasten the dining-room or study windows, or to unscrew the iron bars of his own pantry, none of which is likely, gentlemen—there was but one other way out, and that way was through Bridget Quarles's own room. Now—"

"Ah—that room, that bed, that corpse, that crock!—It is no use, no use," the wretched miscreant added slowly, after his first hurried exclamations; "I did the deed, I did it! guilty, guilty." And, notwithstanding all Mr. Sharp's benevolent interferences, and appeals to judge and jury on the score of mono-mania, and shruggings-up of shoulders at his client's folly, and virtuous indignation at the evident leaning of the court—the murderer detailed what he had done. He spoke quietly and firmly, in his usually stern and tyrannical style, as if severe upon himself, for being what?—a man of blood, a thief, a perjured false accuser? No, no; lower in the scale of Mammon's judgment, worse in the estimate of him whose god is gold; he was now a pauper, a mere moneyless forked animal; a beggared, emptied, worthless, penniless creature: therefore was he stern against his ill-starred soul, and took vengeance on himself for being poor.

It was a consistent feeling, and common with the mercantile of this world; to whom the accidents of fortune are every thing, and the qualities of mind nothing; whose affections ebb and flow towards friends, relations—yea, their own flesh and blood, with the varying tide of wealth: whom a luckless speculation in cotton makes an enemy, and gambling gains in corn restore a friend; men who fall down mentally before the golden calf, and offer up their souls to Nebuchadnezzar's idol: men who never saw harm nor shame in the craftiest usurer or meanest pimp, provided he has thousands in the three per cents.; and whose indulgent notions of iniquity reach their climax in the phrase—the man is poor.

So then, with unhallowed self-revenge, Simon rigidly detailed his crimes: he led the whole court step by step, as I have led the reader, through the length and breadth of that terrible night: of the facts he concealed nothing, and the crowded hall of judgment shuddered as one man, when he came to his awful disclosure, hitherto unsuspected, unimagined, of that second strangulation: as to feelings, he might as well have been a galvanized mummy, an automaton lay-figure enunciating all with bellows and clapper, for any sense he seemed to have of shame, or fear, or pity; he admitted his lie about the door, complimented Burke on the accuracy of his evidence, and declared Roger Acton not merely innocent, but ignorant of the murder.

This done, without any start or trepidation in his manner as formerly, he turned his head over his left shoulder, and said, in a deep whisper, heard all over the court, "And now, Aunt Quarles, I am coming; look out, woman, I will have my revenge for all your hauntings: again shall we wrestle, again shall we battle, again shall I throttle you, again, again!"

O, most fearful thought! who knoweth but it may be true? that spirits of wickedness and enmity may execute each other's punishment, as those of righteousness and love minister each other's happiness! that—damned among the damned—the spirit of a Nero may still delight in torturing, and that those who in this world were mutual workers of iniquity, may find themselves in the next, sworn retributors of wrath? No idle threat was that of the demoniac Simon, and possibly with no vain fears did the ghost of the murdered speed away.

When the sensation of horror, which for a minute delayed the court-business, and has given us occasion to think that fearful thought, when this had gradually subsided, the foreman of the jury, turning to the judge, said,

"My lord, we will not trouble your lordship to sum up; we are all agreed—Guilty."

One word about Mr. Sharp: he was entirely chagrined; his fortunes were at stake; he questioned whether any one in Newgate would think of him again. To make matters worse, when he whispered for a fee to Mr. Jennings (for he did whisper, however contrary to professional etiquette), that worthy gentleman replied by a significant sneer, to the effect that he had not a penny to give him, and would not if he had: whereupon Mr. Sharp began to coincide with the rest of the world in regarding so impoverished a murderer as an atrocious criminal; then, turning from his client with contempt, he went to the length of congratulating Roger on his escape, and actually offered his hand to Ben Burke. The poacher's reply was characteristic: "As you means it kindly, Master Horsehair, I won't take it for an insult: howsomdever, either your hand or mine, I won't say which, is too dirty for shaking. Let me do you a good turn, Master: there's a blue-bottle on your wig; I think as it's Beelzebub a-whispering in your ear: allow me to drive him away." And the poacher dealt him such a cuff that the barrister reeled again; and instantly afterwards took advantage of the cloud of hair-powder to leave the court unseen.

CHAPTER XLVIII.

SENTENCE AND DEATH.

Silence, silence! shouted the indignant crier, and the episodical cause of Burke, *v.* Sharp, was speedily hushed.

The eyes of all now concentred on the miserable criminal; for the time, every thing else seemed forgotten. Roger, Grace, and Ben, grouped together in the midst of many friends, who had crowded round them to congratulate, leaned forward like the rest of that dense hall, as simply thralled spectators. Mr. Grantly lifted up a pair of very moistened eyes behind his spectacles, and looked earnestly on, with his wig, from agitation, wriggled tails in front. The judge (it was good old Baron Parker) put on the black cap to pronounce sentence. There was a pause.

But we have forgotten Simon Jennings—what was he about? did that "cynosure of neighbouring eyes" appear alarmed at his position, anxious at his fate, or even attentive to what was going on? No: he not only appeared, but was, the most unconcerned individual in the whole court: he even tried to elude utter vacancy of thought by amusing himself with external things about him: and, on Wordsworth's principle of inducing sleep by counting

> "A flock of sheep, that leisurely pass by,
> One after one,"

he was trying to reckon, for pleasant peace of mind's sake, how many folks were looking at him. Only see—he is turning his white stareful face in every direction, and his lips are going a thousand and forty-one, a thousand and forty-two, a thousand and forty-three; he will not hurry it over, by leaving out the "thousand:" alas! this holiday of idiotic occupation is all the respite now his soul can know.

And the judge broke that awful silence, saying,

"Prisoner at the bar, you are convicted on your own confession, as well as upon other evidence, of crimes too horrible to speak of. The deliberate repetition of that fearful murder, classes you among the worst of wretches whom it has been my duty to condemn: and when to this is added your perjured accusation of an innocent man, whom nothing but a miracle has rescued, your guilt becomes appalling—too hideous for human contemplation. Miserable man, prepare for death, and after that the judgment; yet, even for you, if you repent, there may be pardon; it is my privilege to tell even you, that life and hope are never to be separated, so long as God is merciful, or man may be contrite. The Sacrifice of Him who died for us all, for you, poor fellow-creature [here the good judge wept for a minute like a child]—for you, no less than for me, is available even to the chief of sinners. It is my duty and my comfort to direct your blood-stained, but immortal soul, eagerly to fly to that only refuge from eternal misery. As to this world, your career of wickedness is at an end: covetousness has conceived and generated murder; and murder has even over-stept its common bounds, to repeat the terrible crime, and then to throw its guilt upon the innocent. Entertain no hope whatever of a respite; mercy in your case would be sin.

"The sentence of the court is, that you, Simon Jennings, be taken from that bar to the county jail, and thence on this day fortnight to be conveyed to the place of execution within the prison, and there by the hands of the common hangman be hanged by the neck——"

At the word "neck," in the slow and solemn enunciation of the judge, issued a terrific scream from the mouth of Simon Jennings: was he mad after all—mad indeed? or was he being strangled by some unseen executioner? Look at him, convulsively doing battle with an invisible foe! his eyes start; his face gets bluer and bluer; his hands, fixed like griffin's talons, clutch at vacancy—he wrestles—struggles—falls.

All was now confusion: even the grave judge, who had necessarily stopped at that frightful interruption, leaned eagerly over his desk, while barristers and serjeants learned in the law crowded round the prisoner: "He is dying! air, there—air! a glass of water, some one!"

About a thimbleful of water, after fifty spillings, arrived safely in a tumbler; but as for air, no one in that court had breathed any thing but nitrogen for four hours.

He was dying: and three several doctors, hoisted over the heads of an admiring multitude, rushed to his relief with thirsty lancets: apoplexy—oh, of course, apoplexy: and they nodded to each other confidentially.

Yes, he was dying: they might not move him now: he must die in his sins, at that dread season, upon that dread spot. Perjury, robbery, and murder—all had fastened on his soul, and were feeding there like harpies at a Strophadian feast, or vultures ravening on the liver of Prometheus. Guilt, vengeance, death had got hold of him, and rent him, as wild horses tearing him asunder different ways; he lay there gurgling, strangling, gasping, panting: none could help him, none could give him ease; he was going on the dark, dull path in the bottom of that awful valley, where Death's cold shadow overclouds it like a canopy; he was sinking in that deep black water, that must some day drown us all—pray Heaven, with hope to cheer us then, and comfort in the fierce extremity! His eye filmed, his lower jaw relaxed, his head dropped back—he was dying—dying—dying—

On a sudden, he rallied! his blood had rushed back again from head to heart, and all the doctors were deceived—again he battled, and fought, and wrestled, and flung them from him; again he howled, and his eyes glared lightning—mad? Yes, mad—stark mad! quick—quick—we cannot hold him: save yourselves there!

But he only broke away from them to stand up free—then he gave one scream, leaped high into the air, and fell down dead in the dock, with a crimson stream of blood issuing from his mouth.

CHAPTER XLIX.

RIGHTEOUS MAMMON.

Thus the crock of gold had gained another victim. Is the curse of its accumulation still unsatisfied? Must more misery be born of that unhallowed store? Shall the poor man's wrongs, and his little ones' cry for bread, and the widows' vain appeal for indulgence in necessity, and the debtor's useless hope for time—more time—and the master's misused bounty, and the murmuring dependants' ever-extorted dues—must the frauds, falsehoods, meannesses, and hardnesses of half a century long, concentrate in that small crock—must these plead still for bloody judgments from on high against all who touch that gold?

No! the miasma is dispelled: the curse is gone: the crimes are expiated. The devil in that jar is dispossessed, and with Simon's last gasp has returned unto his own place. The murderer is dead, and has thereby laid the ghost of his mate in sin, the murdered victim; while that victim has long ago paid by blood for her many years of mean domestic pilfering.

And now I see a better angel hovering round the crock: it is purified, sanctified, accepted. It is become a talent from the Lord, instead of a temptation from the devil; and the same coin, which once has been but dull, unrighteous mammon, through justice, thankfulness, and piety, shineth as the shekel of the temple. Gratefully, as from God, the rightful owner now may take the gift.

For, gold is a creature of God, representing many excellencies: the sweat of honest Industry distils to gold; the hot-spring of Genius congeals to gold; the blessing upon Faithfulness is often showered in gold; and Charities not seldom are guerdoned back with gold. Let no man affect to despise what Providence hath set so high in power. None do so but the man who has it not, and who knows that he covets it in vain. Sour grapes—sour grapes—for he may not touch the vintage. This is not the verdict of the wise; the temptation he may fear, the cares he may confess, the misuse he may condemn: yet will he acknowledge that, received at God's hand, and spent in his service, there is scarce a creature in this nether world of higher name than Money.

Beauty fadeth; Health dieth; Talents—yea, and Graces—go to bloom in other spheres—but when Benevolence would bless, and bless for ages, his blessing is vain, but for money—when Wisdom would teach, and teach for ages, the teacher must be fed, and the school built, and the scholar helped upon his way by money—righteous money. There is a righteous money as there is unrighteous mammon; but both have their ministrations here limited to earth and time; the one, a fruit of heaven—the other, a fungus from below: yet the fruit will bring no blessing, if the Grower be forgotten; neither shall the fungus yield a poison, if warmed awhile beneath the better sun. Like all other gifts, given to us sweet, but spoilt in the using, gold may turn to good or ill: Health may kick, like fat Jeshurun in his wantonness; Power may change from beneficence to tyranny; Learning may grow critical in motes until it overlooks the sunbeam; Love may be degraded to an instinct; Zaccheus may turn Pharisee; Religion may cant into the hypocrite, or dogmatize to theologic hate. Even so it is with money: its power of doing good has no other equivalent in this world than its power of doing evil: it is like fire—used for hospitable warmth, or wide-wasting ravages; like air—the gentle zephyr, or the destroying hurricane. Nevertheless, all is for this world—this world only; a matter extraneous to the spirit, always foreign, often-times adversary: let a man beware of lading himself with that thick clay.

I see a cygnet on the broad Pactolus, stemming the waters with its downy breast; and anon, it would rise upon the wing, and soar to other skies; so, taking down that snow-white sail, it seeks for a moment to rest its foot on shore, and thence take flight: alas, poor bird! thou art sinking in those golden sands, the heavy morsels clog thy flapping wing—in vain—in vain thou triest to rise—Pactolus chains thee down.

Even such is wealth unto the wisest; wealth at its purest source, exponent of labour and of mind. But, to the frequent fool, heaped with foulest dross—for the cygnet of Pactolus and those golden sands, read—the hippopotamus wallowing in the Niger, and smothered in a bay of mud.

CHAPTER L.

THE CROCK A BLESSING.

THERE was no will found: it is likely Mrs. Quarles had never made one; she feared death too much, and all that put her in mind of it. So the next of kin, the only one to have the crock of gold, was Susan Scott, a good, honest, hard-working woman, whom Jennings, by many arts, had kept away from Hurstley: her husband, a poor thatcher, sadly out of work except in ricking time, and crippled in both legs by having fallen from a hay-stack: and as to the family, it was already as long a flight of steps as would reach to an ordinary first floor, with a prospect (so the gossips said) of more in the distance. Susan was a Wesleyan Methodist—many may think, more the pity: but she neither disliked church, nor called it steeple-house: only, forasmuch as Hagglesfield was blessed with a sporting parson, the chief reminders of whose presence in the parish were strifes perpetual about dues and tithes, it is little blame or wonder, if the starving sheep went anywhither else for pasturage and water. So, then, Susan was a good mother, a kind neighbour, a religious, humble-minded Christian: is it not a comfort now to know that the gold was poured into her lap, and that she hallowed her good luck by prayers and praises?

I judge it worth while stepping over to Hagglesfield for a couple of minutes, to find out how she used that gold, and made the crock a blessing. Susan first thought of her debts: so, to every village shop around, I fear they were not a few, which had kindly given her credit, some for weeks, some for months, and more than one for a year, the happy housewife went to pay in full; and not this only, but with many thanks, to press a little present upon each, for well-timed help in her adversity.

The next thought was near akin to it: to take out of pawn divers valued articles, two or three of which had been her mother's; for Reuben's lameness, poor man, kept him much out of work, and the childer came so quick, and ate so fast, and wore out such a sight of shoes, that, but for an occasional appeal to Mrs. Quarles—it was her one fair feature this—they must long ago have been upon the parish: now, however, all the ancestral articles were redeemed, and honour no doubt with them.

Thirdly, Susan went to her minister in best bib and tucker, and humbly begged leave to give a guinea to the school; and she hoped his reverence wouldn't be above accepting a turkey and chine, as a small token of her gratitude to him for many consolations: it pleased me much to hear that the good man had insisted upon Susan and her husband coming to eat it with him the next day at noon.

Fourthly, Susan prudently set to work, and rigged out the whole family in tidy clothes, with a touch of mourning upon each for poor Aunt Bridget, and unhappy brother Simon; while the fifthly, sixthly, and to conclude, were concerned in a world of notable and useful schemes, with a strong resolution to save as much as possible for schooling and getting out the children.

It was wonderful to see how much good was in that gold, how large a fund of blessing was hidden in that crock: Reuben Scott gained health, the family were fed, clad, taught; Susan grew in happiness at least as truly as in girth; and Hagglesfield beheld the goodness of that store, whose curse had startled all Hurstley-cum-Piggesworth.

But also at Hurstley now are found its consequential blessings.

We must take another peep at Roger and sweet Grace; they, and Ben too, and Jonathan, and Jonathan's master, may all have cause to thank an overruling Providence, for blessing on the score of Bridget's crock. Only before I come to that, I wish to be dull a little hereabouts, and moralize: the reader may skip it, if he will—but I do not recommend him so to do.

For, evermore in the government of God, good groweth out of evil: and, whether man note the fact or not, Providence, with secret care, doth vindicate itself. There is justice done continually, even on this stage of trial, though many pine and murmur: substantial retribution, even in this poor dislocated world of wrong, not seldom overtakes the sinner, not seldom encourages the saint. Encourages? yea, and punishes: blessing him with kind severity; teaching him to know himself a mere bad root, if he be not grafted on his God; proving that the laws which govern life are just, and wise, and kind; showing him that a man's own heart's desire, if fulfilled, would probably tend to nothing short of sin, sorrow, and calamity; that many seeming goods are withheld, because they are evils in disguise; and many seeming ills allowed, because they are masqueraded blessings; and demonstrating, as in this strange tale, that the unrighteous Mammon is a cruel master, a foul tempter, a pestilent destroyer of all peace, and a teeming source of both world's misery.

Listen to the sayings of the Wisest King of men:

"As the whirlwind passeth, so is the wicked no more: but the righteous is an everlasting foundation."

"The righteous is delivered out of trouble, and the wicked cometh in his stead."

"He that trusteth in his riches shall fall: but the righteous shall flourish as a branch."

"Better is a little with righteousness, than great revenues without right.'

"The wicked shall be a ransom for the righteous, and the transgressor for the upright."

"A good man leaveth an inheritance to his children's children: and the wealth of the sinner is laid up for the just."

CHAPTER LI.

POPULARITY.

THE storm is lulled: the billows of temptation have ebbed away from shore, and the clouds of adversity have flown to other skies.

"The winter is past; the rain is over and gone; the flowers appear upon the earth; the time of the singing of birds is come, and the voice of the turtle is heard in our land: the fig-tree putteth forth his green figs, and the blossoms of the vine smell sweetly. Arise, and come away."

Yesterday's trial, and its unlooked-for issue, have raised Roger Acton to the rank of hero. The town's excitement is intense: and the little inn, where he and Grace had spent the night in gratitude and prayerful praise, is besieged by carriages full of lords and gentlemen, eager to see and speak with Roger.

Humbly and reverently, yet preserving an air of quiet self-possession, the labourer received their courteous kindnesses; and acquitted himself of what may well be called the honours of that levee, with a dignity native to the true-born Briton, from the time of Caractacus at Rome to our own.

But if Roger was a demi-god, Grace was at the least a goddess; she charmed all hearts with her modest beauty. Back with the shades of night, and the prison-funeral of Jennings, fled envy, hatred, malice, and all uncharitableness; the elderly sisterhood of Hurstley, not to be out of a fashion set by titled dames, hastened to acknowledge her perfections; Calumny was shamed, and hid his face; the uncles, aunts, and cousins of the hill-top yonder, were glad to hold their tongues, and bite their nails in peace: Farmer Floyd and his Mrs. positively came with peace-offerings—some sausage-meat, elder-wine, jam, and other dainties, which were to them the choicest sweets of life: and as for Jonathan, he never felt so proud of Grace in all his life before; the handsome fellow stood at least a couple of inches taller.

Honest Ben Burke, too, that most important witness—whose coming was as Blucher's at Waterloo, and secured the well-earned conquest of the day—though it must be confessed that his appearance was something of the satyr, still had he been Phœbus Apollo in person, he would scarcely have excited sincerer admiration. More than one fair creature sketched his unkempt head, and loudly wished that its owner was a bandit; more than one bright eye discovered beauty in his open countenance —though a little soap and water might have made it more distinguishable. Well—well—honest Ben—they looked, and wisely looked, at the frank and friendly mind hidden under that rough carcase, and little wonder that they loved it.

Now, to all this stream of hearty English sympathy, the kind and proper feeling of young Sir John resolved to give a right direction. His fashionable friends were gone, except Silliphant and Poynter, both good fellows in the main, and all the better for the absence (among others) of that padded old debauchee, Sir Richard Hunt, knight of the order of St. Sapphira—that frivolous inanity, Lord George Pypp—and that professed gentleman of gallantry, Mr. Harry Mynton. The follies and the vices had decamped—had scummed off, so to speak—leaving the more rectified spirits behind them, to recover at leisure, as best they might, from all that ferment of dissipation. So, then, there was now neither ridicule, nor interest, to stand in the way of a young and wealthy heir's well-timed schemes of generosity.

Well-timed they were, and Sir John knew it, though calculation seldom had a footing in his warm and heedless heart; but he could not shut his eyes to the fact, that the state of feeling among his hereditary labourers was any thing but pleasant. In truth, owing to the desperate malpractices of Quarles and Jennings, perhaps no property in the kingdom had got so ill a name as Hurstley: discontent reigned paramount; incendiary fires had more than once occurred; threatening notices, very ill-spelt, and signed by one *soi-disant* Captain Blood, had been dropped, in dead of winter, at the door-sills of the principal farmers; and all the other fruits of long-continued penury, extortion, and mis-government, were hanging ripe upon the bough—a foul and fatal harvest.

Therefore, did the kind young landlord, who had come to live among his own peasantry, resolve, not more nobly than wisely, to seize an opportunity so good as this, for restoring, by a stroke of generous policy, peace and content on his domain. No doubt, the baronet rejoiced, as well he might, at the honourable acquittal of innocence, and the mysteries of murder now cleared up; he made small secret of his satisfaction at the doom of Jennings; and, as for Bridget Quarles, by all he could learn of her from tenants' wives, and other female dependants, he had no mind to wish her back again, or to think her fate ill-timed: nevertheless, he was even more glad of an occasion to vindicate his own good feelings; and prove to the world that bailiff Simon Jennings was a very opposite character to landlord Sir John Devereux Vincent.

To carry out his plan, he determined to redress all wrongs within one day, and to commence by bringing "honest Roger" in triumph home again to Hurstley; following the suggestion of Baron Parker, to make some social compensation for his wrongs. With this view, Sir John took counsel of the county-town authorities, and it was agreed unanimously, excepting only one dissenting vote—a rich and radical Quaker, one Isaac Sneak, grocer, and of the body corporate, who refused to lose one day's service of his shopmen, and thereby (I rejoice to add) succeeded in getting rid of fifteen good annual customers—it was agreed, then, and arranged that the morrow should be a public holiday. All Sir John's own tenantry, as well as Squire Ryle's, and some of other neighbouring magnates, were to have a day's wages without work, on the easy conditions of attending the procession in their smartest trim, and of banqueting at Hurstley afterwards. So, then, the town-band was ordered to be in attendance next morning by eleven at the Swan, a lot of old election colours were shaken from their dust and cobwebs, the bell-ringers engaged, vasty preparations of ale and beef made at Hurstley Hall—an ox to be roasted whole upon the terrace, and a plum-pudding already in the cauldron of two good yards in circumference—and all that every body hoped for that night, was a fine May-day to-morrow.

CHAPTER LII.

ROGER AT THE SWAN.

MEANWHILE, eventide came on: the crowd of kindly gentle-folks had gone their several ways; and Roger Acton found himself (through Sir John's largess) at free quarters in the parlour of the Swan, with Grace by his side, and many of his mates in toil and station round him.

"Grace," said her father on a sudden, "Grace—my dear child—come hither." She stood in all her loveliness before him. Then he took her hand, looked up at her affectionately, and leaned back in the old oak chair.

"Hear me, mates and neighbours; to my own girl, Grace, under God, I owe my poor soul's welfare. I have nothing, would I had, to give her in return:" and the old man (he looked ten years older for his six weeks, luck, and care, and trouble)—the old man could not get on at all with what he had to say—something stuck in his throat—but he recovered, and added cheerily, with an abrupt and rustic archness, "I don't know, mates, whether after all I can't give the good girl something: I can give her—away! Come hither, Jonathan Floyd; you are a noble fellow, that stood by us in adversity, and are almost worthy of my angel Grace." And he joined their hands.

"Give us thy blessing too, dear father!"

They kneeled at his feet on the sanded floor, in the midst of their kinsfolk and acquaintance, and he, stretching forth his hands like a patriarch, looked piously up to heaven, and blessed them there.

"Grace," he added, "and Jonathan my son, I need not part with you —I could not. I have heard great tidings. To-morrow you shall know how kind and good Sir John is: God bless him! and send poor England's children of the soil many masters like him.

"And now, mates, one last word from Roger Acton; a short word, and a simple, that you may not forget it. My sin was love of money: my punishment, its possession. Mates, remember Him who sent you to be labourers, and love the lot He gives you. Be thankful if His blessing on your industry keeps you in regular work and fair wages: ask no more from God of this world's good. Believe things kindly of the gentle-folks, for many sins are heaped upon their heads, whereof their hearts are innocent. Never listen to the counsels of a servant, who takes away his master's character: for of such are the poor man's worst oppressors. Be satisfied with all your lowliness on earth, and keep your just ambitions for another world. Flee strong liquors and ill company. Nurse no heated hopes, no will-o'-the-wisp bright wishes: rather let your warmest hopes be temperately these—health, work, wages: and as for wishing, mates, wish any thing you will—sooner than to find a crock of gold."

CHAPTER LIII.

ROGER'S TRIUMPH.

The steeples rang out merrily, full chime; High street was gay with streamers; the town-band busily assembling; a host of happy urchins from emancipated schools, were shouting in all manner of keys all manner of gleeful noises: every body seemed a-stir.

A proud man that day was Roger Acton; not of his deserts—they were worse than none, he knew it; not of the procession—no silly child was he, to be caught with toy and tinsel; God wot, he was meek enough in self—and as for other pride, he knew from old electioneerings, what a humbling thing is triumph.

But when he saw from the windows of the Swan, those crowds of new-made friends trooping up in holiday suits with flags, and wands, and corporation badges—when the band for a commencement struck up the heart-stirring hymn 'God save the Queen,'—when the horsemen, and carriages, and gigs, and carts assembled—when the baronet's own barouche and four, dashing up to the door, had come from Hurstley Hall for *him*—when Sir John, the happiest of the happy, alighting with his two friends, had displaced them for Roger and Grace, while the kind gentlemen took horse, and headed the procession—when Ben Burke (as clean as soap could get him, and bedecked in new attire) was ordered to sit beside Jonathan in the rumble-tumble—when the cheering, and the merry-going bells, and the quick-march 'British Grenadiers,' rapidly succeeding the national anthem—when all these tokens of a generous sympathy smote upon his ears, his eyes, his heart, Roger Acton wept aloud—he wept for very pride and joy: proud and glad was he that day of his country, of his countrymen, of his generous landlord, of his gentle Grace, of his vindicated innocence, and of God, "who had done so great things for him."

So, the happy cavalcade moved on, horse and foot, and carts and carriages, through the noisy town, along the thronged high road, down the quiet lanes that lead to Hurstley; welcomed at every cottage-door with boisterous huzzas, and adding to its ranks at every corner. And so they reached the village, where the band struck up,

> "See the conquering hero comes,
> Sound the trumpets, beat the drums!"

Is not this returning like a nabob, Roger? Hath not God blest thee through the crock of gold at last, in spite of sin?

There, at the entrance by the mile-stone, stood Mary and the babes, with a knot of friends around her, bright with happiness; on the top of it was perched son Tom, waving the blue and silver flag of Hurstley, and acting as fugleman to a crowd of uproarious cheerers; and beside it, on the bank, sat Sarah Stack, overcome with joy, and sobbing like a gladsome Niobe.

And the village bells went merrily; every cottage was gay with spring garlands, and each familiar face lit up with looks of kindness; Hark! hark!—"Welcome, honest Roger, welcome home again!" they shout: and the patereroes on the lawn thunder a salute; "welcome, honest neighbour;"—and up went, at bright noon, Tom Stableboy's dozen of rockets wrapped around with streamers of glazed calico—"welcome, welcome!"

Good Mr. Evans stood at the door of fine old Hurstley, in wig, and band, and cassock, to receive back his wandering sheep that had been lost: and the school-children, ranged upon the steps, thrillingly sang out the beautiful chant, "I will arise, and go to my Father, and will say unto Him, 'Father, I have sinned against Heaven and before Thee, and am no more worthy to be called thy son!'"

Every head was uncovered, and every cheek ran down with tears.

CHAPTER LIV.

SIR JOHN'S PARTING SPEECH.

THEN Sir John, standing up in the barouche at his own hall-door, addressed the assembled multitude:

"Friends, we are gathered here to-day, in the cause of common justice and brotherly kindness. There are many of you whom I see around me, my tenants, neighbours, or dependants, who have met with wrongs and extortions heretofore, but you all shall be righted in your turn; trust me, men, the old hard times are gone, your landlord lives among you, and his first care shall be to redress your many grievances, paying back the gains of your oppressor."

"God bless you, sir, God bless you!" was the echo from many a gladdened heart.

"But before I hear your several claims in turn, which shall be done to-morrow, our chief duty this day is to recompense an honest man for all that he has innocently suffered. It is five-and-thirty years, as I find by my books, on this very first of May, since Roger Acton first began to work at Hurstley; till within this now past evil month, he has always been the honest steady fellow that you knew him from his youth: what say you, men, to having as a bailiff one of yourselves; a kind and humble man, a good man, the best hand in the parish in all the works of your vocation—a steady mind, an honest heart—what say ye all to Roger Acton?"

There was a whirlwind of tumultuous applause.

"Moreover, men, though you all, each according to his measure and my means, shall meet with liberal justice for your lesser ills, yet we must all remember that Bailiff Acton here had nearly died a felon's death, through that bad man Jennings and the unlucky crock of gold; in addition, extortion has gone greater lengths with him, than with any other on the property; I find that for the last twenty years, Roger Acton has regularly paid to that monster of oppression who is now dead, a double rent—four guineas instead of forty shillings. I desire, as a good master, to make amends for the crimes of my wicked servant; therefore in this bag, Bailiff Acton, is returned to you all the rent you ever paid;" [Roger could not speak for tears;]—"and your cottage repaired and fitted, with an acre round it, is yours and your children's, rent-free for ever."

"Huzzah, huzzah!" roared Ben from the dickey, in a gush of disinterested joy; and then, like an experienced toast-master, he marshalled in due hip, hip, hip order, the shouts of acclamation that rent the air. In an interval of silence, Sir John added,

"As for you, good-hearted fellow, if you will only mend your speech, I'll make you one of my keepers; you shall call yourself licensed poacher, if you choose."

"Blessings on your honour! you've made an honest man o' me."

"And now, Jonathan Floyd, I have one word to say to you, sir. I hear you are to marry our Roger's pretty Grace." Jonathan appeared like a sheep in livery.

"You must quit my service." Jonathan was quite alarmed. "Do you suppose, Master Jonathan, that I can house at Hurstley, before a

Lady Vincent comes amongst us to keep the gossips quiet, such a charming little wife as that, and all her ruddy children?"

It was Grace's turn to feel confused, so she "looked like a rose in June," and blushed all over, as Charles Lamb's Astræa did, down to the ankle.

"Yes, Jonathan, you and I must part, but we part good friends: you have been a noble lover: may you make the girl a good and happy husband! Jennings has been robbing me and those about me for years: it is impossible to separate specially my rights from his extortions: but all, as I have said, shall be satisfied: meanwhile, his hoards are mine. I appropriate one half of them for other claimants; the remaining half I give to Grace Floyd as dower. Don't be a fool, Jonathan, and blubber; look to your Grace there, she 's fainting—you can set up landlord for yourself, do you hear?—for I make yours honestly, as much as Roger found in his now lucky Crock of Gold."

Poor Roger, quite unmanned, could only wave his hat, and—the curtain falls amid thunders of applause.

END OF THE CROCK OF GOLD.

THE TWINS;

A DOMESTIC NOVEL.

BY

MARTIN FARQUHAR TUPPER, A.M., F.R.S.

AUTHOR OF

PROVERBIAL PHILOSOPHY.

HARTFORD:
PUBLISHED BY SILAS ANDRUS & SON.

1851.

THE TWINS.

CHAPTER I.

PLACE: TIME: CIRCUMSTANCE.

BURLEIGH-SINGLETON is a pleasant little watering-place on the southern coast of England, entirely suitable for those who have small incomes and good consciences. The latter, to residents especially, are at least as indispensable as the former: seeing that, however just the reputation of their growing little town for superior cheapness in matters of meat and drink, its character in things regarding men and manners is quite as undeniable for preëminent dullness.

Not but that it has its varieties of scene, and more or less of circumstances too: there are, on one flank, the breezy Heights, with flag-staff and panorama; on the other, broad and level water-meadows, skirted by the dark-flowing Mullet, running to the sea between its tortuous banks: for neighbourhood, Pacton Park is one great attraction—the pretty market-town of Eyemouth another—the everlasting, never-tiring sea a third; and, at high-summer, when the Devonshire lanes are not knee-deep in mire, the nevertheless immeasurably filthy, though picturesque, mud-built village of Oxton.

Then again (and really as I enumerate these multitudinous advantages, I begin to relent for having called it dull), you may pick up curious agate pebbles on the beach, as well as corallines and scarce sea-weeds, good for gumming on front-parlour windows; you may fish *for* whitings in the bay, and occasionally catch them; you may wade in huge caoutchouc boots among the muddy shallows of the Mullet, and shoot *at* cormorants and curlews; you may walk to satiety between high-banked and rather dirty cross-roads; and, if you will scramble up the hedge-row, may get now and then peeps of undulated country landscape.

Moreover, you have free liberty to drop in any where to "tiffin"—Burleigh being very Indianized, and a guest always welcome; indeed, so Indianized is it, so populous in jaundiced cheek and ailing livers, that you may openly assert, without fear of being misunderstood (if you wish to vary your common phrase of loyalty), that Victoria sits upon the "musnud" of Great Britain; you may order curry in the smallest pot-house, and still be sure to get the rice well-cooked; you may call your housemaid "ayah," without risk of warning for impertinence; you may vent your wrath against indolent waiters in eloquence of "jaa, soostee;" and, finally, you may go to the library, and besides the advantage of the day-before-yesterday's Times, you may behold in bilious presence an affable, but authoritative, old gentleman, who introduces himself, "Sir, you see in me the hero of Puttymuddyfudgepoor."

You may even now see such an one, I say, and hear him too, if you will but go to Burleigh; seeing he has by this time over-lived the year or so whereof our tale discourses. He has, by dint of service, attained to the dignity of General H. E. I. C. S., and—which he was still longer coming to—the wisdom of being a communicative creature; though possibly, by a natural rëaction, at present he carries anti-secresy a little too far, and verges on the gossiping extreme. But, at the time to which we must look back to commence this right-instructive story, General Tracy was still drinking "Hodgson's Pale" in India, was so taciturn as to be considered almost dumb, and had not yet lifted up his yellow visage upon Albion's white cliffs, nor taken up head-quarters in his final rest of Burleigh-Singleton.

Nevertheless, with reference to quartering at Burleigh, a certain long-neglected wife of his, Mrs. Tracy, had; and that for the period of at least the twenty-one years preceding: how and wherefore I proceed to tell.

A common case and common fate was that of Mrs. Tracy. She had married, both early and hastily, a gallant lieutenant, John George Julian Tracy, to wit, the military germ of our future general; their courtship and acquaintance previous to matrimony extended over the not inconsiderable space of three whole weeks—commencing with a country ball; and after marriage, honey-moon inclusive, they lived the life of cooing doves for three whole months.

And now came the furlough's end: Mr. Tracy, in his then habitual reserve (a quiet man was he), had concealed its existence altogether: and, for aught Jane knew, the hearty invalid was to remain at home for ever: but months soon slip away; and so it came to pass, that on a certain next Wednesday he must be on his way back to the Presidency of Madras, and—if she will not follow him—he must leave her.

However, there was a certain old relative, one Mrs. Green, a childless widow—rich, capricious, and infirm—whom Jane Tracy did not wish to lose sight of: her money was well worth both watching and waiting for; and the captain, whom a lucky chance had now lifted out of the lieutenancy, was easily persuaded to forego the pleasure of his wife's company till the somewhat indefinite period of her old aunt's death.

How far sundry discoveries made in the unknown regions of each other's temper reconciled him to this retrograding bachelorship, and her to her widowhood-bewitched, I will not undertake to say: but I will hazard the remark, anti-poor-law though it seemeth, that the separation of man and wife, however convenient, lucrative, or even mutually pleasant, is a dereliction of duty, which always deserves, and generally meets, its proper and discriminative punishment. Had the young wife faithfully performed her Maker's bidding, and left all other ties unstrung to cleave unto her lord; had she considered a husband's true affections before all other wealth, and resolved to share his dangers, to solace his cares, to be his blessing through life, and his partner even unto death, rather than selfishly to seek her own comfort, and consult her own interest—the tale of crime and sadness, which it is my lot to tell, would never have had truth for its foundation.

Ill-matched for happiness though they were, however well-matched as to mutual merit, the common man of pleasure and the frivolous woman of fashion, still the wisest way to fuse their minds to union, the likeliest receipt for moral good and social comfort, would have been this course of foreign scenes, of new faces, sprinkled with a seasoning of adventure, hardship, danger, in a distant land. Gradually would they have learned to bear and forbear; the petty quarrel would have been forgotten in the frequent kindness; the rougher edges of temper and opinion would insensibly have smoothed away; new circumstances would have brought out better feelings under happier skies; old acquaintances, false friends forgotten, would have neutralized old feuds: and, by long-living together, though it were perhaps amid various worries and many cares, they might still have come to a good old age with more than average happiness, and more than the common run of love. Patience in dutiful enduring brings a sure reward: and marriage, however irksome a constraint to the foolish and the gay, is still so wise an ordinance, that the most ill-assorted couple imaginable will unconsciously grow happy, if they only remain true to one another, and will learn the wisdom always to hope and often to forgive.

The Tracys, however, overlooked all this, and mutual friends (those invariable foes to all that is generous and unworldly) smiled upon the prudence of their temporary separation. The captain was to come home again on furlough in five years at furthest, even if the aunt held out so long; and this availed to keep his wife in the rear-guard; therefore, Mrs. Tracy wiped her eyes, bade adieu to her retreating lord in Plymouth Sound, and determined to abide, with other expectant dames and Asiatic invalided heroes, at Burleigh-Singleton, until she might go to him, or he return to her: for pleasant little Burleigh, besides its contiguity to arriving Indiamen, was advantageous as being the dwelling-place of aforesaid Mrs. Green;—that wealthy, widowed aunt, devoutly wished in heaven: and the considerate old soul had offered her designing niece a home with her till Tracy could come back.

During the first year of absence, ship-letters and India-letters arrived duteously in consecutive succession: but somehow or other, the regular post, in no long time afterwards, became unfaithful to its trust; and if Mrs. Jane heard quarterly, which at any rate she did through the agent, when he remitted her allowance, she consoled herself as to the captain's well-being: in due course of things, even this became irregular; he was far up the country, hunting, fighting, surveying, and what not; and no wonder that letters, if written at all, which I rather doubt, got lost. Then there came a long period of positive and protracted silence—months of it—years of it; barring that her checks for cash were honoured still at Hancock's, though they could tell her nothing of her lord; so that Mrs. Tracy was at length seriously recommended by her friends to become a widow; she tried on the cap, and looked into many mirrors; but, after long inspection, decided upon still remaining a wife, because the weeds were so clearly unbecoming. Habit, meanwhile, and that still-existing old aunt, who seemed resolved to live to a hundred, kept her as before at Burleigh: and, seeing that a few months after the captain's departure she had presented the world, not to say her truant lord, with twins, she had always found something to do in the way of, what she considered, education, and other juvenile amusement: that is to say, when the gayeties of a circle of fifteen miles in radius left her any time to spare in such a process. The twins—a brace of boys—were born and bred at Burleigh, and had attained severally to twenty years of age, just before their father came home again as brevet-major-general. But both they, and that arrival, deserve special detail, each in its own chapter.

CHAPTER II.

THE HEROES.

Mrs. Tracy's sons were as unlike each other as it is well possible for two human beings to be, both in person and character. Julian, whose forward and bold spirit gained him from the very cradle every prerogative of eldership (and he did struggle first into life, too, so he was the first-born), had grown to be a swarthy, strong, big-boned man, of the Roman-nosed, or, more physiognomically, the Jewish cast of countenance; with melo-dramatic elf-locks, large whiskers, and ungovernable passions; loud, fierce, impetuous; cunning, too, for all his overbearing clamour; and an embodied personification of those choice essentials to criminal happiness—a hard heart and a good digestion. Charles, on the contrary (or, as logicians would say, on the contradictory), was fair-haired, blue-eyed, of Grecian features; slim, though well enough for inches, and had hitherto (as the commonalty have it) "enjoyed" weak health: he was gentle and affectionate in heart, pure and religious in mind, studious and unobtrusive in habits. It was a wonder to see the strange diversity between those own twin-brothers, born within the same hour, and, it is superfluous to add, of the same parents; brought up in all outward things alike, and who had shared equally in all that might be called advantage or disadvantage, of circumstance or education.

Certain is it that minds are different at birth, and require as different a treatment as Iceland moss from cactuses, or bull-dogs from bull-finches: certain is it, too, that Julian, early submitted and resolutely broken in, would have made as great a man, as Charles, naturally meek, did make a good one; but for the matter of educating her boys, poor Mrs. Tracy had no more notion of the feat, than of squaring the circle, or determining the longitude. She kept them both at home, till the peevish aunt could suffer Julian's noise no longer: the house was a Pandemonium, and the giant grown too big for that castle of Otranto; so he must go at any rate; and (as no difference in the treatment of different characters ever occurred to any body) of course Charles must go along with him. Away they went to an expensive school, which Julian's insubordination on the instant could not brook—and, accordingly, he ran away; without doubt, Charles must be taken away too. Another school was tried, Julian got expelled this time; and Charles, in spite of prizes, must, on system, be removed with him: so forth, with like wisdom, all through the years of adolescence and instruction, those ill-matched brothers were driven as a pair. Then again, for fashion's sake, and Aunt Green's whims, the circumspective mother, notwithstanding all her inconsistencies, gave each of them prettily bound hand-books of devotion; which the one used upon his knees, and the other lit cigars withal; both extremes having exceeded her intention: and she proved similarly overreached when she persisted in treating both exactly alike, as to liberal allowances, and liberty of will; the result being, that one of her sons "foolishly" spent his money in a multitude of charitable hobbies; and that the other was constantly supplied with means for (the mother was sorry to say it, vulgar) dissipation. By consequence, Charles did more good, and Julian more evil, than I have time to stop and tell off.

If any thing in this life must be personal, peculiar, and specific, it is education: we take upon ourselves to speak thus dogmatically, not of mere school-teaching only, *musa*, *musæ*, and so forth; nor yet of lectures, on relative qualities of carbon and nitrogen in vegetables; no, nor even of schemes of theology, or codes of morals; but we do speak of the daily and hourly reining-in, or letting-out, of discouragement in one appetite, and encouragement in another; of habitual formation of characters in their diversity; and of shaping their bear's-cub, or that child-angel, the natural human mind, to its destined ends; that it may turn out, for good, according to its several natures, to be either the strong-armed, bold-eyed, rough-hewer of God's grand designs, or the delicate-fingered polisher of His rarest sculptures. Julian, well-trained, might have grown to be a Luther; and many a gentle soul like Charles, has turned out a coxcomb and a sensualist.

The boys were born, as I have said, in the regulation order of things, a few months after Captain Tracy sailed away for India some full score of years, and more, from this present hour, when we have seen him seated as a general in the library at Burleigh; and, until the last year, they had never seen their father—scarcely ever heard of him.

The incidents of their lives had been few and common-place: it would be easy, but wearisome, to specify the orchards and the bee-hives which Julian had robbed as a school-boy; the rebellions he had headed; the monkey tricks he had played upon old fish-women; and the cruel havoc he made of cats, rats, and other poor tormented creatures, who had ministered to his wanton and brutalizing joys. In like manner, wearily, but easily, might I relate how Charles grew up the nurse's darling, though little of his flaunting mother's; the curly-pated young book-worm; the sympathizing, innoffensive, gentle heart, whose effort still it was to countervail his brother's evil: how often, at the risk of blows, had he interposed to save some drowning puppy: how often paid the bribe for Julian's impunity, when mulcted for some damage done in the way of broken windows, upset apple-stalls, and the like: how often had he screened his bad twin-brother from the flagellatory consequences of sheer idleness, by doing for him all his school-tasks: how often striven to guide his insensate conscience to truth, and good, and wisdom: how often, and how vainly!

And when the youths grew up, and their good and evil grew up with them, it were possible to tell you a heart-rending tale of Julian's treachery to more than one poor village beauty; and many a pleasing trait of Charles's pure benevolence, and wise zeal to remedy his brother's mischiefs. The one went about doing ill, and the other doing good: Julian, on account of obligations, more truly than in spite of them, hated Charles; and yet one great aim of all Charles's amiabilities tended continually to Julian's good, and he strove to please him, too, while he wished to bless him. The one had grown to manhood, full of unrepented sins, and ripe for darker crime: the other had attained a like age of what is somewhat satirically called discretion, having amassed, with Solon of old, "knowledge day by day," having lived a life of piety and purity, and blest with a cheerful disposition, that teemed with happy thoughts.

They had, of course, in the progress of human life, been both laid upon the bed of sickness, where, with similar contrast, the one lay muttering discontent, and the other smiling patiently: they had both been in dangers by land and by sea, where Julian, though not a little lacking to himself at the moment of peril, was still loudly minacious till it came too near; while Charles, with all his caution, was more actually courageous, and in spite of all his gentleness, stood against the worst undaunted: they had both, with opposite motives and dissimilar modes of life, passed through various vicissitudes of feeling, scene, society; and the influence of circumstance on their different characters, heightened or diminished, bettered or depraved, by the good or evil principle in each, had produced their different and probable results.

Thus, strangely dissimilar, the twin-brothers together stand before us: Julian the strong impersonation of the animal man, as Charles of the intellectual; Julian, matter; Charles, spirit; Julian, the creature of this world, tending to a lower and a worse: Charles, though in the world, not of the world, and reaching to a higher and a better.

Mrs. Tracy, the mother of this various progeny, had been somewhat of a beauty in her day, albeit much too large and masculine for the taste of ordinary mortals; and though now very considerably past forty, the vain vast female was still ambitious of compliment, and greedy of admiration. That Julian should be such a woman's favourite will surprise none: she had, she could have, no sympathies with mild and thoughtful Charles; but rather dreaded to set her flaunting folly in the light of his wise glance, and sought to hide her humbled vanity from his pure and keen perceptions. His very presence was a tacit rebuke to her social dissipation, and she could not endure the mild radiance of his virtues. He never fawned and flattered her, as Julian would; but had even suffered filial presumption (it could not be affection—O dear, no!) to go so far as gently to expostulate at what he fancied wrong; he never gave her reason to contrast, with happy self-complacence, her own soul's state with Charles's, however she could with Julian's: and then, too, she would indulgently allow her foolish mind—a woman's, though a parent's—to admire that tall, black, bandit-looking son, above the slight build, the delicate features, and almost feminine elegance of his brother: she found Julian alw ys ready to countenance and pamper her gayest wishes, and was glad to make him her escort every where—at balls, and fêtes, and races, and archery parties; while as to Charles, he would be the stay-at-home, the milk-sop, the learned pundit, the pious prayer-monger, any thing but the ladies' man. Yes: it is little wonder that Mrs. Tracy's heart clave to Julian, the masculine image of herself; while it barely tolerated Charles, who was a rarefied and idealized likeness of the absent and forgotten Tracy.

But the mother—and there are many silly mothers, almost as many as silly men and silly maids—in her admiration of the outward form of manliness, overlooked the true strength, and chivalry, and nobleness of mind which shone supreme in Charles. How would Julian have acted in such a case as this?—a sheep had wandered down the cliff's face to a narrow ledge of rock, whence it could not come back again, for there was no room to turn: Julian would have pelted it, and set his bull-dog at it, and rejoiced to have seen the poor animal's frantic leaps from shingly shelf to shelf, till it would be dashed to pieces. But how did Charles act? With the utmost courage, and caution, and presence of mind, he crept down, and, at the risk of his life, dragged the bleating, unreluctant creature up again; it really seemed as if the ungrateful poor dumb brute recognised its humane friend, and suffered him to rescue it without a struggle or a motion that might have endangered both.

Again: a burly costermonger was belabouring his donkey, and the wretched beast fell beneath his cudgel: strange to say, Julian and Charles were walking together that time; and the same sight affected each so differently, that the one sided with the cruel man, and the other with his suffering victim: Charles, in momentary indignation, rushed up to the fellow, wrested the cudgel from his hand, and flung it over the cliff; while Julian was so base, so cowardly, as to reward such generous interference, by holding his weaker brother's arms, and inviting the wrathful costermonger to expend the remainder of his phrensy on unlucky Charles. Yes, and when at home Mrs. Tracy heard all this, she was silly enough, wicked enough, to receive her truly noble son with ridicule, and her other one, the child of her disgrace, with approval.

"It will teach you, Master Charles, not to meddle with common people and their donkeys; and you may thank your brother Julian for giving you a lesson how a gentleman should behave."

Poor Charles! but poorer Julian, and poorest Mrs. Tracy!

It would be easy, if need were, to enumerate multiplied examples tending towards the same end—a large, masculine-featured mother's foolish preference of the loud, bold, worldly animal, before the meek, kind, noble, spiritual. And the results of all these many matters were, that now, at twenty years of age, Charles found himself, as it were, alone in a strange land, with many common friends indeed abroad, but at home no nearer, dearer ties to string his heart's dank lyre withal; neither mother nor brother, nor any other kind familiar face, to look upon his gentleness in love, or to sympathize with his affections, unapprehended, unappreciated: so—while Mrs. Tracy was the showy, gay, and vapid thing she ever had been, and Julian the same impetuous mother's son which his very nurse could say she knew him—Charles grew up a shy and silent youth, necessarily reserved, for lack of some one to understand him; necessarily chilled, for want of somebody to love him.

CHAPTER III.

THE ARRIVAL.

THE young men were thus situated as regards both the world and one another, and Mrs. Tracy had almost entirely forgotten the fact, that she possessed a piece of goods so supererogatory as her husband (a property too which her children had never quite realized), when all on a sudden, one ordinary morning, the postman's knock brought to her breakfast-table at Burleigh-Singleton the following epistle:

"British Channel, Thursday, March 11th, 1842.
"The Sir William Elphinston, E. I. M.

"DEAR JANE: You will be surprised to find that you are to see me so soon, I dare say, especially as it is now some years since you will have heard from me. The reason is, I have been long in an out-of-the-way part of India, where there is little communication with Europe, and so you will excuse my not writing. We hope to find ourselves to-night in Plymouth roads, where I shall get into a pilot-boat, and so shall see you to-morrow. You may, therefore, now expect your affectionate husband,

"J. G. J. TRACY, General H. E. I. C. S.

"P. S. 1.—Remember me to our boy, or boys—which is it?

"P. S. 2.—I bring with me the daughter of a friend in India, who is come over for a year or two's polish at a first-rate school. Of course you will be glad to receive her as our guest.

"J. G. J. T."

This loving letter was the most startling event that had ever attempted to unnerve Mrs. Tracy; and she accordingly managed, for effect and propriety's sake, to grow very faint upon the spot, whether for joy, or sorrow, or fear of lost liberty, or hope of a restored lord, doth not appear; she had so long been satisfied with receiving quarterly pay from the India agents, that she forgot it was an evidence of her husband's existence; and, lo! here he was returning a general, doubtlessly a magnificent moustachioed individual, and she was to be Mrs. General! so that when she came completely to herself, after that feint of a faint, she was thinking of nothing but court-plumes, oriental pearls, and her gallant Tracy's uniform.

The postscripts also had their influence: Charles, naturally affectionate, and willing to love a hitherto unseen father, felt hurt, as well he might, at the "boy, or boys;" while Julian, who ridiculed his brother's sentimentality, was already fancying that the "daughter of a friend" might be a pleasant addition to the dullness of Burleigh-Singleton.

Preparations vast were made at once for the general's reception; from attic to kitchen was sounded the tocsin of his coming. Julian was all bustle and excitement, to his mother's joy and pride; while Charles merited her wrath by too much of his habitual and paternal quietude, particularly when he withdrew his forces altogether from the loud domestic fray, by retreating up-stairs to cogitate and muse, perhaps to make a calming prayer or two about all these matters of importance. As for Mrs. Tracy herself, she was even now, within the first hour of that news, busily engaged in collecting cosmetics, trinkets, blonde lace, and other female finery, resolved to trick herself out like Jezebel, and win her lord once more; whilst the pernicious old aunt, who still lived on, notwithstanding all those twenty years of patience, as vivacious as before, grumbled and scolded so much at this upsetting of her house, that there was really some risk of her altering the will at last, and cutting out Jane Tracy after all.

And the morrow morning came, as if it were no more than an ordinary Friday, and with it came expectancy; and noon succeeded, and with it spirits alternately elated and depressed; and evening drew in, with heart-sickness and chagrin at hopes or prophecies deferred; and night, and next morning, and still the general came not. So, much weeping at that vexing disappointment, after so many pains to please, Mrs. Tracy put aside her numerous aids and appliances, and lay slatternly a-bed, to nurse a head-ache until noon; and all had well nigh forgotten the probable arrival, when, to every body's dismay, a dusty chaise and four suddenly rattled up the terrace, and stopped at our identical number seven.

Then was there scuffling up, and getting down, and making preparation in hot haste; and a stout gentleman with a gamboge face descended from the chaise, exploding wrath like a bomb-shell, that so important an approach had made such slight appearance of expectancy: it was disrespectful to his rank, and he took care to prove he was somebody, by blowing up the very innocent post-boys. This accomplished, he gallantly handed out after him a pretty-looking miss in her teens. Poor Mrs. Tracy, *en papillotes*, looked out at the casement like any one but Jezebel attired for bewitching, and could have cried for vexation; in fact, she did, and passed it off for feeling. Aunt Green, whom the general at first lovingly saluted as his wife (for the poor man had entirely forgotten the uxorial appearance), was all in a pucker for deafness, blindness, and evident misapprehension of all things in general, though clearly pleased, and flattered at her gallant nephew's salutation. Julian, with what grace of manner he could muster, was already playing the agreeable to that pretty ward, after having, to the general's great surprise, introduced himself to him as his son; while Charles, who had rushed into the room, warm-heartedly to fling himself into his father's arms, was repelled on the spot for his affection: General Tracy, with a military air, excused himself from the embrace, extending a finger to the unknown gentleman, with somewhat of offended dignity.

At last, down came the wife: our general at once perceived himself mistaken in the matter of Mrs. Green; and, coldly bowing to the bedizened dame, acknowledged her pretensions with a courteous—

"Mrs. General Tracy, allow me to introduce to you Miss Emily Warren, the daughter of a very particular friend of mine:—Miss Warren, Mrs. Tracy."

For other welcomings, mutual astonishment at each other's fat, some little sorrowful talk of the twenty years ago, and some dull paternal jest about this dozen feet of sons, made up the chilly meeting: and the slender thread of sentimentals, which might possibly survive it, was soon snapt by paying post-boys, orders after luggage, and devouring tiffin.

The only persons who felt any thing at all, were Mrs. Tracy, vexed at her dishabille, and mortified at so cool a reception of, what she hoped, her still unsullied beauties; and Charles, poor fellow, who ran up to his studious retreat, and soothed his grief, as best he might, with philosophic fancies: it was so cold, so heartless, so unkind a greeting. Romantic youth! how should the father have known him for a son?

CHAPTER IV.

THE GENERAL AND HIS WARD.

It is surprising what a change twenty years of a tropical sun can make in the human constitution. The captain went forth a good-looking, good-tempered man, destitute neither of kind feelings nor masculine beauty: the general returned bloated, bilious, irascible, entirely selfish, and decidedly ill-favoured. Such affections as he ever had seemed to have been left behind in India—that new world, around which now all his associations and remembrances revolved; and the reserve (clearly reproduced in Charles), the habit of silence whereof we took due notice in the spring-tide of his life, had now grown, perhaps from some oppressive secret, into a settled, moody, continuous taciturnity, which made his curious wife more vexed at him than ever; for, notwithstanding all the news he must have had to tell her, the company of John George Julian Tracy proved to his long-expectant Jane any thing but cheering or instructive. His past life, and present feelings, to say nothing of his future prospects, might all be but a blank, for any thing the general seemed to care: brandy and tobacco, an easy chair, and an ordnance map of India, with Emily beside him to talk about old times, these were all for which he lived: and even the female curiosity of a wife, duly authorized to ask questions, could extract from him astonishingly little of his Indian experiences. As to his wealth, indeed, Mrs. Tracy boldly made direct inquiry; for Julian set her on to beg for a commission, and Charles also was anxious for a year or two at college; but the general divulged not much: albeit he vouchsafed to both his sons a liberally increased allowance. It was only when his wife, piqued at such reserve, pettishly remarked,

"At any rate, sir, I may be permitted to hope, that Miss Warren's friends are kind enough to pay her expenses;"

That the veteran, in high dudgeon at any imputation on his Indian acquaintances, sternly answered,

"You need not be apprehensive, madam; Emily Warren is amply provided for." Words which sank deep into the prudent mother's mind.

But we must not too long let dock-leaves hide a violet; it is high time, and barely courteous now, to introduce that beautiful exotic, Emily Warren. Her own history, as she will tell it to Charles hereafter, was so obscure, that she knew little of it certainly herself, and could barely gather probabilities from scattered fragments. At present, we have only to survey results in a superficial manner: in their due season, we will dig up all the roots.

No heroine can probably engage our interest or sympathy who possesses the infirmity of ugliness: it is not in human nature to admire her, and human nature is a thing very much to be consulted. Moreover, no one ever yet saw an amiable personage, who was not so far pleasing, or, in other parlance, so far pretty. I cannot help the common course of things; and however hackneyed be the thought, however common-place the phrase, it is true, nevertheless, that beauty, singular beauty, would be the first idea of any rational creature, who caught but a glimpse of Emily Warren; and I should account it little wonder if, upon a calmer gaze, that beauty were found to have its deepest, clearest fountain in those large dark eyes of her's.

Aware as I may be, that "large dark eyes" are nò novelty in tales like this; and famous for rare originality as my pen (not to say genius) would become, if an attempt were herein made to interest the world in a pink-eyed heroine, still I prefer plodding on in the well-worn path of pleasant beauty; and so long as Nature's bounty continues to supply so well the world we live in with large dark eyes, and other feminine perfections, our Emily, at any rate, remains in fashion; and if she has many pretty peers, let us at least not peevishly complain of them. A graceful shape is, luckily, almost the common prerogative of female youthfulness; a dimpled smile, a cheerful, winning manner, regular features, and a mass of luxuriant brown hair—these all heroines have—and so has our's.

But no heroine ever had yet Emily Warren's eyes; not identically only, which few can well deny; but similarly also, which the many must be good enough to grant: and very few heroes, indeed, ever saw their equal; though, if any hereabouts object, I will not be so cruel or unreasonable as to hope they will admit it. At first, full of soft light, gentle and alluring, they brighten up to blaze upon you lustrously, and fascinate the gazer's dazzled glance: there are depths in them that tell of the unfathomable soul, heights in them that speak of the spirit's aspirations. It is gentleness and purity, no less than sensibility and passion, that look forth in such strange power from those windows of the mind: it is not the mere beautiful machine, fair form, and pleasing colours, but the heaven-born light of tenderness and truth, streaming through the lens, that takes the fond heart captive. Charles, for one, could not help looking long and keenly into Emily Warren's eyes; they magnetized him, so that he might not turn away from them: entranced him, that he would not break their charm, had he been able: and then the long tufted eyelashes droop so softly over those blazing suns—that I do not in the least wonder at Charles's impolite, perhaps, but still natural involuntary stare, and his mute abstracted admiration: the poor youth is caught at once, a most willing captive—the moth has burnt its wings, and flutters still happily around that pleasant warming radiance. How his heart yearned for something to love, some being worthy of his own most pure affections: and lo! these beauteous eyes, true witnesses of this sweet mind, have filled him for ever and a day with love at first sight.

But gentle Charles was not the only conquest: the fiery Julian, too, acknowledged her supremacy, bowed his stubborn neck, and yoked himself at once, another and more rugged captive, to the chariot of her charms. It was Caliban, as well as Ferdinand, courting fair Miranda. In his lower grade, he loved—fiercely, coarsely: and the same passion, which filled his brother's heart with happiest aspirations, and pure unselfish tenderness towards the beauteous stranger, burnt him up as an inward and consuming fire: Charles sunned himself in heaven's genial beams, while Julian was hot with the lava-current of his own bad heart's volcano.

It will save much trouble, and do away with no little useless mystery, to declare, at the outset, which of these opposite twin-brothers our dark-eyed Emily preferred. She was only seventeen in years; but an Indian sky had ripened her to full maturity, both of form and feelings: and having never had any one whom she cared to think upon, and let her heart delight in, till Charles looked first upon her beauty wonderingly, it is no marvel if she unconsciously reciprocated his young heart's thought—before ever he had breathed it to himself. Julian's admiration she entirely overlooked; she never thought him more than civil—barely that, perhaps—however he might flatter himself: but her heart and eyes were full of his fair contrast, the light seen brighter against darkness; Charles all the dearer for a Julian. Intensely did she love him, as only tropic blood can love; intently did she gaze on him, when any while he could not see her face, as only those dark eyes could gaze: and her mind, all too ignorant but greedy of instruction, no less than her heart, rich in sympathies and covetous of love, went forth, and fed deliciously on the intellectual brow, and delicate flushing cheek of her noble-minded Charles. Not all in a day, nor a week, nor a month, did their loves thus ripen together. Emily was a simple child of nature, who had every thing to learn; she scarcely knew her Maker's name, till Charles instructed her in God's great love: the stars were to her only shining studs of gold, and the world one mighty plain, and men and women soulless creatures of a day, and the wisdom of creation unconsidered, and the book of natural knowledge close sealed up, till

Charles set out before his eager student the mysteries of earth and heaven. Oh, those blessed hours of sweet teaching! when he led her quick delighted steps up the many avenues of science to the central throne of God! Oh, those happy moments, never to return, when her eyes in gentle thankfulness for some new truth laid open to them, flashed upon her youthful Mentor, love and intelligence, and pleased admiring wonder! Sweet spring-tide of their loves, who scarcely knew they loved, yet thought of nothing but each other; who walked hand in hand, as brother and sister, in the flowery ways of mutual blessing, mutual dependence: alas, alas! how brief a space can love, that guest from heaven, dwell on earth unsullied!

CHAPTER V.

JEALOUSY.

For Julian soon perceived that Charles was no despicable rival. At first, self-flattery, and the habitual contempt wherewith he regarded his brother, blinded him to Emily's attachment: moreover, in the scenes of gayety and the common social circle, she never gave him cause to complain of undue preferences; readily she leant upon his arm, cheerfully accompanied him in morning-visits, noon-day walks, and evening parties; and if pale Charles (in addition to the more regular masters, dancing and music, and other pieces of accomplishment) thought proper to bore her with his books for sundry hours every day, Julian found no fault with that;—the girl was getting more a woman of the world, and all for him: she would like her play-time all the better for such schoolings, and him to be the truant at her side.

But when, from ordinary civilities, the coarse loud lover proceeded to particular attentions; when he affected to press her delicate hand, and ventured to look what he called love into her eyes, and to breathe silly nothings in her ear—he could deceive himself no longer, notwithstanding all his vanity; as legibly as looks could write it, he read disgust upon her face, and from that day forth she shunned him with undisguised abhorrence. Poor innocent maid! she little knew the man's black mind, who thus dared to reach up to the height of her affections; but she saw enough of character in his swart scowling face, and loud assuming manners, to make her dread his very presence, as a thunder-cloud across her summer sky.

Then did the baffled Julian begin to look around him, and took notice of her deepening love of Charles; nay, even purposely, she seemed now to make a difference between them, as if to check presumption and encourage merit. And he watched their stolen glances, how tremblingly they met each other's gaze; and he would often-times roughly break in upon their studies, to look on their confused disquietude with the pallid frowns of envy: he would insult poor Charles before her, in hope to humble him in her esteem; but mild and Christian patience made her see him as a martyr: he would even cast rude slights on her whom he professed to love, with the view of raising his brother's chastened wrath, but was forced to quail and sneak away beneath her quick indignant glance, ere her more philosophical lover had time to expostulate with the cowardly savage.

Meanwhile, what were the parents about? The general had given out, indeed, that he had brought Emily over for schooling; but he seemed so fond of her (in fact, she was the only thing to prove he wore a heart), that he never could resolve upon sending her away from, what she now might well call, home. Often, in some strange dialect of Hindostan, did they converse together, of old times and distant shores; none but Emily might read him to sleep—none but Emily wake him in the morning with a kiss—none but Emily dare approach him in his gouty torments—none but Emily had any thing like intimate acquaintance with that moody iron-hearted man.

As to his sons, or the two young men he might presume to be his sons, he neither knew them, nor cared to know. Bare civilities, as between man and man, constituted all which their intercourse amounted to: what were those young fellows, stout or slim, to him? mere accidents of a soldier's gallantries and of an ill-assorted marriage. He neither had, nor wished to have, any sympathies with them: Julian might be as bad as he pleased, and Charles as good, for any thing the general seemed to heed: they could not dive with him into the past, and the sports of Hindostan: they reminded him, simply, of his wife, for pleasures of Memory; of the grave, for pleasures of Hope: he was older when he looked at them: and they seemed to him only living witnesses of his folly as lieutenant, in the choice of Mrs. Tracy. I will not take upon myself to say, that he had any occasion to congratulate himself on the latter reminiscence.

So he quickly acquiesced in Julian's wish for a commission, and entirely approved of Charles's college schemes. After next September, the funds should be forthcoming: not but that he was rich enough, and to spare, any month in the year: but he would be vastly richer then, from prize-money, or some such luck. It was more prudent to delay until September.

With reference to Emily—no, no—I could see at once that General Tracy never had any serious intention to part with Emily; but she had all manner of masters at home, and soon made extraordinary progress. As for the matter of his sons falling in love with her, attractive in all beauty though she were, he never once had given it a thought: for, first, he was too much a man of the world to believe in such ideal trash as love: and next, he totally forgot that his "boy, or boys," had human feelings. So, when his wife one day gave him a gentle and triumphant hint of the state of affairs, it came upon him overwhelmingly, like an avalanche: his yellow face turned flake-white, he trembled as he stood, and really seemed to take so natural a probability to heart as the most serious of evils.

"My son Julian in love with Emily! and if not he, at any rate Charles! What the devil, madam, can you mean by this dreadful piece of intelligence?—It's impossible, ma'am; nonsense! it can't be true; it shan't, ma'am."

And the general, having issued his military mandates, wrapped himself in secresy once more; satisfied that both of those troublesome sons were to leave home after the next quarter, and the prize-money at Hancock's.

CHAPTER VI.

THE CONFIDANTE.

But Mrs. Tracy had the best reason for believing her intelligence was true, and she could see very little cause for regarding it as dreadful. True, one son would have been enough for this wealthy Indian heiress—but still it was no harm to have two strings to her bow. Julian was her favourite, and should have the girl if she could manage it; but if Emily

Warren would not hear of such a husband, why Charles Tracy may far better get her money than any body else.

That she possessed great wealth was evident: such jewellery, such Trinchinopoli chains, such a blaze of diamonds *en suite*, such a multitude of armlets, and circlets, and ear-rings, and other oriental finery, had never shone on Devonshire before: at the Eyemouth ball, men worshipped her, radiant in beauty, and gorgeously apparelled. Moreover, money overflowed her purse, her work-box, and her jewel-case: Charles's village school, and many other well-considered charities, rejoiced in the streams of her munificence. The general had given her a banker's book of signed blank checks, and she filled up sums at pleasure: such unbounded confidence had he in her own prudence and her far-off father's liberality. The few hints her husband deigned to give, encouraged Mrs. Tracy to conclude, that she would be a catch for either of her sons; and, as for the girl herself, she had clearly been brought up to order about a multitude of servants, to command the use of splendid equipages, and to spend money with unsparing hand.

Accordingly, one day when Julian was alone with his mother, their conversation ran as follows:

"Well, Julian dear, and what do you think of Emily Warren?"

"Think, mother? why—that she's deuced pretty, and dresses like an empress: but where did the general pick her up, eh?—who is she?"

"Why, as to who she is—I know no more than you; she is Emily Warren: but as to the great question of what she is, I know that she is rolling in riches, and would make one of my boys a very good wife."

"Oh, as to wife, mother, one isn't going to be fool enough to marry for love now-a-days: things are easier managed hereabouts, than that: but money makes it quite another thing. So, this pretty minx is rich, is she?"

"A great heiress, I assure you, Julian."

"Bravo, bravo-o! but how to make the girl look sweet upon me, mother? There's that white-livered fellow, Charles—"

"Never mind him, boy; do you suppose he would have the heart to make love to such a splendid creature as Miss Warren: fy, Julian, for a faint heart: Charles is well enough as a Sabbath-school teacher, but I hope he will not bear away the palm of a ladye-love from my fine high-spirited Julian." Poor Mrs. Tracy was as flighty and romantic at forty-five as she had been at fifteen.

The fine high-spirited Julian answered not a word, but looked excessively cross; for he knew full well that Charles's chance was to his in the ratio of a million to nothing.

"What, boy," went on the prudent mother, "still silent! I am afraid Emily's good looks have been thrown away upon you, and that your heart has not found out how to love her."

"Love her, mother? Curses! would you drive me mad? I think and dream of nothing but that girl: morning, noon, and night, her eyes persecute me: go where I will, and do what I will, her image haunts me: d——n it, mother' don't I love the girl?"

[Oh love, love! thou much-slandered monosyllable, how desperately do bad men malign thee!]

"Hush, Julian; pray be more guarded in your language; I am glad to see though that your heart is in the right place: suppose now that I aid your suit a little? I dare say I could do a great deal for you, my son; and nothing could be more delightful to your mother than to try and make her Julian happy."

True, Mrs. Tracy; you were always theatrically given, and played the coquette in youth; so in age the character of go-between befits you still: dearly do you love to dabble in, what you are pleased to call, "*une affaire du cœur.*"

"Mother," after a pause, replied her hopeful progeny, "if the girl had been only pretty, I shouldn't have asked any body's help; for marriage was never to my liking, and folks may have their will of prouder beauties than this Emily, without going to church for it; but money makes it quite another matter: and I may as well have the benefit of your assistance in this matter o' money, eh mother? matrimony, you know: an heiress and a beauty may be worth the wedding-ring; besides, when my commission comes, I can follow the good example that my parents set me, you know; and, after a three months' honey-mooning, can turn bachelor again for twenty years or so, as our governor-general did, and so leave wifey at home, till she becomes a Mrs. General like you."

Now, strange to say, this heartless bit of villany was any thing but unpleasing to the foolish, flattered heart of Mrs. Tracy; he was a chip of the old block, no better than his father: so she thanked "dear Julian" for his confidence, with admiration and emotion; and looking upwards, after the fashion of a Covent Garden martyr, blessed him.

CHAPTER VII.

THE COURSE OF TRUE LOVE, ETC.

"EMILY, my dear, take Julian's arm: here, Charles, come and change with me; I should like a walk with you to Oxton, to see how your little scholars get on." So spake the intriguing mother.

"Why, that is just what I was going to do with Charles," said Emily, "and if Julian will excuse me——"

"Oh, never mind me, Miss Warren, pray; come along with me, will you, mother?"

So they paired off in more well-matched couples (for Julian luckily took huff), and went their different ways: with those went hatred, envy, worldly scheming, and that lowest sort of love that ill deserves the name; with these remain all things pure, affectionate, benevolent.

"Charles, dear," (they were just like brother and sister, innocent and loving), "how kind it is of you to take me with you; if you only knew how I dreaded Julian!"

"Why, Emmy? can he have offended you in any way?"

"Oh, Charles, he is so rude, and says such silly things, and—I am quite afraid to be alone with him."

"What—what—what does he say to you, Emily?" hurriedly urged her half-avowed lover.

"Oh, don't ask me, Charles—pray drop the subject;" and, as she blushed, tears stood in her eyes.

Charles bit his lip and clenched his fist involuntarily; but an instant word of prayer drove away the spirit of hatred, and set up love triumphant in its place.

"My Emily—oh, what have I said? may I—may I call you my Emily? dearest, dearest girl!" escaped his lips, and he trembled at his own presumption. It was a presumptuous speech indeed; but it burst from the well of his affections, and he could not help it.

Her answer was not in words, and yet his heart-strings thrilled beneath the melody; for her eyes shed on him a blaze of love that made him almost faint before them. In an instant, they understood, without a word, the happy truth, that each one loved the other.

"Precious, precious Emily!" They were now far away from Burleigh, in the fields; and he seized her hand, and covered it with kisses.

What more they said I was not by to hear, and if I had been would not have divulged it. There are holy secrets of affection, which those who can remember their first love—and first love is the only love worth mentioning—may think of for themselves. Well, far better than my feeble pencilling can picture, will they fill up this slight sketch. That walk to Oxton, that visit to the village school, was full of generous affections unrepressed, the out-pourings of two deep-welled hearts, flowing forth in sympathetic ecstasy. The trees, and fields, and cottages were bathed in heavenly light, and the lovers, happy in each other's trust, called upon the all-seeing God to bless the best affections of His children.

And what a change these mutual confessions made in both their minds! Doubt was gone; they *were* beloved; oh, richest treasure of joy! Fear was gone; they dared declare their love; oh, purest river of all sublunary pleasures! No longer pale, anxious, thoughtful, worn by the corroding care of "Does she—does she love?"—Charles was, from that moment, a buoyant, cheerful, exhilarated being—a new character; he put on manliness, and fortitude, and somewhat of involuntary pride; whilst Emily felt, that enriched by the affections of him whom she regarded as her wisest, kindest earthly friend, by the acquisition of his love, who had led her heart to higher good than this world at its best can give her, she was elevated and ennobled from the simple Indian child, into the loved and honoured Christian woman. They went on that important walk to Oxton feeble, divided, unsatisfied in heart: they returned as two united spirits, one in faith, one in hope, one in love; both heavenly and earthly.

But the happy hour is past too soon; and, home again, they mixed once more with those conflicting elements of hatred and contention.

"Emily," asked the general, in a very unusual stretch of curiosity, "where have you been to with Charles Tracy? You look flushed, my dear; what's the matter?"

Of course "nothing" was the matter: and the general was answered wisely, for love was nothing in his average estimate of men and women.

"Charles, what can have come to you? I never saw you look so happy in my life," was the mother's troublesome inquiry; "why, our staid youth positively looks cheerful."

Charles's walk had refreshed him, taken away his head-ache, put him in spirits, and all manner of glib reasons for rejoicing.

"You were right, Julian," whispered Mrs. Tracy, "and we'll soon put the stopper on all this sort of thing."

So, then, the moment our guiltless pair of lovers had severally stolen away to their own rooms, there to feast on well-remembered looks, and words, and hopes—there to lay before that heavenly Friend, whom both had learned to trust, all their present joys, as aforetime all their cares—Mrs. Tracy looked significantly at Julian, and thus addressed her ever stern-eyed lord:

"So, general, the old song 's coming true to us, I find, as to other folks, who once were young together:

"'And when with envy Time, transported, seeks to rob us of our joys,
You'll in your girls again be courted, and I'll go wooing in my boys.'"

So said or sung the flighty Mrs. Tracy. It was as simple and innocent a quotation as could possibly be made; I suppose most couples, who ever heard the stanza, and have grown-up children, have thought upon its dear domestic beauty: but it strangely affected the irascible old general. He fumed and frowned, and looked the picture of horror; then, with a fierce oath at his wife and sons, he firmly said—

"Woman, hold your fool's tongue: begone, and send Emily to me this minute: stop, Mr. Julian—no—run up for your brother Charles, and come you all to me in the study. Instantly, sir! do as I bid you, without a word."

Julian would gladly have fought it out with his imperative father: but, nevertheless, it was a comfort to have to fetch pale Charles for a jobation; so he went at once. And the three young people, two of them trembling with affections overstrained, and the third indurated in effrontery, stood before that stern old man.

"Emily, child,"—and he added something in Hindostanee, "have I been kind to you—and do you owe me any love?"

"Dear, dear sir, how can you ask me that?" said the warm-affectioned girl, falling on her knees in tears.

"Get up, sweet child, and hear me: you see those boys; as you love me, and yourself, and happiness, and honour—dare not to think of either, one moment, as your husband."

Emily fainted; Charles staggered to assist her, though he well-nigh swooned himself; and Julian folded his arms with a resolute air, as waiting to hear what next.

But the general disappointed him: he had said his say: and, as volatile salts, a lady's maid, and all that sort of rëinvigoration, seemed essential to Emily's recovery, he rang the bell forthwith: so the pleasant family party broke up without another word.

CHAPTER VIII.

THE MYSTERY.

Our lovers would not have been praiseworthy, perhaps not human, had they not met in secret once and again. True, their regularly concerted studies were forbidden, and they never now might openly walk out unaccompanied: but love (who has not found this out?) is both daring and ingenious; and notwithstanding all that Emily purposed about doing as the general so strangely bade her, they had many happy meetings, rich with many happy words: all the happier no doubt for their stolen sweetness.

There was one great and engrossing subject which often had employed their curiosity; who and what was Emily Warren? for the poor girl did not know herself. All she could guess, she told Charles, as he zealously cross-questioned her from time to time: and the result of his inquiries would appear to be as follows:

Emily's earliest recollections were of great barbaric pomp; huge elephants richly caparisoned, mighty fans of peacock's tails, lines of matchlock men, tribes of jewelled servants, a gilded palace, with its gardens and fountains: plenty of rare gems to play with, and a splendid queenly woman, whom she called by the Hindoo name for mother. The general, too, was there among her first associations, as the gallant Captain Tracy, with his company of native troops.

Then an era happened in her life; a tearful leave-taking with that proud princess, who scarcely would part with her for sorrow; but the captain swore it should be so: and an old Scotch-woman, her nurse, she could remember, who told her as a child, but whether religiously or not she could not tell, "Darling, come to me when you wish to know who made you;" and then Mrs. Mackie went and spoke to the princess, and soothed her, that she let the child depart peacefully. Most of her gorgeous jewellery dated from that earliest time of inexplicable oriental splendour.

After those infantine seven years, the captain took her with him to his station up the country, where she lived she knew not how long, in a strong hill-fort, one Puttymuddyfudgepoor, where there was a great deal of fighting, and besieging, and storming, and cannonading; but it ceased at last, and the captain, who then soon successively became both major and colonel, always kept her in his own quarters, making her his little pet; and, after the fighting was all over, his brother-officers would take her out hunting in their howdahs, and she had plenty of palanquin-bearers, sepoys, and servants at command; and, what was more, good nurse Mackie was her constant friend and attendant.

Time wore on, and many little incidents of Indian life occurred, which varied every day indeed, but still left nothing consequential behind them: there were tiger-hunts, and incursions of Scindian tribes, and Pindarree chieftains taken captive, and wounded soldiers brought into the hospital; and often had she and good nurse Mackie tended at the sick bed-side. And the colonel had the jungle fever, and would not let her go from his sight; so she caught the fever too, and through Heaven's mercy was recovered. And the colonel was fonder of her now than ever, calling her his darling little child, and was proud to display her early budding beauty to his military friends—pleasant sort of gentlemen, who gave her pretty presents.

Then she grew up into womanhood, and saw more than one fine uniform at her feet, but she did not comprehend those kindnesses: and the general (he was general now) got into great passions with them, and stormed, and swore, and drove them all away. Nurse Mackie grew to be old, and sometimes asked her, "Can you keep a secret, child?—no, no, I dare not trust you yet: wait a wee, wait a wee, my bonnie, bonnie bairn."

And now speedily came the end. The general resolved on returning to his own old shores: chiefly, as it seemed, to avoid the troublesome pertinacity of sundry suitors, who sought of him the hand of Emily Warren; for, by this name she was beginning to be called: in her earliest recollection she was Amina; then at the hill-fort, Emily—Emily—nothing for years but Emily: and as she grew to womanhood, the general bade her sign her name to notes, and leave her card at houses, as Emily Warren: why, or by what right, she never thought of asking. But nurse Mackie had hinted she might have had "a better name and a truer;" and therefore, she herself had asked the general what this hint might mean; and he was so angry that he discharged nurse Mackie at Madras, directly he arrived there to take ship for England.

Then, just before embarking, poor nurse Mackie came to her secretly, and said, "Child, I will trust you with a word; you are not what he thinks you." And she cried a great deal, and longed to come to England; but the general would not hear of it; so he pensioned her off, and left her at Madras, giving somebody strict orders not to let her follow him.

Nevertheless, just as they were getting into the boat to cross the surf, the affectionate old soul ran out upon the strand, and called to her "Amy Stuart! Amy Stuart!" to the general's great amazement as clearly as her own; and she held up a packet in her hand as they were pushing off, and shouted after her, "Child—child! if you would have your rights, remember Jeanie Mackie!"

After that, succeeded the monotony of a long sea voyage. The general at first seemed vexed about Mrs. Mackie, and often wished that he had asked her what she meant; however, his brow soon cleared, for he reflected that a discarded servant always tells falsehoods, if only to make her master mischief.

"The voyage over, Charles, with all its cards, quadrilles, doubling the cape, crossing the line, and the wearisome routine of sky and sea, the quarter-deck and cabin, we found ourselves at length in Plymouth Sound; left the Indiaman to go up the channel; and I suppose the post-chaise may be consigned to your imagination."

CHAPTER IX.

HOW TO CLEAR IT UP.

In all this there was mystery enough for a dozen lovers to have crazed their brains about. Emily might be a queen of the East, defrauded of hereditary glories, and at any rate deserved such rank, if Charles was to be judge; but what was more important, if the general had any reason at all for his arbitrary mandate prohibiting their love, it was very possible that reason was a false one.

Meantime, Charles had little now to live for, except his dear forbidden Emily, any more than she for him. And to peace of mind in both, the elucidation of that mystery which hung about her birth, grew more needful day by day. At last, one summer evening, when they had managed a quiet walk upon the sands under the Beacon cliff, Charles said abruptly, after some moments of abstraction, "Dearest, I am resolved."

"Resolved, Charles! what about?" and she felt quite alarmed; for her lover looked so stern, that she could not tell what was going to happen next.

"I'll clear it up, that I will; I only wish I had the money."

"Why, Charles, what in the world are you dreaming about? you frighten me, dearest; are you ill? don't look so serious, pray."

"Yes, Emily, I will; at once too. I'm off to Madras by next packet; or, that is to say, would, if I could get my passage free."

"My noble Charles, if that were the only objection, I would get you all the means; for the kind—kind general suffers me to have whatever sums I choose to ask for. Only, Charles, indeed I cannot spare you; do not—do not go away and leave me; there's Julian, too—don't leave me—and you might never come back, and—and—" all the remainder was lost in sobbing.

"No, my Emmy, we must not use the general's gold in doing what he might not wish; it would be ungenerous. I will try to get somebody to lend me what I want—say Mrs. Sainsbury, or the Tamworths. And as for leaving you, my love, have no fears for me or for yourself; situated as we are, I take it as a duty to go, and make you happier, setting you in rights, whatever these may be; and for the rest, I leave you in His holy keeping who can preserve you alike in body, as in soul, from all things that would hurt you, and whose mercy will protect me in all perils, and bring me back to you in safety. This is my trust, Emmy."

"Dear Charles, you are always wiser and better than I am: let it be so then, my best of friends. Seek out good nurse Mackie, I can give you many clues, hear what she has to say; and may the God of your own poor fatherless Emily speed your holy mission! Yet there is one thing, Charles; ought you not to ask your parents for their leave to go? You are better skilled to judge than I can be, though."

"Emmy, whom have I to ask? my father? he cares not whither I go nor what becomes of me; I hardly know him, and for twenty years of my short life of twenty-one, scarcely believed in his existence; or should I ask my mother? alas—love! I wish I could persuade myself that she would wish me back again if I were gone; moreover, how can I respect her judgment, or be guided by her counsel, whose constant aim has been to thwart my feeble efforts after truth and wisdom, and to pamper all ill growths in my unhappy brother Julian? No, Emily; I am a man now, and take my own advice. If a parent forbade me, indeed, and reasonably, it would be fit to acquiesce; but knowing, as I have sad cause to know, that none but you, my love, will be sorry for my absence, as for your sake alone that absence is designed, I need take counsel only of us who are here present—your own sweet eyes, myself, and God who seeth us."

"True—most true, dear Charles; I knew that you judged rightly."

"Moreover, Emmy, secresy is needful for the due fulfilment of my purpose." (Charles little thought how congenial to his nature was that same secresy.) "None but you must know where I am, or whither I am gone. For if there really is any mystery which the general would conceal from us, be assured he both could and would frustrate all my efforts if he knew of my design. The same ship that carried me out would convey an emissary from him, and nurse Mackie never could be found by me. I must go then secretly, and, for our peace sake, soon; how dear to me that embassy will be, entirely undertaken in my darling Emmy's cause!"

"But—but, Charles, what if Julian, in your absence—"

"Hark, my own betrothed! while I am near you—and I say it not of threat, but as in the sight of One who has privileged me to be your protector—you are safe from any serious vexation; and the moment I am gone, fly to my father, tell him openly your fears, and he will scatter Julian's insolence to the winds of heaven."

"Thank you—thank you, wise dear Charles; you have lifted a load from my poor, weak, woman's heart, that had weighed it down too heavily. I will trust in God more, and dread Julian less. Oh! how I will pray for you when far away."

CHAPTER X.

AUNT GREEN'S LEGACY.

At last—at last, Mrs. Green fell ill, and, hard upon the over-ripe age of eighty-seven, seemed likely to drop into the grave—to the unspeakable delight of her expectant relatives. Sooth to say, niece Jane, the soured and long-waiting legatee, had now for years been treating the poor old woman very scurvily: she had lived too long, and had grown to be a burden; notwithstanding that her ample income still kept on the house, and enabled the general to nurse his own East India Bonds right comfortably. But still the old aunt would not die, and as they sought not her, nor her's (quite contrary to St. Paul's disinterestedness), she was looked upon in the light of an incumbrance, on her own property and in her own house. Mrs. Tracy longed to throw off the yoke of dependance, and made small secret of the hatred of the fetter: for the old woman grew so deaf and blind, that there could be no risk at all, either in speaking one's mind, or in thoroughly neglecting her.

However, now that the harvest of hope appeared so near, the legatee renewed her old attentions: Death was a guest so very welcome to the house, that it is no wonder that his arrival was hourly expected with buoyant cheerfulness, and a something in the mask of kindliness: but I suspect that lamb-skin concealed a very wolf. So, Mrs. Tracy tenderly inquired of the doctor, and the doctor shook his head; and other doctors came to help, and shook their heads together. The patient still grew worse—O, brightening prospect!—though, now and then, a cordial draught seemed to revive her so alarmingly, that Mrs. Tracy affectionately urging that the stimulants would be too exciting for the poor dear sufferer's nerves, induced Dr. Graves to discontinue them. Then those fearful scintillations in her lamp of life grew fortunately duller, and the nurse was by her bed-side night and day; and the old aunt became more and more peevish, and was more and more spoken of by the Tracy family—in her possible hearing, as "that dear old soul"—out of it, "that vile old witch."

Charles, to be sure, was an exception in all this, as he ever was: for he took on him the Christian office of reading many prayers to the poor decaying creature, and (only that his father would not hear of such a thing) desired to have the vicar to assist him. Emily also, full of sympathy, and disinterested care, would watch the fretful patient, hour after hour, in those long, dull nights of pain; and the poor, old, perishing sinner loved her coming, for she spoke to her the words of hope and resignation. Whether that sweet missionary, scarcely yet a convert from her own dark creed—(Alas! the Amina had offered unto Juggernaut, and Emily of the strong hill-fort had scarcely heard of any truer God; and the fair girl was a woman-grown before, in her first earthly love, she also came to know the mercies Heaven has in store for us)—whether unto any lasting use she prayed and reasoned with that hard, dried heart, none but the Omniscient can tell. Let us hope: let us hope; for the fretful voice was stilled, and the cloudy forehead brightened, and the haggard eyes looked cheerfully to meet the inevitable stroke of death. Thus in wisdom and in charity, in patience and in faith, that gentle pair of lovers comforted the dying soul.

However, days rolled away, and Aunt Green lingered on still, tenaciously clinging unto life: until one morning early, she felt so much better, that she insisted on being propped up by pillows, and seeing all the household round her bed to speak to them. So up came every one, in no small hope of legacies, and what the lawyers call "*donationes mortis causâ.*"

The general was at her bed's-head, with, I am ashamed to say, perhaps unconsciously, a countenance more ridiculous than lugubrious; though he tried to subdue the buoyancy of hope and to put on looks of decent mourning; on the other side, the long-expectant legatee, Niece Jane, prudently concealed her questionable grief behind a scented pocket-handkerchief. Julian held somewhat aloof, for the scene was too depressing for his taste: so he affected to read a prayer-book, wrong way up, with his tongue in his cheek: Charles, deeply solemnized at the near approach of death, knelt at the poor invalid's bedside; and Emily stood by, leaning over her, suffused in tears. At the further corners of the bed, might be seen an old servant or two; and Mrs. Green's butler and coachman, each a forty years' fixture, presented their gray heads at the bottom of the room, and really looked exceedingly concerned.

Mrs. Green addressed them first, in her feeble broken manner: "Grant—and John—good and faithful—thank you—thank you both; and you too, kind Mrs. Lloyd, and Sally, and nurse—what's-your-name: give them the packets, nurse—all marked—first drawer, desk: there—there—God bless you—good—faithful."

The old servants, full of sorrow at her approaching loss, were comforted too: for a kind word, and a hundred pound note a-piece, made amends for much bereavement: the sick-nurse found her gift was just a tithe of their's, and recognised the difference both just and kind.

"Niece Jane—you've waited—long—for—this day: my will—rewards you."

"O dear—dear aunt, pray don't talk so; you'll recover yet, pray—pray don't:" she pretended to drown the rest in sorrow, but winked at her husband over the handkerchief.

"Julian!" (the precious youth attempted to look miserable, and came as called,) "you will find—I have remembered—you, Julian." So he winked, too, at his mother, and tried to blubber a "thank you."

"Charles—where's Charles? give me your hand, Charles dear—let me feel your face: here, Charles—a little pocket-book—good lad—good lad. There's Emily, too—dear child, she came—too late—I forgot her—I forgot her! general give her half—half—if you love—love—Emi—"

All at once her jaw dropped; her eyes, which had till now been preternaturally bright, filmed over; her head fell back upon the pillow; and the rich old aunt was dead.

Julian gave a shout that might have scared the parting spirit!

Really, the general was shocked, and Mrs. Tracy too; and the servants murmured "shame—shame!" poor Charles hid his face; Emily looked up indignantly; but Julian asked, with an oath, "Where's the good of being hypocrites?" and then added, "now, mother, let us find the will."

Then the nurse went to close the dim glazed eyes; and the other sorrowing domestics slunk away; and Charles led Emily out of the chamber of death, saddened and shocked at such indecent haste.

Meanwhile, the hopeful trio rummaged every drawer—tumbled out the mingled contents of boxes, desk, and escritoire—still, no will—no will: and at last the nurse, who more than once had muttered, "Shame on you all," beneath her breath, said,

"If you want the will, it's under her pillow: but don't disturb her yet, poor thing!"

Julian's rude hand had already thrust aside the lifeless, yielding head, and clutched the will: the father and mother—though humbled and wonder-stricken at his daring—gathered round him; and he read aloud, boldly and steadily to the end, though with scowling brow, and many curses interjectional:

"In the name of God, Amen. I, Constance Green, make this my last will and testament. Forasmuch as my niece, Jane Tracy, has watched and waited for my death these two-and-twenty years, I leave her all the shoes, slippers, and goloshes, whereof I may happen to die possessed: item, I leave Julian, her son, my '*Whole Duty of Man*,' convinced that he is deficient in it all: item, I confirm all the gifts which I intend to make upon my death-bed: item, forasmuch as General Tracy, my niece's husband, on his return from abroad, greeted me with much affection, I bequeath and give to him five thousand pounds' worth of Exchequer bills, now in my banker's hands; and appoint him my sole executor. As to my landed property, it will all go, in course of law, to my heir,

Samuel Hayley, and may he and his long enjoy it. And as to the remainder of my personal effects, including nine thousand pounds bank stock, my Dutch fives, and other matters, whereof I may die possessed (seeing that my relatives are rich enough without my help), I give and bequeath the same, subject as hereinbefore stated, to the trustees, for the time being, of the Westminster Lying-in Hospital, in trust, for the purposes of that charitable institution. In witness whereof, I have hereunto set my hand and seal this 13th day of May, 1840.

"CONSTANCE GREEN."

"Duly signed, sealed, and delivered! d—nation!" was Julian's brief epilogue—"General, let's burn it."

"You can if you please, Mr. Julian," interposed the nurse, who had secretly enjoyed all this, "and if you like to take the consequences; but, as each of the three witnesses has the will sealed up in copy, and the poor deceased there took pains to sign them all, perhaps—"

This settled the affair: and the discomfited expectants made a precipitate retreat. As the general, however, got vastly more than he expected, for his individual merits; and seeing that he loved Emily as much as he hated both Julian and his wife, he really felt well-pleased upon the whole, and took on him the duties of executor with cheerfulness. So they buried Aunt Green as soon as might be.

CHAPTER XI.

PREPARATIONS AND DEPARTURE.

CHARLES's pocket-book was full of clean bank notes, fifteen hundred pounds' worth: it contained also a diamond ring, and a lock of silvery hair; the latter a proof of affectionate sentiment in the kind old soul, that touched him at the heart.

"And now, my Emmy, the way is clear to us; Providence has sent me this, that I may right you, dearest: and it will be wise in us to say nothing of our plans. Avoid inquiries—for I did not say conceal or falsify facts: but, while none but you, love, heed of my departure, and while I go for our sakes alone, we need not invite disappointment by open-mouthed publicity. To those who love me, Emmy, I am frank and free; but with those who love us not, there is a wisdom and a justice in concealment. They do not deserve confidence, who will not extend to us their sympathy. None but yourself must know whither I am bound; and, after some little search for curiosity's sake, when a week is past and gone, no soul will care for me of those at home. With you, I will manage to communicate by post, directing my letters to Mrs. Sainsbury, at Oxton: I will prepare her for it. She knows my love for you, and how they try to thwart us; but even she, however trustworthy, need not be told my destination yet awhile, until 'India' appears upon the post-mark. How glad will you be, dearest one, how happy in our secret—to read my heart's own thoughts, when I am far away—far away, clearing up mine Emmy's cares, and telling her how blessed I feel in ministering to her happiness!"

Such was the substance of their talk, while counting out the pocket-book.

Charles's remaining preparations were simple enough, now his purse was flush of money: he resolved upon taking from his home no luggage whatever: preferring to order down, from an outfitting house in London, a regular kit of cadet's necessaries, to wait for him at the Europe Hotel, Plymouth, on a certain day in the ensuing week. So that, burdened only with his Emmy's miniature, and his pocket-book of bank notes, he might depart quietly some evening, get to Plymouth in a prëconcerted way, by chaise or coach, before the morrow morning; thence, a boat to meet the ship off-shore, and then—hey, for the Indies!

It was as well-devised a scheme as could possibly be planned; though its secresy, especially with a mother in the case, may be a moot point as to the abstract moral thereof: nevertheless, concretely, the only heart his so mysterious absence would have pained, was made aware of all: then, again, secresy had been the atmosphere of his daily life, the breath of his education; and he too sorely knew his mother would rejoice at the departure, and Julian, too—all the more certainly, as both brothers were now rivals professed for the hand of Emily Warren: as to the general, he might, or he might not, smoke an extra cheroot in the excitement of his wonder; and if he cared about it anyways more tragically than tobacco might betray, Emily knew how to comfort him.

With respect to other arrangements, Emmy furnished Charles with letters to certain useful people at Madras, and in particular to the "somebody" who looked after Mrs. Mackie: so, the mystery was easy of access, and he doubted not of overcoming, on the spot, every unseen difficulty. The plan of leaving all luggage behind, a capital idea, would enable him to go forth freely and unshackled, with an ordinary air, in hat and great-coat, as for an evening's walk; and was quite in keeping with the natural reserve of his whole character—a bad habit of secresy, which he probably inherited from his father, the lieutenant of old times. And yet, for all the wisdom, and mystery, and shrewd settling of the plan, its accomplishment was as nearly as possible most fatally defeated.

The important evening arrived; for the Indiaman—it was our old friend Sir William Elphinston—would be off Plymouth, next morning: the goods had been, for a day or two, safely deposited at the Europe, as per invoice, all paid: the lovers, in this last, this happiest, yet by far the saddest of their stolen interviews, had exchanged vows and kisses, and upon the beach, beneath those friendly cliffs, had commended one another to their Father in heaven. They had returned to the unsocial circle of home; all was fixed; the clock struck nine: and Charles, accidentally squeezing Emily's hand, rose to leave the tea-table.

"Where are you going, Mr. Charles?"

"I am going out, Julian."

"Thank you, sir! I knew that, but whither? General, I say, here 's Charles going to serenade somebody by moonlight."

The brandy-sodden parent, scarcely conscious, said something about his infernal majesty; and, "What then?—let him go, can't you?"

"Well, Julian dear, perhaps your brother will not mind your going with him; particularly as Emily stays at home with me."

This Mrs. Tracy spoke archly, intended as a hint to induce Julian to remain: but he had other thoughts—and simply said, in an ill-tempered tone of voice, "Done, Charles."

It was a dilemma for our escaping hero; but glancing a last look at Emily, he departed, and walked on some way as quietly as might be with Julian by his side: thinking, perhaps, he would soon be tired; and suffering him to fancy, if he would, that Charles was bound either on some amorous pilgrimage, or some charitable mission. But they left Burleigh behind them—and got upon the common—and passed it by, far out of sight and out of hearing—and were skirting the high banks of the darkly-flowing Mullet—and still there was Julian sullenly beside him. In vain Charles had tried, by many gentle words, to draw him into common conversation: Julian would not speak, or only gave utterance to some hinted phrase of insult: his brow was even darker than usual, and night was coming on apace, and he still tramped steadily along beside his brother, digging his sturdy stick into the clay, for very spite's sake. At length, as they yet walked along the river's side in that unfrequented place, Julian said, on a sudden, in a low strange tone, as if keeping down some rising rage within him,

"Mr. Charles, you love Emily Warren."

"Well, Julian, and who can help loving her?"

It was innocently said; but still a maddening answer, for he loved her too.

"And, sirrah," the brother hoarsely added, "she—she does not—does not—hate you, sir, as I do."

"My good Julian, pray do not be so violent; I cannot help it if the dear girl loves me."

"But I can, though!" roared Julian, with an oath, and lifted up his stick—it was nearer like a club—to strike his brother.

"Julian, Julian, what are you about? Good Heavens! you would not—you dare not—give over—unhand me, brother; what have I done, that you should strike me? Oh! leave me—leave me—pray."

"Leave you? I will leave you!" the villain almost shouted, and smote him to the ground with his lead-loaded stick. It was a blow that must have killed him, but for the interposing hat, now battered down upon his bleeding head. Charles, at length thoroughly aroused, though his foe must be a brother, struggled with unusual strength in self-preserving instinct, wrested the club from Julian's hand, and stood on the defensive.

Julian was staggered: and, after a moment's irresolution, drawing a pistol from his pocket, said, in a terribly calm voice,

"Now, sir! I have looked for such a meeting many days—alone, by night, with you! I would not willingly draw trigger, for the noise might bring down other folks upon us, out of Oxton yonder: but, drop that stick, or I fire."

Charles was noble enough, without another word, to fling the club into the river: it was not fear of harm, but fear of sin, that made him trust himself defenceless to a brother, a twin-brother, in the dark: he could not be so base, a murderer, a fratricide! Oh! most unhallowed thought! Save him from this crime, good God! Then, instantaneously reflecting, and believing he decided for the best, when he saw the ruffian glaring on him with exulting looks, as upon an unarmed rival at his mercy, with no man near to stay the deed, and none but God to see it, Charles resolved to seek safety from so terrible a death in flight.

Oxton was within one mile; and, clearly, this was not like flying from danger as a coward, but fleeing from attempted crime, as a brother and a Christian. Julian snatched at him to catch him as he passed: and, failing in this, rushed after him. It was a race for life! and they went like the wind, for two hundred yards, along that muddy high-banked walk.

Suddenly, Charles slipped upon the clay, that he fell; and Julian, with a savage howl, leapt upon him heavily.

Poor youth, he knew that death was nigh, and only uttered, "God forgive you, brother! oh, spare me—or, if not me, spare yourself—Julian, Julian!"

But the monster was determined. Exerting the whole force of his herculean frame, he seized his scarce-resisting victim as he lay, and, lifting him up like a child, flung his own twin-brother head foremost into that darkly-flowing current!

There was one piercing cry—a splash—a struggle; and again nothing broke upon the silent night, but the murmur of that swingeing tide, as the Mullet hurried eddying to the sea.

Julian listened a minute or two, flung some stones at random into the river, and then hastily ran back to Burleigh, feeling like a Cain.

CHAPTER XII.

THE ESCAPE.

But the overruling hand of Him whose aid that victim had invoked, was now stretched forth to save! and the strong-flowing tide, that ran too rapidly for Charles to sink in it, was commissioned from on High to carry him into an angle of that tortuous stream, where he clung by instinct to the bushes. Silence was his wisdom, while the murderer was near: and so long as Julian's footsteps echoed on the banks, Charles stirred not, spoke not, but only silently thanked God for his wonderful deliverance. However, the footsteps quickly died away, though heard far off clattering amid the still and listening night; and Charles, thankfully, no less than cautiously, drew himself out of the stream, very little harmed beyond a drenching: for the waters had recovered him at once from the effects of that desperate blow.

It was with a sense of exultation, freedom, independence, that he now hastened scatheless on his way; dripping garments mattered nothing, nor mud, nor the loss of his demolished hat: the pocket-book was safe, and Emmy's portrait, (how he kissed it, then!) and luckily a travelling cap was in his great-coat pocket: so with a most buoyant feeling of animal delight, as well as of religious gratitude, he sped merrily once more upon his secret expedition. Thank Heaven! Emmy could not know the peril he had past: and wretched Julian would now have dreadful reason of his own for this mysterious absence: and it was a pleasant thing to trudge along so freely in the starlight, on the private embassy of love. Happy Charles! I know not if ever more exhilarated feelings blessed the youth; they made him trip along the silent road, in a gush of joyfulness, at the rate of some six miles an hour; I know not if ever such delicious thoughts of Emily's attachment, and those gorgeous mysteries in India, of adventure, enterprise, escape, had heretofore caused his heart to bound so lightsomely within him, like some elastic spring. I know not if ever strong reliance upon Providential care, more earnest prayers, praises, intercessions (for poor Julian, too,) were offered on the altar of his soul. Happy Charles!

So he went on and on—long past Oxton, and Eyemouth, and Surbiton, and over the ferry, and through the sleeping turnpikes, and past the bridge, and along the broad high-road, until gray of morning's dawn revealed the suburbs of Plymouth.

Of course he missed the mail by which he intended to have gone—for Julian's dread act delayed him.

Long before his journey's end, his clothes were thoroughly dried, and violent exercise had shaken off all possible rheumatic consequence of that fearful plunge beneath the waters: five-and-twenty miles in four hours and three-quarters, is a tolerable recipe for those who have tumbled into rivers. We must recollect that he had gone as quick as he could, for fear of being late, now the coach had passed. At a little country inn, he brushed, and washed, and made toilet as well as he was able, took a glass of good Cognac, both hot and strong; and felt more of a man than ever.

Then, having loitered awhile, and well-remembered Emily in his prayers, at about eight in the morning he presented himself among his luggage at the Europe in gentlemanly trim, and soon got all on board the pilot boat, to meet the Indiaman just outside the breakwater. We may safely leave him there, happy, hopeful Charles! Sanguine for the future, exulting in the present, and thankful for the past: already has he poured out all his joys before that Friend who loves her too, and invoked His blessing on a scheme so well designed, so providentially accomplished.

I had almost forgotten Julian: wretched, hardened man, and how fared he? The moment he had flung his brother into that dark stream, and the waters closed above him greedily that he was gone—gone for ever, he first threw in stones to make a noise like life upon the stream, but that cheatery was only for an instant: he was alone—a murderer, alone! the horrors of silence, solitude, and guilt, seized upon him like three furies: so his quick retreating walk became a running; and the running soon was wild and swift for fear; and ever as he ran, that piercing scream came upon the wind behind, and hooted him: his head swam, his eyes saw terrible sights, his ears heard terrible sounds—and he scoured into quiet, sleeping Burleigh like a madman. However, by some strange good luck, not even did the slumbering watchman see him: so he got in-doors as usual with the latch-key (it was not the first time he had been out at night), crept up quietly, and hid himself in his own chamber.

And how did he spend those hours of guilty solitude? in terrors? in remorse? in misery? Not he: Julian was too wise to sit and think, and in the dark too; but he lit both reading lamps to keep away the gloom, and smoked and drank till morning's dawn to stupify his conscience.

Then, to make it seem all right, he went down to breakfast as usual, though any thing but sober, and met unflinchingly his mother's natural question—

"Good morning, Julian—where's Charles?"

"How should I know, mother; isn't he up yet?"

"No, my dear; and what is more, I doubt if he came home last night."

"Hollo, Master Charles! pretty doings these, Mr. Sabbath-teacher! so he slept out, eh, mother?"

"I don't know—but where did you leave him, Julian?"

"Who! I? did I go out with him? Oh! yes, now I recollect: let's see, we strolled together midway to Oxton, and, as he was going somewhat further, there I left him?"

How true the words, and yet how terribly false their meaning!

"Dear me, that's very odd—isn't it, general?"

"Not at all, ma'am—not at all; leave the lad alone, he'll be back by dinner-time: I didn't think the boy had so much spirit."

Emily, to whom the general's hint was Greek, looked up cheerfully and in her own glad mind chuckled at her Charles's bold adventure.

But the day passed, off, and they sent out men to seek for him: and another—and all Burleigh was a-stir: and another—and the coast-guards from Lyme to Plymouth Sound searched every hole and corner: and another—when his mother wept five minutes: and another—when the wonder was forgotten.

However, they did not put on mourning for the truant: he might turn up yet: perhaps he was at Oxford.

Emily had not much to do in comforting the general for his dear son's loss; it clearly was a gain to him, and he felt far freer than when wisdom's eye was on him. Charles had been too keen for father, mother, and brother; too good, too amiable: he saw their ill, condemned it by his life, and showed their dark too black against his brightness. The unnatural deficiency of mother's love had not been overrated: Julian had all her heart; and she felt only obliged to the decamping Charles for leaving Emily so free and clear to his delightful brother. She never thought him dead: death was a repulsive notion at all times to her: no doubt he would turn up again some day. And Julian joked with her about that musty proverb "a bad penny."

As to our dear heroine, she never felt so happy in all her life before as now, even when her Charles had been beside her; for within a day of his departure he had written her a note full of affection, hope, and gladness; assuring her of his health, and wealth, and safe arrival on board the Indiaman. The noble-hearted youth never said one single word about his brother's crime: but he did warn his Emmy to keep close beside the general. This note she got through Mrs. Sainsbury; that invalid lady at Oxton, who never troubled herself to ask or hear one word beyond her own little world—a certain physic-corner cupboard.

And thou—poor miserable man—thou fratricide in mind—and to thy best belief in act, how drags on now the burden of thy life? For a day or two, spirits and segars muddled his brain, and so kept thoughts away: but within a while they came on him too piercingly, and Julian writhed beneath those scorpion stings of hot and keen remorse: and when the coast-guards dragged the Mullet, how that caitiff trembled! and when nothing could be found, how he wondered fearingly! The only thing the wretched man could do, was to loiter, day after day, and all day long, upon the same high path which skirts the tortuous stream. Fascinated there by hideous recollections, he could not leave the spot for hours: and his soft-headed, romantic mother, noticing these deep abstractions, blessed him—for her Julian was now in love with Emily.

CHAPTER XIII.

NEWS OF CHARLES.

Ay—in love with Emily! Fiercely now did Julian pour his thoughts that way; if only hoping to forget murder in another strong excitement. Julian listened to his mother's counsels; and that silly, cheated woman playfully would lean upon his arm, like a huge, coy confidante, and fill his greedy ears (that heard her gladly for very holiday's sake from fearful apprehensions), with lover's hopes, lover's themes, his Emily's perfection. Delighted mother—how proud and pleased was she! quite in her own element, fanning dear Julian's most sentimental flame, and scheming for him interviews with Emily.

It required all her skill—for the girl clung closely to her guardian: he, unconscious Argus, never tired of her company; and she, remembering dear Charles's hint, and dreading to be left alone with Julian, would persist to sit day after day at her books, music, or needle-work in the study, charming General Tracy by her pretty Hindoo songs. With him she walked out, and with him she came in; she would read to him for hours, whether he snored or listened; and, really, both mother and son were several long weeks before their scheming could come to any thing. A *tête-à-tête* between Julian and Emily appeared as impossible to manage, as collision between Jupiter and Vesta.

However, after some six weeks of this sort of mining and countermining (for Emily divined their wishes), all on a sudden one morning the general received a letter that demanded his immediate presence for a day or two in town; something about prize-money at Puttymuddyfudgepoor. Emily was too high-spirited, too delicate in mind, to tell her guardian of fears which never might be realized; and so, with some forebodings, but a cheerful trust, too, in a Providence above her, she saw the general off without a word, though not without a tear; he too, that stern, close man, was moved: it was strange to see them love each other so.

The moment he was gone, she discreetly kept her chamber for the day, on plea of sickness; she had cried very heartily to see him leave her—he had never yet left her once since she could recollect—and thus she really had a head-ache, and a bad one.

Next morning, she would gladly have found any just excuse for absence from the breakfast-table—fever, small-pox, cholera, any thing: for Julian's attentions were more dreaded than them all. But she was quite recovered now, and a ship-letter, that morning arrived from Charles, all well, and merrily bounding over the salt sea, had put her in such high spirits, that, with something of just pride and matronly fortitude, she determined to confront Mrs. Tracy and her son. Verily, her frank and cheerly trustfulness quite staggered the conspiring pair: for Emily had been strengthened by prayerful trust towards God, and felt happy in her well-requited love.

She was the first to speak. "Good-morrow, Mrs. Tracy; how do you do, Julian? I am afraid to say, you don't look quite so well as usual."

Indeed, he did not; for ghastly fears racked him, and unsatisfied desires: he was pale, wasted, miserable. So he awkwardly answered her address with a common "how d'ye do?"

"Julian has lost his spirits lately very much, my dear: I dare say you can guess the cause?" As if either of them could!

"The cause, Mrs. Tracy? I am sure I cannot; at least," she added, somewhat mischievously, "unless he is anxious about Charles."

"What about Charles?" hurriedly asked Julian, in a wild and nervous way.

"Why, we all know he is missing, don't we, Julian? and has been for these six weeks: I am sure it does you credit to seem so altered since he went."

"Went? whither?" earnestly asked the mother, who really had begun to find out that she loved her now lost child: "whither, dearest Emily? oh, do you know? do you know? tell me—tell me."

To Emily's great surprise, Mrs. Tracy shed real tears of evident affection and sorrow; though a silly and weak one, she was a mother still, and Charles a son, although too good for her.

Accordingly Emily, in the fullness of her sympathy, and with some natural exultation of spirits, now that Charles had got a fair start (he was at the Cape by this time), gayly answered—

"Dear Mrs. Tracy, I rejoice to be able to assure you, that you need not entertain a fear or doubt of Charles's welfare; though I am a woman, I can keep a secret, you see;" (the dear girl was babbling it all the while, quite unconscious of her contradiction;) "Charles is gone to India, to find out who I am, and I heard from him this morning—all well at St. Helena!"

Julian Tracy gave such a start, that he knocked off a cheffonier of rare china and glass standing at his elbow; and the smash of mandarins and porcelain gods would have been enough, at any other time, to have driven his mother crazy.

"Charles alive?" shouted he.

"Yes, Julian—why not? You saw him off, you know: cannot you remember?"

Now to that guilty wretch's mind the fearful notion instantaneously occurred, that Emily Warren was in some strange, wild way bantering him; she knew his dreadful secret—"he *had* seen him off." He trembled like an aspen as she looked on him.

"Oh yes, he remembered, certainly; but—but where was her letter?"

"Never mind that, Julian; you surely would not read another person's letters, Monsieur le Chevalier Bayard?"

Emily was as gay at heart that morning as a sky-lark, and her innocent pleasantry proved her strongest shield. Julian dared not ask to see the letter—scarcely dared to hope she had one, and yet did not know what to think. As to any love scene now, it was quite out of the question, notwithstanding all his mother's hints and management; a new exciting thought entirely filled him: was he a Cain, a fratricide, or not? was Charles alive after all? And, for once in his life, Julian had some repentant feelings; for thrilling hope was nigh to cheer his gloom.

It really seemed as if Emily, sweet innocent, could read his inmost thoughts. "At any rate," observed she, playfully, "Bayard may take the postman's privilege, and see the outside."

With that, she produced the ship-letter that had put her in such spirits, legibly dated some twenty-two days ago. Yes, Charles's hand, sure enough! Julian could swear to it among a thousand. And he fainted dead away.

What an astonishing event! how Mrs. Tracy praised her noble-spirited boy! How the bells rang! and hot water, and cold water, and salts, and rubbings, and *eau de Cologne*, and all manner of delicate attentions, long sustained, at length contributed to Julian's restoration. Moreover, even Emily was agreeably surprised; she had never seen him in so amiable a light before; this was all feeling, all affection for his brother —her dear—dear Charles. And when Mrs. Tracy heard what Emily said of Julian's feeling heart, she became positively triumphant; not half so much at Charles's safety, and all that, as at Julian's burst of feeling. She was quite right, after all; he was worthy to be her favourite, and she felt both flattered and obliged to him for fainting dead away. "Yes—yes, my dear Miss Warren, depend upon it Julian has fine feelings, and a good heart." And Emily began to condemn both Charles and herself for lack of charity, and to think so too.

CHAPTER XIV.

THE TETE-A-TETE.

No sooner had "dear Julian" recovered, which he really had not quite accomplished until the day had begun to wear away (so great a shock had that intelligence of Charles been to his guilty mind), than the gratified and prudent mother fancied this a famous opportunity to leave the young couple to themselves. It was after dinner, when they had retired to the drawing-room; and I will say that Emily had never seemed so favourably disposed towards that rough, but generous, heart before. So then, on some significant pretence, well satisfied her favourite was himself again, as bold, and black, and boisterous as ever, the masculine mother kissed her hand to them, as a fat fairy might be supposed to do, and operatically tripped away, coyly bidding Emily "take care of Julian till she should come back again."

The momentary gleam of good which glanced across that bad man's heart has faded away hours ago; his repentant thoughts had been occasioned more from the sudden relief he experienced at running now no risks for having murdered, than for any better feeling towards his brother, or any humbler notions of himself. Nay, a strong rëaction occurred in his ideas the moment he had seen his brother's writing; and when he fainted, he fainted from the struggle in his mind of manifold exciting causes, such as these:—hatred, jealousy, what he called love, though a lower name befitted it, and vexation that his brother was —not dead. Oh mother, mother! if your poor weak head had but been wise enough to read that heart, would you still have loved it as you do? Alas—it is a deep lesson in human nature this—she would! for Mrs. General Tracy was one of those obstinate, yet superficial characters, whom no reason can convince that they are wrong, no power can oblige to confess themselves mistaken. She rejoiced to hear him called "her very image;" and predominant vanity in the large coquette extended to herself at second-hand; self was her idol substance, and its delightful shadow was this mother's son.

The moment Mrs. Tracy left the room, Julian perceived his opportunity: Charles, detested rival, far away at sea; the guardian gone to London; Emily in an unusual flow of affability and kindness, and he—alone with her. Rashly did he bask his soul in her delicious beauty, deliberately drinking deep of that intoxicating draught. Giving the rein to passion, he suffered that tumultuous steed to hurry him whither it would, in mad unbridled course. He sat so long silently gazing at her with the lack-lustre eyes of low and dull desire, that Emily, quite thrown off her guard by that amiable fainting for his brother, addressed him in her innocent kind-heartedness,

"Are you not recovered yet, dear Julian?"

The effect was instantaneous: scarcely crediting his ears that heard her call him "dear," his eyes, that saw her winning smile upon him, he started from his chair, and trembling with agitation, flung himself at her feet, to Emily's unqualified astonishment.

"Why, Julian, what's the matter?—unhand me, sir! let go!" (for he had got hold of her wrist.)

The passionate youth seized her hand—that one with Charles's ring upon it—and would have kissed it wildly with polluting lips, had she not shrieked suddenly "Help! help!"

Instantly his other hand was roughly dashed upon her mouth—so roughly that it almost knocked her backwards—and the blood flowed from her wounded lip; but by a preternatural effort, the indignant Indian queen hurled the ruffian from her, flew to the bell, and kept on ringing violently.

In less than half a minute all the household was around her, headed by the startled Mrs. Tracy, who had all the while been listening in the other drawing-room: butler, footmen, house-maids, ladies'-maids, cook, scullions, and all rushed in, thinking the house was on fire.

No need to explain by a word. Emily, radiant in imperial charms, stood, like inspired Cassandra, flashing indignation from her eyes at the cowering caitiff on the floor. The mother, turning all manner of colours, dropped on her knees to "poor Julian's" assistance, affecting to believe him taken ill. But Emily Warren, whose insulted pride vouchsafed not a word to that guilty couple, soon undeceived all parties, by addressing the butler in a voice tremulous and broken—

"Mr. Saunders—be so good—as to go—to Sir Abraham Tamworth's—in the square—and request of him—a night's—protection—for a poor—defenceless, insulted woman!"

She could hardly utter the last words for choking tears: but immediately battling down her feelings, added, with the calmness of a heroine—

"You are a father, Mr. Saunders—set all this before Sir Abraham strongly, but delicately.

"Footmen! so long as that wretch is in the room, protect me, as you are men."

And the stately beauty placed herself between the two liveried lacqueys, as Zenobia in the middle of her guards.

"Marguerite!"—the pretty little Française tripped up to her—"wipe this blood from my face."

Beautiful, insulted creature! I thought that I looked upon some wounded Boadicea, with her daughters extracting the arrow from her cheek.

"And now, kind Charlotte, fetch my cloak; and follow me to Prospect House, with what I may require for the night. Till the general's return, I stay not here one minute."

Then, without a syllable, or a look of leave-taking, the wise and noble girl—doubtless unconsciously remembering her early Hindoo braveries, the lines of matchlock men, the bowing slaves, the processions, and her jewelled state of old—marched away in magnificent beauty, accompanied in silence by the whole astonished household.

Mrs. Tracy and her son were left alone: the silly, silly mother thought him "hardly used." Julian, whose natural effrontery had entirely deserted him, looked like what he was—a guilty coward: and the mother, who had pampered up her "fine high-spirited son" to his full-grown criminality by a foolish education, really—when she had time to think of any thing but him—was excessively frightened. The general would be back to-morrow, and then—and then!—she dreaded to picture that explosion of his wrath.

CHAPTER XV.

SATISFACTION.

Sir Abraham Tamworth, G. C. B.—a fine old Admiral of the White, who somewhat looked down upon the rank of General, H. E. I. C. S.—was astonished, as well he might be, at Mr. Saunders, and his message: and, of course, most gladly acquiesced in acting as poor Emily's protector. Accordingly, however jealous Lady Tamworth and her daughters might heretofore have felt of that bright beauty at the balls, they were now all genuine sympathy, indignation, and affection. Emily, I need hardly say, went straight up stairs to have her cry out.

"Whom are you writing to, George, in such a hurry?" asked the admiral, of a fine moustachioed son, George St. Vincent Tamworth, of the Royal Horse Guards, who had just got six months' leave of absence for the sake of marriage with his cousin.

The gallant soldier tossed a billet to his father, who mounted his spectacles, and quietly read it at the lamp.

"Captain Tamworth desires Mr. Julian Tracy's company to-morrow morning, at seven o'clock, in the third meadow on the Oxton road. The captain brings a friend with him; also pistols and a surgeon; and he desires Mr. Tracy to do the like: Prospect House, Thursday evening."

"So, George, you consider him a gentleman, do you? I am afraid it's a poor compliment to our fair young friend." And he quietly crumpled up the challenge in his iron hand.

"Really, sir!—you surprise me;—pardon me, but I will send that note: mustn't I chastise the fellow for this insufferable outrage?"

"No doubt, George, no doubt of it at all: when a lady is insulted, and a man (not to say a queen's officer) stands by without taking notice of it, he deserves whipping at the cart's-tail, and Coventry for life. I've no patience, boy, with such mean meekness, as putting up with bullying insolence when a woman 's in the case. Let a man show moral courage, if he can and will, in his own affront; I honour him who turns on his heel from common personal insult, and only wish my own old blood was cool enough to do so: but the mother, wife, and sister, ay, George, and the poor defenceless one, be she lady, peasant, or menial, who comes to us for safety in a woman's dress, we must take up their quarrel, or we are not men!—"

"Don't interrupt him, George," uxoriously suggested Lady Tamworth, "your father hasn't done talking yet." For George was getting terribly impatient; he knew, from sad experience, how much the admiral was given to prosing. However, the oration soon proceeded to our captain's entire satisfaction, after his progenitor had paused awhile for breath's sake in his eloquence.

"—Take up their quarrel, or we are not men. Nevertheless, boy, I cannot see the need of pistols. The only conceivable case for violent redress, is woman's wrong: and he who wrongs a woman, cannot be a gentleman; therefore, ought not to be met on equal terms. For other causes of duello, as hot-headed speeches, rudenesses, or slights, forgive, forbear to fan the flame, and never be above apologizing: but in an outrage such as this, let a fine-built fellow, such as you are, George (and the women should show wisdom in their choice of champions), let a man, and a queen's officer as you are, treat this brute, Julian Tracy, as a martinet huntsman would a hound thrown out. As for me, boy, I'm going to call on Mrs. Tracy at eleven o'clock to-morrow morning—and, without presuming to advise a six foot two of a son, I think—I think, if I were you, I would be dutiful enough to say—'Father, I will accompany you—and take a horsewhip with me.'"

"Agreed, agreed, sir!" replied the well-pleased son, and her ladyship too vouchsafed her approbation.

Emily had gone to bed long ago, or rather to her chamber; where the three Misses Tamworth had been all kindness, curiosity, and consolation. So, Sir Abraham and his lady, now the speech was finished, followed their example of retirement: and the captain newly blood-knotted his hunting-whip, *con amore*, not to say *con spirito*, overnight.

Nobody will wonder to hear, that when the gallant representatives of army and navy called next morning at number seven, Mrs. Tracy and her son were "not at home:" and of course it would be far too Julian-like a proceeding, for true gentleman to think of forcing their company on the probably ensconced in-dwellers. Accordingly, they marched away, without having deigned to leave a card; the captain taking on himself the duty of perambulating sentinel, while his father proceeded to the library as usual. Judge of the glad surprise, when, within ten minutes, our vindictive George perceived the admiral coming back again, full-sail, with the mother and son in tow, creeping amicably enough up the terrace. Sir Abraham had given her his arm, and precious Mr. Julian was a little in the rear: for the old folks were talking confidentially.

George St. Vincent, placing his whip in the well-known position of "Cane, a mystery," advanced to meet them; and, just after passing his father, with whom he exchanged a very comfortable glance, discovered that the heroic Julian, who had caught a glimpse of the ill-concealed weapon, was slinking quickly round a corner to avoid him. It was certainly undignified to run, but the gallant captain did run, nevertheless; and soon caught the coward by the collar.

Then, at arm's length, was the hunting-whip applied, full-swing; up the terrace, and down the parade, and through High-street, and Smith-street, and Oxton-road, and aristocratical Pacton-square, and the well-thronged plebeian market-place; lash, lash, lash, in furious and fast succession on the writhing roaring culprit; to the universal excoriation of Mr. Julian Tracy, and the amazement of an admiring and soon-collected crowd—the rank, beauty, and fashion—of Burleigh Singleton. Julian was strong indeed, and a coal-heaver in build, but conscience had unnerved him; and the coarse noisy bully always is a coward: therefore, it was a pleasant thing to see how easy came the captain's work to him—he had nothing to do but to lash, lash, lash, double-thonged, like a slave-driver: and, except that he made the caitiff move along, to be a spectacle to man and woman, up and down the town, he might as well, for any difficulty in the deed, have been employed in scarifying a gate-post.

At last, thoroughly exhausted with having inflicted as much punishment as any three drummers at a soldier's whipping-match, and spying out his "tiger" in the throng, our gallant Avenging Childe tossed the heavy whip to the trim cockaded little man, that he might carry home that instrument of vengeance, deliberately wiped his wet mustachios, and giving Julian one last kick, let the fellow part in peace.

CHAPTER XVI.

HOW CHARLES FARED.

Having thus found protectors for poor Emily, and disposed of her assailant to the entire satisfaction of all mankind, let us turn seawards, and take a look at Charles.

Now, "no earthly power,"—as a certain ex-chancellor protested—shall induce me to do so mean a thing as to open Charles's letters, and spread them forth before the public gaze. Doubtless, they were all things tender, warm, and eloquent; doubtless, they were tinted rosy hue, with love's own blushes, and made glorious with the golden light of unaffected piety. I only read them myself in a reflected way, by looking into Emily's eyes; and I saw, from their ever-changing radiance, how feelingly he told of his affections; how fervently he poured out all his heart upon the page; how evidently tears and kisses had made many words illegible; how wise, sanguine, happy, and religious, was her own devoted Charles.

Of the trivial incidents of voyaging, his letters said not much: though cheerful and agreeable in his floating prison, with the various exported marrying-maidens and transported civil officers, who constitute the average bulk of Indian cargoes outward bound, Charles mixed but little in their society, seldom danced, seldom smoked, seldom took a hand at whist, or engaged in the conflicts of backgammon. Sharks, storms, water-spouts; the meeting divers vessels, and exchanging post-bags; tar-barrelled Neptune of the line, Cape Town with its mountain and the Table-cloth, long-rolling seas; and similar common-places, Charles did not think proper to enlarge upon: no more do I. Life is far too short for all such petty details: and, more pointedly, a wire-drawn book is the just abhorrence of a generous public.

The letters came frequently: for Charles did little else all day but write to Emmy, so as always to be ready with a budget for the next piece of luck—a home-bound ship. He had many things to teach her yet, sweet student; and it was a beautiful sight to see how her mind expanded as an opening flower before the sun of tenderness and wisdom. Each letter, both in writing and in reading, was the child of many prayers: and even the loveliness of Emily grew more soft, more elevated, "as it had been the face of an angel," when feeding in solitary joy on those effusions of her lover's heart.

Of course, he could not hear from her, until the overland mail might haply bring him letters at Madras: so that, as our Irish friends would say, with all her will to tell him of her love, "the reciprocity must needs be all on one side." But Emily did write too; earnestly, happily: and poured her very heart out in those eloquent burning words. I dare say Charles will get the letter now within a day or two: for the roaring surf of Madras is on the horizon, almost within sight.

Nevertheless, before he gets there, and can read those letters—precious, precious manuscripts—it will be my painful duty, as a chronicler of (what might well be) truth, to put the reader in possession of one little hint, which seemed likeliest to wreck the happiness of these two children of affection.

I am Emily's invisible friend: and as the dear girl ran to me one morning, with tears in her eyes, to ask me what I thought of a certain mysterious paragraph, I need not scruple to lay it straight before the reader.

At the end of a voluminous love-letter, which I really did not think of prying into, occurred the following postscript, evidently written at the last moment of haste.

"Oh! my precious Emmy, I have just heard the most fearful rumour of ill that could possibly befall us: the captain of our ship—you will remember Captain Forbes, he knew you and the general well, he said—has just assured me that—that—! I dare not, cannot write the awful words. Oh! my own Emmy—Heaven grant you be my own!—pray, pray, as I will night and day, that rumour be not true: for if it be, my love, both God and man forbid us ever to meet again! How I wish I could explain it all, or that I had never heard so much, or never written it here, and told it you, though thus obscurely: for I can't destroy this letter now, the ships are just parting company, and there is no time to write another. Yet will I hope, love, against hope. Who knows? through God's good mercy, it may all be cleared up still. If not—if not—strive to forget for ever, your unhappy "CHARLES.

"Perhaps—O, glorious thought!—Nurse Mackie may know better than the captain, after all; and yet, he seems so positive: if he is right, there is nothing for us both but Wo! Wo! Wo!"

Now, to say plain truth, when Emily showed me this, I looked very blank upon it. That Charles had heard some meddlesome report, which (if true) was to be an insuperable barrier to their future union, struck me at a glimpse. But I had not the heart to hint it to her; and only encouraged hope—hope, in God's help, through the means of Mrs. Mackie and her papers.

As for the poor girl herself, she asked me, in much humility, and with many sobs, if I did not fear that her Hindoo mystery was this:—she was the vilest of the vile, a Pariah, an outcast, whose very presence is contamination!

Beautiful, loving, heavenly-hearted creature! so humble in the midst of her majestic loveliness! how touching was the thought, that she thus readily acquiesced in any the deepest humiliation holy Providence had seen fit to send her; and though the sentence would have crushed her happiness for ever, till the day of death, that she could still look up and say, "Be it to thine handmaid even as thou wilt."

As I had no better method of explaining the matter, and as her infantine reminiscences and prejudices about caste were strong, I even let her think so, if she would: it was a far better alternative than my own sad thoughts about the business: and, however painful was the process, it was something consolatory to observe, that this voluntary humiliation mellowed and chastened her own character, subduing tropical fires, and tempering the virgin gold by meekness.

Oh! Charles, Charles, my poor fellow, "who have cast your all upon a die, and must abide the issue of the throw," I most fervently hope that gossiping Captain Forbes spoke falsely: it is a comfort to reflect that the world is often very liberal in attributing the honours of paternity to some who really do not deserve them. And if a rich old bachelor looks kindly on a foundling, is it not pure malice on that sole account of charity to hail him father? Besides—there's Nurse Mackie.—Speed to Madras, poor youth, and keep your courage up.

CHAPTER XVII.

THE GENERAL'S RETURN.

In a most unwonted flow of animal spirits, and an entire affability which restored him at once to the rank of a communicative creature, General Tracy came back on Friday night. He had met with marvellous prosperity; for Hancock's had been paying off the prize-money; and his own lion's share, as general, in the easy process of dethroning half a dozen diamond-hilted rajahs and nabobs, amounted to something like four lacs of rupees, nearly half a crore! Such a flush of wealth, and he was rich already without it, exhilarated the bilious old gentleman so strangely, that positive peonies were blooming in his cheeks; and, as if this was not miracle enough, he had brought his wife as a present Maurice's '*Antiquities of India*,' gloriously bound, and had even been so superfluous as to purchase a new pair of double-barrelled pistols for Julian: the lad was a fine young fellow after all, and ought to be encouraged in snuffing out a candle; as for Emily's *petit cadeau*, it was a fifty guinea set of cameos, the choicest in their way that Howell and James's had to show him. Moreover, he had sent a Bow-street officer to Oxford, to make inquiries after Charles: actually, good fortune had made him at once humanized and happy.

So the chaise rattled up, and the general bounded out, and flew into the arms of his wondering wife, as Paris might have flown to Helen, or Leander to his heroine—the only feminine Hero, whom grammar recognises. It was past eleven at night: therefore he did not think to ask for Julian; no doubt the boy was gone to bed.

Indeed, he had; and was tossing his wealed body, full of pains, and aches, and bruises, as softly as he could upon the feather-bed: he had need of poultices all over, and a quart of Friar's Balsam would have done him little good: after his well-merited thrashing, the flogged hound had slunk to his kennel, and locked himself sullenly in, without even speaking to his mother. Tobacco-fumes exuded from the key-hole, and I doubt not other creature-comforts lent the muddled man their aid.

However, after the first rush of news to Mrs. Tracy, her lord, who had every moment been expecting the door to fly open, and Emily to fall into his arms—for strangely did they love each other—suddenly asked,

"But, where's Emmy all this time! she knows I'm here?—not got to bed, is she?—knew I was coming?—"

"Oh! general, I'll tell you all about it to-morrow morning."

"About what, madam? Great God! has any harm befallen the child? Speak—speak, woman!"

"Dear—dear—Oh! what shall I say?" sobbed the silly mother. "Emily—Emily, poor dear Julian—"

"What the devil, ma'am, of Julian?" The general turned white as a sheet, and rang the bell, in singular calmness; probably for a dram of brandy. Saunders answered it so instantly, that I rather suspect he was waiting just outside.

The moment Mrs. Tracy saw the gray-headed butler, anticipating all that he might say, she brushed past him, and hurriedly ran up-stairs.

"What's all this, Mr. Saunders? where's Miss Warren?" And the poor old guardian seemed ready to faint at his reply: but he heard it out patiently.

"I am very sorry to say, general, that Miss Emily has been forced to take refuge at Sir Abraham Tamworth's: but she 's well, sir, and safe, sir; quite well and safe," the good man hastened to say, "only I 'm afraid that Mr. Julian had been taking liberties with—"

I dare not write the general's imprecation: then, as he clenched the arms of his easy-chair, as with the grasp of the dying, he asked, in a quick wild way—

"But what was it?—what happened?"

"Nothing to fear, sir—nothing at all, general;—I am thankful to say, that all I saw, and all we all saw, was Miss Emily pulling at the bell-rope with blood upon her face, and Mr. Julian on the floor: but I took the young lady to Sir Abraham's immediately, general, at her own desire."

The father arose sternly; his first feeling was to kill Julian; but the second, a far better one, predominated—he must go and see Emily at once.

So, faintly leaning on the butler's arm, the poor old man (whom a moiety of ten minutes, with its crowding fears, had made to look some ten years older,) proceeded to the square, and knocked up Sir Abraham at midnight, and the admiral came down, half asleep, in dressing-gown and slippers, vexed at having been knocked up from his warm berth so uncomfortably: it put him sorely in remembrance of his hardships as a middy.

"Kind neighbour, thank you, thank you; where 's Emmy? take me to my Emmy;" and the iron-hearted veteran wept like a driveller.

Sir Abraham looked at him queerly: and then, in a cheerful, friendly way, replied—

"Dear general, do not be so moved: the girl 's quite safe with us; you 'll see her to-morrow morning. All 's right; she was only frightened, and George has given the fellow a proper good licking: and the girl 's a-bed, you know; and, eh? what?"—

For the poor old man, like one bereaved, said, supplicatingly—

"In mercy take me to her—precious child!"

"My dear sir—pray consider—it 's impossible; fine girl, you know;—Lady Tamworth, too—can't be, can't be, you know, general."

And the mystified Sir Abraham looked to Saunders for an explanation—

"Was his master drunk?"

"I must speak to her, neighbour; I must, must, and will—dear, dear child: come up with me, sir, come; do not trifle with a breaking heart, neighbour!"

There was a heart still in that hard-baked old East Indian.

It was impossible to resist such an appeal: so the two elders crept up stairs, and knocked softly at her chamber-door. Clearly, the girl was asleep: she had sobbed herself to sleep; the general had been looked for all day long, and she was worn with watching; he could hardly come at midnight; so the dear affectionate child had sobbed herself to sleep.

"Allow me, Sir Abraham." And General Tracy whispered something at the key-hole in a strange tongue.

Not Aladdin's "open Sesame" could have been more magical. In a moment, roused up suddenly from sleep, and forgetting every thing but those tender recollections of gentle care in infancy, and kindness all through life, the child of nature startled out of bed, drew the bolt, and in beauteous disarray, fell into that old man's arms!

It was enough; he had seen her eye to eye—she lived: and the white-haired veteran suffered himself to be led away directly from the landing, like a child, by his sympathizing neighbour.

"My heart is lighter now, Sir Abraham: but I am a poor weak old man, and owe you an explanation for this outburst; some day—some day, not now. O, if you could guess how I have nursed that pretty babe when alone in distant lands; how I have doated on her little winning ways, and been gladdened by the music of her prattle; how I have exulted to behold her loveliness gradually expanding, as she was ever at my side, in peril as in peace, in camp as in quarters, in sickness as in health, still—still, the blessed angel of a bad man's life—a wicked, hard old man, kind neighbour—if you knew more—more, than for her sake I dare tell you—and if you could conceive the love my Emmy bears for me, you would not think it strange—think it strange—" He could not say a syllable more; and the admiral, with Mr. Saunders, too, who joined them in the study, looked very little able to console that poor old man. For they all had hearts, and trickling eyes to tell them.

Then having arranged a shake-down for his master in Sir Abraham's study—for the guardian would not leave his dear one ever again—Saunders went home, purposing to attend with razors in the morning.

CHAPTER XVIII.

INTERCALARY.

The Tamworths did not altogether live at Burleigh Singleton—it was far too petty a place for them; dullness all the year round (however pleasant for a month or so, as a holiday from toilsome pleasures) would never have done for Lady Tamworth and her daughters: but they regularly took Prospect House for six weeks in the summer season, when tired of Portland Place, and Huntover, their fine estate in Cheshire: and so, from constant annual immigration, came as much to be regarded Burleighites, as swifts and swallows to be ranked as British birds. I only hint at this piece of information, for fear any should think it unlikely, that grandees of Sir Abraham's condition could exist for ever in a place where the day-before-yesterday's '*Times*' is first intelligence. Moreover, as another interjectional touch, it is only due to my life-likenesses to record, that Mrs. Green's, although a terrace-house, and ranked as humble number seven, was, nevertheless, a tolerably spacious mansion, well suited for the dignity of a butler to repose in: for Mrs. Green had added an entire dwelling on the inland side, as, like most maritime inhabitants, she was thoroughly sick of the sea, and never cared to look at it, though living there still, from mere disinclination to stir: so, then, it was quite a double house, both spacious and convenient. As for the inglorious incident of Julian's latch-key, I should not wonder if many wide street-doors to many marble halls are conscious of similar convenient fastenings, if gentlemen of Julian's nocturnal tastes happen to be therein dwelling. Another little matter is worth one word. The house had been Mrs. Green's, a freehold, and was, therefore, now her heir's; but the general, as an executor, remained there still, until his business was finished; in fact, he took his year's liberty.

He had returned from India rolling in gold; for some great princess or other—I think they called her a Begum or a Glumdrum, or other such like Gulliverian appellative—had been singularly fond of him, and had loaded him in early life with favours—not only kisses, and so forth, but jewellery and gold pagodas. And lately, as we know, Puttymuddy-fudgepoor, with its radiating rajahs and nabobs, had proved a mine of wealth: for a crore is ten lacs, and a lac of rupees is any thing but a lack of money—although rupees be money, and the "middle is distributed;" in spite of logic, then, a lack means about twelve thousand pounds: and four of them, according to Cocker, some fifty thousand. It would appear then, that with the produce of the Begum's diamonds, converted into money long ago, and some of them as big as linnet's eggs—and not to take account of Mrs. Green's trifling pinch of the five Exchequer bills, all handed over at once to Emily—the General's present fortune was exactly one hundred and twenty-three thousand pounds.

Of course, *he* wasn't going to bury himself at Burleigh Singleton much longer; and yet, for all that stout intention of houses and lands, and carriages and horses, in almost any other county or country, it is as true as any thing in this book, that he was a resident still, a leaseholder of Aunt Green's house, long after the *dénouement* of this story; in many things an altered man, but still identical in one; the unchangeable resolve (though never to be executed) of leaving Burleigh at farthest by next Michaelmas. Most folks who talk much, do little; and taciturn as the general now is, and has been ever throughout life, it will surprise nobody who has learned from hard experience how silly and harmful a thing is secresy (exceptionables excepted), to find that he grew to be a garrulous old man, gossipping for ever of past, present, future, and, not least, about his deeds at Puttymuddyfudgepoor.

General Tracy is by this time awake again; if ever indeed he slept on that uncomfortable shakedown; and, after Mr. Saunders and the razor-strop, has greeted brightly-beaming Emily with more than usual tenderness. Her account of the transaction made his very blood boil; especially as her pretty pouting lips were lacerated cruelly inside: that rude blow on the mouth had almost driven the teeth through them. How confidingly she told her artless tale; how gently did her fond protector kiss that poor pale cheek; and how sternly did he vow full vengeance on the caitiff! Not even Emily's intercession could avail to turn his wrath aside. He could hardly help flying off at once to do something dreadful; but common courtesy to all the Tamworth family obliged him to defer for an hour all the terrible things he meant to do. So he began to bolt his breakfast fiercely as a cannibal, and saluted Lady Tamworth and her daughters with such savage looks, that the captain considerately suggested:

"Here, general," (handing him a most formidable carving-knife,) "charge that boar's head, grinning defiance at us on the side-board; it will do you good to hew his brawny neck. My mother, I am sure, for one, will thank you to do the honours there instead of me. Isn't it a comfort now, to know that I broke the handle of my hunting-whip across the fellow's back, and wore all the whip-cord into skeins. Come, I say, general, don't eat us all round; and pray.have mercy on that poor, flogged, miserable sinner."

This banter did him good, especially as he saw Emily smiling; so he relaxed his knit brow, condescended to look less like Giant Blunderbore, soon became marvellous chatty, and ate up two French rolls, an egg, some anchovies, a round of toast, and a mighty slice of brawn; these, washed down with a couple of cups of tea, soothed him into something like complacency.

CHAPTER XIX.

JULIAN'S DEPARTURE.

Long before the general got home, still in exalted dudgeon (indeed soon after the general had left home over night), the bird had flown; for the better part of valour suggested to our evil hero, that it would be discreet to render himself a scarce commodity for a season; and as soon as ever his mother had run up to his room-door to tell him of his danger, when her lord was cross-questioning the butler, he resolved upon instant flight. Accordingly, though sore and stiff, he hurried up, dressed again, watched his father out, and tumbling over Mrs. Tracy, who was sobbing on the stairs, ran for one moment to the general's room; there he seized a well-remembered cash-box, and instinctively possessed himself of those new, neat, double-barrelled pistols: a bully never goes unarmed. These brief arrangements made, off he set, before his father could have time to return from Pacton Square.

Therefore, when the general called, we need not marvel that he found him not; no one but the foolish mother (so neglected of her son, yet still excusing him) stood by to meet his wrath. He would not waste it on her; so long as Julian was gone, his errand seemed accomplished; for all he came to do was to expel him from the house. So, as far as regarded Mrs. Tracy, her husband, wotting well how much she was to blame, merely commanded her to change her sleeping-room, and occupy Mr. Julian's in future.

The silly woman was even glad to do it; and comforted herself from time to time with prying into her own boy's exemplary manuscripts, memoranda of moralities, and so forth; with weeping, like Lady Constance, over his empty "unpuffed" clothes; with reading ever and anon his choice collection of standard works, among which '*Don Juan*' and Mr. Thomas Paine were by far the most presentable; and with tasting, till it grew to be a habit, his private store of spirituous liquors. Thus did she mourn many days for long-lost Julian.

I am quite aware what became of him. The wretched youth, mad for Emily's love, and tortured by the tyranny of passion, had nothing else to live for or to die for. He accordingly took refuge in the hovel of a smuggler, an old friend of his, not many miles away, disguised himself in fisherman's costume, and bode his opportunity.

Beauteous girl! how often have I watched thee with straining eyes and aching heart, as thou wentest on thy summer's walk so oftentimes to Oxton, there to exercise thy bountiful benevolence in comforting the sick, gladdening the wretched, and lingering, with love's own look, in Charles's village school; how often have I prayed, that guardian angels might be about thy path as about thy bed! For the prowling tiger was on thy track, poor innocent one, and many, many times nothing but one of God's seeming accidents hath saved thee. Who was that strange man so often in the way? At one time a wounded Spanish legionist, with head bound up; at another, an old beggar upon crutches; at another, a floury miller with a donkey and a sack; at another, a black looking man, in slouching sailor's hat and fishing-boots?

Fair, pure creature! thou hast often dropped a shilling in that beggar's hand, and pitied that poor maimed soldier; once, too, a huge gipsy woman would have had thee step aside, and hear thy fortunes. Heaven guarded thee then, sweet Emily; for both girl and lover though thou art, thou would'st not listen to the serpent's voice, however fair might be the promises. And Heaven guarded thee ever, bidding some one pass along the path just as the ruffian might have gagged thy smiling mouth, and hurried thee away amongst his fellows; and more than once, especially, those school children, bursting out of Charles's school at dusk, have unconsciously escorted thee in safety from the perils of that tiger on thy track.

CHAPTER XX.

ENLIGHTENMENT.

THE general could not now be kept in ignorance of Charles's expedition; in fact, he had found his heart, and began resolutely to use it. So, the very day on which he had lost Julian, he intended very eagerly to seek out Charles; for the Oxford search had failed, and no wonder. Now, though Emily had told, as we well know, to both mother and son her secret, the father was not likely to be any the wiser; for he now never spoke to his wife, and could not well speak to his son. However, one day, an hour after an overland letter, a very exhilarating one, dated Madras, whereof we shall hear anon, fair Emily, in the fullness of her heart, could not help saying,

"Dearest sir, you are often thinking of poor lost Charles, I know; and you are very anxious about him too, though nobody but myself, who am always with you, can perceive it: what if you heard he was safe and well?"

"Have you heard any tidings of my poor boy, Emmy?"

She looked up archly, and said, "Why not?" her beautiful eyes adding, as plainly as eyes could speak, "I love him, and you know it; of course I have heard frequently from dear, dear Charles."

But the guardian met her looks with a keen and chilling answer: "Why not! why not! Does he dare to write to you, and you to love him? Oh, that I had told them both a year ago! But where is he now, child? Don't cry, I will not speak so angrily again, my Emmy."

"I hardly dare to tell you, dearest sir: you have always been as a father to me, and I never knew any other; but there are things I cannot explain to myself, and I was very wretched; and so, kind guardian, Charles—Charles was so good—"

"What has he done?—where has he gone?" hastily asked his father.

"Oh, don't, don't be angry with us; in a word, he is gone to Madras, to find out Nurse Mackie, and to tell me who I am."

The poor old man, who had treasured up so long some mystery, probably a very diaphanous one, for Emily's own dear sake in the world's esteem, and from the long bad habit of reserve, fell back into his chair as if he had been shot; but he did not faint, nor gasp, nor utter a sound; he only looked at her so long and sorrowfully, that she ran to him, and covered his pale face with her own brown curls, kissing him, and wiping from his cheek her starting tears.

"Emmy, dear—I can tell you—and I—no, no, not now, not now; if he comes back—then—then; poor children! Oh, the sin of secresy!"

"But, dearest sir, do not be so sad; Charles has happy news, he says."

"Happy, child? Good Heaven! would it could be so!"

"Indeed, indeed, a week ago he was as miserable as any could be, and so was I; for he heard something terrible about me—I don't know what—but I feared I was a—Pariah! However, now he is all joy, and coming home again as soon as possible."

The general shook his head mournfully, as physicians do when hope is gone; but still he looked perplexed and thoughtful.

"You will show me the letters, dear, I dare say: but I do not command you, Emmy; do as you like."

"Certainly, my own kindest guardian—all, all, and instantly."

And flying up to her room, she returned with as much closely-written mauuscript as would have taken any but a lover's eye a full week to decipher. The general, not much given to literary matters, looked quite scared at such a prospect.

"Wait, Emmy; not all, not all; show me the last."

I dare say Emily will forgive me if I get it set up legibly in print. May I, dear?

CHAPTER XXI.

CHARLES AT MADRAS.

Luckily enough for all mankind in general, and our lovers in particular, Charles's last letter was very unlike some that had preceded it; for instead of the usual "Oh, my love"'s, "sweet, sweet eyes," "darling"'s, and all manner of such chicken-hearted nonsense, it was positively sensible, rational, not to say utilitarian: though I must acknowledge that here and there it degenerates into the affectionate, or Stromboli-vein of letter-writing, at opening especially; and really now and then I shall take leave to indicate omitted inflammations by a *.

"Dearest, dearest Emmy,

* * * * * * * *

[and so forth, a very galaxy of stars to the bottom of this page; enough to put the compositor out of his terrestrial senses.]

"You see I have recovered my spirits, dearest, and am not now afraid to tell you how I love you. Oh, that detestable Captain Forbes! let him not cross my path, gossiping blockhead! on pain of carrying about 'til deth,' in the middle of his face, a nose two inches longer. I heartily wish I had never listened for an instant to such vile insinuations; and when I look at this red right hand of mine, that dared to pen the trash in that black postscript, I look at it as Cranmer did, and (but that it is yours, Emmy, not mine), could wish it burnt. But no fears now, my girl, huzza, huzza! I believe every one about me thinks me daft; and so I am for very joyfulness; notwithstanding, let me be didactic, or you will say so too. I really will endeavour to rein in, and go along in the regular hackney trot, that you may partly comprehend me. Well, then, here goes; try your paces, Dobbin.

"On the morning of Sunday, April 11th, 1842, the good ship Elphinston—(that's the way to begin, I suppose, as per ledger, log-book, and midshipman's epistles to mamma)—in fact, dear, we cast anchor just outside a furious wall of surf, which makes Madras a very formidable place for landing; and every one who dares to do so certain of a watering. There lay the city, most invitingly to storm-tost tars, with its white palaces, green groves, and yellow belt of sand, blue hills in the distance, and all else *coleur de rose*. But—but, Emmy, there was no getting at this paradise, except by struggling through a couple of miles of raging foam, that would have made mince-meat of the Spanish Armada, and have smashed Sir William Elphinston to pieces. How, then, did we manage to survive it? for, thank God always, here I am to tell the tale. Listen, Emmy dear, and I will try not to be tedious.

"We were bundled out of the rolling ship into some huge flat-bottomed boats, like coal-barges, and even so, were grated and ground several times by the churning waves on the ragged reefs beneath us: and, just as I was enjoying the see-saw, and trying to comfort two poor drenched women-kind who were terribly afraid of sharks, a huge, cream-coloured breaker came bustling alongside of us, and roaring out 'Charles Tracy,' gobbled me up bodily. Well, dearest, it wasn't the first time I had floundered in the waters [noble Charles! noble Charles! he had long forgiven Julian]; so I was battling on as well as I could, with a stout heart and a steady arm, when—don't be afraid—a *Catamaran* caught me! If you haven't fainted (bless those pretty eyes of your's, my Emmy!) read on; and you will find that this alarming sort of animal is neither an albatross nor an alligator, but simply—a life-boat with a

Triton in the stern. Yes, God's messenger of life to me and happiness to you, my girl, came in the shape of a kindly, chattering, blue-skinned, human creature, who dragged me out of the surf, landed me safely, and, I need not say, got paid with more than hearty thanks. So, I scuffled to the custom-house to look after my traps and fellow-passengers, like a dripping merman.

"'Who is that miserable old woman, bothering every body?' asked I of a very civil searcher, profuse in his salaams.

"'Oh, Sahib, you will know for yourself, presently: she's always hanging about here, to get news of somebody in England, I believe—and to try to find a charitable captain who will take her all the way for nothing: rather too much of a good thing, you know, Sahib.'

[We really cannot undertake to scribble broken English: so we will translate any thing that may mysteriously have been chatted by havildars, and coolies, and all manner of strange names.]

"'Poor old soul—she looks very wretched: what's her name?' asked I, carelessly.

"'Oh, I never troubled to inquire, Sahib: I believe she was an old servant left behind as lumber, and she pesters every one, day by day, about some 'bonnie bonnie bairn.''

"In a moment, Emmy, I had seized on dear nurse Mackie!

"Very old, very deaf, very infirm—she fancied I was driving her away, as many others might have done; and, with a truly piteous face, pleaded—

"'Gude sir, have mercy on a puir auld soul—and let her ask for her sweet young mistress, only once, sir—only once more.'

"'Emily Warren?' said I.

Her wrinkled face brightened over as with glory—and she answered—

"'Bless the mouth that spake it, and these ears that hear her name! yes—yes—yes—they call her so; where is she? how is she? have you seen her? is she yet alive?'

"Leading away the affectionate old soul from the crowd that was collecting round us, I left orders about luggage as a traveller should, and then told her all I knew: and I know you pretty well, I think, my Emmy.

"Her joy was like a mad woman's: the dear old Hecate pranced, and danced, and sung, and shouted like nothing but a mother when she finds her long-lost child: not that she's your mother, Emmy dear. No—no—matters are better than that: all she vouchsafes, though, to tell me is, that you are a lady born and bred, and—for I cannot find the words to inform your pure mind clearer—that 'you are not what he thinks you.'"

[Here followeth another twinkling universe of stars;

* * * * * * * *

and thereafter our cavalier condescendeth again to matters of fact.]

"Nurse Mackie of course comes back with me next packet; this letter goes by the overland mail more quickly than we can; gladly would I go too, but the old woman, whose life is essential to your rights, would die of fatigue by the way; as it is, I am obliged to coddle her, and feed her, and ptisan her, like a sick baby, bless her dear old heart that loves my darling Emmy! She has a pack of papers with her, which she will not open, till the general is by her side: if she unfortunately dies before we can return, I am to have them, and all will be right. But the old soul is so afraid of being left behind (as you throw away the orange-peel after you have squeezed it), that she will not tell me a word about them yet; so, I only gather what I can from her cautious garrulity, hints about a Begum and a captain, and the Stuarts, and a Putty-what-d'ye-call-it. And it is all in document, as well as *viva-voce* (this means 'gossip,' dear). So now you may be expecting us, as soon as ever we can get to you. Tell the general all this, and give him my best love, next after your's Emmy; for he is my father still, and my very heart yearns after him: O, that he were kinder with me as I see he is with you, dear, and more open with us all! Also, kiss, if she will let you, my mother for me, and I hope you will have hinted to her long ago, that I am only playing truant. How is poor—poor Julian? he will understand me, if you tell him I forgive him, and will never say one word about our little tiff. And now dearest Emmy—"

[The remainder of this letter must, believe me, be as starry as before.]

* * * * * * * *

CHAPTER XXII.

REVELATIONS.

General Tracy gave a long-drawn sigh: and tears—tears of true affection—stood in those most fish-like eyes, as he mournfully said, "Bless him, bless dear Charles, almost as much as you, my own sweet

Emmy. Heaven send it be true—for Heaven can work miracles. But without a miracle, Emily, in sober sadness I declare it, you must forget —*your brother Charles, my daughter!*"

Emily fell flat upon her face, so cold, so white, that he believed her dead.

Oh! that he had never—never said that word: or better still, poor father, that you had never kept the dreadful secret from them. The adultery, indeed, was sin; but years of ill-concealings have multiplied its punishment. Wretched father—wretched children! that must bear an erring father's curse.

Oh! that Jeanie Mackie may have reasons, proofs; and be not an impostor after all, dressing up a tale that over-sanguine Charles may bring her back again to Scotland. Well—well! I am full of sadness and perplexities: but we shall hear it out anon. Heaven help them!

Emily was taken very ill, and had a long fit of sickness. Day and night—night and day, did her poor wasting anxious father watch by her bed-side, gentle as the gentlest nurse—tender as the tenderest of mothers. And, indeed, the Lord of Life and Wisdom was gracious to them both; raising up the poor weak child again; and teaching that old man, through this daughter of his shame and sin in youth, that religion is a cure for all things. Ay, "the blessed angel of a bad man's life," indeed—indeed was she; and he humbly knelt, as little children kneel, that hard and dried old man; and his eyes caught the ray of Heaven's mercy, looking up in joy to read forgiveness; and his heart was bathed in penitence—the rock flowed out amain; and his mind was quickened into faith—he lived, he breathed "a new-born babe," that poor and bad old man, given to the prayers of his own daughter!

All this while, Mrs. Tracy, thrown upon her own resources, has been continually tasting dear Julian's store, and finding out excuses for his trivial peccadilloes. And when, from the recesses of his desk, she had routed out (in company with sundry more, rather contrasting with a mother's pure advice) a few of her own letters, which had not yet been destroyed, she would doat by the hour on these proofs of his affection. And then, her spirits were so low; and his choice smuggled Hollands so requisite to screw them up to par again; and no sooner had they rallied, than they would once more begin to droop; so she cried a good deal, and kept her bed; and very often did not remember exactly, whether she was lying down there, or figuring on the Esplanade with Julian, and —all that sort of thing: accordingly, it is not to be wondered at if, in

Aunt Green's double-house, the general and Emily saw very little of her, and during all this illness, had almost forgotten her existence. Nevertheless, she was alive still, and as vast as ever—though a course of strong waters had shattered her nerves considerably; even more so, than her real mother's grief at Julian's protracted absence.

Never had he been heard of since he left, hard heart; though he might have guessed a mother's sorrow, and was not far away, and often lingered near the house in strange disguises. It would have been easy for him, in some clever way or other, latch-key and all, to have gained access to her, and comforted her, and given her some real proof, that all the love she had shed on him had not been utterly thrown away; but he didn't—he didn't; and I know not of a darker trait in Julian's whole career; he was insensible to love—a mother's love.

For love is the weapon which Omnipotence reserved to conquer rebel man, when all the rest had failed. Reason he parries; Fear he answers blow to blow; future interest he meets with present pleasure; but Love, that sun against whose melting beams the Winter cannot stand, that soft-subduing slumber which wrestles down the giant, there is not one human creature in a million—not a thousand men in all earth's huge quintillion, whose clay-heart is hardened against love.

Yet was Julian one of those select ones; an awful instance of that possible, that actual, though happily that scarcest of all characters, a man,

"Black, with *no* virtue, and a thousand crimes."

The amiable villain—one whose generosity redeems his guilt, whose kindliness outweighs his folly, or whose beauty charms the eye to overlook his baseness—this too common hero is an object, an example fraught with perilous interest. Charles Duval, the polite; Paul Clifford, the handsome; Richard Turpin, brave and true; Jack Sheppard, no ignoble mind and loving still his mother; these, and such as these, with Schiller's '*Robbers*' and the like, are dangerous to gaze on, as Germany, if not England too, remembers well. But, not more true to life, though far less common to be met with, is Julian's incorrigible mind: one, in whose life are no white days; one, on whose heart are no bright spots; when Heaven's pity spoke to him, he ridiculed; as, when His threatenings thundered, he defied. Of this world only, and tending to a worse, appetite was all he lived for: and the core of appetite is iron selfishness.

The filched cash-box proved to be too well-filled for him to trouble himself with thinking of his mother yet awhile: and his smuggling acquaintances, a rough-featured, blasphemous crew, set him as their chief, so long as he swore loudest, drank deepest, and had money at command. He hid the money, that they should not secretly steal from him that to which he owed his bad supremacy; and his double-barrels, shotted to the muzzle, were far too formidable for any hope of getting at it by open brute force. Nevertheless, they were "fine high-spirited" fellows those, bold, dark men, of Julian's own kidney; who toasted in their cups each other's crimes, and the ghost or two that ought to have been haunting them.

CHAPTER XXIII.

CONVALESCENCE.

VERY slowly did Emily recover, for the blow had been more than she could bear: nothing but religion gave her any chance at all: and the phials, blisterings, bleedings, would have been in vain, in vain—she must have died long ago—had it not been for the remembrance of God's love, resignation to His will, and trust in the wisdom of his Providence. But these specific remedies gradually brought her round, while the kind-eyed doctors praised their own prescriptions: and after many rallyings and relapses, delirious ramblings, and intervals of hallowed Christian peace, the eye of Love's meek martyr brightened up once more, and health flushed again upon her cheek.

She recovered, God be praised! for her death would have been poor Charles's too; and the same grave that yawned for her and him would have closed upon their father also. Even as it was, when she arose from off the weary bed of sickness, it was to be a nurse herself, and watch beside that patient, weak old man. He could not bear her out of his sight all the fever through; but eagerly would listen to her hymns and prayers, joining in them faintly like a dying saint. With the saddening secret, which had so long pressed upon his mind, he seemed to have thrown off his old nature, as a cast skin: and now he was all frankness for reserve, all piety for profaneness, all peacefulness for blusterings and wrath.

He remembered then poor Julian and his mother: taking blame to himself, justly, deeply, for neglected duties, chilling lack of sympathy, and that dull domestic sin, that still continued evil of unnatural omissions —stern reserve. And he would gladly have seen Julian by his bedside, to have freely forgiven the lad, and welcomed him home again, and begun once more, in openness and charity, all things fair and new: but Julian was not to be found, though rewards were offered, and placards posted up, and emissaries from the Detective Police-force sought him far and wide. Alas! the bold bad man had heard with scorn of his father's penitence, and knew that be would gladly have received him;—but what cared he for kindnesses or pardons? He only lived to waylay Emily.

As for Mrs. Tracy, she was seldom in a state to appear; but one day she managed to refrain a little, and came to see her husband, almost sober. I was, authorially speaking, behind the door, and saw and heard as follows:

The old man, worn and emaciate, was weakly sitting up in bed, and Emma by his side, with the Bible in her lap: she casually shut it as the mother entered.

"Well, Miss Warren, there 's a time for all things; but this is neither morning, noon, nor night: nor Sunday either, nor holiday, that I know of; it 's eleven o'clock on Tuesday, Miss—and I think you might as well leave the general at peace, without troubling him for ever with your prayer-books and your Bibles."

"Jane, my dear, I requested it of Emily; come and sit by me, and take my hand, wife."

"Thank you, sir, you are very obliging: not while that young woman is in the room.—You ought to be ashamed of yourself, General Tracy.

Poor Emmy ran away to weep. It seems that, in her delirium, she had spoken many things, and the servants blabbed them out to Mrs. Tracy.

"Ah, my poor wife, indeed I am: both ashamed and sorry—heartily sorry. But God forgives me, Jenny, and I hope that you will too."

"Upon, my word, general, you carry it off with a high hand: and, not content, sir, with insulting me in my own home by bringing here your other women's children, you have expelled poor dear, dear Julian."

"Jane, if you will remember, he ran away himself; and you know that now I gladly would receive him: we are all prodigal sons together, and if God can bear with us, Jane, we ought to look kindly on each other."

"Ha! that 's always the way with old sinners like you—canting hypocrites! Be a man, General Tracy, if you can, and talk sense. I never did any harm or sin in all my life yet, and don't intend to: and my poor boy Julian's well enough, if they'd only let him alone; but nobody understands his heart but me. Good boy, I'm sure there's virtue enough left in him, if he loves his mother."—*If* he loves his mother.

"Jane, dear, I sent for you to kiss you; for I could not die in peace, nor live in peace (whichever God may please), without your pardon, Jane, for a thousand unkindnesses—but, especially for the sin that gave me Emily. Forgive me this, my wife."

"Never, sir!" rejoined that miserable mind; and fancied that she was acting virtuously. She thrust aside the kindly proffered hand; scowled at him with darkened brow; drew up her commanding height; and, calling Mrs. Siddons to remembrance, brushed away in the indignant attitude of a tragedy queen.

Emmy ran again to her father, and the vain bad mother to her bottle; we must leave them to their various avocations.

CHAPTER XXIV.

CHARLES DELAYED.

Few things could well be more unlikely than that Emily should hear of Charles again before she saw him: for, having left Madras as speedily as might be, now that his mission was so easily, yet so naturally, accomplished—having posted, as we know, his overland letter—and having got on board the fast-sailing ship Samarang, Captain Trueman, Charles, in the probable course of things, if he wrote at all, must have been his own postman. But the Fates—(our Christianity can afford to wink now and then at Clotho, Lachesis, and Atropos; for, at any rate, they are as reasonable creatures as Chance, Luck, and Accident,)—the Fates willed it otherwise: and, accordingly, it is in my power to lay before the reader another genuine lucubration of Charles Tracy.

A change had come over the spirit of their dream, those youthful lovers: and agonizing doubt must rack their hearts, threatening to rend them both asunder. It is evident to me that Charles's letter (which Emily showed to me with a melancholy face) was on principle less warm, less dottable with stars, and more conversant with things of this world; high, firm, honourable principle; intending very gently, very gradually, to wean her from him, if he could; for his faith in Jeanie Mackie had been shaken, and—but let us hear him tell us of it all himself.

"I. E. M. Samarang. St. Helena.

"You will wonder, my dear Emily, to hear again before you see me: but I am glad of this providential opportunity, as it may serve to prepare us both. Naturally enough you will ask, why Charles cannot accompany this letter? I will tell you, dear, in one word—Mrs. Mackie is now lying very ill on shore; and, as far as our poor ship is concerned, you shall hear about it all anon. Several of the passengers, who were in a hurry to get home, have left us, and gone in the packet-boat that takes you this letter: gladly, as you know, would I have accompanied them, for I long to see you, poor dear girl; but it was impossible to leave the old woman, upon whom alone, under God, our hopes of earthly happiness depend: if, alas! we still can dream about such hopes.

"Oh, Emily—I heartily wish that, having finished my embassage by that instantaneous finding of the old Scotch nurse, I had never been so superfluous as to have left those letters of introduction, wherewith you kindly supplied me, in an innocent wish to help our cause. But I felt solitary too, waiting at Madras for the next ship to England; and in my folly, forgetful of the single aim with which I had come, Jeanie Mackie, to wit, I thought I might as well use my present opportunities, and see what I could of the place and its inhabitants.

"With that view, I left my letters at Government House, at Mr. Clarkson's, Colonel Bunting's, Mrs. Castleton's, and elsewhere, according to direction; and immediately found answer in a crowd of invitations. I need not vex you nor myself, Emmy, writing as I do with a heavy, heavy heart, by describing gayeties in which I felt no pleasure, even when amongst them, for my Emmy was not there: splendour, prodigality, and red-hot rooms, only made endurable by perpetually fanning punkahs: pompous counsellors, authorities, and other men in office, and a glut of military uniforms: vulgar wealth, transparent match-making, and predominating dullness: along with some few of the charities and kindnesses of life (Mrs. Bunting, in particular, is an amiable, motherly, good-hearted woman), all these you will readily fancy for yourself.

"My trouble is deeper than any thing so slight as the common satiations of *ennui:* for I have heard in these circles in which your—my—the general, I mean, chiefly mixed, so much of that ill-rumour that it cannot all be false: they knew it all, and were certain of it all, too well, Emily, dear. And I have been pestering Nurse Mackie night and day; but the old woman is so afraid of being left behind any where, or thrown overboard, or dropped upon some desert rock, that she is quite cross, and won't say a single word in answer, even when I tell her all these terrible tales. Her resolution is, not to reveal one syllable more, until she sets foot on England; and several people at Madras annoyed me exceedingly by saying, that this kind of thing is an old trick with people who wish to be sent home again. She has hidden away her papers somewhere; not that I was going to steal them: but it shows how little trust she puts in any thing, or any one, except the keeping of her own secret. However, she does adhere obstinately, and hopefully for us, to her original hint, 'you are not what he thinks you;' although she will not condescend to any single proof, or explanation, against the mighty mass of evidence, which probabilities, and common rumour, and the general's own belief, have heaped together. When I call you Emmy, too—the old soul, in her broad Scotch way, always corrects me, and invokes a blessing upon 'A-amy:' so there is a mystery somewhere: at least, I fervently hope there is: and, if the old woman has been playing us false, let us resign ourselves to God, my girl; for our fate will be that matters are as people say they are—and then my old black postscript ends too truly with a wo, wo, wo—!

"But I must shake off all this lethargy of gloom, dearest, dearest girl—how can I dare to call you so? Let me, therefore, rush for comfort into other thoughts; and tell you at once of the fearful dangers we have now mercifully escaped; for the Samarang lies like a log in this friendly port, dismasted, and next to a wreck.

"I proceed to show you about it; perhaps I shall be tedious—but I do it as a little rest, my own soul's love, from anxious, earnest, heart-distracting prayers continually, continually, that the sorrow which I spoke of be not true. Sometimes, a light breaks in, and I rejoice in the most sanguine hope: at others, gloom—

"But a truce to all this, I say. Here shall follow didactically the cause why the good ship Samarang is not by this time in the Docks.

"We were lying somewhere about the tropical belt, Capricorn you know, (O, those tender lessons in geography, my Emmy!) quite becalmed; the sea like glass, and the sky like brass, and the air in a most stagnant heat: our good ship motionless, dead in a dead blue sea it was

'Idle as a painted ship upon a painted ocean.'

"The sails were hanging loosely in the shrouds: every one set, from sky-scraper to stud-sail, in hopes to catch a breath of wind. My fellow-passengers and the crew, almost melted, were lying about, as weak as parboiled eels: it was high-noon, all things silent and subdued by that intolerable blaze; for the vertical sun, over our multiplied awnings and umbrellas, burnt us up, fierce as a furnace.

"I was leaning over the gangway, looking wistfully at the cool, clear, deep sea, wherefrom the sailors were trying to persuade a shark to come on board us, when, all at once, in the south-east quarter, I noticed a little round black cloud, thrown up from the horizon like a cricket-ball. As any thing is attractive in such sameness as perpetual sea and sky, my discovery was soon made known, and among the first to our captain.

"Calling for his Dolland, and bidding his second lieutenant run quick to the cabin and look at the barometer, he viewed the little cloud in evident anxiety, and shook his head with a solemn air: more than one light-hearted woman thinking he was quizzing them.

"Up came Lieutenant Joyce, looking as if he had seen a ghost in the cabin.

"'The mercury, sir, is falling just as rapidly as it would rise if you plunged it into boiling water: an inch a minute or so!"

"Our captain saw the danger instantly, and, brave as Trueman is, I never saw a man look paler.

"To drive all the passengers below, and pen them in with closed hatches and storm-shutters, (so hot, Emmy, that the black-hole of Calcutta must have been an ice-house to it: how the foolish people abused our wise skipper, and more than one pompous old Indian threatened him with an action for false imprisonment!) this huddling away was the first effort; and simultaneously with it, the crew were all over the rigging, furling sails, hurriedly, hurriedly.

"Meanwhile (for I was last on deck), that little cloud seemed whirling within itself, and many others gathered round it, all dancing about on the horizon, as if sheaves of mischief tossed about by devils: I don't wish to be poetical, Emmy, for my heart is very, very sad; but if ever the powers of the air sow the wind and reap the whirlwind, they were gathering in their harvest at that door. Underneath the skipping clouds, which came on quickly, leaping over each other, as when the wain is loaded by a score of hands, I noticed a sea approaching, such as Pharaoh must have seen, when the wall of waters fell upon him; and premonitory winds came whistling by, and two or three sails were flapping in them still, and I was hurried down stairs after all the rest of us.

"Then, on a sudden, it appeared not winds, nor waves, nor thunder, but as if the squadroned cavalry of heaven had charged across the seas, and crushed our battered ship beneath their horse-hoofs! We were flung down flat on our beam ends; and the two or three unfurled sails, bursting with the noise of a cannon, were scattered miles away to leeward as if they had been paper. As for the poor fellows in the rigging, the spirit of the storm had already made them his: twenty of our men were swept away by that tornado.

"Then there was hewing and cleaving on deck, the clatter of many axes and hatchets: for we were in imminent danger of being capsized, keel uppermost, and our only chance was to cut away the masts.

"The muscles of courage were tried then, my Emmy, and the strength which religion gives a man. I felt sensibly held up by the Everlasting Arms: I could listen to the still small Voice in the midst of a crash which might have been the end of all things: though in darkness, God had given me light; though in uttermost peril, my peace was never calmer in our little village school.

"And the billows were knocking at the poor ship's side like sledge hammers; and the lightnings fell around us scorchingly, with forked bolts, as arrows from the hand of a giant; the thunders overhead, close overhead, crashing from a concave cloud that hung about us heavily—a dense, black, suffocating curtain—roared and raved as nothing earthly can, but thunder in the tropics; the rain was as a cataract, literally rushing in a mass: the winds appeared not winds, nor whirlwinds, but legions of emancipated demons shrieking horribly, and flapping their wide wings; a flock of night-birds flying from the dawn; and all else was darkness, confusion, rolling and rocking about, the screams of women, the shouts of men, curses and prayers, agony, despair, and—peace, deep peace.

"On a sudden, to our great astonishment, all was silent again, oppressively silent; and, but for the swell upon the seas, all still. The tornado had rushed by: that troop of Tartar horse, having sacked the village, are departed, now in full retreat: the blackness and the fury are beheld on our lee, hastening across the broad Atlantic to Cuba or Jamaica: and behold, a tranquil temperate sky, a kindly rolling sea, a favouring breeze, and—not a sail, but some slight jury-rig, to catch it.

"Many days we drifted like a log upon the wave; provisions running short, and water—water under tropical suns—scantily dealt out in tea-cups. Then, poor old Mackie's health gave way; and I dreaded for her death: one living witness is worth a cart-load of cold documents. So I nursed and watched her constantly: till the foolish folks on board began to say I was her son: ah! me, for your sake I wish it had been so.

"And at length, just as some among the sailors were hinting at a mutiny for spirits, and our last case of Gamble's meat was opened for the sick, our look-out on the jury-mast gave the welcome note of 'Land!' and soon, to us on deck, the heights of St. Helena rose above the sea. Towed in by friendly aid, here we are, then, precious Emily, refitting: and, as it must be a week yet before we can be ready, I have taken my old woman to a lodging upon land, and rejoice (what have I to do with joy?) to see her speedily recovering."

The remainder of Charles's long letter is so stupid, so gloomy, so loving, and so little to the purpose, that I take an editor's privilege, and omit it altogether. Of course he was coming home again, as soon as the Samarang and Jeanie Mackie would permit.

CHAPTER XXV.

TRIALS.

THE general recovered; as slowly, indeed, as Emily had, but it is gratifying to add, as surely. And now that loving couple might be seen, weakly creeping out together, when the day was finest: tottering white December leaning on a sickly fragile May. There were no concealments now between them, no reservings, and heart-stricken Emily heard from her repentant father's lips the story of her birth: she was, he said, his own daughter by a native princess, the Begum Dowlia Burruckjutli.

A bitter—bitter truth was that: the destruction of all her hopes, pleasures, and affections. It had now become to her a sin to love that dearest one of all things lovely on this earth: duty, paramount and stern, commanded her, without a shadow of reprieve, to execute on herself immediately the terrible sentence of banishing her own betrothed: nay, more, she must forget him, erase his precious image from her heart, and never, never see that brother more. And Charles must feel the same, and do

20

the like; oh! sorrow, passing words! and their two commingled souls must be violently wrenched apart; for such love in them were crime.

Dear children of affection—it is a dreadful lesson this for both of you; but most wise, most needful—or the hand that guideth all things, never would have sent it. Know ye not for comfort, that ye are of those to whom all things work together for good? Know ye not for counsel, that the excess of love is an idolatry that must be blighted? It is well, children, it is well, that ye should thus carry your wounded hearts for balm to the altar of God; it is well that ye should bow in meekness to His will, in readiness to His wisdom. Ye are learning the lesson speedily, as docile children should; and be assured of high reward from the Teacher who hath set it you. Poor Charles! white and wan, thy cheek is grown transparent with anxiety, and thy blue eye dim with hope deferred: poor Emmy, sick and weak, thou weariest Heaven with thy prayers, and waterest thy couch with thy tears. Yet, a little while; this discipline is good: storm and wind, frost and rushing rains, are as needful to the forest-tree as sun and gentle shower; the root is strengthening, and its fibres spreading out: and loving still each other with the best of human love, ye justly now have found out how to anchor all your strongest hopes, and deepest thoughts, on Him who made you for himself. Who knoweth? wisely acquiescing in His will, humbly trusting to His mercy, and bringing the holocaust of your inflamed affections as an offering of duty to your God—who knoweth? Cannot He interpose? will He not befriend you? For His arm is power, and His heart is love.

Days rolled on in dull monotony, and grew to weeks more slowly than before; earthly hopes had been levelled with the dust; life had forgotten to be joyous: there was, indeed, the calm, the peace, the resignation, the heavenly ante-past, and the soul-entrancing prayer; but human life to Emily was flat, wearisome, and void; she felt like a nun, immolated as to this world: even as Charles, too, had resolved to be an anchorite, a stern, hard, mortified man, who once had feelings and affections. The rëaction in both those fond young hearts had even overstept the golden mean: and Mercy interposed to make all right, and to bless them in each other once again.

Only look at this *billet-doux* from Charles, just come in, and dated Plymouth:

"Huzzah—for Emily and England: huzzah for the land of freedom! no secrets now—dear, dear old Jeanie Mackie has given me proofs positive: all I have to wish is that she could move: but she is very ill; so, as we touched here on the voyage up channel, I landed her and myself, thinking to kiss, within a day, my darling Emmy. But I cannot get her out of bed this morning, and dare not leave her: though an hour's delay seems almost insupportable. If I possibly can manage it, I will bring the dear old faithful creature, wrapped in blankets, by chaise to-morrow. Tell my father all this: and say to him—he will understand, perhaps, though you may not, my blessed girl—say to him, that 'he is mistaken, and all are mistaken—you are not what they think you.' A thousand kisses. Expect, then, on bright to-morrow to see your happy, happy

"CHARLES."

"P.S. Hip! hip! hip!—huzzah!"

Dearest Emily had taken up the note with fears and trembling: she laid it down, as they that reap in joy; and I never in my life saw any thing so beautiful as her eyes at that glad minute; the smile through the tear, the light through the gloom, the verdure of high summer springing through the Alpine snows, the mild and lustrous moon emerging from a baffled thunder-cloud.

And, although the general mournfully shook his head, distrustfully and despondingly; though he only uttered, "Poor children—dear children—would to Heaven that it could be so;"—and he, for one, was evidently innoculated, as before, with all the old thoughts of gloom, sadness, and anxiety;—still Emily hoped—for Charles hoped—and Jeanie Mackie was so certain.

CHAPTER XXVI.

JULIAN.

NEXT day, a fine summer afternoon, when our feeble convalescents had gone out together, they found the fresh air so invigorating, and themselves so much stronger, that they prolonged their walk half-way to Oxton. The pasture-meadows, rich and rank, were alive with flocks and herds; the blue sea lazily beat time, as, ticking out the seconds, it melodiously broke upon the sleeping shore; the darkly-flowing Mullet swept sounding to the sea between its tortuous banks; and upon that old high foot-path skirting the stream, now shady with hazels, and now flowery with meadow-sweet, crept our chastened pair.

Just as they were nearing a short angle in the river, the spot where Charles had been preserved, they noticed for the first time a rough-looking fisherman, who, unseen, had tracked their steps some hundred yards; he had a tarpaulin over his shoulder, very unnecessarily, as it would seem, on so fine and warm a day; and a slouching sou'-wester, worn askew, flapped across the strange man's face.

He came on quickly, though cautiously, looking right and left; and Emily trembled on her guardian's feeble arm. Yes—she is right; the fisherman approaches—she detects him through it all: and now he scorns disguise; flinging off his cap and the tarpaulin, stands before them—Julian!

"So, sir—you tremble now, do you, gallant general: give me the girl." And he levelled at his father one of those double-barrelled pistols, full-cock.

"Julian, my son, I forgive you, Julian; take my hand, boy."

"What—coward? now you can cringe, and fawn, eh? back with you! —the girl, I say." For poor Emily, wild with fear, was clinging to that weak old man.

Julian levelled again; indeed, indeed it was only as a threat; but his hand shook with passion—the weapon was full-cock, hair-triggered—shotted heavily as always—hark, hark!—And his father fell upon the turf, covered with blood!

When a wicked man tampers with unintended crime, even accident falls out against him. Many a one has richly merited death for many other sins, than that isolated, haply accidental one, which he has hanged for.

Julian, horror-stricken, pale and trembling, flew instinctively to help his father: but Emily has circled him already with her arms; and listen, Julian—your dying father speaks to you.

"Boy, I forgive—I forgive: but—Emily, no, no, cannot, cannot be—Julian—she—she is your *sister!*" and the old man swooned away, from loss of blood and the excitement of that awful scene.

Not a word in reply said that poor sinner, maddened with his life-long crimes, the fratricide in will, the parricide in deed, and all for—a sister. But growing whiter as he stood, a marble man with bristling hair, he slowly drew the other pistol from his pocket, put the muzzle to his mouth, and, firing as he fell, leapt into the darkly-flowing Mullet!

The current, all too violent to sink in, and uncommissioned now to save, hurried its black burden to the sea; and a crimson streak of gore marked the track of the suicide.

The old man was not dead; but a brace of bullets taking effect upon his feeble frame—one through the shoulder, and another which had grazed his head—had been quite enough to make him seem so. Forgetful of all but that dear sufferer, and totally ignorant of Julian's fate—for she neither saw nor heard any thing, nor feared even for her own imminent peril, while her father lay dying on the grass—Emily had torn off her scarf, and bound up, as well as she could, the ghastly scored head and broken shoulder. She succeeded in staunching the blood—for no great vessel had been severed—and so simple an application as grass dipped in water, proved to be a good specific. Then, to her exceeding joy, those eyes opened again, and that dear tongue faintly whispered—"Bless you."

Oh, that blessing! for it fell upon her heart: and fervently she knelt down there, and thanked the Great Preserver.

And now, for friendly help; there is no one near: and it is growing dusk; and she dared not leave him there alone one minute—for Julian—dreaded Julian, may return, and kill him. What shall she do? How to get him home? Alas, alas! he may die where he is lying.

Hark, Emmy, hark! The shouts of happy children bursting out of school! See, dearest—see: here they come homewards merrily from Oxton.

Thus, rewarded through the instrumentality of her own benevolence, help was speedily obtained; and Mrs. Sainsbury's invalid-chair, hurried to the spot by an escort of indignant rustics, soon conveyed the recovering patient to the comforts of his own home, and the appliances of medical assistance.

CHAPTER XXVII.

CHARLES'S RETURN; AND MRS. MACKIE'S EXPLANATION.

And now the happy day was come at length; that day formerly so hoped-for, latterly so feared, but last of all, hailed with the joy that trembles at its own intensity. The very morning after the sad occurrence it has just been my lot to chronicle—while the general was having his wounds dressed, slight ones, happily, but still he was not safe, as inflammation might ensue—while Mrs. Tracy was indulging in her third tumbler, mixed to whet her appetite for shrimps—and while Emily was deciphering, for the forty thousandth time, Charles's sanguine *billet-doux* —lo! a dusty chaise and smoking posters, and a sun-burnt young fellow springing out, and just upon the stairs—they were locked in each other's arms!

Oh, the rapture of that instant! it can but happen once within a life. Ye that have loved, remember such a meeting; and ye that never loved, conceive it if you can; for my pen hath little skill to paint so bright a pleasure. It is to be all heart, all pulse, all sympathy, all spirit—but the warm soft kiss, that rarified bloom of the Material.

How the sick old nurse got out, cased in many blankets; how she was bundled up stairs, and deposited safely on a sofa, no poet is alive to sing: to those who would record the payment of postillions, let me leave so sweet a theme.

The first fond greeting over, and those tumults of affection sobered down, Charles rejoiced to find how lovingly the general met him; the kind and good old man fell upon his neck, as the father in the parable. Many things were then to be made known: and many questions answered, as best might be, about a mother and a brother; but well aware of all things ourselves, let us be satisfied that Charles heard in due time all they had to tell him; though neither Emily nor the general could explain what had become of Julian after that terrible encounter. In their belief, he had fled for very life, thinking he had killed his father. Poor wretched man, thought Charles—on that same spot, too, where he would have murdered me! And for his mother—why came she not down eagerly and happily, as mothers ever do, to greet her long-lost son? Do not ask, Charles; do not press the question. Think her ill, dying, dead—any thing but—drunken. He ran to her room-door; but it was locked—luckily.

Now, Charles—now speedily to business; happy business that, if I may trust the lover's flushing cheek, and Emily's radiant eyes; but a mournful one too, and a fearful, if I turn my glance to that poor old man, wounded in body and stricken in mind—who waits to hear, in more despondency than hope, what he knows to be the bitter truth—the truth that must be told, to the misery of those dear children.

Faint and weak though she appeared, Jeanie Mackie's waning life spirited up for the occasion; her dim eye kindled; her feeble frame was straight and strong; energy nerved her as she spoke; this hour is the errand of her being.

Long she spoke, and loudly, in her broad Scotch way; and the general objected many things, but was answered to them all; and there was close cross-questioning, slow-caution, keen examination of documents and letters: catechisms, solecisms, Scottisms; reminiscences rubbed up, mistakes corrected; and the grand result of all, Emily a Stuart, and the general not her father! I am only enabled to give a brief account of that important colloquy.

It appears, that when Captain Tracy's company was quartered to the west of the Gwalior, sent thither to guard the Begum Dowlia against sundry of her disaffected subjects, a certain Lieutenant James Stuart was one among those welcome brave allies. That our gallant Tracy was the beautiful Begum's favourite soon became notorious to all; and not less so, that the Begum herself was precisely in the same interesting situation as Mrs. James Stuart. The two ladies, Pagan and Christian, were, technically speaking, running a race together. Well, just as times drew nigh, poor Lieutenant Stuart was unfortunately killed in an insurrection headed by some fanatics, who disapproved of foreign friends, and perhaps of their princess's situation. His death proved fatal also to that kind and faithful wife of his—a dark Italian lady of high family, whose love for James had led her to follow him even into Central Hindoostan: she died in giving birth to a babe; and Jeanie Mackie, the lieutenant's own foster-mother, who waited on his wife through all their travels, assisted the poor orphan into this bleak world, and loved it as her own.

Two days after all this, the Begum herself had need of Mrs. Mackie: for it was prudent to conceal some things, if she could, from certain Brahmins, who were to her what John Knox had erstwhile been to Mary: and Jeanie Mackie, burdened with her little Amy Stuart, aided in the birth of a female Tracy-Begum. So, the nurse tended both babes; and more than once had marvelled at their general resemblance; Amy's mother looked out again from those dark eyes; there was not a shade between the children.

Now, Mrs. Mackie perceived, in a very little while, how fond both Christian and Pagan appeared of their own child; and how little notice was taken by any body of the poor Scotch gentleman's orphan. Accordingly, with a view to give her favourite all worldly advantages, she adroitly changed the children; and, while she was still kind and motherly to the little Tracy-Begum, she had the satisfaction to see her pet supposititiously brought up in all the splendours of an Eastern court.

Years wore away, for Captain Tracy was quite happy, the Begum being a fine showy woman, and the pretty child his playmate and pastime: so he never cared to stir from his rich quarters, till the company's orders forced him: and then Puttymuddyfudgepoor hailed him accumulatively both major and colonel.

When he found that he must go, he insisted on carrying off the child; and the Begum was as resolute against it. Then Mrs. Mackie, eager to expedite little Stuart in her escape, went to the princess, told her how that, in anticipation of this day, she had changed the children, and got great rewards for thus restoring to the mother her own offspring.

The remainder of that old Scotch nurse's very prosy tale may be left to be imagined: for all that was essential has been stated: and the documents in proof of all were these—

First: The marriage certificates of James Stuart and Ami di Romagna, duly attested, both in the Protestant and Romanist forms.

Secondly: Divers letters to Lieutenant Stewart from his friends at Glenmuir; others to Mrs. Stuart, from her father, the old Marquis di Romagna, at Naples: several trinkets, locks of hair, the wedding-ring, &c.

Thirdly: A grant written in the Hindoostanee character, from the Begum Dowlia, promising the pension of thirty rupees a month to Jeanie Mackie, for having so cleverly preserved to her the child: together with a regular judicial acknowledgement, both from several of Tracy's own sepoys, and from the Begum herself, that the girl, whom Captain Tracy was so fond of, was, to the best of their belief, Amy Stuart.

Fourthly: A miniature of Mrs. James Stuart, exactly portraying the features of her daughter—this bright, beautiful, dark-eyed face—our own beloved Emily Warren.

And to all that accumulated evidence, Jeanie Mackie bore her living testimony; clearly, unhesitatingly, and well assured, in the face of God and man.

Doubt was at an end; fear was at an end; hope was come, and joy. Happy were the lovers, happy Jeanie Mackie, but happiest of all appeared the general himself. For now she might be his daughter indeed, sweet Emmy Tracy still, dear Charles's loving wife. And he blessed them as they knelt, and gave them to each other; well-rewarded children of affection, who had prayed in their distress!

CHAPTER XXVIII.

JULIAN TURNS UP: AND THERE'S AN END OF MRS. TRACY.

There is a muddy sort of sand-bank, acting as a delta to the Mullet, just where it spreads from deep to shallow, and falls into the sea. Strange wild fowl abound there, coming from the upper clouds in flocks; and at high water, very little else but rushes can be seen, to testify its sub-marine existence.

A knot of fishermen, idling on the beach, have noticed an uncommon flight of Royston crows gathered at the island, with the object, as it would appear, of battening on a dead porpoise, or some such body, just discernible among the rushes. Stop—that black heap may be kegs of whiskey;—where 's the glass?

Every one looked: it warn't barrels—and it warn't a porpoise: what was it, then? they had universally nothing on earth to do, so they pushed off in company to see.

I watched the party off, and they poked among the rushes, and heaved out what seemed to me a seal: so I ran down to the beach to look at the strange creature they had captured. Something wrapped in a sail; no doubt for exhibition at per head.

But they brought out that black burden solemnly, laying it on the beach at Burleigh: a crowd quickly collected round them, that I could not see the creature: and some ran for a magistrate, and some for a parson. Then men in office came—made a way through the crowd, and I got near: so near, that my foolish curiosity lifted up the sail, and I beheld—what had been Julian.

O, sickening sight: for all which the pistol had spared of that swart and hairy face, had been preyed upon by birds and fishes!

There was a hurried inquest: the poor general and Emily deposed to what they knew, and the rustics, who escorted him from Oxton. The verdict could be only one—self-murder.

So, by night, on that same swampy island, when the tide was low, they buried him, deeply staked into the soil, lest the waves should disinter him, without a parting prayer. Such is the end of the wicked.

In a day or two, I noticed that a rude wooden cross had been set over the spot: and it gratified me much to hear that a rough-looking crew of smugglers had boldly come and fixed it there, to hallow, if they could, a comrade's grave.

However, these poor fellows had been cheated hours before: Charles's brotherly care had secured the poor remains, and the vicar winked a blind permission: so Charles buried them by night in the church-yard corner, under the yew, reading many prayers above them.

Two fierce-looking strange men went to that burial with reverent looks, as it were chief mourners; and when all the rites were done, I heard them gruffly say to Charles, "God bless you, sir, for this!"

When the mother heard those tidings of her son, she was sobered on the instant, and ran about the house with all a mother's grief, shrieking like a mad woman. But all her shrieks and tears could not bring back poor Julian; deep, deep in the silent grave, she cannot wake him—cannot kiss him now. Ah well! ah well!

Then did she return to his dear room, desperate for him—and Hollands; once, twice, thrice, she poured out a full tumbler of the burning fluid, and drank it off like water; and it maddened her brain: her mind was in a phrensy of delirium, while her body shook as with a palsy.

Let us draw the curtain; for she died that night.

They buried her in Aunt Green's grave: what a meeting theirs will be at the day of resurrection!

CHAPTER XXIX.

THE OLD SCOTCH NURSE GOES HOME.

Six months at least—this is clearly not a story of the unities—six months' interval must now elapse before the wedding-day. Charles and Emmy—for he called her Emmy still, though Jeanie Mackie would persist in mouthing it to "Aamy,"—wished to have it delayed a year, in respect for the memory of those who, with all their crime and folly, were not the less a mother and a brother: but the general would not hear of such a thing; he was growing very old, he said; although actually he seemed to have taken out a new lease of life, so young again and buoyant was the new-found heart within him; and thus growing old, he was full of fatherly fear that he should not live to see his children's happiness. It was only reasonable and proper that our pair of cooing doves should acquiesce in his desire.

Meanwhile, I am truly sorry to say it, Jeanie Mackie died; for it would have been a good novel-like incident to have suffered the faithful old creature to have witnessed her favourite's wedding, and then to have been forthwith killed out of the way, by—perishing in the vestry. However, things were ordered otherwise, and Jeanie Mackie did not live to see the wedding: if you wish to know how and where she died, let me tell you at once.

Scotland—Argyleshire—Glenmuir; this was the focus of her hopes and thoughts—that poor old Indian exile! She had left it, as a buxom bright-haired lassie: but oaks had now grown old that she had planted acorns; and grandmothers had died palsied, whom she remembered born; still, around the mountains and the lakes, those changeless features of her girlhood's rugged home, the old woman's memory wandered; they were pictured in her mind's eye hard, and clear, and definite as if she looked upon them now. And her soul's deep hope was to see them once again.

There was yet another object which made her yearn for Scotland. Lieutenant Stuart had been the younger of two brothers, the eldest born of whom became, upon his father's, the old laird's, death, Glenmuir and Glenmurdock. Now, though twice married, this elder brother, the new laird, never had a child; and the clear consequence was, that Amy Stuart was likely to become sole heiress of her ancestor's possessions. The lieutenant's marriage with an Italian and a Romanist had been, doubtless, any thing but pleasant to his friends; the strict old Presbyterians, and the proud unsullied family of Stuart, could not palate it at all. Nevertheless, he did marry the girl, according to the rites of both churches, and there was an end of it; so, innumerable proverbs coming to their aid about "curing and enduring" and "must be's," and the place where "marriages are made," &c., the several aunts and cousins were persuaded at length to wink at the iniquity, and to correspond both with Mrs. James and her backsliding lieutenant. Of the offspring of that marriage, and her orphaned state, and of Mrs. Mackie's care, and the indefinite detention in central Hindostan, they had heard often-times; for, as there is no corner of the world where a Scot may not be met with, so, with laudable nationality, they all hang together; and Glenmuir was written to frequently, all about the child, through Jeanie Mackie, "her mark," and a scholarly sergeant, Duncan Blair.

Amy's rights—or Emmy let us call her still, as Charles did—were now, therefore, the next object of Mrs. Mackie's zeal; and all parties interested willingly listened to the plan of spending one or two of those weary weeks in rubbing up relationships in Scotland; the general also was not a little anxious about heritage and acres. Accordingly, off they set in the new travelling-carriage, with due notice of approach, heartily welcomed, to Dunstowr Castle, the fine old feudal stronghold of Robert Stuart, Laird of Glenmuir and Glenmurdock.

The journey, the arrival, and the hearty hospitality; and how the gray old chieftain kissed his pretty niece; and how welcome her betrothed Charles and her kind life-long guardian, and her faithful nurse were made; and how the beacons blazed upon the hill-tops, and the mustering clan gathered round about old Dunstowr; and how the laird presented to them all their beautiful future mistress, and how Jeanie Mackie and her documents travelled up to Edinburgh, where writers to the signet pestered her heart-sick with over-caution; and how the case was all cleared up, and the distant disappointed cousin, who had irrationally hoped to be the heir, was gladdened, if not satisfied, with a pension and a cantle of Glenmuir; and how all was joyfulness and feasting, when Amy Stuart was acknowledged in her rights—the bagpipes and the wassail, salmon, and deer, and black-cock, with a river of mountain dew: let others tell who know Dunstowr; for as I never was there, of course I cannot faithfully describe it. Should such an historian as I condescend to sheer inventions?

With respect to Jeanie Mackie, I could learn no more than this: she was sprightly and lively, and strong as ever, though in her ninetieth year, till her foster-child was righted, and the lawyers had allowed her her claim. But then there seemed nothing else to live for; so her life gradually faded from her eye, as an expiring candle; and she would doze by the hour, sitting on a settle in the sun, basking her old heart in the smile of those old mountains. None knew when she died, to a minute; for she died sitting in the sun, in the smile of those old mountains.

They buried her, with much of rustic pomp, in the hill-church of Glenmuir, where all her fathers slept around her; and Emily and Charles, hand-in-hand, walked behind her coffin mournfully.

CHAPTER XXX.

FINAL.

GLADLY would the laird have had the marriage at Dunstower, and have given away the beauteous bride himself: but there must still be two months more of decent mourning, and the general had long learned to sigh for the maligned delights of Burleigh Singleton. So, Glenmuir could only get a promise of rëappearance some fine summer or other · and, after another day's deer-stalking, which made the general repudiate telescopes from that day forth (the poor man's eyes had actually grown lobster-like with straining after antlers)—the travelling-carriage, and four lean kine from Inverary, whisked away the trio towards the South.

And now, in due time, were the Tamworths full of joy—congratulating, sympathizing, merrymaking; and the three young ladies behaved admirably in the capacity of pink and silver bridesmaids; while George proved equally kind in attending (as he called it) Charles's "execution," wherein he was "turned off;" and the admiral, G. C. B. was so hand-in-glove with the general, H. E. I. C. S., that I have reason to believe they must have sworn eternal friendship, after the manner of the modern Germans.

How beautiful our Emmy looked—I hate the broad Scotch Aamy—how bright her flashing eyes, and how fragrantly the orange-blossoms clustered in her rich brown hair; let him speak lengthily, whose province it may be to spin three volumes out of one: for me, I always wish to recollect that readers possess, on the average, at least as much imagination as writers. And why should you not exercise it now? Is not Emmy in her bridal-dress a theme well worth a revery?

For a similar reason, I must clearly disappoint feminine expectation, by forbearing to descant upon Charles's slight but manly form, and his Grecian beauty, &c., all the better for the tropics, and the trials and the troubles he had passed.

When Captain Forbes, just sitting down to his soup in the Jamaica Coffee-house, read in the *Morning Post*, the marriage of Charles Tracy with Amy Stuart, he delivered himself mentally as follows:

"There now! Poets talk of 'love,' and I stick to 'human nature.' When that fine young fellow sailed with me, hardly a year ago, in the Sir William Elphinston, he was over head and heels in love with old

Jack Tracy's pretty girl, Emily Warren: but I knew it wouldn't last long: I don't believe in constancy for longer than a week. It does one's heart good to see how right one is; here's what I call proof. My sentimental spark kisses Emily Warren, and marries Amy Stuart." The captain, happier than before, called complacently for Cayenne pepper, and relished his mock-turtle with a higher gusto.

It is worth recording, that the same change of name mystified slanderous friends in the Presidency of Madras.

And now, kind-eyed reader, this story of '*The Twins*' must leave off abruptly at the wedding. As in its companion-tale, '*The Crock of Gold*,' one grand thesis for our thoughts was that holy wise command, "Thou shalt not covet," and as its other comrade '*Heart*' is founded on "Thou shalt not bear false witness," so in this, the seed-corn of the crop, were five pure words, "Thou shalt not commit adultery." Other morals doubtless grew up round us, for all virtue hangs together in a bunch: the harms of secresy, false witness, inordinate affections, and red murder: but in chief, as we have said.

Moreover, I wish distinctly to make known, for dear "domestic" sake, that so far from our lovers' happiness having been consummated (that is, finished) in the honey-moon—it was only then begun. How long they are to live thus happily together, Heaven, who wills all things good, alone can tell; I wish them three score years. Little ones, I hear, arrive annually—to the unqualified joy, not merely of papa and mamma, but also of our communicative old general, his friend the G. C. B., and (all but most of any) the Laird of Glenmuir and Glenmurdock, whose heart has been entirely rejoiced by Charles Tracy having added to his name, and to his children's names, that of Stuart.

Mr. and Mrs. Tracy Stuart are often at Glenmuir; but oftener at Burleigh, where the general, I fancy, still resides. He protests that he never will keep a secret again: long may he live to say so!

END OF THE TWINS.

HEART;

A SOCIAL NOVEL.

BY

MARTIN FARQUHAR TUPPER, A. M., F. R. S.

AUTHOR OF

PROVERBIAL PHILOSOPHY.

HARTFORD:
PUBLISHED BY SILAS ANDRUS & SON.

1851.

HEART.

CHAPTER I.

WHEREIN TWO ANXIOUS PARENTS HOLD A COLLOQUY.

"Is he rich, ma'am? is he rich? ey? what—what? is he rich?"

Sir Thomas was a rapid little man, and quite an epicure in the use of that luscious monosyllable.

"Is he rich, Lady Dillaway? ey? what?"

"Really, Thomas, you never give me time to answer," replied the quintescence of quietude, her ladyship; "and then it is perpetually the same question, and—"

"Well, ma'am, can there be a more important question asked? I repeat it, is he rich? ey? what?

"You know, Sir Thomas, we never are agreed about the meaning of that word; but I should say, very."

As Lady Dillaway always spoke quite softly in a whisper, she had failed to enlighten the knight; but he seemed, notwithstanding, to have caught her intention instinctively; for he added, in his impetuous, imperious way,

"No nonsense now, about talents and virtues, *and all such trash*; but quick, ma'am, quick—is the man rich?"

"In talents, as you mention the word, certainly, very rich; a more clever or accomplished—"

"Cut it short, ma'am—cut it short, I say—I'll have no adventurers, who live by their wits, making up to my daughter—pedantic puppies, good for ushers, nothing else. What do they mean by knowing so much? ey? what?"

"And then, Sir Thomas, if you will only let me speak, a man of purer morals, finer feelings, higher Christian—"

"Bah! well enough for curates: go on, ma'am—go on, and make haste to the point of all points—is he rich?"

"You know I never will make haste, Thomas, for I never can have patience, and you shall hear; I am little in the habit of judging people entirely by their purses, not even a son-in-law, provided there is a sufficiency on the one side or the other for—"

"Quick, mum—quick—rich—rich? will the woman drive me mad?" and Sir Thomas Dillaway, Knight, rattled loose cash in both pockets more vindictively than ever. But the spouse, nothing hurried, still crept on in her *sotto voce adantino* style,

"Mr. Clements owes nothing, has something, and above and beside all his good heart, good mind, good fame, good looks, good family, possesses a contented—"

"Pish! contented, bah!" our hasty knight's nose actually curled upwards in utter scorn as he added, "Now, that 's enough—quite enough. I 'll bet a plum the man 's poor. Contented indeed! did you ever know a rich man yet who was contented—ey? mum—ey? or a poor one that wasn't—ey? what? I 've no patience with those contented fellows: it 's my belief they steal away the happiness of monied men. If this Mr. Clements was rich—rich, one wouldn't mind so much about talents, virtues, and contentment—work-house blessings; but the man 's poor, I know it—poo-o-or!"

Sir Thomas had a method quite his own of pronouncing those contradictory monosyllables, rich and poor: the former he gave out with an unctuous, fish-saucy gusto, and the word seemed to linger on his palate as a delicious morsel in the progress of delightful deglutition; but when he uttered the word poor, it was with that "mewling and puking" miserable face, appropriated from time immemorial to the gulping of a black draught.

"No, Lady Dillaway, right about 's the next word I shall say to that smooth-looking pauper, Mr. Henry Clements—to think of his impudence, making up to my daughter, indeed! a poo-o-o-r man, too."

"I did not tell you he was poor, Sir Thomas: you have run away with that idea on your own account: the young man has enough for the present, owes nothing for the past, and reasonable expectations for the—

"Future, I suppose, ey? what? I hate futures, all the lot of 'em: cash down, ready money, bird in the hand, that 's my ticket, mum: expectations, indeed! Well, go on—go on; I 'm as patient as a—as a mule, you see; go on, will you; I may as well hear it all out, Lady Dillaway."

"Well, Sir Thomas, since you think so little of the future, I will not insist on expectations; though I really can only excuse your methods of judging by the fancy that you are far too prudent in fearing for the future: however, if you will not admit this, let me take you on your own ground, the present; perhaps Mr. Clements may not possess quite as much as I could wish him, but then surely, dear Thomas, our daughter must have more than—"

I object to seeing oaths in print; unless it must be once in a way, as a needful point of character: probably the reader's sagacity will supply many omissions of mine in the eloquence of Sir Thomas Dillaway and others. But his calm spouse, nothing daunted, quietly whispered on—

"You know, Thomas, you have boasted to me that your capital is doubling every year; penny-postage has made the stationery business most prosperous; and if you were wealthy when the old king knighted you as lord mayor, surely you can spare something handsome now for an only daughter, who—"

"Ma'am!" almost barked the affectionate father, "if Maria marries money, she shall have money, and plenty of it, good girl; but if she will persist in wedding a beggar, she may starve, mum, starve, and all her poverty-stricken brats too, for any pickings they shall get out of my pocket. Ey? what? you pretend to read your Bible, mum—don't you know we're commanded to 'give to him that hath, and to take away from him that—'"

"For shame, Sir Thomas Dillaway!" interrupted the wife, as well she might, for all her quietude: she was a good sort of woman, and her better nature aroused its wrath at this vicious application of a truth so just when applied to morals and graces, so bitterly iniquitous in the case of this world's wealth. I wish that our ex-lord mayor's distorted text may not be one of real and common usage. So, silencing her lord, whose character it was to be overbearing to the meek, but cringing to any thing like rebuke or opposition, she forthwith pushed her advantages, adding—

"Your income is now four thousand a-year, as you have told me, Thomas, every hour of every day, since your last lucky hit in the government contract for blue-elephants and whitey-browns. We have only John and Maria; and John gets enough out of his own stock-brokering business to keep his curricle and belong to clubs—and—alas! my fears are many for my poor dear boy—I often wish, Thomas, that our John was not so well supplied with money: whereas, poor Maria—"

"Tush, ma'am, you're a fool, and have no respect at all for monied men. Jack's a rich man, mum—knows a trick or two, sticks at nothing on 'Change, shrewd fellow, and therefore, of course I don't stint him: ha! he's a regular Witney comforter, that boy—makes money—ay, for all his seeming extravagance, the clever little rogue knows how to keep it, too. If you only knew, ma'am, if you only knew—but we don't blab to fools."

I dare say "fools" will hear the wise man's secret some day.

"Well, Thomas, I am sure I have no wish to pry into business transactions; all my present hope is to help the cause of our poor dear Maria."

"Don't call the girl 'poor,' Lady Dillaway; it's no recommendation, I can tell you, though it may be true enough. Girls are a bad spec, unless they marry money. If our girl does this, well; she will indeed be to me a dear Maria, though not a poo-o-o-r one; if she doesn't, let her bide, and be an old maid; for as to marrying this fellow Clement's, I'll cut him adrift to-morrow."

"If you do, Sir Thomas, you will break our dear child's heart."

"Heart, ma'am! what business has my daughter with a heart?" [what, indeed?] "I hate hearts; they were sent, I believe, purposely to make those who are plagued with 'em poo-o-o-r. Heart, indeed! When did heart ever gain money? ey? what? It'll give, O yes, plenty—plenty, to charities, and churches, and orphans, and beggars, and any thing else, by way of getting rid of gold; but as to gaining—bah! heart indeed—pauperizing bit of muscle! save me from wearing under my waistcoat what you're pleased to call a heart. No, mum, no; if the girl has got a heart to break, I've done with her. Heart indeed! she either marries money and my blessing, or marries beggary and my curse. But I should like to know who wants her to marry at all? Let her die an old maid."

Probably this dialogue need go no farther: in the coming chapter we will try to be didactic. Meantime, to apostrophize ten words upon that last heartless sentence:

"Let her die an old maid." An old maid! how many unrecorded sorrows, how much of cruel disappointment and heart-cankering delay, how often-times unwritten tragedies are hidden in that thoughtless little phrase! O, the mass of blighted hopes, of slighted affections, of cold neglect, and foolish contumely, wrapped up in those three syllables! Kind heart, kind heart, never use them; neither lightly as in scorn, nor sadly as in pity: spare that ungenerous reproach. What! canst thou think that from a feminine breast the lover, the wife, the mother, can be utterly sponged away without long years of bitterness? Can Nature's wounds be cicatrized, or her soft feelings seared, without a thousand secret pangs? Hath it been no trial to see youthful bloom departing, and middle age creep on, without some intimate one to share the solitude of life? Ay, and the coming prospect too—hath it greater consolations than the retrospect? How faintly common friends can fill that hollow of the heart! how feebly can their kindness, at the warmest, imitate the sympathies and love of married life! And in the days of sickness, or the hour of death—to be lonely, childless, husbandless, to be lightly cared for, little missed—who can wonder that all those bruised and broken yearnings should ferment within the solitary mind, and sometimes sour up the milk of human kindness? Be more considerate, more just, more loving to that injured heart of woman; it hath loved deeply in its day; but imperative duty or untoward circumstances nipped those early blossoms, and often generosity towards others, or the constancy of youthful blighted love, has made it thus alone. There was an age in this world's history, and may be yet again (if Heart is ever to be monarch of this social sphere), when those who lived and died as Jephthah's daughter, were reckoned worthily with saints and martyrs. Heed thou, thus, of many such, for they have offered up their hundred warm yearnings, a hecatomb of human love, to God, the betrothed of their affections; and they move up and down among this inconsiderate world, doing good, Sisters of Charity, full of pure benevolence, and beneficent beyond the widow's mite. Heed kinder then, and blush for very shame, O man and woman! looking on this noble band of ill-requited virgins; remember all their trials, and imitate their deeds; for among the legion of that unreguarded sisterhood whom you coldly call old maids, are often seen the world's chief almoners of warm unselfish sympathy, generous in mind, if not in means, and blooming with the immortal youth of charity and kindliness.

CHAPTER II.

HOW THE DAUGHTER HAS A HEART; AND, WHAT IS COMMONER, A LOVER.

YES, Maria Dillaway, though Sir Thomas's own daughter, had a heart, a warm and good one: it was her only beauty, but assuredly at once the best adornment and cosmetic in the world. The mixture of two such conflicting characters as her father and mother might (with common Providence to bless the pair) unitedly produce heart; although their plebeian countenances could hardly be expected without a direct miracle to generate beauty. Maria inherited from her father at once his impetuosity and his little button-nose: although the latter was neither purple nor pimply, and the former was more generous and better directed: from her mother she derived what looked to any one at first sight very like red hair, along with great natural sweetness of disposition: albeit her locks had less of fire, and her sweetness more of it: sympathy was added to gentleness, zeal to patience, and universal tenderness to a general peace with all the world; for that extreme quietude, almost apathy, alluded to before, having been superseded by paternal impetuosity, the result of all was Heart. She doated on her mother; and (how she contrived this, it is not quite so easy to comprehend) she found a great deal loveable even in her father. But in fact she loved every body. Charity was the natural atmosphere of her kind and feeling soul—always excusing, assisting, comforting, blessing; charity lent music to her tongue, and added beauty to her eyes—charity gave grace to an otherwise ordinary figure, and lit her freckled cheek with the spirit of loveliness. Let us be just—nay, more: let us be partial, to the good looks of poor dear Maria. Notwithstanding the snub nose (it is not snub; who says it is snub?—it is *mignon*, personified good nature)—notwithstanding the carroty hair (I declare, it was nothing but a fine pale auburn after all)—notwithstanding the peppered face (oh, how sweetly rayed with smiles!) and the common figure (gentle, unobtrusive, full of delicate attentions)—yes, notwithstanding all these unheroinals, no one who had a heart himself could look upon Maria without pleasure and approval. She was the very incarnation of cheerfulness, kindness, and love: you forgot the greenish colour of those eyes which looked so tenderly at you, and so often-times were dimmed with tears of unaffected pity; her smile, at any rate, was most enchanting, the very sunshine of an amiable mind; her lips dropped blessings; her brow was an open plain of frankness and candour; sincerity, warmth, disinterested sweet affections threw such a lustre of loveliness over her form, as well might fascinate the mind alive to spiritual beauty: and altogether, in spite of natural defects and disadvantages—*nez retroussé*, Cleopatra locks, and all—no one but those constituted like her materialized father and his kind, ever looked upon Maria without unconsciously admiring her, he scarcely knew for what. Though there appeared little to praise, there certainly was every thing to please; and faulty as in all pictorial probability was each lineament of face and line of form, taken separately and by detail, the veil of universal charity softened and united them into one harmonious whole, making of Maria Dillaway a most pleasant, comfortable, wife-like little personage.

At least, so thought Henry Clements. Neither was it any sudden fortnight's fancy, but the calm consideration of two full years. Maria's was a character which grew upon your admiration gradually—a character to like at first just a little; then to be led onwards imperceptibly from liking to loving; and thence from fervid summer probably to fever heat. She dawned upon young Henry like the blush of earliest morn, still shining brighter and fairer till glorious day was come.

He had casually made her acquaintance in the common social circle, and even on first introduction had been much pleased, not to say captivated, with her cordial address, frank unsophisticated manners, and winsome looks; he contrasted her to much advantage with the affected coquette, the cold formal prude, the flippant woman of fashion, the empty heads and hollow hearts wherewithal society is peopled. He had long been wearied out with shallow courtesies, frigid compliments, and other conventional hypocrisies, up and down the world; and wanted something better to love than mere surface beauty, mere elegant accomplishment—in a word, he yearned for Heart, and found the object of his longings in affectionate Maria.

This first casual acquaintance he had of course taken every opportunity to improve as best he might, and happily found himself more and more charmed on every fresh occasion. How heartily glad she was to see him! how unaffectedly sincere in her amiable joy! how like a kind sister, a sympathizing friend, a very true-love—a dear, cheerful, warm-hearted girl, who would make the very model for a wife!

It is little wonder that, with all external drawbacks, now well-nigh forgotten, the handsome Henry Clements found her so attractive; nor that, following diligently his points of advantage, he progressed from acquaintanceship to intimacy, and intimacy to avowed admiration; and thence (between ourselves) to the resolute measure of engagement.

I say between ourselves, because nobody else in the world knew it but the billing pair of lovers; and even they have got the start of us only by a few hours. As for Henry Clements, he was a free man in all senses, with nobody to bias his will or control his affections—an orphan, unclogged by so much as an uncle or aunt to take him to task on the score of his attachment, or to plague him with impertinent advice. His father, Captain Clements of the seventieth, had fallen "gloriously" on the bloody field of Waterloo, and the pensioned widow had survived her gallant hero barely nine winters; leaving little Henry thrown upon the wide world at ten years of age, under the nominal guardianship of some very distant Ulster cousin of her own, a Mackintosh, Mackenzie, or Macfarlane—it is not yet material which; and as for the lad's little property, his poor patrimony of two hundred a-year had hitherto amply sufficed for Harrow and for Cambridge (where he had distinguished himself highly), for his chambers in the Temple, and his quiet bachelor-mode of life as a man of six-and-twenty.

Accordingly, our lover took counsel of nobody but Maria's beaming eyes, when he almost unconsciously determined to lay siege to her: he really could not make up his mind to the preliminary formal process of storming Sir Thomas in his counting-house, at the least until he had made sure that Maria's kind looks were any thing more particular than universal charity; and as to Lady Dillaway, it was impossible to broach so delicate a business to her till the daughter had looked favourably as aforesaid, set aside her ladyship's formidable state of quiescence, and apparent (though only apparent) lack of sympathy. So the lover still went on sunning his soul from time to time in Maria's kindly smiles, until one day, that is, yesterday, they mutually found out by some happy accident how very dear they were to each other; and mutually vowed ever to continue so. It was quite a surprise this, even to both of them—an extemporary unrehearsed outburst of the heart; and Maria discovered herself pledged before she had made direct application to mamma about the business. However, once done, she hastened to confide the secret to her mother's ear, earnestly requesting her to break it to papa. With how little of success, we have learnt already.

CHAPTER III.

PATERNAL AMIABILITIES.

Maria, as we know, loved her father, for she loved every thing that breathes; but she would not have been human had she not also feared him. In fact, he was to her a very formidable personage, and one would have thought any thing but an amiable one. Over Maria's gentle kindness he could domineer as loftily as he would cringe in cowardly humiliation to the boisterous effrontery of that unscrupulous and wily stockjobber, "my son Jack." With the tyranny proper to a little mind, he would trample on the neck of a poor meek daughter's filial duty, desiring to honour its parent by submission; and then, with consistent meanness, would lick the dust like a slave before an undutiful only son, who had amply redeemed all possible criminalities by successful (I did not say honest) gambling in the funds, and otherwise.

Yes! John Dillaway was rich; and, climax to his praise, rich by his own keen skill, independent of his father, though he condescended still to bleed him. In this "money century," as Kohl, the graphic traveller, has called it, riches "cover the multitude of sins;" leaving poor Maria's charity to cover its own naked virtues, if it can. So John was the father's darling, notwithstanding the very heartless and unbecoming conduct he had exhibited daily for these thirty years, and the marked scorn wherewithal he treated that pudgy city knight, his dear progenitor; but then, let us repeat it as Sir Thomas did—Jack was rich—rich, and such a comfort to his father; whereas Maria, poor fool, with all her cheap unmarketable love and duty, never had earned a penny—never could, but was born to be a drain upon him. Therefore did he scorn her, and put aside her kindnesses, because she could not "make money."

For what end on earth should a man make money! It is reasonable to reply, for the happiness' sake of others and himself; but, in the frequent case of a rich and cold Sir Thomas, what can be the object in such? Not to purchase happiness therewith himself, nor yet to distribute it to others; a very dog in the manger, he snarls above the hay he cannot eat, and is full of any thoughts rather than of giving: whilst, as for his own pleasure, he manifestly will not stop a minute to enjoy a taste of happiness, even if he finds it in his home; nay, more, if it meets him by the way, and wishes to cling about his heart, he will be found often to fling it off with scorn, as a reaper would the wild sweet corn-flower in some handful of wheat he is cutting. O, Sir Thomas! is not poor Maria's love worth more than all your rich rude Jack's sudden flush of money? is it not a deeper, higher, purer, wiser, more abundant source of pleasure? You have yet to learn the wealth of her affections, and his poverty of soul.

It was not without heart-sickness, believe me, sore days and weeping nights, that affectionate Maria saw her father growing more and more estranged from her. True, he had never met her love so warmly that it was not somewhat checked and chilled; true, his nature had reversed the law of reason, by having systematically treated her with less and less of kindness ever since the nursery; she did seem able to remember something like affection in him while she was a prattling infant; but as the mental daylight dawned apace, and she grew (one would fancy) worthier of a rational creature's love, it strangely had diminished year by year; moreover, she could scarcely look back upon one solitary occasion, whereon her father's voice had instructed her in knowledge, spoken to her in sympathy, or guided her footsteps to religion. Still, habituated as she long had now become to this daily martyrdom of heart, and sorely bruised by coarse and common worldliness as had been every fibre of her feelings, she could not help perceiving that things got worse and worse, as the knight grew richer and richer; and often-times her eyes ran over bitterly for coldness and neglect. There was, indeed, her mother to fly to; but she never had been otherwise than a very quiet creature, who made but little show of what feeling she possessed; and then the daughter's loving heart was affectionately jealous of her father too.

"Why should he be so cold, with all his impetuosity? so formal, in spite of his rapidity? so little generous of spirit, notwithstanding all his wonderful prosperity?"

Ah, Maria, if you had not been quite so unsophisticated, you would have left out the latter "notwithstanding." Nothing hardens the heart, dear child, like prosperity; and nothing dries up the affections more effectually than this hot pursuit of wealth. The deeper a man digs into the gold mine, the less able—ay, less willing—is he to breathe the sweet air of upper earth, or to bask in the daylight of heaven: downward, downward still, he casts the anchor of his grovelling affections, and neither can nor will have a heart for any thing but gold.

Moreover, have you wondered, dear Maria, at the common fact (one sees it in every street, in every village), that parental love is oftenest at its zenith in the nursery, and then falls lower and lower on the firmament of human life, as the child gets older and older? Look at all dumb brutes, the lower animals of this our earth; is it not thus by nature's law with them? The lioness will perish to preserve that very whelp, whom she will rend a year or two hence, meeting the young lion in the forest; the hen, so careful of her callow brood, will peck at them, and buffet them away, directly they are fully fledged; the cow forgets how much she once loved yonder well-grown heifer; and the terrier-bitch fights for a bit of gristle with her own two-year-old, whom she used to nurse so tenderly, and famished her own bowels to feed. And can you expect that men, who make as little use as possible of Heart, that unlucrative commodity—who only exercise Reason for shrewd purposes of gain, not wise purposes of good, and who might as well belong to Cunningham's "City of O," for any souls they seem to carry about with them—can you expect that such unaffectioned, unintelligent, unspiritualized animals, can rise far above the brute in feeling for their offspring? No, Maria; the nursery plaything grows into the exiled school-boy; and the poor child, weaned from all he ought to love, soon comes to be regarded in the light of an expensive youth; he is kept at arm's length, unblest, uncaressed, unloved, unknown; then he grows up apace, and tops his father's inches; he is a man now, and may well be turned adrift; if he can manage to make money, they are friends; but if he can only contrive to spend it, enemies. Then the complacent father moans about ingratitude, for he did his duty by the boy in sending him to school.

O, faults and follies of the by-gone times, which lingered even to a generation now speedily passing away!—ye are waning with it, and a better dawn has broken on the world. Happily for man, the multiplication of his kind, and pervading competition in all manner of things mercantile, are breaking down monopolies, and hindering unjust accumulation, with its necessary love of gain. "Satisfied with little" is young England's cry; a better motto than the "Craving after much" of their fathers. No longer immersed, single-handed, in a worldly business, which seven competitors now relieve him of; no longer engrossed with the mint of gold gains, which a dozen honest rivals now are sharing with him eagerly, the parent has leisure to instruct his children's minds, to take an interest in their pursuits, and to cultivate their best affections. Home is no longer the place perpetually to be driven from; the voices of paternal duty and domestic love are thrillingly raised to lead the tuneful chorus of society; and fathers, as well as mothers, are beginning to desire that their children may be able to remember them hereafter as the ever-sympathizing friend, the wisely indulgent teacher, the guide of their religion, and the guardian of their love; quite as much as the payer of their bills and the filler of their purses.

The misfortune of a past and passing generation has been, too much money in too few hands; its faults, neglect of duty; its folly, to expect therefrom the too-high meed of well-earned gratitude; and from this triple root has grown up social selfishness, a general lack of Heart. No parent ever yet, since the world was, did his duty properly, as God intended him to do it, by the affections of the mind and the yearnings of the heart, as well as by the welfare of the body with its means, and lived to complain of an ungrateful child. He may think he did his duty; oh yes, good easy man! and say so too, very, very bitterly; and the world may echo his most partial verdict, crying shame on the unnatural Goneril and Regan, bad daughters who despise the Lear in old age, or on the dissolute and graceless youth, whose education cost so much, and yields so very little. But money cannot compensate that maiden or that youth for early and habitual injustice done to their budding minds, their sensitive hearts, their craving souls, in higher, deeper, holier things than even cash could buy. "Home affections"—this was the magic phrase inscribed upon the talisman they stole from that graceless youth; and the loss of home affections is scantily counterbalanced at the best by a critical acquaintance with '*Dawes's Canons,*' and '*Bos on Ellipses,*' in his ardent spring of life, and by a little more of the paternal earnings which the legacy-office gives him in his manhood.

But let us not condemn generations past and passing, and wink at our own-time sins; we have many motes yet in our eyes, not to call them very beams. The infant school, the factory, the Union, and other wholesale centralizations, ruin the affections of our poor. O, for the spinning-wheel again within the homely cottage, and those difficult spellings by the grand-dame's knee! There is wisdom and stability in a land thick-set with such early local anchorages; but the other is all false, republican, and unaffectioned. So, too, the luxurious city club has cheated many a young pair of their just domestic happiness, for the husband grew dissatisfied with home and all its poor humilities; whilst a bad political philosophy, discouraging marriage and denouncing offspring, has insidiously crept into the very core of private families, setting children against parents and parents against children, because a cold expediency winks at the decay of morals, and all united social influences strike at the sacrifice of Heart.

We are forgetting you, poor affectionate Maria, and yet will it comfort your charity to listen. For the time is coming—yea, now is—when a more generous, though poorer age will condemn the Mammon phrensy of that which has preceded it. Boldly do we push our standards in advance, pressing on the flying foe, certain that a gallant band will follow. Fearlessly, here and there, is heard the voice of some solitary zealot, some isolated missionary for love, and truth, and philanthropic good, some dauntless apostle in the cause of Heart, denouncing selfish wealth as the canker of society: and, hark! that voice is not alone; there is a murmur on the breeze as the sound of many waters; it comes, it comes! and the young have caught it up; and manhood hears the thrilling strain that sinks into his soul; and old age, feebly listening, wonders (never too late) that he had not hitherto been wiser; and the whole social universe electrically touched from man to man, I hear them in their new-born generosities, penitently shouting "God and Heart!" even louder than they execrate the memory of Dagon.

CHAPTER IV.

EXCUSATORY.

It really may be numbered among doubts whether it is possible to exaggerate the dangers into which a fictionist may fall. My marvel is, that any go unstabbed. How on earth did Cervantes continue to grow old, after having pointed the finger of derision at all grave Spain? There is Boccaccio, too; he lived to turn threescore, in spite of the thousand husbands and wives, who might pretty well imagine that he spoke of them. Only consider how many villains, drawn to the life, Walter Scott created. What! were there no heads found to fit his many caps, hats, helmets, and other capillary properties? What! are we so blind, so few of friends, that we cannot each pick out of our social circles Mrs. Gore's Dowager, Mrs. Grey's Flirt, Mrs. Trollope's Widow, and Boz's Mrs. Nickleby? Who can help thinking of his lawyer, when he makes acquaintance with those immortal firms Dodson and Fogg, or Quirk, Snap, and Gammon? Is not Wrexhill libellous, and Dr. Hookwell personal? Arise! avenge them both, ye zealous congregations! Why slumber pistols that should damage Bulwer? Why are the clasp-knives sheathed, which should have drunk the blood of James? Hath every "[dash] good-natured friend" forgotten to be officious, and neglected to demonstrate to relations and acquaintances that this white villain is Mr. A., and that old virgin poor Miss B.? Speak, Plumer Ward, courageous veteran, Have the critics yet forgiven Mr. John Paragraph—forgotten, is impossible? and how is it no house-keeper has arsenicked my soup, O rash recruit, for the mysteries of perquisite divulged in Mrs. Quarles?

A dangerous craft is the tale-wright's, and difficult as dangerous. Human nature goes in casts, as garden-pots do. Lo, you! the crowd of thumb-pots; mean little tiny minds in multitudes, as near alike as possible. Then there are the frequent thirty-twos, average "clever creatures" in this mental age, wherein no one can make an ordinary how-d'ye-do acquaintance without being advertised of his or her surprising talents: and to pass by all intermediate sizes, here and there standing by himself, in all the prickly pride of an immortal aloe, some one big pot monopolizes all the cast of earth, domineering over the conservatory as Brutus's colossal Cæsar, or his metempsychosis in a Wellington.

Again: no painter ever yet drew life-likeness, who had not the living models at least in his mind's eye: but no good painter ever yet betrayed the model in his figure; unless (though these instances are rarish too) we except, *pace* Lawrence, the mystery of portraiture. He takes indeed a line here and a colour there; but he softens this and heightens that; so that none but he can well discover any trace of Homer's noble head in yonder sightless beggar, or Juno's queenly form in the Welsh woman trudging with her strawberry load to Covent Garden market.

Flatter not thyself, fair Helen, I have not pictured thee in gentle Grace: tremble not, my little white friend Clatter, thou art by no means Simon Jennings. Dark Caroline Blunt, it is true thou hast fine eyes; nevertheless, in nothing else (I am sorry to assure thee) art thou at all like Emily Warren. Flaunting Lady Busbury, be calm; if you had not been so wrathful, I never should have thought of you—undoubtedly you are not the type of Mrs. Tracy.

Why will all these people don my imaginary characters? Truly, it may seem to be a compliment, as proving that they speak from heart to heart, of universal human nature, not unaptly; still is their inventor or creator embarrassed terribly by such unwelcome honours; your precious balms oppress him, gentle friends; lift off your palm branches; indeed, he is unworthy of these petty triumphs; and, to be serious, he detests them.

No: once and for all, let a plain first person say it, I abjure personalities; my arrows are shot at a venture; and if they hit any one at all, it is only that he stands in my shaft's way, and the harness of his conscience is unbuckled. The target of my feeble aim is general—to pierce the heart of evil, evil in the form of social heartlessness: it is no fault of mine, if some alarmed particulars will crowd about the mark.

Ideal characters, ideal incidents, ideal scenes—to these I honestly pledge myself: but as most men have two eyes, being neither naturally monocular nor triocular, so most men of their own special cast have similar distinguishable sympathies.

The overweening love of money is a seed, a soil, and a sun that generates a certain crop: the aim of my poor husbandry is only to reap this; but my sickle does not wish to wound the growers: let them stand aside; or, better far, let them help me cut those rank and clogging tares, and bind them up in bundles to be burned. Heart is a sweet-smelling shrub, ill to stand against the chilling breath of worldliness: my small care desires to cherish this; gather round it, friends! shelter it beside me. How many fragrant flowers now are bursting into beauty! how cheering is their scent! how healthful the aroma of their bloom! Pluck them with me; they are sweet, delicate, and lustrous to look upon, even as the night-blowing cereus.

Henceforth then, social circle, feel at peace with such as I am, whose public parable would teach, without any thought of personality, entirely disclaiming private interpretations: there are other people stout besides one's uncle, other people deaf besides one's aunt. Sir Thomas Dillaway is not Alderman Bunce, nor any other friend or foe I wot of; a mere creature of the counting-house, he is a human ledger-mushroom: rub away the mildew from your hearts, if any seem to see yourselves in him: neither have I ventured to transplant Miss Cassiopeia Curtis's red hair to dear Maria's head: imitate her graces, if you will, maiden; but charge me not with copying your locks. Though "my son Jack" be a boisterous big rogue, on 'Change, and off it—let not mine own honest stock-broker put that hat upon his head, in the mono-mania that it fits him, because he may heretofore have been both bull and bear; and as for any other heroes yet to come upon this scene, to enact the tragedy or comedy of Heart—"Know all men by these presents,"—your humble servant's will is to smite bad principles, not offending persons; to crusade against evil manners, not his guilty fellow-men.

Wo is me! who am I, that I should satirize my brethren?—Yet, wo is me—if I silently hide the sin I see. Make me not an offender for a word, seeing that my purposes are good. Be not hypercritical, for Heart's sake, against a man whose aim it is to help the cause of Heart. Neither count it sufficient to answer me with an inconclusive "*tu quoque:*" I know it, I feel it, I confess it, I would away with it. Heaven send to him that writes, as liberally as to those who read (yea, more, according to his deeper needs and failings) the grace to counteract all mammonizing blights, and to cultivate this garden of the Heart.

CHAPTER V.

WHEREIN A WELL-MEANING MOTHER ACTS VERY FOOLISHLY.

Returned from her unsuccessful embassage, Lady Dillaway determined—kind, calm soul—to hide the bitter truth from poor Maria, that her father was inexorably adverse. A scene was of all things that indentical article least liked by the quiescent mother; and that her warm-hearted daughter would enact one, if she heard those echoes of paternal love, was clearly a problem requiring no demonstration.

Accordingly, with well-intentioned kindliness, but shallowish wisdom, and most questionable propriety, Maria was persuaded to believe that her father had hem'd and haw'd a little, had objected no doubt to Henry's lack of money, but would certainly, on second thoughts, consider the affair more favourably:

"You know your father's way, my love; leave him to himself, and I am sure his better feeling will not fail to plead your cause: it will be prudent, however, just for quiet's sake, to see less of Henry Clements for a day or two, till the novelty of my intelligence blows over. Meantime, do not cry, dear child; take courage, all will be well; and I will give you my free leave to console your Henry too."

"Dearest, dearest mamma, how can I thank you sufficiently for all this? But why may I not now at once fly to papa, tell him all I feel and wish cordially and openly, and touch his dear kind heart? I am sure he would give us both his sanction and his blessing, if he only knew how much I love him, and my own dear Henry."

"Sweet child," sighed out mamma, "I wish he would, I trust he would, I believe indeed he will some day: but be advised by me, Maria, I know your father better than you do; only keep quiet, and all will come round well. Do not broach the subject to him—be still, quite still; and, above all, be careful that your father does not yet awhile meet Mr. Clements."

"But, dearest mamma, how can I be so silent when my heart is full? and then I hate that gloomy sort of secresy. Do let me ask papa, and tell him all myself. Perhaps he himself will kindly break the ice for me, now that your dear mouth has told him all, mamma. How I wish he would!"

"Alas, Maria, you always are so sanguine: your father is not very much given, I fear, to that sort of sociality. No, my love; if you only will be ruled by me, and will do as I do, managing to hold your tongue, I think you need not apprehend many conversational advances on your father's part."

Poor Maria had more than one reason to fear all this was true, too true; so her lip only quivered, and her eyes overflowed as usual.

Thereafter, Lady Dillaway had all the talk to herself, and she smoothly whispered on without let or hindrance; and what between really hoping things kindly of her husband's better feelings, and desiring to lighten the anxieties of dear Maria's heart, she placed the whole affair in such a calm, warm, and glowing Claude-light, as apparently to supply an emendation (no doubt the right reading) to the well known aphorism—

"The course of true love never did run smooth-*er*."

In fine, our warm and confiding Maria ran up to her own room quite elated after that interview; and she heartily thanked God that those dreaded obstacles to her affection were so easily got over, and that her dear, dear father had proved so kind.

It is quite a work of supererogation to report how speedily the welcome news were made known, by *billet-doux*, to Henry Clements; but they rather smote his conscience, too, when he reflected that he had not yet made formal petition to the powers on his own account. To be sure, they (the lovers, to wit) were engaged only yesterday, quite in an unintended, though delightful, way: and, previously to that important *tête-à-tête*, however much he may have thought of only dear Maria—however frequently he found himself beside her in the circle of their many mutual friends—however happily he hoped for her love—however foolishly he reveried about her kindness in the solitude of his Temple garret—still he never yet had seen occasion to screw his courage to the sticking point, and boldly place his bliss at hard Sir Thomas's disposal. Some day—not yet—perhaps next week, at any rate not exactly to-day—these were his natural excuses; and they availed him even to the other side of that social Rubicon, engagement. Nevertheless, now at length something must decidedly be done; and, within half an hour, Finsbury's deserted square echoed to the heroic knock of Mr. Henry Clements, fully determined upon claiming his Maria at her father's hands.

The knight was out; probably, or rather certainly, not yet returned from his counting-house in St. Benet's Sherehog. So, perforce, our hero could only have an audience with his lady.

The same glossing over of unpalatable truths—the same quiet-breathing counsel—the same tranquil sort of hopefulness—fully satisfied the lover that his cause was gained. How could he think otherwise? In the father's absence, he had broached that mighty topic to the mother, who even now hailed him as her son, and promised him his father's favour. What could be more delicious than all this? and what more honourable, while prudent, too, and filial, than to acquiesce in Lady Dillaway's fears about her husband's nervousness at the sight of one who was to take from him an only and beloved daughter? It was delicacy itself—charming; and Henry determined to make his presence, for the first few days, as scarce as possible in the sight of that affectionate father.

And thus it came to pass that two open and most honourable minds, pledged to heartiest love, could not find one speck of sin in loving on clandestinely. Nay, was it clandestine at all? Is it, then, merely a legal fiction, and not a religious truth, that husband and wife are one? and is it not quite as much a matrimonial as a moral one that father and mother are so too? Was it not decidedly enough to have spoken to the latter, especially when she undertook to answer for the former? Sir Thomas was a man engrossed in business; and, doubtless, left such affairs of the Heart to the kinder keeping of Lady Dillaway. No; there was nothing secret nor clandestine in the matter; and I entirely absolve both Henry and Maria. They could not well have acted otherwise; if any harm should come to it, the mother is to blame.

Lady Dillaway, without doubt, should have known her husband better; but her tranquil love of our dear Maria seemed to have infatuated her into simply believing—what she so much wished—her happiness secure. She heeded not how little sympathy Sir Thomas felt with lovers; and only encouraged her innocent child to play the dangerous game of unconscious disobedience. Accordingly, consistent with that same quiet kindness of character which had smoothed away all difficulties hitherto, the indulgent mother now allowed the loving pair to meet alone, for the first time permissively, to tell each other all their happiness. Lady Dillaway left the drawing-room, and sent Maria to the heart that beat with hers.

Who shall describe the beauty of that interview—the gush of first affections bursting up unchecked, unchidden, as hot springs round the Hecla of this icy world! They loved and were beloved—openly, devotedly, sincerely, disinterestedly. Henry had never calculated even once how much the city knight could give his daughter; and as for Maria, if she had not naturally been a girl all heart, the home wherein she was brought up had so disgusted her of still-repeated riches, that (it is easy of belief) the very name of poverty would be music to her ears. Accordingly, how they flew into each other's arms, and shed many happy tears, and kissed many kindest kisses, and looked many tenderest things, and said many loving words, "let Petrarch's spirit in heroics sing:" as for our present prosaical Muse, shé delights in such affections too naturally and simply to wish to cripple them with rhymes, or confine them in sonnets; she despises decoration of simple and beautiful Nature —gilding gold, and painting lilies; and she loves to throw a veil of secret sanctity over all such heaven-blest attachments. "Hence! ye profane," —these are no common lovers: I believe their spirits, still united in affections that increase with time, will go down to the valley of death unchangeably together; and will thence emerge to brighter bliss hand in hand throughout eternity—a double Heart with one pulse, loving God, and good, and one another!

CHAPTER VI.

PLEASANT BROTHER JOHN.

"Ho, ho! I suspected as much; so this fellow Clements has been hanging about us at parties, and dropping in here so often, for the sake of Miss Maria, ey?"—For the door had noisily burst open to let in Mr. John Dillaway, who under grumbled as above.

"Dear John, I am so rejoiced to see you; I am sure it will make you as happy as myself, brother, to hear the good news: papa and mamma are so kind, and —— I need not introduce to you my —— you have often met him here, John—Mr. Henry Clements."

"Sir, your most obedient." The vulgar little purse-proud citizen made an impudent sort of distant bow, and looked for all the world like a coated Caliban sarcastically cringing to a well-bred Ferdinand.

Poor Henry felt quite taken aback at such frigid formality; and dear Maria's very heart was in her mouth: but the brother tartly added, "If Mr. Clements wishes to see Sir Thomas—that's his knock: he was following me close behind: I saw him; but, as I make it a point never to walk with the governor, perhaps it's as well for you two I dropped in first by way of notice, ey?"

It was a dilemma, certainly—after all that Lady Dillaway had said and recommended: fortunately, however, her lord the knight, when the street door was opened to him, hastened straightway to his own "study," where he had to consult some treatise upon tare and tret, and a recent pamphlet upon the undoubted social duty, '*Run for Gold;*' so that awkward rencounter was avoided; and Mr. Clements, taking up his hat, was enabled to accomplish a dignified retreat.

"Dear John, your manner grieves me; I wish you had been kinder to my—to Henry Clements."

"Oh, you do, do you? does the governor know of all this? the fellow 's a beggar."

"For shame, John! you shall not call my noble Henry such names: of course papa has heard all."

"And approves of all this spooneying, ey, miss?"

"Brother, brother, do be gentler with me: mamma's great kindness has smoothed away all objections, and surely you will be glad, John, to have at last a brother of your own to love you as I do."

"Ey? what? another thief to go shares with me when the governor cuts up? Thank you, miss, I'd rather be excused. You are quite enough, I can tell you, for you make my whole a half; nobody wants a third: much obliged to you, though." [Interjections may as well be understood.]

"O, dear brother, you hurt me, indeed you do: I am sure (if it were right to say so) I would not wish to live a minute, if poor Maria's death could—could make you any happier;—O John, my heart will——" [Her tears can as readily be understood as his interjections.]

If a domestic railroad could have been cleverly constructed to Maria's chamber from every room in that great house, it would have stood her in good stead; for every day, from some room or other, this poor girl of feeling had to rush up stairs in a torrent of grief. Yearning after sympathy and love, neither felt nor understood by the minds with whom she herded, a trio of worldliness, apathy, and coarse brutality, her bosom ached as an empty void: treated with habitual neglect and cold indifference, made various (as occasion might present) by stern rebuke or bitter sarcasm, her heart was sore within its cell, and the poor dear child lived a life of daily martyrdom, her feelings smitten upon the desecrated altar of home by the "foes of her own household."

And not least hostile in the band of those home-foes was this only brother, John. Look at him as he stands alone there, muttering after her as she ran up stairs, "Plague take the girl!" and let me tell you what I know of him.

That thick-set form, with its pock-marked face, imprisons as base a spirit as Baal's. He was a chip of the old block, and something more. If the father had a heart with "gold" written on it, the son had no heart at all, but gold was in its place. Thoroughly unscrupulous as to ways and means, and simply acting on the phrase "*quocunque modo rem*," he seemed to have neither conscience of evil, nor dread of danger. In two words, he was a "bold bad" man, divested equally of fear and feeling. The memoirs of his past life hitherto, without controversy very little edifying, may be guessed with quite sufficient accuracy for all characteristic purposes from the coarse, sensual, worldly, and iniquitous result now standing for his portraiture before us. We will waste on such a type of heartlessness as few words as possible: let his conduct show the man.

Just now, this worthy had risen into high favour with his father: we already know why; he had suddenly got rich on his own account, and for that very sufficient reason drew any additional sums he pleased on "the governor's." The trick or two, whereat Sir Thomas hinted, and which so wise a man would not have blabbed to fools, are worthy of record; not merely as illustrative of character, but (in one case at least, as we may find hereafter) for the sake of ulterior consequences.

John Dillaway's first exploit in the money-making line was a clever one. He managed to possess himself of a carrier-pigeon of the Antwerp breed, one among a flock kept for stock-jobbing purposes, by a certain great capitalist; and he contrived that this trained bird should wheel down among the merchants just at noon one fine day in the Royal Exchange. The billet under its wing contained certain cabalistic characters, and the plain-spoken intelligence, "*Louis Philippe est mort!*" In a minute after these most revolutionizing news, French funds, then at one hundred and twelve, were toppling down below ninety, and our prudent John was buying stock in all directions: nay, he even made some considerable bargains at eighty-seven. There was a complete panic in the market, and wretched was the man who possessed French fives. The afternoon's work so beautifully finished, John spent that night as true-born Britons are reported to have done before the battle of Hastings, rioting in drunken bliss, and panting for the morrow; and when the morrow came, and the Paris post with it, I must leave it to be understood with what complacency of triumph our enterprising stock-jobber hastened to sell again at one hundred and fourteen, pocketing, in the aggregate, a difference of several thousand pounds. It was a feat altogether to ravish a delighted father's heart, and no wonder that he counted John so great a comfort.

Trick number two had been at once even more lucrative and more dangerous. As a stock-broker, this enterprising Mr. Dillaway had peculiar opportunities of investigating closely certain records in the office for unclaimed dividends: he had an object in such close inspection, and discovered soon that one Mrs. Jane Mackenzie, of Ballyriggan, near Belfast, was a considerable proprietor, and had made no claim for years. Why should so much money lie idle? Was the woman dead? Probably not; for in that case executors or administrators would have touched it. Legatees and next of kin are little apt to forget such matters. Well, then, if this Mrs. Jane Mackenzie is alive, she must be a careless old fool, and we'll try if we can't kill her on paper, and so come in for spoils instead of kith and kin. "Shrewd Jack," as they called him in the Alley, chuckled within himself at so feasible a plot.

Accordingly, in an artful and well-concocted way, which we may readily conceive, but it were weary to detail, John Dillaway managed to forge a will of Jane Mackenzie aforesaid; and inducing some dressed-up "ladies" of his acquaintance to personate the weeping nieces of deceased (doubtless with no lack of Irish witnesses beside, competent to swear to any thing), he contrived to pass probate at Doctors' Commons, and get twelve thousand two hundred and forty-three pounds, bank annuities transferred, as per will, to the two ladies legatees. As the munificent *douceur* of a thousand pounds a-piece had (for the present) stopped the mouths of those supposititious nieces, who stipulated for not a farthing more nor less, clever John Dillaway a second time had the filial opportunity of rejoicing his father's heart by this wholesale money-making. Ten thousand pounds bank stock was manifestly another good day's work; and seeing our John had not appeared at all in the transaction, even as the ladies' stock-broker, things were made so safe, that the chuckling knight, when he heard all this (albeit he did tenderly fy, fy a little at first), was soon induced to think "my son Jack" the very best boy and the very cleverest dog in Christendom: at once a parent's pride and joy. Yes, Lady Dillaway—such a comfort! And the worshipful stationer apostrophized "rich Jack" with lips that seemed to smack of Creasy's Brighton sauce, whilst his calm spouse appeared to acquiesce in her amiable John's good fortune. The mystified mother little guessed that it was felony.

This good son's new-born wealth, besides the now liberal paternal largess (for his allowance grew larger in proportion as he might seem to need it less), of course availed to introduce him to some fashionable and estimable circles of society, whither it might not at all times be discreet in us to follow him; amongst other places, whether or not the Pandemonium in Jermyn street proved to him another gold mine, we have not yet heard; but John Dillaway was often there, the intimate friend of many splendid cavaliers who lived upon their industry, familiar with a whole rookery of blacklegs, patron of two or three pigeonable city sparks, and, on the whole, flusher of money than ever. His quiet mother, if she cared about her son at all, and probably she did care when her health permitted, might well be apprehensive on the score of that increasing wealth which made the father's joy.

However, with all his prosperity Mr. John as yet professed himself by no means satisfied; he was far too greedy of gain, and ever since he had come to man's estate, had amiably longed to be an only child. Not that he heeded a monopoly of the parental feelings and affections, nor even that he meditated murdering Maria—oh dear, no: rather too troublesome that, and quite unnecessary; it would be entirely sufficient if he could manage so to influence his father as to cut that superfluous sister Maria very short indeed in the matter of cash. With this generous and amiable view, he now for a course of sundry years had whispered, backbitten, and lied; he had, as occasion offered, taken mean advantages of Maria's outspeaking honesty, had set her warm-hearted sayings and charitable doings in the falsest lights, and had entirely "mildewed the ear" of her listening papa. The knight in truth listened unreluctantly; it was consolation, if not happiness to him, if he could make or find excuses for harshness to a being who would not worship wealth; it would be joy and pride, and an honour to his idol, if he should keep Maria pretty short of cash, and so make her own its preciousness; triumphant would he feel, as a merely-moneyed man, to see troublesome, obtrusive Heart, with all its win-ways, and whimperings, and incomprehensible spirituality, with its sermons and its prayers, bending before him "for a bit of bread." Yes, poor loving disinterested Maria ran every chance of being disinherited, from the false witness of her brother, simply because she gave him antecedent opportunities, by her honest likings and dislikings, by her bold rebuke of wrong and open zeal for right, by her scorn of hypocrisies as to what she did feel, or did not feel, and by the unpopular fact that she wore a heart, and refused to be the galley-slave of gold.

"Oh, ho, then!" said our crafty John, "we shall soon set this all right with our governor; thank you for the chance, Miss Maria. If father doesn't kick out this Clements, and cut you off with a shilling, he is not Sir Thomas, and I am not his son."

CHAPTER VII.

PROVIDENCE SEES FIT TO HELP VILLANY.

"Now that's what I call bones."

It was a currish image, suggestive of the choicest satisfaction. Let us try to discover what good news such an idiosyncrasy as that of John Dillaway would be pleased to designate as "bones." He had forthwith gone to his father's room as merry at the chance of ousting poor Maria, as the heartlessness of avarice could make him; and omnipresent authorship jotted down the dialogue that follows:

"So, governor, there's to be a wedding here, I find; when does it come off?"

"Ey? what? a wedding? whose?"

"Oh, ho! you don't know, ey? I guessed as much: what do you think now of our laughing, and crying, and kissing, and praying Miss Maria with—

"Not that beggar Clements? Ey? what? d——" &c., &c.

"Ha, ha, ha, ha! I thought so; why not, governor? Are you an old mole, that you haven't seen it these six weeks? Are you stone deaf, that all their pretty speeches have been wasted on you? All I can say is, that if Mr. and Mrs. Clements an't spliced, it's pretty well time they should be, and—

Sir Thomas Dillaway rattled out so terrible an oath about Maria's disinheritance if she ventured upon a marriage, that even John was staggered at such a dreadful curse; nevertheless, an instantaneous reflection soon caused that curse to be viewed metaphorically as a "bone;" and the generous brother cautiously proceeded—

"Why, governor, all this is very odd, must say; when I caught 'em kissing up there ten minutes ago, they were sharp enough to swear that you knew all about it, and that you were so 'very, very kind.'"

How is it possible, intelligent reader, to avoid perpetual allusion to an oath? We must not pare the lion's claws, and give bad men soft speeches: pr'ythee, supply an occasional interjection, and believe that in this place Sir Thomas swore most awfully; then, in a complete phrensy, he vowed that he "would turn Maria out of house and home this minute." This was another "bone," clearly.

But it was now becoming politic to calm him. Shrewd Jack was well aware that Maria would relinquish all, and sacrifice, not merely her own heart, but her Henry's too, rather than be guilty of filial disobedience. All this storming, hopeful as it looked, might still be premature, and do no substantial good; nay, if this wrath broke out too soon, Maria would at once give way, become more dutiful than ever, and his golden chance was gone. No: they were not married yet. Let the wedding somehow first take place, and then—! and then!—for now he knew which way the wind blew; so the scheming youth calmed his rising triumphs, and counselled his progenitor as follows:

"Well, governor, I never saw so green a blade in all my born days. Can't you see, now, that it's all cram this, just to put you in spirits, old boy, in case of such things happening? It was wicked too of me to tease you so—but I'm so jolly, governor; such luck in Jermyn street—I knew you'd like a joke served up with such rich sauce as this is, ey? only look!" It was half a hatful of bank notes raked up at the hazard table.

Sir Thomas's gray eyes darted swiftly at the spoil; often as he had warned and scolded Jack about the matter of Jermyn street (for Jack was bold enough never to conceal one of his little foibles), the father had now nothing to object; for, in his philosophy, the end justified the means. With most of this wise world, he looked upon success as in the nature of virtue, and failure as the surest sign of vice; accordingly his ire was diverted on the moment, and blazed in admiration of son Jack: and that estimable creature immediately determined it was wise to speak in tones of unwonted affection respecting his sister.

"Now, governor, I put it to you plump, isn't this hatful enough to *make a man beside himself, so as not to stick at a white lie or two?* Dear Maria there is no more going to become a Mrs. Clements than you are; she cut the fellow dead long ago: so mind, that's a tough old bird, you don't say one word to her about him; it would be just raking up the cinders again, you know, and you might be fool enough to raise a flame. No, governor, if it's any consolation to you, that pauper connection has been all at an end this month; not but what the beggar's got my mother's ear still, I fancy; but as to Maria, she detests him. So take my advice, and don't tease the poor girl about the business. Now, then, that this is all settled, and now that you're the merrier for that silly bit of storming at nothing, just listen: the wedding's my own! isn't Jack Dillaway a clever fellow now, to have caught a Right Honourable Ladyship, with a park in Yorkshire, a palace in Wales, and a mansion in Grosvenor square?"

At this *extempore* invention, the delighted parent rained so many blessings on his progeny, that John knew the tide was turned at once. Our ex-lord mayor had high ambitions, dating from the year of glory onwards; so that nothing could be more prudent or well-timed that this ideal aristocratic connection. Jack was a good fellow, a dear boy; and he added to his apparent amiabilities now by reiterating counsels of kindness and silence towards "poor dear sister Maria, whom he had been making the scape-goat all this time;" after which done, our stock-jobber feigned a pressing engagement with some fashionable friends, and left his father to ruminate upon his worth in lonely admiration.

Well; if that clever and gratuitous lie was not another "bone," I am at a loss to know what could be a "bone" to such a hound: therefore it appears that Dillaway had three of them at least to gladden him in solitude; and he went on revealing to wonder-stricken angels, and to us, the secrets of his crafty soul, as he thus soliloquized:

"Yes, marry the fools first, and then for spoils at leisure; it won't be easy though, she's so consummate filial, and he so bloated up with honour. They'll never wed, I'm clear, unless the governor's by to bless 'em; and as to managing that, and the cutting-adrift scheme too, one kills the other. How the deuce to do it? Eh—do I see a light?"

He did. A light lurid sulphurous gleam upon the midnight of his mind seemed to show the way before him, as wisp-fire in a marsh. He did see a light, and its character was this:

Quite aware of his mother's tranquil hopefulness, and that his kind good sister was ingenuous as the day, he soon apprehended the state of affairs; and, resolving to increase those misunderstandings on all sides, he quickly perceived that he could triumph in the keen Machiavellian policy, "*divide et impera.*" The plan became more obvious as he calmly thought it out. Evidently his first step must be to ingratiate himself with both Henry and Maria, as the sympathizing brother, a very easy task among such charitable fools: number two should be to persuade them, as the mother did, that Sir Thomas, generally a reserved unsocial man at home (and that in especial to Maria), was very nervous at the thought of losing his dear daughter, and (while he acquiesced in the common fate of parents and the usual way of the world) begged that his coming bereavement might be obtruded on him as little as possible—Mr. Clements always to avoid him, and Maria to hold her tongue: number three, to amuse his father all the while by the prospect of his own high alliance, so as effectually to hoodwink him from what was going on: and, number four, to send him up to Yorkshire a week hence (on some fool's errand to inquire after the imaginary countess's imaginary mortgages), leaving behind him an autograph epistle (which our John well knew how to write), recommending "that the ceremony be performed immediately and in his absence, to spare his feelings on the spot," mentioning "son John as his worthy substitute to give dear Maria away," and enclosing them at once his "blessing and a hundred pound note to help them on their honey-moon."

"John Dillaway, if craft be a virtue, thou art an archangel: but if Heaven's chief requirement is the heart, thou art very like a devil—very. If selfishness deserves the meed of praise, who more honourable than thou art? But if a heartless man can never reach to happiness, I know who will live to curse the hour of his birth, and is doomed to perish miserably.

It was a clever scheme, and had unscrupulous hands to work it. Mystified by quiet Lady Dillaway as our lovers had been from the first, entirely unsuspicious of all guile, and rejoicing in their brother's marvellous amiability, never surely were such happy days; always together while the knight was at his counting-house, they gladly acquiesced in his beautifully paternal nervousness; it was a delightful trait of character in the dear old man; and a very respectable proof that love is keen-eyed enough to believe what it wishes, but is stone-blind to any thing that might possibly counteract its hopes. Then again, the mother was a close ally; for having set her quiet heart upon the match, Lady Dillaway at once encouraged all John's symyathetic scheme, on the prudent principle of getting the young couple inextricably married first, and then obliging her lord to be reconciled afterwards to what he could not help. Sir Thomas himself, poor blinkered creature, was full of the most aristocratical and wealthy fancies, and only yearned to inspect the acres of his future honourable grand-children. He was, from these fanciful causes, unusually affable and indulgent to Maria; spoke so kindly always that she was all but dissolving thrice a-day; and, from his constant reveries about the countess, appeared perpetually to be brooding over dear Maria's soon approaching loss. Poor girl! more than once she had determined to give it all up, and make her father happy by serving him still in single blessedness: but then, how could she break dear Henry's heart, as well as her own? No, no: they should live very near to Finsbury square, and be in and out constantly, and papa should never miss her: how delightful was all this!

As for John himself, (our heartless model-man, strange contrast to Maria's perfect charity!) he chuckled hugely as his scheme now ripened fast. He had long been putting all things in train for the wedding to-morrow. Every body knew it except Sir Thomas who—what between Jack's prudent watchfulness, his habitual counting-house hours, his usually unsocial silence, and his now asserted wish for "not one word upon the subject,"—was at once kept in total ignorance of all; and yet, as ambassadorial John constantly gave out to Clements and Maria, in an amiable nervous state of natural acquiescence. Next day, then, the besotted father was about to be packed post for Yorkshire; the important letter, with its enclosed bank note, was already written and sealed, as like the governor's hand as possible; a license had been long ago provided, and the clergyman bespoke, by the brotherly officiousness of John; neither Henry Clements, who was too delicate, too unsuspecting for prudent business-papers, nor Maria, whose heart was never likely to have conceived the thought, had even once alluded to a settlement; Lady Dillaway was lying, as her wont was, on her habitual sofa, in tranquil ecstasy, at to-morrow morning's wedding: and Holy Providence, for wise purposes no doubt, had seen fit to aid a villain in his deep-laid treacherous designs.

The Wednesday dawned: Sir Thomas was to be off early, poor man, all agog for right honourable acres; and Maria could no longer restrain the expression of her glad and grateful feelings. Up she got by six, threw herself in her kind dear father's way; and though, to spare his feelings, she said not a word about the marriage, prayed him on her knees for a blessing. The startled parent, believing all this frantic show of feeling was sufficiently to be accounted for by his own long and no doubt dangerous journey, blessed her as devoutly as ever he could; and when the carriage drove away, left her in his study, overcome with joy, affection, and admiration of his fine heart, exquisite sensibilities, and generous feelings. Then, as a crowning-stone to all the bliss, if any lingering doubt existed in the mind of Clements, who had more than once expressed dislike at Sir Thomas's silent and unsatisfying sympathy —the letter—the letter, whereof kind brother John, secretly initiated, had some days forewarned them of its probability—that letter, which explained at once all a father's kind anxieties, and made up for all his cold reserve, was found on Sir Thomas's own table! How amiable, how beautifully sensitive, how liberal too! Lady Dillaway plumed herself in a whispering transport upon her just appreciation of the father's better feelings; a kinder heart manifestly never existed than her husband's, though he did take strange methods of proving it: the bridesmaids, two daughters of a friend and neighbour, privy to the coming mystery three days, approved highly of so unobtrusive an old gentleman: Maria was all pantings, blushings, weepings, and rejoicings; Henry Clements, handsome, pale, and agitated; perhaps, misgiving too, and a little displeased at the father's absence; however, Mr. John Dillaway gave away the bride with a most paternal air; and, just as Sir Thomas was changing horses at Huntingdon, our innocent lovers were indissolubly married.

CHAPTER VIII.

THE ROGUE'S TRIUMPH.

Never was there such a happy couple; nor a more auspicious day. Away they went, in deep delight, too joyful to be merry, in a holy transport of affection, and its dearest hope fulfilled. They seemed to be in love with all the world, for every thing around them wore a lustre of deliciousness: and when the smoking posters left them at Salt hill, and that well-matched husband and wife sat down to their first boiled fowl, it would probably be a bathos to allude to angelic bliss; but they nevertheless were, and knew they were, the happiest of mortals. If any thing could add to Henry's self-complacency at that moment, it was the recollection of his own truly disinterested conduct; for only yesterday he had transferred all his little property to that kind and brotherly fellow John Dillaway, in trust for Maria Clements, should any possible reverse of fortune affect her father's or his own prosperity. Yes; and John had been so wise as to make the two hundred a-year already a third more, by investing (as he said) what had been a few thousands of three per cents. in some capital "independent" bank shares of Australasia—safe as a mountain, and productive as a valley.

All this appeared very prosperous and pleasant: but we of the initiated into the secrets of character, may reasonably apprehend that Henry's little all would have been safer any where than in Dillaway's possession: and "possession," I am sorry to declare, is a word used advisedly; for Mr. John required a largish floating capital to enable him to go to the desperate lengths he did at hazard and *rouge-et-noir;* and I am afraid that if Mr. or Mrs. Clements were to receive any of those so-called Austral dividends, they would only have been taking three hundred pounds a-year out of their principal moneys in John's immaculate keeping.

Leaving then those wedded lovers to their honey-moon of joy, and shrewd Jack gloating not merely over the full success of his nefarious plan, but also over this unexpected acquisition of poor Clement's few thousands, let us return to Sir Thomas—or, to be quite accurate, let us return with him.

In high dudgeon, full of fire and fury, back rushed the knight, sore under the sense of having been made an April-fool of in July; for no one in the place whereto he went, had ever heard of a widow'd Countess of Lancing; and her ladyship's acres, if any where at all, were undoubtedly not in the North Riding. But clever son John, meeting his indignant father on the threshold, soon made all that right by a word.

"Well, if ever! why, stupid, I said Diddlington, not Darlington."

Into the accuracy of this distinction it is needless to inquire: and then the ingenuous youth went on to observe—

"But all's right as it is now; you may as well not have seen the property, and better, too, as things have turned out roughly, governor: the match is off, and you may well congratulate me. Such an escape—I just discovered it, and was barely in time: you hadn't been gone two hours when I found it all out, through a clever devil of a lawyer, who was hired by my father's son to look into incumbrances, and keep a sharp look-out for a mutual settlement; that old harridan of a ladyship is over head and ears in debt; and, it seems, I was to have paid all straight, or *i. e.* you, governor, ey? As to the Yorkshire acres, the old woman had but a life interest in the mere bit that wasn't deeply mortgaged—and not a very long life either, seeing she is seventy. So, bless your clever boy again, old governor, he's free."

The knight had nothing to object: Jack's ready lie had plenty of reasons in it: and so he blessed his clever boy again.

"But I say, governor, I rather think that you've astonished us all: what on earth made you turn so soft of a sudden, and write that letter?"

"What letter? ey? what?"—Sir Thomas might well inquire.

"That's a good joke, governor—you keep it up to the last, I see; what a close old file it is! What letter? why, the letter you wrote to Maria and her lord, telling them to marry."

"Marry? ey? what, Maria? what—what is it all?" The poor old man was thoroughly bewildered.

"Well done, governor—bravo! you can carry it off as cleverly as if you were an actor; do you mean to say now you didn't leave a letter behind you here upon your table, bidding Maria marry in your absence to spare your paternal feelings (kind old boy, it is, too!) and enclosing them one hundred pounds for the honey-moon?"

The mystified father made some inarticulate expression of ignorant amazement, and our stock-jobber went on:

"So of course they're married and off—Mr. and Mrs. Cle———"

A whirlwind of disastrous imprecations cut all short; and then in a voice choked with passion he gasped out—

"But—but are they married—are they married? how do you know it? can't we catch 'em first, ey? what!"

"How do I know it? that's a good un now, father, when I had it under your hand to give the girl away myself instead of you. Do you mean to say you didn't write that letter?"

"Boy, I tell you, I've written nothing—I know nothing; you speak in riddles."

"Well then, governor, if I do, I'll to guess 'em: I begin to see how it was all brought about—but they did it cleverly too, and were quite too many for me. Only listen: that fellow Clements, ay, and Miss Maria too (artful minx, I know her), must have forged a letter as if from you to get poor fools, me and my mother, to see 'em spliced, while you were tooling to Yorkshire."

"Impossible—ey? what? I'll—I'll—I'll—"

"Now, governor, don't stand there doing nothing but denying all I say; only you go yourself, and ask my mother if she didn't see the letter—if they didn't marry upon it, and if that precious sister of mine doesn't richly deserve every thing she 'll some day get from her affectionate, her excellent, her ill-used father?"

Iago's self, or his master, smooth-tongued Belial, could not have managed matters better.

The incredulous knight, scarcely able to discover how far it might not still be all a joke, especially after his Yorkshire expedition, rushed up to Lady Dillaway; on her usual sofa, quietly knitting, and thinking of her Maria's second day of happiness.

"So, ma'am—ey? what? is it true? are they married? is it true? married—ey? what?"

"Certainly, Thomas, they were only too glad, and I will add, so was I, to get your kind—"

"Mine? I give leave? ey? what? Madam, we 're cheated, fooled—I never wrote any letter."

"Most astonishing; I saw it myself, Thomas, your own hand; and our dear John too."

"Ay, ay—he sees through it all, and so do I now—ey? what? that precious pair of rogues forged it! Now, ma'am, what don't they deserve, I should like to know?"

It was quite a blow, and a very hard one, to the poor tranquil mother. Could her dear Maria really have been so base, and that noble-looking Henry too? how dreadfully deceived in them, if this proved true! And how could she think it false? A letter contrived to expedite their marriage in the father's casual absence, which no one could have thought of writing but Sir Thomas himself, or the impatient lovers. So poor Lady Dillaway could only fall a-crying very miserably; whereupon her husband more than half suspected her of being an accomplice in the despicable plot.

"Now then, ma'am, I 'm determined: as they are married, the thing 's at an end; we can't untie that knot—but, once tied, I 've done with the girl; they may starve, for any help they 'll get of me: and as for you, mum, give 'em money at your peril; stay, to make sure of it, Lady Dillaway, I shall stint you to whatever you choose to ask me for out of my own pocket; never draw another cheque on Jones's, do you hear? ey? what? for your cheques shall not be honoured, ma'am. And now, from this hour, you and I have only one child, John.

"Oh, Thomas—Thomas! be merciful to poor Maria! indeed, she was deceived; she believed it all—poor Maria!"

"Ma'am. never mention that woman again—ey? what? deceived?

Yes, she deceived you and me, and John, and all. Wicked wretch! and all to marry a beggar! Well, ma'am, there 's one comfort left; the fellow married her for money, and he 's caught in his own trap; never a penny of mine shall either of them see. Henceforth, Lady Dillaway, we have no daughter; dear John is the only child left us for old age."

In spite of himself, of wrath, and disappointment, the father spoke in a moved and broken manner; and his weeping wife attempted to explain, console, and soothe him; but all in vain—he was inexorable and inveterate against those mean deceivers. To say truth, the poor mother was staggered too, especially when her managing son set all the matter in what he stated to be the right light; for he had, the whole business through, whispered so separately to each, and had seemed to say so little openly (making his mother believe that his sister told him of the coming letter, and a choice variety of other embellishments), that he was now looked upon as the very martyr to roguish plotting, in having been induced to give away his sister. Excellent, mistaken John!

And forthwith John became installed sole heir, proving the most dutiful of sons: how glibly would he tell them any sort of welcome news, original or selected; how many anecdotes could he invent to prove his own merits and certain other folks' deficiencies; how amiably would he fetch and carry slippers and smelling-bottles, and write notes, and read newspapers, and make himself every thing by turns (he devoutly hoped it would be nothing long) to his poor dear parents, as became an only child! It was quite affecting—and both father and mother, softened in spite of themselves at the loss of that Maria, often would talk over the new-found virtues of their most exemplary son. His character came out now with five-fold lustre when contrasted with his former usual ruggedness: no widow ever had a one sick child more tender, more considerate, more dutiful, than rude Jack Dillaway.

He gained his end; saw the new will signed; earwigged the lawyer; and kept a copy of it.

CHAPTER IX.

FALSE-WITNESS KILLS A MOTHER, AND WOULD WILLINGLY STARVE A SISTER.

Day by day, letters, doubtless full of happiness and Heart, were left by the promiscuous and undiscerning postman at the house in Finsbury square, from our excellent calumniated couple; but, seeing that there were always two sieves waiting ready to sift it before it came to Lady Dillaway's turn—to wit, John in the hall, and Sir Thomas in his study, it came to pass that every letter with those malefactors' hand and seal on it got burnt instanter, and unopened.

How many troubles might mankind be spared if they would only stop to hear each other's explanations! How many ailments, both of body and soul, if explanations only came more frequently and freely! Melancholy from that dreadful doubt, and all these cold delays, viewing her daughter as a criminal, the husband as a swindler, and all this long course of silence as very, very heartless and seemingly conclusive of their guilt, the poor mother sickened fast upon her couch: she had for years always been an invalid, wan and wo-begone, living upon ether, gum, and chicken-broth; but her white skin now grew whiter, her faint voice fainter, the energies of life in her debilitated frame weaker than ever; it was no mere hypochondria, or other fanciful malady: her calm heart seemed to be dying down within her, as a plant that has earth-grubs gnawing at its root—she grew very ill. Days, weeks of silence—her heart was sick with hope deferred. How could Maria, with all her seeming warmth, treat her with such utter negligence? But now the honey-moon was coming to an end: they must call and see her some day again, surely; how strangely unkind not to answer those motherly and anxious letters, sent to their first known stage, Salt hill, and thereafter to be forwarded.

O, cold continued crime! Bad man, bad man, thy mother's own hand-writing shall plead against thee at the last dread day. For those coveted letters of affection, often sent on both those loving parts, had been regularly and ruthlessly intercepted, opened, mocked, and burnt! How could the man have stood case-proof against those letters—his mother's anxious outbursts of affection towards a lost, an innocent, a calumniated sister? For selfishness had dried up in that hard and wily man all the milk of human kindness.

And our loving pair, upon their travels, were as much hurt and surprised at this long silence as poor Lady Dillaway herself: it was most mysterious, inexplicable. The only letter they had received ever since they had left home was one—only one, from John, which had frightened them exceedingly. Some practical joker (the bridesmaid's brother was suspected), by way of giving Maria a present on her approaching wedding, as it would seem, had cleverly imitated her father's hand-writing, and—that letter was a forgery! to every body's great amazement. Nobody could, according to his own account, be kinder than John, who had done more than mortal things to appease his father; but the old man remained implacable. It was a meanly-contrived clandestine match, he said; and he never intended to set eyes on them again! As for John, he in that letter had strongly counselled them to keep away, and trust to him for bringing his father round. In the midst of their terrible dilemma, kind brother John seemed as an angel sent by Heaven to assist them.

Dear children of affection and calamity! how innocently did they walk into the snare; and how closely doth the wicked man draw his toils around them. Who can accuse them of any wrong (the hopefulness of love considered) in point either of honour or duty? And shall they not be righted at the last? It may be so—it shall be so: but Holy Providence hath purposes of good in plunging those twin wedded hearts deep beneath the billows of earthly destitution. The wicked must prosper for a while, in this as in a million other cases, and the good for their season struggle with adversity; that the one may be destroyed for ever, and the others may add to this world's wealth the incalculable riches of another.

They had spent the few first weeks of marriage among the pleasant lakes and hills of Westmoreland and Cumberland, wandering together, in delightful interchange of thought, from glen to glen, from tairn to tairn, all about Ambleside, Helvellyn, and Lodore, Ullswater, Saddleback, and Schiddaw. Maria's ever-flickering smile seemed to throw a sun-beam over the darkest moor, even in those darkest hours of doubt, heart-sickening anxiety, and grief at the neglect which they experienced; while Henry's well-informed good sense not only availed to cheer the sad Maria, but made every rock a point of interest, and showed every little flower a miracle of wisdom. There were hundreds of extemporaneous "lover's seats," where they had "rested, to be thankful" for the past, joyful for the present, and hopeful for the future; and every ramble that they took might deservedly take the name, style, and title of a "lover's walk!" Happy times—happy times! but still there might be happier; yes, and happiest, too, they seemed to whisper, if ever they should have a merry little nursery of prattling boys and girls! But I am not so entirely in the confidence of those young folks as to be certain about what they seemed to whisper: in that pretty prattling sentence were they not getting a little beyond the honey-moon? Yes—yes, young Hymen is too full of new-found pleasure to heed those holier joys of calm old marriage; for wedded love is as a coil of line, lengthening with the lapse of years, fitted and intended, day after day, to be continually sounding a lower and a lower deep in the ocean of happiness.

Returned to town, it was the immediate care of our fond, confused, and unfortunate young couple to call at the old house in Finsbury square; where, to their great dismay and misery, they encountered a formal standing order for their non-admission. The domestics were new, had been strictly warned against the name of Clements, and, in effect, were creatures of the worthy John. It was a deplorable business; they did not know what to think, nor how to act. Letters left at the door, couched in whatever terms of humility, kindliness, and just excuse, were equally unavailing; for the Cerberus there was too well sopped by pleasant brother John ever to deliver them to any one but him. It was entirely hopeless—extraordinary—a most wretched state of things. What were they to do? The only practicable mode of getting at Sir Thomas, and, therefore, at some explanation of these mysteries, was obviously to watch for him, and meet him in the street. As for Lady Dillaway, she was very ill, and kept her chamber, which was as resolutely guarded from incursion or excursion as Danae's herself—yea, more so, for gold was added to her guards: Sir Thomas, going to and from his counting-house, appeared to be the only weak point in the enemy's fortifications.

Poor old man! he was, or thought he was, harder, colder, more inveterate than ever: and his duteous son John rarely let him venture out alone, for fear of some such meeting, casual or intended. Accordingly, one day when the Clements and the Dillaways mutually spied each other afar off, and a junction seemed inevitable, John's promptitude bade his father (generously as it looked, for paternal peace of mind's sake) return a few paces, get into a cab, and so slip home, the while he valiantly stepped forward to meet the enemy.

"Mr. Clements! my father (I grieve to say) will hear no reason, nor any excuse whatever; he totally refuses to see you or Mrs. Clements."

"O, dearest John! what have I done—what has Henry done, that papa, and you, and dear mamma, should all be so unkind to us?"

"You have married, Mrs. Clements, contrary to your father's wish and knowledge: and he has cast you off—I must say—deservedly."

"Brother, brother! you know I was deceived, and Henry too. This is cruel, most cruel: let me see my beloved father but one moment!"

"His commands are to the contrary, madam; and I at least obey them. Henceforth you are a stranger to us all."

The poor broken-hearted girl fell into her husband's arms, stone-white: but her hard brother, making no account whatever of all that show of feeling, only took the trouble quietly to address Henry Clements. "Misfortunes never come single, they say; it is no fault of mine if the proverb hits Mr. Henry Clements. I am sorry to have to tell you, sir, that the Austral Independent bank has stopped payment, and is not expected to refund to its depositors or shareholders one penny in the pound."

"Impossible, Mr. Dillaway! You answered for its stability yourself: and the proposition came originally from you. I hope surely, surely, you may have been misinformed of these bad news."

"It is true, sir—too true for you: the wisest man on 'change is often out of reckoning. I have nothing now of yours in my hands, sir: you are aware that no writings passed between us."

"Great Heaven! be just and merciful! Are we, then, to be utterly ruined?"

"Really, sir, you know your own affairs better than I can.—Your servant, Mr. Clements."

O, hard and wicked heart!—what will not such a miscreant do for money? Nothing, I am clear, but the cowardly fear of discovery prevents John Dillaway from becoming a positive parricide by very arsenic or razor, so as to grasp his cheated father's will and wealth. And this assertion will appear not in the least uncharitable, when the reader is in this place reminded that Henry Clements's own little property had never been Australized at all, but was still safe and snug in the coffers of crafty John. Jermyn street—or the sharpers congregated there—had drained him very considerably; all his own ill-got gains had been gradually raked away by the croupier at the gaming-table; and unsuspecting Henry's little trust-fund was to be the next bank on which the brother played.

Poor Henry and Maria! What will they do? where will they go? how will they live? Hard questions all, not to be answered in a hurry.

We shall see. There was one comfort, though, amidst all their misery;—they did not find the adage a true one, which alludes to poverty coming in at the door, and love flying out of the window; for they never loved each other more deeply—more devotedly—than when daily bread was growing a scarcity, and daily life almost a burden. But we are anticipating.

And how fared the parents all this while? was the erring daughter entirely forgotten? No, no. Son John, indeed, took good care to hinder any amicable feelings of relapse to intrude upon his father's resolution. But the old man was not easy, nevertheless; often thought of poor Maria; and could not clearly make out who had forged the letter. Had it not been for that wicked brother John, a meeting—an explanation—a reconciliation—would undoubtedly have taken place: but he was shrewd enough to keep them asunder, and did not take much to heart his father's altered spirits and breaking state of health: his will and wealth were seemingly all the nearer.

And what of that poor stricken mother? Wasted to a shadow, feverish and weak, she lay for weeks, counting the dreary hours, till she heard of dear, though unnatural, Maria. Oh! the heartless caitiff, John! will he thus watch his mother die by inches, when one true word from his lips could restore her to tranquillity and health? Yes, he would—he did—the wretch! She gradually pined—waned—wasted; the candle of her life burnt down into the hollow socket—glimmering awhile—flared and reeled, and then—one night, quietly and suddenly—went out! She entered on the world of spirits, where all secrets show revealed; and there she read, almost before she died—whilst yet the black curtain of eternity was gradually rising to receive her—the innocence of good Maria, and the deep-stained villany of John. Her last words—uttered supernaturally from her quiescence, with the fervour of a visionary whose ken is more than mortal—were "Look, look, Thomas!—beware of John. O poor, poor innocent outcast!—O rich, rich heart of love—Maria! my Mari—a—!"

CHAPTER X.

HOW TO HELP ONE'S SELF.

WHERE then did they live, and how—that noble and calumniated couple? They had done no wrong, nor even, as it seems to us, the semblance of wrong, unless it be by having acquiesced in the foolishness of secresy, and thus aided the contrivance of false witness; for aught else, their only social error had been lack of business caution among business men. Feeling generously themselves, they gave others credit for the like good feeling; acting upon honourable impulse, they believed that other men would act so too. Heart was the hindrance in their way;—too much sensitiveness towards all about them; too swift a surrender of the judgment to the affections: too imprudent a reliance upon other men of the world; though, when they trusted to a father's love, and a brother's honesty, prudence herself might have almost been dispensed with. Machinations of the wicked and the shrewd hemmed them in to their un-doing: and really, they, children more or less of affluent homes, born and bred in plenty, who had moved all their lives long in circles of comparative wealth and wastefulness, now seemed likely to come to the galling want of necessary sustenance. Was it not to teach them deeper feeling for the poor, if ever God again should give them riches? Was it not, by poverty, to try those hearts which had passed so blamelessly through all the ordeals and temptations of wealth, in order that they worthily might wear the double crown given only to such as remain unhardened by prosperity, unembittered by adversity? Was it not to discipline our warm Maria's love, and to chasten her Henry's very gentlemanly pride into the due Christian proportions—self-respect with self-humiliation? Was it not, chiefest and best, to school their hearts for heaven, and, by feeding them on miseries and wrongs a little while, to fix their affections on things above rather than on things of this world? Yes: Providence has many ends in view, and they all tend consistently to one great focus—the ultimate advantage of the good by means of the confusion of the wicked.

Meanwhile came trouble on apace. Henry Clements justly felt aggrieved, insulted; and the sentiment of pride, improper only from excess, determined him to make no more advances: all that man could do, that is, which a gentleman ought to do, he had done; but letters and visits proved equally unavailing. He had come to the resolution that he would make no more efforts himself, nor scarcely let Maria make any. As for her, poor soul! she was now in grievous tribulation, with sad, sufficient reason for it too; seeing that, in addition to her father's anger, still protracted—in addition to that vile forgery imputed to her craft, and whereof she had been made the guilty victim—in addition to their own soon pressing money-wants, and that heartless fraud of John's against her husband's little all (though she counted of it only as a luckless speculation)—she had just become acquainted, through the public prints, of her dear good mother's death, even before she had heard of any illness. What bitter pangs were there for her, poor child! That she should have lost that mother just then, without forgiveness, without blessing—whilst all was unexplained, and their whole conduct of affections without guile, wore the hideous mask of base, undutiful contrivance! Cheer up, Maria; cheer up! only in this bad world can innocence be sullied with a doubt: cheer up! the spirit of that mother whom you loved on earth knows it well already; learned it while yet she was leaving the body of her death: cheer up! she is still near you both—dear children of affliction and affection! and God has commissioned her for good to be your ministering angel.

With reference to means of living, they appeared limited at once to a little ready money, and a few personal chattels and trinkets; without so much as one pound of capital to back the young house-keepers, or a shilling's-worth of interest or dividend or earnings coming in for weekly bills. Clements had been utterly confounded in all his economical arrangements by that sudden bitter breach of trust; and, albeit (as we have hinted), his aim in marriage was not money; still, without much of worldly calculation, he might prudently have looked for some provision on Maria's part at least equal to his own: in fact, the fond young couple had reasonably set their hearts upon that golden mean—four hundred a-year to begin with. Now, however, by two fell swoops—brother John's dishonesty and Sir Thomas's resolve of disinheritance—all this rational and moderate expectation had been dashed to atoms; and the cottage of contented competence appeared but as a castle in the clouds—a mere airy matter of undiluted moonshine. Thus, when that happiest of honeymoons had dwindled down the hundred-pound bank-note (shrewd John's well-expended bait) to the fractional part of a ten, and our newly-married pair came to put together their united resources, wherewithal to travel through the world, they could muster but very little:—considering, too, the future, and the promise of an early increase to provide for, forty-seven pounds was not quite a fortune; and a few articles of jewellery did not much increase it.

We need not imagine that Henry calmly acquiesced without a struggle in the roguish fraud which had impoverished him; but, notwithstanding all his best endeavours, he found, to his dismay, that the case was irremediable: the transfer-books, indeed, were evidence; and equity would give credit for the trust: but that the "Independent bank" had failed was a simple fact; and so long as John stood ready to swear he had invested in it, there was an end to the business. Be sure, shrewd Jack was not likely to leave any thing dubious or unsatisfactory in the affair. Austral papers were easily got at now, cheap as whitey-brown; and for any help the law could give him, poor Henry Clements might as well engage the wind-raising services of a Lapland witch.

He must put his shoulder to the wheel without delay; manifestly, his profession of the law, however unlucrative till now, must be the mighty lever that should raise him quickly to the summit of opulence and fame: and he vigorously set to work, as the briefless are forced to do, inditing a new law-book, which should lift him high in honour with those magnates on the bench; being, as he was, a court-counsel, not a chamber one, an eloquent pleader too (if the world would only give him a hearing), he unluckily took for his thesis the questionable '*Doctrine of Defence;*' combating magnanimously on the loftiest moral grounds all manner of received opinions, time-honoured fictions, legitimated quibbles, and other things which (as he was pleased to put it) "render the majesty of the law ridiculous to the ears of common sense, and iniquitous in the sight of Christian judgment." Rash youth! forensic Quixote! better had you plodded on, without this extra industry and skill, in the hopeless idleness and solitude of your Temple garret—better had you burnt your wig and gown outright, with all the airy briefs to come that fluttered round them, than have owned yourself the author of that heretical piece of moral mawkishness—'*The Doctrine of Defence*, by Henry Clements.'

He had with difficulty found a publisher—a chilling incident enough in itself, considering an author's feelings for his book-child; and when found, the scarcely satisfactory arrangement was insisted on, of mutual participation in profit and loss: in other parlance, the bookseller pocketing the first, and the author unpocketing the second. Thus it came to pass, that after three months' toil and enormous collation of cases—after extravagant indulgence of the most ardent hopes—glory, good, and gold, consequent instantaneously on this happy publication—after reasonably expecting that judges would quote it in their ermine, and sergeants consult it in their silk—that London would be startled by the event from the humdrum of its ordinary routine—and the wondering world applaud the name of Henry Clements—O, heart-sickening reality! what was the result of his exertions?

"So, that puppy Clements has taken upon himself to put us all to school about whom we may defend, and how, I see——Hang the fellow's impudence!" grunted a fat Old Bailey counsel to his peers, well aware that the luckless author sat nervously within ear-shot.

"I know whose junior that modest swain shall never be;" simpered Sergeant Tiffin.

"The fellow's done for himself," was the simultaneous verdict of a well-wigged band of brothers. And what else they might have added in their charity poor Clements never knew, for he crept away to his garret, stricken with disappointment. There he must encounter other trials of the heart: two or three reviews and newspapers lay upon his table, just sent in by the bookseller, as per order; for they contained, in spirit-stirring print, notices of '*Clements on Defence.*' Unluckily for his present peace of mind, poor fellow, the periodicals in question were none of the humaner sort; no kindly encouraging '*Literary Register*,' no soft-spoken '*Courtier*,' no patient '*Investigator*,' no generously-indulgent '*Critical Gazette*:' these more amiable journals would be slower in the field—some six weeks hence, perhaps, creeping on with philanthropic sloth: but fiercer prints, which dart hebdomadal wrath at every trembling seeker of their parsimonious praise, had whipt up their malice to deliver the first swift blow against our hapless neophyte in print. Thus, when, with nervous preboding, Henry took up the '*Watchman*,' in eager hope for favour to his poor dear book, he turned quite sick at heart to find the lying verdict run as follows, though the small type in which it spake was a comfort too:

"A careless compilation of insignificant cases, clumsily thrown together, and calculated to set its author high indeed upon the rolls of fame; proving to the world that a Mr. Henry Clements can reason very feebly; that his premises are habitually false; and that presumptuous preaching is the natural accompaniment of extreme ignorance."

By all that worries man, but this was too bad: "careless?"—every word had been a care to him: "clumsy?"—in composition it was Addison's own self: "feeble?"—if he was good for any thing, he was good for logic: "false?"—not one premise but stood on adamant, not one conclusion but it was fixed as fate: "presumptuous?"—it was bold and masculine, certainly, but humble too; here and there almost deferential: "ignorant?"—ye powers that live in looks, testify by thousands how Clements had been studying!—And yet this most lying sentence, a congeries or sorites of untruths, hastily penned by some dyspeptic scribe, who perhaps had barely dipped into the book, was at the moment circulating in every library of the kingdom, proclaiming our poor barrister a fool!

O, thou watchful scribe, forbear! for it is cowardly—they cannot smite again: forbear! for it is cruel—the hearts of wife and mother and lover ache upon your idle words: forbear! it is unreasonable—for often-times a word would prove that Rhadamanthus' self is wrong: forbear, calumnious scribe! and heed the harms you do, when you rob some poor struggler of his character for sense, and make the bread of the hungry to fail.

'*The Corinthian*,' another snarling watch-dog in the courts of the temple of Fame, followed instinctively the same injurious wake: it was a leisurely sarcastic anatomization, quite enough to blight any young candidate's prospects, supposing that mankind respected such a verdict; if not to make him cut his throat, granting that the victim should be sensitive as Keats. The generous review in question may be judged of by its first line and last sentence; as Hercules from his advancing foot, or Cuvier's Megatherium from the relics of its great toe. Thus it commenced:

"When a disappointed man, intolerant of fortune," &c., &c., and it wound up many stinging observations with this grateful climax following:

"We trust we have now said enough to prove that if a man will be bold enough to 'depreciate censure,'—will attack what he is pleased to consider abuses, however countenanced by high authority—and will obtrude his literary eloquence into our solemn courts of law, he deserves —what does he not deserve?—to be addressed henceforth by a name suggestive at once of ignorance, presumption, and conceit, as Mr. Henry Clements."

Now, will it be believed that a trivial error of the press mainly conduced to occasion this hostility? Our poor author had been weak enough to "deprecate censure" in his penny-wise humility, and the printer had negatived his meaning as above: "*hinc illæ lachrymæ*." Oh, but how the ragged tooth of calumny gnawed his very heart!

'*The Legal Recorder*' was another of those early unfavourables; being as a matter of course adverse too, and not very disinterestedly either: for it played the exalted part of pet puffer to a rival publisher, who wanted no other reason for condemning this book of Mr. Clements than that it came from the legal officina of an opponent in his trade. There was another paper or two, but Clements felt so utterly disheartened that he did not dare to look at them. I wish he had; they would have comforted him, pouring balm upon his wounded pride by their kind and cordial praises: but ill-luck ruled the hour, so he burnt them forthwith, and lost much literary comforting.

To sauce up all this pleasantry with a smack of concreted pleasure itself, the last and only remaining document upon the table was a civil note from Mr. Wormwood, publisher and bookseller, enclosing the following items with his compliments:

To 500 copies '*Doctrine of Defence,*' . .	£124 3
To advertising ditto, ...	25 0
To 10 per cent. on sales, ...	&c.
Supplied to author, 12 copies, ...	&c.
Given to periodicals for review, 15 copies, . .	&c.

Against all which was the solitary offset of "three copies sold;" leaving as our Henry's *share* of now certain loss a matter of eighty pounds: which, between ourselves, was only a very little more than the whole cost of that untoward publication. Mr. Wormwood hoped to hear from Mr. Clements at his earliest convenience, as a certain sum was to be made up on a certain day, and the book-trade never had been at a lower ebb, and prompt payment would be esteemed a great accommodation, and—all that stereotyped sort of thing.

Poor Clements—reviled author, ruined lawyer, almost reckless wight—here was an extinguisher indeed to the morning's brilliant hopes! What an overwhelming debt to that ill-used couple in their altered circumstances! How entirely by his own strong effort had he swamped his legal expectations! Just as a man who cannot swim splashes himself into certain suffocation; whereas, if he would but lie quite still, he was certain to have floated on as safe as cork.

Well: to cut a long story short, our unlucky author found that he must pay, and pay forthwith, or incur a lawyer's bill for his debt to Mr. Wormwood: so he gave up his Temple garret, sold his books, nicknacks, and superfluous habiliments, added to the proceeds their forty pounds of capital, and a neck-chain of Maria's; and, at tremendous sacrifices, found himself once more out of danger, because out of debt. But it was a bad prospect truly for the future—ay, and for the present too; a few pounds left would soon be gone—and then dear Maria's confinement was approaching, and a hundred wants and needs, little and great: accordingly, they made all haste to get rid of their suburban dwelling in the City Road, collected their few valuables remaining, and retreated with all economical speed to a humble lodging in a cheap back street at Islington.

That little parlor was a palace of love: in the midst of her deep sorrow, sweet Maria never failed of her amiable charities—nay, she was even cheerful, hopeful—happy, and rendering happy: a thousand times a day had Henry cause to bless his "wedded angel." And, showing his love by more than words, he resolutely set about another literary enterprise, anonymous this time for very fear's sake; but Providence saw fit to bless his efforts with success. He wrote a tragedy, a clever and a good one too; though '*The Watchman*' did sneer about "modern Shakspeares," and '*The Corinthian*,' pouncing on some trifling fault, pounded it with would-be giant force: nevertheless, for it was a famous English theme, he luckily got them to accept it at the Haymarket, and '*Boadicea*' drew full houses; so the author had his due ninth night, and pocketed, instead of fame (for he grimly kept his secret) enough to enable him to print his tragedy for private satisfaction; and that piece of vanity accomplished, he still found himself seven pounds before-hand with the world.

CHAPTER XI.

FRAUD CUTS HIS FINGERS WITH HIS OWN EDGED TOOLS.

UNPLEASANT as it is to feel obliged to be the usher of ill company, I must now introduce to the fastidious public a brace of characters any thing but reputable. It were possible indeed to slur them over with a word; but I have deeper ends in view for a glance so superficial: we may learn a lesson in charity, we may gain some schooling of the heart, even from those "ladies-legatees."

Do you remember them, the supposititious nieces, aiders and abetters in our stock-jobber's forged will? Two flashy, showy women, *not* of easy virtue, but of none at all—special intimates of John Dillaway, and the genus of his like, and habitual frequenters of divers choice and pleasant places of resort.

The reason of their introduction here is two-fold: first, they have to play a part in our tale—a part of righteous retribution; and, secondly, they have to instruct us incidentally in this lesson of true morals and human charity—dread, denounce, and hate the sin, but feel a just compassion for the sinner. Let us take the latter object first, and bear with the brief epitome of facts which have blighted those unfortunates to what they are.

Look at these two women, impudent brawlers, foul with vice: can there be any excuses made for them, considered as distinct from their condition? God knoweth: listen to their histories; and fear not that thy virtuous glance will be harmed or misdirected, or a minute of thy precious time ill-spent.

Anna Bates and Julia Manners (their latest *noms de guerre* will serve all nominative purposes as well as any other) had arrived at the same lowest level of female degradation by very different downward roads. Anna's father had been a country curate, unfortunate through life, because utterly imprudent, and neither too wise a man nor too good a one, or depend upon it his orphan could not have come to this: "Never saw I the righteous forsaken, nor his seed begging their bread." But the father died carelessly as he had lived—in debt, with all his little affairs at sixes and sevens; and his widow with her budding daughter, saving almost nothing from the wreck, set up for milliners at Hull. Then did the mother pique herself upon playing her cards cleverly; for gallant Captain Croker was quite smitten with the girl. Poor child —she loved, listened, and was lost; a more systematic traitor of affection never breathed than that fine man; so she left by night her soft intriguing broken-spirited mother, followed her Lothario from barrack to barrack, and at last—he flung her away! Who can wonder at the reckless and dissolute result? Whom had she to care for her—whom had she to love? She must live thus, or starve. Without credit, character, or hope, or help, the friendless unprotected wretch was thrown upon the town. When the last accounts are opened, oblivious General Croker will find an ell-long score of crimes laid to his charge, whereof he little reckons in his sear and yellow leaf. The trusting victim of seduction has a legion of excuses for the wretched one she is.

Again; for another case whereon the better-favoured heart may ruminate in charity. Miss Julia Manners had a totally different experience; but man can little judge how mainly the iron hand of circumstance confined that life-long sinner to the ways and works of guilt. In the nervous language of the Bible—(hear it, men and women, without shrinking from the words)—that poor girl was "the seed of the adulterer and the whore:" born in a brothel, amongst outcasts from a better mass of life—brought up from the very cradle amid sounds and scenes of utter vice (whereof we dare not think or speak one moment of the many years she dwelt continuously among them)—educated solely as a profligate, and ignorant alike of sin, righteousness, and a judgment to come—had she then a chance of good, or one hopeful thought of being better than she was? The water of holy baptism never bedewed that brow; the voice of motherly counsel never touched those ears; her eyes were unskilled to read the records of wisdom; her feet untutored to follow after holiness; her heart unconscious of those evils which she never knew condemned; her soul—she never heard or thought of one! Oh, ye well-born, well-bred, ye kindly, carefully, prayerfully instructed daughters of innocence and purity, pause, pause, ere your charity condemns: hate the sin, but love the sinner: think it out further, for yourselves, in all those details which I have not time to touch, skill to describe, nor courage to encounter; think out as kindly as ye may this episode of just indulgence; there is wisdom in this lesson of benevolence, and after-sweetness too, though the earliest taste of it be bitter; think it out; be humbler of your virtue, scarcely competent to err; be more grateful to that Providence which hath filled your lot with good; and be gentler-hearted, more generous-handed unto those whose daily life is—all temptation.

Now, these two ladies (who extenuates their guilt, caviller? who breathes one iota of excuse for their wicked manner of life? who does not utterly denounce the foul and flagrant sin, whilst he leaves to a secret-searching God the judgment of the sinner?)—these two ladies, I say, had of late become very sore plagues to Mr. John Dillaway. They had flared out their hush-money like duchesses, till the whole town rang about their equipage and style; and now, that all was spent, they pestered our stock-jobber for more. They came at an unlucky season, a season of "ill luck!" such a miraculous run of it, as nothing could explain to any rational mind but loaded dice, packed cards, contrivance and conspiracy. Nevertheless, our worthy John went on staking, and betting, and playing, resolute to break the bank, until it was no wonder at all to any but his own shrewd genius, that he found himself one feverish morning well nigh penniless. At such a moment then, called our ladies-legatees, clamorous for hush-money.

As a matter most imperatively of course, not a farthing more should be forthcoming, and many oaths avouched that stern determination. They ought to be ashamed of themselves, after such an enormous bribe to each—as if shame of any kind had part or lot in those feminine accomplices: it was a sanguine thought of Mr. John Dillaway. But the ladies were not ashamed, nor silenced, nor any thing like satisfied. So, having thoroughly fatigued themselves with out-swearing and out-threatening our sneerful stock-jobber, they resolved upon exposing him, come what might. For their own guilty part in that transaction of Mrs. Jane Mackenzie's pseudo-will, good sooth, the wretched women had no characters to lose, nor scarcely aught else on which one could set a value. Danger and the trial would be an excitement to their pallid spirits, possible transportation even seemed a ray of hope, since any thing was better than the town; and in their sinful recklessness, liberty or life itself was little higher looked on than a dice's stake. Moreover, as to all manner of personal pains and penalties, there was every chance of getting off scot-free, provided they lost no time, went not one before the other, but doubly turned queen's evidence at once against their worthy coadjutor and employer. In the hope, then, of ruining him, if not of getting scathelessly off themselves, these ladies-legatees mustered once more from the mazes of St. Giles's the pack of competent Irish witnesses, collected whatever documentary or other evidence looked likeliest to help their ends, and then one early day presented themselves before the lord-mayor, eager to destroy at a blow that pleasant Mr. Dillaway.

The proceedings were long, cautious, tedious, and secret: emissaries to Belfast, Doctors' Commons, and the bank: the stamp office was stirred to its foundations; and Canterbury staggered at the fraud. Thus within a week the proper officials were in a condition to prosecute, and the issue of immense examinations tended to that point of satisfaction, the haling Mr. Dillaway to prison on the charge of having forged a will.

CHAPTER XII.

HEART'S CORE.

THEY were come into great want, poor Henry and Maria: they had not wherewithal for daily sustenance. The few remaining trinkets, books, clothes, and other available moveables had been gradually pledged away, and to their full amount—at least, the pawnbroker said so. That unlucky publication of the law book, so speedily condemned and heartlessly ridiculed, had wrecked all Henry's possible prospects in the courts; and as for help from friends—the casual friends of common life—he was too proud to beg for that—too sensitive, too self-respectful. Relations he had none, or next to none—that distant cousin of his mother's, the Mac-something, whom he had never even seen, but who, nevertheless, had acted as his guardian.

Much as he suspected Dillaway in the matter of that bitter breach of trust, he had neither ready money to proceed against him, (nor, when he came to think it over) any legal grounds at all to go upon; for, as we have said before, even granting there should be evidence adduced of the transfer of stock from the name of Clements to that of Dillaway, still it was a notorious fact that the "Independent bank" had failed, whereto the stock-broker could swear he had intrusted it. In short, shrewd Jack had managed all that affair to admiration; and poor Clements was ruined without hope, and defrauded without remedy.

Then, again, we already know how that Lady Dillaway was dead, so help from her was simply impossible; and the miserable father Sir Thomas was kept too closely up to the mark of resolute anger by slanderous John, to give them any aid, if they applied to him; but, in truth, as to personal application, Henry would not for pride, and Maria now could not, for her near-at-hand motherly condition. Her frequent letters, as we may be sure, were intercepted; and, even if Sir Thomas now and then yearned after his lost child, it had become a matter of physical impossibility to find out where she lived. Thus were they hopelessly sinking, day by day, into all the bitter waves of want. Not but that Henry strived, as we have seen, and shall yet see: still his endeavours had been very nearly fruitless—and, perchance, till all available moveables had been pawned outright, very feeble too. Now, however, that Maria, in her sorrow and her need, must soon become a mother, the state of things grew terrible indeed; their horizon was all over black with clouds.

No: not all over. There is light under the darkness, a growing light that shall dispel the darkness; a precious light upon their souls, the early dawn of Heaven's eternal day; God's final end in all their troubles, the reaping-time of joy for their sowing-time of tears.

Without cant, affectation, or hypocrisy, there is but one panacea for the bruised or broken heart, available alike in all times, all places, and all circumstances: and he who knows not what that is, has more to learn than I can teach him. That pure substantial comfort is born of Heaven's hope, and faith in Heaven's wisdom; it is a solid confidence in God's great love, but faintly shadowed out by all the charities of earth. Human affections in their manifold varieties are little other than an echo of that Voice, "Come unto me; Comfort ye, comfort ye; I will be a Father unto you, and ye shall be my sons and my daughters; thy Maker is thy Husband; he hath loved thee with an everlasting love; when thou goest through the fire, I will be with thee, through the waters, they shall not overflow thee; eye hath not seen, nor ear heard, neither hath it entered into the mind of man to conceive the blessings which His love hath laid in store for *thee*."

Heart's-ease in heart's-affliction—this they found in God; turning to Him with all their hearts, and pouring out their hearts before Him, they trusted in Him heartily for both worlds' good. Therefore did He give them their heart's desire, satisfying all their mind: wherefore did they love each other now with a newly-added plenitude of love, mutually in reference to Him who loved them, and gave Himself for them: therefore did they feel in their distresses more gladness at their hearts, than in the days of luxury and affluence, the increase of their oil and their wine.

For this is the great end of all calamities. God doth not willingly afflict: trouble never cometh without an urgent cause; and though man in his perverseness often misses all the prize of purity, whilst he pays all the penalty of pain; still the motive that sent sorrow was the same—O, that there were a better heart in them!

In many modes the heart of man is tried, as gold must be refined, by many methods; and happiest is the heart, that, being tried by many, comes purest out of all. If prosperity melts it as a flux, well; but better too than well, if the acid of affliction afterwards eats away all unseen impurities; whereas, to those with whom the world is in their hearts, affluence only hardens, and penury embitters, and thus, though burnt in many fires, their hearts are dross in all. Like those sullen children in the market-place, they feel no sympathies with heaven or with earth: unthankful in prosperity, unsoftened by adversity, well may it be said of them, Hearts of stone, hearts of stone!

Not of such were Henry and Maria: naturally warm in affections and generous in sympathies, it needed but the pilot's hand to steer their hearts aright: the energies of life were there, both fresh and full, lacking but direction heavenwards; and chastisement wisely interposed to wean those yearning spirits from the brief and feverish pursuits of unsatisfying life, to the rest and the rewards of an eternity. Then were they wedded indeed, heart answering to heart; then were they strong against all the ills of life, those hearts that were established by grace; then spake they often one to another out of the abundance of their hearts; and in spite of all their sorrows, they were happy, for their hearts were right with God.

Let the grand idea suffice, unincumbered by the multitude of details. Whatsoever things are true, honest and just; whatsoever things are pure, lovely, or of good report; if there be any virtue, and if there be any praise—believe of those twin hearts that God had given them all. Patience, hope, humility; faith, tenderness, and charity; prayer, trust, benevolence, and joy: this was the lot of the afflicted! It was good for them that they had been in trouble; for they had gained from it a wealth that is above the preciousness of rubies, deservedly dearer to their hearts than the thousands of gold and silver.

What a contrast then was shown between God's kindness and man's coldness! No one of their fellows seemed to give them any heed: but He cared for them, and on Him they cast their cares. Former friends appeared to stand aloof, self-dependent and unsympathizing; but God was ever near, kindly bringing help in every extremity, which always seemed at hand, yet ever kept away: smoothing the pillow of sickness, comforting the troubled spirit, and treading down calamity and calumny and care; as a conqueror conquering for them. So, they learned the priceless wisdom which adversity would teach to all on whom she frowneth; when earthly hopes are wrecked, to anchor fast on God; and if affluence should ever come again, to aid the poor afflicted with heartiness, beneficence, and home-taught sympathy.

CHAPTER XIII.

HOPE'S BIRTH TO INNOCENCE, AND HOPE'S DEATH TO FRAUD.

John Dillaway's sudden loss of property, his character exploded as a monied man, and the strong probability of his turning out a felon, had a great effect on the spirits of Sir Thomas. He had called upon his promising son in prison, had found him very sulky, disinclined for social intercourse, and any thing but filial; all he condescended to growl, with a characteristic d—— or two interlarding his eloquence, was this taunting speech:

"Well, governor, I may thank you and your counsels for this. Here 's a precious end to all my clever tricks of trade! I wish you joy of your son, and of your daughter too, old man. Who wrote that letter? What, not found out yet? and does she still starve for it? Who gained money as you bade him—never mind how? And is now going to do honour to the family all round the world, ey?—Ha, ha, ha!"

The poor unhappy father tottered away as quickly as he could, while yet the brutal laughter of that unnatural son rang upon his ears. He was quite miserable, let him turn which way he would. On 'Change the name had been disgraced—posted up for scorn on the board of degradation: at home, there was no pliant son and heir, to testify against Maria, and to close the many portals of a wretched father's heart. He grew very wretched—very mopy; determined upon cutting adrift shrewd Jack himself, as a stigma on the name which had once held the mace of mayoralty; made his will petulantly, for good and all, in favour of Stationer's hall, and felt very like a man who had lived in vain. "Cut it down; why cumbereth it the earth?"

Meanwhile, in those two opposite quarters of the world of London, Newgate and Islington, Sir Thomas's two discarded children were bearing in a different way their different privations. Poor Maria's hour of peril had arrived; and amidst all those pains, dangers, and necessities, a soft and smiling babe was born into the world; gladness filled their hearts, and praise was on their tongues, when the happy father and mother kissed that first-born son. It was a splendid boy, they said, and should redeem his father's fortunes: there was hope in the future, let the past be what it may; and this new bond of union to that happy wedded pair made the present—one unclouded scene of gratitude and love. Who shall sing of the humble ale-caudle, and those cheerful givings to surrounding poor, scarcely poorer than themselves? Who shall record how kind was Henry, how useful was the nurse, how liberal the doctor, how sympathizing all? Who shall tell how tenderly did Providence step in with another author's night of that same tragedy, and how other avenues to literary gain stood wide open to industry and genius? It was happiness all, happiness, and triumph: they were weathering the storm famously, and had safely passed the breakers of False-witness

Amidst the other part of London sate a sullen fellow, quite alone, in Newgate, looking for his trial on the morrow, and prophesying accurately enough how some two days hence, he, John Dillaway, of Broker's alley, son and heir of the richest stationer in Europe, was to appear in the character of a convicted felon, and be probably condemned to transportation for life. A pleasant retrospect was his, a pleasanter aspect, and a pleasanter prospect; all was pleasure assuredly.

And the morrow duly came; with those implacable approvers, those accurate Irish witnesses, those tell-tale documents, that prosecuting crown and bank, that dogged jury, and that sentencing recorder: so then, by a little after noon, to the scandal of Finsbury square, John Dillaway discovered that the "wise man's trick or two in the money market" was about to be rewarded with twenty-one years of transportation.

Of this interesting fact Henry Clements became acquainted by an occasional peep into the public prints; and he perceived to his astonishment, that the defrauded Mrs. Jane Mackenzie, of Ballyriggan, near Belfast, could surely be none other than his mother's Ulster cousin, the nominal guardian of his boyhood! To be sure, it mattered little enough to him, for the old lady had never been much better than a stranger to him, and at present appeared only in that useless character to an expectant, a person despoiled of her money; nevertheless, of that identical money, certain sanguine friends had heretofore given him expectations in the event of her death, seeing that she had nobody to leave it to, except himself and the public charities of the United Kingdom: clearly, this cousin must have been the defrauded bank annuitant, and he could not help feeling more desolate than ever; for John Dillaway's evil influences had robbed him now of name, fame, fortune, and what hope regards as much as any—expectations. Yet—must not the bank of England bear the brunt of all this forgery, and account for its stock to that innocent depositor? Old Mrs. Jane was sinking into dotage, probably had plenty of other money, and scarcely seemed to stir about the business; therefore, legitimately interested as Henry indubitably was, he took upon him to write to his antiquated relative, and in so doing managed to please her mightily: renewed whatever interest she ever might have felt in him, enabled her to enforce her just claim, and really stood a likelier chance than ever of coming in for competency some day. However, for the present, all was penury still. Clements had been too delicate for even a hint at his deplorable condition: and his distant relative's good feeling, so providentially renewed, served indeed to gild the future, but did not avail to gingerbread the present. So they struggled on as well as they could: both very thankful for the chance which had caused a coalition between sensitiveness and interest; and Maria at least more anxious than ever for a reconciliation with her father, now that all his ardent hopes had been exploded in son John.

CHAPTER XIV.

PROBABLE RECONCILIATION.

It was no use—none at all. Nature was too strong for him; and a higher force than even potent Nature. In vain Sir Thomas pish'd, and tush'd' and bah'd; in vain he buried himself chin-deep amongst the century of ledgers that testified of gainful years gone by, and were now mustily rotting away in the stagnant air of St. Benet's Sherehog: interest had lost its interest for him, profits profited not, speculation's self had dull, lack-lustre eyes, and all the hard realities of utilitarian life were become weary, flat, and stale. Sir Thomas was a miserable man—a bereaved old man—who nevertheless clung to what was left, and struggled not to grieve for what was lost: there was a terrible strife going on secretly within him, dragging him this way and that: a little lightning flash of good had been darted by Omnipotence right through the stone-built caverns of his heart, and was smouldering a concentred flame within its innermost hollow; a small soft-skinned seed had been dropped by the Father of Spirits into that iron-bound soil, and it was swelling day by day under the case-hardened surface, gradually with gentle violence, despite of all the locks and gates, and bolts and bars, a silent enemy had somehow crept within the fortress of his feelings, ready at any unguarded moment to fling the portals open. The rock had a sealed fountain leaping within it, as an infant in the womb. The poor old man, the worldly cold old man, was giving way.

Happy misery! for his breaking heart revealed a glorious jewel at the core. Oh, sorrow beyond price! for natural affections, bursting up amid these unsunned snows, were a hot-spring to that Iceland soul. Oh, bitter, bitter penitence most blest! which broke down the money-proud man, which bruised and kneaded him, humbled, smote, and softened him, and made him come again a little child—a loving, yearning, little child—a child with pity in its eyes, with prayer upon its tongue, with generous affection in its heart. "Oh, Maria! precious, cast-off child, where art thou, where art thou, where art thou—starving? And canst thou, blessed God, forgive? And will not thy great mercy bring her to me yet again? Oh, what a treasury of love have I mis-spent; what riches of the Heart, what only truest wealth, have I, poor prodigal, been squandering! Unhappy son—unhappy father of the perjured, heartless, miserable John! Wo is me! Where art thou, dear child, my pure and best Maria?"

We may well guess, far too well, how it was that dear Maria came not near him. She had been, prior to confinement, very, very ill: nigh to death: the pangs of travail threatened to have seized upon her all too soon, when wasted with sorrow, and weakened by want. She lay, long weeks, battling for life, in her little back parlour, at Islington, tended night and day by her kind, good husband.

But did she not often (you will say) urge him, earnestly as the dying ask, to seek out her father or brother (she had not been told of his conviction), and to let them know this need? Why, then, did he so often put her off with faint excuses, and calm her with coming hopes, and do any thing, say any thing, suffer any thing, rather than execute the fervent wish of the affectionate Maria? It is easily understood. With, and notwithstanding, all the high sentiments, strong sense, and warm feelings of Henry Clements, he was too proud to seek any succour of the Dillaways. Sooner than give that hard old man, or, beforetime, that keen malicious young one, any occasion to triumph over his necessitous condition, he himself would starve: ay, and trust to Heaven his darling wife and child; but not trust these to them. Never, never—if the heart-divorcing work-house were their doom—should that father or that brother hear from him a word of supplication, or one murmur of complaint. Nay; he took pains to hinder their knowledge of this trouble: all the world, rather than those two men. Let penury, disease, the very parish-beadle triumph over him, but not those two. It was a natural feeling for a sensitive mind like his—but in many respects a wrong one. It was to put away, deliberately, the helping hand of Providence, because it bade him kiss the rod. It was a direct preference of honour to humility. It was an unconsciously unkind consideration of himself before those whom he nevertheless believed and called more dear to him than life—but not than honour. Therefore it was that the hand-bills he had so often seen pasted upon walls were disregarded, that the numerous newspaper advertisements remained unanswered, and that all the efforts of an almost frantic father to find his long-lost daughter were in vain.

Meanwhile, to be just upon poor Clements, who really fancied he was doing right in this, he left no stone unturned to obtain a provision for his beloved wife and child. Frequently, by letters (as little urgent as affection and necessity would suffer him), he had pressed upon some powerful friends for that vague phantom of a gentlemanly livelihood—"something under government;" a hope improbable of accomplishment, indefinite as to view, but still a hope: especially, since very civil answers came to his request, couched in terms of official guardedness. He had called anxiously upon "old friends," in pretty much of his usual elegant dress (for he was wise enough, or proud enough, never to let his poverty be seen in his attire), and they made many polite inquiries after "Mrs. Clements," and "Where are you living?" and "How is it you never come our way?" and "Clements has cut us all dead," and so forth. It was really entirely his own fault, but he never could contrive to tell the truth: and when one day, in a careless tone of voice, he threw out something about "Do you happen to have ten pounds about you?" to a dashing young blood of his acquaintance—the dashing young blood affected to treat it as a joke—"You married men, lucky dogs, with your regular establishments, are too hard upon us poor bachelors, who have nothing but clubs to go to. I give you my honour, Clements, ten pounds would dine me for a fortnight:—spare me this time, there's a fine fellow: take the trouble to write a cheque on your bankers—here's paper—and my tiger shall get it cashed for you while you wait: we poor bachelors are never flush." But Clements had already owned it was a mere "*obiter dictum*,"—nothing but a joke of prudent marriage against extravagant bachelorship.

Ah, what a bitter joke was that! On the verge of that yes or no, to be uttered by his frank young friend, trembled reluctant honour; home-affections were imploring in that careless tone of voice; hunger put that off-hand question. It was vain; a cruel killing effort for his pride: so Henry Clements never asked again; withdrew himself from friends; grew hopeless, all but reckless; and his only means of living were picked up scantily from the by-ways of literature. An occasional guinea from a magazine, a copy of that luckily anonymous tragedy now and then sold by him from house to house (he always disguised himself at such times), a little indexing to be done for publishers, and a little correcting of the press for printers—these formed the trifling and uncertain pittance upon which the pale family existed. Poor Henry Clements, proud Henry Clements, you had, indeed, a dose of physic for your pride: bitter draughts, bitter draughts, day after day; but, for all that weak and wasted wife, dearly, devotedly beloved; for all the pining infant, with its angel face and beautiful smiles: for all the strong pleadings of affection, yea, and gnawing hunger too, the strong man's pride was stronger. And had not God's good providence proved mercifully strongest of them all, that family of love would have starved outright for pride.

But Heaven's favour willed it otherwise. By something little short of miracle, where food was scant and medicine scarce, the poor emaciated mother gradually gained strength—that long, low fever left her, health came again upon her cheek, her travail passed over prosperously, the baby too thrived, (oh, more than health to mothers!) and Maria Clements found herself one morning strong enough to execute a purpose she had long most anxiously designed. "Henry was wrong to think so harshly of her father. She knew he would not spurn her away: he must be kind, for she loved him dearly still. Wicked as it doubtless was of her [dear innocent girl] to have done any thing contrary to his wishes, she was sure he would relieve her in her utmost need. He could not, could not be so hard as poor dear Henry made him." So, taking advantage of her husband's absence during one of his literary pilgrimages, she took her long-forgotten bonnet and shawl, and, with the baby in her arms, flew on the wings of love, duty, penitence, and affection to her dear old home in Finsbury square.

CHAPTER XV.

THE FATHER FINDS HIS HEART FOR EVER.

He had been at death's door, sinking out of life, because he had nothing now to live for. He still was very weak in bed, faint, and worn, and white, propped up with pillows—that poor, bereaved old man. Ever since Lady Dillaway's most quiet death he had felt alone in the world. True, while she lived she had seemed to him a mere tranquil trouble, a useless complacent piece of furniture, often in his way; but now that she was dead, what a void was left where she had been—mere empty space, cold and death-like. She had left him quite alone.

Then again—of John, poor John, he would think, and think continually—not about the little vulgar pock-marked man of 'change, the broker, the rogue, the coward—but of a happy curly child, with sparkling eyes —a merry-hearted, ruddy little fellow, romping with his sister—ay, in this very room; here is the identical China vase he broke, all riveted up; there is the corner where he would persist to nestle his dormice. Ah, dear child! precious child! where is he now?—Where and what indeed! Alas, poor father! had you known what I do, and shall soon inform the world, of that bad man's awful end, one more, one fiercest pang would have tormented you: but Heaven spared that pang. Nevertheless, the bitter contrast of the child and of the man had made him very wretched—and to the widower's solitude added the father's sadness.

And worst of all—Maria's utter loss—that dear, warm-hearted, innocent, ill-used, and yet beloved daughter. Why did he spurn her away? and keep her away so long?—oh, hard heart, hard heart! Was she not innocent, after all? and John, bad John, too probably the forger of that letter, as the forger of this will? And now that he should give his life to see her, and kiss her, and—no, no, not forgive her, but pray to be forgiven by her—"Where is she? why doesn't she come to hold up my poor weak head—to see how fervently my dead old heart has at last learnt to love—to help a bad, and hard, a pardoned and penitent old man to die in perfect peace—to pray with me, for me, to God, our God, my daughter! Where is she—how can I find her out—why will she not come to me all this sorrowful year? Oh come, come, dear child—our Father send thee to me—come and bless me ere I die—come, my Maria!"

Magical, or contrived, as it may seem to us, the poor old man was actually bemoaning himself thus, when our dear heroine of the Heart faintly knocked at her old home door. It opened; a faded-looking woman, with a baby in her arms, rushed past the astonished butler: and, just as her father was praying out aloud for Heaven to speed her to him, that daughter's step was at the bed-room door.

Before she turned the handle (some house-maid had recognised her on the stairs, and told her, with an impudent air, that "Sir Thomas was ill a-bed"), she stopped one calming instant to gain strength of God for that dreaded interview, and to check herself from bursting in upon the chamber of sickness, so as to disquiet that dear weak patient. So, she prayed, gently turned the handle, and heard those thrilling words—"Come, my Maria!"

It was enough; their hearts burst out together like twin fountains, rolling their joyful sorrows together towards the sea of endless love, as a swollen river that has broken through some envious and constraining dam! It was enough; they wept together, rejoiced together, kissed and clasped each other in the fervour of full love: the babe lay smiling and playing on the bed: Maria, in a torrent of happiest tears, fondled that poor old man, who was crying and laughing by turns, as little children do—was praising God out loud like a saint, and calling down blessings on his daughter's head in all the transports of a new-found Heart. What a world of things they had to tell of—how much to explain, excuse, forgive, and be forgiven, especially about that wicked letter—how fervently to make up now for love that long lay dormant—how heartily to bless each other, and to bless again! Who can record it all? Who can even sketch aright the heavenly hues that shone about that scene of the affections? Alas, my pen is powerless—yea, no mortal hand can trace those heavenly hues. Angels that are round the penitent's, the good man's bed—ye alone who witness it, can utter what ye see: ye alone, rejoicingly with those rejoicing, gladly speed aloft frequent ambassadors to Him, the Lord of Love, with some new beauteous trait, some rare ecstatic thought, some pure delighted look, some more burning prayer, some gem of Heaven's jewellery more brilliant than the rest, which raises happy envy of your bright compeers. I see your shining bands crowding enamoured round that scene of human tenderness; while now and then some peri-like seraph of your thronging spiritual forms will gladly wing away to find favour of his God for a tear, or a prayer, or a holy thought dropped by his ministering hands into the treasury of Heaven.

But the cup of joy is large and deep: it is an ocean in capacity: and mantling though it seemeth to the brim, God's bounty poureth on.

Another step is on the stairs! You have guessed it, Henry Clements. Returning home wearily, after a disheartening expedition, and finding his wife, to his great surprise, gone out, sick and weak, as still he thought her, he had calculated justly on the direction whereunto her heart had carried her; he had followed her speedily, and, with many self-compunctions, he had determined to be proud no more, and to help, with all his heart, in that holy reconciliation. See! at the bed-side, folding Maria with one arm, and with his other hand tightly clasped in both of that kind and changed old man's, stands Henry Clements.

Ay, changed indeed! Who could have discovered in that joy-illumined brow, in those blessing-dropping lips, in those eyes full of penitence, and pity, and peace, and praise, and prayer, the harsh old usurer—the crafty money-cankered knave of dim St. Benet's Sherehog—the cold husband—the cruel father—the man without a heart? Ay, changed—changed for ever now, an ever of increasing happiness and love. Who or what had caused this deep and mighty change? Natural affection was the sword, and God's the arm that wielded it. None but he could smite so deeply; and when he smote, pour balm into the wound: none but He could kill death, that dead dried heart, and quicken life within its mummied caverns: none but the Voice, which said "Let there be light," could work this common miracle of "Let there be love."

He grew feebler—feebler, that dying kind old man: it had been too much for him, doubtlessly; he had long been ill, and should long ago have died; but that he had lived for this; and now the end seemed near. They never left his bed-side then for days and nights, that new-found son and daughter: physicians came, and recommended that the knight be quite alone, quite undisturbed: but Sir Thomas would not, could not—it were cruelty to force it; so he lay feebly on his back, holding on either side the hands of Henry and Maria.

It was not so very long: they had come almost in the nick of time: a few days and hours at the most, and all will then be over. So did they watch and pray.

And the old man faintly whispered:

"Henry—son Henry: poor John, forgive him, as you and our God have now forgiven me; poor John—when he comes back again from those long years of slavery, give him a home, son—give him a home, and enough to keep him honest; tell him I love him, and forgive him; and remind him that I died, praying Heaven for my poor boy's soul.

"Henry and Maria—I had, since my great distresses, well nigh forgotten this world's wealth; but now, thank God, I have thought of it all for your sakes: in my worst estate of mind I made a wicked will. It is in that drawer—quick, give it me.

"Thanks—thanks—there is time to tear it; and these good friends, Dr. Jones and Mr. Blair, take witness—I destroy this wicked will; and my only child, Maria, has my wealth in course of law. Wealth, yes—if well used, let us call it wealth; for riches may indeed be made a mine of good, and joy, and righteousness. I am unworthy to use any of it well, unworthy of the work, unworthy of the reward: use it well, my holier children, wisely, liberally, kindly: God give you to do great good with it; God give you to feel great happiness in all your doing good. My hands that saved and scraped it all, also often-times by evil hardness, now penitently washed in the Fountain of Salvation, heartily renounce that evil. Be ye my stewards; give liberally to many needy. Oh me, my sin! children, to my misery you know what need is: I can say no more; poor sinful man, how dare I preach to others? Children, dearest ones, I am a father still; and I would bless you—bless you!

"I grow weak, but my heart seems within me to grow stronger—I go—I go, to the Home of Heart, where He that sits upon the throne is Love, and where all the pulses of all the beings there thrill in unison with him, the Great Heart of Heaven! I, even I, am one of the redeemed—my heart is fixed, I will sing and give praise; I, even I, the hardest and the worst, forgiven, accepted! Who are ye, bright messengers about my bed, heralds of glory? I go—I go—one—one more, Maria—one last kiss; we meet—again—in Heaven!"

Had he fainted? yes—his countenance looked lustrous, yet diminishing in glory, even as a setting sun; the living smile faded gradually away, and a tranquil cold calm crept over his cheeks: the angelic light which made his eyes so beautiful to look at, was going out—going out: all was peace—peace—deep peace.

O death, where is thy victory? O grave, where is thy sting?

CHAPTER XVI.

A WORD ABOUT ORIGINALITY AND MOURNING.

When a purely inventive genius concocts a fabulous tale, it is clearly competent to him so to order matters, that characters shall not die off till his book is shortly coming to an end: and had your obedient servant now been engaged in the architecture of a duly conventional story, arranged in pattern style, with climax in the middle and a brace of ups and downs to play supporters, doubtless he might easy have kept alive both father and mother to witness the triumph of innocence, and have produced their deaths at the last as a kind of "sweet sorrow," or honied sting, wherewithal to point his moral. Such, however, was not my authorship's intention; and, seeing that a wilful pen must have its way, I have chosen to construct my own veracious tale, respecting the incidents of life and death, much as such events not unfrequently occur, that is, at an inconvenient season: for though such accessories to the fact of dying, as triumphant conversion, or a tranquil going out, may appear to be a little out of the common way, still the circumstance of death itself often in real life seems to come as out of time, as your wisdom thinks in the present book of Heart. People will die untowardly, and people will live provokingly, notwithstanding all that novelists have said and poets sung to the contrary: and if two characters out of our principal five have already left the mimic scene, it will now be my duty only to show, as nature and society do, how, of those three surviving chief *dramatis personæ*, two of them—to wit, our hero and heroine of Heart—gathered many friends about their happy homestead, did a world of good, and, in fine, furnish our volume with a suitable counterpoise to the mass of selfish sin, which (at its height in the only remaining character) it has been my fortune to record and to condemn as the opposite topic of heartlessness.

If writers will be bound by classic rules, and walk on certain roads because other folks have gone that way before them, needs must that ill-starred originality perish from this world's surface, and find refuge (if it can) in the gentle moon or Sirius. Therefore, let us boldly trespass from the trodden paths, let us rather shake off the shackles of custom than hug them as an ornament approved: and, notwithstanding both parental deaths, seemingly ill-timed for the happiness of innocence, let us acquiesce in the facts, as plain matters of history, not dubious thoughts of fiction; and let us gather to the end any good we can, either from the miserable solitude of a selfish Dillaway, or from the hearty social circle of our happy married pair.

Need I, sons and daughters, need I record at any length how Maria mourned for her father? If you now have parents worthy of your love, if you now have hearts to love them, I may safely leave that theme to your affections: "now" is for all things "the accepted time," now is the day for reconciliations: our life is a perpetual now. However unfilial you may have been, however stern or negligent they, if there is now the will to bless, and now the heart to love, all is well—well at the last, well now for evermore—thank Heaven for so glad a consummation. Oh, that my pen had power to make many fathers kind, many children trustful! Oh, that by some burning word I could thaw the cold, shame sarcasms, and arouse the apathetic! Oh that, invoking upon every hearth, whereto this book may come, the full free blaze of home affections, my labour of love be any thing but vain, when God shall have blessed what I am writing!

Yes, children, dear Maria did mourn for her father, but she mourned as those who hope; his life had been forgiven, and his death was as a saints's: as for her, rich rewarded daughter at the last, one word of warm acknowledgement, one look of true affection, one tear of deep contrition, would have been superabundant to clear away all the many clouds, the many storms of her past home-life: and as for our Maker, with his pure and spotless justice, faith in the sacrifice had passed all sin to him, and love of the Redeemer had proved that faith the true one. How should a daughter mourn for such a soul? With tears of joy; with sighs—of kindred hopefulness; with happiest resolve to live as he had died; with instant prayer that her last end be like his.

There is a plain tablet in St. Benet's church, just within the altar-rail, bearing—no inscription about Lord Mayoralty, Knighthood, or the Worshipful Company of Stationers—but full of facts more glorious than every honour under heaven; for the words run thus:

SORROWFUL, YET REJOICING,
A DAUGHTER'S LOVE HAS PLACED THIS TABLET
TO THE MEMORY OF
THOMAS DILLAWAY;
A MAN WHO DIED IN THE FAITH OF CHRIST,
IN THE LOVE OF GOD, AND IN THE HOPE OF HEAVEN.

Noble epitaph! Let us so live, that the like of this may be truth on our tomb-stones. Seek it, rather than wealth, before honour, instead of pleasure; for, indeed, those words involve within their vast significancy riches unsearchable, glory indestructible, and pleasure for evermore! Hide them, as a string of precious pearls, within the casket of your hearts.

I had almost forgotten, though Maria never could, another neighbouring tablet to record the peaceful exit of her mother; however, as this had been erected by Sir Thomas in his life-time, and was plastered thick with civic glories and heathen virtues, possibly the transcript may be spared: there was only one sentence that looked true about the epitaph, though I wished it had been so in every sense; but, to common eyes, it had seemed quite suitable to the physical quietude of living Lady Dillaway, to say, "Her end was peace;" although, perhaps, the husband little thought how sore that mother's heart was for dear Maria's loss, how full of anxious doubts her mind about Maria's sin. Poor soul, however peaceful now that spirit has read the truth, in the hour of her departure it had been with her far otherwise: her dying bed was as a troubled sea, for she died of a broken heart.

Yearly, on the anniversaries of their respective deaths, the growing clan of Clements make a solemn pilgrimage to their grand paternal shrine, attending service on those days (or the holiday nearest to them), at St. Benet's Shere-hog; and Maria's eyes are very moist on such occasions; though hope sings gladly too within her wise and cheerful heart. She does not seem to have lost those friends; they are only gone before.

CHAPTER XVII.

THE HOUSE OF FEASTING.

But in fact, with our happy married folks an anniversary of some sort is perpetually recurring: wedding-days, birth-days, and all manner of festival occasions, worthy (as the old Romans would have said) to be noted up with chalk, happened in that family of love weekly—almost daily. They cultivated well the grateful soil of Heart, by a thousand little dressings and diggings; courting to it the warm sunshine of the skies, the zephyrs of pleasant recollections, and the genial dews of sympathy. And very wise were all those labours of delight; for their sons and their daughters grew up as the polished corners in the temple; moulded with delicate affections, their moral essence sharp, and clearly edged with sensitive feelings, as if they had sprung fresh from the hands of God, their sculptor, and the world had not rubbed off the master-touches of His chisel. For, in this dull world, we cheat ourselves and one another of innocent pleasures by the score, through very carelessness and apathy: courted day after day by happy memories, we rudely brush them off with this indiscriminating besom, the stern material present: invited to help in rendering joyful many a patient heart, we neglect the little word that might have done it, and continually defraud creation of its share of kindliness from us. The child made merrier by your interest in his toy; the old domestic flattered by your seeing him look so well; the poor, better helped by your blessing than your penny (though give the penny too); the labourer, cheered upon his toil by a timely word of praise; the humble friend encouraged by your frankness; equals made to love you by the expression of your love; and superiors gratified by attention and respect, and looking out to benefit the kindly—how many pleasures here for any hand to gather; how many blessings here for any heart to give! Instead of these, what have we rife about the world? Frigid compliment—for warmth is vulgar; reserve of tongue—for it is folly to be talkative; composure, never at fault—for feelings are dangerous things; gravity—for that looks wise; coldness—for other men are cold; selfishness—for every one is struggling for his own. This is all false, all bad; the slavery chain of custom riveted by the foolishness of fashion; because there ever is a band of men and women, who have nothing to recommend them but externals—their looks or their dresses, their rank or their wealth—and in order to exalt the honour of these, they agree to set a compact seal of silence on the heart and on the mind; lest the flood of humbler men's affections, or of wiser men's intelligence, should pale their tinsel-praise; and the warm and the wise too softly acquiesce in this injury done to heartiness shamed by the effrontery of cold calm fools, and the shallow dignity of an empty presence. Turn the tables on them, ye truer gentry, truer nobility, truer royalty of the heart and of the mind; speak freely, love warmly, laugh cheerfully, explain frankly, exhort zealously, admire liberally, advise earnestly—be not ashamed to show you have a heart: and if some cold-blooded simpleton greet your social effort with a sneer, repay him—for you can well afford a richer gift than his whole treasury possesses—repay him with a kind good-humoured smile: it would have shamed Jack Dillaway himself. If a man persists to be silent in a crowd for vanity's sake, instead of sociable, as good company expects, count him simply for a fool; you will not be far wrong; he remembers the copy-book at school, no doubt, with its large-text aphorism, "Silence is wisdom;" and thinking in an easy obedience to gain credit from mankind by acting on that questionable sentence, the result is what you perpetually see—a self-contained, self-satisfied, selfish, and reserved young puppy. Hint to such an incommunicative comrade, that the fashion now is coming about, to talk and show your wisdom; not to sit in shallow silence, hiding hard your folly; soon shall you loosen the flood-gates of his speech; and society will even thank you for it; for, bore as the chatterer may oft-times be, still he does the frank companion's duty; and at any rate is vastly preferable to the dull, unwarmed, unsympathetic watcher at the festal board, who sits there to exhibit his painted waistcoat instead of the heart that should be in it, and patiently waits, with a snakish eye and a bitter tongue, to aid conversation with a sarcasm.

Henry and Maria had many hearty friends to keep their many anniversaries. They were well enough for wealth, as we may guess without much trouble; for the knight had left three thousand a-year behind him, and Maria, as sole heiress, had no difficulty in establishing her claim to it; but it may be well to put mankind in memory how hospitably, how charitably, how wisely, and how heartily they stewarded it. I need not stop to tell of local charities assisted, good societies supported, and of philanthropic good done by means of their money, both at home and abroad: nor detail their many dinners, and other festal opportunities, rivets in the lengthening chain of ordinary friendship: but I do wish to make honourable mention of one happiest anniversary, which, while it commemorated fine young Master Harry's birth, rejoiced the many poor of Lower-Sack street, Islington.

The birth-day itself was kept at home with all the honours, in their old house at Finsbury square; Maria would not leave that house, for old acquaintance sake. Master Harry, a frank-faced, open-hearted, curly-headed boy of ten (at least when I dined there, for he has probably grown older since), was of course the happy hero of the feast, ably supported by divers joyful brothers and sisters, who had all contributed to their elder brother's triumph on that day, by the contribution of their various presents—one a little scent bag, another a rude drawing, another a book-marker, and so forth, all probably worthless in the view of selfish calculation, but inestimable according to the currency of Heart. Half-a-dozen choice old friends closed the list of company; and a noisy rout of boys and girls were added in the early evening, full of negus, and sponge-cake, snap-dragon, and blindman's-buff, with merry music, and a golden-flood of dances and delight.

We dined early; and, to be very confidential with you, I thought (until I found out reasons why), that the bill-of-fare upon the table was inordinately large, not to say vulgar; for the board was overloaded with solid sweets and savouries: so, in my uncharitable mind, I set all that down to the uncivilized hospitality asserted of a citizen's feast, and (for aught I know) still rife in St. Mary Axe and Finsbury square.

Never mind how the dinner passed off, nor how jovially the children kept it up till near eleven: for I learnt, in an incidental way, what was regularly done upon the morrow; and I am sure it will gratify my readers to learn it too, as a trait of considerate kindness which will gladden man and woman's heart.

On the seventh of April in every year (Harry's birth-day was the sixth), Henry and Maria used to go on an humble pilgrimage to Lower Sack street, Islington. Not to shame the poor by fine clothes or their usual equipage, they sedulously donned on that occasion the same now faded suits they had worn in their adversity, and made their progress in a hackney-coach. They would have walked for humility's sake and sympathy, but that the coach in question was crammed full of eatables and drinkables, nicely packed up in well-considered parcels, consisting of the vast *débris* of yesterday's overwhelming feast, with a sackful of tea and sugar added. Their pockets also, as I took the liberty of inquiring at Sack street afterwards, must have been well stored, for their largess was munificent. Then would they go to that identical lodgings of years gone by, where they had so struggled with adversity, now in the happy contrast of wealth and peace and thankfulness to Heaven, and of joy at doing good. That parlour was right liberally hired for the day, and all the poor in Sack street were privileged to call, where Mrs. Clements held her levee. They came in an orderly stream, clean for the occasion, and full of gratitude and blessings; and, to be just upon the poor, no impostor had ever been known to intrude upon the privilege of Sack street. As for dear Maria, she regularly broke down just as the proceedings commenced, and Henry's manlier hand had to give away the spoil; whilst Maria sobbed beside him, as if her heart would break. Then did the good old nurse come in for a cold round of beef, with tea, sugar, and a sovereign; and the bed-ridden neighbour up-stairs for jellied soup, and other condiments, with a similar royal climax; and the cobbler over the way carried off ham and chickens, with apple-puffs and a bottle of wine: and so some thirty or forty families were gladdened for the hour, and made wealthy for a week. Altogether they divided amongst them a coachful of comestibles, and a pocketful of coin.

It would be impertinent in us to intrude so far on privacy, as to record how Henry and Maria passed much time in prayer and praise on that interesting anniversary; it is unnecessary too, for in fact they did not stop for anniversaries to do that sort of thing. Be sure that good thoughts and good words are ever found preceding good and grateful deeds. It is quite enough to know that they did God service in doing good to man.

CHAPTER XVIII.

THE END OF THE HEARTLESS.

There is plenty of contrast in this poor book, if that be any virtue. Let us turn our eyes away from those scenes of love and cheerfulness, of benevolence and peace. Let us leave Maria in her nursery, hearing the little ones their lessons; and Henry cutting the leaves of a nice new book, fresh from the press, while his home-taught son and heir is playing at pot-hooks and hangers in a copy-book beside him. Let us recollect their purity of mind, their holiness of motive, and their happiness of life; these are the victims of false-witness. And how fares the wretch that would have starved them?

The fate of John Dillaway is at once so tragical, so interesting, and so instructive, that it will be well for us to be transported for awhile, and give this rogue the benefit of honest company.

For many months I had seen a sullen lowering fellow, with cropped head, ironed-legs, and the motley garments of disgrace, driven forth at early morning with his gang of bad compeers; a slave, toiling till nightfall in piling cannon-balls, and chipping off the rust with heavy hammers; a sentinel stood near with a loaded musket; they might not speak to each other, that miserable gang; hope was dead among them; life had no delights; they wreaked their silent hatred on those hammered cannon-balls. The man who struck the fiercest, that sullen convict with the lowering brow, was our stock-jobber, John Dillaway.

Soon after that foretaste of slavery at Woolwich, the ship sailed, freighted with incarnate crime; her captain was a ruffian; (could he help it with such cargoes?) her crew, the offscouring of all nations; and the Chesapeake herself was an old rotten hull, condemned, after one more voyage, to be broken up; a creaking, foul, unsafe vessel, full of rats, cockroaches, and other vermin.

The sun glared ungenially at that blot upon the waters, breeding infectious disease; the waves flung the hated burden from one to the other, disdainful of her freight of sin; the winds had no commission for fair sailing, but whistled through the rigglng crossways, howling in the ears of many in that ship, as if they carried ghosts along with them: the very rocks and reefs butted her off the creamy line of breakers, as sea-unicorns distorting; no affectionate farewell blessed her departure; no hearty welcomes await her at the port.

And they sailed many days as in a floating hell, hot, miserable, and cursing; the scanty meal was flung to them like dog's-meat, and they lapped the putrid water from a pail; gang by gang for an hour they might pace the smoking deck, and then and thence were driven down to fester in the hold for three-and-twenty more. O, those closed hatches by night! what torments were the kernel of that ship! Suffocated by the heat and noxious smells; bruised against each other, and by each other's blows, as the black unwieldy vessel staggered about among the billows, the wretched mass of human misery wore away those tropical nights in horrid imprecation; worse than crowded slaves upon the Spanish Main, from the blister of crime upon their souls, and their utter lack of hopefulness for ever.

And now, after all the shattering storms, and haggard sufferings, and degrading terrors of that voyage, they neared the metropolis of sin; some town on Botany Bay, a blighted shore—where each man, looking at his neighbour, sees in him an outcast from heaven. They landed in droves, that ironed flock of men; and the sullenest-looking scoundrel of them all was John Dillaway.

There were murderers among his gang; but human passions, which had hurried them to crime, now had left them as if wrecked upon a lee shore—humbled and remorseful, and heaven's happier sun shed some light upon their faces: there were burglars; but the courage which could dare those deeds, now lending strength to bear the stroke of punishment, enabled them to walk forth even cheerily to meet their doom of labour: there was rape; but he hid himself, ashamed, vowing better things: fiery arson, too, was there, sorry for his rash revenge: also, conspiracy and rebellion, confessing that ambition such as theirs had been wickedness and folly; and common frauds, and crimes, and social sins; bad enough, God wot, yet hopeful; but the mean, heartless, develish criminality of our young Dagon beat them all. If to be hard-hearted were a virtue, the best man there was Dillaway.

And now they were to be billeted off among the sturdy colonists as farm-servants, near a-kin to slaves; tools in the rough hands of men who pioneer civilization, with all the vices of the social, and all the passions of the savage. And on the strand, where those task-masters congregated to inspect the new-come droves, each man selected according to his mind: the rougher took the roughest, and the gentler, the gentlest; the merry-looking field farmer sought out the cheerful, and the sullen backwoods settler chose the sullen. Dillaway's master was a swarthy, beetled-browed caitiff, who had worn out his own seven years of penalty, and had now set up tyrant for himself.

As a hewer of wood and a drawer of water, in a stagnant little clearing of the forest, our convict toiled continually—continually—like Caliban: all days alike; hewing at the mighty trunk and hacking up the straggling branches; no hope—no help—no respite; and the iron of servile tyranny entered into his very soul. Ay—ay; the culprit convicted, when he hears in open court, with an impudent assurance, the punishment that awaits him on those penal shores, little knows the terrors of that sentence. Months and years—yea, haply to gray hairs and death, slavery unmitigated—uncomforted; toil and pain; toil and sorrow; toil, and nothing to cheer; even to the end, vain tasked toil. Old hopes, old recollections, old feelings, violently torn up by the roots. No familiar face in sickness, no patient nurse beside the dying bed: no hope for earth, and no prospect of heaven: but, in its varying phases, one gloomy glaring orb of ever-present hell.

It grew intolerable—intolerable; he was beaten, mocked, and almost a maniac. Escape—escape! Oh, blessed thought! into the wild free woods! there, with the birds and flowers, hill and dale, fresh air and liberty! Oh, glad hope—mad hope! His habitual cunning came to his aid; he schemed, he contrived, he accomplished. The jutting heads of the rivets having been diligently rubbed away from his galling fetter by a big stone—a toil of weeks—he one day stood unshackled, having watched his time to be alone. An axe was in his hand, and the saved single dinner of pea-bread. That beetled-browed task-master slumbered in the hut; that brother convict—(why need he care for him, too? every one for himself in this world)—that kinder, humbler, better man was digging in the open; if he wants to escape, let him think of himself: John Dillaway has enough to take care for. Now, then; now, unobserved, unsuspected; now is the chance! Joy, life, and liberty! Oh, glorious prospect—for this inland world is unexplored.

He stole away, with panting heart, and fearfully exulting eye; he ran—ran—ran, for miles—it may have been scores of them—till nightfall, on the soft and pleasant greensward under those high echoing woods. None pursued; safe—safe; and deliciously he slept that night beneath a spreading wattle-tree, after the first sweet meal of freedom.

Next morning, waked up like the starting kangaroos around him (for John Dillaway had not bent the knee in prayer since childhood), off he set triumphant and refreshed: his arm was strong, and he trusted in it, his axe was sharp, and he looked to that for help; he knew no other God. Off he set for miles—miles—miles: still that continuous high acacia wood, though less naturally park-like, often-times choked with briars, and here and there impervious a-head. Was it all this same starving forest to the wide world's end? He dug for roots, and found some acrid bulbs and tubers, which blistered up his mouth; but he was hungry, and ate them; and dreaded as he ate. Were they poisonous? Next to it, Dillaway; so he hurried eagerly to dilute their griping juices with the mountain streams near which he slept: the water was at least kindly cooling to his hot throat; he drank huge draughts, and stayed his stomach.

Next morning, off again: why could he not catch and eat some of those half-tame antelopes? Ha! He lay in wait hours—hours, near the torrent to which they came betimes to slake their thirst: but their beautiful keen eyes saw him askance—and when he rashly hoped to hunt one down afoot, they went like the wind for a minute—then turned to look at him afar off, mockingly—poor, panting, baffled creeper.

No; give it up—this savoury hope of venison; he must go despondently on and on; and he filled his belly with grass. Must he really starve in this interminable wood! He dreamt that night of luxurious city feasts, the turtle, turbot, venison, and champagne; and then how miserably weak he woke. But he must on wearily and lamely, for ever through this wood—objectless, except for life and liberty. Oh, that he could meet some savage, and do him battle for the food he carried; or that a dead bird, or beast, or snake lay upon his path; or that one of those skipping kangaroos would but come within the reach of his oft-aimed hatchet! No: for all the birds and flowers, and the free wild woods, and hill, and dale, and liberty, he was starving—starving; so he browsed the grass as Nebuchadnezzar in his lunacy. And the famished wretch would have gladly been a slave again.

Next morning, he must lie and perish where he slept, or move on: he turned to the left, not to go on for ever; probably, ay, too probably, he had been creeping round a belt. Oh, precious thought of change! for within three hours there was light a-head, light beneath the tangled underwood: he struggled through the last cluster of thick bushes, longing for a sight of fertile plain, and open country. Who knows? are there not men dwelling there with flocks and herds, and food and plenty? Yes—yes, and Dillaway will do among them yet. You envious boughs, delay me not! He tore aside the last that hid his view, and found that he was standing on the edge of an ocean of sand—hot yellow sand to the horizon!

He fainted—he had like to have died; but as for prayer—he only muttered curses on this bitter, famishing disappointment. He dared not strike into the wood again—he dared not advance upon that yellow sea exhausted and unprovisioned: it was his wisdom to skirt the wood; and so he trampled along weakly—weakly. This liberty to starve is horrible!

Is it, John Dillaway? What, have you no compunctions at that word starve? no bitter, dreadful recollections? Remember poor Maria, that own most loving sister, wanting bread through you. Remember Henry Clements, and their pining babe; remember your own sensual feastings and fraudulent exultation, and how you would utterly have starved the good, the kind, the honest! This same bitter cup is filled for your own lips, and you must drink it to the dregs. Have you no compunctions, man? nothing tapping at your heart? for you must *starve!*

No! not yet—not yet! for chance (what Dillaway lyingly called chance)—in his moments of remorse at these reflections, when God had hoped him penitent at last, and, if he still continued so, might save him —sent help in he desert! For, as he reelingly trampled along on the rank herbage between this forest and that sea of sand, just as he was dying of exhaustion, his faint foot trod upon a store of life and health! It was an Emeu's ill-protected nest; and he crushed, where he had trodden, one of those invigorating eggs. Oh, joy—joy—no thanks—but sensual joy! There were three of them, and each one meat for a day; ash-coloured without, but the within—the within—full of sweet and precious yolk! Oh, rich feast, luscious and refreshing: cheer up—cheer up: keep one to cross the desert with: ay—ay, luck will come at last to clever Jack! how shrewd it was of me to find those eggs!

Thus do the wicked forget thee, blessed God! thou hast watched this bad man day by day, and all the dark nights through, in tender expectation of some good: Thou hast been with him hourly in that famishing forest, tempting him by starvation to—repentance; and how gladly did Thine eager mercy seize this first opportunity of half-formed penitence to bless and help him—even him, liberally and unasked! Thanks to Thee—thanks to Thee! Why did not that man thank Thee? Who more grieved at his thanklessness than Thou art? Who more sorry for the righteous and necessary doom which the impenitence of heartlessness drags down upon itself?

And Providence was yet more kind, and man yet more ungrateful; mercy abounding over the abundant sin. For the famished vagrant diligently sought about for more rich prizes; and, as the manner is of those unnatural birds to leave their eggs carelessly to the hatching of the sunshine, he soon stumbled on another nest. "Ha—ha!" said he, "clever Jack Dillaway of Broker's alley isn't done up yet: no—no, trust him for taking care of number one; now then for the desert; with these four huge eggs and my trusty hatchet, deuce take it, but I'll manage somehow!"

Thus, deriving comfort from his bold hard heart, he launched unhesitatingly upon that sea of sand: with aching toil through the loose hot soil he ploughed his weary way, footsore, for leagues—leagues—lengthened leagues; yellow sand all round, before, and on either hand, as far as eye can stretch, and behind and already in the distance that terrible forest of starvation. But what, then, is the name of this burnt plain, unwatered by one liquid drop, unvisited even by dews in the cold dry night? Have you not yet found a heart, man, to thank Heaven for that kind supply of recreative nourishment, sweet as infant's food, the rich delicious yolk, which bears up still your halting steps across this world of sand? No heart—no heart of flesh—but a stone—a cold stone, and hard as yonder rocky hillock.

He climbed it for a view—and what a view! a panorama of perfect desolation, a continent of vegetable death. His spirit almost failed within him; but he must on—on, or perish where he stood. Taking no count of time, and heedless as to whither he might wander, so it be not back again along that awful track of liberty he longed for, he crept on by little and little, often resting, often dropping for fatigue, night and day—day and night: he had made his last meal; he laid him down to die—and already the premonitory falcon flapped him with its heavy wing. Ha! what are all those carrion fowls congregated there for? Are they battening on some dead carcase? O, hope—hope! there is the smell of food upon the wind: up, man, up—battle with those birds, drive them away, hew down that fierce white eagle with your axe; what right have they to precious food, when man, their monarch, starves? So, the poor emaciated culprit seized their putrid prey, and the scared fowls hovered but a little space above, waiting instinctively for this new victim: they had not left him much—it was a feast of remnants—pickings from the skeleton of some small creature that had perished in the desert—a wombat, probably, starved upon its travels; but a royal feast it was to that famishing wretch: and, gathering up the remainder of those priceless morsels, which he saved for some more fearful future, again he crept upon his way. Still the same, night and day—day and night—for he could only travel a league a-day: and at length, a shadowy line between the sand and sky—far, far off, but circling the horizon as a bow of hope. Shall it be a land of plenty, green, well-watered meadows, the pleasant homes of man, though savage, not unfriendly? O hope, unutterable! or is it (O despair!) another of those dreadful woods, starving solitude under the high-arched gum-trees.

Onward he crept; and the line on the horizon grew broader and darker: onward, still; he was exulting, he had conquered, he was bold and hard as ever. He got nearer, now within some dozen miles; it was an indistinct distance, but green at any rate; huzza—never mind night-fall; he cannot wait, nor rest, with this Elysium before him: so he toiled along through all the black night, and a friendly storm of rain refreshed him, as his thirsty pores drank in the cooling stream. Aha! by morning's dawn he should be standing on the edge of that green paradise, fresh as a young lion, and no thanks to any one but his own shrewd indomitable self.

Morning dawned—and through the vague twilight loomed some high and tangled wall of green foliage, stretching seemingly across the very world. Most sickening sight! a matted, thorny jungle, one of those primeval woods again, but closer, thicker, darker than the park-like one before, rank and prickly herbage in a rotting swamp, crowding up about the stately trees. Must he battle his way through? Well, then, if it must be so, he must and will; any thing rather than this hot and blistering sand. If he is doomed by fate to starve, be it in the shade, not in that fierce sun. So, he weakly plied his hatchet, flinging himself with boldness on that league-thick hedge of thorns; his way was choked with thorns; he struggled under tearing spines, and through prickly underwood, and over tangled masses of briery plants, clinging to him every where around, as with a thousand taloned claws; he is exhausted, extrication is impossible; he beats the tough creepers with his dulled hatchet, as a wounded man vainly; ha! one effort more—a dying effort—must he be impaled upon these sharp aloes, and strange-leafed prickly shrubs; they have caught him there, those thirsty poisoned hooks, innumerable as his sins; his way, whichever way he looks, is hedged up high with thorns—thick-set thorns—sturdy, tearing thorns, that he cannot battle through them. Emaciated, bleeding, rent, fainting, famished, he must perish in the merciless thicket into which hardheartedness had flung him!

Before he was well dead, those flapping carrion fowls had found him out; they were famishing too, and half forgot their natural distaste for living meat. He fought them vainly, as the dying fight; soon there were other screams in that echoing solitude, besides the screeching falcons! and when they reached his heart (if its matter aptly typified its spirit), that heart should have been a very stone for hardness.

So let the selfish die! alone, in the waste howling wilderness; so let him starve uncared-for, whose boast it was that he had never felt for other than himself—who mocked God, and scorned man—whose motto throughout life, one sensual, unsympathizing, harsh routine, was this: "Take care of the belly, and the heart will take care of itself!"—who never had a wish for other's good, a care for other's evil, a thought beyond his own base carcase; who was a man—no man—a wretch, without a heart. So let him perish miserably; and the white eagles pick his skeleton clean in yonder tangled jungle!

CHAPTER XIX.

WHEREIN MATTERS ARE CONCLUDED.

CERTAIN folks at Ballyriggan, near Belfast, observe to me, with not a little Irish truth, that it is by no means easy to conclude a history never intended to be finished. It so happens that my good friends the clan Clements are still enjoying life and all it sweets, beneficent in their generation; and as for their hearts' affections, that story without an end will still be heard, ringing on its happy changes, in the presence of God and of his immortal train, when every reader of these records shall have been to this world dead. Out of the heart are the issues of life, and within, it is life's well-spring. Death is but a little narrow gate, in a dark rough pass among the mountains, where each must go alone, one by one, in solemn silence, for the avalanches hanging overhead; one by one, in breathless caution, for there is but barely a footing; one by one, for none can help his brother on the track: the steady eye of faith, the firm foot of righteousness, the staff of hope to comfort and support—these be the only helps. And each one carries with him, as his sole possession on that lonely journey, no heaps of wealth—no trappings of honour; these burdens of the camel must all be lifted off, ere he can struggle through that gully in the rocks—"The Needle's Eye;" but the sole possession which every wayfarer must take with him into those broad plains where only Spirit can be seen, and Sin no longer can be hid, is the shrine of his affections, the casket of his precious pearls in life—his Heart, unmantled and unmasked. And if in time it had been a well of love, flowing towards God in penitence, and irrigating this world's garden with charities and blessed works, that little sparkling stream shall then burst forth from this rocky portal of the grave, a river of joy and peace, to gladden even more the sunny provinces of heaven. For the heart with its affections, never dieth: they may, indeed, flow inward, and corrupt to selfishness; becoming then, in lieu of fountains of waters, gushing forth to everlasting life, a bottomless volcano of hot lava, tempestuous and involved, setting up the creature as his own foul god, and living the perpetual death-bed of the damned; or they may nobly burst the banks of self, and, rising momentarily higher and higher, till every Nilometer is drowned, will seek for ever, with expanding strength, to reach the unapproachable level of that source in the Most

Highest whence they originally sprung. For this cause, the kindest fatherly word which ever reached man's ear, the surest scheme for happiness that ever touched his reason, was one from God's own heart—"My son, give me thy heart."

They lived upon the blessing of that Word, our noble, kindly pair. To enlarge upon the thought as respects a better world is well for those who will: for if He that made the eye and framed the ear, by the stronger argument Himself must see and hear, so he that fashioned loveliness and moulded the affections, how well-deserving must that Beautiful Spirit be of his rational creature's heart! Away with mawkish cant and stale sentimentalities! let us think, and speak, and feel as men, framed by nature's urgent law to the lovely and to hate the vile. Oh, that the advocates for Him, the Good One, would oftener plead His cause by the human affections—by generosity, by sympathy, by gentleness and patience, by self-denying love, and soul absolving beauty; for these are of the essence of God, and their spiritual influence on reaso child writes upon his heart that warmer code of morals, which the iron tool of threatening availeth not to grave upon the rock, while the voice of love can change that rock into a spring of water.

But we must descend from our altitudes, and speak of lower things; for the time and space forbid much longer intrusion on your courtesy. A few ravelling threads of this our desultory tale have yet to be gathered up, as tidily as may be. Suffer, then, such mingling of my thoughts: the web I weave has many threads, woven with divers colours. Human nature is nothing if not inconsistent; and I have no more notion of irreverence in turning from a high topic to a low one, than a bee may be fancied to have of irrelevant idleness in flitting from the sweet violet to the scented dahlia. We may gather honey out of every flower. Have you not often noticed, that riches generally come to a man, when he least stands in need of them? Directly a middle-aged heir succeeds to his long-expected heritage, half-a-dozen aunts and second cousins are sure to die off and leave him super-abounding legacies, any one of which would have helped his poverty stricken youth, and made him of independent mind throughout his servile manhood. The other day (the idea remains the same, though the fact is to be questioned) the richest lord in Europe dug up a chest of hoarded coins, many thousand pound's worth, simply because he didn't want it: and, if such particularization were not improper or invidious, you or I might name a brace of friends a-piece, who, having once lacked bread in the career of life, suddenly have found themselves monopolizing two or three great fortunes. As too few things are certain, novel writers less like truth in their descriptions, than where ample wealth falls upon the hero just in the nick of time. Providence intends to teach by penury: yes, and by prosperity too: and we almost never see the reward given, or the no less reward withheld, just as the scholar has begun to spell his lesson, and before he has had the chance of getting it by heart.

That another death should occur, in the progress of this tale, must be counted for no fault of mine; especially as I am not about to introduce another death-bed. One need not have the mummy always at our feasts. Surely, too, these deaths have ever been on fit occasion: one broken heart; one bereaved, yet comforted; and one which perished in its sin of uttermost hard-heartedness. And here, if any insurance clerk, or other interested person, will show cause why Mrs. Jane Mackenzie should not die at the age of ninety-two, I would keep her alive if I could; but the fact is, I cannot: she died. Henry Clements never saw her, any more that I, nor dear Maria. But that was no earthly reason wherefore—

First, Maria should not bewail the dear old relative's loss with all her heart and eyes, and children and household in mourning.

Nor, *secondly*, wherefore Mrs. Jane Mackenzie, aforesaid, of Ballyriggan, province of Ulster, should not leave her estate of Ballyriggan, aforesaid, and a vast heap of other property, to the only surviving though distant scion of her family, Henry Clements.

Nor, *thirldy*, wherefore I should not record the fact, as duly bound in my capacity of honest historian.

Tnis accession of property was large, almost overwhelming, when added to Maria's patrimony of three thousand a-year, the produce of St. Benet's Sherehog: for besides and beyond a considerable breadth of Irish acres, sundry houses in Belfast, and an accumulation of half-forgotten funds, the Bank of England found itself necessitated (from particular circumstances of ill-caution in its servants) to refund the whole of that twelve thousand forty-three pounds bank annuities, which Jack Dillaway and his ladies had already made away with.

Rich, however, as Clements had become, he felt himself only as a great lord's steward to help a needy world; and I never heard that he spent a sixpence more upon himself, his equipage, or his family, from being some thousands a-year richer: though I certainly did hear that, owing to this legacy, every tenant upon Ballyriggan, and a vast number of struggling families in Spitalfields and round about St. Benet's, had ample cause to bless Heaven and the good man of Finsbury square. As for dear Maria, it rejoiced her generous heart to find that Henry (whose gentlemanly pride had all along been reproaching him for pauperism) was now become pretty well her equal in wealth; even as her humility long had known him her superior in mind, good looks, and good family.

Another thread in my discourse, hanging loosely on the world, concerns our lady-legatees. What became of Miss Julia, after the safe and successful issue of that vengeful trial, I never heard: and, perhaps, it may be wise not to inquire: if she changed her name, she did not change her nature: and is probably still to be numbered among the sect of Strand peripatetics.

But of Anna Bates I have pleasanter news to tell. With respect to repentance, let us be charitable, and hope, even if we cannot be so sanguine as firmly to believe; but at any rate we may rest assured of an outward reformation, and an honest manner of life. The miracle happened thus: After the trial and condemnation of Dillaway, poor Anna Bates felt entirely disappointed that she had not the chance of better things presented to her mind by transportation; the two approvers, to her dismay—poor thing!—were graciously pardoned for their evidence; and, whereas, the one of them returned to her old courses more devotedly than ever, the other resolved to make one strong effort to extricate her loathing self from the gulf in which she lay. Fortunately for her, our Maria had the heart to pity and to help a frail and fallen sister; and when the poor disconsolate woman, finding her to be the sister of that evil paramour, came to Mrs. Clements in distress, revealing all her past sins and sorrows, and pleading for some generous hand to lift her out of that miserable state, she did not plead in vain. Maria spurned her not away, nor coldly disbelieved her promise of amendment; but, taking counsel of her husband, she gave the poor woman sufficient means of setting up a milliner's shop at Hull, where, under her paternal name of Stellingburne, our Fleet street lady-legatee still survives, earning a decent livelihood, and little suspected amongst her kindly neighbours of ever having been much worse than a strictly honest woman.

For another thread, if the reader, in his ample curiosity, wishes to be informed how it became possible for me to learn the fate of Dillaway, let him know, that up to the hour of escape, I derived it easily from living witnesses; and thereafter, that certain settlers, having set out to explore the country, found a human skeleton stretched upon a thicket which, from the *débris* of convicts' clothes, and the hatchet stamped with his initials, was easily decided to be that bad man's. It always had struck me, as a remarkable piece of retribution, that whereas John made Austral shares a plea for ruining Henry Clements, a howling Austral wilderness was made the means of starving him. Maria never heard what became of her brother; but still looks for his return some day with affectionate and earnest expectation.

Another little matter to be mentioned is the fact, that Henry Clements, in his leisure from business, and freedom from care, resolved to attain some literary glories; and first, he published his now-renowned tragedy of '*Boadicea*,' with his name at length, giving a mint of proceeds to that very proper charity the Theatrical Fund. Secondly, he followed up his tragic triumph by a splendid '*Caractacus*,' by way of a companion picture. Thirdly, he turned to his maligned law-treatise on *Defence*, and boldly published a capital vindication thereof, flinging down his gauntlet to the judges both of law and literature. It was strange, by the way, and instructive also, to find with what a deferential air the wealthy writer now was listened to; and how meekly both '*Watchman*' and '*Corinthian*' kissed the smiling hand of the literary genius, who—gave such sumptuous dinners; for Henry, of his mere kindness, (not bribery—don't imagine him so weak,) now that he was known as a Mæcenas amongst authors, made no invidious distinctions between literary magnates, but effectually overcame evil with good by his hearty hospitality to '*Corinthian*' and '*Watchman*' editors, as well as to other potent wielders of the pen of fame, who had erst-while favoured the productions of his genius.

The last dinner he gave, I, an old friend of the family, was present; and when the ladies went up-stairs, I had, as usual, the honour of enacting vice. It was according to Finsbury taste and custom, to produce toasts and speeches; whether cold high-breeding would have sanctioned this or not, little matters: it was warm and cordial, and we all liked it; moreover, finding ourselves at Rome, we unanimously did as other Romans do: and this I take to be politeness. Among the speeches, that which proposed the health of the host and hostess caused the chiefest roar of clamorous joy: it was a happy-looking friend who spoke, and what he said was much as follows:

"Clements, my dear fellow, you are the happiest man I know—except myself; at least, in one thing I am happier—for I can call you friend, whereas you can only return the compliment with such a sorry substitute as I am."

[This ingenious flattery was much ridiculed afterwards; but I pledge my word the man intended what he said; moreover, he went on, utterly regardless of surrounding critics, in all the seeming egotism of a warm and open heart.]

"Clements—I cannot help telling you how heartily I love you;" (Hear, hear!) "and I wish I had known you thirty years instead of three, to have said so with the unction of my earliest recollections: but we cannot help antiquity, you know. Let us all the rather make up now by heartiness for all lost time. I think, nay, am sure, that I speak the language of all present in telling you I love you:" (an enormous hear-hearing, which rose above the drawing-room floor; Harry Clements singularly distinguished himself, in proving how he loved his father; a fine young fellow he grows too, and I wish, between ourselves, to catch him for a son-in-law some day;)—"Yes, Clements, I do love you, and your children, and your wife, for there is the charm of heart about you all: in yourself, in your Maria, in that fine frank youth, and those dear warm girls up stairs" (every word was bravoed to the echo), "in every one of you, all the charities and amenities, all the kindnesses and the cheerfulness of life appear to be embodied; you love both God and man; the rich and the poor alike may bless you, Clements, and your admirable Maria; whilst, as for yourselves, you may both well thank God, whose mercy made you what you are."

Clements hid his face, and Harry sobbed with joyfulness.

"Friends! a toast and sentiment, with all the honours: 'This happy family! and may all who know them now, or come to hear of them in future, cultivate as they do all the home affections, and acknowledge that there is no wealth of man's, which may compare with riches of the heart.'"

28

THE END OF HEART.

AN AUTHOR'S MIND;

THE BOOK OF TITLE-PAGES:

"A BOOKFUL OF BOOKS," OR "THIRTY BOOKS IN ONE."

EDITED BY

M. F. TUPPER, ESQ., M. A.

En un mot, mes amis, je n'ai entrepis de vous contenter tous en general; ainsi, uns et autres en particulier; et par special, moymême."—PASQUIER.

HARTFORD:
PUBLISHED BY SILAS ANDRUS & SON.

1851.

ANNOUNCEMENT.

BY THE EDITOR.

The writer of this strange book (a particular friend of mine) came to me a few mornings ago with a very happy face and a very blotty manuscript. "Congratulate me," he began, "on having dispersed an armada of head-aches hitherto invincible, on having exorcised my brain of its legionary spectres, and brushed away the swarming thoughts that used to persecute my solitude; I can now lie down as calmly as the lamb, and rise as gayly as the lark; instead of a writhing Laocoon, my just-found Harlequin's wand has changed me into infant Hercules brandishing his strangled snakes; I have mowed, for the nonce, the docks, mallows, hogweed, and wild-parsley of my rank field, and its smooth green carpet looks like a rich meadow; I am free, happy, well at ease: argal, an thou lovest me, congratulate."

Wider and wider still stared out my wonder, to hear my usually sober friend so voluble in words and so profuse of images: I saw at once it was a set speech, prepared for an impromptu occasion; nevertheless, as he was clearly in an enviable state of disenthraldom from thoughtfulness, I graciously accorded him a sympathetic smile. And then this more than Gregorian cure for the head-ache! here was an anodyne infinitely precious to one so brain-feverish as I: had all this pleasure and comfort arisen from such common-place remedials as a dear young lover's courtesy or a deceased old miser's codicil, I should long ago have heard all about it; for, between ourselves, my friend was never known to keep a secret. There was evidently more than this in the discovery; and when my curiosity, provoked by his laughing silence, was naturally enough exhibiting itself in a "What on earth——?" he broke out with the abruptness of an Abernethy, "Read my book."

Well, I did read it; and, in candid disparagement, as amicably bound, can readily believe what I was told afterwards, that, to except a very small portion of older material, it had been at chance intervals rapidly thrown off in a couple of months, (the old current-quill style,) chiefly with the view of relieving a too prolific brain: it appeared to me a mere idle overflowing of the brimful mind; an honest, indeed, but often useless exposure of multifarious fancies—some good, some bad, and not a few indifferent; an incautious uncalled-for confession of a thousand thoughts, little worth the printing, if the very writing were not indeed superfluous. Nevertheless, with all its faults, I thought the book a novelty, and liked it not the less for its off-hand fashion; it had something of the free, fresh, frank air of an old-school squire at Christmas-tide, suggestive as his misletoe, cheerful as his face, and careless as his hospitality. Knowing then that my friend had been more than once an author—indeed, he tells us so himself —and perceiving, from innumerable symptoms, that he meditated putting also this before the world, I thought kindly to anticipate his wishes by proposing its publication: but I was rather curtly answered with a "Did I suppose these gnats were intended to be shrined in amber? these mere minnows to be treated with the high consideration due only to potted char and white bait? these fleeting thoughts fixed in stone before that Gorgon-head, the public? these ephemeral fancies dropped into the true elixir of immortality, printer's-ink? these——" I stopped him, for this other mighty mouthful of images betrayed the hypocrite—"Yes, I did." An involuntary smile assured me he did too, and the cause proceeded thus: first, a promise not to burn the book; then a Bentley to the rescue, with accessory considerations; and then, the due administration of a little wholesome flattery: by this time we had obtained permission, after modest reluctance pretty well enacted, to transform the deformity of manuscript into the well-proportioned elegance of print. But, this much gained, our author would not yield to any argument we could urge upon the next point, viz: leave to produce the volume, duly fathered with his name. "Not he indeed; he loved quiet too well; he might, it was true, secretly like the bantling, but cared not to acknowledge it before a populous reading-world, every individual whereof esteems himself and herself competent to criticize!" Mr. Publisher, deeply disinterested, of course, bristled up at the notion of any thing anonymous; and the only alternative remaining was the stale expedient of an editor; that editor, in brief, to be none other than myself, a very palpable-obscure: and let this excuse my name upon the title-page.

Now, as editor, I have had to do—what seems, by the way, to be regarded by collective wisdom as the best thing possible—nothing: my author would not suffer the change of a syllable, for all his seeming carelessness about the THING, as he called it; so, I had no more for my part than humbly to act the Helot, and try to set decently upon the public tables a genuine mess of Spartan porridge.

M. F. T.

Albury, Guildford.

AN AUTHOR'S MIND:

THE

BOOK OF TITLE-PAGES.

A RAMBLE.

In these days of universal knowledge, schoolmaster and scholars all abroad together, quotation is voted pedantry, and to interpret is accounted an impertinence; yet will I boldly proclaim, as a mere fact, clear to the perceptions of all it may concern, "This book deserves richly of the Sosii." And that for the best of reasons: it is not only a book, but a book full of books; not merely a new book, but a little-library of new books; thirty books in one, a very harvest of epitomized authorship, the cream of a whole fairy dairy of quiescent post-octavos. It is not—O, mark ye this, my Sosii, (and by the way, gentle ladies, these were worshipful booksellers of old, the Murrays and the Bentleys of imperial Rome,)—it is not the dull concreted elongation of one isolated hackneyed idea—supposing in every work there *be one,* a charitable hypothesis—wire-drawn, and coaxed, and hammered through three regulation volumes; but the scarcely-more-than-hinted abstractions of some forty thousand flitting notions—hasty, yet meditative Hamlets; none of those lengthy, drawling emblems of Laertes—driven in flocks to the net of the fowler, and penned with difficult compression within these modest limits. So "goe forth, littel boke," and make thyself a friend among those good husbandmen, who tend the trees of knowledge, and bring their fruit to the world's market.

Now, reader, one little preliminary parley with you about myself: here beginneth the trouble of authorship, but it is a trouble causing ease; ease from thoughts—thoughts—thoughts, which never cease to make one's head ache till they are fixed on paper; ease from dreams by night and reveries by day, (thronging up in crowds behind, like Deucalion's children, or a serried host in front, like Jason's instant army,) harassing the brain, and struggling for birth, a separate existence, a definite life; ease, in a cessation of that continuous internal hum of aërial forget-me-nots, clamouring to be recorded. O, happy unimaginable vacancy of mind, to whistle as you walk for want of thought! O, mental holiday, now as impossible to me, as to take a true school-boy's interest in rounders and prisoner's base! An author's mind—and remember always, friend, I write in character, so judge not as egotistic vanity merely the well playing of my *rôle*—such a mind is not a sheet of smooth wax, but a magic stone indented with fluttering inscriptions; no empty tenement, but a barn stored to bursting: it is a painful pressure, constraining to write for comfort's sake; an appetite craving to be satisfied, as well as a power to be exerted; an impetus that longs to get away, rather than a dormant dynamic: thrice have I (let me confess it) poured forth the alleviating volume as an author, a real author—real, because for very peace of mind, involuntarily; but still the vessel fills; still the indigenous crop springs up, choking a better harvest, seeds of foreign growth; still those Lernæan necks sprout again, claiming with many mouths to explain, amuse, suggest, and controvert—to publish invention, and proscribe error. Truly, it were enviable to be less apprehensive, less retentive; to be fitted with a colander-mind, like that penal cask which forty-nine Danaïdes might not keep from leaking; to be, sometimes at least, suffered for a holiday to ramble brainless in the paradise of fools. Memory, imagination, zeal, perceptions of men and things, equally with rank and riches, have often cost their full price, as many mad have known; they take too much out of a man—fret, wear, worry him; to be irritable, is the conditional tax laid of old upon an author's intellect; the crowd of internal imagery makes him hasty, quick, nervous as a haunted hunted man: minds of coarser web heed not how small a thorn rends one of so delicate a texture; they cannot estimate the wish that a duller sword were in a tougher scabbard; the river, not content with channel and restraining banks, overflows perpetually; the extortionate exacting armies of the Ideal and the Causal persecute MY spirit, and I would make a patriot stand at once to vanquish the invaders of my peace: I write these things only to be quit of them, and not to let the crowd increase; I have conceived a plan to destroy them all, as Jehu and Elijah with the priests of Baal; I feel Malthusian among my mental nurselings; a dire resolve has filled me to effect a premature destruction of the literary populace superfœtating in my brain—plays, novels, essays, tales, homilies, and rhythmicals; for ethics and poetics, politics and rhetorics, will I display no more mercy than sundry commentators of maltreated Aristotle: I will exhibit them in their state chaotic; I will addle the eggs, and the chicken shall not chirp; I will reveal, and secrets shall not waste me; I will write, and thoughts shall not batten on me.

The world is too full of books, and I yearn not causelessly to add more than this involuntary unit: bottles, bottles—invariable bottles—was the one idea of a most clever Head at Nieder-Selters; books, books—accumulating books—press upon my conscience in this literary London: despairing auctioneers hate the sound, ruined publishers dread it, surfeited readers grumble at it, and the very cheese-monger begins to be an epicure as to which grand work is next to be demolished. Friendships and loves tremble at the daily recurrence of "Have you read this?" and "Mind you buy that;" wise men shun a blue-belle, sure that she will recommend a book; and the yet wiser treat themselves to solitary confinement, that they may not have to meet the last new batch of authors, and be obliged to purchase, if not to peruse, their never-ending books. I fear to increase the plague, to be convicted an abettor of great evils, though by the measure of a little one. I am infected, and I know it: but for science-sake I break the quarantine, and in my magnanimity would be victimized unknown, consigning to a speedy grave this useless offspring, together with its too productive parent, and saving of a race so hopeless little else than their prĕdetermined names—in fact, their title-pages.

But is that indeed little? Speak, authors with piles of ready-written copy, is not the theme (so often carried out beyond, or beside, or even against its original purpose) less perplexing than the after-thought thesis? Bear witness, readers, bit by a mysterious advertisement in the '*Morning Post*,' are names, indeed, not matters of much weight? Press forward, Sosii aforesaid, and answer me truly, is not a title-page the better part of many books? Cheap promises of stale pleasure, false hopes of dull interest, imprimaturs of deceived fancy, lying visions of the future unfulfilled, title-pages still do good service to the cause of—bookselling.

And, to commence, let me elucidate mine own—I mean the first, the head and front of this offending phalanx—mine own, *par excellence*, '*An Authors Mind*:' such in sooth it shall be found, for richer or poorer, for better or for worse; not of selfish, but of common application; not so much individually of mine own, as generically of authors; a medley of crudities; an undigested mass, as any in the maw of Polypheme; a fermenting hotchpotch of half-formed things, illustrative, among other matters, of the Lucretian theory, those close-cohering atoms; a farrago of thoughts, and systems of thoughts, in most admired disorder, which would symbolize the Corpernican astronomy, with its necessary clash of whirling orbs, about as well as the intangible chaos of Berkeleyan metaphysics.

So much then on the moment for the monosyllable "Mind;"—whereof followeth, indeed, all the more hereafter; but—"An author's?"—what author's? You would see my patent of such rank, my commission to wear such honourable uniform. Pr'ythee be content with simple assurance that it is so; consider the charm of unsatisfied curiosity, and pry not; let me sit unseen, a spectator; for this once I would go *in domino.* Heretofore, "credit me, fair Discretion, your Affability" hath achieved glory, and might Solomonize on its vanity at least as well as poor discomfited, discovered Sir Piercie Shafton: heretofore, I have stood forth in good causes, with helm unbarred, and due proclamation of name, style, and title, an avowed author; and might sermonize thus upon success, that a little censure loseth more friends than much praise winneth enemies. So now, with visor down, and a white shield, as a young knight-candidate unknown, it pleases my leisure to take my pastime in the tourney: and so long as in truthful prowess I bear me gallantly and gently, who is he that hath a right to unlatch my helmet, or where is the herald that may challenge my rank? Nevertheless, inquisitive, consider the mysteries that lie in the Turkish-looking *sobriquet* of "Mufti;" its vowels and its consonants are full of strict intention: I never saw cause why the most charming of essayists hid himself in "Elia," but he may for all that have had pregnant reasons; even so, (but that slender wit could read my riddle,) you shall perhaps find fault with my Mussulman agnomen; still you and I equally participate in this shallow secret, and within so brief a word is concealed the key to unlock the casket that tempts your curiosity: however, the less said of so diaphanous a mystery, the better.

And let me remark this of the mode anonymous; a mode, indeed, to purposes of shame, and slander, and falsity of all kinds too often prostituted: for the present, bear with it; sometimes it is well to go disguised, and the voice of one unseen lacks not eager listeners; we address your judgment, unbiased by the prejudice or sanction of a name: we put forth, lightly and negligently, those lesser matters which opportunity hath not yet matured; we escape the nervous pains, the literary perils of the hardier acknowledged. Only of this one thing be sure; we—(no, I; why should unregal, unhierarchal I affect pluralities?)—I hope to keep inviolate, as much when masked as when avowed, the laws of truth, charity, sincerity, and honour; and, although, among my many booklets, the grave and the gay will be found in near approximation, I trust—will it offend any to tell them that I pray?—to do no ill service at any time to the cause of that true religion which resents not the neighbourhood of innocent cheerfulness. I show you, friend, my honest mind.

I by itself, I; odious mono-literal; thinnest, feeblest, most insignificant of letters, I dread your egotistic influence as my bane; they will not suffer you, nor bear with a book so speckled with your presence. Still, world, hear me; mercifully spare a poor grammarian the penance of perpetual third persons; let an individual tender conscience escape censure for using the true singular in preference to that imposing lie, the plural. Suffer a humble unit to speak of himself as I, and, once for all, let me permissively disclaim intentional self-conceit in the needful usage of isolated I-ship.

These few preliminaries being settled, though I fear little to the satisfaction of either party concerned, let us proceed—further to preliminarize; for you will find, even to the end, as you may have found out already from the beginning, that your white knight is mounted rather on an ambling preambling palfrey, than on any determinate charger; curveting and prancing, and rambling and scrambling at his own unmanaged will: scorning the bit and bridle, too hot to bear the spur, careless of listing laws, and wishing rather playfully to show his paces, than to tilt against a foe.

An author's mind, *quà* author, is essentially a gossip; an oral, ocular, imaginative, common-place-book: a *pot pourri* mixed from the *hortus siccus* of education, and the greener garden of internal thought that springs in fresh verdure about the heart's own fountain; a compound of many metals flowing from the mental crucible as one—perchance a base alloy, perchance new, and precious, and beautiful as the fine brass of Corinth; an accidental meeting in the same small chamber of many spiritual essences that combine, as by magnetism into some strange and novel substance; a mixture of appropriations, made lawfully a man's own by labour spent upon the raw material; corn-clad Egypt rescued from a burnt Africa by the richness of a swelling Nile—the black forest of pines changed into a laughing vineyard by skill, enterprise, and culture—the mechanism of Frankenstein's man of clay, energized at length by the spark Promethean.

And now, reader, do you begin to comprehend me, and my title? '*An Author's Mind*' is first in the field, and, as with root and fruit, must take precedence of its booklets; bear then, if you will, with this desultory anatomization of itself yet a little longer, and then in good time and moderate space you will come to the rudiments—bones, so to speak—of its many members, the frame-work on which its nerves and muscles hang, the names of its unborn children, the title-pages of its own unprinted books.

Philosophers and fools, separately or together, as the case may be—for folly and philosophy not seldom form one Janus-head, and Minerva's bird seems sometimes not ill-fitted with the face of Momus—these and their thousand intermediates have tried in all ages to define that quaint enigma, Man: and I wot not that any pundit of literature hath better succeeded than the nameless, fameless man—or woman, was it?—or haply some innocent shrewd child—who whilom did enunciate that MAN IS A WRITING ANIMAL: true as arithmetic, clear as the sunbeam, rational as Euclid, a discerning, just, exclusive definition. That he is "capable of laughter," is well enough even for thy deathless fame, O Stagyrite! but equally (so Buffon testifies) are apes and monkeys, horses and hyenas; whether perforce of tickling or sympathy, or native notions of the humorous, we will not stop to contend. That he actually is "an animal whose best wisdom is laughter," hath but little reason in it, Democrite, seeing there are such obvious anomalies among men as suicidal jesters and cachinating idiots; nevertheless, my punster of Abdera, thy whimsical fancy, surviving the wreck of dynasties, and too light to sink in the billows of oblivion, is now become the popular thouhgt, the fashionable dress of heretofore moping wisdom: crow, an thou wilt, jolly old chanticleer, but remember thee thou crowest on a dung-hill; man is not a mere merry-andrew. Neither is he exclusively "a weeping animal," lugubrious Heraclite, no better definer than thy laughter-loving foe: that man weeps, or ought to weep, the world within him and the world without him indeed bear testimony: but is he the only mourner in this valley of grief, this travailing creation? No, no; they walk lengthily in black procession: yet is this present writing not the fit season for enlarging upon sorrows; we must not now mourn and be desolate as a poor bird grieving for its pilfered young—is Macduff's lamentable cry for his lost little ones, "All—what, all?" more piteous? —we must now indulge in despondent fears, like yonder hard-run stag, with terror in his eye, and true tears coursing down his melancholy face: we must not now mourn over cruelty and ingratitude, like that poor old worn-out horse, crying—positively crying, and looking imploringly for merciful rest into man's iron face; we must not scream like the wounded hare, nor beat against our cage like the wild bird prisoned from its freedom. Moreover, Heraclite, even in thine own day thou mightest well have heard of the classic wailings of Philomel for Atys, or of consumptive Canens, that shadow of a voice, for her metamorphosed Pie, and have known that very crocodiles have tears: pass on, thy desolate definition hath not served for man.

With flippant tongue a mercantile cosmopolite, stable in statistics and learned in the leger, here interposes an erudite suggestion: "Man is a calculating animal." Surely, so he is, unless he be a spendthrift; but he still shares his quality with others; for the squirrel hoards his nuts, the aunt lays in her barley-corns, the moon knoweth her seasons, and the sun his going down: moreover, Chinese slates, multiplying rulers, and, as their aggregated wisdom, Babbage's machine, will stoutly contest so mechanical a fancy. Savoury steams, and those too smelling strongly of truth, assault the nostrils, as a Vitellite—what a name of hungry omen for the imperial devourer!—plausibly insinuates man to be "a cooking animal." Who can gainsay it? and wherewithal, but with domesticated monkeys, does he share this happy attribute? It is true, the butcher-bird spits his prey on a thorn, the slow epicurean boa glazes his mashed antelope, the king of vultures quietly waits for a gamey taste and the rapid roasting of the tropics: but all this care, all this caloric, cannot be accounted culinary, and without a question, the kitchen *is* a sphere where the lord of creation reigns supreme: still, thou best of practical philosophers, caterer for daily dinners—man—MAN, I say, is not altogether a compact of edible commons, a Falstaff pudding-bag robbed of his seasoning wit, a mere congeries of food and pickles; moreover, honest Gingel of "fair" fame hath (or used to have, "in my warm youth, when George the Third was king,") automatons, [pray, observe, Sosii, I am not pedant or wiseacre enough to indite *automata;* we conquering Britons stole that word among many others from poor dead Greece, who couldn't want it; having made it ours in the singular, why be bashful about the plural! So also of memorandums, omnibuses, [you remember Farren's *omni*BI!] necropolises, gymnasiums, eukeirogeneions, and other unlegacied property of dear departed Rome and Greece. All this, as you see, is clearly parenthetical;] well, then, Gingel has automatons, that will serve you up all kinds of delicate viands, pleasant meats, and choice cates by clock-work, to say nothing of Jones' patent all-in-a-moment-any-thing-whatsoever cooking apparatus: no mine Apiciite, Heliogabalite, Sardanapalite, Seftonite, Udite, thou of extravagant ancestry and indifferent digestion; little, indeed, as you may credit me, man is not all stomach, nor altogether formed alone for feeding. Remember Æsop's parable, the belly and the members; and, above them all, do not overlook the head.

What think you then of "a featherless biped?" gravely suggests a rusty Plinyite. Absolute sir, and most obsolete Roman, doubtless you never had the luck to set eyes upon a turkey at Christmas; the poor bare *bipes implumis*, a forked creature, waiting to be forked supererogatively; ay, and *risibilis* to boot, if ever all concomitants of the hearty old festival were properly provocative of decent mirth. Thus then return we to our muttons, and time enough, quotha: literary pundit, (whose is the notable saying?) thy definition is bomb-proof, thy fancy unscaleable, thy thought too deep for undermining; that notion is at the head of the poll, a candidate approved of Truth's most open borough; for, in spite of secretary-birds with pens stuck clerk-like behind their ears (as useless an emblem of sinecure office as gold keys, silver, and coronation armour)—in spite of whole flights of geese, capable enough of saving capitols, but impotent to wield one of their own all-conquering quills—in spite, also, (keen-eyed categorists, be to my faults in ratiocination a little blind, for very cheerfulness,) in spite, I say, of copying presses, manifold inditers, and automaton artists, MAN IS A WRITING ANIMAL.

Wearily enough, you will think, have we disposed of this one definition: but recollect, and take me for a son of leisure, an amateur tourist of Parnassus, an idling gatherer of way-side flowers in the vale of Thessaly, a careless, unbusied, "contemplative man," recreating himself by gentle craft on the banks of much-poached Helicon; and if you, my casual friend, be neither like-minded in fancy nor like-fitted in leisure, courteously consider that we may not travel well together: at this station let us stop, freely forgiving each other for mutual misliking; to your books, to your business, to your fowling, to your feasting, to your mummery, to your nunnery—go: my track lays away from the high-road, in and out between yonder hills, among thickets, mossy rocks, green hollows, high fern, and the tangled hair of hiding river-gods; I meet not pedlers and bagsmen, but stumble upon fawns just dropped, and do not scare their doting mothers; I quench not my noonday thirst with fiery drams from a brazen tap, but, lying over the cold brook, drink to its musical Naiades; I walk no dusty roads of a working-day world, but flit upon the pleasant places of one made up of holidays.

A truce to this truancy, and method be my maxim: let us for a moment link our reasonings, and solder one stray rivet; man being a writing animal, there still remains the question, what is writing? Ah, there's the rub: a very comfortable definition would it be, if every pen-holder and pen-wiper could truly claim that kingship of the universe—that imagery of his Maker—that mystical, marvellous, immortal, intellectual, abstraction, manhood: but, what then is WRITING? Ye tons of invoices, groaning shelves of incalculable legers, parchment abhorrences of rare Charles Lamb, we think not now of you; dreary piles of unhealthy-looking law-books, hypochondriacal heaps of medical experiences, plodding folios of industrious polemics, slow elaborations of learned dullness, we spare your native dust; letters unnumbered, in all stages of cacography, both physical and metaphysical, alack! most of you must slip through the meshes of our definition yet unwove; poor deciduous leaves of the forest, that, at your best, serve only—it is yet a good purpose—to dress the common soil of human kindness, without attaining to the praise of wreaths and chaplets ever hanging in the Muses' temple; flowers withered on the stalk, whose blooming beauty no lover's hand has dropped upon the sacred waters of Siloa, like the Hindoo's garland on her Ganges; prolix, vain, ephemeral letters (especially enveloped penny-posters)—and sparing only some few redolent of truth, wisdom, and affection—your bulky majority of flippant trash, staid advices, dunnings, hoaxings, lyings, and slanderings, degrade you to a lower rank than that we take on us to designate as "writing."

And what, O what—"how poor is he that hath not patience!"—shall we predicate of the average viscera of circulating libraries?—abominable viscera!—isn't that the word, my young Hippocrates?—A parley—a parley! and the terms of truce are these: If this present pastime of mine (for pastime it is, so spurn not at its logic,) be mercifully looked on by you, lady novelists and male dittoes—yet truly there are giants in your ranks, as Scott, and Ward, and Hugo, and Le Sage, towering above ten thousand pigmies)—if I be spared your censures well-deserved, interchangeably as toward your authorships will I exercise the charitable wisdom of silence: a white flag or a white feather is my best alternative in soothing or avoiding so terrible a host; and verily, to speak kinder of those whose wit, and genius, and graphic powers have so smoothed this old world's wrinkled face of care, many brilliant, many clever, many well-intended caterers to public amusement, throng your ill-ordered ranks: still, there are numbered to your shame as followers of the fool's-cap standard, the huge corrupting mass of depraved moralists, meagre trash-inditers, treacherous scandal-mongers, men about town who immortalize their shame, and the dull, pernicious school of feather-brained Romancists: and take this sentence for a true one, a *verum-dictum.* But enough, there are others, and those not few, even far less veniable; ye priers into family secrets—fawning, false guests at the great man's open house, eagerly jotting down with paricidal pen the unguarded conversation of the hospitable board—shame on your treason, on its wages, and its fame! ye countless gatherers and disposers of other men's stuff; chiels amang us takin' notes, an' faith, to prent 'em too, perpetually, without mitigation or remorse; ye men of paste and scissors, who so often falsely, feebly, faithlessly, and tastelessly are patching into a Harlequin whole the *disjecta membra* of some great hacked-up reputation; can such as ye are tell me what it is to write? Writing is the concreted fruit of thinking, the original expression of new combinations of idea, the fresh chemical product of educational compounds long simmering in the mind, the possession of a sixth sense, distinguishing intelligence, and proclaiming it to the four winds; writing is not labour, but ease; not care, but happiness; not the petty pilferings of poverty, but the large overflowings of mental affluence; it begs not on the highway, but gives great largess, like a king; it preys not on a neighbour's wealth, but enriches him; it may light, indeed, a lamp, at another's candle, but pays him back with brilliancy; it may borrow fire from the common stock, but uses it for genial warmth and noble hospitality.

Remember well, good critic, (for verily bad there be,) my purposes in this odd volume—this queer, unsophisticate, uncultivated book: to empty my mind, to clear my brain of cobwebs, to lift off my head a porters's load of fancy articles; and as in a bottle of bad champaign, the first glass, leaping out hurryskurry, at a railroad pace boiling a gallop, carries off with it bits of cork and morsels of rosin, even such is the first ebullition of my thoughts: take them for what they are worth, and blame no one but your discontented self that they are no better. Do you suppose, keen sir, that I am not quite self-conscious of their shallowness, utter contempt of subordination and selection, their empty reasoning and pellucid vanity?—There I have saved you the labour of a sentence, and present you with a killing verdict for myself. After a little, perhaps, your patience may find me otherwise; of clearer flow, but flatter flavour: these desultorinesses must first of all be immolated, for in their Ariel state they vex me, but I bind them down like slaving Calibans, by the magic of a pen; and glad shall I be to victimize my monsters, eager to dissipate my musquito-like tormentors; yea, I would "take up arms against a sea"—["Arms against a sea?" dearest Shakspeare, would that Theobald, or Johnson's stock-butt, "the Oxford Editor," had indeed interpolated that unconscionable image! It has been sapiently remarked by some hornet of criticism, that "Shakspeare was a clever man;" but cleverer far must that champion stand forth who wars with any prospect of success upon seas; perhaps Xerxes might have thought of it—or your Astley's brigand, who rushes sword in hand on an ocean of green baize. Who shall cure me of parentheses?]—well, "a sea of troubles, [thoughts trouble us more than things—I sin again; close it;] and by opposing, end them;" that is, by setting forth these troublous thoughts opposite, in stately black and white, I clip their wings, and make them peck among my poultry, and not swarm about my heaven. But soon must I be more continuous; turn over to my future title-pages, and spare your objurgation; a little more of this medley while the fit lasts, and afterward a staid course of better accustomed messes; a few further variations on this lawless theme of authorship, and then to try simpler tunes; briefly, and yet to be grandiloquent, as a last round of this giddy climax, after noisy clashing Chaos there shall roll out, "perfect, smooth, and round," green young worldlets, moving in quiet harmony, and moulded with systematic skill.

As an author, meanwhile, let man be most specifically characterized: a real author, voluntary in his motives, but involuntary as regards his acts authorial; full of matter, prolific of images and arguments, teeming, bursting, with something, much, too much, to say, and well witting how to say it: none of your poor devils compulsory from poverty—Plutus help them!—whose penury of pocket is (pardon me) too often equitably balanced by their emptiness of head; and far less one of the lady's-maid school, who will glory in describing a dish of cutlets at Calais, or an ill-trimmed bonnet, or the contents of an old maid's reticule, or of a young gentleman's portmanteau, or those rare occasions for sentimentality, moonlight, twilight, arbours, and cascades, in the moderate space of an hour by Shrewsbury clock: but a man who has it weightily upon his mind to explain himself and others, to insist, refute, enjoin: a man—frown not, fair helpmates; the controversial pen, as the controversial sword, be ours; we will leave your flower-beds and sweeter human nurseries, despotism over cooks and Penelobean penance upon carpet-work; nay, a trip to Margate prettily described, easy lessons and gentle hymns in behalf of those dear prattlers, and for the more cœrulean sort, "lyrics to the Lost one," or stanzas on a sickly geranium, miserably perishing in the mephitic atmosphere of routs—these we masculine tyrants, we Dionysii of literature, ill-naturedly have accounted your prerogatives of authorship. But who then are Sévigné and Somerville, Edgeworth and De Staël, Barbauld and Benger, and Aikin, and Jameson, Hemans, Landon, and a thousand more, not less learned, less accomplished, nor less useful? Forgive, great names, my half-repeated slander: riding with the self-conceited *cortège* of male critics, my boasted loyalty was well-nigh guilty of *lèze majesté:* but I repudiate the thought; my verdict shall have no reproach in it, as my championship no fear: how much has man to learn from woman! teach us still to look on humanity in love, on nature in thankfulness, on death without fear, on heaven without presumption; fairest, forgive those foolish and ungallant calumnies of my ruder sex, who boast themselves your teachers—making yet this wise use of the slander: never be so bold in authorship, as to hazard the loss of your sweet, retiring, modest, amiable, natural dependence: never stand out as champions on the arena of strife, but if you will, strew it with poises for the king of the tournament; it ill becomes you to be wrestlers, though a Lycurgus allowed it, and Atalanta, another Eve, was tripped up by an apple in the foot-race. So digressing, return we to our author; to wit, a man, *homo*—a human, as they say in the west —with news of actual value to communicate, and powers of pen competent to do so graphically, honestly, kindly, boldly.

Much as we may emulate Homer's wordy braggadocios in boasting ourselves far better than our fathers, still, great was the wisdom of our ancestors: and that time-tried wisdom has given us three things that make a man; he must build a house, have a child, write a book: and of this triad of needfuls, who perceives not the superior and innate majesty of the last requisite?—"Build a house?" I humbly conceive, and steal my notion from the same ancestral source, that, in nine cases out of ten, fools build houses for wise men to live in; besides, if houses be made a test of supreme manhood, your modern wholesale runner-up of lath and plaster tenements, warranted to stand seven years—provided quadrilles be excluded, and no larger flock of guests *than six* be permitted to settle on one spot—such a jackal for surgeons, such a reprobate provider for accident-wards as this, would be among our heroes, a prizeman, the flower of the species. "Children" too?—very happy, beautiful, heart-gladdening creations—God bless them all, and scatter those who love them not!—but still for a proof of more than average humanity, somewhat common, somewhat overwhelming: rabbits beat us here, with all our fecundity, so offensive to Martineau and Malthus. But as to "books"—common enough, too, smirks gentle reader: pardon, courteous sir, most rare—at least in my sense; I speak not of flat current shillings, but the bold medallions of ancient Syracuse; I heed not the dull thousands of minted gold and silver, but the choice coin-sculptures of Larissa and Tarentum. There do indeed flow hourly, from an ever-welling press, rivers of words; there are indeed shoaling us up on all sides a throng of well-bound volumes—novels, histories, poems, plays, memoirs, and so forth—to all appearance, books: but if by "books" be intended originality of matter, independent arguments, water turned wine, by the miracle of right-thinking, and not a mere re-decantering of dregs from other vessels—these many masqueraded forms, these multiplied images of little-varied likenesses, these Protean herds, will not stay to be counted, nor abide judgment, nor brook scrutiny, but will merge and melt by thousands into the one, or the two, real, original, sterling books. We live in a monopolylogue of authorship: an idea goes forth to the world's market-place well dressed from the wardrobe of some master-mind; it greets the public with a captivating air, and straightway becomes the rage; it seems epidemical; it comes out simultaneously as a piece of political economy, a cookery-book, a tragedy, a farce, a novel, a religious experience, an abstract *ism*, or a concrete *ology;* till the poor worn-out, dissipated shadow of a thought looks so feeble, thin, fashionably affected and fashionably infected, that its honest, bluff old father, for very shame, disowns it. Thus has it come to pass, that one or two minds, in this golden age of scribbling, have, to speak radically, been the true originators of a million volumes, which haply shall have sprung from the seed of some singular book, or of books counted in the dual.

Indignant authors, be not merciless on my candour: I confess too much whereof I hold you guilty; I am one of yourselves, and I question not that few of you can beat me in a certain sort of—I will say, unintended, plagiarism; you are thieves—patience—I thieve from thieves; Diogenes cannot see me any more than you; you copy phrases, I am perpetually and unconsciously filching thoughts; my entomological netted-scissors, wherewith I catch those small fowl on the wing, are always within reach; you will never find me without well-tenanted pill-boxes in my pocket, and perhaps a buzzing captive or two stuck in spinning thraldom on my castor; you are petty larceners, I profess the like *métier* of intellectual abstractor; you pilfer among a crowd of volumes, manuscripts, rare editions, conflicting commentators, and your success depends upon rëusage of the old materials; whereas I sit alone and bookless in my dining-parlour, thinking over bygone fancies, rëconsidering exploded notions, appropriating all I find of lumber in the warehouse of my memory, and, if need be, without scruple, quietly digesting, as my special provender, the thoughts of others, originated ages ago.

Is it necessary to remind you—dropping this lightsome vein for a precious moment—that I am penning away my "crudites," off-hand, at the top of my speed? that my set intention is, if possible, to jot down instanter my heavy brainful, and feel for once light headed?—I stick to my title, '*An Author's Mind*,' and that with a laudable scorn of concealment, and an honest purpose not to pretend it better or wiser than it is; then let no one blame me on the score of my fashion of speech, or my sarcasms mingled with charity; for consistency with me were inconsistent.

Neither let me, poor innocent, be accused of giving license to what a palled public and dyspeptical reviewers will call for the thousandth time a *cacoethes;* word of cabalistic look, unknown to Dr. Dilworth. Truly, my masters, though disciple I be of venerable Martinus the Scribbler; though, for aught I know, himself in progress of transmigration; still, I submit, my cornucopia is not crammed with leaves and chopped straw; and if, in utter carelessness, the fruit is poured out pell-mell after this desultory fashion, yet, I wot, it *is* fruit, though whether ripe or crude, or rotten, my husbandry takes little thought: the mixture serves for my cider-press, and, fermentation over, the product will be clarified. Judge me too, am I not consecutive? I've shown man to be a writing animal; and writing, what it is and is not; and meanwhile have been routing recreatively at pen's point whims, and fancies, and ideas, and images, pulled in manfully by head and shoulders: and now—after an episode, quite relevant and quite Herodotean, concerning the consequences of a bit of successful authorship on a man's scheme of life, to illustrate yet more the "author's mind"—I shall proceed to tell all men how many books I might, could, should, or would have written, but for reiterated and legitimated *buts*, and how near of kin I must esteem myself to the illustrious J. of nursery rhymes, being, as he is or was, "Mister Joe Jenkins, who played on the fiddle, and began twenty tunes, but left off in the middle." Moreover, no one can be ignorant of the close consanguinity recognised in every age and every dictionary between I and J. But now for the episode:

If ever a toy were symbolical of life, that toy was a kaleidoscope: the showy bits of tinsel, coloured glass, silk, beads, and feathers, with here and there perchance a stray piece of iridescent ore or a pin, each, in its turn of ideal multiplication, filling successively the field of vision; the trifling touch that will disenchant the fairest patterns; the slightest change, as in chemical arithmetic, that will make the whole mixture a poison or a cordial. A man is vexed, the nerve of his equanimity thrillingly touched at the tender elbow, and forthwith his whole wholesome body writhes in pain; while, to speak morally, those useful reminders of life's frailty, the habitual side-thorns—spurs of diligence, incentives to better things—are exaggerated into sixfold spears, and terribly stop the way, like long-lanced Achæans: a careless fit succeeds to one of spleen, and vanity well spangled, pretty baubles, stars and trinkets and trifles, fill their cycle, to magnetize with folly that rolling world the brain: another twist, and love is lord paramount, a paltry bit of glass, casually rose-coloured, shedding its warm blush over all the reflective powers: suddenly an overcast, for that marplot, Disappointment, has obtruded a most vexatiously reiterated morsel of lamp-black: again Hope's little bit of blue paint makes azure rainbows all about the firmament of man's own inner world; and at last an atom of gold-dust specks all the glasses with its lurid yellow, and haply leaves the old miser to his master-passion. So, ever changing day by day, every man's life is but a kaleidoscope. Stay; this simile is somewhat of the longest, but the whim is upon me, and I must have my way; the fit possesses me to try a sonnet, and I shall look far for a fairer thesis; he that hates verse—and the Muses now-a-days are too old-maidish to look many lovers—may skip it, and no harm done; but one or two may like this stave on

LIFE.

I saw a child with a kaleidoscope,
  Turning at will the tesselated field;
  And straight my mental eye became unseal'd,
I learnt of life, and read its horoscope:
  Behold, how fitfully the patterns change!
The scene is azure now with hues of Hope;
  Now sobered gray by Disappointment strange;

With Love's own roses blushing, warm and bright;
  Black with Hate's heat, or white with Envy's cold;
Made glorious by Religion's purple light;
  Or sicklied o'er with yellow lust of Gold;
So, good or evil coming, peace or strife,
  Zeal when in youth, and Avarice when old,
In changeful, chanceful phases passeth life.

It is well I was not stopped before my lawful fourteenth rhyme by yonder prosaic gentleman, humbly listening in front, who asks, with somewhat of malicious triumph, whereto does all this lead?—Categorically, sir, [there is no argument in the world equal to a word of six syllables,] categorically, sir, to this: of all life's turns and twists, few things produce more change to the daring *debutant* than successful authorship; it is as if, applying our simile, a fragment of printed bookishness among those kaleidoscopic morsels, having worked its way into the field of vision, had there got stereotyped by a photogenic process: in fact, it fixes on it a prëdestinated "author's mind."

An author's mind! what a subject for the lights and shadows of metaphysical portraiture! what a panorama of images! what a whirling scene of ever-changing incidents! what a store-house for thoughts! what a land of marvels! what untrodden heights, what unexplored depths of an ever-undiscovered country! That strange world hath a structure and a furniture all its own; its chalcedonic rocks are painted with rare creatures floating in their liquid-seeming hardness; forms of other spheres lie buried in its lias cliffs; seeds of unknown plants, relics of unlimned reptiles, fragments of an old creation, the ruins of a fanciful cosmogony, lie hid until the day of their requiral beneath its fertile soil: and then its lawless botany; flowers of glorious hue hung upon the trees of its forests; luscious fruits flung liberally among the mosses of its banks; air-plants sailing in its atmosphere; unanchored water-lilies dancing in its bright cascades; and this, too, a world, an inner secret world, peopled with unthought images, specimens of a peculiar creation; outlandish forms are started from its thickets, the dragon and the cherub are numbered with its winged inhabitants, and herds of uncouth shape pasture on its meadows. Who can sound its seas, deep calling unto deep? who can stand upon the hill-tops, height beckoning unto height? who can track its labyrinths? who can map its caverns? A limitless essence, an unfailing spring, an evergreen fruit-tree, a riddle unsolved, a quaint museum, a hot-bed of inventions, an over-mantling tankard, a whimsical motley, a bursting volcano, a full, independent, generous—a poor, fettered, jealous, Anomaly, such—bear witness—is an author's mind. O, theme of many topics! chaos of ill-sorted fancies! Let us come now to the jealousies, the real or imaginary wrongs of authorship: hereafter treat we this at lengthier; "for the time present" —I quote the facetious Lord Coke, when writing on that highly exhilerating topic, the common-law—"hereof let this little taste suffice." Is it not a wrong to be taken for a mere book-merchant, a mercenary purveyor of learning and invention, of religion and philosophy, of instruction, or even of amusements, for the sole consideration of value received, as one would use a stalking-horse for getting near a stag? this, too, when ten to one some cormorant on the tree of knowledge, some staid-looking publisher in decent mourning, is complacently pocketing the profits, and modestly charging you with loss? and this, moreover and more poignantly, when the flame of responsibility on some high subject is blazing at your heart, and the young Elihu, even if he would, cannot keep silence? Is it not a wrong to find pearls unprized, because many a modern, like his Celtic progenitors, (for I must not say like swine,) would sooner crush an acorn? to know your estimation among men ebbs and flows according to the accident of success, rather than the quality of merit? to be despised as an animal who must necessarily be living on his wits in some purlieu, answering to that antiquated reproach, a Grub-street attic; or suspected among gentler company in this most mercantile age for a pickpocket, a pauper, a *chevalier d'industrie?* And then those hounds upon the bleeding flanks of many a hunted author, those open-mouthed inexorable critics, (I allude to the Pariah class, not to the higher caste brethren,) how suddenly they rend one, and fear not! Only for others do I speak, and in no degree on account of having felt their fangs, as many have done, my betters; gentle and kind, as domesticated spaniels, have reviewers in general been to your humble confessor, and for such courtesies is he their debtor. But who can be ignorant how frequently some hapless writer is impaled alive on the stake of ridicule, that a flagging magazine may be served up with *sauce piquante,* and pander to the world for its waning popularity by the malice of a pungent article? who, while as a rule he may honour the bench of critics for patience, talent, and impartiality, is not conusant of those exceptions, not seldom of occurence, where obvious rancour has caused the unkindly condemnation; where personal inveteracy aims from behind the Ajax shield of anonymous reviewing, and shoots, like a cowardly Teucer, the foe fair-exposed whom he dares not fight with?—But, as will be seen hereafter, I trespass on a title-page, and here will add no more than this: Is it not a wrong of double edge, that while the world makes no excuse for the writhing writer, on the reasonable ground that after all he may be innocent of what his critics blame him for, the same good-natured world, on almost every occasion of magazine applause, believes either that the author has written for himself the favourable notice, or that pecuniary bribes have made the honest editor his tool? Verily, my public, thou art not generous here; ay, and thou art grievously deceived, as well as sordid: for by careless praise, causeless censure, credit given for corrupt bribery, and no allowance made for unamiable criticisms, poor maltreated authors speak to many wrongs: and of them more anon.

What moreover shall we say of chilling friendships, near estrangements, heartless lovers loitering behind, shy acquaintance dropping off? Verily, there is a mighty sifting: you have dared to stand alone, have expounded your mind in imperishable print, have manifested wit enough to outface folly, sufficient moral courage to condemn vice, and more than is needful of good wisdom to shame the oracles of worldliness: and so some dread you, some hate, and many shun: the little selfish asterisks in that small sky fly from your constellatory glories: you are independent, a satellite of none: you have dared to think, write, print, in all ways contrary to many; and if wise men and good be loud in their applause, you arrive at the dignity of manifold hatreds; but if those and their inferiors condemn, you sink into the bathos of multiplied contempts. Of other wrongs somewhen and where, hereafter; meanwhile, a better prospect glows on the kaleidoscopic field—a flattering accession of new and ardent friends: "Sir," said an old priest to a young author, "you have made a soft pillow for your head when it comes to be as white as mine is;" a pretty saying of sweet charity, and such sink deep: as for the younger and the warmer, being mostly of the softer sex, some will profess admiring sensations that border not a little on idolatries; others, gayer, will appear in the dress of careless, unskillful admiration; not a few, both men and women, go indeed weakly along with the current stream of popularity, but, to say truth, look happiest when they find some stinging notice that may mortify the new bold candidate for glory; while, last and best, a fewer, a very much fewer, do handsomely the liberal part of friends, commending where they can, objecting where they must, sincere in sorrow for a fault, rejoicing without envy for a virtue.

Many like phenomena has authorship: a certain class of otherwise humanized and well-intentioned people begin to regard your scribe as a monster—not a so-called "lion" to be sought, but some strange creature to be dreaded: Perdition! what if he should be cogitating a novel or a play, and means to make free with our characters? what if that libellous cöpartnership of Saunders and Ottley is permitted to display our faults and foibles, flimsily disguised, before a mocking world? Disappointed maidens that hover on the verge of forty, and can sympathize with Jephtha's daughter in her lonely mournings, causelessly begin to fear that a mischievous author may appropriate their portraits; venerable bachelors, who have striven to earn some little local notoriety by the diligent use of an odd phrase, a quaint garment, or an eccentric fling in the peripatetic, dread a satirist's powers of retributive burlesque; table orators suddenly grow dumb, for they suspect such a caitiff intends cold-blooded plagiarisms from their eloquence; the twinkling stars of humble village spheres shun him for an ominous comet, whose very trail robs them of light, or as paling glow-worms hide away before some prying lantern; and all who have in one way or another prided themselves on some harmless peculiarity, avoid his penetrating glance as the eye of a basilisk. Then, again, those casual encounters of witlings in the world authorial, so anticipated by a hostess, so looked-forward-to by guests! In most cases, how forlorn they be! how dull, constrained, suspicious! like rival traders, with pockets instinctively buttoned up, and glaring each upon the other with most uncommunicative aspects; not brothers at a banquet, but combatants and wrestlers, watching for solecisms in the other's talk, or toiling to drag in some laboured witticism of their own, after the classical precedent of Hercules and Cerberus: those feasts of reason, how vapid! those flows of soul, how icily congealing! those Attic nights, how dim and dismal! Once more; and, remember me, I speak in a personated character of the general, and not experimentally; so, flinging self aside, let me speak what I have seen: grant that the world-without crown a man with bays, and lead him to his Theban home with tokens of rejoicing; is the victor there set on high, chapleted, and honoured as Nemean heroes should be? or does he not rather droop instantly again into the obscure unit among a level mass, only the less welcome for having stood up, a Saul or a Musæus, with his head above his fellows? Verily, no man is a proph—Enough, enough! for ours is a prerogative, a glorious calling, and the crown of barren leaves is costlier than his of Rabbah; enough, enough! sing we the praises, count we well the pleasures of fervent, overflowing authorship. There, in perfect shape before the eyes—there, well born in beauty—there perpetually (so your fondness hopes) to live —slumbers in her best white robe the mind's own fairest daughter; the Minerva has sprung in panoply from that parental aching head, and stands in her immortal independence; an Eve, his own heart's fruit, welcomes delighted Adam. You have made something, some good work, bodily; your communion has commenced with those of times to come; your mind has produced a witness to its individuality; there is a tablet sacred to its memory standing among men for ever.

A thinker is seldom great in conversation, and the glib talkers who have silenced such a one frequently in clamorous argument, founder in his deep thoughts, blundering, like Stephanos and Trinculos—(let Caliban be swamped;) such generous revenge is sweet: a writer often unexplained, because speaking little, and that little foolishly mayhap, and lightly for the holiday's sake of an unthoughful rest, finds his opportunities in printing, and gives the self-expounding that he needs; such heart-emptyings yield heart-ease: an author, who has done his good work well—for such a one alone we speak—while, privately, he scarce could have refreshed mankind by petty driblets—in the perpetuity, publicity, and universal acceptation of his high and honourable calling, does good by wholesale, irrigates countries, and gladdens largely the large heart of human society. And are not these unbounded pleasures, spreading over life, and comforting the struggles of a death-bed? Yes: rising as Ezekiel's river from ankle to knee, from knee to girdle, from girdle to the overflowing flood—far beyond those lowest joys, which many wise have trampled under foot, of praise, and triumph, and profit—the authorship of good, that has made men better; that has consoled sorrow, advanced knowledge, humbled arrogance, and blest humanity; that has *sent the guilty to his prayers, and has gladdened the Christian in his* praises—the authorship of good, that has shown God in his loveliness, and man in his dependence; that has aided the cause of charity, and shamed the face of sin—this high beneficence, this boundless good-doing, hath indeed a rich recompense, a glorious reward!

But we must speed on, and sear these hydra-necks, or we shall have as many heads to our discourse, and as puzzling, as any treatise of the Puritan divinity. Let us hasten to be practical; let us not so long forget the promised title-pages; let it at length satisfy to show, more than theoretically, how authorship stirs up the mind to daily-teeming projects, and then casts out its half-made progeny; how scraps of paper come to be covered with the cabala of half-written thoughts, thenceforward doomed to suffer the dispersion-fate of Sibylline leaves; how stores of mingled information gravitate into something of order, each seed herding with its fellows; and how every atom of mixed metal, educationally held in solution by the mind, is sought out by a keen precipitating test, gregariously building up in time its own true crystal.

Hereabouts, therefore, and hereafter, in as frank a fashion as heretofore, artlessly, too, and, but for crowding fancies, briefly shall follow a full and free confession of the embryo circulating library now in the book-case of my brain; only premising, for the last of all last times, that while I know it to be morally impossible that all should be pleased herewith, I feel it to be intellectually improbable that any one mind should equally be satisfied with each of the many parts of a performance so various, inconsistent, and unusual; premising, also, that wherein I may have stumbled upon other people's titles, it is unwittingly and unwillingly; for the age breeds books so quickly, that a man must read harder than I do to peruse their very names; and premising this much farther, that I profess to be a sort of dog in the manger, neither using up my materials myself, nor letting any one else do so; and that, whether I shall happen or not, at any time future to amplify and perfect any of these matters, I still proclaim to all bookmakers and booksellers, STEAL NOT; for so surely as I catch any one thus behaving—and truly, my masters, the temptation is but small—I will stick a "*Sic vos, non vobis,*" on his brazen forehead.

Wait! there remaineth yet a moment in which to say out the remnant of my mind, "an author's mind," its last parting speech, its dying utterances before extreme unction. I owe all the world apologies; I would pray a catholic forgiveness. Authors and reviewers, critics, and the undiscriminating many, fair women, honest men, I cry your pardons universally! I do confess the learning of my mind to lie, strangely and Pisa-like, inveterately as at Welsh Caërphilli, out of the perpendicular of truth; it is my disposition to make the most of all things, for good or for evil; I write, speak, and think, as if I were but an unhallowed special pleader; I colour highly, and my outlines are too strong; I am guilty on all sides of unintentional misstatements, consequent on the powerful gusts of feeling that burst upon my irritable breast; my heart is no smooth Dead Sea, but the still vexed Bermoothes: therefore I would print my penitence; I would publish my confessions; I would not hide my humbleness; and it pleases me to pour out in sonnet-form my unconventional

APOLOGY TO ALL.

—For I have sinn'd; oh! grievously and often;
Exaggerated ill, and good denied;
Blacken'd the shadows only born to soften;
And Truth's own light unkindly misapplied:
Alas! for charities unloved, uncherish'd,
When some stern judgment, haply erring wide,
Hath sent my fancy forth, to dream and tell
Other men's deeds all evil! Oh, my heart!
Renew once more thy generous youth, half perish'd;
Be wiser, kindlier, better than thou art!
And first, in fitting meekness, offer well
All earnest, candid prayers, to be forgiven
For worldly, harsh, unjust, unlovable
Thoughts and suspicions against man and Heaven!

Friends all, let this be my best amendment: bear with the candour, homely though it may be, of your author's mind; and suffer its further revelations of unborn manuscript with charitable listening; for they would come forth in real order of time, the first having priority, and not the best, ungarnished, unweeded, uncared-for, humbly, and without any further flourish of trumpets.

Serjeant Ion—I beg his pardon, Talfourd—somewhere gives it as his opinion, that most people, in any way troubled with a mind, have at some time or other meditated a tragedy. Truly, too, it *is* a fine vehicle for poetical solemnities, a stout-built vessel for an author's graver thoughts; and the bare possibility of seeing one's own heart-stirring creation visually set before a crowded theatre, the preclusive echoes of anticipated thundering applause, the expected thrilling silence attendant on a pet scene or sentiment, all the tangible accessories of painting and music, clever acting and effective situation, and beyond and beside these the certain glories of the property-wardrobe, make most young minds press forward to the little-likely prize of successful tragedy. That at one weak period I was bitten, my honesty would scorn to deny; but fortunately for my peace of mind, "Melpomene looked upon me with an aspect of little favour," and sturdy truth-telling Tacitus made me at last but lightly regardful of my subject. Moreover, my Pegasus was visited with a very abrupt pull-up from other causes; it has been my fatality more than once or twice, as you will ere long see, to drop upon other people's topics—for who can find any thing new under the sun?—and I had already been mentally delivered of divers fag-ends of speeches, stinging dialogues, and choice tit-bits of scenes, (all of which I will mercifully spare you,) when a chance peep into Johnson '*Lives of the Poets*' showed me mine own fine subject as the work of some long-forgotten bard! This moral earthquake demolished in a moment my goodly aërial fabric; the fair plot burst like a meteor; and an after-recollection of a certain French tragedy-queen, Agrippina, showed me that the ground was still further prëoccupied. But it is high time to tell the destined name of my abortive play; in four letters, then,

NERO;

A CLASSICAL TRAGEDY:

IN SEVEN SCENES.

AND now, in pity to an afflicted parent, hear for a while his offspring's Roscian capabilities. First of all, however, (and you know how I rejoice in all things preliminary,) let me clear my road by explanations: we must pioneer away a titular objection, "in seven scenes," and an assumed merit, in the term "classical." I abhor scene-shifters; at least, their province lies more among pantomimes, farces, and comedies, than in the region of the solemn tragic muse; her incidents should rather partake of the sculpture-like dignity of *tableaux*. My unfashionable taste approves not of a serious story being cut up into a vast number of separate and shuffled sections; and the whistle and sliding panels detract still more from the completeness of illusion: I incline as much as is possible to the classic unities of time, place, and circumstances, wishing, moreover, every act to be a scene, and every scene an act; with a comfortable green curtain, that cool resting-place for the haggard eye, to be the grass-like drop, mildly alternating with splendid crime and miserable innocence: away with those gaudy intermediates, and, still worse, some intruded ballet; bring back Garrick's baize, and crush the dynasty of head-aches.

But onward: let me further extenuate the term, seven scenes; the utterance seven "acts" would sound horrific, full of extremities of weariness; but my meaning actually is none other than seven acts of one scene each: for the number seven, there always have been decent reasons, and ours may best appear as we proceed, less than a brief seven seeming insufficient, and more, superfluous; again, so mystical a number has a staid propriety, and a due double climax of rise and fall. Now, as to our adjective "classical:" Why not, in heroic drama, have something a-kin to the old Greek chorus, with its running comment upon motives and moralities, somewhat as the mighty-master has set forth in his truly patriotic '*Henry the Fifth?*'—However, taking other grounds. the epithet is justified, both by the subject and the proposed unmodern method of its treatment: but of all this enough, for, on second thoughts, perhaps we may do without the chorus.

It is obvious that no historical play can strictly preserve the true unity of time; cause and effect move slower in the actual machinery of life, than the space of some three hours can allow for: we must unavoidably clump them closer; and so long as a circumstance might as well have happened at one time as at another, I consider that the poet is justified in crowding prior events as near as he may please towards the goal of their catastrophe. If then any slight inaccuracy as to dates arrests your critical ken, believe that it is not ignorantly careless, but learnedly needful. One other objection, and I have done. No man is an utter inexcusable, irremediable villain; there is a spot of light, however hidden, somewhere; and, notwithstanding the historian's picture, it may charitably be doubted whether we have made due allowance for his most reasonable prejudice even in Nero's case. Human nature has produced many monsters; but, amongst a thousand crimes, there has proverbially lingered in each some one seedling of a virtue; and when we consider the corruption of manners in old Rome, the idolatrous flatteries hemming in the prince, the universal lie that hid all things from his better perceptions, we can fancy some slight extenuation for his mad career. Not that it ever was my aim, in modern fashion, to excuse villany, or to gild the brass brow of vice; and verily, I have not spared my odious hero; nevertheless, in selecting so unamiable a subject, (or rather emperor,) I wished not to conceal that even in the worst of men there is a soil for hope and charity; and that if despotism has high prerogatives, its wealth and state are desperate temptations, whose dangers mightily predominate, and whose necessary influences, if quite unbiased, tend to utter misery.

Now to introduce our *dramatis personæ*, with their "cast,"—for better effect—rather unreasonably presumed. *Nero*—(Macready, who would impersonate him grandly, and who, moreover, whether complimented or not by the likeness, wears a head the very counterpart of Nero's, as every Numismatist will vouch,)—a naturally noble spirit, warped by sensuality and pride into a very tyrant; liberal in gifts, yet selfish in passion; not incapable of a higher sort of love, yet liable to sudden changes, and at times tempestuously cruel. *Nattalis*—(say Vandenhoff,)—his favourite and evil genius, originally a Persian slave, and still wearing the Eastern costume: a sort of Iago, spiriting up the willing Nero to all varieties of wickedness, getting him deified, and otherwise mystifying the poor besotted prince with all kinds of pleasure and glory, to subserve certain selfish ends of rapine, power, and licentiousness, and to avenge, perhaps, the misfortunes of his own country on the chief of her destroyers. *Marcus Manlius*—(who better than Charles Kean?—supposing these artistic combinations not to be quite impossible,)—a fine young soldier, of course loving the heroine, captain of Nero's body-guard, chivalrous, honourable, noble, and faithful to his bad master amid conflicting trials. *Publius Dentatus*—(any *bould* speaker; besides, it would be rather too much to engage all the actors yet awhile;)—a worthy old Roman, father of the heroine. *Galba*, the chief mover in the catastrophe, as also the opener of its causes, an intriguing and fierce, but well-intentioned patriot, who ultimately becomes the next emperor. With *Curtius* a tribune, senators, conspirators, soldiers, priests, flamens, &c. And so, after the ungallant fashion of theatrical play-wrights, as to a class inferior to the very &c. of masculines—(of less intention withal than one of those &cs. of crabbed Littleton, like an old shoe fricasséed into savourings of all things by its inimitable Coke,)—come we to the women-kind. *Agrippina*, (one of the school of Siddons,) empress-mother, a strong-minded, Lady-Macbeth sort of woman, and the only person in the world who can awe her amiable son. *Lucia*, (*you* cannot be spared here, clever Helen Faucit)—the heroine, secretly a Christian affianced to Manlius; a character of martyr's daring and woman's love. *Rufa*, a haggard old sibyl, with both private and public reasons for detesting Nero and Nattalis: and all the fitting female attendants to conclude the list.

Each scene, in which each act will be included, should be pictorially, so to speak, a *tableau* in the commencement, and a *tableau* of situation in the end. Let us draw up upon scene *the first*. Back-ground, Rome burning; in front, ruins of fine Tuscan villa, still smoking; and a terminal altar in the garden. Plebs. running to and fro, full of conventional little speeches, with goods, parents, penates, and other lumber, rescued from the flames; till a tribune, (hight Curtius,) in a somewhat incendiary oration concerning poor men's calamities, and against the powers that be, sends them to the capitol with a procession of flamines Diales and vestals, dirging solemnly a Roman hymn [some "*Ad Capitolium, Ad Jovis solium,*" and so forth] to good music. At the end of the train come in Publius and Lucia, to whom from opposite hurriedly walks Galba, full of talk of omens, direful doings, patriotism, and old Rome's ruin. To these let there be added—to speak mathematically—open-hearted Manlius; and let there follow certain disceptatious converse about Nero, Manlius excusing him, extenuating his vices by his temptations, giving military anecdotes of his earlier virtues, and in fact striving to make the most of him, a very gentle monster: Galba throwing in, sarcastically, blacker shadows. After disputation, the father and lovers walk off, leaving Galba alone for a moment's soliloquy; and, from behind the terminal altar, unseen Sibyl hails him Cæsar; he, astonished at the airy voice so coincident with his own feelings, thinks it ideal, chides his babbling thoughts, and so forth: then enter to him suddenly chance-met noble citizens, burnt out of house and home, who declaim furiously against Nero. Sibyl, still unseen from behind the altar, again hails Galba as future Cæsar; who, no longer doubting his ears, and all present taking the omen, they conspire at the altar with drawn swords, and as the Sibyl suddenly presides—*tableau*—and down drops the soft green baize. This first act, you perceive, is stirring, introductory of many characters; and the picture of the seven-hilled-city, seen in a transparent blaze, might give the followers of Stanfield a triumph.

Second: The senate scene, producing another monstrous crime of Nero's, also inaccurately dated. In the full august assembly, Nero discovered enthroned, not unmajestic in deportment, yet effeminately chapleted, and holding a lyre: suppose him just returned from Elis, a pancratist, the world's acknowledged champion. Nattalis, ever foremost in flatteries, after praising the prince's exploits in Greece, avows that, like Paris in Troy, and Alexander at Persepolis, Nero *had* gloriously fired Rome; he found it wood, and wished to leave it marble; (so, the catafalque at the Invalides of the twice-buried Corsican;) in destroying, as well as blessing, he had asserted his divinity; and after due allusions to Phœnixes, and fire-kingships, and *coups-de-soliel* falling from the same Apollo so great upon the guitar, Nattalis moves that Nero should be worshipped, and calls on the priest of Jupiter to set a good example. None dare refuse, and the senate bend before him; whereupon enter, in clerical procession, augurs, and diviners, men at arms with pole-axes, and coronaled white bulls, paraded before sacrifice: all this pandering to present love of splendour and picturesque effect. In the midst of these classical preparations, enters, with a bevy of attendants, the haughty queen-like Agrippina, whom Nero, having sent for to complete his triumph, commands to bend too; but she stoutly refusing, and taking him fiercely to task, objurgating likewise Rome's degenerate gray-beards—great bustle—senate broken up hurriedly—and she, with a "*feri ventrem,*" dragged off to be killed by her son's order. Nero alone with Nattalis by imperial command; his momentary compunction nullified by the wily Iago, who turns off the subject smoothly to a new object of desire: Publius was the only senator not in his place, and Publius has a daughter, the fairest in Rome, Lucia—had not the emperor noticed her among Agrippina's women? Nero, charmed with any scheme of novelty that may change remorseful thoughts, is induced, nothing loth, to attempt the subtle abduction of the heroine; a body-guard, headed as always by Manlius, ready in the vestibule to escort him, and exit. Nattalis, alone for a minute, betrays his own selfish schemes concerning Lucia, who had refused him before, and alludes to his secret reasons for urging on the maddened Nero to the worst excesses.

Third scene (or part, or *act,* if it must be so), expounds, in fitting contrast to the foregoing, the tender loves of Lucia and Manlius; a gentle home-scene, a villa and its terraced gardens: also, as Lucia is a Christian, we have, poetically, and not puritanically, an insight into her scruples of conscience as to the heathenism of her lover: and also into *his* consistent nobility of character, not willing to surrender the religion of his fathers unconvinced. To them rushes in Publius, who has been warned by friend Galba of the near approach of Nattalis and a guard, to seize Lucia for disreputable Nero: no possible escape, and all urge Lucia to imitate Virginia, Lucretia, and others of like Dian fame, by cowardly self-murder; she is high-principled, and won't: then they—the father and lover—request leave to kill her; conflicting passions and considerable stage effect; Lucia, who with calm courage derides the dastard sacrifice, standing unharmed between those loving thirsty swords: in a grand speech, she makes her quiet departure a test of Manlius' love, and her ultimate deliverance to be a proof to him that her God is the true God, the God who guards the innocent. Manlius, struck with her martyr-like constancy, professes that if indeed she is saved out of this great trouble, he will embrace her faith, renounce his own, and so break down the only difference between them: just after which, Nattalis and guard burst in; then ensue much scornful parley, and a storm of quarrel, which Lucia allays, and she walks off confident in virtue. Publius and Manlius left alone in despair, until—bright thought—the latter considers that, as Nero's body-captain, he can always hover round the safety of his beloved; and though his soldier's oaths, and notions of sacred sovereignty, forbid him to slay Nero, yet he comforts himself with the thought that in the last resort of unavoidable dishonour, he can rush in, and kill his own Lucia.

The fourth scene is a climacter, as old Browne would say—the heroine's extremity: Nero's golden house, the roof rolling like the spheres to soft music, and a gorgeous marble avenue, ending with the colossal statue of the emperor, of gold, with incense burning before it: a scene, true to history, that might pale Aladdin's lamp, and dazzle the eyes of the groundlings: consider well then this my possible tragedy, ye that cater for theatric banquets. Lucia discovered alone, soliloquizing: suddenly enters, unattended, the buskined Nero; [who was believed to have been then out hunting with Nattalis on a new white steed, which the favourite had, to serve his purpose, given him, but had stolen secretly from the chase, as he wisely tells Lucia, to track up fairer game.] A grand scena between them, to be managed with as much delicacy as possible, of fawning entreaty, indignant refusal, imperious command, and dignified rebuke; ending in Nero forcibly seizing her, and Lucia's involuntary ejaculation "that the God of the Christians might protect her!" at this word, Nero's love is turned into burning hate; he falls into one of Macready's magnificent passions, and, howling for his body-guard, he commits Lucia, as an odious victim for the stake, unconscious of their acquaintance, into the hands of Manlius!—Nero, considerably disgusted, retires alone to a tapestried couch at the side:—and now (all due care being taken to prevent the incident being farcical,) in creeps Nattalis, also secretly from the chase, merry at having outwitted Nero on that runaway white hunter; of course, he proceeds to make sure of his presumably sleeping prize, the fair Lucia; so, much praising his lucky stars, he draws the envious tapestry, and—only conceive the huge fracas between Nero and Nattalis, the struggle of two such demons! They cross swords, and while fighting furiously, in rushes a guard; and, Nero being wounded, Nattalis escapes in the scuffle, and, like all other disappointed friends, assumes the metamorphosis of his deadliest enemy.

Fifth scene: the Sibyl's cave, a fine bit of witchcraft-rites, and moonlight, in the neighbourhood of lake Avernus. Galba and conspirators are met together by appointment; reasonable complaints against Nero's crimes, crowned by the murder of his mother, the burning of Rome, and (after having openly avowed it, and sung the fall of Ilium to its crackling accompaniment,) his excessive lying meanness in now accusing those poor fools, the Nazarenes. Incantations meanwhile brewing, with witch in the rear. Enters dishevelled Nattalis, with bloody sword, at first to their infinite consternation, soon changed to joy. He is sworn among them, although they distrust him, and secretly resolve that he and Nero shall die together, as master and man should: moreover, the Sibyl, who lets out her private reasons for this by accusing, in a strain of retributive justice, Nattalis of having ruined heretofore her own two daughters, and driven her—her, a high-born Roman matron—to be the thing she now is for vengeance-sake, oracularly denounces him to die simultaneously with Nero. The rascal shows his cowardly nature by humiliating prayers, and miserably repents his double treachery; but those Tartars will not let him go, the conspirators keep him in their well-armed company; so he wretchedly foresees his fate, and resolves, as some last act of what he considers virtue, to die, since he must, in ridding the world of that monster, the emperor.

The sixth is a palace scene, with a throne behind: Nero discovered alone, a victim to horrible remorse, and half resolved to turn penitent; the voice of his mother's ghost heard at intervals, as torturing his conscience, and speaking close to him, palpably, though unseen. The murder of his kind old tutor Seneca, also afflicting him, to say nothing of poor Poppæa. His fears of solitude, and equal dread of company, incidentally revealing that under his imperial vest he wears secret armour; for, now that Nattalis has failed him, whom can he trust? some traits of human kindness, even to tears, in his recollections of Nattalis. A courtier, after this, announces that Publius demands audience of the emperor: the court come in, Nero assumes state, mounts the throne, and enter Publius. A most heart-rending intercession of the father for his daughter's life, which Nero's iron heart, chagrined at his discomfiture, derides: this failing, Publius changes his tone, and, with many hints of what he, an old man, has gained in wisdom by his years, and especially (perhaps) of what he has heard from one Saul or Paul, a captive, professes he can tell Nero of a new pleasure, a secret he withholds if denied his daughter's life; the graphic description of happiness to be gained thereby, rouses Nero's selfish curiosity; threats, cajolery, and promises of wealth and rank, are alike thrown away upon Publius; at last, the prince promises; and when Publius, after a burst of earnest eloquence, proclaims the new pleasure to consist in *showing mercy*, Nero's utter wrath, his hurricane of hate, revoking that hasty promise, and hurrying away old Publius to die at the same stake with his daughter.

Seventh: the catastrophe scene lies in the Coliseum amphitheatre; (I mean the older one, anterior to Vespasian's:) bloody games pictured behind, and those "human torches" at fiery intervals. Nero, enthroned in side front, surrounded by a brilliant court, amongst whom are some of the conspirators: at other side Publius and Lucia, tied at one stake in white robes, back to back, to die before Nero's eyes, Manlius and soldiers guarding them: he, Manlius, having nobly resolved to test miraculous assistance to the last, but now tremblingly believing the chance of a Providence interfering, since Lucia's escape from Nero at the golden house. Just as the emperor, after a sarcastic speech, characteristically interlarded with courtier conversation, is commanding the fagot to be lighted, and Lucia's constant faith has bade Manlius *do it*—a rush of Nattalis with attendant conspirators and Rufa the Sibyl, up to Nero; Nattalis strikes him, but the sword breaks short off on the hidden armour; Nero's majestic rising for a moment, asserting himself Cæsar still, the inviolable majesty;—suddenly stopped by a centripetal rush of the conspirators; who kill him, (after he has vainly attempted in despair to kill himself,) and Galba sits on the throne, while Nero, unpitied and unhelped, gasps out in the middle his dying speech. Meanwhile, at the other side, Manlius has killed Nattalis for his treachery, cut the bonds of Publius and Lucia, and all ends in moral justice for the triumph of good, and the defeat of evil; Manlius and Lucia, hand in hand, Publius with white head and upraised hands blessing them, Nero, a mangled corpse, Nattalis in his dying agonies persecuted by the vindictive Rufa, and Galba hailed as Cæsar by the assembled Romans. So, upon a magnificent *tableau*, slowly falls the lawny curtain.

Patient reader, what think you of my long-winded tragedy? No quibbling about Nero having really died in a drain, four years after the murder of Aggrippina; no learned disquisitions, if you please, as to his innocence of Rome's fire, a counterpart to our slander on the Papacy in the matter of London's; spare me, I pray you, learned pundit, your suspicions about Galba's too probable *alibi* in Spain. Tell me rather this: do I falsify history in any thing more important than mere accidental anachronisms and anatopisms? do I make an untrue delineation of character, blackening the good, or white-washing the wicked? Do I not, by introducing Nero's three greatest crimes so near upon his assassination, merely accelerate the interval between causes and effect? And is not tragic dignity justified in varnishing, with other compost than the dregs of Rome, the exit of the last true Cæsar of the Augustan family? For all the rest, good manager, provide me actors, and I am even now uncertain —such is my weakness—whether this skeleton might not at some time be clad with flesh and skin, and a decent Roman toga. I fear it will yet haunt me as a '*Midsummer Night's Dream*,' destroying my quiet with involuntary shreds and patches of long-metred blank; the notion is still vivacious, albeit scotched: Alexandrine though the synopsis appear, it must not be thrown on the highroad as a dead snake; nay, let me cherish it yet on my hearth, and not hurl it away like a *bonum waviatum;* a little more boiling up of Roman messes in my brain, and my tragedy might flow forth spontaneously as lava. What if this book be, after all, a sort of pilot-balloon, to show my huge Nassau the way the wind blows —a feeler as to which and which may please? Whether or not this be so, I will still confess on, emptying my brain of booklets, and, if by happy possibility I can keep my secret, shall hear unsuspected, friend, *your* verdict.

I MUST rather hope, than expect, that my next bit of possible authorship is not like the last, a subject forestalled. Scribbling as I find myself for very listlessness in a dull country-house, there's not a publisher's index within thirty miles; so, for lack of evidence to the contrary, I may legitimately, for at least a brief period of self-delusion, imagine the intoxicating field my own. And yet so fertile, important, interesting a subject, cannot have been quite overlooked by the corps of professed literary labourers: the very title-page would insure five thousand readers (especially with a Brunswicker death's-head and marrow-bones added underneath).

OPIUM;

A HISTORY;

standing alone in single blackiness: Opium, a magnificent theme, warranted to fill a huge octavo: and certain, from sheer variety of information, to lead into the captivity of admiring criticism minds of every calibre. Its natural history, with due details of all manner of poppies, their indigenous habitats, botanical characters, ratios of increase, and the like; its human history, discovery as a drug; how, when, where, and by whom cultivated; dissertations as to the possibility of Chaldean, Pharaonic, Grecian, or Roman opium eating, with most erudite extracts out of all sorts of scribes, from Sanchoniathon down to Juvenal, on these topics; its medicinal uses, properties, accidents, and abuses; as to whether it might not be used homœopathically or in infinitesimal doses, to infuse a love of the pleasures of imagination into clodpoles, lawyers' clerks, and country cousins; its intellectual possibilities of usefulness, stimulating the brain; its moral ditto, allaying irritability; together with a dreadful detail of its evils in excess, idiotizing, immoralizing, ruining soul and body. Plenty of stout unquestionable statistics, from all crannies of the globe, to corroborate all the above to the extreme satisfaction of practical men, with causes and consequences of its insane local popularity. All this, moreover, at present, with especial reference to China and the East; added to the moral bearings of the Opium-war, and our national responsibilities relative to that unlucky traffic. The metaphysical question stated and answered, whether or not prohibition of any thing does not lead to its desire; showing the increasing appetency of those sottish Serics for the forbidden vice, and illustrating Gay's fable of the foolish young cock, who ne'er had been in that condition, but for his mother's prohibition: moreover, how is it, that so captivating a form of intoxication is so little rife among our drunken journeymen? queries, however, as to this; and whether or not the humbug of teetotalism (a modern speculation, got up by and for the benefit of grocers and sugar-planters on the one side, schismatics and conspiring demagogues on the other,) has already substituted opium-eating, drinking, or smoking, for the wholesomer toddies, among factory folk and the finest pisantry. Millions of anecdotes regarding Eastern Rajahs, Western Locofocos, Southern Moors, and North-country Muscovites, as to the drug in its abuses: strange cures (if any) of strange ailments of mind or body by its prudent use: how to wean men and nations from those deleterious chewings and smokings; with true and particular accounts of such splendid self-conquests as Coleridge and De Quincey, and—shall I add another, a living name?—have attained to. Then, again, what a field for poetical vagaries, and madnesses of imagination, would be afforded by the subject of opium-dreams! Now, strictly speaking, in order to hallucinate honestly, your opium-writer ought to have had some practical knowledge of opium-eating: then could he descant with the authority of experience—yea, though he write himself thereby down an ass—on its effects upon mind and body; then could he tell of luxuries and torments in true Frenchified detail; then could he expound its pains and pleasures with all the eloquence of personal conviction. But, as to such real risk of poisoning myself, and of making I wot not how actual a mooncalf, of my present sound mind and body, I herein would reasonably demur: and, if I wanted dreams, would tax my fancy, and not my apothecary's bill. Dreams? I need not whiff opium, nor toss off laudanum negus, to imagine myself—a young Titan, sucking fiery milk from the paps of a volcano; a despot so limitless and magnificent, as to spurn such a petty realm as the Solar System, with Cassiopeia, Boötes, and his dog, to boot; an intellect, so ravished, that it feels all flame, or a mass of matter so inert, that it lies for ages in the silent depths of ocean, a lump of primeval metal: Madness, with the red-hot iron hissing in his brain: Murder, with the blood-hound ghost, over land, over sea, through crowds, deserts, woods, and happy fields, ever tracking silently in horrid calmness; the oppression of indefinite Guilt, with that Holy Eye still watching; the consciousness of instant danger, the sense of excruciating pain, the intolerable tyranny of vague wild fear, without will or power to escape: spurring for very life on a horse of marble: flying upward to meet the quick-falling skies—O, that universal crash!—greeted in a new-entered world with the execrations of the assembled dead—that hollow, far-echoing, malicious laughter—that hurricane-sound of clattering skulls; to be pent up, stifling like a toad, in a limestone rock for centuries; to be haunted, hunted, hooted; to eat off one's own head with its cruel madly crunching under-jaw; to—but enough of horrors: and as to delights, all that Delcroix suggests of perfume, and Mahomet of Houris, and Gunter of cookery, and the German opera of music: all Camilla-like running unexertive, all that sea unicorns can effect in swift swimming, or storm-caught condors in things aërial; all the rapid travellings of Puck from star to star, system to system, all things beauteous, exhilarating, ecstatic—ages of all these things, warranted to last. Now, multiply all these several alls by forty-nine, and the product will serve for as exaggerated a statement as possible of opium pandering to pleasure; yes, by forty-nine, by seven times seven at the least, that we be not accused of extenuating so fatal an excitement; for it is competent to conceive one's self expanded into any unlimited number of bodies, seven sevens being the algebraic *n*, and if so, into their huge undefined aggregate; a giant's pains are throes indeed, a giant's pleasures indeed flood over. But, we may do harm to morality and truth, by falsely making much of a faint, fleeting, paltry, excitation. The brain waltzing intoxicated, the heart panting as in youth's earliest affection, the mind broad, and deep, and calm, a Pacific in the sunshine, the body lapped in downy rest, with every nerve ministering to its comfort; what more can one, merely and professedly of this world of sensualism—an opium-eater for instance—conceive of bliss? Such imaginative flights as these, with its pungent final interrogatory, suggestive to man's selfishness of joys as yet untried, might tempt to tamper with the dear delight; whereas the plain statement of the most that opium could minister to happiness, as contrasted with those false vain views of it, remind me of Tennyson's poetical '*Timbuctoo*,' gorgeous as a new Jerusalem in Apocalyptic glories, and the mean filth-obstructed kraals dotted on an arid plain, to which, for very truthfulness, his soaring fancy drops plumbdown, as the shot eagle in '*Der Freischutz*.'

Let this then serve as a meagre sketch of my defunct treatise on opium: think not that I love the subject, curious and fertile though it be; perhaps, philosophically regarded, it is not a better one than *gin;* but ears polite endure not the plebeian monosyllable, unless indeed with a rĕduplicated *n*, as Mr. Lane *will* have it our whilom genie should be spelt: accordingly, I magnanimously give up the whole idea, and am liberal enough, in this my dying determination, to sign a codicil, bequeathing opium to my executors.

NOVELISM is a field so filled with copy-holders, so populously tenanted in common, that it requires no light investigation to find a site unoccupied, and a hero or heroine waiting to be hired. Nevertheless, I seem to myself to have lighted on a rich and little-cultivated corner; imagining that the subject is a good one, because still untouched, founded on facts, and with amplifiable variations that border on the probable. He that lionizes Stratford-on-Avon, will remember in one of the Shakspearian museums of that classic town, the pictured trance of hapless

CHARLOTTE CLOPTON,

as it was limned in death-seeming life. He will be shown the tombs of her ancient family in Stratford church, and the door of that fatal vault;

he will hear something of her noble birth—her fine character—her fascinating beauty—her short, innocent, eventful life—her horrible death. Consider, too, the age and locality in which she lived, Elizabethan, Shakspeare's; the great contemporary characters that might be casually introduced; the mysterious suicide, in that dim dreadful pool at the end of the terraced walk among the cropped yews, of her poor only sister, Margaret; equalled only in the miserable interest by that of Charlotte herself. And then for a plot: some darkly hinted parricide of years agone, in the generation but one preceding, has dropt its curse upon the now guiltless, but, by the law of Providence, still-not-acquitted family; a parricide consequent on passionate love, differing religions, and the Montague-and-Capulet-school of hating feudal fathers—Theodore Clopton having been a Catholic, Alice Beauvoir a Protestant; an introductory recountal of old Beauvoir's withering curse on the Clopton family for Theodore's abduction of his daughter, followed by the tragic event of the father and son, Cloptons', mutual hatred, and the former found in his own park with the broken point of his son's sword in him, the latter flying the realm: the curse has slept for a generation; and now two fair daughters are all that remain to the high-bred Sir Clement and his desponding lady, on whom the Beauvoir descendant, a bitterest enemy, takes care to remind them the hovering curse must burst. This Rowland Beauvoir is the villain of the story, whose sole aim it is, after the fulfilment of his own libertine wishes, to see the curse accomplished: and Charlotte's love for a certain young Saville, whom Beauvoir hates as his handsome rival in court patronage, as well as her pointed refusal of himself, gives new and present life to his ancestral grudge. The lovers are espoused, and to make Sir Clement's joy the greater, Saville has interest sufficient to meet the old knight's humour of keeping up the ancient family name, by getting it added to his own; so that the Beauvoir hatred and parricidal curse seem likely to be frustrated. But—the first hindrance to their union is poor sister Margaret's secret and infatuated love for that scheming villain Rowland, her then too probable seduction, melancholic madness, and suicide: successively upon this follow the last illnesses and deaths of the heart-broken old people, whom Rowland's dreadful ubiquity terrifies in their very chamber of disease; and as the too likely consequence of such accumulated sorrows on a creature of exquisite sensibility, Charlotte, the only remaining heiress of that ancient lineage, gradually, and with all the semblance of death, falls into her terrible trance. Rowland, who, through his intimacy with Margaret, knows all the secret passages and sliding panels of the old mansion, and who thereby gets mysterious admission whenever he pleases, comes into that silent chamber, and finds Saville mourning over his dead-seeming bride: she, all the while, though unable to move, in an agony of self-consciousness; and at last, when Rowland in fiendish triumph pronounces the curse complete, to the extreme horror of both, by an effort of tortured mind over apparently inanimate matter, rolls her glazed eyes, and gives an involuntary groan: having thus to all appearance confirmed the curse, she lies more marble-white, more corpse-like, more entranced than ever. Then, after long lingering, draws on the horrible catastrophe: a catastrophe, alas! as far at least as regards the heroine, *quite true*. Fully aware of all that is going on—the preparations for burial, the misery of her lover, the gratified malice of her foe—she is placed in the coffin: the rites proceed, her heart-stricken espoused takes his last long leave, she is carried to the grave, locked in the family vault under Stratford church, and there left alone, fearfully buried alive! And then, after a day or two, how shrieks and groans are heard in the church-yard by truant school-boys, and are placed to the account of the curse: how, at last, her despairing lover demands to have the vault opened; and the wretch Rowland—partly from curiosity, partly from malice—determined to be there to see. As they and some church-followers come near the door of the vault, they hear knockings, and desperate plunges within; Saville swoons away, the crowd falls back in terror, and the hardened Rowland alone dares unlock the door. Instantly, in her shroud, mad, starved, with the flesh gnawed from her own fair shoulders, rushes out the maniac Charlotte: in phrensied half-reason she has seized Rowland by the throat, with the strength of insanity has strangled him, and then falls dead upon the steps of the vault! Of Saville—who, as having swooned, is spared all this scene of horror, and who leaves the country for ever—little or nothing is more said: and Clopton Hall remains a ruin, tenanted by ghosts and bats.

P. S. If thought fit, after the fashion of Parisian charcoal-burners in ill-ventilated bed-rooms, Charlotte may have recorded her experiences in the vault, by writing with a rusty nail on the coffin-plates.

Now, the gist of this Victor-Hugo tale of terror is its general truth: a true end of a truly-named family, in its own neighbourhood, and long since extinct: the house, now rĕbuilt and rĕstyled—the vault—the picture of that poor unfortunate, (how unsearchable in real life often are the ways of Providence! how frequently the innocent suffer for the guilty!)—the gloomy well—and something extant of the story—remains still, and are known to some at Stratford. To do the thing graphically, one should go there, and gain materials on the spot: and nothing could be easier than to mix with them fifteenth-and-sixteenth-century costumes, modes of thought, and historical allusions; accessories of the humorous, if the age demands it, might relieve the pathetic; Charlotte's own innocence and piety might be made to soften her hard fate, with the assurance of a better life; Saville might become a wisely-resigned recluse; and while the sins of the fathers are not gently, though justly, visited on the children, the villain of the story meets his full reward.

Behold, then, hungry novel-monger, what grist is here for the mill! Behold, Sosii, what capabilities of orders from every library in the kingdom!—As doomed ones, and denounced ones, and undying ones, and unseen ones, seem to be such taking titles, what think you of the *Buried-alive-one!*—is it not new, thrilling, terrible? Who is he that would pander to the popular taste for details of dreadful, cruel, criminal, and useless abominations? "Should such a one as I?" In emptying my head of the notion, I have ministered too much already: but the sample of henbane is poured out, an offering to the infernal manes, and poisons no longer the current of my thoughts. Thy ghost, poor beautiful Charlotte! shall not be disturbed by me; thy misfortunes sleep with thee. Nevertheless, this tale about a more amiable Charlotte than Werter's, so naturally also falling into the orthodox three-volume measure, is capable of being fabricated into something of deep, romantic, tragical interest; such a character, in such circumstances, in such an age, and such a place: I commend it to those of the Anglo-Gallic school, who love the domestically horrible, and delight in unsunned sorrows: but, I throw not any one topic away as a waif, for the casual passer-by to pick up on the highway. Shadows, indeed, are flung upon the waters, but Phulax still holds the substance with tenacious teeth.

Stop awhile, my dog and shadow, and generously drop the world a morsel; be not quite so bold when no one thinks of robbing you, and spare your gasconade: the expediency of a sample has been cleverly suggested, and WE *ego et canis meus*, royal in munificence, do graciously accede. Will this serve the purpose, my ever-pensive public? At any rate, with some aid of intellect in readers, it is happily an extract which explains itself—the death of poor infatuated Margaret: we will suppose preliminaries, and hazard the abrupt.

* * * * * * * *

"That bitter speech shot home; it had sped like an arrow to her brain: it had flown to her heart like the breath of pestilence: for Rowland to be rough, uncourteous, unkind, might cause indeed many a pang; but such conduct had long become a habit, and woman's charitable soul excused moroseness in him, whom she loved more than life itself, more than honour. But now, when the dread laugh of a seemingly more righteous world was daily, hourly, to be feared against her—when the cold finger of scorn was preparing to be pointed at her fading beauty, and her altered form—now, when indulgence is most due, and cruelty has a sting more scorpion than ever—to be taunted with that once-kind tongue with having rightfully inherited *a curse*—to be told, in a sort of fiendish triumph, that some ancient family grudge, forsooth, against her father's fame, certainly as much as the selfish motives of a libertine professed, had warped the will of Rowland to her ruin—to know, to hear, yea, from his own lips, that the oft-repented crime of her warm and credulous youth—of her too free, unsuspicious affection—had calmly been contrived by the heart she clung to for her first, her only love—here was misery, here was madness!

"Rowland, at the approach of footsteps, had hastily slunk away behind the accustomed panel, and alone in the chamber was left poor Margaret: his last sneering speech, the mockery of his sarcastic pity, were still haunting her ear with echoes full of wretchedness; and she had uttered one faint cry, and sunk swooning on a couch, when her sister entered.

"Charlotte, gentle Charlotte, had nothing of the hardness of a heroine; her mind, as her most fair body, was delicate, nervous, spiritualized; but the instinct of imperious duty ever gave her strength in the day of trial. Long with an elder sister's eye had she watched and feared for Margaret; she had palliated natural levity by evident warmth of disposition, and excused follies of the judgment by kindness of the heart. Charlotte was no child; in any other case, she had been keener of perception; but in that of a young, generous, and most loving sister, suspicion had been felt as a wickedness, and had long been lulled asleep: now, however, it awaked in all its terrors; and, as Margaret lay fainting, the sorrowful condition of one soon to be a mother who never was a wife, was only too apparent. She touched her, sprinkled water on her pale face, and, as the fixed eyes opened suddenly, Charlotte started at their strange wild glare: they glittered with a freezing brilliancy, and stared around with the vacuity of an image. Could Margaret be mad? *She bit her tender lips with sullen rage, and a gnashing desperation; her* cheek was cold, white, and clammy as the cheek of a corpse; her hair, still woven with the strings of pearl she often wore, hung down loose and dishevelled, except that on her flushing brow the crisp curls stood on end, as a nest of snakes. And now a sudden thought seemed to strike the brain; her eyes were set in a steady horror; slowly, with dread determination, as if inspired by some fearful being, other than herself, uprose Margaret; and, while her frightened sister, shuddering, fell back, she glided, still gazing on vacancy, to the door: so, like a ghost through the dark corridor, down those old familiar stairs, and away through the Armory-hall; Charlotte now more calmly following, for her father's library, where his use was to study late, opened out of it, and surely the conscience-stricken Margaret was going in her penitence to him. But, see! she has silently passed by; her hand is on the lock of the hall-door; with one last look of despairing recklessness behind her, as taking an eternal leave of that awe-struck sister, the door turns upon its hinge, and she, still with slow solemnity, goes out. Whither, oh God!—whither? The night is black as pitch, rainy, tempestuous; the old knight's guests at Clopton Hall have gladly and right wisely preferred even such questionable accommodation as the blue chamber, the dreary white apartment looking on the moat—nay, the haunted room of the parricide himself—to encountering the dangers and darkness of a night-return so desperate; but Margaret, in her gayest evening attire, near upon so foul a midnight in November, stalks like a spectre down the splashy steps. Charlotte follows, calls, runs to her—but cannot rescue from some settled purpose, horribly suggested, that gentle fearful creature, now so changed. Suddenly in the dark she has lost her. Which way did the maniac turn?—whither in that desolate gloom shall Charlotte fly to find her? Guided by the taper still twinkling in her father's study, she rushes back in terror to the hall; and then—Help, help!—torches, torches! The household is roused, dull lanterns glance among the shrubberies; pine-lights, ill-shielded from wind and rain by cap or cloak, are seen dotting the park in every direction, and dance about through the darkness, like sportive wild-fires: Sir Clement in moody calmness looks prepared for any thing the worst, like a man who anticipates evil long-deserved; the broken-hearted mother is on her knees at the cold door-steps, striving to pierce the gloom with her eyes, and ejaculating distracted prayers: and so the live-long night—that night of doubt, and dread, and dreariness—through bitter hours of confusion and dismay, they sought poor Margaret—and found her not!

"But, with morning's light came the awful certainty. At the end of a terraced walk, mournfully shaded by high-cropped yews, stood an arbour, and behind it, half-hidden among rank weeds, was an old half-forgotten fountain; there, on many a sultry summer night, had Rowland met with Margaret, and there had she resolved in terrible remorse to perish. With the seeming fore-thought of reason, and the resolution of a phrensied fortitude, she had bound a quantity of matted weeds about her face, and twisted her hands in her fettering garments, that the shallow pool might not in cruel kindness fail to drown her; she lay scarcely half immersed in those waters of death; a few lazy tench floating sluggishly about, appeared to be curiously inspecting their ghastly, uninvited guest; and the fragments of an enamelled miniature, with some torn letters in the hand-writing of Rowland Beauvoir, were found scattered on the overflowing margin of the pool."

Well, unkindly whelp, if your bone has no pickings better than this, not a cur shall envy you the sorry banquet. Yet, had my genius been better educated in the science of French cookery, this might have been served up with higher seasoning as a savoury *ragout:* but you get it in simplicity, scarce grilled; and in sooth, good world, it is easier to sneer at a novel than to imagine one; and far more self-complacency may be gained by manfully affecting to despise the novelist, than by adding to his honours in the compliment of humble imitation.

THINGS supernatural have every where and every when exercised mortal curiosity. Fear and credulity support the arms of superstition, fierce as city griffins, rampant as the lion and the unicorn; and forasmuch as no creature, Nelson not excepted, can truly boast of having never known fear, and no man also—from polite Voltaire, shrewd Hume, Leviathan Hobbes, and erudite Gibbon, down to the most stultified Van-Diemanite—can honestly swear himself free from the influence of some sort of faith, for thus much the marvellous and the terrible meet with universal popularity. Now, one or two curious matters connected with those "more things in heaven and earth, Horatio, than are dreamt of in your philosophy," which have even occurred to mine own self, (whereof, to gratify you, shall be a little more anon), have heretofore induced me to touch upon sundry interesting points, which, like pikemen round their chief, throng about the topic of

THE MARVELLOUS.

A BOOK, so simply titled, with haply underneath a gigantic note of admiration between two humble queries (?!?) would positively, my worthy publisher, make your worship's fortune. For it should concern ghosts, dreams, omens, coincidences, good-and-bad luck, warnings, and true vaticinations: no childish collection, however, of unsupported trumpery, but authenticated cases staidly evidenced, and circumstantially detailed; no Mother Goose-cap's tales, no Dick the Ploughman's dreams, no stories from the '*Terrific Register*,' nor fancies of hysterical females in Adult asylums; even Merlin witch-finders, and Taliesins should be excluded: and, in lieu of all such common-places, I should propose an anecdotic treatise in the manner scientifical. Macnish's '*Philosophy of Sleep*,' Scott's '*Demonology*,' treatises on Apparitions, and many a rare black-letter alchemical pamphlet, might lend us here their aid; the British Museum is full of well-attested ghost-stories, and there are very few old ladies unable to add to the supply: then, this ghost department might be climaxed by the author's own experience; forasmuch as he is ready to avouch that a person's fetch was heard by many, and seen by some, in an old country-house, a hundred miles away from the place of death, at the instant of its happening.

As to omens, aforesaid witness deposes that the sceptre, ball, and cross were struck by lightning out of King John's hand, in the Schools quadrangle at Oxford, immediately on the accession of William the Reformer; and all the world is cognusant that York Minster, the Royal Exchange, and the Houses of Parliament were destroyed by fire near about the commencement of open hostility, among ruling powers, to our church, commerce, and constitution; and I myself can tell a tale of no less than eight remarkable warnings happening one day to a poor friend, who died on the next, which none could be expected to believe unless I delivered it on oath as having been an eye-witness to the facts. Dreams also—strange, vague, mysterious word; there is a gloomy look in it, a dreary intonation that makes the very flesh creep: the records of public justice will show many a murder revealed by them, as instance the Red Barn; more than one poor client, in the clutch of a "respectable" attorney, has been helped to his rights by their influence; from Agamemnon and Pilate, down to Napoleon, the oppressors of mankind have in those had kindly warning. Dreams—how many millions false and foolish, for the one proving to be true!—but that one, how clear, determinate, and lasting, as ministered by far other agency than imagination taking its sport while reason slumbers! Who has not tales to tell of dreams? A warning not to go on board such and such a ship—which founders; a strange unlikely scene fixed upon the mind, concerning friends and circumstances miles away, exactly in the manner and at the time of its occurrence; the fore-shown coming of an unexpected guest; the pourtrayed visage of a secret enemy: these, and others like these, many can attest, and I not least. And of other marvels, though here left unconsidered, yet might much be said: truths so strange, that the pages of romance would not trench on such extravagance; combinations so unlikely, that thrice twelve cast successively by proper dice, were but probability to those. Thus, in authorial fashion, has the marvellous dwelt upon my mind; and thus would I suggest a hand-book thereof to catering booksellers and the insatiable public.

Against bears in a stage-coach, pointers in a drawing-room, lap dogs in a *vis-à-vis*, and monkeys in a lady's boudoir, my love of comfort and propriety enters strong protest; an emancipated parrot attracts my sympathy far less than bright-eyed children feeding their testy pet, for I dread the cannibal temptation of those soft fair fingers, when brought into collision with Polly's hook and eye; gigantic Newfoundlanders dragging their perpetual chains, larks and linnets trilling the faint song of liberty behind their prison bars, cold green snakes stewing in a school-boy's pocket, and dormice nestling in a lady's glove, summon my antipathies; a cargo of five hundred pigs, with whom I had once the honour of sailing from Cork to London, were far from pleasant as *compagnons de voyage;* neither can I sleep with kittens in the room. Nevertheless, no one can profess truer compassion, truer friendship (if you will) for the animal creation: often have I walked on in weariness, rather than increase the strain upon the Rosinantes of an omnibus; and my greatest school scrape was occasioned by thrashing the favoured scion of a noble house for cruelty to a cat. Such and such-like—for we learn from Æsop (Fable eighty-eight, to wit) that trumpeters deserve to be unpopular—is my physical zeal in the cause of poor dumb brutes: nor is my regard for them the less in matters metaphysical. Bishop Butler, we may all of us remember, in 'THE *Analogy*,' argues that the objector against a man's immortality must show good cause why that which exists, should ever cease to exist; and, until that good cause be shown, the weight of probability is in favour of continual being. Now, for my part, I wish to be informed why this probability should not be extended to that innocent maltreated class, whom God's merey made with equal skill, and sustains with equal care, as in the case of man, and—dare we add?—of angels. Doth He not feed the ravens? Do the young lions not gather what He giveth? Doth a sparrow fall to the ground without Our Father? and is not the unsinning multitude of Nineveh's young children climaxed with "much cattle?" It is true, there may be mighty difference between "the spirit of a man that goeth upward, and the spirit of a beast that goeth downward in the earth:" but mark this, there *is* a spirit in the beast; and as man's eternal heaven may lie in some superior sphere, so that temporarily designed for the lower animals may be seen in the renovated earth. It is also true, that St. Paul, arguing for the temporal livelihood of Christian ministers from the type of "not muzzling the ox that treadeth out the corn," asks, "Doth God care for oxen?"—or, in effect, doth He legislate (I speak soberly, though the sublime treads on the ridiculous,) for a stable?—and the implication is, "To thy dutiful husbandry, O man! such lesser cares are left." Sorry, righteously sorry, would it make any good man's heart to think that the Creator had ceased to care for the meanest of his creatures: in a certain sense

"He sees with equal eye, as God of all,
A hero perish, or a sparrow fall;"

and, assured that carelessness in a just Creator of his poor dependent creatures must be impossible, I submit that, critically speaking, some laudable variation might be made in that text by the simple consideration that μελει is not so strictly rendered "care for" as κεδεται. Scripture, then, so far from militating against the possible truth, that animals have souls, would seem, by a side-long glance, to countenance the doctrine: and now let us for a passing moment turn and see what aid is given to us by moral philosophy.

No case can be conceived more hard or more unjust than that of a sentient creature (on the hypothesis of its having no soul, no conscience, necessarily quite innocent), thrown into a world of cruelty and tyranny, without the chance of compensation for sufferings undeserved. Neither can any good government be so partial, as (limiting the whole existence of animals to an hour, a day, a year,) to allow one of a litter to be pampered with continual luxuries, and another to be tortured for all its little life by blows, famine, disease—and in its lingering death by the scientific scalpels of a critical Majendie or a cold-blooded Spallanzani. Remember, that in the so-called parallel case of partialities among men—the this-world's choice of a Jacob, the this-world's rejection of an Esau—the answer is obvious: there are two scales to the balance, there is yet another world. Far be it from us to think that all things are not then to be cleared up; that the innocent little ones of Kedar and the exterminated Canaanites will not then be heard one by one, and no longer be mingled up indiscriminately in an overwhelming national judgment; that the pleas of evil education and example, of hereditary taint and common usage, will be then thrown aside as vain excuse; and that eventual justice will not with facility explain every riddle in the moral government of God. But in the case of soulless extinguished animals, there is, there can be no compensation, no explanation; whether in pain or pleasure, they have lived and they have died forgotten by their Maker, and left to the casual kindness or cruelty of, towards them at least, irresponsible masters. How different the view opened to us by the possibility of soul being apportioned in various measure among the lower animals: there is a clue given "to justify the ways of God to"—brutes: we need not then consider, with a certain French abbé, that they are fallen angels, doing penance for their sins; we need not, with old Pythagoras and latter Brahmins, account them stationed lodges, homes of transmigration for the spirits of men in process of being purged from their offences: we need not regard them as Avatars of Vishnu, or incarnations of Apis, visible deities craving the idolatries of India and Egypt. The truth commends itself by mere simplicity: nakedness betrays its Eve-like innocence of guile or error: those living creatures whom we call brutes and beasts, have, in their degree, the breath of God within them, as well as His handiwork upon them. And, candid theologian, tell me why—in that Millenium so long looked-for, when, after a fiery purgation, this earth shall have its sabbath, and when those who for a time were "caught up into the air," descending again with their Lord and his ten thousand saints, shall bodily dwell with others risen in the flesh for that happy season on this renovated globe—tell me why there should not be some tithe of the animal creation made to rise again to minister in pleasure, as they once ministered in pain? And for the rest, the other nine, what hinders them from tenanting a thousand happy fields in other of the large domains of space? What hinders those poor dumb slaves from enjoying some emancipate existence—we need not perhaps accord them more of immortality than justice demands for compensation—for a definite time, a millenium let us think, in scores of those million orbs that twinkle in the galaxy?

> Space stretches wide enough for every grain
> Of the broad sands that curb our swelling seas,
> Each separate in its sphere, to stand apart
> As far as sun from sun.

Shall I then say what hinders?—the littleness of man's mind, refusing possibility of room for those countless quadrillions; and the selfishness of his pride, scorning the more generous savage, whose doctrine (certainly too lax in liberality) raises the beast to a level with mankind, and

> "Who thinks, admitted to that equal sky,
> His faithful dog shall bear him company."

Truly, the Creator's justice, and mercy, and the majesty of his kingdom, give hope of after-life to all creation: Saint Antony of Padua did waste time in homilizing birds, beasts, and fishes; but may they not find blessings, though ignorant of priests?—And now, suffer me, in my current fashion, to glance at a few other considerations affecting this topic. It will be admitted, I suppose, that the lower animals possess, in their degree, similar cerebral or at least nervous mechanism with ourselves; in their degree, I say; for a zoöphyte and a caterpillar have brains, though not in the head; and to this day Waterton does not know whether he shot a man or a monkey, so closely is his nondescript linked with either hand to the grovelling Australian and the erect orang outang. Brutes are nerved as we are, and uncivilized man possesses instincts like them: all we can with any show of reason deny them is moral sense, and in our arbitrary refusal of this, and our summary disposal of what we are pleased to term instinct, we take credit to ourselves for exclusive participation in that immaterial essence which is called Soul. But is it, in candour, true that brutes have no moral sense? Obviously, since moral sense is a growing thing, and ascending in the scale of being, and since man is its chief receptacle on earth, we ought to be able to take the best instances of animal morals from those creatures which have come most within the influence of human example; as pets of every kind, but mainly dogs. Does not a puppy, that has stolen a sweet morsel from some butcher's stall, fly, though none pursue him? Is a fox-hound not conscience-stricken for his harry of the sheep-fold? and who will deny some sense of duty, and no little strength of affection, in a shepherd's dog? Have not Cowper's now historic hares displayed an educated and unnatural confidence; and many a gray parrot, though limited in speech, said many a witty thing?—Again, read some common collection of canine anecdotes: What essential difference is there between the affectionate watch kept by man over his brother's bed of sickness, and that which has been known of more than one poor cur, whose solicitude has extended even to dying on his master's grave? The soldier's faithful poodle licks his wounds upon the stormy battle-field; and Landseer's colley-dog tears up the turf, and howls the shepherd's requiem. What real distinction can we make between a high sense of duty in the captain who is the last to leave his sinking ship, and that in the watchful terrier, whom neither tempting morsels nor menaced blows can induce to desert the ploughman's smock committed to his care? Once more: Who does not recognise individuality of character in animals? A dog, or a horse, or a tame deer, or, in fact, any domesticated creature, will act throughout life, in a certain course of disposition, at least as consistently as most masters: it will also have its whims and ways, likings and dislikings, habits, fears, joys, and sorrows; and, verily, in patience, courage, gratitude, and obedience, will put its monarch to the blush.

But upon this theme—meagre as the sketch may be, fanciful, illogical —my cursory notions have too long detained you. I had intended barely to have introduced a black-looking Greek composite, serving for name to an unwritten essay which we will imagine in existence as

PSYCHOTHERION,

AN INCONCLUSIVE ARGUMENT ON THE SOULS OF BRUTES;

And my thoughts have run on thus far so little conclusively (I humbly admit to you), that we will, to save trouble, leave the riddle as unsolved as ever, and gain no better advantage than thus having loosely adverted to another fancy of your author's mind.

Not yet is my mind a simple freeman, a private, unincumbered, individual self-possessor: its slaves are not yet all manumitted; I lack not subjects; I am no lord of depopulated regions; albeit my aim is indeed akin to that of old Rufus, and Goldsmith's tyrannical Squire of Auburn;

I wish to clear my hunting-grounds, to make a solitude, and call it peace. Slowly, but still surely, am I working out that will. Meanwhile, however, there is no need to advertise for heroes; they are only too rife, clinging like bats to the curtains of my chambers of imagery, or with attendant satellites hanging in bunches, as swarming bees about their monarch, to the rafters of my brain. Selection is the hardest difficulty; here is the labour, here the toil; because for just selection there should be good reasons. Now, amongst other my multitudinous authorial projects, this perhaps is not the worst; namely, by a series of dissimilar novels, psychological rather than religious, and for interest's sake laid in diverse ages and countries, to illustrate separately the most rampant errors of the Papacy. For example, say that Lewis's '*Monk*' is a strong delineation of the evils consequent on constrained and unchosen celibacy; though its colouring be meretricious, though its details offend the moralities of nature, still it is a book replete to thoughtful minds with terrible teaching—be not high-minded, but fear. In like manner, guilty thoughts dropped upon innocent young hearts in that foul corner,

THE CONFESSIONAL,

might make a stirring tale, or haply a series of them: the cowled hypocrite suggesting crime to those whose answer is all innocence; his schemes of ambition, or avarice, or lust, slowly elaborated by the fiend-like purposes to which he puts his ill-used knowledge of the human heart; his sacrilegious violation of the holy grievings made by mistaken penitence. History should bring its collateral assistance: the Medicean Queens, Venice, bloody Spain, hard-visaged monks calmly directing the engines of torture, the poison of anonymous calumny, and dread secrets more dreadfully betrayed, could furnish much of truthful precedent. The bad obstructions placed between the sinner and his God by selfish priestcraft; the souls that would return again, like Noah's weary dove, enticed by ravens to forsake the ark, mate with them, and feed on their banquet of corruption; the social, religious, philosophic, and eternal harms brought out in full detail; the progress of this world's misery in the lives of the confessing, and of studious crime in the heart of the absolver: a scene laid among the high Alps, and the sunny plains they topple over; the time, that of some murderous Simon de Montfort; the actors, Waldensian saints, and demon inquisitors; the prominent characters, a plausible intriguing friar, (as of old a monk of Cluni,) whose ambition is the popedom, and whose conscience has no scruple about means, bloody, bad, vindictive, atheistic; and then his victims, a youth that he trains from infancy to the sole end of poisoning, subtly and slowly, all who stand in his path; a girl who loves this youth, and who, flying from the foul friar in the day of temptation, betakes her to the mountains, and ultimately saves her lover from his terrible destination in guilt, by hiding him in her own haven of refuge, the persecuted little church; and with these materials to work upon, I need hardly detail to you an intricate plot and an obvious *dénouement.*

This class of theme, it is probable, has exercised the talents of many; but as the evils of confessing to deceitful man, and of blind trust in his deleterious advice, have not specifically met my eye, the subject is new to me, and may be so to others. Still, I stay not now further to enlarge upon it; I must press on; and will not cruelly encourage the birth of thoughts brought forth only to be destroyed, like father Saturn's babes —the anthropophagite.

A good reason for selection at last presents itself. Sundry collateral ancestors of mine [every body from Cain downwards must have had ancestors; so no quibbling, please, nor quarrelling about so exploded an absurdity as family-pride,] were lucky enough in days lang syne to appropriate to themselves, amongst other matters, a respectable allowance of forfeited monastic territory; and I know it by this token: that in yonder venerable chest of archives and muniments, rest in their own dust of ages, duly and clearly assorted, all those abbey deeds from the times of Henry Beauclerc. Here 's a fine unlooked-for opportunity of making dull ancestral spots classic ground, famous among men; here 's a chance of immortalizing the crumbling ruins of an obscure, but interesting, abbey-church; here 's a fair field for dragging in all that one knows or does not know, all that parchments can prove, or fancy can invent, of redoubtable or reprobate progenitors, and investing the place of their possessions with a glory beyond heraldry. Much is on my mind of the desperate evils consequent on the Romish rule of idol-worship: and why not lay my scene on the wild banks of the Swale, among the bleak, rough moors that stand round Richmond, and the gullies that run between the Yorkshire hills? Why not talk about those names of gentle blood, familiar to the ear as household words, Uvedale and Scrope, Vavasour and Ratcliffe? Why not press into the service of instructive novelism truths stranger than fiction, among characters more marked, and names of higher note, than the whole hot-pressed family of the Fitzes?

All this might be accomplished, were it worth the worry, in

THE PRIOR OF MARRICK.

And now for a story of idolatry. It seems an absurdity, an insanity; it is one—both. But think it out. Is it quite impossible, quite incredible? Let me sketch the outline of so strange infatuation. Our prior was once a good man—an easy, kind, and amiable: he takes the cowl in early youth, partly because he is the younger son of an unfighting family, and must, partly because he is melancholy, and will. And wherefore melancholy? There was brought up with him, from the very nursery, a fair girl, the weeping orphan of a neighbouring squire, who had buckled on his harness, and fallen in the wars: they loved, of course, and the deeper, because secretly and without permission: they were too young to marry, and indeed had thought little of the matter; still, substance and shadow, body and soul, were scarcely more needful to each other, or more united. But—a hacking cough—a hectic cheek —a wasting frame, were to blue-eyed Mary the remorseless harbingers of death, and Eustace, standing on her early grave, was in heart a widower: henceforth he had no aim in life; the cloister was—so thought he, as many do—his best refuge, to dream upon the past, to soothe his present sorrows, and earn for a future world the pleasures lost in this. Time, the best anodyne short of what Eustace could not buy at Rome —true-healing godliness—alleviates his grief, and makes him less sad, but not wiser; years pass, the desire of prëeminence in his own small world has hitherto furnished incentives to existence, and he find himself a prior too soon; for he has nothing more to live for. Yes: there is an object; the turmoil of small ambition with its petty cares is past, and the now motiveless man lingers in yearning thought on the only white spot in his gloomy journey, the green oasis of his desert life, that dream of early love. He has long loved the fair, quiet image of our Lady of Marrick, unwittingly, for another Mary's sake; half-oblivious of the past in scheming for the present, he has knelt at midnight before that figure of the Virgin-mother, and knew not why he trembled; he thought it the ecstacy of devotion, the warm-gushing flood of calmness, which prayer confers upon care confessed. But now, he sees it, he knows it; there is, indeed, good cause: how miraculously the white marble face grows into resemblance with *hers!* the same sainted look of delicate unearthly beauty, the same white cheek, so still and unruffled even by a smile, the same turn of heavenly triumph on the lip, the same wild compassion in the eye! Great God—he loves again!—that staid, grave, melancholy man, loves with more than youthful fondness; the image is now dearer than the most sacred; there is a halo round it, like light from heaven: he adores its placid, eternal, changeless aspect; if it could move, the charm would half dissolve; he loves it—as an image! And then how rapturously joins he with the wondering choir of more stagnant worshippers, while they yield to this substantial form, this stone-transmigration of his love, this tangible, unpassionate, abiding, present deity, the holy hymns of praise, due only to the unseen God! How gladly he sings her titles, ascribing all excellence to her! How tenderly falls he at her feet, with eyes lighted as in youth! How earnestly he prays to his fixed image—*to* it, not *through* it, for his heart is *there!* How zealously he longs for her honour, her worship among men—hers, the presiding idol of that Gothic pile, the hallowed Lady, the goddess-queen of Marrick! Stop—can he do nothing for her, can he venture nothing in her service? Other shrines are rich, other images decked in gold and jewels; there is yet an object for his useless life, there are yet ends to be attained, ends—that can justify the means. He longs for wealth, he plots for it, he dares for it: he plans lying miracles, and thousands flock to the shrine; he waylays dying men, and, by threatened dread of torments of the damned, extortionizes conscience into unjust riches for himself; he accuses the innocent, and reaps the fine; he connives at the guilty, and fingers the bribe. So wealth flows in, and the altar of his idol is hung with cloth of gold, her diadem is alight with gems, costly offerings deck her temple, bending crowds kneel to her divinity. Is he not happy? Is he not content? Oh, no: an insatiate demon has possessed him; with more than Pygmalion's insanity, he loves that image; he dreams, he thinks of that one unchanging form. The marvelling brotherhood, credulous witnesses of such deep devotion, hold him for a saint; and Rome, at the wish of the world, sends him, as to a living St. Eustatius, the patent of canonization: they praise him, honour him, pray to him; but he contemptuously (and they take it for humility) spurns a gift which speaks of any other heaven than the presence of that one fair, beautiful, beloved statue. A thought fills him, and that with joy: he has heard of sacrifices in old time, immolations, offerings up of self, as the highest act of a devout worshipper; he cares not for earth nor for heaven; and one night, in his enthusiastic vigils, the phrensy of idolatry arms that old man's own weak hand against himself, and he falls at the statue's feet, self-murdered, *its* martyr.

Here were scope for psychology; here were subtle unwindings of motive, trackings of reason, intricate anatomizations of the heart. All ages, before these last in which we live, have been worshippers, even to excess, of "unknown gods," "too superstitious:" we, upon whom the ends of the world are fallen, may be thought to be beyond a danger into which the wisest of old time were entrapped: we scarcely allow that the Brahmin may, notwithstanding, be a learned man and a shrewd, when we see him fall before his monster; we have not wits to understand how the Babylonian, Persian, Grecian, and Roman dynasties could be so besotted. For this superior illumination of mind, let us thank not ourselves, but the Light of the world; and, warned by the history of ages, let us beware how we place created things to mediate between us and the most High; let us be shy of symbolic emblems—of pictures, images, observances—lest they grow into forms that engross the mind, and fill it with a swarm of substantial idols.

Now, this tale of the '*Prior of Marrick*' would, but for the present premature abortion, have seen daylight in the form of an auto-biography —the catastrophe, of course, being added by some brother-monk, who winds up all with his moral: and to get at this auto-biographical sketch —a thing of fragments and wild soliloquies, incidentally laying bare the heart's disease, and the poisonous breathings of idolatrous influence—I could easily, and after the true novelist fashion, fabricate a scheme, somewhat as follows: Let me go gayly to the Moors by rail, coach, or cart, say for a sportsman's pastime, a truant vicar's week, or an audit-clerk's holiday: I drop upon the ruined abbey, now indeed with scarcely a vestige of its former beauty remaining, but still used as a burial-place; being a bit of an antiquary, I rout up the sexton, (sexton, cobbler, and general huckster,) resolved to lionize the old desecrated precinct: I find the sexton a character, a humourist; he, cobbler-like, looks inquisitively at my caoutchouc shooting-shoes, and hints that he too is an artist in the water-proof line; then follows question as how, and rejoinder as thus. Our sexton has got a name among his neighbours for his capital double-leather brogues, warranted to carry you dry-shod through a river; and, warmed by my brandy-flask and *bonhomie*, considering me moreover little likely to set up a rival shop, cunningly communicates his secret: he puts parchment between the leathers!—Parchment, my good man? where can you get your parchment hereabouts? I spoke innocently, for I thought only of ticketing some grouse for my friends southward: but the question staggered my sexton so sensibly, that I came to the uncharitable conclusion—he had stolen it. And then follows confession: how, among the rubbish in a vault, he had found a small oak chest—broke it open—no coins, no trinkets, "no nothing,"—except parchment; a lot of leaves tidily written, and—warranted to keep out the wet. A few shillings and a tankard make the treasure mine, I promising as extra to send a huge bundle of ancient indentures in place of the precious manuscript. Thus, in the way of Mackenzie's '*Man of Feeling*,' we become fragmentary where we fear to be tedious; and so, in a good historic epoch, among the wars of the Roses, surrounded by friars and nuns, outlaws and border-riders, chivalrous knights and sturdy bowyers, consign I to the oblivescent firm of Capulet and Co. my happily destroyed '*Prior of Marrick.*'

A crank boat needs ballast; and of happy fortune is it for a disposition towards natural levity, when educational gravity has helped to steady it. Upon the vivacious, let the reflective supervene: to the gay, suffer in its season the addition of the serious. Amongst other wholesome topics of of meditation—for wholesome it is to the healthy spirit, although of some little danger to the presumptuous and inflated—the study of the sure word of Prophecy has more than once excited the writing propensity of your author's mind. On most matters it has been my fate, rather from habits of incurable revery than from any want of opportunities, to think more than to read; and therefore it is, with very due diffidence, that as far as others and their judgments are concerned, I can ever hope to claim originality or novelty. To my own conscience, however, these things are reversed; for contemplation has produced that as new to my own mind, which may be old to others deeper read, and has thought those ideas original, which are only so to its own fancy. Very little, then, must such as I reasonably hope to add on Prophetical Interpretation; the Universal Wisdom of two millenaries cannot be expected to gain any thing from the passing thought of a hodiernal unit: if any fancies in my brain are really new, and hitherto unbroached upon the subject, it can scarcely be doubted but that they are false; so very little reliance do principles of catholicity allow to be placed upon "private interpretations."

With thus much of apology to those alike who will find, and those who will not find, any thing of novelty in my notions, I still do not withhold them. By here a little and there a little, is the general mind instructed: it would be better for the world if every mighty tome really contributed its grain.

The prophecies of Holy Writ appear to me to have one great peculiarity, distinguishing them from all other prophecies, if any, real or pretended; and that peculiarity I deferentially conceive to be this: that, whereas all human prophecies profess to have but one fulfilment, the divine have avowedly many true fulfilments. The former may indeed light upon some one coincidence, and may exult in the accident as a proof of truth; the latter bounds as it were (like George Herbert's sabbaths) from one to another, and another, through some forty centuries, equally fulfilled in each case, but still looking forward with hope to some grander catastrophe: it is not that they are loosely suited, like the Delphic oracles, to whatever may turn up, but that they, by a felicitous adaptation, sit closely into each era which the Architect of Ages has arranged. Pythonic divination may be likened to a loose bag, which would hold and involve with equal ease almost any circumstance; biblical prophecy to an exact mould, into which alone, though not all similar in perfection, its own true casts will fit: or again, in another view of the matter, accept this similitude: let the All-seeing Eye be the centre of many concentric circles, beholding equally in perspective the circumference of each, and for accordance with human periods of time measuring off segments by converging radii: separately marked on each segment of the wheel within wheel, in the way of actual fulfilment, as well as type and antitype, will appear its satisfied word of prophecy, shining onward yet as it becomes more and more final, until time is melted in eternity. Thus, it is perhaps not impossible that every interpretation of wise and pious men may alike be right, and hold together; for different minds travel on the different peripheries. So our Lord (to take a familiar instance) speaks of his second advent in terms equally applicable to the destruction of one city, of the accumulated hosts at Armageddon, and of this material earth: Antiochus and Antichrist occur prospectively within the same pair of radii at differing distances; and, in like manner and varying degrees, may, for aught we can tell, such incarnations of the evil principle as papal Rome, or revolutionary Enrope, or infidel Cosmopolitism; or, again, such heads of parties, such indexes of the general mind, as a Cæsar, an Attila, a Cromwell, a Napoleon, a—whoever be the next. So also of hours, *days, years,* eras; all may and do cöexist in harmonious and mutual relations. Good men, those who combine prayer with study, need not fear necessary difference of result, from holding different views; the grand error is too loosely generalizing; a little circle suits our finite ken; we cannot, as yet, mentally span the universe. These crude and cursory remarks may serve to introduce a likely-looking idea to which my thoughts have given entertainment, and which, with others of a similar sort, were once to have come forth in an essay-form, headed

THE SEVEN CHURCHES;

moreover, for aught that has come across my reading, to be additionally styled '*A New Interpretation, for these Latter Days.*' Without desiring to do other than quite confirm the literal view, as having related primarily to those local churches of old times, geographically in Asia Minor; without attempting to dispute that they may have an individual reference to varieties of personal character, and probably of different Christian sects; I imagine that we may discover, in the Apocalyptic prospect of these seven churches, an historical view of Christianity, from the earliest ages to the last: beginning as it did, purely, warmly, and laboriously, with the apostolic emblematic Ephesus, and to end with the "shall He find faith on earth" of luke-warm Laodicea: thus Smyrna would symbolize the state of the church under Diocletian, the "tribulation ten days:" Pergamus, perhaps the Byzantine age, "where Satan's seat is" the Balaam and Balak of empire and priesthood; Thyatira, the avowed commencement of the Papacy, "Jezebel," &c.; Sardis, the dreary void of the dark ages, the "ready to die;" Philadelphia, the rise of Protestantism, "an open door, a little strength;" and Laodicea, (the riches of civilization choking the plant of Christianity,) its decline, and, but for the Founder's second coming, its fall; if, indeed, this were possible.

The elucidation of these several hints might show some striking confirmations of the notion; which, as every thing else in this book, would humbly claim your indulgence, reader, for my sketches must be rapid, and their descriptions brief. Concurrently, however, with this, (which I know not whether any prophetic scholiasts have mentioned or not,) there may be deduced a still further interpretation, equally, as far as I am concerned, underived from the lucubrations of others. This other interpretation involves a typical view of the general characteristics of Christendom's seven true churches, as they are to be found standing at the coming of their Lord; the Asiatic seven may be assimilated, in their religious peculiarities, with the national Protestant churches of modern Europe: what order should be preserved in this assimilation, unless indeed it be that of eldership, it might be difficult to decide; but, excluding those communities which idol-worship has unchurched, and leaving out of view such anomalies as America presents, having no national religion, we shall find seven true churches now existing, between which and the Asiatics many curious parallels might be run: the seven are, those of England, Scotland, Holland, Prussia, perhaps Switzerland, Sweden, and Germany. Without professing to be quite confident as to the list, the idea remains the same: it is but a light hint on a weighty subject, demanding more investigation than my slender powers can at present compass. It is merely thrown out as undigested matter; a crude notion let it rest: if ever I aspire to the dignity and dogmatism of a theological teacher, it must be after more and deeper inquiry of the Newtons, Faber, Frere, Croly, Keith, and other learned interpreters, than it is possible or proper to make in a hurry: volumes have been, and volumes might be again, written for and against any prophecy unfulfilled; it is dangerous to teach speculations; for, if found false, they tend to bring holy truths into disrepute. Let me then put upon the shelf, as a humble layman should, my hitherto unaccomplished prophetical treatise; and receive its mention for little more than my true revelation of another phase of authorship.

And many like attempts have been hazarded by me in the mode theological; though, from some cause or other, they have mostly fallen abortive. Were mention here made of the more completed efforts of your author's mind, in this walk of literature, or of others, it might too evidently lay bare the mystery of my mask; a piece of secret information intended not as yet to be bestowed. But this book—purporting to be the medley of my mind, the *bonâ fide* emptying of its multifarious fancies—must of necessity, if honest, pourtray all the wanings and waxings of an ever-changing lunar disposition: so, haply you shall turn from a play to a sermon, from a novel to a moral treatise, from a satire or an epigram to a religious essay. Such and so inconsistent is authorial man. Here then, in somewhat of order, should have followed lengthily various other writings of serious import, half-fashioned, and from conflicting reasons left—perhaps for ever—half-finished. But considering the crude and apparently careless nature of this present book, and taking into account the solemn and responsible manner in which such high topics ought invariably to be treated, I have struck out, without remorse or mercy, all except a mere mention of the subjects alluded to. The contiguity of lighter matter demands this sacrifice; not that I am one of those who deem a cheerful face and a prayerful heart incongruous: there is danger in a man, however religious, when his brow lowers, and his cheek is stern; so did Cromwell murder Charles; so did Mary (though bigoted, sincere,) consign Cranmer to the flames and Jane to the scaffold: innocence and mirth are near of kin, and the tear of penitence is no stranger to the laughter-loving eye. But I ramble as usual. Let it suffice to say, that in accordance with common prejudices, I suffer my mind to be shorn of its consecrated rays; for albeit my moral censor has spared the prophetical ideas, and one or two other serious sobrieties, on the ground that, although they are mere hints, they are at all events hints of good, still more experimental and more hazardous pieces of biblical criticism have been not unwisely immolated. The full cause of this will appear in the mere title of the first of these half-attempted essays, viz:

THE WISDOM OF REVISION;

whereof my predication shall be simply and strictly *nil.*

The next piece of serious study, as yet little more than a root in my mind, was to have fructified in the form of

HOMELY EXPOSITIONS,

or domestic readings in Scripture for daily use in family worship, with an easy, sensible, useful sort of commentary; a book calculated expressly for the understandings, wants, vices, temptations, and peculiarities of household servants, and quite opposed to the usual plans of injuriously raising doubts to lay them, of insisting upon obsolete Judaisms, of strict theological controversy, of enlarging to satiety on the meaning of passages too obvious to require explanation, and ingeniously slurring over those which really need it; indeed, of pursuing the courses generally adopted by the mass of commentators.

A further notion extended to

LAY SERMONS.

whereof are many written: their principal peculiarities consist in being each of a quarter-hour length, as little as possible regarding Jews and their didactic histories, and, as much as might be, crowding ideas, and images, and out-of-the-way knowledge of all sorts, into the good service of illustrating Gospel truths.

Another religious essay has been relinquished, although to a great degree effected, from the apprehension that it may suggest matter fanciful or false: also, in part, from the material being perhaps of too slender a character to insist upon. Its name stood thus,

SCRIPTURAL PHYSICS;

being an attempt to vindicate the wisdom of Holy Writ in matters of natural science; for example, cosmogony, geology, the probable centre of the earth, the vitality and circulation of the blood, hints of magnetism and electricity, a solar system, a plurality of worlds, the earth's shape, inclined axis, situation in space, and connection with other spheres, the separate existence of disembodied life, the laws of optics, much of recondite natural history:—all these can be easily proved to be alluded to in detached, or ingeniously compared, passages of the Hebrew Scriptures. It is very likely, however, that Huntington has anticipated some of this, although I have never met with his writings; and a great deal more of it is mentioned in notes and sermons which many have read or heard. Until, therefore, I become surer of neither invading the provinces of others, nor of detracting from their wisdom, let those ill-written fancies still lie dormant in my desk.

A fifth tractate on things theological, still in the egg state, was to have been indued with the rather startling appellation of

AN APOLOGY FOR HEATHENISM;

especially as contrasted with practical atheism, which, truth to tell, is the contradictory sort of religion most universally professed among the moderns: working out the idea, that any-how it is better to have many objects of veneration than none, and that, although idol-worship is a dreadful sin, still it is not so utterly hopeless as actual ungodliness. That, among the heathens, temporal judgment ever vindicated the true Divinity; whereas the consummation of the more modern unworshiping world will be an eternal one: so, by the difference in punishments comparing that of their criminalities. Showing also that, however corrupted afterwards by impure rites and fatuous iniquities, heathenism was, in its most ancient form, little more than the hieroglyphic dress of truth: this exemplified by Moses and the brazen serpent, by interpretations of Grecian mythology, shown, after the manner of perhaps too ingenious Lord Bacon, to be consistent with philosophy and religion; by the way, in which Egyptian priests satisfied so good and shrewd, though credulous, a mind as that of Herodotus; by Hesiod's '*Theogony*;' by the practical testimony of the whole educated world in earliest times to the deep meaning involved in idolatrous rites; by the mysteries of Eleusis in particular; by the characters of all most enlightened heathens—as Cicero, Socrates, and Plato—(half-convinced of the Godhead's unity, and still afraid to disavow His plurality,) contrasted with those of the school of Pyrrho, and Lucretius, and the later Epicureans. The possibility of early allusions to the Trinity, as "Let us make man," *etc.*, having led to the idea of more than one God; and if so, in some sort, its veniality.

All the above might be applied with some force, and, if so, with no little value, to modern false semblances of religion, and non-religion; to Roman Catholicism, with its images, its services in an unknown tongue, its symbols, its adoption of heathen festivals, its actual placing of many Gods in the throne of One; to Mammonism, as practically a religion as if the golden calf of Babylon were standard at Cornhill; to Voluptatism—if I may fabricate a name for pleasure-hunters, following still, with Corybantic fury, the orgic revels of Osiris or Astarte: in brief, to all the shades of human heresy, on this side or on that of the golden mean, the worship of one true God, as revealed to us in His three mysterious characters.

But, query? Has not all this, and the very title, for any thing I know, been done already by another, by a wiser? and, if so, by whom?—Speak, some friend: it is the misfortune of mere thinkers (and this present amygdaloid mass, this breccia book, exemplifies it well) to stumble frequently upon fancies too good not to have been long ago appropriated by others like-minded. A read, or heard, hint may be the unerring clue, and we vainly imagine some old labyrinth to be our new discovery: education renders up the master-key, and we come to regard ancient treasuries as wealth of our own amassing, from which we deem it our right to filch as recklessly as he from the mint of Crœsus, who so filled his pockets—ay, his mouth—that we read he ἰβεβυστο. Who, in this age of literature, can be fully condemned, or heartily acquitted of plagiarism? An age—and none so little in advance or in arrear of it as I—of easy writing and discursive reading, of ideas unpatented, and books that have outlived copy-right. But this has detained us long enough: for the present, my brain is quit of its heathenish exculpations: let us pass on; many regiments are yet to be reviewed; their uniforms [*Hibernicè*] are various, but their flag is one.

A last serious subject—(they grow tedious)—is a fair field for ingenious explanation and Oriental poetry,

THE SIMILES OF SCRIPTURE:

(of course "similes" is an English word: the author of a recent '*Essay on Magna Charta*' has been *learned* enough to write it "similæ," for which original piece of Latinity let him be congratulated; I safely follow Johnson, who would have roared like a lion at "similia;" and, though Shakspeare does write it "similies," it may stoutly be contended that this is of mixed metal, and that Matthew Prior's "similes" is the purer sample: all the above being a praiseworthy parenthesis.)

The similes of Scripture, then, were to have been demonstrated apt and happy: for there is indeed both majesty, and loveliness, and propriety, and strict resemblance in them. "As a rolling thing before the whirlwind,"—"as when a standard-bearer fainteth"—"as the rushing of mighty waters,"—"as gleaning grapes when the vintage is done,"—"as a dream,"—"as the morning dew,"—"as"—but the whole book is a garden of similitudes; they are "like the sand upon the sea-shore for multitude." It is, however, too true, that often-times the baldness of translation deprives poetry, Eastern especially, of its fervour, its glow, its gush, and blush of beauty: to quote Aristotle's example, it too frequently converts the rosy-fingered Morn into the red-fisted; and so the poetry of dawning-day, with its dew-dropped flowers, its healthy refreshment, its "rosy-fingers" drawing aside the star-spangled curtain of night, falls at once into the low notion of a foggy morning, and is suggestive only of red-fisted Abigails struggling continuously with the deposits of a London atmosphere. In like manner, (for all this has not been an episode beside the purpose,) many a roughly rendered similitude of Scripture might be advantageously vindicated; local diversities and Orientalisms might be explained in such a treatise: for example, in the '*Canticles*,' the "beloved among the sons," is compared with an apple-tree among the trees of the wood:" now, amongst us, an apple-tree is stunted and unsightly, and always degenerates in a wood; whereas the Eastern apple-tree, probably one of the citron class, (to be more correct,) may be a magnificent monarch of the forest. "Camphire," to a Western mind, is not suggestive of the sweetest perfume, and perhaps the word may be amended into the marginal "cypress," or cedar, or some other: as "a bottle in the smoke," loses its propriety for an image, until shown to be a wine-skin. "Who is this that cometh out of the wilderness, like pillars of smoke?"—probably intending the swiftly-rushing columns of *sand* flying on the wings of the whirlwind. "Thine eyes are like the fish-pools in Heshbon," might well be softened into fountains—tearful, calm, resplendent, and rejoicing; and in showing the poetic fitness of comparing the bride to a landscape, it might clearly be set out how emblematic of Jewish millennial prosperity and of Christian universality, that bride was; while comparisons of a like un-European imagery might be taken from other Eastern poets, who will not scruple to compare that rare beauty, a straight Grecian nose, with a tower, and admire above all things the Cleopatra-coloured hair which they call purple, and we auburn. Very much might be done in this vein of literature, but it must be by a man at once an Oriental scholar and a natural poet: the idioms of ancient and modern times should be more considered, and something of apologetic explanation offered to an English ear for phrases such as "the mountains skipping like rams," "the horse swallowing the ground with fierceness," and represented as being afraid as a grasshopper." A thousand like instances could be displayed with little searching; let the above be taken as they are meant, for good, and as of zeal for showing the best of books to the best advantage: but it will appear that this essay trenches on the former one so slenderly hinted at, as '*The Wisdom of Revision*,' and therefore has been stated too much at length already. Let it then rest on the shelf till a better season. For this time, good reader, I, following up the object of self-relieving, thank you for your patience, and will turn to other themes of a more sublunary aspect.

ONE of the most natural and indigenous productions of a true author's mind, is, by common consent, an epic poem: verily, a wearisome, unnecessary, unfashionable bit of writing. Nevertheless, let my candour humbly acknowledge that, for the larger canticle of two mortal days, I was brooding over, and diligently brewing up, a right happy, capital, and noble-minded thesis, no other than

HOME.

ALAS, for the epidemy to which, few can doubt, ideas are subject! Alas, for the conflict of prolific geniuses, wherewith the world's quiet is disturbed! not impossibly, this very book now in progress of inditing will come to be classed as a "Patch-work," an "Olla Podrida," a "Book without a name," or some other such like *rechauffée* publication; whereas I protest its idea to be exclusively mine own, and conceived long before its seeming congeners saw the light in definite advertisements—at least to my beholding. And similarly went it with my poor epic: scarcely had a general plan suggested itself to my musings, and divers particular morsels thereof assumed "their unpremeditative lay;" scarcely had I jotted down a staid synopsis, and a goodly array of metrical specimens; when some intrusive newspaper displayed to me in black and white a good-natured notice of somebody else's '*Home, an Epic.*' So, as in the case of '*Nero,*' and haply of other subjects, had it come to pass, that my high-mettled racer had made another false start; that my just-discovered island, so gladly to have been self-appropriated, was found to have, sticking on one corner of it, the flag of another king; that the havoc of my brain, subsiding calmly into the pendulum regularities of metre, was much ado about nothing; and all those pretty fancies were the catalogued property of another. Such a subject, too! intrinsically worthy of a niche in the temple of Fame, besides Hope, Memory, and Imagination, *if* only one could manage it well enough to be named in the same breath with Campbell, Rogers, and Akenside. Well, it was a mental mortification; for I am full of moral land-marks, and would not (poetically speaking) for the world move rooted termini into other people's grounds. Whether the field has been well or ill pre-occupied I wot not, having neither seen the poem nor heard its maker's name: therefore shall my charity hope well of it, and mourn over the unmerited oblivion which generally greets modern poetry—yea, upon its very natal-day. Nevertheless, as an upright man will never wish barefacedly to steal from others, so does he determine at all times to claim independently his own: to be robbed, and not resent it (I speak foolishly), is the next mean thing after pilfering itself; and rash will be thy daring, O literary larcener! (can such things be?) if thou art found unpermissively appropriating even such sorry spoil as these poor seedlings of still possible volumes.

Prose and verse are allowed to have some disguising differences, at least in termination; and as we must not—so hints the public taste—spoil honest prose, bad as it may be, with too much intermixture of worse verse, it will be prudent in me to be sparing of my specimens. Yet, who will endure so *staccato* a page of jerking sentences as a confirmed synopsis?—"Well, any thing rather than poetry," says the world; so, for better or worse, I will jot down prosaically a few of my all but impromptu imaginings on Home.

After some general propositions, it would be proper to indulge the orthodoxy of invocation; not to Muses, however, but to the subject itself; for now-a-days, in lieu of definite deities, our worship has regard to theories, doctrines, and other abstract idolisms: and thereafter should follow at length an historical retrospect of domestic life, from the savage to the transition states of hunters and warriors; Nimrods and New Zealanders; Actæons and Avanese, Attilas, Roderics, and all the Ercles' vein or that of mad Cambyses, Hindoos and Fuegians, Greece, Egypt, Etruria, and Troy, in those old days when funds and taxes were not invented, but people had to fight for their dinner, and be their own police: so in a due course of circumconsideration to more modern conditions, from ourselves as central civilization, to Cochin China, and extreme Mexico, to Archangel and Polynesia.

Divers national peculiarities of the *physique* of homes; as, Tartars' tents, Esquimaux snow-pits, Caffre kraals, Steppe huts, South-sea palm-thatch, tree-villages, caves, log-cabins, and so forth. Then, a wide view of the homes of higher society, first Continental, afterwards British; through all the different phases of comfort to be found in heath-hovels, cottages, ornées, villas, parsonage-houses, squirealities, seats, town mansions, and royal palaces. Thus, with a contrastive peep or two about the feverish neighbourhood of a factory, up this musty alley, and down that winding lane, we should have considered briefly all the external accidents of home. The miserable condition of the homeless, whether rich or poor; an oak with its tap-root broken, a house on wheels, a boat without a compass, and all that sort of thing: together with due declamation about soldiers spending twenty years in India, shipwrecked Robinson Crusoes far from native Hull, cadets going out hopelessly for ever, emigrants, convicts, missionaries, and all other absentees, voluntary or involuntary. Tirades upon abject poverty, wanton affluence, poor laws, mendicancy, and Ireland; not omitting some thrilling cases of barbaric destitution.

Now come we lawfully to descant upon matters more mental and sentimental—the *metaphysique* of the subject—the pleasures and pains of Home. As thus, most cursorily: the nursery, with its dear innocent joys; the school-boy, holiday feelings and scholastic cruelties; the desk-abhorring clerk; the over-worked milliner; the starving family of factory children, and of agricultural labourers, and of workers in coal mines and iron furnaces, with earnest exhortations to the rich to pour their horns of plenty on the poor. England, once a safer and a happier land, under the law of charity: now fast verging into a despotic centralized system, kept together by bayonets and constables' staves. Home a refuge for all; for queens and princes from their cumbrous state, as well as for clowns from their hedging and ditching. The home of love, and its thousand blessings, founded on mutual confidence, religion, openheartedness, communion of interest, absence of selfishness, and so on: the honoured father, due subordination, and results; the loving wife, obedient children, and cheerful servants. Absolute, though most kind, monarchy the best government for a home; with digressions about Austria and China, and such laudable paternal rule; and *contra*, bitter castigation of republican misrule, its evils and their results, for which see Old Athens and New York, and certain spots half-way between them.

The pains of home: most various indeed, caused by all sorts of opposite harms—too much constraint or too little, open bad example or impossible good example, omissions and commissions, duty relaxed by indulgence, and duty tightened into tyranny; but mainly and generally attributable to the non-assertion or other abuse of parental authority. The spoiled child, and his progress of indulgence, unchecked passions, dissipation, crime, and ruin. Interested interlopers, as former friends, relatives, flatterers, and busy parasites, undermining that bond of confidence without which home falls to pieces; the gloomy spirit of reserve, discouraging every thing like generous open-heartedness; menial influences lowering their subject to their own base level; discords, religious, political, and social; the harmful consequence of over-expenditure to ape the hobbies or grandeur of the wealthier; foolish education beyond one's sphere, as the baker's daughter taking lessons in Italian, and opera-stricken butcher's-boys strumming the guitar; immoral tendencies, gambling, drinking, and other dissipations; and the aggregate of discomforts, of every sort and kind; with cures for all these evils; and to end finally by a grand climax of supplication, invocation, imprecation, resignation, and beatification, in the regular crash of a stout-expiring overture.

It's all very well, objects reader, and very easy to consider this done; but the difficulty is—not so much to do it, answers writer, as to escape the bother of prolixity by proving how much has been done, and how speedily all might be even completed, had poor poesy in these ticketing times only a fair field and no disfavour; for there is at hand good grist, ready ground, baked and caked, and waiting for its eaters. But in this age of prose-devouring and verse-despising, hardy indeed should I be, if I adventured to bore the poor, much-abused, uncomplaining public with hundreds of lines out of a dormant epic; the very phrase is a lullaby; it's as catching as a yawn; well will it be for me if my thread-bare domino conceals me, for whose better fame could brook the scandal of having fathered or fostered so slumbering an embryo?—Let then a few shreds and patches suffice—a brick or two for the house: and verily I know they will, be they never so scanty; for what man of education does not now entertain a just abhorrence of the Muses, the nine antiquated maiden aunts destined for ever to be pensioned on that money-making nice young man, Mammon's great heir-at-law, Prose Prose, Esq.?

With humblest fear, then, and infinite apology, behold, in all sober seriousness, what the labour of such a file as I am might betimes work into a respectable commencement; I don't pretend it *is* one; but *valeat quantum*, take it as it stands, unweeded, unpruned, uncared-for, unaltered.

Home, happy word, dear England's ancient boast,
Thou strongest castle on her sea-girt coast,
Thou full fair name for comfort, love, and rest,
Haven of refuge found and peace possest,
Oasis in the desert, star of light
Spangling the dreary dark of this world's night,
All-hallowed spot of angel-trodden ground
Where Jacob's ladder plants its lowest round,
Imperial realm amid the slavish world,
Where Freedom's banner ever floats unfurl'd,
Fair island of the blest, earth's richest wealth,
Her plague-struck body's little all of health,
Home, gentle name, I woo thee to my song,
To thee my praise, to thee my prayers belong:
Inspire me with thy beauty, bid me teem
With gracious musings worthy of my theme:
Spirit of Love, the soul of Home thou art,
Fan with divinest thoughts my kindling heart;
Spirit of Power, in pray'rs thine aid I ask,
Uphold me, bless me to my holy task;
Spirit of Truth, guide thou my wayward wing;
Love, Power, and Truth, be with me while I sing.

V'la: my consolation is that somewhere may be read, in hot-pressed print, too, many worse poeticals than these, which, however, nine readers out of ten will have had the worldly wisdom to skip; and the tenth is soon satiated: yet a tithe is something, at least so think the modern Levites; so, then, on second thoughts, a victim who is so good a listener must not be let off quite so cheaply. However, to vary a little this melancholy musing, and to gild the compulsory pill, Reserve shall be served up sonnet-wise. (P. S. I love the sonnet, maligned as it is both by ill-attempting friend and semi-sneering foe: of course, in our epic, Reserve ambles not about in this uncertain rhyme, but duly stalks abroad in the uniform dress; iambically still, though extricated from those involutions, time out of mind the requisite of sonnets.) Stand forth to be chastised, unpopular

RESERVE.

THOU chilling, freezing fiend, Love's mortal bane,
  Lethargic poison of the moral sense,
Killing those high-soul'd children of the brain,
  Warm Enterprise and noble Confidence,
  Fly from the threshold, traitor—get thee hence!
Without thee, we are open, cheerful, kind;
Mistrusting none but self, injurious self,
  Of and to others wishing only good;
With thee, suspicions crowd the gloomy mind,
  Suggesting all the world a viperous brood
That acts a base bad part in hope of pelf:
  Virtue stands shamed, Truth mute misunderstood,
Honour unhonoured, Courage lacking nerve,
Beneath thy dull domestic curse, Reserve.

Without professing much tendency to the uxorious, all may blamelessly confess that they see exceeding beauty in a good wife; and we need never apologize for the unexpected company of ladies: at off-hand then let this one sit for her portrait. Enduring listener, will the following serve our purpose in striving worthily to apostrophize

THE WIFE.

BEHOLD, how fair of eye, and mild of mien,
Walks forth of marriage yonder gentle queen:
What chaste sobriety whene'er she speaks,
What glad content sits smiling on her cheeks,
What plans of goodness in that bosom glow,
What prudent care is throned upon her brow,
What tender truth in all she does or says,
What pleasantness and peace in all her ways!

For ever blooming on that cheerful face
Home's best affections grow divine in grace;
Her eyes are ray'd with love, serene and bright;
Charity wreathes her lips with smiles of light;
Her kindly voice hath music in its notes;
And heav'n's own atmosphere around her floats!

Thus, wife-like, for better or worse, is the above *portrait charmant* consigned to the dingy digits of an undistinguishing printer's-devil; so doth Cæsar's dust come to stop a bung-hole. One morsel more, about children, blessed children, and for this bout I shall have tilted sufficiently in the Muses' court; or, if it must be so said, unhandsome critic, stilted to satiety in false heroics: stay—not false; judge me, my heart. Suppose then an imaginary parent thus to speak about his

INFANT DAUGHTERS.

Oh ye, my beauteous nest of snow-white doves,
What wealth could price for me your guileless loves?
My earthly cherubim, my precious pearls,
My pretty flock of loving little girls,
My stores of happiness with least alloy,
My treasuries of hope and trembling joy!
Yon toothless darling, nestled soft and warm
On a young yearning mother's cradling arm;
The soft angelic smiles of natural grace
Tinting with love that other little face;
And the sweet budding of this sinless mind
In winning ways, that round my heart-strings wind,
Dear winning ways—dear nameless winning ways,
That send me joyous to my God in praise.

Enough! not heartlessly, but to shame the heartlessness of YOUR *ennui*, let me veil those holiest affections; yes, even at the risk of leaving nominatives widowed of their faithful verbs, will I, until required, epicise no more. Let these mauled bits be intimations of what a little care might have made a little better. Gladly will I keep all the remainder in a state quiescent, even to doubling Horace's wholesome prescription of nine years: for it is impossible but that your fervent poet, in the heat of inspiration, (credit me, lack-wits, there is such a thing,) should blurt out many an unpalatable bit of advice, rebuke, or virtuous indignation against homes in general, for the which sundry conscience-stricken particulars might uncharitably arraign him. But divers other notions are crowding into the retina of my mind's-eye: I must leave my epic as you see it, and bid farewell, a long farewell, to '*Home.*' Still shall my egotism have to appear for many weary pages a most impartial and universal friend to the world of bibliopolists; I cater multifariously for all varieties of the literary profession: booksellers at least must own me as their friend, though the lucky purse of Fortunatus saves me from being impaled upon the point of poor Goldsmith's epigram, and I leave to [——] the questionable praise of being their hack. For Bentley and Hatchard, alike with Rivington and Frazer, for Colburn and Nisbet, as well as Knight, Tilt, Tyas, Moxon, and Murray, I seem to be gratuitously pouring out in equal measure my versatile meditations; at this sign all customers may be suited; only, shop-lifters will be visited with the utmost rigour of that obnoxious monosyllable.—Well, poor Epic, good night to you, and my benison on those who love you.

To any one, much in the habit of thoughtful revery, how very unsatisfactory those notions look in writing. He can't half unravel the chaotic cobwebs of his mind; as he plods along penning it, a thousand fancies flit about him too intangibly for fixed words, and his ever-teeming hot imagination cannot away with the slow process of concreted composition. For me, I must write impromptu, or not at all; none of your conventional impromptus, toils of half-a-day, as little instantaneous as sundry patent lights; no working-up of laborious epigrams, sedulously sharpened antitheses, or scintillative trifles, diligently filed and polished; but the positive impromptu of longing to be an adept at short-hand-writing, by way of catching as they fly those swift-winged thoughts; not quick enough by half; most of those bright colours unfixed; most of those fair semi-notions unrecorded. To say nothing of reasons of time, there being other things to do, and reasons of space, there being other things to write. And thus, good friend, affectionately believe the best of these crude intimations of things intellectual, which the husbandry of good diligence, and the golden shower of Danæ's enamoured, and the smiles of the Sun of encouragement might heretofore have ripened into authorship; nay, more, perhaps may still: believe, generously, that if I could coil off quietly, like unwrapped cocoons, all these epics, tragics, theologics, pathetics, analytics, and didactics, they would show in fairer forms, and better-defined proportions: believe, also, truly, that I could, if I would, and that I would, if the game were worth its candle.

But, sooth to say, the over-gorged public may well regard that small-

tomed author with most favourable eye, who condenses himself within the narrowest limits; a *diable boiteux*, not the huge spirit of the Hartz; concentrated meat-lozenges, not *soup maigre ;* pocket-pistols of literature, not lumbering parks of its artillery. Verily, there is a mightier mass of typography than of readers; and the reading world, from very brevity of life, must rush, at a Bedouin pace, over the illimitable plains of newspaper publication, while the pyramids of dusty folio are left to stand in solitary proud neglect. The cursory railroad spirit is abroad: we abhor that old painful ploughing through axle-deep ruts: the friend who will skate with us, is welcomer than he who holds us freezing by the button; and the teacher, who suggestively bounds in his balloon on the tops of a chain of arguments, is more popular in lecturing than he of the old school, who must duteously and laboriously struggle up and down those airy promontories.

I love an avenue, though, like Lord Ashburton's magnificent mile of yew-trees, it may lead to nothing, and therefore have not expunged this unnecessary preface: rather, will I bluntly come upon a next subject, another work in my unseen circulating library,

THE SEVEN SAYINGS OF GRECIAN WISDOM,

ILLUSTRATED IN SEVEN TALES.

Cordially may this theme be commended to the more illuminating booksellers: well would it be greeted by the picture-loving public. It might come out from time to time as a periodical, in a classical wrapper: might be decorated with the sages' physiognomies, copied from antique gems, with the fancied passage in each one's life that provoked the saying, and with specific illustrations of the exemplifying story. There should be a brilliant preface, introducing the seven sages to each other and the reader, after the ensample of Plutarch. and exhausting all the antiquarianism, all the memoirism, and all the varia-lectionism of the subject. The different tales should be of different countries and ages of the world, to insure variety, and give an easier exit to *ennui*. As thus: Solon's "Know thyself" might be fitted to an Eastern favourite raised suddenly to power, or a poor and honest Glasgow weaver all upon a day served as heir to a Scotch barony, when he forthwith falls into fashionable vices. Chilo's "Note the end of life" might concern the merriment of the drunkard's career, and its end—delirium tremens. or spontaneous combustion: better, perhaps, as less vulgarian, the grandeur and assassination of some Milanese ducal tyrant. The "Watch your opportunity" of Pittacus could be shown in the fortunes of some Whittington of trade, some Washington of peace, or some Napoleon of war. Bias's uncharitable bias, believing the worst of the world, might seem to some a truism, to others a falsehood, according as their fellows have served them well or ill; but a brief history of some hypocrite's life, some misanthrope's experience, or some Arabian Stylobatist's resolve to be perched above this black earth on a column like a stork, might help to prove that "the majority are wicked." As for Periander's aphorism, that "to industry all things are possible," pyramid-building old Egypt, or the Druids of Stonehenge, or Scottish proverbial perseverance in Australian sheep rearing and Canadian timber clearing, will carry the point by acclamation. Cleobulus, praising "moderation in all things," would glorify a moral warning of universal application, as to pleasures, riches, and rank; or especially perhaps as preferring true temperance before its modern tee-total false pretences; or lauding some Richard Cromwell's choice of a quiet country life, before the turbulent honours of a proffered Protectorate; while Thales, with his all but old English proverb of "more haste, less speed," would apply admirably to Sultan Mahmoud's ruinous reforms; or to the actual injury gulled Britain has done to the condition of negroes in general by a vastly too precipitate abolition of the slave-trade: a vile evil, indeed, but a cancer of too long creeping to be cured in a day, a rottenness too deeply seated in the frame-work of the world to be extirpated by such caustic surgery as fire and sword; or to be quacked into health by patent gold-salve.

Seven such tales, shrewdly setting out their several aims, and illustrative of good moral maxims which wise heathens live by, would (I trow and trust) be somewhat better, more original—ay, and more entertaining, too—than the common run of magazine adventures. It may not here be fair to particularize further than in the way of avowing my unmitigated contempt for the exploits of highwaymen, swindlers, men about town, and ladies of the *pavé*. I protest against gilding crimes, and palliating follies. Serve the public tables with better food, good Pandarus. Those commentators on the Newgate calendar, those bringers-into-fashion of the mysteries of vice, must not be quite acquitted of the evils they have caused: brilliancy of dialogue, and graphic power of delineation, are only weapons in a madman's hand, if the moral be corrupting and profane. To cheerful, hearty, care-dispelling humour, to such merry faces as Pickwick and Co.—inimitable Pickwick—hail, all hail! but triumphs of burglary, and escapes of murderers, aroint ye!

Why then should I throw this cargo overboard?—Friend, my ship is too full; *if* I could only do one thing at a time, and could finish it within the limits of its originating fit, these things all might be less abortive. But I doubt if my glorification of Greek aphorisms ever reaches any higher apotheosis than the airy castles sketchily built above.

Similar in idea with these last tales, but essentially more sacred as to character, would be an illustrative elucidation of the seven last sayings of our Blessed Lord, when dying in the crucifixion. The Romish Church, in some of her imposing ceremonies, has caused the sayings to be exhibited on seven banners, which are occasionally carried before the holy cross: from this I probably derived the idea of detaching these sentences from the frame-work of their contexts, and regarding them in some sort as aphorisms. For a name, not to be tautologous, should be proposed a Græco-Anglicism,

THE HEPTALOGIA;

OUR SAVIOUR'S SEVEN LAST SAYINGS.

The addition of "hagia" might be rather too Attic for English ears; and I know not whether "the Sacred Heptalogia" would not also be too mystical. This series of tales is capable of like illustration with the last, except in the matter of portraits, unless indeed some eminent fathers of the church, or some authenticated enamels, gems, or coins, (if any,) displaying our Lord's likeness, served the purpose; and of course the character of the stories should not be much in dissonance with the sacredness of the text. The first might well enforce forgiveness of enemies, especially if their hatred springs from misapprehension. "Father, forgive them; for they know not what they do:" many a true story of religious persecution, as of Inquisitorial torture, exacted by sincere bigotry, and endured by equally sincere conviction, would illustrate the prayer, and the scene might be laid among Waldensian saints and the friars of Madrid. The second tale might enlarge upon a promised Paradise, the assurance of pardon, and the efficacy of repentance: the certainty of hope and life being co-extensive, so that it might still be said of the seeming worst, the brigand and the blasphemer, "To-day shalt thou be with me in Paradise;" a story to check presumption, while it encourages the humility of pentitent hope; the details of a prodigal's career and his return, say a falsely philosophizing German student, or the excesses of some not ungenerous outburst of youthful wantonness; haply, a fair and passionate Neapolitan. The third might well regard filial piety: "Behold thy son—behold thy mother:" illustrated perhaps by a slave scene in Morocco, or the last adieus between a Maccabæan mother, and her noble children rushing on duteous death; or the dangers of a son, during the Reign of Terror, protecting his proscribed parents; or allusive to the case of many razed and fired homes in the Irish rebellion. The fourth, necessarily a tale of overwhelming calamity ultimately triumphant, "My God, my God, why hast thou forsaken me?"—the confidence of *my* God still, even in His recognised judgments trusted in as merciful: the history of many an unrecorded Job; a parent bereaved of his fair dear children; an aged merchant beggared by the roguery of others, and his very name blamelessly dishonoured; the extremity of a martyr's sufferings; or some hunted soul's temptation. The fifth, "I thirst;" which might be commented on, either morally only, as referring to a thirst after religion, virtue, and knowledge—or physically also, in some story of well-endured miseries at sea on a wrecking craft; or of Christian resignation even to the horrible death of drought among the torrid sands of Africa; or some noble act, like that of Sir Philip Sidney on the battle-field, or David's libation of that desired draught from the well of Bethlehem. I need not remark that all these sayings might primarily be applied to their Good Utterer, if it seemed more advisable to shape the publication into seven sermons: but this, it will at once be perceived, is not the present object; the word "sermons" has to most men a repulsive sound, and a tale, similar in disguised motive, may win, where an orderly discourse might unhappily repel: a teacher's best influences are the indirect: like the conquering troops at Culloden, his charge will be oblique; his weapon will strike the unguarded flank, and not the opposing target. The sixth, "It is finished;" perhaps, not only as a fact on the true, the necessary value of the Christian scheme of redemption being so completed; but, more generally, to display the evils and dangers of leaving mental, spiritual, or even worldly good designs unfinished: a tale of natural procrastination conquered, difficulties overcome, prejudices broken down, and gigantic good effected: a Russian Peter, a literary Johnson, a missionary Neff, a Wesley, or a Henry Martyn. The seventh, descanting upon noble patience, and agonies vanquished by faith, the death and glorious expectance of a martyr, the end of one of Fox's heroes;

"Father, into Thy hands I commend my spirit." Of necessity in these Christian tales there would be more of sameness than in those heathen; because it would be improper and impolitic, with such theses, to enter much into the lower human passions and the common events of life. But my intentions of further proceeding in this matter have, as at present, very sensibly subsided; for many wise and many good might reasonably object to making those holy last dying words mere pegs to hang moral tales upon. The idea might please one little sect, and anger half the world; I care not to behold it accomplished, and question my own capabilities; only, as it has been an authorial project heretofore conceived by me, suffer it to boast this brief existence.

It is scandalously reported of some folks that they are not musical, a calumny that has been whispered of myself: and, though against my own convictions, (who will confess he "has not music in his soul?") I partly acquiesce; that is to say—for, of such a charge, self-defence claims to explain a little—although I *am* charmed with all manner of music, still for choice I prefer a German chorus to an Italian solo, and an English glee to a French jig. Accordingly the operatic world have every reason to despise my taste: especially if I add that Welsh songs, and Scotch and Irish national melodies—[where are our English gone?]—rejoice my heart beyond Mozart and Rossini. And now this next little notion is scarcely of substance sufficient to assume the garb of authorship: it is little more than a passing whim, but I choose for the very notion's sake to make it better known. Except in a very few instances—as Hadyn's '*Seasons*,' e. g.—Oratorios, from some conventional idea of Lent, we may suppose, seem obligated to concern matters sacred. Of course, every body is aware of the prayerful meaning of the name; but we know also that a madrigal has long ago put off its monkish robe of a hymn to the Virgin, and worn the more laic habit of a love song. Now, it is a fact, that very many good men who delight in Handel's melody, and of course cannot object to psalms and anthems, entertain conscientious objections to hearing the Bible set to music in a concert-room; and sure may we all be, that, unless the whole thing be regarded as a religious service, (in a mixed gay company who think of sound more than sense, not very easy,) the warbling of sacred phrases, and variations on the summoning trumpet, and imitated angelic praise, and the unfelt expressions of musical repentance, and unfearing despondency of guilt in recitative, are any thing but congenial to a mind properly attuned. I hope I am neither prudish, nor squeamish, nor splenetic, but speak only what many feel, and few care to express. Now, the cure in future for all this would be very simple: Why not have some lay oratorios? Protestants have appropriated the madrigal, and listen, delighted with its melody, without the needless offence of seeming to countenance idolatry; why should they not have solemn music, new or ancient as may be adapted, administering to their patriotism, or their tragic interests, or historic recollections, without grating against their feelings of religious veneration?—To be specific, let me suggest a subject, and show, for the benefit of any Pindar of this day, its musical capabilities: we are, or ought to be as Englishmen, all stirred at the name of

ALFRED;

and he would minister as well to the harmonies of an oratorio as Abel, or Jephtha, Moses, or St. Paul—nay, as the Messiah, or the last dread Judgment. Remember, our Alfred was a proficient himself, and spied the Danish forces in the character of a harper. What scope were here for gentle airs, and stirring Saxon songs! He harangues his patriot band, and a manly Phillips would personify with admirable taste the truly royal bard: he leaves Athel-switha his wife, and a fair flock of children in sanctuary, while he rushes to the battle-field: the churchmen might receive their queenly charge with music: the Danes riot in their unguarded camp with drinking-snatches, and old-country-staves: a storm might occur, with elemental crash: the succeeding silence of nature, and distant coming on of the patriot troops at midnight; their war-songs and marches nearer and nearer; the invaders surprised in their camp and in their cups; the hurlyburly of the fight—a hail-stone chorus of arrows, a clash of thousand swords, trumpets, drums, and clattering horse-hoofs; a silent interval, to introduce a single combat between Alfred and Hubba the Dane, with Homeric challenges, tenor and bass; the routed foe, in clamorous and discordant staccato; the conquerors pressing on in steady overwhelming concord; how are the mighty fallen—and praise to the God of battles!

Most briefly, then, thus: there is religion enough to keep it solemn, without being so experimental as to intrude upon personal prejudice. The notion is too slight, and too slenderly worked out, even for admission here, if I were not still, my shrewd and mindful reader, sedulously endeavouring to get rid of all my brain-oppressing fancies: and this, happening to come uppermost as I write, finds itself caught, to my comfort. It is commended, if worth any thing, to the musical proficient: for I might as well think of adding a note to the gamut as of trying to compose an oratorio.

The authorial mind is infinitely versatile: books and book-making are indeed its special privilege, forte, and distinguishing peculiarity; but still its thoughts and regards are ever cast towards originality of idea, though unwritten and unprinted, in all the multitudinous departments of science and of art. Thus, mechanical invention, chemical discovery, music as above, painting as elsewhere, sculpture as below, give it exercise continually. The authorial mind never is at rest, but always to be seen mounted and careering on one hobby-horse or other out of its untiring stud. If the coin of some rude Parthian, or the fragments of some old Ephesian frieze, serve not as a scope for its present ingenuities, it will break out in a new method of grafting raspberries on a rose-bush, in the comfortable cut of a pilot-coat, or the safest machinery for a steamer. *Ne sutor ultra crepidam* is a rule of moderation it repudiates; incessant energy provokes unabated meddling, and its intuitive qualities of penetration, adaptation, and concentration, are only hindered by the accidents of life from carrying any one thing out to the point at least of respectable attainment. Look at Michael Angelo; poet, painter, sculptor, architect, and author: and if indeed we are not told of Milton having modeled, or Horace having built up other monuments than his own imperishable fame, still nothing but manual habit and the world's encouragement were wanting to perfect, in the concrete, the conceptions of those plastic minds. Who will deny that Hogarth was a novelist and play-wright, if not indeed a heart-rending tragedian? Who will refuse to those nameless monastic architects who planned and fashioned the fretted towers of Gloucester, the stern solidity of Durham, the fairy steeple of Strasburg, or the delicate pinnacles of Milan, the praise due to them of being genuine poets of the immortal Epic? Phidas and Praxiteles, Canova and Thorswaldsen, are in this view real authors, as undoubtedly as Homer or Dante, Sallust or Racine; and to rise highest in this argument, the heavens and the earth are but mighty scrolls of an Omniscient Author, fairly written in a universal tongue of grandeur and beauty, of skill, poetry, philosophy, and love.

But let me not seem to prove too much, and so leap over my horse instead of vaulting into the saddle: though authorship may claim thus extensively every master-mind, from the Adorable Former of all things down to the humblest potter at his wheel fashioning the difficult ellipse; still, in human parlance, must we limit it to common acceptations, and think of little more than scribe, in the name of author. Nevertheless, let such seeds of thought as here are carelessly flung out, nurtured in the good soil of charity, and not unkindly forced into foolish accusations of my own conceit, whereas their meaning is general, (as if forsooth selfishly dibbled in with vain particularity, and not liberally broadcast that he may run that reads,)—let such crude considerations excuse my own weak and uninjurious invasion of the provinces of other men. The wisdom for social purposes of infinitesimal division of labour, may be proved good by working well; but its lowering influences on the individual mind cannot be doubted: that an intelligent man should for a life-time be doomed to watch a valve, or twist pin-heads, or wind cotton, or lacquer coffin-nails, cannot be improving; and while I grant great evil in my desultory excesses, still I may make some use of that argument in the converse, and plead that it is good to exercise the mind on all things. Thus, in my assumed métier of authorship, let notions be extenuated that popularly concern it little, and yield admittance to any thought that may lead to that Athenian desideratum, "some new thing."

While the echoes of the name of Alfred still linger on the mind, and our patriotism looks back with gratitude on his thousand virtues unsullied by a fault, (at least that History, seldom so indulgent, has recorded,) —while we reflect that in him were combined the wise king, the victorious general, the enlightened scholar, the humble Christian, the learned author, the excellent father, the admirable MAN in all public and private relations, in domestic alike with social duties, I cannot help wishing that forgetful England had raised some architectural trophy, as a worthy testimonial of Alfred the noble and the good. Whether Oxford, his pet child—or Westminster Hall, as mindful of the code he gave us—or Greenwich, as the evening resting-place of those sons of thunder whom the genius of Alfred first raised up to man our wooden walls—should be the site of some great national memorial, might admit of question; but there can be none that something of the kind has been owing now near upon a thousand years, and that it will well become us to claim boastingly for England so true, so glorious a hero. With a view to expedite this object, and strictly to bear upon the topic in author-fashion, it has come into my thought how much we want a

LIFE OF ALFRED:

my little reading knows of none, beyond what dictionaries have gathered from popular history and vague tradition, rather than manuscripts of old time, and Asser, the original biographer. Of this last work, written originally in Saxon, and since translated into Latin, I submit that a popular English version is imperatively called for; a translation from a translation being never advisable, (compare Smollett's Anglo-Gallified dilution of '*Don Quixote*,') the primary source should be again consulted; and seeing that profound ignorance of the ancient Saxon coupled with, as now, total indifference about its acquisition, place me in the list of incapables, I leave the good suggestion to be used by pundits of the Camden or Roxburghe or other book-learned society. If it may have been already done by some neglected scribe, bring it to the light, and let us see the bright example set to all future ages by that early Crichton; if never yet accomplished, my zeal is over-paid should the hint be ever acted on; and if, which is still possible, an English version of the life of Alfred should be positively rife and common among the reading public, your humble ignoramus has nothing for it but to pray pardon of its author for not having known him, and to walk softly with the world for writing so much before he reads.

But this is an accessory—an episode; I plead for a statue to King Alfred: and—(now for another episode; is there *no* cure for these desperate parentheses?)—*apropos* of statues, let me, in the simple untaught light of nature, suggest a word or two with regard to some recent undertakings. Notwithstanding classical precedents, whereof more presently, it does seem ridiculous to common sense, to set a man like a scavenger-bird at Calcutta, or a stork at Athens, or a sonorous Muezzin, or a sun-dried Simeon Stylites, on the top of a column a hundred feet high: sculpture imitates life, and who would not shudder at such an unguarded elevation? sculpture imitates life, and who can recognise a countenance so much among the clouds? Again for the precedents: I presume that Pompey's pillar, (which, indeed, perhaps never had any thing on its summit except some Egyptian emblem, as the cap and throne of higher and lower Egypt, or a key of the Nile as likely as any thing,) is the most notable, if not the first, of solitary columns: now, Pompey, or, as some prefer, Diocletian, and others Alexander Severus, had that fine pillar ferried over from the quarries of Lycian Xanthus; at least, this is a good idea, seeing that near that place still lie three or four other columns of like gigantic dimensions, unfinished, and believed to have been intended to support the triglyph of some new temple. Pompey's idea was to fix the pillar up as a sea-mark, for either entering the harbour of Alexandria, or to denote shallows, anchorage, or the like; but apart from this actual utility, and apart also from its acknowledged ornament as a sentinel on that flat strand, I take it to be an architectural absurdity to erect a regular-made column with little or nothing to support: an obelisk now, or a naval trophy, or a tower decorated with shields, or a huge stele or cippus, or a globe, or a pyramid, or a Waltham-cross sort of edifice, (of course all these supporting nothing on their apices,) in fact, *any thing but* a Corinthian or Tuscan, or other regular pillar, seems to be permissable; but for base, shaft, and capital to have nothing to do but lift a telescopic man from earth's maternal surface, does look not a little unreasonable; and therefore as much out of taste, as for the marble arch at Buckingham Palace to spend its energies in supporting a flag-staff.

The magnificent column of Trajan is exempted from this hasty bit of criticism, (as also of course is its modern counterpart, Napoleon's,) because it is, both from decoration and proportions, out of the recognised orders of architecture; it partakes rather of the character of a triumphal tower, than of one among many pillars separated chiefly from the rest; the man is a superlative accessory, a climax to his positive exploits; he does not stand a-top, as if dropt from a balloon, but like a gallant climber treading on his conquests: and, as to Phocas's column at Rome, I shall only say, that it illustrates my meaning, except in so far as an immense base to the super-imposed statuere deems it from the jockey imputation of carrying too light a weight, Now, with respect to the Nelson memorial, your meddlesome scribe had an unexhibited notion of his own. Mehemet Ali is understood to have given certain two obelisks respectively to the French and English nations: the Parisians appropriated theirs, and have set it up, thorn-like, in their midst, perhaps as an emblem of what African conquest has been in the heartside of France; but we English, less imaginative, and therefore less antiquarian, have permitted our *petit cadeau* to lie among its ruins of Luxor or Karnac, unclaimed and unconsidered.

Nelson of the Nile might have had this consecrated to his honour: and if, as is probable, it be of insufficient elevation, I should have proposed a high flight of steps and a base, screened all round by shallow Egyptian entrances, with an Etruscan sarcophagus just within the principal one, (Egypt and Etruria were cousins germane,) and an alto-relievo of Nelson dying, but victorious, recumbent on the lid: the globe and wings, emblems alike of Nelson's rapidity, his universal fame, and his now-emaciated spirit, might be sculptured over each entrance; a sphinx, or a Prudhoe lion, being allusive to England as well as Egypt, should sit guardiant at each corner of the steps; and the three remaining doorways would be represented closed, and carved externally with some allegorical personations of Nelson's career, of the Nile, Copenhagen, and Trafalgar. This, then, had it been strictly in my métier, (a happy métier mine of literary leisure,) should have been my limnèd outline for the Nelson testimonial: the real interesting antique needle, rising from the midst of its solid Egyptian architecture, and pointing to the skies; not a steeple, however, but merely the obelisk raised upon a heavy base, only hollowed far enough to admit of an interior alto-relievo.

It is probable that the exhibition of designs, which an *alibi* prevented me from seeing, included several obelisks; but the peculiarities I should have insisted on, would have been first to make good use of the real thing, the rarely carved old Egypt's porphyry; and, next, to have had our hero's likeness within reasonable distance of the eye.

But to return from this other desperate digression: Alfred, the great and wise, deserves his Saxon cross; or let him lie enshrined in a grove of florid Gothic pinnacles, a fretted roof on clustered columns reverently keeping off the rain; or, best of all, let him stand majestic in his own-time costume, colossal bronze on a cube of granite, and so put to shame the elegancies of a Windsor uniform, and the absurdity of sticking heroes, as at St. George's, Bloomsbury, and elsewhere, on the summit of a steeple. So, friend, let all this tirade serve to introduce a most unlikely and chaotic treatise on

NATIONAL MEMORIALS.

Politics are a sore temptation to any writer, and of dalliance with a Delilah so seductive it is futile to declare that I am innocent. My principles positively are known to myself; which is a measure of self-knowledge, in these any-thing-arian days, of that cabinet coin-climax the "8th degree of rarity;" and that those choice principles may not be concealed from so kind an eye as yours, friend reader, hear me profess myself honestly—if you approve, or shamelessly—if you *will* so think it—"a rabid Tory!" At least, by such a nomenclature sundry veracious journals, daily leaders of the public opinion, would call me, were such a groundling as I prominent enough to attract their indignation; and, from all that can be gathered from their condemnatory clauses against others like minded, I have no little reason to be proud of the title. For, on collation of such clauses with their causes, I find, and therefore take (under correction always) the rabid Tory to be—a temperate lover of order, whom his mother has taught to "fear God," his father to "honour the king," and his pastor to "meddle not with them who are given to change." A rabid Tory, in matters of national expenditure, remembers to have heard an old unexploded proverb, "There is that scattereth, and yet increaseth, and there is that withholdeth what is due, but it tendeth to poverty;" and he is by no means sure that a certain mismanaged nation is not immolating her prosperity to what actuaries would call economical principles. A rabid Tory is bigoted enough to entertain a ridiculous fear of that generation abstraction, Catholic Rome, whom further he is sufficiently vulgar-minded to consider as a lady of easy virtue arrayed in the colours of a cardinal: he thinks one Luther to be somewhat more than a renegade monk; and is childish enough to venerate, when a man, the same Liturgy which his grandmother had taught him when a boy. For other matters, the higher born, the better bred, the more classically educated, and the more extensively possessed of moneys and lands our honest-spoken Tory may be, ten to one the more is he afflicted with this rabbies: and his mad propensities become positively criminal, when, as a magistrate or a captain of dragoons, he thinks himself bound in honourable duty to quell the enthusiasm of some disinterested patriots, whose innocent wishes rise no higher than to subvert the existing order of things, to secure for themselves a reasonable share of parks, palaces, and pocket-money, and (as the very justifiable means for so happy an end) manfully to sacrifice in the temple of Freedom the rogues who would object to being robbed, and the tyrants who would be bloody enough to fight for life and liberty.

A rabid Tory—you see it is a pet name of mine—feels no little contempt for a squeezable character; and he is well assured, from history as well as on his own conviction, that the noble army of martyrs lived and died upon his principles: whereas the retrograde regiment of cow-ards, whom the wisdom of providing for personal safety has in battle induced to run away, *relictis non bene parmulis*—the clamorous cohort of bullies, whom the necessities of impending castigation have sensibly induced to eat their words—the volunteer company of light-heeled swindlers, whom nature instructs that they must live, and honesty has neglected to inform how—every one, in short, whose grand maxim (*quocunque modo rem*) is temporizing expediency, and with whom the cogent argument "you shall" has more force than the silly conscience-whisper of "you ought,"—contributes to swell the band which the professor of Toryism, the abstracted follower of principles and not of men, has the honour of beholding in the angle of his diagram, inscribed "contradictory." Not that your true Tory believes so ill of *all* his adversaries; there are some few geese among the cranes; an Abdiel here and there, who has long felt irksome in the host, but for false shame is there still; sundry men, having ambitious or illuminated wives, and too amiable, or too prudent, to attempt a breach of peace at home; some thronging the opposite benches, because their fathers and grandfathers topographically occupied those same seats—a decent reason, supposing similarity of places and names, to insure similarity of principles and practice; and some—I dislike them not for honesty—confessing and upholding the republican extremes, upon a belief that all short of these are but an unsatisfactory part of a great and glorious experiment. Now, the rabid Tory prefers an open foe to a false friend; but your go-between, your midway sneak, your shuttlecock, your perjured miser who will swear to any thing for an extra per centage—all these are his detestation: and although he will readily acknowledge some good and some wise in the adversary's ranks, still he recognises that tri-coloured banner as the one under which all naturally fight, who are poor in both worlds—with neither money nor religion. Thus much of my reasonable rabies.

One may hate principles without hating men; and for this sentiment we have the Highest Example. Things are either right or wrong; if right, do; if wrong, forbear: nothing can be absolutely indifferent, and to do a little actual evil in order to compass great hypothetical good, is false morality, and therefore bad government. Why should not honesty and plain-dealing be as inviolable publicly as privately? Why be guilty of such mean self-stultification as to say one thing and do another? It is criminal in rulers to give a helping hand to the evil which they deem unavoidable; let them, in preference, cease to rule, and imitate the noble threat of that king for half a century whose conscience bade him abdicate rather than do wrong.

But to come abruptly on a title-page: often-times, in reading deleterious leading articles in wrong-sided newspapers, have I longed to set before the world of faction

A MANUAL OF GOOD POLITICS,

which indeed has already been half-done, if decently begun be synonymous. With this view has my author's mind heretofore thought over many scriptural texts, characters, doctrines, and usages; yet, let me freely confess the upshot of those efforts to be little satisfactory: for I fear much, that though there be grounds enough to go upon for one who is already fixed in right political principle, [orthodoxy being, as is common among arguers, *my* doxy,] there may not be sufficient so to reason from as to convince the thousands, ready and willing to gainsay them: and Locke's utter annihilation of poor ridiculous well-intentioned Filmer, makes one wary, of taking up and defending a position so little tenable, as, for instance, Adam's primary grant for the foundation of absolute monarchy, or of attempting to nullify natural freedom by the dubious succession of patriarchal power. At the same time, (competency for so great a task being conceded—no small supposition, by the way,) much remains to be done in this field of discourse; as, the fearful example made of Korah, Dathan, and Abiram, for conduct very analogous with numberless instances of modern Liberalism; the rights of rulers, as well as of the governed; of kings, as well as people; the connexion subsisting now, as through all former ages, between church and state—well indeed and deeply argued out already by such great minds as Coleridge and Gladstone, but perhaps, for general usefulness, requiring a more brief and popular discourse; the question of passive obedience; the true though unfashionable doctrine of man's general depravity invalidating the consignment of power to the masses; and so forth. There are, however, if Scripture is to be held a constitutional guide, some examples to a certain extent contrary to the argument: as, elective monarchy in the case of Saul; non-legitimate succession in families even where election is omitted, as in the case of Solomon; and, honestly to say it, many other difficulties of a like nature. In fact, upon the whole, this distinction might be drawn; that although the Bible at large favours what we may, for shortness' sake, term Conservative politics, still it would not be easy to deduce from its page as code of rules, so necessarily of a social, temporary, and accidental nature: The principle is given, but little of the practice; the seed of true and undefiled religion produces among other good fruit what we will call Conservatism, but we must be very microscopic to detect that fruit in the seed: of this admission let my *Liberal* adversary make—as indeed he will—the most; but let him remember that truth has always been most economically distributed. It is a material too costly to be broadcast before swine; and in slender evidence lurks more of moral test, than in stout arguments and open miracles. At any rate, as unfitted for the task, I leave it. For any thing mine un-book-learned ignorance can tell, the very title may be as old as Christianity itself; it is a good name, and a fair field.

This manual was commenced in the form of familiar letters to a radical acquaintance, whom I had resolved to convert triumphantly; but John Locke disarmed me, without, however, having gained a convert: he made me drop my weapon as Prospero with Ferdinand; but the fault lay with Ferdinand, for want of equal power in the magic art.

"Measures, not men" is, as we have hinted already, the groundwork of a true Tory's political creed; and measures themselves only in so far as they expound and are consistent with principles. A man may fail; the stoutest partisan become a renegado; and the pet measure of a doughtiest champion may after all prove traitorous, unwise, unworthy: but principle is eternally an unerring guide, a master to whose words it is safe to swear, a leader whose flag is never lowered in compromise, nor sullied by defeat. Defalcations of the generally upright, derelictions of duty by the usually noble-minded, shake not that man's faith which is founded on principle: for the cowardice, or rashness, or dishonesty of some individual captain, he may feel shame, but never for the *cause* in which such hold commissions; he may often find much fault with *soi-disant* Tories, but never with the 'ism they profess. We overstep their follies; we disclaim their corruptions; we date above their faults; we wash our hands of their abuses. An abstracted student in his chamber, building up his faith from the foundations, and trying every stone of the edifice, takes little heed of who is for him, and who against him, so Conscience is the architect, and the Master of the house looks on approving. A man's mind is but one whole; be it palace or hovel, feudal stronghold or Italian villa, it is all of a piece: a duly subordinated spirit bears no superstructure of the Radical, and the friable soil of discontented Liberalism, is too sandy a foundation for ponderous fanes of the religious.

I rejoice in being accounted one of those unheroic, and therefore more useful, members of society, who profess to be by no means ambitious of reigning. A plain country gentleman, with a mind (thank Heaven!) well at ease, and things generally, both external and internal, being in his case consentaneous with happiness, would appear to have reached the acme of human felicity; and no one but a fool cares, in any world, to exemplify the dog's preference for the shadow. Unenvious, therefore, of royalty, and fully crediting that *never-quoted* sentiment of Shakspeare's "Uneasy," &c., my motto, within the legitimate limits of right reason, and in common with that of some ridiculed philosopher of Roundhead times, is the prudent saying, "Whoever's king, I'll be subject!"—ay, and for the masculine I place the epicene. While, however, in sober practice of right subordination, and under existing circumstances of just rule, we gladly would amplify the maxim, (as in courtesy, gallantry, loyalty, and honest kind feeling strongly bound,) still in mere speculation, and irrespectively of things as they are, our abstract musings tended to approve the original word in its unextended gender. Every one of Edmund Burke's school would honour the ensign of Divine vice-regency wherever he found it; but, apart from this uninquisitive respect, he will claim to be reasonably patriotic, patriotically rational; habit encourages to practice one thing, but theory may induce to think another. Now, little credence as so unenlightened so illiberal an integer as I give to an equalization in the rights of man, certainly on many accounts my blindness gives less to the rights of women with man, and very far less to those rights over man: it might be inconvenient to be specific as to reason; but the working of an ultra-republican scheme, in which females should ballot as well as males, would briefly illustrate my meaning. Barbarism makes gentle woman our slave; right civilization raises her into a loving helpmate; but what kind of wisdom exalts her into mastery?

Readily, however, shall sleep in dull suppression sundry comments on a certain Rhenish law, whereof my author's mind had at one time studiously cogitated a grave and wholesome homily. For our censor of the press, one strait-laced Mr. Better Judgment, has, "with his abhorred shears," clipped off the more eloquent and spirited portion of a trenchant argument concerning—the revealed doctrine of a superior sex, the social evils of female domination, church-headships considered as to type and antitype, improper influences, necessary hindrances, anomalous example, feminine infirmities, and an infinitude more such various objections springing out of this fertile subject. Thereafter might have come the historical view, evils and perils, for the majority of instances, following in the wake of such mastery. However, to leave these questionable matters quiescent, the principles of passive obedience mildly interpose, forbidding to stir the waters of commotion, although with healing objects, for the sake of an abstract theory; there is ill-meant change enough afloat, without any call for well-intentioned meddlers to launch more. So, judicious after-thought resolves rather to strengthen too-much-weakened authority, in these ungovernable times, than attempt to prove its weaknesses inherent; to look obstinately at the golden side only of the double-wielded shield: instead of picking away at a soft stone in constitutional foundations, our feeble wish magnanimously prefers to prop it and plaster it, flinging away that injurious pick-axe. The title of this once-considered lucubration is far too suggestive to carping minds of more than the much that it means, to be without objection: nevertheless, I did begin, and therefore, always under shelter of a domino, and protesting against any who would move my mask, I confess to

WOMAN, A SUBJECT:

it was a mere speculative argument; a flock of fancies now roaming unregarded in some cloudy limbo. Let them fly into oblivion—"black, white, and gray, with all their trumpery."

Notwithstanding these present hostile argumentations, politics are to me what they doubtless are to many others, subjects and disquisitions little short of hateful; perpetual mulligatawney; curried capsicums; a very heating, unsatisfactory, unwholesome sort of food. How many pleasant dinner-parties have been abruptly broken up by the introduction of this dish! How many white waistcoats unblanched by projectile wine-glasses on account of this impetuous theme! How many little-civil wars produced from the pips of this apple of contention! Yes, I hate it; and for this cause, good readers, (who may chance to have been used scurvily, some six pages back, in respect of your opinions, honest as my own, though fixed in full hostility—and so, courteously be entreated for your pardons,) for this cause of hate, I beseech you to regard me as sacrificing my present inclination to my future quiet. We have heard of women marrying men they may detest, in order to get rid of them: even with such an object is here indited the last I ever intend to say about politics. The shadows of notions fixed upon this page will cease to haunt my brain; and let no one doubt but that after relief from these pent-up humours, I shall walk forth less intolerant, less unamiable, less indignant than as heretofore. But, meanwhile, suffer with all brevity that I say out this small say, and deliver my patriotic conscience; for many a head-ache has obfuscated your author's mind in consequence of other abortive bits of political common-place. Every successive measure of small triumphant Whiggery, every piece of what my view of the case would designate non-government or mis-government, has pinched, vexed, bruised, and stung my fervent country's love day by day, session after session. Like thousands of others, I have been a greyhound in the leash, a bolt in the bow, longing to take my turn on the arena: eager as any Shrovetide 'prentice for a fling at negligence, peculation and injustice, and other the long black catalogue of British injuries. Socialism, Chartism, Ribandism; Spain, Canada, China; freed criminals, and imprisoned poverty; penny wisdom, and pound folly; the universal centralizing system, corrupting all generous individualities: patriotism ridiculed, and questionable loyalty patted on the back; vice in full patronage, and virtue out of countenance; Protestantism discouraged, Popery taken by the hand; Dissent of *any* kind preferred to sober Orthodoxy; and, fitting climax, all this done under pretences of perfect wisdom, and most exquisite devotion to the crown and the constitution:—these things have made me too often sympathize in Colonel Crockett's humour, tiger-like, with a dash of the alligator. Accordingly let me not deny having once attempted a bitter diatribe, in petto, surnamed

FALSE STEPS;

BRITAIN'S HIGHROAD TO RUIN;

a production of the pamphlet class, and, like its confraternity, destined at longest to the life ephemeral. But, to say truth, I found all that sort of thing done so much better, spicier, cleverer, in numberless newspaper articles, than my lack of the particular knowledge requisite, and my little practice in controversy, could have managed, that I wisely drew in my horns, sheathed my toasting-iron, and decided upon not proceeding political pamphelteer, till, on awaking some fine morning, I find myself returned to parliament for an immaculate constituency.

Patient reader, of whatever creed, do not hate me for my politics, nor despise the foolish candour of confession. Henceforth, I will not trouble you, but abjure the subject; except, indeed, my sturdy friend "the Squire," soon to be introduced to you, insists upon his after-dinner topic: but we will cut him short; for, in fact, nothing can be more provoking, tedious, useless, and causative of ill-blood, than this perpetual intermeddling of private ignoramuses, like him and me, with matters they do not understand, nor can possibly ameliorate.

A POET is born a poet, as all the world is well aware; and your thorough-paced lawyer is not less born a lawyer; while the junction of these two most militant incompatibles clearly bears out the hackneyed quotation as above, with the final misfit, that is, "*non fit.*" Your poetaster at the bar is that grotesque ideal, which Flaccus thought so funny that his friends *must* laugh; (although really, Romans, it *is* possible to contemplate a sort of sphinx figure, "a human head to a horse's neck," and so on, varied plumes and all, without much chance of a guffaw;) and yonder sickly-looking clerk, perched upon his high stool, penning "stanzas while he should engross," is the lugubrious caricature of Apollo on his Pegassus, with Helicon for inkstand.

It may be nothing extraordinary that, jostled in so wide a theatre as ours of the world, chance-comers should not, at once or at all, comfortably find their proper places; but that wise-looking chaperons, having with prospective caution duly taken a box, should by malice prepense thrust all the big people in front, and all the little folks behind, is rather hard upon the latter, and not a little foolish in itself. Even so in life: who does not wish a thousand times he could help some people to change places? Look at this long fellow, fit for Frederick of Prussia's regiment of giants: his parents and guardians have bent him double, broken his spirit, and spoiled his paces, by cramming him, a giraffe in the stable, between that frigate's gun-decks as a middy: while yonder martial little bantam, by dint of exaggerated heels, and exalted bear-skin, peeps about among his grenadiers, much as Brutus and Cassius did with their collossal

Cæsar. So also of minds: look at brilliant Burns, the exciseman; and quaintly versatile Lamb, the common city clerk: Look at—had you only patience, you should have examples by the gross; but, to make a shorter tale of it, (I presume this shows the etymology of cur-tail,) just think over the pack of your acquaintance, and see if you could not shuffle those kings, queens—yes, and knaves too—more to your satisfaction, and their own advantage: at least, so most folks imagine, silly meddlers as they are; for, after all, what with human versatility, and the fact of a probationary state, and the influence of habit, and the drudging example set by others, things work so kindly as they are, that, notwithstanding misfits, the wiser few must be of Pope's mind, "whatever is, is right;"—ay, that it is.

A year or two ago—if your author is little better than one of the foolish now, what in charity must he have been then?—I took it upon me to indite an innocent, stingless satire, whereof for samples take the following. Skip them one and all; you will, if you are wise, for they bear the ban of rhyme, are peevish, dull, ill-reasoned; but if you are not wise, (and, strange to say, malicious people tell me there are many such,) you may wish to see in print a metred inconclusive grumble. Take it, then, if you will, as I do, merely for a change; at any rate, your manciple has furnished this buttery of yours with ample choice of viands; and omnivoracious as man may be—gormandizing, with gusto, fat moths in Australia, cockchafers at Florence, frogs in France, and snails in Switzerland, equally as all less objectionable meats, drinks, fruits, roots, composites, and simples—still, in reason, no one can be expected or expect himself to like every thing: have charity, for what suits not one man's taste may please the palate of another; so hear me complacently turn

"KING'S EVIDENCE,"

and give heed to certain confessions, extorted under the *peine forte et dure* of a whilom state legal. Yet, when I come to consider of this, (*mihi cogitanti*, as school themes invariably commenced,) it strikes my memory that all confessions, short of the last dying one, are weak and foolish impertinences; whether Jean Jacques or Mr. Adams thought so, or caused others to think so, are separate topics beside the question: for myself, I will spare you a satire dotted with as many I's as an Argus pheasant; and, without exacting upon good-nature by troublesome contributions, will hazard a few couplets concerning Blackstone's cast-off mistress, the

Law. One word more though: undoubting of thine amiability, friend that hast walked with me hitherto in peace, I will be tame as a purring cat, and sheathe my talons; therefore are you still unteased by divers sly speeches and sarcastic hints, of and concerning innumerable black sheep that crowd about a woolsack; especially of certain "highly respectables," whom the omnipotence of parliament (no less power presumably being competent) commands to be accounted "gentlemen." Should then my meagre sketches seem but little spiteful, accord me credit for tolerance at the expense of wit, (yea, in mine own garbled satire, hear it Juvenal!) and view them kindly in the same light as you would sundry emasculated extracts from a discreet Family Shakspeare. Indignation ever speaks in short sharp queries; and it is well for the printer's pocket that the self-experience hereof was considered inadmissible, for a new fount of notes of interrogation must have been procured: as it is, we are sailing quietly on the Didactic Ocean, and have, I fear, been engaged some time upon topics actionable on a charge of *scandalum magnatum.* Hereof then just a little sample: let us call it '*A Judgment in the Rolls Court;*' or in any other; I care not.

PRECEDENT's slave, this mountebank decides
As great Authority, not Reason, guides.
" 'Tis not for him, degenerate wight, to say
Faults can be mended at this time of day,
For Coke himself declared—no matter what—
Can Justice suffer what Lord Coke would not?
And if 1 Siderfin, p. 10, you scan,
Lord Hoax has fixed the rule, that learned man:
I cannot, dare not, if I would, be just,
My hands are tied, and follow Hoax I must;
That *very* learned Lord could not be wrong.
Besides, in fact, it has been settled long,
For the great case of Hitchcock versus Bundy
Decided—(Cro. Eliz. per Justice Grundy),
That [black was white];—and so, what can I say?
Landmarks are things must not be moved away:
I cannot put the clock of Wisdom back,
And solemnly pronounce that black *is* black.
Though plaintiff has the right, I grant it clear,
I must be ruled by Hoax and Hitchcock here:
Equity follows, does not mend the laws:
Therefore declare, defendant gains the cause."

Then, as virtuously bound, Indignation interrogates sundry ejeculations; or, if you like it better, ejaculates sundry interrogations: as thus, take a brace:

If right and reason both combine in one,
Why, in God's name, should justice not be done?
If law be not a lie, and judgments jokes,
Why not *be just*, and cut adrift Lord Hoax?

After a vast deal more in this vein of literature—for you perceive my present purpose is dissection in part of this ancient rhyme—we arrive at a magnanimous—

No! Right shall have his own, put off no longer
By rule of Former, or by whim of Stronger;
Nor, because Jack goes tumbling down the hill,
Shall precedent create a tumbling Jill.
Public opinion soon shall change the scene,
And wash the Law's Augæan stable clean;
Sweep out the Temple, drive the sellers thence,
And lead, in novel triumph, Common Sense.

Verily, this is of the dullest, but it is brief: endure it, and pray you consider the deadliness of the topic, and the barbarous cruelty wherewith courtesy has clipped the wings of my poor spite. Let us turn to other title-pages; assuring all the world that no specific mountebank has been here intended, and that nothing more is meant than a nerveless blow against legal cant, quainter than Quarles's, and against that well-known species of Equity, which must have been so titled from like antiquated reasons with those that induced Numa and his company to call a dark grove, lucus.

How many foes, in this utilitarian era, has that very unwarrantable vice, called Poetry! All who despise love and love-making, all who prefer billiards to meditation, all who value hard cash above mental riches, feel privileged to hate it; while really, typographers, the illegible diamond print in which you generally set it up, whether in book, or newspaper, or handbill, or magazine, induces many an indifferent peruser to skip the poem for the sake of his eye-sight. I presume that the monosyllable, rhyme, comprehends pretty nearly all that the world at large intends by poetry; and, in the same manner as certain critics have sneered at Livy—no, it was Tacitus—for commencing his work with a bad hexameter, so many a reader will now-a-days condemn a whole book, because it is somewhere found guilty of harbouring a distich. But poetry, friend World, means far other than rhyme; its etymology would yield "creation," or "fabrication," of sense as well as sound, and of melody for the eye as well as melody for the ear. So did [*epoiese*] Milton; and so did not——Well, I myself, if you will. Yet, in fact, there are fifty other kinds of poetries, beside the poetry of words: as the poetry of life—affection, honour, and hope, and generosity; the poetry of beauty—never mind what features decorate the Dulcinea, for this species of poetry is felt and seen almost only in first love; the poetry of motion, as first-rates majestically sailing, furiously scudding waves, bending corn-fields, and, briefly, all things moveable but railway-trains; the poetry of rest, as pyramids, a tropical calm, an arctic winter, and generally all things quiescent but a slumbering alderman; the poetry of music, heard oftener in a country milkmaid's evening song, than in many a concert-room; the poetry of elegance, more natural to weeping willows, unbroken colts, flames, swans, ivy-clad arches, grey-hounds, yea, to young donkeys, than to those *pirouette*-ing and *very* active *danseuses* of the opera; the poetry of nature, as mountains, waterfalls, storms, summer evenings, and all manner of landscapes, except Holland and Siberia; the poetry of art, acqueducts, minarets, Raphael's colouring, and Poussin's intricate designs; the poetry of ugliness, well seen in monkeys and Skye terriers; and the poetry of awkwardness, whereof the brightest example is Mr. trans-Atlantic Rice. And, verily, many other poetries there be, as of impudence (for which consult the experience of swindlers); of prose, (for which see Addison); of energy, of sleep, of battle and of peace: for it is an easy-seeming artfulness, the most fascinating manner of doing as of saying, complication simplified, and every thing effected to its bravest advantage. Poetry wants a champion in these days, who will save her from her friends: O, namby-pamby "lovers of the Nine!" your innumerous dull lyrics—ay, and mine—your unnatural heroics—I too have sinned thus—your up-hill sonnets—that labour of folly have I known as well—in brief, your misnamed poetry, hath done grievous damage to the cause you toil for. Yet I would avow thus much, for I believe it: as an average, we have beaten our ancestors; seldom can we take up a paper or a periodical which does not show us verses worthy of great names; the age is full of highly respectable, if not superlative poetry; and truly may we consider that the very abundance of good versification has lowered the price of poets, and therefore, in this marketing world, has robbed them of proper estimation. Doubtless, there have been mighty men of song higher in rank, as earlier in time, than any now who dare to try a chirrup: but there are also many of our anonymous minstrels, with whom the greater number of the so-called old English poets could not with advantage to the ancients justly be compared. Look at '*Johnson's Lives.*' Who can read the book, and the specimens it glorifies, without rejoicing in his prose, and thoroughly despising their poetry?—With a few brilliant exceptions, of course, (for ill-used Milton, Pope—and shall we in the same sentence put Dryden? —are there,) a more wretched set of halfpenny-a-liners never stormed mob-trodden Parnassus. The poetry of Queen Anne's time and thereabouts, I judge to have been at the lowest bathos of badness; all satyrs, and swains, fulsome flattery of titles, and foolish adoration of painted shepherdesses: poor weak hobbling lines, eked out by 'eds and expletives, often terminated by false rhymes, and made lamer by triplets and dreary Alexandrines; ill-selected subjects, laboured, indelicate, or impossible similes, passions frigid as Diana, wit's weapons dull as lead. Yet these (many exceptions doubtless there were, and many redeeming *morceaux* even in the worst, charitable reader, but as of the rule we speak not falsely), these are the poets of England, the men our great grandfathers delighted to honour, the feared, the praised, the pensioned, and those whom we their children still denominate—the poets! Praise, praise your stars, ye lucky imps of Fame! who could tolerate you now-a-days?—You lived in golden times, when Dorset, Harley, Bolingbroke, Halifax, and Company, gave away places of a thousand a-year, as but justly due to any man who could pen a roaring song, fabricate a fulsome sonnet, or bewail in meagre elegiacs the still-resisting virtue of some persecuted Stella! Happy fellows, easy conquisitors of wealth and fame, autocrats of coffee-houses, fêted and favoured by town-bred dames! In those good old times for the fashionable Nine, an epic was sure to lead to a Ministry-of-State, and even an epigram produced its pension: to be a poet, or reputed so, was to be—eligible for all things; and the fortunate possessor of a rhyming dictionary might have governed Europe with his metrical protocols. But these halcyon times are of the past—and so, verily, are their heroes. Farewell, a long farewell, children of oblivion! farewell, Spratt, Smith, Duke, Hughes, King, Pomfret, Phillips, and Blackmore: ye who, in that day of very small things, just rose, as your Leviathan biographer so often testifies, "to a degree of merit above mediocrity:" ye who—but (Candor and good Charity, I thank you for the hint,) limited indeed is my knowledge of your writings, ye long-departed poets, whom I thus am base enough to pilfer of your bays; and therefore, if any man among you penned aught of equal praise with "*My Mind to me a Kingdom is*," or "*No Glory I covet, no Riches I want*," humbly do I cry that good man's pardon. Believe that I have only seen the château of your fame, but never the rock on which it rested; and therefore candidly consider, if I might not with reason have accounted it a castle in the air?

Now, after this wholesale species of poetical massacre, this rifling of old Etruscan tombs of their honourable spoil, a very pleasant ninny would that poetaster stand forth, whose inanely conceited daring exhibited specimens from his own mint, as medals in fit contrast with those slandered "things of base alloy." No, as with politics, so with poetry; in public I abjure and do renounce the minx: and although privately my author's mind is so silly as to doat right lovingly on such an ancient mistress, and has wasted much time and paper in her praise or service, still that mind is sufficiently self-possessed in worldly prudence, as to set seemingly little store on the worth of an acquaintance so little in the fashion. Therefore I disown and disclaim

A VOLUME OF POETICS,

ill-fated offspring of a foolish father; miscellaneous collection of occasionals and fugitives, longer or shorter, as the army of Bombastes. Poetical as in verity I must confess to have been, (using the word "poetical" as most men use it, and the words "have been" in the sense of Troy's existence,) there must have lingered in me, even at that hallucinating period, some little remnant of prosaic wisdom; for it is now long since that I consigned to the most voracious of elements all the more love-sick rhythmicals, and all the more hateful satiricals. Now, I will maintain that act of incremation to be one of true heroism, nearly equal to the judgment of Brutus; nor less is it matter of righteous boasting to have immolated (warned by Charles Lamb's ghost) divers albuminous preparations, which to have to do, were, Clio knows, little pleasure, and to have done, we all know, as little praise. Such light follies are like skeins of cotton, or adjectives, or babies, unfit to stand alone; haply, well enough, times and things considered, but totally unworthy to be dragged out of their contexts into the imperishability of print; it is to take flies out of treacle, and embalm them in clear amber.

As to sonnets, what real author's mind will not, if honest, confess to the almost daily recurrence of that symptom of his disease? With mine, at least, they have increased, and are increasing; yea, more—as a certain statesman suggested of Ireland's multitudinous *pisantry*, or as tavern patriots declare of the power of the crown—they ought to be diminished. Nevertheless, resolutely do I hope that some of these at least are little worthy of the days of good Queen Anne.

In matters of the sacred muse, lengthily as others have I trespassed heretofore; the most protracted *fytte*, however, made a respectable inroad on a new metrical version of the '*Psalms*,' attempting at any rate closer accuracy from the Hebrew than Brady's, and juster rhymes than Sternhold's: but this has since been better done by another bard. On the whole budget of exploded poeticals is now legibly inscribed "to be kept till called for," a period rather more indefinite than the promise of a spendthrift's payment. Let them rest in peace, those unfortunate poetics!

There are also in the bundle, if I rightly do remember me, sundry metricals of the humorous sort, which may be considered as really *waste-failures* as any tainted hams that ever were yclept Westphalias. For of all dreary and lugubrious perpetrations in print, nothing can be more desolate than laboured witticism. A pun is a momentary spark dropt upon the tinder-box of social intercourse; and to detach such a sentence from its producing circumstances, is about as efficacious a method of producing laughter, as the scintillatory flint and steel struck upon wet grass would be of generating light. Few things are less digestible than abortive efforts at the humorous; the stream of conversation instantly freezes up; the disconcerted punster wears the look of his well-known kinsman, the detected pickpocket; and a scribe, so mercilessly suicidal as regards his better fame, deserves, when a plain blunt jury comes to sit upon the body, to be found in mystical Latin, *felo de se*, or in plain English "a fellow deceased."

"There shall come in the last days, scoffers;" those same last days in which "many shall run to and fro, and knowledge shall be increased." It is true that these phrases (quoted with the deepest reverence, though found in lighter company) are forcibly taken from their context; but still, the judgment of many wise among us will agree that they present a remarkable coincidence: in this view of the case, and it is a most serious one, the concurrent notoriety of humour having just arisen like a phœnix from its ashes, of railroads and steamboats having partially annihilated space, and of the strides which education, if not intellect, has made upon the highroad of human improvement, assumes an importance greater than the things themselves deserve. To a truly philosophic ken, there is no such thing as a trifle; the ridiculous is but skin-deep, papillæ on the surface of society; cut a little deeper, you will find the veins and arteries of wisdom. Therefore will a sober man not deride the notion that comic almanacs, comic Latin grammars, comic hand-books of sciences and arts, and the great prevalence of comicality in popular views taken of life and of death, of incident and of character, of evil and of good, are, in reality, signs of the times. These straws, so thick upon the wind, and so injuriously mote-like to the visual organs, are flying forward before a storm. As symptoms of changing nationality, and of a disposition to make fun of all things ancient and honourable, and wise, and mighty, and religious, they serve to evidence a state of the universal mind degenerated and diseased. Still, let us not be too severe; and, as to individual confessions, let not me play the hypocrite. Like every thing else, good in its good use, and evil only in abuse of its excesses, humour is capable of filling, and has filled, no lightly-estimable part in the comedy of temporal happiness. What a good thing it is to raise an innocent and cheerful laugh; to inoculate moroseness with hearty merriment; to hunt away misbelieving care, if not with better prayers, at the lowest with a pack of yelping cachinations; to make pain forget his head-ache by the anodyne of mirth! Truly, humour has its laudable and kindly uses: it is the mind's play-time after office-drudgery—an easy recreation from thought, anxiety, or study. Only when it usurps, or foolishly attempts to usurp, the office of more than a temporary alleviation; when it affects to set up as an atheistic panacea; when it professes to walk as an abiding companion, lighting you on your way with injurious gleams (as that dreadful figure in Dante, who lanterns his path by the glaring eyes of his own truncated head); and when it ceases to become merely the casual scintillation, the flitting *ignus fatuus* of a summer evening—then only is wit to be condemned. Often, for mine own poor part in this most mirthful age, have I had

HEARTY LAUGHS,

IN PROSE AND VERSE;

but take no thought of preserving their echoes, or of shrining them in the eternal basalt of print, like to the oft-repeated cries of Lurley's hunted in-dweller. The humorous infection caught also me, as a thing inevitable; but the case, I wot, proved an unfavourable one: and who dare enter the arena of contention with these mighty men of Momus, these acknowledged sages of laughter, (pardon me for omitting some fifty more,) so familiar to the tickled ear, as Boz, and Sam Slick, Ingoldsby, and Peter Plymley, Titmarsh, Hood, Hook; not to mention —(but that artists are authors)—laughter-loving Leech, Pickwickian Phiz, and inimitable Cruikshank? Nevertheless, let a tender conscience penitently ask, is it quite an innocent matter to lend a hand in rendering the age more careless than perchance, but for such ministrations, it would cease to be? Is it quite wise in a writer, by following in that wake, to be reputed at once to help in doing harm, and help to do harm to his own reputation? There are professors enough in this quadrangle of the college of amusement, popular and extant in flourishing obesity, without so dull a volunteer as Mr. Self intruding his humours on the world: and surely the far-echoing voices of a couple of cannons, thundering their mirth throughout Europe from the jolly quarters of St. Paul's, may well frighten into silence a poor solitary pop-gun, which, as the frog with the bull, might burst in an attempt at competition, or, like Bottom's Numidian lion, could imitate the mighty roar only as gently as your sucking-dove.

Grapho-mania, or the love of scribbling, is clearly the great distinguishing characteristic of an author's mind; pen and ink are to it, what bread and butter are to its lodging-house the body: observe, we do not hazard a remark so false as that the one produces the other—their relations are far from being mutual; but we only suggest that the mind, as well as the body, hobbles like a three-legged Œdipus, resting on its proper staff of life. And what can be more provocative of scribbling than travel? How eagerly we hasten to describe unheard-of adventures, how anxiously record exaggerated marvels! to prove some printed hand-book *quite wrong* in the number of steps up a round-tower: or to crush, as a wicked vender of execrable wines, the once fair fame of some over-charging inn-keeper! Then, again, how pleasant to immortalize the holiday, and read in after-years the story of that happy trip langsyne; how pleasant to gladden the kind eyes of friends, that must stay at home, with those wonder-telling journals, and to taste the dulcet joys of those first essays at authorship. A great charm is there in jotting down the day's tour, and in describing the mountains and museums, the lakes and lazzaroni, the dishes and disasters that have made it memorable: moreover, for fixing scenery on the mental retina, as well as for comparison of notes as to an *alibi*, for duly remembering things heard and seen, as well as for being humbled in having (as a matter inevitable) left unseen just the best lion of the whole tour, journals are a most praise-worthy pastime, and usually rank among the earliest efforts of an embryo author's mind.

It is a thing of commonest course, that, in this age of inveterate locomotion, your present humble friend, now talking in this candid fashion with your readership, has been every where, seen every thing, and done his touristic devoirs like every body else about him: also, as a like circumstance of etymological triviality, that he has severally, and from time to time, recorded for self-amusement and the edification of others all such matters as holiday-making school-boys and boarding-misses, and government-clerks in their swift-speeding vacation, and elderly gentlemen vainly striving to enjoy their first fretful continental trip, usually think proper to descant upon. Of such manuscripts the world is clearly full; no catacomb of mummies more fertile of papyri; no traveller so poor but he has by him a packet of precious notes, whereon he sets much store: every tourist thinks he can reasonably emulate clever Basil Hall, in his eloquent fragments of voyages and travels; and I, for my part, a truth-teller to my own detriment, am ashamed to confess the existence of

A DECADE OF JOURNALS;

which of olden time my *cacoethes* produced as regularly as recurred the summer solstice. Unlike that of Livy's, I am satisfied that this poor Decade be irrevocably lost; but, for dear recollection's sake of days gone by, intend it at least to be spared from malicious incremation. Records of roamings in romantic youth, witnesses of wayward wayside wanderings, gayly with alliterative titles might your contents, *à la Roscoe*, be set forth. But—what conceivable news can be told at this time of day about the trampled Continent, and the crowded British isles? Had my luck led me to Lapland or Formosa, to Mexico or Timbuctoo, to the top of Egyptian pyramids or the bottom of Polish salt-mines, my authorship would long since have publicly declared, in common with many a monkey, that it had "seen the world." As things are, to Bruce,

Buckingham, Belzoni, and that glorious anomaly, the blind brave Holman, let us leave the harvest of praise, worthy to be reaped as their own by modern travellers.

More, yet more, most exemplary of listeners; and a web or webs of very various texture. *Let any man tell truths of himself, and seem to* be consistent, if he can. From grave to gay, from simple to severe, is the line most expressive of such foolish versatility as mine; *varium et mutabile semper*, to one thing constant never. I have heard, or read, among the experiences of a popular preacher, that one of his most vexatious petty temptations, was the rise of humorous notions in his mind the moment he stepped into the pulpit; and it is well known that many a comic actor has been afflicted with the blackest melancholy while supporting right facetiously his best, because most ludicrous character. Let such thoughts then as these, of the frailties incident to man, serve to excuse the present juxtaposition of fancies in themselves diametrically opposite.

It is proper to preamble somewhat of apology before announcing the next presumptuous tractate; presumptuous, because affecting to advise some thousands of men whose office alike and average character are sacred, and just, and excellent. Why then intrude such unrequired counsel? Read the next five pages, and take your answer. Zealously inflamed for the cause of truth, if not also charitably wroth against sundry lukewarm cumber-earth incumbents, and certainly more in love with the Church-of-England prayer-book than with her no-ways-extenuated evils of omission or commission, I wrote, not long since, [and truly, not long since, for few things in this book can boast of higher antiquity than a most modern existence, some things being the birth of an hour, some of a day, a week, or a month; and not more than one or two above a twelve month's age.—Alas, for Horace's forgotten counsels! —alas, for Pope's and Boileau's reiterated prescription of revisal for—*morbleu et parbleu*—nine years!] I wrote then a good cantle of an essay addressed to the clergy on some matters of judicious amelioration, which we will call, if you please—and if the word hints be not objectionable—

LAY HINTS.

Now, as to the unclerical authorship of this, it is wise that it be done out of métier. Laymen are more likely to gain attention in these matters, from the very fact of their influence being an indirect one, speaking as they do rather from the social arm-chair, the high-stool of the counting-house, or the benches of whilom St. Stephen's, than *ex cathedrâ* as of office and of duty.

It would be a fair exemplification of the stolid prowess of a Quixote tilting against, yea, stouter foes than wind-mills, were I to have commenced with an attack upon external church architecture: this topic let us leave to the fraternity of builders; only asking by what rule of taste an obelisk-like spire, is so often stuck upon the roof of a Grecian temple, and by what rule of convenience gigantic columns so commonly and resolutely sentinel the narrowest of exits and entrances. Let us be more commonly contented, as well we may, with our grand, appropriate, and impressive indigenous kind of architecture—Gothic, Norman, and Saxon: the temple of Ephesus was not suitable to be fitted up with galleries, nor was the Parthenon meant to be surmounted by a steeple. But all this is useless gossip.

Similarly Quixotic would be any tirade against pews, those pet strongholds of snug exclusive selfishness; bad in principle, as perpetually separating within wooden walls members of the same communion; unwholesome in practice, confining in those antre-like parallelograms the close-pent air; unsightly in appearance, as any one will testify, whose soul is exalted above the iron beauties of a plain conventicle; expensive in their original formation, their fittings and repairs; and, when finished, occupying perhaps one-fourth of the area of a church already ten times too small for its neighbouring population. Fixed benches, or a strong muster of chairs, or such modes of congregational accommodation as public meeting-rooms and ordinary lecture-rooms present, seems to me more consistent and more convenient. But all this again is vain talking—a very empty expenditure of words; we must be satisfied with churches as they are; and, after all, let me readily admit that steeples are imposing in the distance, and of use as belfries; (probably of like intent were the strange columnar towers of Ireland;) and with regard to pews, let me confess that practice finds perfect what theory condemns as wrong, so—let these things pass.

Nevertheless, let me begin upon the threshold with the extortionate and abominable race of pew-women, beadles, clerks, vergers, bell-ringers, and other fee-hungry ravens hovering around and about almost every hallowed precinct: pray you, reform all that, and copy railroad companies in forbidding those begrudged gratuities to mendicant and ever-grumbling menials. Next, give more sublunary heed, we beseech you, to the comforts or discomforts incidental to doors, windows, stoves, paint, dust, dirt, and general ventilation; consider the cold, fevers, lumbagos, rheums, life-long aches, and fatal pains too often caught helplessly and needlessly by the devout worshipper in a town or country church. Look to your organist, that he wot something of the value of time and the mysteries of tune; or, if a country parson, drill cleverly that insubordinate phalanx of *soi-disant* musicians, a rustic orchestra; and exclude from the latter, at all mortal hazards, the huntsman's horn, the volunteer fiddle, and the shrill squeaking of the wry-necked pipe. Much is being now done for congregational psalmody; but when will country folks give up their murderous execution of the fugue-full anthem, and when will London congregations understand that the singing-psalms are not set apart exclusively for charity-children? When shall Bishop Kenn's '*Awake my soul*,' cease to be our noonday exhortation; and a literal invocation for sweet sleep to close our eye-lids no longer be the ill-considered prelude to an afternoon discourse? Take some trouble to improve and educate, or get rid of, if possible, your generally vulgar, illiterate, ill-conditioned clerk; insist upon his v's and h's: let him shut up his shoe-stall; and raise in the scale of society one of the leaders of its worship: as, at present, these stagnant, recreant, ignorant clerks are sad stumbling-blocks; no help to the congregation, and a nuisance to its minister. In reading—suffer this foolishness, my masters—fight against the too frequent style of dogged, dormant, dull formality; we take you for earnest living guides to our devotion, not mere dead organs of an oft-repeated service; quicken us by your manner; a psalm so spoken is better than the sermon. In more fitting places has your author long ago delivered his mind concerning matters of a character more directly sacred than shall here find room; as, the sacrament with its holy mysteries, and the many things amendable in ordinary preachments; but for these my unseasonable Wisdom shrouds itself in Silence: therefore, to do away with details, and apply a general rule, above all things, and in all things, strive by judicious acquiescence with human wants, and likings, and failings too, if conscientiously you can, as well as by spirited and true devotion, to break down the sluggish mounds of needful uniformity, and to build up round the church a rampart of good sense: and so, Heaven bless your labours! A word more: if it be possible, take no fees at a baptism, and let it not be thought, by either rich or poor, that an entrance into Christ's fold must be paid for; no, nor at a burial; but let the service for the Christian dead be accorded freely, without money and without price. To a wedding, the same ideas are not perhaps so closely applicable; therefore we will generously suffer that you keep your customs there; but on the introduction of a little one to the bosom of the church, or restoring the body of a saint to Him who made it of the dust, nothing can be more repulsive to right religious feelings than to be bothered by a fee-seeking clerk, thrusting in your face an itching palm: to the poor, these things are more than a mere annoyance; they amount to a hardship and a hindrance; for such demands at such seasons are often nothing less than a bitter extortion upon the self-denial of conscientious duty.

More might be added; but enough, too much has been alluded to. Nothing would strengthen the bulwarks of our Zion more than such easy reforms as these: recent happy revivals in our church would thus be more solidified; and where, as now, many have been lulled to slumber, many grieved, many become disgusted or Dissenters, our sons and our daughters would grow up as the polished corners of the temple, and crowds would throng the courts of our holy and beautiful House.

Suffer thus far, clerical and lay, these crude hints: in all things have I studied brevity, throughout this little bookful; therefore are you spared a perusal of my reasons, and so be indulgent for their absence. I "touch your ears" but lightly; be you for charity, as in old Rome, my favourable witnesses.

My before-mentioned Censor of the press had a very considerable mind to dock all mention of the following intended *brochure*. But I answered, Really, Mr. Judgment, (better or worse, as occasion may register your Agnomen,) you must not weigh trifles in gold-assaying scales; be not so particular as to the polish of a thumb-nail; endure a little incoherent pastime; count not the several stems of hay, straw, stubble—but suffer them to be pitch-forked *en masse*, and unconsidered: it is their privilege, in common with that of certain others—lightnesses that froth upon the surface of society. Moreover, let me remind your worship's classicality that no one of mortals is sapient at all times. Item, that if friend Flaccus be not a calumniator, even the rigid virtue of the antiquer Cato delighted in so stimulant a vanity as wine hot. So give the colt his head, and let it go: remembering always that this same colt, as straying without a responsible rider, is indeed liable to be impounded by any who can catch him; but still, if he be found to have done great damage to his master's character, or to a neighbour's fences, the estray shall rather be abandoned than acknowledged. Let then this unequal work, this ill-assorted bundle of dry book-plants, this undirected parcel of literary stuff, be accounted much in the same situation as that of the wanton caitiff-colt, so likely to bait a-pound, and afterwards to be sold for payment of expenses, in true bailiff-sense of justice. And let thus much serve as discursive prolegomena to a notion, scarcely worth recording, but for the wonder, that no professed writer (at least to my small knowledge) has entered on so common-sense a field. Paris, I remember, some years ago was inundated with copies of a treatise on the important art of tying the cravat; every shop-window displayed the mystic diagrams, and every stiff neck proclaimed its popularity. This was my yesterday's-conceived precedent for entertaining the bright hope of illuminating London on the subject of shaving:

ANTI-XURION;

A CRUSADE AGAINST RAZORS,

should have been my taking title; and perchance the learned treatise might have been characteristically illustrated with steel cuts. Shaving is a wider topic than most people think for; it is a species of insanity that has afflicted man in all ages, deprived him of nature's best adornment in every country under heaven. So contradictorily too; as thus: the Spanish friar shaves all but a rim round his head, which rim alone sundry North American aborigines determine to extirpate; John Chinaman nourishes exclusively a long cue, just on that same inch of crown-land which the P. P. sedulously keeps as bare as his palm: all the Orientals shave the head, and cherish the beard; all the Occidentals immolate the beard, and leave the honours of the head untouched. Then, again, the strange successive fashions in this same unnatural, unneedful depilation; look at the vagaries of young France: not to descend also to savage men, and their clumsy shell-scrapings; and to devote but little time to the voluminous topic of wigs, male and female, cavàlier and caxon, Marlborough and monstrous maccaroni—from the plaited Absalom-looking periwig of a Pharaoh in the British Museum, to Truefitt's last patent self-adjuster. Of all these follies, and their root a razor, might we show the manifest absurdity: we might argue upon Eastern stupidity as caused by thickness of the skull, such thickness being the substitute for thatchy hair suggested by kind ill-used Nature as the hot brain's best protection: we might reason upon the average sheepishness of this peaceful West, as due to having shorn the lion of his mane, Phœbus of his glory, man of his majestic beard. Then the martyrdom it is to many! who stoically, day after day, persist in scratching to the quick their irritable chins, and after all to little better end than the diligent earning of tooth-aches, ear-aches, colds, sore throats, and unbecoming blank faces. Habit, it is true, makes us deem that a comfort, and our better halves (or those we would fain have so) think that a beauty, which our forerunners of old time would have held a plague, a disgrace, a deformity, a mortification: prisoned paupers in the Union think it an insufferable hardship to go bearded, and King David's ambassadors would have given their right eyes *not* to have been shaved; so much are we the slaves of custom: Sheffield also, it is equally true, is a town that humane men would not wish to ruin; by razors they of Sheffield live, and shaving is their substance. But, as in the case of the smoother and softer sex, we are convinced that the wand of fashion would presently convert their heterodox anti-barbal prejudices: so, in the case of harder-ware Sheffield, while we hope to live to see razors regarded as antiquarian rarities, (even as a watchman's rattle, or the many-caped coats of the semi-extinct class *Welleria coachmanensis* are now some time become,) still we desire all possible multiplication to the tribe of trimming scissors. Like Ireland, we shout for long-denied justice; give us our beards. That reasonable indulgence shall never be abused; our Catholic emancipation of moustache and imperial, whisker and the rest, shall not be a pretence for lion's manes, or the fringe of goats and monkeys: we would not so far follow unsophisticated nature as to relapse into barbarous wild men; but diligently squaring, pointing, combing, and perfuming those natural manly decorations, after the most approved modes of Raleigh, Walsingham, and Shakspeare, and heroical Edward the Black Prince, and venerable apostolic Bede, we will encroach little further than to discard our comfortless starched collars and strangling stocks, to adopt once more in lieu thereof open necks and vandyke borders.

Of course, (here, priest-like, we take our ell,) there must follow upon this a grand and glorious revolution in male attire. This present close-fitting, undignified set of habiliments, which no chisel dare imitate—this cumbersome, unbecoming garb—might, should, ought to be, and would be, superseded by slashed gay jerkins, and picturesque nether garments:

cap and feather throwing into shade the modern hat, ugliest of all imaginable head-dresses; and in lieu of the smock-frock Macintosh, or coarse-featured bear-skin, Ciceronian mantles flowing from the shoulders, or lighter capes of the elegant olden-time Venitian. By way of distinguisihng the now confused classes of society, my radical reform in dress would go to recommend that nobles and gentry wear their own heraldic colours and livery buttons; and humbler domesticated creatures walk, as modest gentlefolks do now, in what sundry have presumed to call "Mufti." To be briefer; in dress, if nothing more, let us sensibly retrograde to the days of good Queen Bess: I will not say, copy a Sir Piercie Shafton, who boasts of having "danced the salvage man at the mummery of Clerkenwell, in a suit of flesh-coloured silk, trimmed with fur;" neither, under these dingy skies, would I care to walk abroad with Sir Philip Sidney in satin boots, or with Oliver Goldsmith in a peach-coloured doublet: but still, for very comfort's sake, let us break our bonds of cloth and buckram, and, in so far as adornment is concerned, let us exchange this staid funeral monotony for the gallant garb of our ancestors, the brave costumes of our Edwards and the bluff King Hal.

Behold, too scornful friend, how my Tory rabies reaches to the wardrobe. The modern dress of illuminated Europe has, in my humble opinion, gone far to weaken the old empire of the Porte, to denationalize Egypt, to degenerate the Jews, to mammonize once generous Greece, and carry republican equality into the great prairies of America: it is the undistinguishing, humiliating, unchivalrous livery of our cold cosmopolites. But enough of this: pews and spires are to my Quixotism not more unextinguishable foes, than coats, cravats, waistcoats, and unnameables.

And now an honest word at parting, about such trivialities of authorship. Why should a poor shepherd of the Landes for ever wear his stilts? Or a tragic actor, like some mortified La Trapist, never be allowed to laugh? Or Mr. Green be denied any other carriage than the wicker car of his balloon? Even so, dear reader, pr'ythee suffer a serious sort of author sometimes to take off his wig and spectacles, and condescend to think of such minor matters as the toilet and its still-recurring duties. And, if you *should* find out the veritable name of your weak confessing scribe, think not the less kindly of his graver volumes; this one is his pastime, his holiday laugh, his purposely truant, lawless, desultory recreance: impute not folly to the face of cheerfulness; be charitable to such mixtures of alternate gayety and soberness as in thine own mind, if thou searchest, thou shalt find; let me laugh with those that laugh, as well as sympathize with weepers; and cavil not at those inconsistencies, which of a verity are man's right attributes.

IDEAS lie round about us, thick as daisies in a summer meadow. For my own part, I know not what a walk, or a talk, or a peep into a book may lead me to. Brunel hit upon the notion of a tunnel-shield, from the casual sight of a certain water-beetle, to whom the God of Nature had given a protecting buckler for its head. Newton found out gravitation, by reasoning on the fall of an apple from the tree. Almost every invention has been the suggestion of an accident. Even so, to descend from great things to small, did a solitary stroll in most-English Devonshire hint to me the next fair topic. It was while wandering about the Pyrenean neighbourhood of Linton and Ly'mouth not many months ago, that my reveries became concentrated for divers hallucinating hours on a very pretty book, with a very pretty title. And here let me remark episodically, that I pride myself on titles; what compositors call "monkeyfying the title-page" is known to be a talent of itself, and one moreover to which in these days of advertisements and superficialities many a meagre book has owed its popular acceptance. The titles of generations back seemed not to have been regarded honest, if they did not exhibit on their face a true and particular table of contents; whereas in these sad times, (with many, not with me,) mystery is a good rule, but falsehood is a better. Again, those honest-speaking authors of the past scrupled not to designate their writings as '*A Most Erudite Treatise*' on so-and-so, or a "*A Right Ingenious Handling of the Mysteries*' of such-and-such, whereas modern hypocrisy aims at under-rating its own pet work; and more than one book has been ruined in the market, for having been carelessly titled by the definite THE; as if, forsooth, it were the world's arbiter of that one topic, self-constituted pundit of, e. g., title-pages. And this word brings me back: consider the truly English music of this one:

THE SQUIRE,

AND HIS BEAUTIFUL HOME,

a fine old country gentleman, pleasantly located, affluent, noble-minded, wise, and patriotic. This was to have been shown forth, in wish at least, as somewhat akin to, or congenerous with '*The Doctor, &c.*,'—that rambling wonder of strange and multifarious reading: or '*The Rectory of Valehead*,' or '*Vicar of Wakefield*,' or '*The Family Robinson Crusoe*,' still unwrecked; or many another hearty, cheerful or pathetic tale of home, sweet home: and yet as to design and execution strictly original and unplagiaristic. The first chapters (simple healthy writing, redolent of green pastures, and linchened rocks, and dew-dropt mountains,) might introduce localities; the beautiful home itself, an Elizabethan mansion, with its park, lake, hill and valley scenery; a peep at the blue mile-off sea, brawling brooks, oak-woods, conservatories, rookery, and all such pleasant adjuncts of that most fortunate of pleasure-hunters, a country squire, with a princely rent-roll. Then should be detailed, circumstantially, the lord of the beautiful home, a picture of the hospitable virtues; the wife of the beautiful home, a portraiture of happy domesticity, admirable also as a mother, a nurse, a neighbour, and the poor's best friend: children must abound, of course, or the home is a heaven uninhabited; and shrewd hints might hereabouts be dropped as to the judicious or injudicious in matters educational: servants, too, both old and young, with discussions on their modern treatment, and on that better class of bygones, whom kindness made not familiar, and the right assertion of authority provoked not into insolence; whose interest for the dear old family was never merged in their own, and whose honesty was as unsuspected as that of young master himself, or sweet little mistress Alice.

After all this, might we descant upon the squire's characteristics. Take him as a politician: liberal, that is to say, (for his frown is on me at a phrase so doubtful,) generous, tolerant, kind, and manly; but none of your low-bred slanderers of that noble name, so generally tyrants at home and cowardly abroad—mean agitating fellows, the scum of disgorging society, raised by turbulence and recklessness from the bottom to the surface: oh no, none of these; but, for all his just liberality, an honest, honourable, loyal, church-going, uncompromising Tory: with a detail of his reasons, notions, and practices thereabouts, inclusive of his conduct at elections, his wholesome influence over an otherwise unguided or ill-guided tenantry, and as concerning other miscalled corruptions: his open argumentation of the representative doctrine, that it ought to stop short as soon as ever the religion, the learning, and the wealth of a country are fairly represented; that in fact the poor man thinks little of his vote, unless indeed in worse cases looking for a bribe; and that the principle is pushed into ruinous absurdities when the destitution, the crime, and the ignorance of a nation demand their proper representatives; that, almost as a consequence of human average depravity, the greater the franchise's extension, the worse in all ways become those who impersonate the enfranchised; and so, after due condemnation of Whiggery, to stultify Chartism, and that demoralizing lie, the ballot. Then as to the squire's religion; and certain confabulations with his parson, his household, his harvest-home tenantry, and local preachers of dissent and schism; his creed, practice, and favourable samples of daily life. Moreover, our squire should have somewhat to tell of personal history and adventures; a youth of poor dependence on a miser uncle; a storm-tost early manhood, consequent on his high uncompromising principles; then the miser's death, without the base injustice of that cruel will, which an eleventh-hour penitence destroyed: the squire comes to his property, marries his one old flame, effects reformations, attains popularity, happiness, and other due prosperities. Anecdotes of particular passages, as in affliction or in joy; his son lamed for life, or his house half burnt down, his attack by highwaymen, or election for parliament. The squire's general confidence in man, sympathy with frailties, and success in regenerating long-lost characters. His discourse on field sports, displaying the amiable intellectuality of a Gilbert White as opposed to the blood-thirsty Nimrodism and Ramrodism of a mad Mytton. A marriage; a funeral; a disputed legacy of some eccentric relative; with its agreeable concomitants of heartless selfish strife, rebuked by the squire's noble example: the conventicle gently put down by dint of gradual desertions, and church-going as tenderly extended; vestry demagogues and parochial incendiaries chastised by our squire; and divers other adventures, conversations, situations, and conditions, illustrative of that grand character, a fine old English gentleman, all of the olden time.

Altogether, if well managed, a book like this would be calculated to do substantial good in these days of no principle or bad principle. A captivating example well applied—witness the uses of biography—is infectious among the well-inclined and well-informed. But—but—but —I fancy there may exist, and do exist already, admirable books of just this character. I have heard of, but not seen, '*The Portrait of a Christian Gentleman*,' and another '*of a Churchman*:' doubtless, these, combined with a sort of Mr. Dovedale in that clever impossible '*Floreston*,' or an equally unnatural and charming Sir Charles Grandison, with a dash of scenery and a sprinkle of anecdote, would make up, far better than I could fabricate, the fair fine character that once I thought to sketch. Moreover, to a plain gentleman, living in the country, of perfectly identical ideas with hose of the squire on all imaginable topics, gifted too (we will not say with quite his princely rent-roll, but at any rate) with sundry like advantages in the way of decent affluence, pleasant scenery, an old house, a good wife, and fair children—with plenty of similar adventures and circumstantials—and the necessary proportion of highwaymen, radicals, rascals, and schismatics dotted all about his neighbourhood, the idea would seem, to say the least, somewhat egotistic. But why may not humble individualities be generalized in grander shapes? why not glorify the picture of a cottage with colouring of Turner's most imaginative palette? An author, like an artist, seldom does his work well unless he has nature before him: exalted and idealized, the Roman beggar goes forth a Jupiter, and country wenches help a Howard to his Naiads. Nevertheless, let the Squire and his train pass us by, indefinite as Banquo's progeny: let his beautiful home be sublimely indistinct; even such are Martin's ætherial cities: the thought shall rest unfructified at present—a mummied, vital seed. The review is over, and the Squire's troop of yeomanry not required: so let them wait till next year's muster.

Few novelties are more called for, in this halcyon age of authorship, this summer season for the Sosii, this every-day-a-birth-day for some five-and-twenty books, than the establishment of a recognised literary tribunal, some judgment-hall of master spirits, from whose calm, unhurried, unbiased verdict, there should be no appeal. Far, very far be it from me to arraign modern reviewers either of partialities or incapacity; indeed, it is probable that few men of high talent, character, and station, have not, at some time or other, temporarily at least contributed to swell their ranks: moreover, from one they have treated so magnanimously, they shall not get the wages of ingratitude; they have been kind to my dear book-children, and I—*don't be so curious*—thank them for their courtesy with all a father's feeling toward the liberal friends of his sons and daughters. Speaking generally, (for, not to flatter any class of men, truly there are rogues in all,) I am bold to call them candid, honest, clever men; quite superior, as a body, to every thing like bribery and corruption, and, with human limitations, little influenced by motives, either of prejudice or favour. For indefatigable industry, unexampled patience, and powers of mind very far above what are commonly attributed to them, I, for my humble judgment, would give our periodical journalists their honourable due: I am playing no Aberdeenshire game of mutual scratching; I am too hardened now in the ways of print to be much more than indifferent as to common praise or censure; that honey-moon is over with me, when a laudatory article in some kindly magazine sent a thrill from eye to heart, from heart to shoe-sole understanding: I no longer feel rancorous with inveterate wrath against a poor editor whose faint praise, impotent to d—, has yet abundant force to induce a hearty return of the compliment: like some case-nardened rock, so little while ago but soft young coral, the surges may lash me, but leave no mark; the sun may shine, but cannot melt me. Argal, as the clown says, is my verdict honest: and further now to prove it so, shall come the limitations.

With all my gratitude and right good feeling to our diurnal and hebdomadal amusers and instructors, I cannot but consider that gazette and newspaper reviewers are insufficient and unsatisfactory judges of literature, if not indeed sometimes erring guides to the public taste; the main cause of this consisting in the essential rapidity of their composition. There is not—from the multiplicity of business to be got through, there cannot be—adequate time allowed for any thing like justice to the claims of each author. Periodicals that appear at longer intervals are in all reason more or less excepted from this objection; but by the daily and weekly majority, the labours of a life-time are cursorily glanced at, hastily judged from some isolated passage, summarily found laudable or guilty; and this weak opinion, strongly enough expressed as some compensation in solid superstructure for the sandiness of its foundations, is circulated by thousands over all corners of the habitable world. To say that the public (those so-called reviewers of reviews, but wiser to be looked on only as perusers,) balance all such false verdicts, might indeed be true in the long run, but unfortunately it is not: for first, no run at all, far less a long one, is permitted to the persecuted production; and next, it is notorious, that people think very much as they are told to think Now, I have already stated at too much length that I have no personalities to complain of, no self-interests to serve: for the past I have been well entreated; and for the future, supposing such an unlikelihood as more hypothetical books, I am hard, bold, sanguine, stoical; while, as for the present, though I refuse not my gauntlet to any man, my visor shall be raised by none. But I enter the list for others, my kinsmen in composing. Authors, to speak it generally, are an ill-used race, because judged hastily, often superciliously, for evil or for good. It is impossible for the poor public, (who, besides having to earn daily bread, have to wade through all the daily papers,) from mere lack of hours in the day, to entertain any opinions of their own about a book or books: the money to buy them is one objection, the time to read them another; to say less of the capacity, the patience, and the will. Without question, they are guided by their teachers; and the grand fault of these is, their everlasting hurry.

At another necessary failing of reviewers I would only delicately hint. The royal We is very imposing; for example, the king of magazines, No. 134, (need I name it?) informs us, p. 373, "We happen to have now in wear a good long coat of imperial gray," &c.; and some fifteen lines lower down, "We are now mending our pen with a small knife," and so forth: now all this grandiloquence serves to conceal the individual; and to reduce my other great objection to a single letter, let us only recollect that this powerful, this despotic We, is, being interpreted, nothing but an I by itself, a simple scribe, a single and plebeian number one. A mere unit, an anonymous, irresponsible unit, dissects in a quarter of an hour the grand result of some ten years; and this momentary influence on one man's mind, (perhaps wearied, or piqued, or biased, or haply unskilled in the point at issue, but at all events inevitably in a hurry to jump at a conclusion,) this light accidental impression is sounded forth to the ends of the earth, and leads public opinion in a verdict of thunder. And as for yon impertinent parenthesis—or pertinent, as some will say—give me grace thus blandly to suggest a possibility. The mighty editorial We, upon whose authoritative tones the world's opinion will probably be pivoted—whose pen by casual ridicule or as casual admiration makes or mars the fortune of some pains-taking literary labourer—whose dictum carelessly dispenses local honour or disgrace, and has before now by sharp sarcasms, speaking daggers though using none, even killed more than one over-sensitive Keats—this monarchic We is but a frail mortal, liable at least to "some of the imperfections of our common nature, gentlemen," as, for example, to be morose, impatient, splenetic, and the more if over-worked. Neither should I waive in this place, in this my rostrum of blunt, plain speech, the many censurable cases, unhappily too well authenticated, where personal enmity has envenomed the reviewing pen against a writer, and stabs in the dark have wounded good men's fame. Neither, again, those other instances where reviewers, not being omniscient, (yet is their knowledge most various and brilliant,) having been from want of specific information incompetent to judge of the matters in question, have striven to shroud their ignorance of the greater topic in clamorous attacks of its minor incidents; burrowing into a mound if they cannot force a breach through the rampart; and mystifying things so cleverly with doubts, that we cannot see the blessed sun himself for very fog.

Now really, good folk, all this should be amended: would that the WE were actually plural; would that we had a well-selected bench of literary judges; would that some higher sort of Stationers' Hall or Athenæum were erected into an acknowledged tribunal of an author's merits or demerits; would that, to wish the very least, the wholesome practice of a well-considered imprimatur were revived! Let famous men, whose reputation is firm-fixed—our Wordsworths, Hallams, Campbells, Crolys, Wilsons, Bulwers, and the like—decide in the case of at least all who desire such decision. I suppose, as no one in these selfish times will take trouble without pay, that either the judges should be numbered among state pensioners, or that each work so calmly examined must produce its regular fee: but these are after-considerations; and be sure no writer will grudge a guinea for calm, unbought, unsuspected justice bestowed upon his brain-child. Let all those members of the tribunal, deciding by ballot, (here in an assembly where all are good, great, and honest, I shrink not from that word of evil omen,) judge, as far as possible, together and not separately, of all kinds of literature: I would not have poets sentencing all the poetry, historians all the history, novelists all the novels, and theologists all the works upon religion; for humanity is at the best infirm, and motives little searchable; but let all judge equally in a sort of open court. The machinery might be difficult, and I cannot show its workings in so slight an essay; but surely it is a strange thing in civilization, and a stranger when we consider what literature does for us, blessing our world or banning it—it is a wonder and a shame that books of whatever tendency are so cast forth upon the waters to sink or swim at hazard. I acknowledge, friend, your present muttering, Utopian! Arcadian! Formosan! to be not ill-founded: the sketch is a hasty one; but though it may have somewhat in common with the vagaries of Sir Thomas More, Sir Philip Sidney, and that king in impudence, George Psalmanazar, still I stand upon this ground, that many an ill-used author wants protection, and that society, for its own sake as well as his, ought to supply a court for literary reputation. Some poor man the other day, and in a reputable journal too, had five new-born tragedies strangled and mangled in as many lines: we need not suppose him a Shakspeare, but he might have been one for aught of evidence given to the contrary; at any rate, five at once, five mortal tragedies, (so puppy-fashion born and drowned,) must, however carelessly executed, have been the offspring of no common mind. Again, how often is not a laborious historiographer, particularly if of contrary politics, dismissed with immediate contempt, because, perchance, in his three full volumes, he has admitted two false dates, or haply mistakes the christened name of some Spanish admiral! Once more, how continually are not critical judgments falsified by the very extracts on which they rest! how often the pet passage of one review is the stock butt of another! Here you will say is cure and malady together, like viper's fat and fang: I trow not; mainly because not one man in a thousand takes the trouble to judge for himself. But it is needless to enumerate such instances; every man's conscience or his memory will supply examples wholesale: therefore, maltreated authors, bear witness to your own wrongs: jealously regarded by a struggling brotherhood, cruelly baited by self-constituted critics, the rejected of publishers, the victimized by booksellers, the garbled in statement, misinterpreted in meaning, suspected of friends, persecuted by foes—"O that mine enemy would write a book!" It is to put a neck into a noose, to lie quietly in the grove of Dr. Guillot's humane prescription: or, if not quite so tragical as this, it is at least to sit voluntarily in the stocks with Sir Hudibras, and dare the world's contempt; while fashionable—or unfashionable idiots, who are scarcely capable of a grammatical answer to a dinner invitation, (those formidably confounded he's and him's!)—think themselves privileged to join some inane laugh against a clever, but not yet famous, author, because, forsooth, one character in his novel may be an old acquaintance, or one epithet in a long poem may be weak, indelicate, tasteless, or foolish, or one philosophical fact in an essay is misstated, or one statistical conclusion seems to be exaggerated. It is perfectly paltry to behold stupid fellows, whose intellects against your most ordinary scribe vary from a rush-light to a "long four," as compared with a roasting, roaring kitchen-fire, affecting contemptuously to look down upon some unjustly neglected or mercilessly castigated labourer in the brick-fields of literature, for not being—can he help it?—a first-rate author, or because one reviewer in seven thinks he might have done his subject better justice. Take my word for it—if indeed I can be a fair witness —the man who has written a book, is above the unwriting average, and, as such, should be ranked mentally above them: no light research, and tact, and industry, and head-and-hand labour, are sufficient for a volume; even certain stolid performances in print do not shake my judgment; for arrant blockheads as sundry authors undoubtedly are, the average (mark, not all men, but the average) unwriting man is an author's intellectual inferior. All men, however well capable, have not perchance the appetite, nor the industry, nor the opportunity to fabricate a volume; nor, supposing these requisites, the moral courage (for moral courage, if not physical, must form part of an author's mind,) to publish the lucubration: but "I magnify mine office" above the unnumbered host of unwriting, uninformed, loose, unlettered gentry, who (as full of leisure as a cabbage, and as overflowing with redundant impudence as any Radical mob,) mainly tend to form by their masses the average penless animal-man, who could not hold a candle to any the most mediocre of the Marsyas-used authors of haply this week's journals. Spare them, victorious Apollos, spare! if libels that diminish wealth be punishable, is there no moral guilt in those legalized libels that do their utmost to destroy a character for wisdom, wit, learning, industry, and invention?—Critical flayer, try thou to write a book; learn experimentally how difficult, yet relieving; how nervous, yet gladdening; how ungracious, yet very sweet; how worldly-foolish, yet most wise; how conversant with scorn, yet how noble and ennobling an attribute of man, is —authorship.

All this rhetoric, impatient friend—and be a friend still, whether writer, reviewer, or unauthorial—serves at my most expeditious pace, opposing notions considered, to introduce what is (till to-morrow, or perhaps the next coming minute, but at any rate for this flitting instant of time,) my last notion of possible, but not probable, authorship: a rhodomontade oration, rather than an essay, after my own desultory and yet determinate fashion, to have been entituled—so is it spelled by act of parliament, and therefore let us in charity hope rightly—to have been entituled then,

THE AUTHOR'S TRIBUNAL;

A COURT OF APPEAL AGAINST AMATEUR AND CONNOISSEUR CRITICISMS:

and (the present being the next minute whereof I spake above) there has just hopped into my mind another taking title, which I generously present to any smarting scribe who may meditate a prose version of '*English Bards and Scotch Reviewers'—videlicet,*

ZOILOMASTRIX.

At length then have I liberty to yawn—a freedom whereof doubtless my readers have long been liverymen: I have written myself and my inkstand dry as Rosamond's pond; my brain is relieved, recreated, emptied; I go no longer heavily, as one that mourneth; and with gleeful face can I assure you that your author's mind is once again as light as his heart: but when crowding fancies come thick upon it, they bow it, and break it, and weary it, as clouds of pigeons settling gregariously on a trans-Atlantic forest; and when those thronging thoughts are comfortably fixed on paper, one feels, as an apple-tree may be supposed to feel, all the difference between the heavy down-dragging crop of autumn and the winged aërial blossom of sweet spring-tide. An involuntary author, just eased for the time of ever-exacting and accumulating notions, can sympathize with holiday-making Atlas, chuckling over a chance so lucky as the transfer of his pack to Hercules; and can comprehend the relief it must have been to that foolish sage in Rasselas, when assured that he no longer was afflicted with the care of governing a galaxy of worlds.

Some people are born to talk, with an incessant tongue illustrating perpetuity of motion in the much-abused mouth; some to indite solid continuous prose, with a labour-loving pen ever tenanting the hand; but I clearly was born a zoölogical anomaly, *with a pen in my mouth*, a sort of serpent-tongue. Heaven give it wisdom, and put away its poison!

Such being my character from birth, a paper-gossip, a writer from the cradle, I ought not demurely to apologize for nature's handicraft, nor excuse this light affliction of chattering in print.—Who asks you to read it?—Neither let me cast reflections on your temper or your intellect by too humble exculpation of this book of many themes; or must I then regard you as those sullen children in the market-place, whom piping cannot please, and sorrow cannot soften?

And now, friend, I've done. Require not, however shrewd your guess, my acknowledgment of this brain-child; forgive all unintended harms; supply what is lacking in my charities; politically, socially, authorially, think that I bigotize in theoretic fun, but am incarnate Tolerance for practical earnest. And so, giving your character fairer credit than if I feared you as one of those captious cautious people who make a man offender for an ill-considered word; commending to the cordial warmth of Humanity my unhatched score and more of book-eggs, to perfect which I need an Eccaleobion of literature; and scorning, as heartily as any Sioux chief, to prolong palaver, when I have nothing more to say; suffer me thus courteously to take of you my leave. And forasmuch as Lord Chesterfield recommends an exit to be heralded by a pungent speech, let me steal from quaint old Norris the last word wherewith I trouble you: "These are my thoughts; I might have spun them out into a greater length, but that I think a little plot of ground, thick-sown, is better than a great field, which for the most part of it lieth fallow."

APPENDIX.

AN AFTER-THOUGHT.

It will be quite in keeping with your author's mind, and consistently characteristic of his desultory indoles—(not indolence, pray you, good Anglican, albeit thereunto akin,)—if after having thus formally taken his *congé* with the help of a Petronius so redoubtable as Chesterfield, he just steps back again to induce you to have another last ramble. Now, the wherefore of this might sentimentally be veiled, were I but little honest, in professed attachment for my amiable reader, as though with Romeo I cried, "Parting in such sweet sorrow, that I could say farewell till it be morrow;" or it might be extenuated cacoethically, as though a new crop of fancies were sprung up already, an after-math rank and wild, before the gladdening shower of commendation has yet freshened-up my brown hay-field: or it might be disguised falsely, as if a parcel of precious MSS. had been lost by penny-postage, or stolen in the purlieus of Shoe-lane; but, instead of all these unworthy subterfuges, the truth shall be told plainly; we are yet too short by a sheet (so hints our publishing Procrustes) of the marketable volume. Accordingly, whether or not in this booklet your readership has already found seed sufficient for cyclopædias, I am free to admit that the expectant butterman at least has not his legitimate post-octavo allowance of three hundred pages; and to fill this aching void as cleverly and quickly as I can, is my first object in so rapid a return. That honesty is the best policy, deny who dare?

Still it is competent for me to confess worthier objects, (although, in point of their arising, they were secondary,) as further illustrative of my '*Author's Mind*' shown in other specimens; for example, a linsey-woolsey tapestry of many colours shall be hung upon the end of this arcade; the last few trees in this poor avenue shall bear the flowers of poetry as well as the fruit of prose; my swan (O, dub it not a goose!)

would, like a *prima-donna*, go off this theatre of fancy, singing. And again, suffer me, good friend, to think your charity still willing to be pleased: many weary pages back, I offered you to part with me in peace, if you felt small sympathies with a rambler so whimsical and lawless; surely, having walked together kindly until now, we shall not quarrel at the last.

Empty, however—empty, and rejoicing in its unthoughtful emptiness—have I boasted this my head but a page or two ago; and that boast, for all the critic's sneer, that no one will deny it, shall not be taken from me by renewal of determined meditations; now that my house is swept and garnished, I would not beckon back those old inhabitants. Neither let me heed so lightly of your intellect, as to hope to satisfy its reading with the scanty harvest of a *soil effete;* this license of writing up to measure shall not show me sterile, any more than that emancipation shall, by indulgence of thought, be disenchanted. And now to solve the problem: not to think, for my mind is in a regimen of truancy; not to fail in pleasing, if it be possible, the great world's implacable palate, therefore to eschew dilution of good liquor; and yet to render up in fair array the fitting tale of pages: well, if I may not metaphysically draw upon internal resources, I can at least externally and physically resort to yonder—desk; (drawer would have savoured of the Punic, which Scipio and I blot out with equal hate;) for therein lie *perdus* divers poeticals I fain would see in print; yea, start not at "poeticals," carp not at the threatening sound, for verily, even as carp—so called from *carpere*, to catch if you can, and the Saxon capp, to cavil, because when caught they don't pay for mastication—even as carp, a muddy fish, difficult to hook, and provocate of hostile criticism, conceals its lack of savour in the flavour of port-wine—even so shall strong prose-sauce be served up with my poor dozen of sonnets: and ye who would uncharitably breathe that they taste stronger of Lethe's mud than of Helicon's sweet water, treat me to a better dish, or carp not at my fishing.

Imagination, as I need not tell psychologists by this time, is my tyrant; I cannot sleep, nor sit out a sermon, nor remember yesterday, nor read in peace, (how calm in blessed quiet people seem to read!) without the distraction of a thousand fancies: I hold this an infirmity, not an accomplishment; a thing to be conquered, not to be coveted: and still I love it, suffering those chains of gossamer to wind about me, that seductive honey-jar yet again to trap me, like some poor insect; thus then my foolish idolatry heretofore hath hailed

IMAGINATION.

MY fond first love, sweet mistress of my mind,
Thy beautiful sublimity hath long
Charm'd mine affections, and entranced my song,
Thou spirit-queen, that sit'st enthroned, enshrined
Within this suppliant heart; by day and night
My brain is full of thee: ages of dreams,
Thoughts of a thousand worlds in visions bright,
Fear's dim terrific train, Guilt's midnight schemes,
Strange peeping eyes, soft smiling fairy faces,
Dark consciousness of fallen angels nigh,
Sad converse with the dead, or headlong races
Down the straight cliffs, or clinging on a shelf
Of brittle shale, or hunted thro' the sky!—
O, God of mind, I shudder at myself!

Now, friend reader, you have accustomed yourself to think that every thing in rhyme, *i. e.*, poetry, as you somewhat scornfully call it, must be false: and I am sorry to be obliged to grant you that a leaning towards plain matter-of-fact, is no wise characteristic of metrical enthusiasts. But believe me for a truth-teller; that sonnet (did you read it?) hints at some fearful verities; and that you may further apprehend this sweet ideal mistress of your author's mind, suffer me to introduce to your acquaintance

IMAGINATION PERSONIFIED.

DREAD Monarch-maid, I see thee now before me,
Searching my soul with those mysterious eyes,
Spell-bound I stand, thy presence stealing o'er me,
While all unnerved my trembling spirit dies:
Oh, what a world of untold wonder lies
Within thy silent lips! how rare a light
Of conquer'd joys and ecstasies repress'd
Beneath thy dimpled cheek shines half-confess'd!
In what luxuriant masses, glossy bright,
Those raven locks fall shadowing thy fair breast!
And, lo! that bursting brow, with gorgeous wings,
And vague young forms of beauty coyly hiding
In thy crisp curls, like cherubs there abiding—
Charmer, to thee my heart enamour'd springs.

Such, then, and of me so well beloved, is that abstracted Platonism. But verily the fear of imagination would far outbalance any love of it, if crime had peopled for a man that viewless world with spectres, and the Medusa-head of Justice were shaking her snakes in his face. And, by way of a parergon observation, how terrible, most terrible, to the guilty soul must be the solitary silent system now so popular among those cold legislative schemers, who have ground the poor man to starvation, and would hunt the criminal to madness! How false is that political philosophy which seeks to reform character by leaving conscience caged up in loneliness for months, to gnaw into its diseased self, rather than surrounding it with the wholesome counsels of better living minds. It is not often good for man to be alone: and yet in its true season, (parsimoniously used, not prodigally abused,) solitude does fair service, rendering also to the comparatively innocent mind precious pleasures: religion prĕsupposed, and a judgment strong enough of muscle to rein-in the coursers of Imagination's car, I judge it good advice to prescribe for most men an occasional course of

SOLITUDE.

THEREFORE delight thy soul in solitude,
Feeding on peace; if solitude it be
To feel that million creatures, fair and good,
With gracious influences circle thee;
To hear the mind's own music; and to see
God's glorious world with eyes of gratitude,
Unwatch'd by vain intruders. Let me shrink
From crowds, and prying faces, and the noise
Of men and merchandise; far nobler joys
Than chill Society's false hand hath given,
Attend me when I'm left alone to think.
To think--alone?—Ah, no, not quite alone;
Save me from that—cast out from earth and heaven,
A friendless, Godless, isolated ONE!

But of these higher metaphysicals, these fancy-bred extravagations, perhaps somewhat too much: you will dub me dreamer, if not proser —or rather, poet, as the more modern reproach. Let us then, by way of clearing our mind at once of these hallucinations, go forth quickly into the fresh green fields, and expatiate with glad hearts on these full-blown glories of

SUMMER.

WARM summer! Yes, the very word is warm;
The hum of bees is in it, and the sight
Of sunny fountains glancing silver light,
And the rejoicing world, and every charm
Of happy nature in her hour of love,
Fruits, flowers, and flies, in rainbow-glory bright:
The smile of God glows graciously above,

And genial earth is grateful; day by day
Old faces come again with blossoms gay,
Gemming in gladness meadow, garden, grove:
Haste with thy harvest, then, my softened heart,
Awake thy better hopes of better days,
Bring in thy fruits and flowers of thanks and praise,
And in creation's pæan take thy part.

How different in sterner beauty was the landscape not long since! The energies of universal life prisoned up in temporary obstruction; every black hedge-row tufted with woolly snow, like some Egyptian mother mourning for her children; shrubs and plants fettered up in glittering chains, motionless as those stone-struck feasters before the *head of Gorgon; and the dark-green fir-trees swathed in heavy curtains* of iridescent whiteness. Contrast is ever pleasurable; therefore we need scarcely apologize for an ice in the dog-days—I mean for this present unseasonable introduction of dead

WINTER.

As some fair statue, white and hard and cold,
Smiling in marble, rigid, yet at rest,
Or like some gentle child of beauteous mould,
Whose placid face and softly swelling breast
Are fixed in death, and on them bear impress
His magic seal of peace—so, frozen, lies
The loveliness of nature: every tree
Stands hung with lace against the clear blue skies;
The hills are giant waves of glistering snow;
Rare and northern fowl, now strangely tame to see,
With ruffling plumage cluster on the bough,
And tempt the murderous gun; mouse-like, the wren
Hides in the new-cut hedge; and all things now
Fear starving Winter more than cruel men.

Ay, "cruel men:" that truest epithet for monarch-man must be the tangent from which my Pegasus shall strike his hoof for the next flight. Who does not writhe while reading details of cruelty, and who would not rejoice to find even there somewhat of

CONSOLATION?

SCHOLAR of Reason, Grace, and Providence,
Restrain thy bursting and indignant tears;
With tenderest might unerring Wisdom steers
Through those mad seas the bark of Innocence.

Doth thy heart burn for vengeance on the deed—
  Some barbarous deed wrought out by cruelty
On woman, or on famish'd childhood's need,
Yea, on these fond dumb dogs—doth thy heart bleed
  For pity, child of sensibility?
Those tears are gracious, and thy wrath most right
  Yet patience, patience; there is comfort still;
The Judge is just; a world of love and light
  Remains to counterpoise the load of ill,
  And the poor victim's cup with angel's food to fill.

For, as my Psycotherion has long ago informed you, I hope there is some sort of heaven yet in reserve for the brute creation: if otherwise, in respect of costermongers' donkeys, Kamskatdales' gaunt starved dogs, the Guacho's horse, spurred deep with three-inch rowels, the angler's worm, Strasburgh geese, and poor footsore curs harnessed to ill-balanced trucks—for all these and many more I, for one, sadly stand in need of consolation. Meanwhile, let us change the subject. After a dose of cruel cogitations, and this corrupting converse with Phalaris and Domitian, what better sweetener of thoughts than an "olive-branch" in the waters of Marah? Spend a moment in the nursery; it is happily fashionable now, as well as pleasurable, to sport awhile with Nature's prettiest playthings; the praises of children are always at the tip of my—pen, that is, tongue, you remember, and often have I told the world, in all the pride of print, of my fond infantile predilections: then let this little Chanson be added to the rest; we will call it

MARGARET.

A song of gratitude and cheerful prayer
  Still shall go forth my pretty babes to greet,
As on life's firmament, serenely fair,
  Their little stars arise, with aspects sweet
Of mild successive radiance: that small pair,
  Ellen and Mary, having gone before
In this affection's welcome, the dear debt
Here shall be paid to gentle Margaret:
  Be thou indeed a pearl—in pureness, more
Than beauty, praise, or price; full be thy cup,
  Mantling with grace, and truth with mercy met,
  With warm and generous charities flowing o'er;
And when the Great King makes his jewels up,
  Shine forth, child-angel, in His coronet!

And while hovering about this fairy-land of sweet-home scenery, and confessing thankfully to these domestic affections, your author knows one heart at least that will be gladdened, one face that will be brightened by the following

BIRTH-DAY PRAYER.

Mother, dear mother, no unmeaning rhyme,
  No mere ingenious compliment of words,
My heart pours forth at this auspicious time:
  I know a simple honest prayer affords
  More music on affection's thrilling cords,
More joy, than can be measured or express'd
  In song most sweet, or eloquence sublime.
Mother, I bless thee! God doth bless thee too!
In these thy children's children thou *art* blest,
  With dear old pleasures springing up anew:
And blessings wait upon thee still, my mother!
  Blessings to come, this many a happy year;
For, losing thee, where could we find another
  So kind, so true, so tender, and—so dear?

Is it an impertinence—I speak etymologically—to have dropped that sonnet here?—Be it as you will, my Zoilus; let me stand convicted of honesty and love: I ask no higher praise in this than to have pleased my mother.

Penman as I am, have been, and shall be, innumerable letters have grown beneath my goose-quill. Who cannot say the same indeed? For in these patriotic days, for mere country's love and post-office prosperity, every body writes to every body about every thing, or, as oftener happens, about nothing. Nevertheless, I wish some kind pundit would invent a corrosive ink, warranted to consume a letter within a week after it had been read and answered: then should we have fewer of those ephemeral documents treasured up in pigeon-holes, and docketed correspondence for possible publication. Not Byron, nor Lamb, nor West, nor Gray, with all their epistolary charms, avail to persuade my prejudice that it is honest to publish a private letter: if written with that view, the author is a hypocrite in his friendships; if not so, the decent veil of privacy is torn from social life, confidence is rebuked, betrayed, destroyed; and the suspicion of eaves-droppings and casual scribblings to be posthumously printed, makes silence truly wisdom, and grim reserve a virtue. This public appetite for secret information, and, if possible, for hinted scandal—this unhallowed spirit of outward curiosity trespassing upon the sacred precincts of a man's own circle—is to the real author's mind a thing to be feared, if he is weak—to be circumspectly watched, if he is wise. Such is the present hunger for this kind of reading, that it would be diffidence, not presumption, in the merest school-boy to dread the future publication of his holiday letters; who knows—I may jump scathless from the Monument, or in these Popish times become excommunicated by special bull, or fly round the world in a balloon, or attain to the authorship of forty volumes, or be half-smothered by a valet-de-place, or get indicted for inveterate Toryism, or any how, I may—notwithstanding all present obscurities that intervene—wake one of these fine mornings, and find myself famous: and what then? The odds at Tattersall's would be twelve to one that sundry busy-bodies, booksellers or otherwise, would scrape together with malice prepense, and keep *câchet* for future print, a multitude of careless scrawls that should have been burnt within an hour of the reading. Now, is not this a thing to be exclaimed against? And, utterly improbable on the ground of any merit in themselves as I should judge their publication (but for certain stolidities of the same sort, that often-times have wearied me in print), I choose to let my author's mind here enter its eternal protest against any such treachery regarding private

LETTERS.

TEAR, scatter, burn, destroy—but keep them not;
  I hate, I dread those living witnesses
Of varying self, of good or ill forgot,
  Of altered hopes, and withered kindnesses.
  Oh! call not up those shadows of the dead,
Those visions of the past, that idly blot
  The present with regret for blessings fled:
  This hand that wrote, this ever-teeming head,
This flickering heart is full of chance and change;
  I would not have you watch my weaknesses,
Nor how my foolish likings roam and range,
  Nor how the mushroom friendships of a day
  Hastened in hot-bed ripeness to decay,
Nor how to mine own self I grow so strange.

So anathema to editors, maranatha to publishers of all such hypothetical post-obits!

Every one can comprehend something of an author's ease, when he sees his manuscript in print: it is safe; no longer a treasure uninsurable, no longer a locked-up care: it is emancipated, glorified, incapable of real extermination; it has reached a changeless condition; the chrysalis of illegible cacography has burst its bonds, and flies living through the world on the wings of those true Dædali, Faust, and Gutemberg: the transition-state is passed; henceforth for his brain-child set free from that nervous slumber, its parent calmly can expect the oblivion of no more than a death-like sleep, if he be not indeed buoyed up with certain hope of immortality. "'Tis pleasant sure to see one's self in print," is the adequate cause for ninety books out of a hundred; and, though zeal might be the ostentatious stalking-horse, my candour shall give no better excuse for the fourteen lines that follow; they require but this preface: a most venerable chapel of old time, picturesque and full of interest, is dropping to decay, within a mile of me; where it is, and whose the fault, are askings improper to be answered: nevertheless, I cast upon the waters this meagre morsel of

APPEAL.

SHAME on thee, Christian, cold and covetous one!
The laws (I praise them not for this) declare
That ancient, loved, deserted house of prayer
As money's worth a layman landlord's own.
Then use it as thine own; thy mansion there
Beneath the shadow of this ruinous church
Stands new and decorate; thine every shed
And barn is neat and proper; I might search
Thy comfortable farms, and well despair
Of finding dangerous ruin overhead,
And damp unwholesome mildew on the walls:
Arouse thy better self: restore it; see,
Through thy neglect the holy fabric falls!
Fear, lest that crushing guilt should fall on thee.

I fear much, poor book, this finale of jingling singing will jar upon the public ear; all men must shrink from a lengthy snake with a rattle in its tail: and this ballast a-stern of over-ponderous poetry may chance to swamp so frail a skiff. But I have promised a dozen sonnets in this after-thought Appendix; yea, and I will keep that promise at all mortal hazards, even to the superadded unit proverbial of dispensing Fornarinas. Ten have been told off fairly, and now we come upon the gay court-cards. After so much of villanous political ferment, society returns at length to its every-day routine, heedful of other oratory than harangues from the hustings, and glad of other reading than figurative party-speeches. Yet am I bold to recur, just for a thought or two, to my whilom patriotic hopes and fears: fears indeed came first upon me, but hopes finally out-voted them: briefly, then, begin upon the worst, and endure, with what patience you possess, this croaky stave of bitter

POLITICS.

CHILL'D is the patriot's hope, the poet's prayer:
  Alas for England, and her tarnish'd crown,
  Her sun of ancient glory going down,
Her foes triumphant in her friends' despair:
What wonder should the billows overwhelm
  A bark so mann'd by Comus and his crew,
"Youth at the prow, and pleasure at the helm?"
Yet, no!—we will not fear; the loathing realm
  At length has burst its chains; a motley few,
  The pseudo-saint, the boasting infidel,
The demagogue, and courtier, hand in hand
  No more besiege our Zion's citadel:
But high in hope comes on this nobler band
For God, the sovereign, and our father-land.

That last card, you may remember, must reckon as the knave; and therefore is consistently regarding an ominous trisyllable, which rhymes to "knavish tricks" in the national anthem; our suit now leads us in regular succession to the queen, a topic (it were Milesian to say a subject) whereon now, as heretofore, my loyalty shall never be found lacking. In old Rome's better antiquity, a slave was commissioned to whisper counsel in the ear of triumphant generals or emperors; and, in old England's less enlightened youth, a baubled fool was privileged to blurt out verities, which bearded wisdom dared not hint at. Now, I boast myself free, a citizen of no mean city—my commission signed by duty—my counsel guarantied by truth: and if, O still intruding Zoilus, the liberality of your nature provokes you to class me truly in the family of fools, let your antiquarian ignorance of those licensed Gothamites blush at its abortive malice; the arrow of your sarcasm bounds from my target blunted; pick up again the harmless reed: for, not to insist upon the prevalence of knaves, and their moral postponement to mere lack-wits, let me tell you that wise men, and good men, and shrewd men, were those ancient baubled fools: therefore would I gladly be thought of their fraternity.

But our twelfth sonnet is waiting, save the mark! Stay: there ought to intervene a solemn pause; for your author's mind, on the spur of the occasion, pours forth an unpremeditated song of free-spoken, uncompromising, patriotic counsel; let its fervency atone for its presumption

BOLD in my freedom, yet with homage meek,
  As duty prompts and loyalty commands,
To thee, O, queen of empires! would I speak.

Behold, the most high God hath giv'n to thee
Kingdoms and glories, might and majesty,
Setting thee ruler over many lands;
Him first to serve, O monarch, wisely seek:
And many people, nations, languages,
Have laid their welfare in thy sovereign hands;
Them next to bless, to prosper and to please,
Nobly forget thyself, and thine own ease:
Rebuke ill-counsel; rally round thy state
The scattered good, and true, and wise, and great:
So Heav'n upon thee shed sweet influences!

And now for my Raffaellesque disguise of a vulgar baker's twelve, the largess muffin of Mistress Fornarina: thirteen cards to a suit, and thirteen to the dozen, are proverbially the correct thing; but, as in regular succession I have come upon the king card, I am free to confess—(pen, why will you repeat again such a foolish, stale Joe-Millerism?)—the subject a dilemma. Natheless, my good nature shall give a royal chance to criticism most malign: whether candour acknowledge it or not, doubtless the author's mind reigns dominant in the author's book; and, notwithstanding the self-silence of blind Mæonides, (a right notable exception,) it holds good as a rule that the majority of original writings, directly or indirectly, concern a man's own self; his whims and his crotchets, his knowledge and his ignorance, wisdom and folly, experiences and suspicions, therein find a place prepared for them. Scott's life naturally produced his earlier novels; in the '*Corsair*,' the '*Childe*,' and the '*Don*,' no one can mistake the hero-author; Southey's works, Shelley's, and Wordsworth's, are full of adventure, feeling, and fancy, personal to the writers, at least equally with the sonnets of Petrarch or of Shakspeare. And as with instances illustrious as those, so with all humbler followers, the skiffs, pinnaces, and heavy barges in the wake of those gallant ships: an author's library, and his friends, his hobbies and amusements, business and pleasure, fears and wishes, accidents of life, and qualities of soul, all mingle in his writings with a harmonizing individuality; nay, the very countenance and hand-writing, alike with choice of subject and style and method of their treatment, illustrate, in one word, the author's mind. These things being so, what hinders it from occupying, as in honesty it does, the king's place in this pack of sonnets? Nevertheless, forasmuch as by such occupancy an ill-tempered sarcasm might charge it with conceit; know then that my humbler meaning here is to put it lowest and last, even in the place of wooden-spoon; for this also (being mindful of the twelve apostle-spoons from old time antecedent) is a legitimate thirteener: and so, while in extricating my muse from the folly of serenading a non-existent king, I have candidly avowed the general selfishness of printing, believe that, in this avowal, I take the lowest seat, so well befitting one of whom it may ungraciously be asked, Where do fools buy their logic?

List, then, oh list! while generically, not individually I claim for authorship

THE CATHEDRAL MIND.

TEMPLE of truths most eloquently spoken,
Shrine of sweet thoughts veiled round with words of power,
The '*Author's Mind,*' in all its hallowed riches,
Stands a cathedral: full of precious things;
Tastefully built in harmonies unbroken,
Cloister, and aisle, dark crypt, and aëry tower:
Long-treasured relics in the fretted niches,
And secret stores, and heap'd-up offerings,
Art's noblest gems, with every fruit and flower,
Paintings and sculpture, choice imaginings,
Its plenitude of wealth and praise betoken:
An ever-burning lamp portrays the soul;
Deep music all arouud enchantment flings;
And God's great Presence consecrates the whole.

Now at length, in all verity, I have said out my say: nor publisher nor printer shall get more copy from me: neither, indeed, would it before have been the case, for all that Damastic argument, were it not that many beginnings—and you remember my proverbial preliminarizing—should, for mere antithesis' sake, be endowed with a counterpoise of many endings. So, in this second parting, let me humbly suggest to gentle reader these: that nothing is at once more plebeian and unphilosophical than—censure, in a world where nothing can be perfect, and where apathy is held to be good-breeding; *item*, (I am quoting Scott,) that "it is much more easy to destroy than to build, to criticise than to compose;" *item*, (Sir Walter again, *ipsissima verba*, in a letter to Miss Seward,) that there are certain literary "gentlemen who appear to be a sort of tinkers, who, unable to *make* pots and pans, set up for *menders* of them, and often make two holes in patching one;" *item*, that in such possible cases as "exercise" for "exorcise," "repeat" for repent," "depreciate" for "deprecate," and the like, an indifferent scribe is always at the mercy of compositors; and lastly, that if it is, by very far, easier to read a book than to write one, it is also, by at least as much, worthier of a noble mind to give credit for good intentions, rather than for bad, or indifferent, or none at all, even where hypercriticism may appear to prove that the effort itself has been a failure.

PROBABILITIES;

AN AID TO FAITH.

BY THE

AUTHOR OF "PROVERBIAL PHILOSOPHY.'

ALMOST THOU PERSUADEST ME TO BE A CHRISTIAN."

HARTFORD:

PUBLISHED BY SILAS ANDRUS & SON.

1851.

PROBABILITIES.

AN AID TO FAITH.

The certainty of those things which most surely are believed among us, is a matter quite distinct from their antecedent probability or improbability. We know, and take for facts, that Cromwell and Napoleon existed, and are persuaded that their characters and lives were such as history reports them: but it is another thing, and one eminently calculated to disturb any disbeliever of such history, if a man were enabled to show, that, from the condition of social anarchy, there was an antecedent likelihood for the use of military despots; that, from the condition of a popular puritanism, or a popular infidelity, it was previously to have been expected that such leaders should have the several characteristics of a bigoted zeal for religion, or a craving appetite for worldly glory; that, from the condition liable to revolutions, it was probable to find such despots arising out of the middle class; and that, from the condition of rëaction incidental to all human violences, there was a clear expectability that the power of such military monarchs should not be continued to their natural heirs.

Such a line of argument, although in no measure required for the corroboration of facts, might have considerable power to persuade *à priori* the man, who had not hitherto seen reason to credit such facts from posterior evidence. It would have rolled away a great stone, which to such a mind might otherwise have stood as a stumbling-block on the very threshold of truth. It would have cleared off a heavy mist, which might prevent him from discerning the real nature of the scene in which he stood. It would have shown him that, what others know to be fact, is, even to him who does not know it, become antecedently probable; and that Reason is not only no enemy to Faith, but is ready and willing to acknowledge its alliance.

Take a second illustration, by way of preliminary. A woodman, cleaving an oak, finds an iron ball in its centre; he sees the fact, and of course believes; some others believing on his testimony. But a certain village-pundit, habitually sceptical of all marvels, is persuaded that the wonder has been fabricated by our honest woodman; until the parson, a good historian, coming round that way, proclaims it a most interesting circumstance, because it was one naturally to have been expected; for that, here was the spot where, two hundred years ago, a great battle had been fought: and it was no improbability at all that a carbine-bullet should have penetrated a sapling, nor that the tree should thereafter have grown old with the iron at its heart. How unreasonable then would appear the pundit's incredulity, if persisted in: how suddenly enlightened the rational faith of the rustic: how seasonable would be felt the useful learning of him, whose knowledge well applied can thus unfetter truth from the bandages of ignorance.

Illustrations, if apt, are so well adapted to persuade towards a particular line of argument, that, at the risk of diffuseness, and because minds being various are variously touched, one by one thought and one by another, I think fit to add yet more of a similar tendency: in the hope that, by a natural induction, such instances may smoothe our way.

When an eminent living geologist was prosecuting his researches at Kirkdale cave, Yorkshire, he had calculated so nicely on the antecedent probabilities, that his commands to the labourers were substantially these: "Take your mattocks, and pick up that stone flooring; then take your basket, and fill it—with the bones of hyænas and other creatures which you will find there." We may fancy the ridicule wherewith ignorance might have greeted science: but lo, the triumph of philosophy, when its mandate soon assumed a bodily shape in—bushels of bones gnawed as by wild beasts, and here and there a grinning skull that looked like a hyæna's! Do we not see how this bears on our coming argument? Such a deposit was very unlikely to be found there in the eyes of the unenlightened: but very likely to the wise man's ken. The real probabilities were in favour of a strange fact, though the seeming probabilities were against it.

Take another. We are all now convinced of the existence of America; and so, some three or four hundred years back, was Christopher Columbus—but nobody else. Alone, he proved that mighty continent so probable, from geometrical measurements, and the balance of the world, and tides, and trade-winds, and casual floatsams driven from some land beneath the setting sun, that he was antecedently convinced of the fact: and it would have been a shock to his reason, as well as to his faith, had he found himself able to sail due west from Lisbon to China, without having struck against his huge probability. I purposely abstain from applying every illustration, or showing its specific difference regarding our theme. It is better to lead a mind to think for itself than to endeavour to forestall every notion.

Another. A Kissoor merchant in Timbuctoo is told of the existence of water hard and cold as marble. All the experience of his nation is against it. He disbelieves. However, after no long time, the testimony of two native princes who have been *fêted* in England, and have seen ice, shakes his once not unreasonable incredulity: and the additional idea brought soon to his remembrance, that, as lead cools down from hot fluidity to a solid lump, so, in the absence of solar heat, in all probability would water—corroborates and makes acceptable by analogous likelihood the doctrine simultaneously evidenced by credible witnesses.

Yet one more illustration for the last. Few things in nature appear more unlikely to the illiterate, than that a living toad should be found prisoned in a block of limestone; nevertheless, evidence goes to prove that such cases are not uncommon. Now, if, instead of limestone, which is a water-product, the creature had been found embedded in granite, which is a fire-product; although the fact might have been from eyesight equally unimpeachable, how much more unlikely such a circumstance would have appeared in the judgment of science. To the rustic, the limestone case is as stout a puzzle as the granite one; but *à priori*, the philosopher—taking into account the aqueous fluidity of such a matrix at a period when reptiles were abundant, the torpid qualities of the toad itself, and the fact that time is scarcely an element in the absence of air—arrives at an antecedent probability, which comforts his acceptance of the fact. The granite would have staggered his reason, even though his own experience or the testimony of others were sufficient, nay, imperative, to assure his faith: but in the case of limestone, Reason even helps Faith; nay, anticipates and leads it in, by suggesting the wonder to be previously probable. How truly, and how strongly this bears upon our theme, let any such philosophizing mind consider.

But enough of illustrations: although these, multipliable to any amount, might bring, each in its own case, some specific tendency to throw light upon the path we mean to tread: it is wiser perhaps, as implying more confidence in the reader's intellectual powers, to leave other analogous cases to the suggestion of his own mind; also, not to vex him in every instance with the intrusive finger of an obvious application.

Meanwhile, it is a just opportunity to clear the way at once of some obstructions, by disposing of a few matters personal to the writer; and by touching upon sundry other preliminary considerations.

1. The line of thought proposed is intended to show it probable that any thing which has been or is, might, viewed antecedently to its existence, by an exercise of pure reason, have by possibility been guessed: and on the hypothesis of sufficient keenness and experience, that this idea may be carried even to the future. Any thing, meaning every thing, is a word not used unadvisedly; for this is merely a suggestive treatise, starting a rule capable of infinite application: and, notwithstanding that we have here and now confined its elucidation to some matters of religious moment only, as occupying a priority of importance, and at all times deserving the lead; still, if knowledge availed, and time and space permitted, I scarcely doubt that a vigorous and illuminated intellect might so far enlarge on the idea, as to show the antecedent probability of every event which has happened in the kingdoms of nature, providence, and grace: nay, of directing his guess at coming matters with no uncertain aim into the realms of the immediate future. The perception of cause in operation enables him to calculate the consequence, even perhaps better than the prophecy of cause could in the prior case enable him to suspect the consequence. But, in this brief life, and under its disturbing circumstances, there is little likelihood of accomplishing in practice all that the swift mind sees it easy to dream in theory: and if other and wiser pens are at all helped in the good aim to justify the ways of God with man, and to clear the course of truth, by some of the notions broadcast in this treatise, its errand will be well fulfilled.

2. Whether or not the leading idea, so propounded, is new, or is new in its application as an auxiliary to Christian evidences, the writer is unaware: to his own mind it has occurred quite spontaneously and on a sudden; neither has he scrupled to place it before others with whatever ill advantage of celerity, because it seemed to his own musings to shed a flood of light upon deep truths, which may not prove unwelcome nor unuseful to the doubting minds of many. It is true that in this, as in most other human efforts, the realization of idea in concrete falls far short of its abstract conception in the mind: there, all was clear, quick, and easy; here, the necessity of words, and the constraints of an unwilling perseverance, clog alike the wings of fancy and the feet of sober argument: insomuch that the difference is felt to be quite humiliating between the thoughts as they were thought, and the thoughts as they are

written. Minerva, springing from the head of Jove, is not more unlike the heavily-treading Vulcan.

3. Necessarily, that the argument be (so to speak) complete, and on the wise principle that no fortresses be left untaken in the rear, it must be the writer's fate to attempt a demonstration of the anterior probability of truths, which a child of reason can not only now never doubt as fact, but never could have thought improbable. Instance the first effort, showing it to have been expectable that there should, in any conceived beginning, have existed a Something, a Great Spirit, whom we call God. To have to argue of the mighty Maker, that HE was an antecedent probability, would appear a most needless attempt; if it did not occur as the first link in a chain of arguments less open to objection by the thoughtless. With our little light to try to prove *à priori* the dazzling mystery of a Divine Tri-unity, might (unreasonably viewed) be assailed as a presumptuous and harmful thing; but it is our wise prerogative, if and when we can, to "Prove all things." Moreover, we live in a world wherein Truth's greatest enemy is the man who shrinks from endeavouring at least to clear away the mists and clouds that veil her precious aspect; and at a time when it behooves the reverent Christian to put on his panoply of faith and prayer, and meet in argument, according to the grace and power given to him—not indeed the blaspheming infidel, for such a foe is unreasonable and unworthy of an answer, but—the often candid, anxious, and involuntary doubter; the mind, which, righteously vexed with the thousand corruptions of truth, and sorely disappointed at the conduct of its herd of false disciples, from a generous misconception is embracing error: the mind, never enough tenderly treated, but commonly taunted as a sceptic which yet with a natural manliness asserts the just prerogative of thinking for itself: fairly enough requiring, though rarely finding, evidence either to prop the weakness of a merely educational faith, or to argue away the objections to Christianity so rife in the clashing doctrines and unholy lives of its pseudo-sectaries. One of our poets hath said, "He has no hope who never had a fear:" it is quite as true (and take this saying for thy comfort, any harassed misbelieving mind), He has no faith, who never had a doubt. There is hope of a mind which doubts, because it thinks; because it troubles itself to think about what the mass of nominal Christians live threescore years and die of very mammonism, without having had one earnest thought about one difficulty, or one misgiving: there is hope of a man, who, not licentious nor scornful, from simple misconception, misbelieves; there is just and

reasonable hope that (the misconception once removed) his faith will shine forth all the warmer for a temporary state of winter. To such do I address myself: not presumptuously imagining that I can satisfy by my poor thoughts all the doubts, cavils and objections of minds so keen and curious; not affecting to sail well among the shoals of metaphysics, nor to plumb unerringly the deeper gulphs of reason; but asking them for awhile to bear with me and hear me to the end patiently; with me, convinced of what (κατ' ἐξοχήν) is Truth, by far surer and stronger arguments than any of the less considerations here expounded as auxiliary thereto; to bear with me, and prove for themselves at this penning of my thoughts (if haply I am helped in such high enterprise), whether indeed those doctrines and histories which the Christian world admit, were antecedently improbable, that is, unreasonable: whether, on the contrary, there did not exist, prior to any manifestation of such facts and doctrines, an exceeding likelihood that they would be so and so developed: and whether on the whole, led by reason to the threshold of faith, it may be worth while to encounter other arguments, which have rendered probabilities now certain.

4. It is very material to keep in memory the only scope and object of this essay. We do not pretend to add one jot of evidence, but only to prepare the mind to receive evidence: we do not attempt to prove facts, but only to accelerate their admission by the removal of prejudice. If a bed-ridden meteorologist is told that it rains, he may or he may not receive the fact from the force of testimony; but he will certainly be more prĕdisposed to receive it, if he finds that his weatherglass is falling rather than rising. The fact remains the same, it rains; but the mind—precluded by circumstances from positive personal assurance of such fact, and able only to arrive at truth from exterior evidence—is in a fitter state for belief of the fact from being already made aware that it was probable. Let it not then be inferred, somewhat perversely, that because antecedent probabilities are the staple of our present argument, the theme itself, Religion, rests upon hypotheses so slender: it rests not at all upon such straws as probabilities, but on posterior evidence far more firm. What we now attempt is not to prop the ark, but favourably to prĕdispose the mind of any reckless Uzzah, who might otherwise assail it; not to strengthen the weak places of religion, but to annul such disinclination to receive Truth, as consists in prejudice and misconception of its likelihood. The goodly ship is built upon the stocks, the platforms are reared, and the cradle is ready; but mistaken prĕconceptions may scatter the

incline with gravel-stones rather than with grease, and thus put a needless hindrance to the launching: whereas a clear idea that the probabilities are in favour, rather than the reverse, will make all smooth, lubricate, and easy. If, then, we fail in this attempt, no disservice whatever is done to Truth itself; no breach is made in the walls, no mine sprung, no battlement dismantled; all the evidences remain as they were; we have taken nothing away. Even granting matters seemed anteriorily improbable, still, if evidence proved them true, such anterior unlikelihood would entirely be merged in the stoutly proven facts. Moreover, if we be adjudged to have succeeded, we have added nothing to Truth itself; no, nor to its outworks. That sacred temple stands complete, firm and glorious from corner-stone to top-stone. We do but sweep away the rubbish at its base; the drifting desert sands that choke its portals. We only serve that cause (a most high privilege), by enlisting a prĕjudgment in its favour. We propose herein an auxiliary to evidence, not evidence itself; a finger-post to point the way to faith; a little light of reason on its path. The risk is really nothing; but the advantage, under favour, may be much.

5. It is impossible to elude the discussion of topics, which in their direct tendencies, or remoter inferences, may, to the author at least, prove dangerous or disputable ground. If a "great door and effectual" is opened to him, doubtless he will raise or meet with many adversaries. Besides mere haters of his creed, despisers of his arguments, and protestors, loud and fierce against his errors; he may possibly fall foul of divers unintended heresies; he may stumble unwittingly on the relics of exploded schisms; he may exhume controversies in metaphysical or scholastical polemics, long and worthily extinct. If this be so, he can only plead, *Mea culpa, mea culpa, mea maxima culpa.* But it is open to him also to protest against the common critical folly of making an offender for a word: of driving analogies on all four feet, and straining thoughts beyond their due proportions. Above all, never let a reader stir one inch beyond, far less against, his own judgment: if there seem to be sufficient reasons, well: if otherwise, let me walk uncompanied. The first step especially is felt to be a very difficult one; perhaps very debatable: for aught I know, it may be merely a vain insect caught in the cobweb of metaphysics, soon to be destroyed, and easily to be discussed at leisure by some Aranean logician. However, it seemed to my midnight musings a probable mode of arriving at truth, though somewhat unsatisfactorily told from poverty of thought and language.

Moreover, it would have been, in such *à priori* argument, ridiculous to have commenced by announcing a posterior conclusion: for this cause did I do my humble best to work it out anew: and however supererogatory it may seem at first sight to the majority of readers, those keener minds whom I mainly address, and whose interests I wish to serve, will recognise the attempt as at least consistent: and will be ready to admit that if the arduous effort prove anteriorly a First Great Cause, and His attributes, be futile (which, however, I do not admit), it was an attempt unneeded on the score of its own merits; albeit, with an obvious somewhat of justice, pure reason may desire to begin at the beginning. No one, who thinks at all upon religion, however misbelieving, can entertain any mental prejudice against the existence of a Deity, or against the received character of His attributes. Such a man would be merely in a savage state, irrational: whilst his own mind, so speculating, would stand itself proof positive of an Intellectual Father; either immediately, as in the first man's case, or mediately, as in our own, it must have sprung out of that Being, who is emphatically the Good One—God. But if, as is possible, a mind, capable of thinking, and keen to think on other themes, from any cause, educational or moral, has neglected this great track of mediation, has "forgotten God," and "had him *not* in all his thoughts," such an one I invite to walk with me; and, in spite of all incompleteness and insufficiency, uncaptious of much that may haply be fanciful or false, briefly and in outline to test with me sundry probabilities of the Christian scheme, considered antecedently to its elucidation.

A GOD: AND HIS ATTRIBUTES.

I WILL commence with a noble, and, as I believe, an inspired sentence: than which no truth uttered by philosophers ever was more clearly or more sublimely expressed. "In the beginning was the Word: and the Word was with God; and the Word was God." In its due course, we will consider especially the difference between the Word and God; likewise the seeming contradiction, but true concord, of being simultaneously God, and with God. At present, and previously to the true commencement of our *à priori* thoughts, let us, by a word or two, paraphrase that brief but comprehensive sentence, "In the beginning was the Word." Eternity has no beginning, as it has no end: the clock of Time is futile there: it might as well attempt to go in vacuo. Nevertheless, in respect to finite intelligences like ourselves, seeing that eternity is an idea totally inconceivable, it is wise, nay it is only possible, to be presented to the mind piecemeal. Even our deepest mathematicians do not scruple to speak of points "infinitely remote;" as if in that phrase there existed no contradiction of terms. So, also, we pretend in our emptiness to talk of eternity past, time present, and eternity to come; the fact being that, muse as a man may, he can entertain no idea of an existence which is not measurable by time: any more than he can conceive of a colour unconnected with the rainbow, or of a musical note beyond the seven sounds. The plain intention of the words is this: place the starting-post of human thought as far back into eternity as you will, be it what man counts a thousand ages, or ten thousand times ten thousand, or be these myriads multiplied again by millions, still, in any such Beginning, and in the beginning of all beginnings (for so must creatures talk)—then was God. He Was: the scholar knows full well the force of the original term, the philological distinctions between εἰμί and γίγνομαι: well pleased, he reads as of the Divinity ἦν, He self-existed; and equally well pleased he reads of the humanity ἐγεννήθη, he was born. The thought and phrase ἦν sympathizes, if it has not an identity, with the Hebrew's unutterable Name. He then, whose title, amongst all others likewise denoting excellence supreme and glory underivative, is essentially "I am;" He who, relatively to us as to all creation else, has a new name wisely chosen in "the Word,"—the great expression of the idea of God; this mighty Intelligence is found in any such beginning self-existent. That teaching is a mere fact, known posteriorly from the proof of all things created, as well as by many wonderful signs, and the clear voice of revelation. We do not attempt to prove it; that were easy and obvious: but our more difficult endeavour at present is to show how antecedently propable it was that God should be: and that so being, He should be invested with the reasonable attributes, wherewithal we know His glorious Nature to be clothed.

Take then our beginning where we will, there must have existed in that "originally" either Something, or Nothing. It is a clear matter to prove, *à posteriori*, that Something did exist; because something exists now: every matter and every derived spirit must have had a Father; *ex nihilo nihil fit*, is not more a truth, than that creation must have had a Creator. However, leaving this plain path (which I only point at by the way for obvious mental uses), let us now try to get at the great antecedent probability that in the beginning Something should have been, rather than Nothing.

The term, Nothing, is a fallacious one: it does not denote an existence, as Something does, but the end of an existence. It is in fact a negation, which must prësuppose a matter once in being and possible to be denied; it is an abstraction, which cannot happen unless there be somewhat to be taken away; the idea of vacuity must be posterior to that of fullness; the idea of no tree is incompetent to be conceived without the previous idea of *a* tree; the idea of nonentity suggests, *ex vi termini*, a pre-existent entity; the idea of Nothing, of necessity, prësupposes Something. And a Something once having been, it would still and for ever continue to be, unless sufficient cause be found for its removal; that cause itself, you will observe, being a Something. The chances are forcibly in favour of continuance, that is of perpetuity; and the likelihoods proclaim loudly that there should be an Existence. It was thus, then, antecedently more probable, than in any imaginable beginning from which reason can start, Something should be found existent, rather than Nothing. This is the first probability.

Next; of what nature and extent is this Something, this Being, likely to be?—There will be either one such being, or many: if many, the many either sprang from the one, or the mass are all self-existent; in the former case, there would be a creation and a God: in the latter, there would be many Gods. Is the latter antecedently more probable?—let us see. First, it is evident that if many are probable, few are more probable, and one most probable of all. The more possible gods you take away, the more do impediments diminish; until, that is to say, you arrive at that One Being, whom we have already proved probable. Moreover, many must be absolutely united as one; in which case the many is a gratuitous difficulty, because they may as well be regarded for all purposes of worship or argument as one God: or the many must have been in essence more or less disunited; in which case, as a state of any thing short of pure concord carries in itself the seeds of dissolution, needs must that one or other of the many (long before any possible beginnings, as we count beginnings, looking down the past vista of eternity), would have taken opportunity by such disturbing causes to become absolute monarch: whether by peaceful persuasion, or hostile compulsion, or other mode of absorbing disunions, would be indifferent; if they were not all improbable, as unworthy of the God. Perpetuity of discord is a thing impossible; every thing short of unity tends to decomposition. Any how then, given the element of eternity to work in, a one great Supreme Being was, in the created beginning, an *à priori* probability. That all other assumptions than that of His true and eternal Oneness are as false in themselves as they are derogatory to the rational views of deity, we all now see and believe; but the direct proofs of this are more strictly matters of revelation than of reason: albeit reason too can discern their probabilities. Wise heathens, such as Socrates and Cicero, who had not our light, arrived nevertheless at some of this perception; and thus, through conscience and intelligence, became a law unto themselves: because that, to them, as now to any one of us who may not yet have seen the light, the anterior likelihood existed for only one God, rather than more; a likelihood which prepares the mind to take as a fundamental truth, "The Lord our God is one Jehovah."

Next; Self-existence combined with unity must include the probable attribute, or character, Ubiquity; as I now proceed to show. On the same principle as that by which we have seen Something to be likelier than Nothing, we conclude that the same Something is more probable to be every where, than the same Nothing (if the phrase were not absurd), to be any where: we may, so to speak, divide infinity into spaces, and prove the position in each instance: moreover, as that Something is essentially—not a unit as of many, but—unity involving all, it follows as most probable that this Whole Being should be ubiquitous; in other parlance, that the one God should be every where at once: also, there being no limit to what we call Space, nor any imaginable hostile power to place a constraint upon the One Great Being, this Whole Being must be ubiquitous to a degree strictly infinite: "HE is in every place, beholding the evil and the good."

Such a consideration (and it is a perfectly true one) renders necessary the next point, to wit, that God is a Spirit. No possible substance can be every where at once: essence may, but not substance. Corporeity in any shape must be local; local is finite; and we have just proved the anterior probability of a One great Existence being (notwithstanding unity of essence) infinite. Illocal and infinite are convertible terms: spirit is illocal; and, as God is infinite—that is, illocal—it is clear that "God is a Spirit."

We have thus (not attempting to build up faith by such slight tools, but only using them to cut away prejudice) arrived at the high probability of a God invested with His natural qualities or attributes; Self-existence, Unity, the faculty of being every where at once and that every where Infinitude; and essentially of a Spiritual nature, not material. His moral, or accidental attributes (so to speak), were, ante cedently to their expression, equally easy of being proved probable. First, with respect to Power: given no disturbing cause—(we shall soon consider the question of permitted evil, and its origin; but this, however disturbing to creatures, will be found not only none to God, but, as it were, only a ray of His glory suffered to be broken for prismatic beauty's sake, a flash of the direction of His energies suffered to be diverted for the superior triumph of good in that day when it shall be shown that "God hath made all things for himself, yea, even the wicked for the time of visitation")—with the *datum* then of no disturbing cause obstructing or opposing, an infinite being must be able to do all things within the sphere of such infinity: in other phrase, He must be all-powerful. Just so, an impetus in vacuity suffers no check, but ever sails along among the fleet of worlds; and the innate Impulse of the Deity must expand and energize throughout that infinitude, Himself. For a like reason of ubiquity, God must know all things: it is impossible to escape from the strong likelihood that any intelligent being must be conversant of what is going on under his very eye. Again; in the case both of Power and Knowledge, alike with the coming attributes of Goodness and Wisdom—(wisdom considered as morally distinct from mere knowledge or awaredness; it being quite possible to conceive a cold eye seeing all things heedlessly, and a clear mind knowing all things heartlessly)—in the case, I say, of all these accidental attributes, there recurs for argument, one analogous to that by which we showed the anterior probability of a self-existence. Things positive must precede things negative. Sight must have been, before blindness is possible; and before we can arrive at a just idea of no sight. Power must be precursor to an abstraction from power, or weakness. The minor-existence of ignorance is an impossibility, unless you prëallow the major-existence of wisdom; for it amounts to a debasing or a diminution of wisdom. Sin is well defined to be, the transgression of law; for without law, there can be no sin. So, also, without wisdom, there can be no ignorance; without power, there can be no weakness; without goodness, there can be no evil.

Furthermore. An affirmative—such as wisdom, power, goodness—can exist absolutely; it is in the nature of a Something: but a negative—such as ignorance, weakness, evil—can only exist relatively; and it would, indeed, be a Nothing, were it not for the previous and now simultaneous existence of its wiser, stronger, and better origin. Abstract evil is as demonstrably an impossibility as abstract ignorance, or abstract weakness. If evil could have self-existed, it would in the moment of its eternal birth have demolished itself. Virtue's intrinsic concord tends to perpetual being: vice's innate discord struggles always with a force towards dissolution. Goodness, wisdom, power have existences, and have had existences from all eternity, though gulphed within the Godhead; and that, whether evidenced in act or not: but their corruptions have had no such original existence, but are only the same entities perverted. Love would be love still, though there were no existent object for its exercise: Beauty would be beauty still, though there were no created thing to illustrate its fairness: Power would be power still, though there be no foe to combat, no difficulty to be overcome. Hatred, ill-favour, weakness, are only perversions or diminutions of these. Power exists independently of muscles or swords or screws or levers; love, independently of kind thoughts, words, and actions; beauty, independently of colours, shapes, and adaptations. Just so is Wisdom philosophically spoken of by a truly royal and noble author:

"I, wisdom, dwell with prudence, and find out the knowledge of clever inventions. Counsel is mine, and sound wisdom; I am understanding; I have strength. The Lord possessed me in the beginning of his way, before his works of old. I was set up from everlasting, from the beginning, or ever the earth was. When there were no depths, I was brought forth; before the mountains were fixed, or the hills were made. When He prepared the heavens, I was there; when he set a compass upon the face of the depth; when he established the clouds above; when he strengthened the foundations of the deep: Then was I by him, as one brought up with him: and I was daily his delight, rejoicing always before him; rejoicing in the habitable parts of his earth; and my delights were with the sons of men."

King Solomon well knew of Whom he wrote thus nobly. Eternal wisdom, power, and goodness, all prospectively thus yearning upon man, and incorporate in One, whose name, among his many names, is Wisdom. Wisdom, as a quality, existed with God; and, constituting full pervasion of his essence, was God.

But to return, and bind to a conclusion our ravelled thoughts. As, originally, the self-existent being, unbounded, all-knowing, might take up, so to speak, if He willed, these eternal affirmative excellences of wisdom, power, and goodness; and as these, to every rational apprehension, are highly worthy of his choice, whereas their derivative and inferior corruptions would have been most derogatory to any reasonable estimate of His character; how much more likely was it that He should prefer the higher rather than the lower, should take the affirmative before the negative, should "choose the good, and refuse the evil,"—than endure to be endowed with such garbled, demoralizing, finite attributes as those wherewith the heathen painted the Pantheon. What high antecedent probability was there, that if a God should be (and this we have proved highly probable too)—He should be One, ubiquitous, self-existent, spiritual: that He should be all-mighty, all-wise, and all-good?

THE TRIUNITY.

ANOTHER deep and inscrutable topic is now to engage our thoughts—the mystery of a probable Triunity. While we touch on such high themes, the Christian's presumption ever is, that he himself approaches them with reverence and prayer; and that, in the case of an unbeliever, any such mind will be courteous enough to his friendly opponent, and wise enough respecting his own interest and safety lest these things be true, to enter upon all such subjects with the seriousness befitting their importance, and with the restraining thought that in fact they may be sacred.

Let us then consider, antecedently to all experience, with what sort of deity pure reason would have been satisfied. It has already arrived at Unity, and the foregoing attributes. But what kind of Unity is probable? Unity of Person, or unity of Essence? A sterile solitariness, easily understandable, and presumably incommunicative? or an absolute oneness, which yet relatively involves several mysterious phases of its own expansive love? Will you think it a foregone conclusion, if I assert the superior likelihoods of the latter, and not of the former? Let us come then to a few of many reasons. First: it was by no means probable to be supposed anteriorly, that the God should be clearly comprehensible: yet he must be one: and oneness is the idea most easily apprehended of all possible ideas. The meanest of intellectual creatures could comprehend his Maker, and in so far top his heights, if God, being truly one in one view, were yet only one in every view: if, that is to say, there existed no mystery incidental to his nature: nay, if that mystery did not amount to the difficulty of a seeming contradiction. I judge it likely, and with confidence, that Reason would prërequire for his God, a Being, at once infinitely easy to be apprehended by the lowest of His spiritual children, and infinitely difficult to be comprehended by the highest of His seraphim. Now, there can be guessed only two ways of compassing such a prërequirement: one, a moral way; such as inventing a deity who could be at once just and unjust, every where and no where, good and evil, powerful and weak; this is the heathen phase of Numen's character, and is obviously most objectionable in every point of view: the other would be a physical way; such as requiring a God who should be at once material and immaterial, abstraction and concretion; or, for a still more confounding paradox to Reason (considered as antagonist to Faith, in lieu of being strictly its ally), an arithmetical contradiction, an algebraic mystery, such as would be included in the idea of Composite Unity; one involving many, and many collapsed into one. Some such enigma was probable in Reason's guess at the nature of his God. It is the Christian way; and one entirely unobjectionable: because it is the only insuperable difficulty as to His Nature which does not debase the notion of Divinity. But there are also other considerations.

For, secondly. The self-existent One is endowed, as we found probable, with abundant loving-kindness, goodness overflowing and perpetual. Is it reasonable to conceive that such a character could for a moment be satisfied with absolute solitariness? that infinite benevolence should, in any possible beginning, be discovered existent in a sort of selfish only-oneness? Such a supposition is, to the eye of even unenlightened Reason, so clearly a *reductio ad absurdum*, that men in all countries and ages have been driven to invent a plurality of Gods, for very society sake: and I know not but that they are anteriorly wiser and more rational than the man who believes in a Benevolent Existence eternally one, and no otherwise than one. Let me not be mistaken to imply that there was any likelihood of many cöexistent gods: that was a reasonable improbability, as we have already seen, perhaps a spiritual impossibility: but the anterior likelihood of which I speak goes to show, that in One God there should be more than one cöexistence: each, by arithmetical mystery, but not absurdity, pervading all, cöequals, each being God, and yet not three Gods, but one God. That there should be a rational difficulty here—or, rather, an irrational one—I have shown to be Reason's prërequirement: and if such a one as I, or any other creature, could now and here (ay, or any when or any where, in the heights of highest heaven, and the far-stretching distance of eternity) solve such intrinsic difficulty, it would demonstrably be one not worthy of its source, the wise design of God: it would prove that riddle read, which uncreate omniscience propounded for the baffling of the creature mind. No. It is far more reasonable, as well as far more reverent, to acquiesce in Mystery, as another attribute inseparable from the nature of the God-head; than to quibble about numerical puzzles, and indulge unwisely in objections which it is the happy state of nobler intelligences than man on earth is, to look into with desire, and to exercise withal their keen and lofty minds.

But we have not yet done. Some further thoughts remain to be thrown out in the third place, as to the prëconceivable fitness or propriety of that Holy Union, which we call the trinity of Persons who constitute the Self-existent One. If God, being one in one sense, is yet likely to appear, humanly speaking, more than one in another sense; we have to inquire anteriorly of the probable nature of such other intimate Being or Beings: as also, whether such addition to essential oneness is likely itself to be more than one or only one. As to the former of these questions: if, according to the presumption of reason (and according also to what we have since learned from revelation; but there may be good policy in not dotting this book with chapter and verse)—if the Deity thus loved to multiply Himself; then He, to whom there can exist no beginning, must have so loved, so determined, and so done from all eternity. Now, any conceivable creation, however originated, must have had a beginning, place it as far back as you will. In any succession of numbers, however infinitely they may stretch, the commencement at least is a fixed point, one. But, this multiplication of Deity, this complex simplicity, this intricate easiness, this obvious paradox, this sub-division and con-addition of a One, must have taken place, so soon as ever eternal benevolence found itself alone; that is, in eternity, and not in any imaginable time. So then, the Being or Beings would probably not have been creative, but of the essence of Deity. Take also for an additional argument, that it is an idea which detracts from every just estimate of the infinite and all-wise God to suppose He should take creatures into his eternal counsels, or consort, so to speak, familiarly with other than the united sub-divisions, persons, and cöequals of Himself. It was reasonable to prëjudge that the everlasting companions of Benevolent God, should also be God. And thus, it appears antecedently probable that (what from the poverty of language we must call) the multiplication of the one God should not have been created beings; that is, should have been divine; a term, which includes, as of right, the attribution to each such Holy Person, of all the wondrous characteristics of the Godhead.

Again: as to the latter question; was it probable that such so-called sub-divisions should be two, or three, or how many? I do not think it will be wise to insist upon any such arithmetical curiosity as a perfect number; nor on such a toy as an equilateral triangle and its properties; nor on the peculiar aptitude for sub-division in every thing, to be discerned in a beginning, a middle, and an end; nor in the consideration that every fact had a cause, is a constancy, and produces a consequence: neither, to draw any inferences from the social maxim that for counsel, companionship, and conversation, the number three has some special fitness. Some other similar fancies, not altogether valueless, might be alluded to. It seems preferable, however, on so grand a theme, to attempt a deeper dive, and a higher flight. We would then, reverently as always, albeit equally as always with the free-born boldness of God's intellectual children, attempt to prëjudge how many, and with what distinctive marks, the holy beings into whom (ὡς ἔπος ειπέιν) God, for very Benevolence sake, pours out Essential Unity, were likely to be.

Let us consider what principles, as in the case of a forthcoming creation, would probably be found in action, to influence such creation's Author.

First of all, there would be Will, a will energized by love, disposing to create: a phase of Deity aptly and comprehensively typified to all minds by the name of a universal Father: this would be the primary impersonation of God. And is it not so?

Secondly: there would be (with especial reference to that idea of creation which doubtless at most remote beginnings occupied the Good One's contemplation), there would be next, I repeat, in remarkable adaptation to all such benevolent views, the great idea of principle, Obedience; conforming to a Father's righteous laws, acquiescing in his just will, and returning love for love: such a phase could not be better shadowed out to creatures than by an Eternal Son; the dutiful yet supreme, the subordinate yet cöequal, the amiable yet exalted Avatar of our God. This was probable to have been the second impersonation of Deity. And is it not so?

Thirdly: Springing from the conjoint ideas of the Father and the

Son, and with similar prospection to such instantly creative universe, there would occur the grand idea of Generation; the mighty cöequal, pure, and quickening Impulse: aptly announced to men and angels as the Holy Spirit. This was to have been the third impersonation of Divinity. And is it not so?

Of all these—under illumination of the fore-known fact, I speak, in their aspect of anterior probability. With respect to more possible Persons, I at least cannot invent one. There is, to my reflection, neither need nor fitness for a fourth, or any further Principle. If another can, let him look well that he be not irrationally demolishing an attribute and setting it up as a principle. Obedience is not an attribute; nor Generation; nor Will: whilst the attribute of Love, pervading all, sets these only possible three Principles going together as One in a mysterious harmony. I would not be misunderstood; persons are not principles; but principles may be illustrated and incorporative in persons. Essential Love, working distinctively throughout the Three, unites them instinctively as One: even as the attribute Wisdom designs, and the attribute Power arranges all the scheme of Godhead.

And now I ask Reason, whether, prësupposing keenness, he might not have arrived by calculation of probabilities at the likelihood of these great doctrines: that the nature of God would be an apparent contradiction: that such contradiction should not be moral, but physical; or rather verging towards the mëtaphysical, as immaterial and more profound: that God, being One, should yet, in his great Love, marvellously have been companioned from eternity by Himself: and that such Holy and United Confraternity should be so wisely contrived as to serve for the bright unapproachable exemplar of love, obedience, and generation to all the future universe, such Triunity Itself existing uncreated.

THE GODHEAD VISIBLE.

We have hitherto mused on the Divinity, as on Spirit invested with attributes: and this idea of His nature was enough for all requirements antecedently to a creation. At whatever beginning we may suppose such creation to have commenced, whether countless ages before our present κόσμος, or only a sufficient time to have prepared the crust of earth; and to whatever extent we may imagine creation to have spread, whether in those remote periods originally to our system alone and at after eras to its accompanying stars and galaxies and firmaments; or at one and the same moment to have poured material existence over space to which our heavens are as nothing: whatever, and whenever, and wherever creation took place, it would appear to be probable that some one person of the Deity should, in a sort, become more or less concretely manifested; that is, in a greater or a minor degree to such created minds and senses visible. Moreover, for purposes at least of a concentrated worship of such creatures, that He should occasionally, or perhaps habitually, appear local. I mean, that the King of all spiritual potentates and the subordinate Excellencies of brighter worlds than ours, the Sovereign of those whom we call angels, should will to be better known to and more aptly conceived by such His admiring creatures, in some usual glorious form, and some wonted sacred place. Not that any should see God, as purely God; but, as God relatively to them, in the capacity of King, Creator, and the Object of all reasonable worship. It seems anteriorly probable that one at least of the Persons in the Godhead should for this purpose assume a visibility; and should hold His court of adoration in some central world, such as now we call indefinitely Heaven. That such probability did exist in the human forecast, as concerns a heaven and the form of God, let the testimony of all nations now be admitted to corroborate. Every shape from a cloud to a crocodile, and every place from Æther to Tartarus, have been peopled by man's not quite irrational device with their so-called gods. But we must not lapse into the after-argument: previous likelihood is our harder theme. Neither, in this section, will we attempt the probabilities of the place of heaven: that will be found at a more distant page. We have here to speak of the antecedent credibility that there should be some visible phase of God; and of the shape wherein he would be most likely, as soon as a creation was, to appear to such his creatures. With respect, then, to the former. Creatures, being finite, can only comprehend the infinite in his attribute of unity: the other attributes being apprehended (or comprehended partially) in finite phases. But, unity being a purely intellectual thought, one high and dry beyond the moral feelings, involves none of the requisites of a spiritual, that is an affectionate, worship; such worship as it was likely that a beneficent Being would, for his creatures' own elevation in happiness, command and inspire towards Himself. In order, therefore, to such worship and such inspiration acting through reason, it would appear fitting that the Deity should manifest Himself especially with reference to that heavenly Exemplar, the Three Divine Persons of the One Supreme Essence already shown to have been probable. And it seems likeliest and discreetest to my thinking, that, with this view, the secondary phase, loving Obedience, under the dictate of the primary phase, a loving Will, and energized by the tertiary or conjoining phase a loving Quickening Entity, should assume the visbile type of Godhead, and thus concentrate unto Himself the worship of all worlds. I can conceive no scheme more simply profound, more admirably suited to its complex purposes, than that He, in whom dwelt the fullness of the Godhead, bodily, should take the form of God, in order that unto Him every knee should bow, of things in heaven, and things in earth, and things in regions under the earth. Was not all this reasonably to have been looked for? and tested afterwards by Scripture, in its frequent allusions to some visible phase of Deity, when the Lord God walked with Adam, and Enoch, and Abraham, and Peter, and James, and John—I ask, is it not the case?

The latter point remaining to be thus briefly touched upon, respects the probable shape to be assumed and worn, familiarly enough to be recognised as His, by Deity thus vouchsafing Himself visible. And here we must look down the forward stream of Time, and search among the creatures whom thereafter God should make, to arrive at some good reason for, some antecedent probability of, the form which he should thus frequently inhabit. Fire, for example, a pure and spirit-like nature, would not have been a guess unworthy of reason: but this, besides its humbler economic uses, would endanger an idolatry of the natural emblem. So also would light be no irrational thought. And it is true that God might, and probably would, invest Himself in one or both of these pure essences, so seemingly congenial to a nature higher than ours: but then there would be some nucleus to the brilliancy and the burning; these would be as a veil to the Divinity; we should have need, before He were truly visible, that the veil were laid aside: we should have to shred away to the nucleus, which (and not the fire or light) would be the form of God. Similar objections, in themselves or in their idolatrizing tendencies, would lie against any such shape as a cloud, or a rainbow, or an angel (whatever such a being may resemble), or in fact any other conceivable creature, whether good as the angelic case or indifferent as that of the cloud, which the Deity, though assuming often, would nevertheless in every instance assume in conjunction with such his ordinary creature, and could not entirely monopolize. I mean; if God had the shape of a cloud, or of a rainbow, common clouds ana rainbows would come to be thought gods too. Reason would anticipate this objection to such created and too-favoured shapes: more; in every case, but one, he would be quite at a loss to look for some type, clearly apt and probable. That one case he might discern to be this. Known unto God are all things from the beginning to the end: and, in His foreknowledge, Reason might have been enlightened to prophesy (as we shall hereafter see) that for certain wise and good ends one great family out of the myriads who rejoice in being called God's children, would in a most marked manner fall away from Him through disobedience; and should thereby earn, if not the annihilation of their being, at least its endless separation from the Blessed. Manifestly, the wisdom and benevolence of God would be eager and swift to devise a plan for the redemption of so lost a race. Why He should permit their fall at all will be reverentially descanted on in its proper section; meanwhile, how is it probable that God, first, by any theory consistently with truth and justice, could, and next by power and contrivance actually would, lift up again this sinful family from the pit of condemnation? Reason is to search the question well: and after much thought, you will arrive at the truth that there was but one way probable. Rebellion against the Great and Self-existent Author of all things, must needfully involve infinite punishment; if only because He is infinite, and his laws of an eternal sanction. The problem then was, how to inflict the unbounded punishment thus claimed by justice for a transgressional condition, and yet at love's demand to set the prisoner free: how to be just, and simultaneously justifier of the guilty. That was a question magnificently solved by God alone: magnificently about to be solved, as according to our argument seemed probable, by God Triune, in wondrous self-involving council. The solution would be rationally this. Himself, in his character of filial obedience, should pay the utter penalty to Himself in his character of paternal authority, whilst Himself in the character of quickening spirit, should restore the ransomed family from death to life, from the power of evil unto good. Was not this a most probable, a most reasonably probable scheme? was it not altogether wise and philosophical, as well as entirely generous and kind to wretched men?

And (returning to our present topic), was it not antecedently to have been expected that God the Son (so to put it) should, in the shape He was thereafter to assume upon earth, appear upon the eternal throne of heaven? In a shape, however glorified and etherealized, with glistening countenance and raiment bright as the light, nevertheless resembling that more humble form, the Son of Man, who was afterwards thus by a circle of probabilities to be made in the form of God; in a shape, not liable, from its very sinfulness, to the deification either of other worlds or of this [hero-worship is another and a lower thing altogether; we speak here of true idolatries:]—was it unlikely, I say, that in such a shape Deity should have deigned to become visible, and have blazed Manifested God, the central Sun of Heaven?—This probability, prior to our forth-flowing thoughts on the Incarnation, though in some measure anticipating them, will receive further light from the views soon to be set forth. I know not but that something is additionally due to the suggestion following; namely: that, raise our swift imagination to what height we may, and stretch our searching reason to the uttermost, we cannot, despite of all inventive energies and powers of mind, conceive any shape more beautiful, more noble, more worthy for a rational intelligence to dwell in, more in one Homeric word θεοειδὴς, than the glorified and etherealized human form divine. Let this serve as Reason's short reply to any charge of anthropomorphism in the doctrines of his creed: it was probable that God should be revealed to His creation; and as to the form of any such revealed essence in any such infinite beginnings of His work, the most likely of all would appear to be that one, wherein He, in the ages then to come, was well resolved to earn the most glorious of all triumphs, the merciful reconciliation of everlasting justice with everlasting love, the wise and wondrous scheme of God forgiving sinners.

THE ORIGIN OF EVIL.

It will now be opportune to attempt elucidation of one of the darkest and deepest riddles ever propounded to the finite understanding; the *à priori* likelihood of evil: not, mind, its eternal existence, which is a false doctrine; but its probable procession from the earliest created beings, which is a true one.

At first sight, nothing could appear more improbable: nothing more inconsistent with the recognised attributes of God, than that error, pain, and sorrow should be mingled in His works. These, the spontaneous offspring of His love, one might (not all wisely) argue, must always be good and happy—because perfect as Himself. Because perfect?—

Therein lies the fallacy, which reason will at once lay bare. Perfection is attributable to no possible creature: perfection argues infinity, and infinity is one of the prerogatives of God. However good, "very good," a creation may be found, still it must, from essential finitude, fall short of that Best, which is in effect the only state purely unexceptionable. For instance, no creature can be imagined of a wisdom undiminished from the single true standard, God's wisdom: in other phrase, every creature must be more or less departed from wisdom, that is, verging towards folly. Again; no creature can be presumed of a purity so spotless as to rank in an equality with that of the Almighty: in other words, neither man, nor angel, nor any other creature, can exist who is not more or less—I will not say impure, positively, but—unpure negatively. Thus, the birth-mark of creation must have been an inclination towards folly, and from purity. The mere idea of creatures would involve, as its great need-be, the qualifying clause that these emanations from perfection be imperfect; and that these children of purity be liable to grow unpure. They must either be thus natured, or exist of the essence of God, that is, be other persons and phases of the Deity: such a case was possible certainly; but, as we have already shown, not probable. And it were possible, that, in consequence of some redemption such as we have spoken of, creatures might by ingraftation into God become so entirely part of Him—bone of bone, and flesh of flesh, and spirit of spirit—that an exhortation to such blest beings should reasonably run, "Be ye perfect." But this infinite munificence of the Godhead in redemption was not to be found among His bounties as Creator. It might indeed arise afterwards, as setting up again the fallen creature in some safe niche of Deity: and we now know it has arisen: "we are complete in Him."

But this, though relevant, is a digression. Returning, and to produce some further argument against all creature perfectness; let us consider how rational it seems to prĕsuppose that the mighty Maker in his boundless love should have willed to form a long chain of classes of existence more and more subordinated each to the other, each good of its kind and happy in its way, but yet all needfully more or less removed from the high standard of uncreate Perfection. These descending links, these graduations downwards, must involve a nearer or remoter approach to evil. Now, we must bear in mind that Evil is not a principle, but a perversion: it amounts merely to a denial, a limitation, a corruption of good, not to the dignity of its abstract antagonism. Familiarly, but fallaciously, we talk of the evil principle, the contradictory to good: we might as well talk of the nosologic principle, the contradictory to health; or the darkness principle, the contradictory to light. They are contraries, but not contradictories: they have no positive, but only a relative existence. Good and evil are verily foes, but originally there was one cemented friendship: slender beginnings consequent on a creation, began to cause the breach: the civil war arose out of a state of primitive peace: images betray us into errors, or I might add with a protest against the risk of being misinterpreted, that like brothers turned to a deadly hate, they nevertheless sprang not originally out of two hostile and opposite hemispheres, but from one paternal hearth. Not, however, in any sense that God is the author of evil; but that God's workmanship, the finite creature, needfully perverted good.

The origin of evil—that is, its birth—is a term true and clear: original evil—that is, giving it no birth but an antedate to all created things, suffering it to run parallel with God and good from all eternity—this is a term false and misty. The probability that good would be warped, and grow deteriorate; that wisdom would be dwindled down into less and less wisdom, or foolishness; and power degenerated more and more towards imbecility; must arise, directly a creature should spring out of the Creator; and that, let astronomy or geology name any date they will: Adam is a definite date; perhaps also the first day's—or period's—work: but the Beginning of Creation is undated. It would then, under this impression of the necessary defalcation of the creature from the strict straight line, be rational to look for deviations: it would be rational to prësuppose that God—just, and good, and pure, and wise—should righteously be able to "charge his angels with folly," should verily declare that "the heavens are not pure in his sight."

Further; it would be a possible chance (which considerations soon succeeding would render even probable) that for a wise humiliation of the reasoning creature, and a just exaltation of the only Source of life and light and all things, one or more of such first created beings, or angels, should be suffered to fall, possibly from the vastest height, and at first by the slenderest beginnings, lower and lower into folly, impurity, and all other derelictions from the excellence of God. The lines, once unparalleled, would, without a check, go further apart for all eternity; albeit, the primal deviation arose in time. The aerolite, dropping slowly at first, increases in swiftness as it multiplies the fathoms of descent: and if the abyss be really bottomless, how impossible a check or a return.

Some such terrible example would amount to a reasonable likelihood, if only for a lesson and a warning: to all intelligent hierarchs, be not high-minded, but fear; to all responsible beings, keep righteousness and reverence, and tempt not God; to all the Virtues, Dominations, Obediences, and due Subordinations of unknown glorious worlds, a loud and living exhortation to exercise, and not to let grow dim their spiritual energies, in efforts after goodness, wisdom, and purity. A creature state, to be happy, must be a progressive state: the capability of progression argues lack, or a tendency from good: and progression itself needs a spur, lest indolence relapse towards evil.

Additionally: we must remember that a creature's excellence before God is the reasonable service which he freely renders: freedom, dangerous prerogative, involves choice: and choice necessitates the possibility of error. The command to a rational intelligence would be, do this, and live; do it not, and die: if thou doest, it is well done, good and faithful servant; thou hast mounted by thine own heaven-blest exertions to a higher approach towards infinite perfection; enter thou into the joy, not merely of a creature, but of thy Lord. But, if thou doest not, it is wo to thee, unworthy hireling; thou hast broken the tie that bound thee to thy Maker—obedience, the root of happiness; thou livest on indeed, because the Former of all things cancelleth not nor endeth his beginning; but henceforth thine existence is, as a river which earthquakes have divorced from its bed, and instead of flowing on for ever through the fair pastures of peace and among the mountain roots of everlasting righteousness, thy downward course is shattery, headlong, turbulent, and destructive; black-throated whirlpools here, miasmatic marshes there, a cataract, a shoal, a rapid; until the remorseless stream, lashing among rocks which its own riot rendered sterile, pours its unresting waters into the thirsty sands of the Sahara.

It was indeed probable (as since we know it to be true) that the generous Giver of all things would in the vast majority of cases minister such secret help to His weaker spiritual children, that, far from failing of continuous obedience, they should find it so unceasingly easier and happier that their very natures would soon come to be imbued with that pervading habit: and that thus, the longer any creature stood upright, the stronger should he rest in righteousness; until, at no very distant period, it should become morally impossible for him to fall. Such would soon be the condition of myriads, perhaps almost the whole, of heaven's innumerable host: and with respect to any darker Unit in that multitude, for the good of all permitted to make early shipwreck of himself, simply by leaving his intelligence to plume its wings into presumptuous flight, and by allowing his pristine goodness or wisdom to grow rusty from non-usage until that sacred panoply were eaten into holes; with respect to any such unhappy one, and all others (if others be) who should listen to his glozing, and make a common cause in his rebellion, where, I ask, is any injustice, or even unkindness done to him by Deity? Where is any moral improbability that such a traitor should be; or any just inconsistency chargeable on the attributes of God in consequence of such his being? Whom can he in reason accuse but himself for what he is? And what misery can such a one complain of, which is not the work of his own hands? And lest the Great Offender should urge against his God, why didst thou make me thus?—Is not the answer obvious, I made thee, but not thus. And on the rejoinder, Why didst thou not keep me as thou madest me? Is not the reply just, I made thee reasonable, I led thee to the starting place, I taught thee and set thee going well in the beginning; thou art intelligent and free, and hast capacities of Mine own giving: wherefore didst thou throw aside My grace, and fly in the face of thy Creator?

On the whole; consider that I speak only of probabilities. There is a depth in this abyss of thought, which no human plummet is long enough to sound; there is a maze in this labyrinth to be tracked by no mortal clue. It involves the truth, How unsearchable are his judgments: Thou hidest thy ways in the sea, and thy paths in the deep waters, and thy footsteps are not known. The weak point of man's argument lies in the suggested recollection, that doubtless the Deity could, if He would, have upheld all the universe from falling by his gracious power; and that the attribute of love concludes that so He would. However, these three brief considerations further will go some way to solve the difficulty, and to strengthen the weak point; first, there are other attributes besides love to run concurrently with it, as truth, justice, and unchangeableness:—Secondly, that grace is not grace, if manifested indiscriminately to all: and thirdly, that to our understanding at least there was no possible method of illustrating the amiabilities of Goodness, and the contrivances of Wisdom, but by the infused permission of some physical and moral evils: Mercy, benevolence, design, would in a universe of best have nothing to do; that universe itself would grow stagnant, as incapable of progress; and the principal record of God's excellences, the book of redemption, would have been unwritten. Is not then the existence of evil justified in reason's calculation? and was not such existence an antecedent probability?

Of these matters, thus curtly: it is time, in a short recapitulation, to reflect, that, from foregoing causes, mysteries were probable around the throne of heaven: and, as I have attempted to show, the mystery of imperfection, a concrete not an abstract, was likely to have sprung out of any creature universe. Reason perceives that a Gordion knot was likely to have become entangled; in the intricate complexities of abounding good to be mingled needfully with its own deficiencies, corruptions, and perversions: and this having been shown by Reason as anteriorly probable, its difficult involvements are now since cut by the sword of conquering Faith.

COSMOGONY.

THESE deep themes having been descanted on, however from their nature unsatisfactorily and with whatever human weakness, let us now endeavour mentally to transport ourselves to a period immediately antecedent to our own world's birth. We should then have been made aware that a great event was about to take place; whereat, from its foreseen consequences, the hierarchies of heaven would be prompt to shout for joy, and the holy ones of God to sing for gratitude. It was no common case of a creation; no merely onemore orb, of third-rate unimportance, amongst the million others of higher and more glorious praise: but it was a globe and a race about to be unique in character and fate, and in the far-spread results of their existence. On it and of its family was to be contrived the scene, wherein, to the admiration of the universe, God himself in Person was going visibly to make head against corruption in creation, and for ever thus to quench that possibility again: wherein He was marvellously to invent and demonstrate how Mercy and Truth should meet together, how Righteousness and Peace should kiss each other. There, was going to be set forth the wonderfully complicated battle-plan, by which, force countervailing force, and design converging all things upon one fixed point, Good, concrete in the creature, should overwhelm not without strife and wounds Evil concrete in the creature, and all things, "even the wicked," should be seen harmoniously blending in the glory of the attributes of God. The mythologic

Pan, το πᾶν the great Universal All, was deeply interested in the struggle: for the seed of the woman was to bruise the serpent's head; not merely as respected the small orb about to be, but concerning heaven itself, the unbounded " haysh hamaim," wherefrom dread Lucifer was thus to be ejected. On the earth, a mere planet of humble lustre, which the prouder suns around might well despise, was to be exhibited this noble and analogous result; the triumph of a lower intelligence, such as man, over a higher intelligence, such as angel: because, the former race, however frail, however weak, were to find their nature taken into God, and should have for their grand exemplar, leader and brother, the Very Lord of all arrayed in human guise; while the latter, the angelic fallen mass, in spite of all their pristine wisdom and excellency, were to set up as their captain him, who may well and philosophically be termed their Adversary.

This dark being, probably the mightiest of all mere creatures as the embodiment of corrupted good and perversion of an archangelic wisdom, was about to be suffered to fall victim to his own overtopping ambitions, and to drag with him a third part of the heavenly host—some tributary monarchs of the stars: thus he, and those his colleagues, should become a spectacle and a warning to all creatures else; to stand for spirits' reading in letters of fire a deeply burnt-in record how vast a gulf there is between the Maker and the made; how impassable a barrier between the derived intelligence and its infinite Creator. Such an unholy leader in rebellion against good—let us call him *A* or *B*, or why not for very euphony's sake Lucifer and Satanas?—such a corrupted excellence of heaven was to meet his final and inevitable disgrace to all eternity on the forthcoming battle-field of earth. Would it not be probable then that our world, soon to be fashioned and stocked with its teeming reasonable millions, should concentrate to itself the gaze of the universe, and, from the deeds to be done in it, should arrogate towards man a deep and fixed attention: that "the morning stars should sing together, and all the sons of God should shout for joy." Let us too, according to the power given to us, partake of such attention antecedently in some detail: albeit, as always, very little can be tracked of the length and breadth of our theme.

What would probably be the nature of such world and of such creatures, in a physical point of view? and what, in a moral point of view? It is not necessary to divide these questions: for the one so bears upon the other, or rather the latter so directs and pervades the former, that we may briefly treat of both as one.

The first probability would be, that, as the creature Man so to be abased and so to be exalted must be a responsible and reasonable being, every thing—with miraculous exceptions just enough to prove the rule—every thing around him should also be responsible and reasonable. In other words, that, with such exceptions as before alluded to, the whole texture of this world should bear to an inquisitive intellect the stamp of cause and effect: whilst for the mass, such cause and effect should be so little intrusive, that their easier religion might recognise God in all things immediately, rather than mediately. For instance: take the cases of stone, and of coal; the one so needful for man's architecture, the other for his culinary warmth. Now, however simple piety might well thank the Maker for having so stored earth with these for necessary uses; they ought, to a more learned, though not less pious ken, to seem not to have been created by an effort of the Great Father *quâ stone*, or *quâ coal.* Such a view might satisfy the ordinary mind: but thinkers would see no occasion for a miracle; when Christ raises Lazarus from the dead, it would have been a philosophical fault to have found the grave-clothes and swathing bandages ready loosened also. Unassisted man can do that: and unhelped common causes can generate stone and coal. The deposits of undated floods, the periodical currents of lava, the still and stagnant lake, and the furious up-bursting earthquake; all these would be called into play, and not the unrequired, I had almost said unreasonable, energies, which we call miracle. An agglutination of shells, once peopled with life; a crystallized lump of segregate minerals, once in a molten state; a mass of carbonated foliage and trunks of tropical trees, buried by long changes under the soil, whereover they had once waved greenly luxuriant; these, and no other, should have been man's stone and coal. This instance affects the reasonableness of such material creation. Take another, bearing upon its analogous responsibilities. As there was to be warred in this world the contest between good and evil, it would be expectable that the crust of man's earth, anteriorly to man's existence on it, should be marked with some traces that the evil, though newly born so far as might regard man's own disobedience, nevertheless had existed antecedently. In other words: it was probable that there should exist geological evidences of suffering and death: that the gigantic ichthyosaurus should be found fixed in rock with his cruel jaws closed upon his prey: that the fearful iguanodon should leave the tracks of having desolated a whole region of its reptile tribes: that volcanoes should have ravaged fair continents prolific of animal and vegetable life: that, in fine, though man's death came by man's sin, yet that death and sin were none of man's creating: he was only to draw down upon his head a prëexistent wo, an ante-toppling rock. Observe then, that these geological phenomena are only illustrations of my meaning: and whether such parables be true or false, the argument remains the same: we never build upon the sand of simile, but only use it here and there for strewing on the floor. Still, I will acknowledge that the introduction of such fossil instances appears to me wisely thrown in as affects their antecedent probability, because ignorant comments upon scriptural cosmogony have raised the absurdest objections against the truth of scriptural science. There is not a tittle of known geological fact, which is not absolutely reconcilable with Genesis and Job. But this is a word by the way: although aimed not without design against one of the poor and paltry weak-holds of the infidel.

ADAM.

Remembering, then, that these are probabilities, and that the whole treatise purports to be nothing but a sketch, and not a finished picture, we have suggestively thus thrown out that the material world, man's home as man, was likely to have been prepared, as we posteriorly know it to be. Now, what of man's own person, circumstances, and individuality? Was it likely that the world should be stocked at once with many several races, or with one prolific seed? with a specimen of every variety of the genus man, or with the one generic type capable of forming those varieties?—Answer. One is by far the likelier in itself, because one thing must needs be more probable than many things: additionally; Wisdom and Power are always economical, and where one will suit the purpose, superfluities are rejected. That this one seed, covering with its product a various globe under all imaginable differences of circumstance and climate, should, in the lapse of ages, generate many species of the genus Man, was antecedently probable. For example, morality, peace and obedience would exercise transforming powers: their opposites the like in an opposite way. We can well fancy a mild and gentle race, as the Hindoo, to spring from the former educationals: and a family with flashing eyes and strongly-visaged natures, as the Malay, from a state of hatred, war, and license. We can well conceive that a tropical sun should carbonize some of that tender fabric the skin, adding also swift blood and fierce passions: while an arctic climate would induce a sluggish, stunted race. And, when to these considerations we add that of promiscuous unions, we arrive at the just likelihood that the whole family of man, though springing from one root, should, in the course of generations, be what now we see it.

Further. How should this prolific original, the first man, be created? and for a name let us call him Adam; a justly-chosen name enough, as alluding to his medium colour, ruddiness. Should he have been cast upon the ground an infant, utterly helpless, requiring miraculous aid and guidance at every turn? Should he be originated in boyhood, that hot and tumultuous time, when the creature is most rash, and least qualified for self-government? or should he be first discerned as an adult, in his prime, equal alike to obedience and rule, to moral control and moral energy?

Add also here; is it probable there would be any needless interval placed to prŏcreations? or rather, should not such original seed be able immediately to fulfil the blank world call upon him, and as the greatly-teeming human father be found fitted from his birth to propagate his kind? The questions answer themselves.

Again. Should this first man have been discovered originally surrounded with all the appliances of an after-civilization, clad, and housed, and rendered artificial? nor rather, in a noble and naturally royal aspect appear on the stage of life as king of the natural creation, sole warder of a garden of fruits, with all his food thus readily concocted, and an eastern climate tempered to his nakedness?

Now, as to the solitariness of this one seed. From what we have already mused respecting God's benevolence, it would seem probable that the Maker might not see it good that man should be alone. The seed, originally one, proved (as was likely) to resemble its great parent, God, and to be partitionable, or reducible into persons; though with reasonable differences as between creature and Creator. Woman—Eve, the living or life-giving—was likely to have sprung out of the composite seed, Man, in order to companionship and fit society. Moreover, it were expectable that in the pattern creature, composite man, there should be involved some apt, mysterious typification of the same creature, after a fore-known fall restored, as in its perfect state of rëunion with its Maker. *A posteriori*, the figurative notion is, that the Redeemed family, or mystical spouse, is incorporated in her husband, the Redeemer:

not so much in the idea of marriage, as (taking election into view) of a cöcreation; as it were rib of rib, and life woven into life, not copulated or conjoined, but immingled in the being. This is a mystery most worthy of deep searching; a mystery deserving philosophic care, not less than the more unilluminate enjoyment of humble and believing Christians. I speak concerning Christ and his church.

THE FALL.

There is a special fitness in the fact, long since known and now to be perceived probable, that if mankind should fail in disobedience, it should rather be through the woman than through the man. Because, the man, *quâ man*, and the deputed head of all inferior creatures, was nearer to his Creator, than the woman; who, *quâ woman*, proceeded out of man. She was, so to speak, one step further from God, *ab origine*, than man was; therefore, more liable to err and fall away. To my own mind, I confess, it appears that nothing is more anteriorly probable than the plain, scriptural story of Adam and Eve: so simple that the child delights in it; so deep that the philosopher lingers there with an equal, but more reasonable joy.

For, let us now come to the probabilities of a temptation; and a fall; and what temptation; and how ordered.

The heavenly intelligences beheld the model-man and model-woman, rational beings, and in all points "very good." The Adversary panted for the fray, demanding some test of the obedience of this new, favourite race. And the Lord God was willing that the great controversy, which he fore-knew, and for wise purposes allowed, should immediately commence. Where was the use of a delay? If you will reply, To give time to strengthen Adam's moral powers: I rejoin, he was made with more than enough of strength infused against any temptation not entering by the portal of his will: and against the open door of will neither time nor habits can avail. Moreover, the trial was to be exceedingly simple; no difficult abstinence, for man might freely eat of every thing but one; no natural passion tempted; no exertion of intelligence requisite. Adam lived in a garden; and his Maker, for proof of reasonable obedience, provides the most easy and obvious test of it—do not eat that apple. Was it, in reality, an improbable test; an unsuitable one? Was it not, rather, the likeliest in itself, and the fittest as addressed to the new-born, rational animal, which imagination could invent, or an amiable fore-knowledge of all things could desire? Had it been to climb some arduous height without looking back, or on no account to gaze upon the sun, how much less apt and easy of obedience! Thus much for the test.

Now, as to the temptation and its ordering. A creature, to be tempted fairly, must be tempted by another equal or lower creature; and through the senses. If mere spirit strives with spirit, plus matter, the strife is unequal: the latter is clogged; he has to fight in the net of Retiarius. But if both are netted, if both are spirit plus matter, (that is, material creatures,) there is no unfairness. Therefore, it would seem reasonable that the Adversary in person should descend from his mere spirituality into some tangible and humbled form. This could not well be man's, nor the semblance of man's: for the first pair would well know that they were all mankind: and, if the Lord God himself was accustomed to be seen of them as in a glorified humanity, it would be manifestly a moral incongruity to invest the devil in a similar form. It must, then, be the shape of some other creature; as a lion, or a lamb, or—why not a serpent? Is there any improbability here? and not rather as apt an avatar of the sinuous and wily rebel, the dangerous, fascinating foe, as poetry at least, nay, as any sterner contrivance could invent? The plain fact is, that Reason—given keenness—might have guessed this also antecedently a likelihood.

A few words more on other details probable to the temptation. Wonderful as it may seem to us with our present experience, in the case of the first woman it would scarcely excite her astonishment to be accosted in human phrase by one of the lower creatures; and in no other way could the tempter reach her mind. Much as Milton puts it, Eve sees a beautiful snake, eating, not improbably, of the forbidden apple. Attracted by a natural curiosity, she would draw near, and in a soft sweet voice the serpent, *i. e.* Lucifer in his guise, would whisper temptation. It was likely to have been keenly managed. Is it possible, O fair and favoured mistress of this beautiful garden, that your Maker has debarred you from its very choicest fruit? Only see its potencies for good: I, a poor reptile, am instantly thereby endued with knowledge and the privilege of speech. Am I dead for the eating?—ye shall not surely die; but shall become as gods yourselves; and this your Maker knoweth.

The marvellous fruit, invested thus with mystery, and tinctured with the secret charm of a thing unreasonably, nay, harmfully, forbidden, would then be allowed silently to plead its own merits. It was good for food: a young creature's first thought. It was pleasant to the eyes: addressing a higher sense than mere bodily appetite, than mental predilection for form and colour which marks fine breeding among men. It was also to be desired to make one wise; here was the climax, the great moral inducement which an innocent being might well be taken with; irrespectively of the one qualification that this wisdom was to be plucked in spite of God. Doubtless, it were probable, that had man not fallen, the knowledge of good would never have been long withheld: but he chose to reap the crop too soon, and reaped it mixed with tares, good, and evil.

I need not enlarge, in sermon form, upon the theme. It was probable that the weaker creature, Woman, once entrapped, she would have charms enough to snare her husband likewise: and the results thus perceived to have been likely, we have long since known for fact. That a depraved knowledge should immediately occasion some sort of clothing to be instituted by the great moral Governor, was likely: and there would be nothing near at hand, in fact nothing else suitable, but the skins of beasts. There is also a high probability that some sort of slaying should take place instantly on the fall, by way of reference to the coming sacrifice for sin; and for a type of some imputed righteousness. God covered Man's evil nakedness with the skins of innocent slain animals: even so, Blessed is he whose unrighteousness is forgiven, and whose sin is covered.

With respect to restoration from any such fall. There seems a remarkable prior probability for it, if we take into account the empty places in heaven, the vacant starry thrones which sin had caused to be untenanted. Just as, in after years, Israel entered into the cities and the gardens of the Canaanite and other seven nations, so it was anteriorly likely, would the ransomed race of Men come to be inheritors of the mansions among heavenly places, which had been left unoccupied by the fallen host of Lucifer. There was a gap to be filled: and probably there would be some better race to fill it.

THE FLOOD.

THEMES like those past and others still to come, are so immense, that each might fairly ask a volume for its separate elucidation. A few seeds, pregnant with thought, are all that we have here space, or time, or power to drop beside the world's highway. The grand outlines of our race command our first attention: we cannot stop to think and speak of every less detail. Therefore, now would I carry my companion across the patriarchal times at once to the era of the Deluge. Let us speculate, as hitherto, antecedently, throwing our minds as it were into some angelic prior state.

If, as we have seen probable, evil (a concretion always, not an abstraction) made some perceptible ravages even in the unbounded sphere of a heavenly creation, how much more rapid and overwhelming would its avalanche (once ill-commenced) be seen, when the site of its infliction was a poor band of men and women prisoned on a speck of earth. How likely was it that, in the lapse of no long time, the whole world should have been "corrupt before God, and filled with wickedness." How probable, that taking into account the great duration of pristine human life, the wicked family of man should speedily have festered up into an intolerable guiltiness. And was this dread result of the primal curse and disobedience to be regarded as the Adversary's triumph? Had this Accuser—the Saxon word is Devil—had this Slanderer of God's attribute then really beaten Good? or was not rather all this swarming sin an awful vindication to the universe of the great need-be that God unceasingly must hold his creature up lest he fall, and that out of Him is neither strength nor wisdom? Was Deity, either in Adam's case or this, baffled—nor rather justified? Was it an experiment which had really failed; nor rather one which, by its very seeming failure, proved the point in question, the misery of creatures when separate from God? Yea, the evil one was being beaten down beneath his very trophies in sad Tarpeian triumph: through conquest and his children's sins heightening his own misery.

Let us now advert to a few of the anterior probabilities affecting this evil earth's catastrophe. It is not competent to us to trench upon such ulterior views as are contained in the idea of types relatively to antitypes. Neither will we take the fanciful or poetical aspect of coming calamity, that earth, befouled with guilt, was likely to be washed

ing calamity, that earth, befouled with guilt, was likely to be washed clean by water. It is better to ask, as more relevant, in what other way more benevolent than drowning could, short of miracle, the race be made extinct? They were all to die in their sins, and swell in another sphere the miserable hosts of Satan. There was no hope for them, for there was no repentance. It was infinitely probable that God's long-suffering had worn out every reasonable effort for their restoration. They were then to die; but how?—in the least painful manner possible. Intestine wars, fevers, famines, a general burning-up of earth and all its millions, were any of these preferable sorts of death to that caused by the gradual rise of water, with hope of life accorded still even to the last gurgle? Assuredly, if "the tender mercies of the wicked are cruel," the judgments of the Good one are tempered well with mercy.

Moreover, in the midst of this universal slaughter there was one good seed to be preserved: and, as Heaven never works a miracle where common cause will suit the present purpose, it would have been inconsistent to have extirpated the wicked by any such means as must demonstrate the good to have been saved only by super-human agency.

The considerations of humanity, and of the divine less-intervention, add that of the natural and easy agency of a long-commissioned comet. No "*Deus e machinâ*" was needed for this effort: one of His ministers of flaming fire was charged to call forth the services of water. This was an easy and majestic interference. Ever since man fell—yea, ages before it—the omniscient eye of God had foreseen all things that should happen: and his ubiquity had, possibly from The Beginning, sped a comet on its errant way, which at a calculated period was to serve to wash the globe clean of its corruptions: was to strike the orbit of earth just in the moment of its passage, and disturbing by attraction the fountains of the great deep, was temporarily to raise their level. Was not this a just, a sublime, and a likely plan? Was it not a merciful, a perfect, and a worthy way? Who should else have buried the carcases on those fierce battle-fields, or the mouldering heaps of pestilence and famine?—But, when at Jehovah's summons, heaving to the comet's mass, the pure and mighty sea rises indignant from its bed, by drowning to cleanse the foul and mighty land—how easy an engulfing of the corpses; how awful that universal burial; how apt their monumental epitaph written in water, "The wicked are like the troubled sea that cannot rest;" how dread the everlasting requiem chanted for the whelmed race by the waves roaring above them: yea, roaring above them still! for in that chaotic hour it seems probable to reason that the land changed place with ocean; thus giving the new family of man a fresh young world to live upon.

NOAH.

When the world, about to grow so wicked, was likely thus to have been cleansed, and so renewed, the great experiment of man's possible righteousness was probable to be repeated in another form. We may fancy some high angelic mind to have gone through some such line of thought as this, respecting the battle and combatants. Were those champions, Lucifer and Adam, really fit to be matched together? Was the tourney just; were the weapons equal; was it, after all, a fair fight?—on one side, the fallen spirit, mighty still, though fallen, subtlest, most unscrupulous, most malicious, exerting every energy to rear a rebel kingdom against God; on the other, a new-born, inexperienced, innocent, and trustful creature, a poor man vexed with appetites, and as naked for absolute knowledge in his mind as for garments on his body. Was it, in this view of the case, an equal contest? were the weapons of that warfare matched and measured fairly?

Some such objection, we may suppose, might seem to have been admissible, as having a show at least of reason: and, after the world was to have been cleansed of all its creatures in the manner I have mentioned, a new champion is armed for the conflict, totally different in every respect; and to reason's view vastly superior.

This time, the Adam of renewed earth is to be the best and wisest, nay, the only good and wise one of the whole lost family: a man, with the experience of full six hundred years upon his hoary brow, with the unspeakable advantage of having walked with God all those long-drawn centuries, a patriarch of twenty generations, recognised as the one great and faithful witness, the only worshipper and friend of his Creator. Could a finer sample be conceived? was not Noah the only spark of spiritual "consolation" in the midst of earth's dark death? and was not he the best imaginable champion to stand against the wiles of the devil? Verily, reason might have guessed, that if Deity saw fit to renew the fight at all, the representative of man should have been Noah.

Before we touch upon the immediate fall of this new Adam also, at a time when God and reason had deserted him, it will be more orderly to allude to the circumstances of his preservation in the flood. How, in such a hurlyburly of the elements, should the chosen seed survive? No house, nor hill-top, no ordinary ship would serve the purpose: still less the unreasonable plan of any cavern hermetically sealed, or any aerial chariot miraculously lifted up above the lower firmament. To use plain and simple words, I can fancy no wiser method than a something between a house and a diving-bell; a vessel, entirely storm-tight and water-tight, which nevertheless for necessary air should have an open window at the top: say, one a cubit square. This, properly hooded against deluging rain, and supplied with such helps to ventilation as leathern pipes, air tunnels and similar appliances, would not be an impracticable method. However, instead of being under water as a diving-bell, the vessel would be better made to float upon the rising flood, and thus continually keeping its level, would be ready to strike land as the waters assuaged.

Now, as to the size of this ark, this floating caravan, it must needs be very large; and also take a great time in building. For, suffering cause and effect to go on without a new creation, it was reasonable to suppose that the man, so launching as for another world on the ocean of existence, would take with him (especially if God's benevolence so ordered it) all the known appliances of civilized life; as well as a pair or two of every creature he could collect, to stock withal the renewed earth according to their various excellences in their kinds. The lengthy, arduous, and expensive preparation of this mighty ark—a vessel which must include forests of timber and consume generations in building; besides the world-be-known collection of all manner of strange animals for the stranger fancy of a fanatical old man; not to mention also the hoary Preacher's own century of exortations: with how great moral force all this living warning would be calculated to act upon the world of wickedness and doom! Here was the great ante-diluvian potentate, Noah, a patriarch of ages, wealthy beyond our calculations—(for how else without a needless succession of miracles could he have built and stocked the ark?)—a man of enormous substance, good report, and exalted station, here was he for a hundred and twenty years engaged among crowds of unbelieving workmen, in constructing a most extravagant ship, which, forsooth, filled with samples of all this world's stores, was to sail with our only good family in search of a better. Moreover, Noah here declares that our dear old mother-earth is to be destroyed for her iniquities by rain and sea: and he exhorts us by a solid evidence of his own faith at least, if by nothing else, to repent, and turn to him, whom Abel, Seth, and Enoch, as well as this good Noah, represent as our Maker. Would not such sneers and taunts be probable: would they not amply vindicate the coming judgment? Was not the "long-suffering of God" likely to have thus been tried "while the ark was preparing?" and when the catastrophe should come, had not that evil generation been duly warned against it? On the whole, it would have been Reason's guess that Noah should be saved as he was; that the ark should have been as we read of it in Genesis; and that the very immensity of its construction should have served for a preaching to mankind. As to any idea that the ark is an unreasonable (some have even said ridiculous) incident to the deluge, it seems to me to have furnished a clear case of antecedent probability.

Lastly: Noah's fall was very likely to have happened: not merely in the theological view of the matter, as an illustration of the truth that no human being can stand fast in righteousness: but from the just consideration that he imported with him the seeds of an impure state of society, the remembered luxuries of that old world. For instance, among the plants of earth which Noah would have preserved for future insertion in the soil, he could not have well forgotten the generous, treacherous Vine. That to a righteous man, little used to all unhallowed sources of exhilaration, this should have been a stepping-stone to a defalcation from God, was likely. It was probable in itself, and shows the honesty as well as the verisimilitude of Scripture to read, that "Noah began to be a husbandman, and planted a vineyard; and he drank of the wine, and was drunken." There was nothing here but what, taking all things into consideration, Reason might have previously guessed. Why then withhold the easier matter of an afterward belief?

BABEL.

THIS book ought to be read, as mentally it is written, with at the end of every sentence one of those *et ceteras*, which the genius of a Coke interpreted so keenly of the genius of a Littleton: for, far more remains on each subject to be said, than in any one has been attempted.

Let us pass on to the story of Babel: I can conceive nothing more *à priori* probable than the account we read in Scripture. Briefly consider the matter. A multitude of men, possibly the then whole human family, once more a fallen race, emigrate towards the East, and come to a vast plain in the region of Shinar, afterwards Chaldæa. Fertile, well-watered, apt for every mundane purpose, it yet wanted one great requisite. The degenerate race "put not their trust in God:" they did not believe but that the world might some day be again destroyed by water: and they required a point of refuge in the possible event of a second deluge from the broken bounds of ocean and the windows of the skies. They had come from the West; more strictly the North-west, a land of mountains, as they deemed them, ready-made refuges: and their scheme, a probable one enough, was to construct some such mountain artificially, so that its top might reach the clouds, as did the summit of Ararat. This would serve the twofold purpose of outwitting any further attempt to drown them, and of making for themselves a proud name upon the earth. So, the Lord God, in his etherealized human form (having taken counsel with His own divine compeers), coming in the guise wherein He was wont to walk with Adam and with Enoch and his other saints of men, "came down and saw the tower:" truly, He needed not have come, for ubiquity was his, and omniscience; but in the days when God and man were (so to speak) less chronologically divided than as now, and while yet the trial-family was young, it does not seem unlikely that He should. God then, in his aspect of the Head of all mankind, took notice of that dangerous and unholy combination: and He made within His Triune Mind the wise resolve to break their bond of union. Omniscience had herein a view to ulterior consequences benevolent to man, and He knew that it would be a wise thing for the future world, as well as a discriminative check upon the race then living, to confuse the universal language into many discordant dialects. Was this in any sense an improbable or improper method of making "the devices of the wicked to be of none effect, and of laughing to scorn the counsels of the mighty?" Was it not to have been expected that a fallen race should be disallowed the combinative force necessary to a common language, but that such force should be dissipated and diverted for moral usages into many tongues?—There they were, all the chiefs of men congregated to accomplish a vast, ungodly scheme: and interposing Heaven to crush such insane presumption—and withal thereafter designing to bless by arranging through such means the future interchange of commerce and the enterprise of nationalities—He, in his Trinity, was not unlikely to have said, "Let us go down, and confound their language." What better mode could have been devised to scatter mankind, and so to people the extremities of earth? In order that the various dialects should crystallize apart, each in its discriminative lump, the nucleus of a nation; that thereafter the world might be able no longer to unite as one man against its Lord, but by conflicting interests, the product of conflicting languages, might give to good a better chance of not being altogether overwhelmed; that, though many "a multitude might go to do evil," it should not thenceforward be the whole consenting family of man; but that, here by one and there by one, the remembrance of God should be kept extant, and evil no longer acquire an accumulated force, by having all the world one nation.

JOB.

Every scriptural incident and every scriptural worthy deserves its own particular discussion: and might easily obtain it. For example; the anterior probability that human life in patriarchal times should have been very much prolonged, was obvious; from consideration of—1, the benevolence of God; 2, the inexperience of man; and 3, the claim so young a world would hold upon each of its inhabitants: whilst Holy Writ itself has prepared an answer to the probable objection, that the years were lunar years, or months; by recording that Arphaxad and Salah and Eber and Peleg and Reu and Serug and Nahor, descendants of Shem, each had children at the average age of two-and-thirty, and yet the lives of all varied in duration from a hundred and fifty years to five hundred. And many similar credibilities might be alluded to: what shall I say of Abraham's sacrifice, of Moses and the burning bush, of Jonah also, and Elisha, and of the prophets? for the time would fail me to tell how probable and simple in each instance is its deep and marvellous history. There is food for philosophic thought in every page of ancient Jewish Scripture scarcely less than in those of primitive Christianity: here, after our fashion, we have only touched upon a sample.

The opening scene to the book of Job has vexed the faith of many very needlessly: to my mind, nothing was more likely to have literally and really happened. It is one of those few places where we get an insight into what is going on elsewhere: it is a lifting off the curtain of eternity for once, revealing the magnificent simplicities constantly presented in the halls of heaven. And I am moved to speak about it here, because I think a plain statement of its sublime probabilities will be acceptable to many: especially if they have been harassed by the doubts of learned men respecting the authorship of that rare history. It signifies nothing who recorded the circumstances and conversations, so long as they were true, and really happened: given power, opportunity, and honesty, a life of Dr. Johnson would be just as fair in fact, if written by Smollett, as by Boswell, or himself. Whether then Job, the wealthy prince of Uz, or Abraham, or Moses, or Elisha, or Eliphaz, or whoever else, have placed the words on record, there they stand, true; and the whole book in all its points was anteriorly likely to have been decreed a component part of revelation. Without it, there would have been wanting some evidence of a godly worship among men through the long and dreary interval of several hundred years: there would never have been given for man's help the example of a fortitude, and patience, and trust in God most brilliant; of a faith in the resurrection and redeemer, signal and definite beyond all other texts in Jewish Scripture: as well as of a human knowledge of God in his works beyond all modern instance. However, the excellences of that narrative are scarcely our theme: we return to the starting-post of its probability, especially with reference to its supernatural commencement. What we have shown credible, many pages back, respecting good and evil and the denizens of heaven, finds a remarkable after-proof in the two first chapters of Job; and for some such reason, by reference, these two chapters were themselves anteriorly to have been expected.

Let us see what happened:

"There was a day when the sons of God came to present themselves before the Lord, and Satan came also among them. And the Lord said unto Satan, whence comest thou? Then Satan answered the Lord, and said, From going to and fro in the earth, and from walking up and down in it. And the Lord said unto Satan, Hast thou considered my servant Job, that there is none like him in the earth, a perfect and an upright man, one that feareth God and escheweth evil? Then Satan answered the Lord, and said, Doth Job fear God for naught? Hast thou not made a hedge about him, and about his house, and about all that he hath on every side? Thou hast blessed the work of his hands, and his substance is increased in the land. But put forth thine hand now, and touch all he hath, and he will curse thee to thy face. And the Lord said unto Satan, Behold, all that he hath is in thy power; only upon himself put not forth thine hand. So Satan went forth from the presence of the Lord."—[Job 1. 6–13.]

It is a most stately drama: any paraphrase would spoil its dignity, its quiet truth, its unpretending, yet gigantic lineaments. Note: in allusion to our views of evil, that Satan also comes among the sons of God: note, the generous dependence placed by a generous Master on his servant well-upheld by that Master's own free grace: note, Satan's constant imputation against piety when blessed of God with worldly wealth, Doth he serve for naught? I can discern no cause wherefore all this scene should not have truly happened; not as in vision of some holy man, but as in fact. Let us read on, before further comment:

"Again, there was a day when the sons of God came to present themselves before the Lord, and Satan came also among them to present himself before the Lord. And the Lord said unto Satan, Whence comest thou? And Satan answered the Lord, and said, From going to and fro in the earth, and from walking up and down in it. And the Lord said unto Satan, Hast thou considered my servant Job, that there is none like him in the earth, a perfect and an upright man, one that feareth God and escheweth evil? and still he holdeth fast his integrity, although thou movedst me against him, to destroy him without cause. And Satan answered the Lord, and said, Skin for skin, yea, all that a man hath will he give for his life. But put forth thine hand now, and touch his bone and his flesh, and he will curse thee to thy face. And the Lord said unto Satan, Behold, he is in thine hand; but save his life. So Satan went forth from the presence of the Lord, and smote Job with sore boils, from the sole of his foot unto his crown."

Some such scene, displaying the devil's malice, slandering sneers, and permitted power, recommends itself to my mind as antecedently to have been looked for: in order that we might know from what quarter many of life's evils come; with what aims and ends they are directed; what limits are opposed to our foe; and Who is on our side. We needed some such insight into the heavenly places; some such hint of what is continually going on before the Lord's tribunal; we wanted this plain and simple setting forth of good and evil in personal encounter, of innocence awhile given up to malice for its chastening and its triumph. Lo, all this so probable scene is here laid open to us, and many, against reason, disbelieve it!

Note, in allusion to our after-theme, the *locus* of heaven, that there is some such usual place of periodical gathering. Note, the open unchiding loveliness dwelling in the Good One's words, as contrasted with the subtle, slanderous hatred of the Evil. And then the vulgar proverb, Skin for skin: this pious Job is so intensely selfish, that let him lose what he may, he heeds it not; he cares for nothing out of his own skin. And there are many more such notabilities.

Why did I produce these passages at length? For their Doric simplicity; for their plain and masculine features; for their obvious truthfulness; for their manifest probability as to fact, and expectability previously to it. Why on earth should they be doubted in their literal sense? and were they not more likely to have happened than to have been invented? We have no such geniuses now as this writer must have been, who by the pure force of imagination could have created that tableau. Milton had Job to go to. Simplicity is proof presumptive in favour of the plain inspiration of such passages: for the plastic mind which could conceive so just a sketch, would never have rested satisfied, without having painted and adorned it picturesquely. Such rare flights of fancy are always made the most of.

One or two thoughts respecting Job's trial. That he should at last give way, was only probable: he was, in short, another Adam, and had another fall; albeit he wrestled nobly. Worthy was he to be named among God's chosen three, "Noah, Daniel, and Job:" and worthy that the Lord should bless his latter end. This word brings me to the point I wish to touch on; the great compensation which God gave to Job.

Children can never be regarded as other than individualities: and notwithstanding Eastern feelings about increase in quantity, its quality is, after all, the question for the heart. I mean that many children to be born, is but an inadequate return for many children dying. If a father loses a well-beloved son, it is small recompense of that aching void that he gets another. For this reason of the affections, and because I suppose that thinkers have sympathized with me in the difficulty, I wish to say a word about Job's children, lost and found. It will clear away what is to some minds a moral and affectionate objection. Now, this is the state of the case.

The patriarch is introduced to us as possessing so many camels, and oxen, and so forth; and ten children. All these are represented to him by witnesses, to all appearance credible, as dead; and he mourns for his great loss accordingly. Would not a merchant feel to all intents and purposes a ruined man, if he received a clear intelligence from different parts of the world at once that all his ships and warehouses had been destroyed by hurricanes and fire? Faith given, patience follows: and the trial is morally the same, whether the news be true or false. Remarkably enough, after the calamitous time is past, when the good man of Uz is discerned as rewarded by heaven for his patience by the double of every thing once lost—his children remain the same in number, ten. It seems to me quite possible that neither camels, &c., nor children, really had been killed. Satan might have meant it so, and schemed it; and the singly-coming messengers believed it all, as also did the well-enduring Job. But the scriptural word does not go to say that these things happened; but that certain emissaries said they happened. I think the devil missed his mark: that the messengers were scared by some abortive diabolic efforts; and that, (with a natural increase of camels, &c., meanwhile,) the patriarch's paternal heart was more than compensated at the last, by the restoration of his own dear children. They were dead, and are alive again; they were lost, and are found. Like Abraham returning from Mount Calvary with Isaac, it was the Resurrection in a figure.

If to this view objection is made, that, because the boils of Job were real, therefore, similarly real must be all his other evils; I reply, that in the one temptation, the suffering was to be mental; in the other, bodily. In the latter case, positive, personal pain, was the gist of the matter: in the former, the heart might be pierced, and the mind be overwhelmed, without the necessity of any such incurable affliction as children's deaths amount to. God's mercy may well have allowed the evil one to overreach himself; and when the restoration came, how double was the joy of Job over those ten dear children.

Again, if any one will urge that, in the common view of the case, Job at the last really has twice as many children as before, for that he has ten old ones in heaven, and ten new ones on earth: I must, in answer, think that explanation as unsatisfactory to us, as the verity of it would have been to Job. Affection, human affection, is not so numerically nor vicariously consoled: and it is, perhaps, worth while here to have thrown out (what I suppose to be) a new view of the case, if only to rescue such wealth as children from the infidel's sneer of being confounded with such wealth as camels. Moreover, such a paternal reward was anteriorly more probable.

JOSHUA.

How many of our superficial thinkers have been staggered at the great miracle recorded of Joshua; and how few, even of the deeper sort, comparatively, may have discerned its aptness, its science, and its anterior likelihood: "Sun! stand thou still upon Gibeon; and thou, moon, in the valley of Ajalon." Now, consider, for we hope to vindicate even this stupendous event from the charge of improbability.

Baal and Ashtaroth, chief idols of the Canaanites, were names for sun and moon. It would manifestly be the object of God and His ambassador to cast utter scorn on such idolatry. And what could be more apt than that Joshua, commissioned to extirpate the corrupted race, should miraculously be enabled, as it were, to bind their own gods to aid in the destruction of such votaries?

Again: what should Joshua want with the moon for daylight, to help him to rout the foes of God more fiercely? Why not, according to the astronomical ignorance of those days, let her sail away, unconsorted by the sun, far beyond the valley of Ajalon? There was a reason, here, of secret, unobtruded science: if the sun stopped, the moon must stop *too; that is to say, both apparently: the fact being that the earth must*, for the while, rest on its axis. This, I say, is a latent, scientific hint; and so, likewise, is the accompanying mention as a fact, that the Lord immediately "rained great stones out of heaven" upon the flying host. For would it not be the case that, if the diurnal rotation of earth were suddenly to stop, the impetus of motion would avail to raise high into the air by centrifugal force, and fling down again by gravity, such unanchored things as fragments of rock?

Once more: our objector will here perhaps inquire, Why not then command the earth to stop—and not the sun and moon? if thus probably Joshua or his Inspirer knew better? Answer. Only let a reasonable man consider what would have been the moral lesson both to Israelite and to Canaanite, if the great successor of Moses had called out, incomprehensibly to all, "Earth, stand thou still on thine axis;"—and lo! as if in utter defiance of such presumption, and to vindicate openly the neathen gods against the Jewish, the very sun and moon in heaven stopped, and glared on the offender. I question whether such a noon-day miracle might not have perverted to idolatry the whole believing host: and almost reasonably too. The strictly philosophical terms would have entirely nullified the whole moral influence. God in his word never suffers science to hinder the progress of truth: a worldly philosophy does this almost in every instance, darkening knowledge with a cloud of words: but the science of the Bible is usually concealed in some neighbouring hint quite handy to the record of the phenomena expressed in ordinary language. In fact, for all common purposes, no astronomer finds fault with such phrases as the moon rising, or the sun setting: he speaks according to the appearance, though he knows perfectly well that the earth is the cause of it, and not the sun or moon. Carry this out in Joshua's case.

On the whole, the miracle was very plain, very comprehensible, and very probable. It had good cause: for Canaan felt more confidence in the protection of his great and glorious Baal, than stiff-necked Judah in his barely-seen divinity: and surely it was wise to vindicate the true but invisible God by the humiliation of the false and far-seen idol. This would constitute to all nations the quickly-rumoured proof that Jehovah of the Israelites was God in heaven above as well as on the earth beneath. And, considering the peculiar idolatries of Canaan, it seems to me that no miracle could have been better placed and better timed—in other words, anteriorly more probable—than the command of obedience to the sun and to the moon. I suppose that few persons who read this book will be unaware, that the circumstance is alluded to as well in that honest heathen, old Herodotus, as in the learned Jew Josephus. The volumes are not near me for reference to quotations: but such is fact: it will be found in Herodotus, about the middle of Euterpe, connected with an allusion to the analogous case of Hezekiah.

No miracles, on the whole (to take one after-view of the matter), could have been better tested: for two armies (not to mention all surrounding countries) must have seen it plainly and clearly: if then it had never occurred, what a very needless exposure of the falsity of the Jewish Scriptures! These were open, published writings, accessible to all: Cyrus and Darius and Alexander read them, and Ethiopian eunuchs; Parthians, Medes, and Elamites, with all other nations of the earth, had free access to those records. Only imagine if some recent history of England, Adolphus's, or Stebbing's, contained an account of a certain day in George the Fourth's reign having had twenty-four hour's daylight instead of the usual admixture; could the intolerable falsehood last a minute? Such a placard would be torn away from the records of the land the moment a rash hand had fixed it there. But, if the matter were fact, how could any historian neglect it?—In one sense, the very improbability of such a marvel being recorded, argues the probability of it having actually occurred.

Much more might here be added: but our errand is accomplished, if any stumbling-block had been thus easily removed from some erring thinker's path. Surely, we have given him some reason for faith's due acceptance of Joshua's miracle.

THE INCARNATION.

In touching some of the probabilities of our blessed Lord's career, it would be difficult to introduce and illustrate the subject better, than by the following anecdote. Whence it is derived, has escaped my memory; but I have a floating notion that it is told of Socrates in Xenophon or Plato. At any rate, by way of giving fixity thereto and picturesqueness, let us here report the story as of the Athenian Solomon:

Surrounded by his pupils, the great heathen Reasoner was being questioned and answering questions: in particular respecting the probability that the universal God would be revealed to his creatures. "What a glorious King would he appear!" said one, possibly the brilliant Alcibiades: "What a form of surpassing beauty!" said another, not unlikely the softer Crito. "Not so, my children," answered Socrates. "Kings and the beautiful are few, and the God, if he came on earth as an exemplar, would in shape and station be like the greater number." "Indeed, Master? then how should he fail of being made a King of men, for his goodness, and his majesty, and wisdom?" "Alas! my children," was pure Reason's just rejoinder," *οἱ πλείονες κακοί*, most men are so wicked that they would hate his purity, despise his wisdom, and as for his majesty, they could not truly see it. They might indeed admire for a time, but thereafter (if the God allowed it), they would even hunt and persecute and kill him." "Kill him!" exclaimed the eager group of listeners; "kill Him? how should they, how could they, how dare they kill God?" "I did not say, kill God," would have been wise Socrates's reply, "for God existeth ever: but men in enmity and envy might even be allowed to kill that human form wherein God walked for an ensample. That they could, were God's humility: that they should, were their own malice: that they dared, were their own grievous sin and peril of destruction. Yea," went on the keen-eyed sage, "men would slay him by some disgraceful death, some lingering, open, and cruel death, even such as the death of slaves!"—Now slaves, when convicted of capital crime, were always crucified.

Whatever be thought of the genuineness of the anecdote, its uses are the same to us. Reason might have arrived at the salient points of Christ's career, and at His crucifixion!

I will add another topic: How should the God on earth arrive there? We have shown that His form would probably be such as man's; but was he to descend bodily from the atmosphere at the age of full-grown perfection, or to rise up out of the ground with earthquakes and fire, or to appear on a sudden in the midst of the market-place, or to come with legions of his heavenly host to visit his Temple? There was a wiser way than these, more reasonable, probable, and useful. Man required an exemplar for every stage of his existence up to the perfection of his frame. The infant, and the child, and the youth, would all desire the human-God to understand their eras; they would all, if generous and such as he would love, long to feel that He has sympathy with them in every early trial, as in every later grief. Moreover, the God coming down with supernatural glories or terrors would be a needless expense of ostentatious power. He, whose advent is intended for the encouragement of men to exercise their reason and their conscience; whose exhortation is "he that hath ears to hear, let him hear;" that pure Being, who is the chief preacher of Humility, and the great teacher of man's responsible condition—surely, he would hardly come in any way astoundingly miraculous, addressing his advent not to faith, but to sight, and challenging the impossibility of unbelief by a galaxy of spiritual wonders. Yet, if He is to come at all—and a word or two of this hereafter—it must be either in some such strange way; or in the usual human way; or in a just admixture of both. As the first is needlessly overwhelming to the responsible state of man, so the second is needlessly derogatory to the pure essence of God; and the third idea would seem to be most probable. Let us guess it out. Why should not this highest Object of faith and this lowest Subject of obedience be born, seemingly by human means, but really by divine? Why should there not be found some unspotted holy virgin, betrothed to a just man and soon to be his wife, who, by the creative power of Divinity, should miraculously conceive the shape divine, which God himself resolved to dwell in? Why should she not come of a lineage and family which for centuries before had held such expectation? Why should not the just man, her affianced, who had never known her yet, being warned of God in a dream of this strange, immaculate conception, "fear not to take unto him Mary his wife," lest the unbelieving world should breathe slander on her purity, albeit he should really know her not until after the Holy Birth. There is nothing unreasonable here; every step is previously credible: and invention's self would be puzzled to devise a better scheme. The Virgin-born would thus be a link between God and man, the great Mediator: his natures would fulfil every condition required of their double and their intimate conjunction. He would have arrived at humanity without its gross beginnings, and have veiled his Godhead for a while in a pure though mortal tenement. He would have participated in all the tenderness of woman's nature, and thus have reached the keenest sensibilities of men.

Themes such as these are inexhaustible: and I am perpetually conscious of so much left unsaid, that at every section I seem to have said next to nothing. Nevertheless, let it go; the good seed yet shall germinate. "Cast thy bread upon the waters, and thou shalt find it after many days."

It may to some minds be a desideratum, to allude to the anterior probability that God should come in the flesh. Much of this has been anticipated under the head of Visible Deity and elsewhere; as this treatise is so short, one may reasonably expect every reader to take it in regular course. For additional considerations: the Benevolent Maker would hardly leave his creatures to perish, without one word of warning or one gleam of knowledge. The question of the Bible is considered further on: but exclusively of written rules and dogmas, it was likely that Our Father should commission chosen servants of his own, orally to teach and admonish; because it would be in accordance with man's reasonable nature, that he should best and easiest learn from the teaching his brethren. So then, after all lesser ambassadors had failed, it was to be expected that He should send the highest one of all, saying, "They will reverence my Son." We know that this really did occur by innumerable proofs, and wonderful signs posterior: and now, after the event, we discern it to have been anteriorly probable.

It was also probable in another light. This world is a world of incarnations; nothing has a real and potential existence, which is not embodied in some form. A theory is nothing; if no personal philosopher, no sect, or school of learners, takes it up. An opinion is mere air; without the multitude to give it all the force of a mighty wind.

An idea is mere spiritual light; if unclad in deeds, or in words written or spoken. So, also, of the Godhead: He would be like all these. He would pervade words spoken, as by prophets or preachers: He would include words written, as in the Bible: He would influence crowds with spirit-stirring sentiments: He would embody the theory of all things in one simple, philosophic form. As this material world is constituted, God could not reveal himself at all, excepting by the aid of matter. I mean; even granting that He spiritually inspired a prophet, still the man was necessary: he becomes an inspired man; not mere inspiration. So, also, of a book; which is the written labour of inspired men. There is no doing without the Humanity of God, so far as this world is concerned, any more than His Deity can be dispensed with, regarding the worlds beyond worlds, and the ages of ages, and the dread for ever and ever.

MAHOMETANISM.

It seems expedient that, in one or two instances, I should attempt the illustration of this rule of probability in matters beyond the Bible. As very fair ones, take Mahometanism and Romanism. And first of the former.

At the commencement of the seventh century, or a little previously to that era, we know that a fierce religion sprang up, promulgated by a false prophet. I wish briefly to show that this was antecedently to have been expected.

In a moral point of view, the Christian world, torn by all manner of schisms, and polluted by all sorts of heresies, had earned for the human race, whether accepting the gospel or refusing it, some signal and extensive punishment at the hands of Him, who is the Great Retributor as well as the Munificent Rewarder. In a physical point of view, the civilized kingdoms of the earth had become stagnant, arguing that corrupt and poisonous calm which is the herald of a coming tempest. The heat of a true religion had cooled down into lukewarm disputations about nothings, scholastical and casuistic figments; whilst at the same time the prevalence of peaceful doctrines had amalgamated all classes into a luxurious indolence. Passionate Man is not to be so satisfied; and the time was fully come for the rise of some fierce spirit, who should change the tinsel theology of the crucifix for the iron religion of the sword: who should blow in the ears of the slumbering West the shrill war-blast of Eastern fervencies; who should exchange the dull rewards of canonization due to penance, or an after-life voluntary humiliation under pseudo-saints and angels, for the human and comprehensible joys of animal appetite and military glory: who should enlist under his banner all the frantic zeal, all the pent-up licentiousness, all the heart-burning hatreds of mankind, stifled either by a positive barbarism, or the incense-laden cloud of a scarcely-masked idolatry.

Thus, and then, was likely to arise a bold and self-confiding hero, leaning on his own sword: a man of dark sentences, who, by judiciously pilfering from this quarter and from that shreds of truth to jewel his black vestments of error, and by openly proclaiming that Oneness of the object of all worship which besotted Christendom had then, from undue reverence to saints and martyrs, virgins and archangels, well nigh forgotten; a man who, by pandering to human passions and setting wide as virtue's avenue the flower-tricked gates of vice; should thus, like Lucifer before him, in a comet-like career of victory, sweep the startled firmament of earth, and drag to his erratic orbit the stars of heaven from their courses.

Mahomet; his humble beginnings; his iron perseverance under early probable checks; his blind, yet not all unsublime, dependence on fatality; his ruthless, yet not all undeserved, infliction of fire and sword upon the cowering coward race that filled the western world;—*these*, and all whatever else besides attended his train of triumphs, and all whatever besides has lasted among Moors, and Arabs, and Turks, and Asiatics, even to this our day—constitute to a thinking mind (and it seems not without cause) another antecedent probability. Let the scoffer about Mahomet's success, and the admirer of his hotchpot Koran; let him to whom it is a stumbling-block that error (if indeed, quoth he, it be more erroneous than what Christendom counts truth) should have had such free course and been glorified, while so-called Truth, *pede claudo*, has limped on even as now cautiously and ingloriously through the well-suspicious world; let him who thinks he sees in Mahomet's success an answer to the foolish argument of some, who test the truth of Christianity by its Gentile triumphs; let him ponder these things. Reason, the God of his idolatry, might, with an archangel's ken, have prophesied some Mahomet's career: and, so far from such being in the nature of any objection to Faith, the idea thus thrown out, well-mused upon, will be seen to lend Faith an aid in the way of previous likelihood.

"There is one God, and Mahomet is his prophet!" How admirably calculated such a war-cry would be for the circumstances of the seventh century. The simple sublimity of Oneness, as opposed to school-theology and catholic demons: the glitter of barbaric pomp, instead of tame observances: the flashing scimetar of ambition to supersede the cross: a turban aigretted with jewels for the twisted wreath of thorns. As human nature is, and especially in that time was, nothing was more expectable (even if prophetic records had not taught it), than the rise and progress of that great False Prophet, whose waving crescent even now blights the third part of earth.

ROMANISM.

We all know how easy it is to prophesy after the event: but it would be uncandid and untrue to confound this remark with another, cousin-germane to it; to wit: how easy it is to discern of any event, after it has happened, whether or not it were antecedently likely. When the race is over, and the best horse has won (or by clever jockey-management, the worst), how obviously could any gentleman on the turf, now in possession of particulars, have seen the event to have been so probable, that he would have staked all upon its issue.

Carry out this familiar idea; which, as human nature goes, is none the weaker as to illustration, because it is built upon the rule "*parvis componere magna*." Let us sketch a line or two of that great foreshadowing cartoon, the probabilities of Romanism.

That our blessed Master, even in His state as man, beheld its evil characteristics looming on the future, seems likely not alone from both His human keenness and His divine omniscience, but from here and there a hint dropped in his biography. Why should He, on several occasions, have seemed, I will say with some apparent sharpness, to have rebuked His virgin mother.—"Woman, what have I to do with thee?"—"Who are my mother and my brethren?"—"Yea—More blessed than the womb which bare me, and the paps that I have sucked, is the humblest of my true disciples." Let no one misunderstand me: full well I know the just explanations which palliate such passages;

and the love stronger than death which beat in that Filial heart. But, take the phrases as they stand; and do they not in reason constitute some warning and some prophecy that men should idolize the mother? Nothing, in fact, was more likely than that a just human reverence to the most favoured among women should have increased into her admiring worship: until the humble and holy Mary, with the sword of human anguish at her heart, should become exaggerated and idealized into Mother of God—instead of Jesus's human matrix, Queen of heaven, instead of a ransomed soul herself, the joy of angels—in lieu of their lowly fellow-worshipper, and the Rapture of the blessed—thus dethroning the Almighty.

Take a second instance: why should Peter, the most loving, most generous, most devoted of them all, have been singled out from among the twelve—with a "Get thee behind me, Satan?"—it really had a harsh appearance; if it were not that, prophetically speaking, and not personally, he was set in the same category with Judas, the "one who was a devil." I know the glosses, and the contexts, and the whole amount of it. Folios have been written, and may be written again, to disprove the text; but the more words, the less sense: it stands, a record graven in the Rock; that same Petra, whereon, as firm and faithful found, our Lord Jesus built his early Church: it stands, a mark indelibly burnt into that hand, to whom were intrusted, not more specially than to any other of the saintly sent, the keys of the kingdom of heaven: it stands, along with the same Peter's deep and terrible apostacy, a living witness against some future Church, who should set up this same Peter as the Jupiter of their Pantheon: who should positively be idolizing now an image christened Peter, which did duty two thousand years ago as a statue of Libyan Jove! But even this glaring compromise was a matter probable, with the data of human ambitions, and a rotten Christianity.

Examples such as these might well be multiplied: bear with a word or two more, remembering always that the half is not said which might be said in proof; nor in answering the heap of frivolous objections.

Why, unless relics and pseudo-sacred clothes were to be prophetically humbled into their own mere dust and nothing-worthiness, why should the rude Roman soldiery have been suffered to cast lots for that vestment, which, if ever spiritual holiness could have been infused into mere matter, must indeed have remained a relic worthy of undoubted worship? It was warm with the Animal heat of the Man inhabited by God: it was half worn out in the service of His humble travels, and had even, on many occasions, been the road by which virtue had gone out; not of it, but of Him. What! was this wonderful robe to work no miracles? was it not to be regarded as a sort of outpost of the being who was Human-God? Had it no essential sacredness, no *noli-me-tangere* quality of shining away the gambler's covetous glance, of withering his rude and venturous hand, or of poisoning, like some Nessus' shirt, the lewd ruffian who might soon thereafter wear it? Not in the least. This woven web, to which a corrupted state of feeling on religion would have raised cathedrals as its palaces, with singing men and singing women, and singing eunuchs too, to celebrate its virtues; this coarse cloth of some poor weaver's, working down by the sea of Galilee or in some lane of Zion, was still to remain, and be a mere unglorified, economical, useful garment. Far from testifying to its own internal mightiness, it probably was soon sold by the fortunate Roman die-thrower to a second-hand shop of the Jewish metropolis; and so descended from beggar to beggar till it was clean worn out. We never hear that, however easy of access so inestimable relic might then have been considered, any one of the numerous disciples, in the fervour of their earliest zeal, threw away one thought for its redemption. Is it not strange that no St. Helena was at hand to conserve such a desirable invention? Why is there no St. Vestment to keep in countenance a St. Sepulchre and a St. Cross? The poor cloth, in primitive times, really was despised. We know well enough what happened afterwards about handkerchiefs imbued with miraculous properties from holy Paul's body for the nonce: but this is an inferior question, and the matter was temporary; the superior case is proved, and besides the rule *omne majus continet in se minus* there are differences quite intelligible between the cases, whereabout our time would be less profitably employed than in passing on and leaving them unquestioned. Suffice it to say, that "God worked those special miracles," and not the unconscious "handkerchiefs or aprons." "Te Deum laudamus!" is Protestantism's cry; "Sudaria laudemus!" would swell the Papal choirs.

Let such considerations as these then are in sample serve to show how evidently one might prove from anterior circumstances, (and the canon of Scripture is an anterior circumstance,) the probability of the rise and progress of the Roman heresies. And if any one should ask, how was such a system more likely to arise under a Gentile rather than a Jewish theocracy? why was a St. Paul, or a St. Peter, or a St. Dunstan, or a St. Gengulphus, more previously expectable than a St. Abraham, a St. David, a St. Elisha, or a St. Gehazi? I answer, from the idea of idolatry, so adapted to the Gentile mind, and so abhorrent from the Jewish. Martyred Abel, however well respected, has never reached the honours of a niche beside the altar. Jephtha's daughter, for all her mourned virginity, was never paraded, (that I wot of,) for any other than a much-to-be-lamented damsel. Who ever asked, in those old times, the mediation of St. Enoch? Where were the offerings, in jewels or in gold, to propitiate that undoubted man of God and denizen of heaven, St. Moses? what prows, in wax, of vessels saved from shipwreck, hung about the dripping fane of Jonah? and where was, in the olden time, that wretched and insensate being, calling himself rational and godly, who had ventured to solicit the good services of Isaiah as his intercessor, or to plead the merits of St. Ezekiel as the make-weight for his sins?

It was just this, and reasonably to have been expected; for when the Jew brought in his religion, he demolished every false god, broke their images, slew their priests, and burnt their groves with fire. But, when a worldly Christianity came to be in vogue, when emperors adorned their banners with the cross, and the poor fishermen of Galilee, (in their portly representatives,) came to be encrusted with gems, and rustling with seric silk; then was made that fatal compromise; then it was likely to have been made, which has lasted even until now: a compromise which, newly baptizing the damned idols of the heathen, keeps yet St. Bacchus and St. Venus, St. Mars and St. Apollo, perched in sobered robes upon the so-called Christian altar; which yet pays divine honours to an ancyle or a rusty nail; to the black stones at Delphi, or the gold-shrined bones at Aix; which yet sanctifies the chickens of the capitol, or the cock that startled Peter; which yet lets a wealthy sinner, by his gold, bribe the winking Pythoness, or buy dispensing clauses from "the Lord our God, the Pope."

There is yet a swarm of other notions pressing on the mind, which tend to prove that Popery might have been anticipated. Take this view. The religion of Christ is holy, self-denying; not of this world's praise, and ending with the terrible sanction of eternity for good or evil: it sets up God alone supreme, and cuts down creature-merit to a point perpetually diminishing; for the longer he does well, the more he owes to the grace which enabled him to do it.

Now, man's nature is, as we know, diametrically opposite to all this: and unable to escape from the conviction of Christian truth in some sense, he would bend his shrewd invention to the attempt of warping that stern truth to shapes more consistent with his idiosyncrasies. A religious plan might be expected, which, in lieu of a difficult, holy spirituality, should exact easy, mere observances; to say a thousand Paters with the tongue, instead of one "Our Father," from the heart; to exact genuflections by the score, but not a single prostration of the spirit; to write the cross in water on the forehead often-times, but never once to bear its mystic weight upon the shoulder. In spite of self-denial, cleverly kept in sight by means of eggs, and pulse, and hair-cloth, to pamper the deluded flesh with many a carnal holiday; in contravention of a kingdom not of this world, boldly to usurp the temporal dominion of it all: instead of the overwhelming incomprehensibility of an eternal doom, to comfort the worst with false assurance of a purgatory longer or shorter; that after all, vice may be burnt out; and who knows but that gold, buying up the prayers and superfluous righteousness of others, may not make the fiery ordeal an easy one? In lieu of a God brought near to his creatures, infinite purity in contact with the grossest sin, as the good Physician loveth; how sage it seemed to stock the immeasurable distance with intermediate numia, cycle on epicycle, arc on arc, priest and bishop and pope, and martyr, and virgin, and saint, and angel, all in their stations, at due interval soliciting God to be (as if His blessed Majesty were not so of Himself!) the sinner's friend. How comfortable this to man's sweet estimation of his own petty penances; how glorifying to those "filthy rags," his so-called righteousness: how apt to build up the hierarchist power; how seemingly analogous with man's experience here, where clerks lay the case before commissioners, and commissioners before the government, and the government before the sovereign.

All this was entirely expectable: and I can conceive that a deep Reasoner among the first apostles, even without such supernal light as "the Spirit speaking expressly," might have so calculated on the probabilities to come, as to have written, long ago, words akin to these: "In the latter times some shall depart from the faith, giving heed to seductive doctrines, and fanciful notions about intermediate deities, (δαιμονίων,) perverting truth by hypocritical departures *from it, searing conscience* against its own cravings after spiritual holiness, forbidding marriage, (to invent another virtue,) and commanding abstinence from God's good gifts, as a means of building up a creature-merit by voluntary humiliation." At the likelihood that such "profane and old wives' fables" should thereafter have arisen, might Paul without a miracle have possibly arrived.

Yet again: take another view. The Religion of Christ, though intended to be universal in some better era of this groaning earth, was, until that era cometh, meant and contrived for any thing rather than a Catholicity. True, the Church is so far Catholic that it numbers of its blessed company men of every clime and every age, from righteous Abel down to the last dear babe christened yester-morning; true, the commission is "to all nations, teaching them:" but, what mean the simultaneous and easily reconciled expressions—come out from among them, little flock, gathered out of the Gentiles, a peculiar people, a church militant, and not triumphant, here on earth? Thus shortly of a word much misinterpreted: let us now see what the Romanist does, what, (on human principles,) he would be probable to do, with this discriminating religion. He, chiefly for temporal gains, would make it as expansive as possible: there should be room at that table for every guest, whether wedding-garmented or not; there would be sauces in that poisonous feast, fitted to every palate. For the cold, ascetical mind, a cell and a scourge, and a record kept of starving fancies as calling them ecstatic visions vouchsafed by some old Stylite to bless his favoured worshipper; for the painted demirep of fashionable life, there would be a pretty pocket-idol, and the snug confessional well tenanted by a not unsympathizing father; for the pure girl, blighted in her heart's first love, the papist would afford that seemingly merciful refuge, that calm and musical and gentle place, the irrevocable nunnery; a place, for all its calmness, and its music, and its gentle reputations, soon to be abhorred of that poor child as a living tomb, the extinguisher of all life's aims, all its duties, uses and delights: for the bandit, a tythe of the traveller's gold would avail to pay away the murder, and earn for him a heap of merits kept within the cash-box: the educated, high-born and finely-moulded mind might be well amused with architecture, painting, carving, sweet odours, and the most wondrous music that has ever cheated man, even while he offers up his easy adorations, and departs, equally complacent at the choral remedies as at the priestly absolution; while, for those good few, the truly pious and enlightened children of Rome, who mourn the corruptions of their church, and explain away, with trembling tongue, her obvious errors and idolatries, for these the wily scheme, so probable, devised an undoubted mass of truth to be left among tne rubbish. True doctrines, justly held by true martyrs and true saints, holy men of God who have died in that communion; ordinances and an existence which creep up, (heedless of corruption though,) step by step, through past antiquity, to the very feet of the Founder; keen casuists, competent to prove any point of conscience or objection, and that indisputably, for they climax all by the high authority of Popes and councils that cannot be deceived: pious treatises and manuals, verily of flaming heat, for they mingle the yearnings of a constrained celibacy with the fervencies of worship and the cravings after God. Yes, there is meat here for every human mouth; only that, alas for men! the meat is that which perisheth, and not endureth unto everlasting life. Rome, thou wert sagely schemed; and if Lucifer devised thee not for the various appetencies of poor, deceivable, Catholic Man, verily it were pity, for thou art worthy of his handiwork. All things to all men, in any sense but the right, signifies nothing to anybody: in the sense of falsehoods, take the former for thy motto; in that of single truth, in its intensity, the latter.

Let not then the accident—the probable accident—of the Italian superstition place any hindrance in the way of one whose mind is all at sea because of its existence. What, O man with a soul, is all the world else to thee? Christianity, whatever be its broad way of pretences, is but in reality a narrow path: be satisfied with the day of small things, stagger not at the inconsistencies, conflicting words, and hateful strifes of those who say they are Christians, but "are not, but are of the synagogue of Satan." Judge truth, neither by her foes nor by her friends but by herself. There was one who said (and I never heard that any writer, from Julian to Hobbes, ever disputed his human truth or wisdom) "Needs must that offences come; but wo be to that man by whom the offence cometh. If they come, be not shaken in faith: lo, I have told you before. And if others fall away, or do ought else than my bidding, what is that to thee? follow thou ME."

THE BIBLE.

WHILST I attempt to show, as now I desire to do, that the Bible should be just the book it is, from considerations of anterior probability, I must expand the subject a little; dividing it, first, into the likelihood of a revelation at all; and secondly, into that of its expectable form and character.

The first likelihood has its birth in the just Benevolence of our heavenly Father, who without dispute never leaves his rational creatures unaided by some sort of guiding light, some manifestation of himself so needful to their happiness, some sure word of consolation in sorrow, or of brighter hope in persecution. That it must have been thus an *à priori* probability, has been all along proved by the innumerable pretences of the kind so constant up and down the world: no nation ever existed in any age or country, whose seers and wise men of whatever name have not been believed to hold commerce with the Godhead. We may judge from this, how probable it must ever have been held. The Sages of old Greece were sure of it from reason: and not less sure from accepted superstition those who reverenced the Brahmin, or the priest of Heliopolis, or the medicine-man among the Rocky Mountains, or the Llama of old Mexico. I know that our ignorance of some among the most brutalized species of mankind, as the Bushmen in Caffraria, and the tribes of New South Wales, has failed to find among their rites any thing akin to religion: but what may we not yet have to learn of good even about such poor outcasts? how shall we prove this negative? For aught we know, their superstitions at the heart may be as deep and as deceitful as in others; and, even on the contrary side, the exception proves the rule: the rule that every people concluded a revelation so likely, that they have one and all contrived it for themselves.

Thus shortly of the first: and now, secondly, how should God reveal himself to men? In such times as those when the world was yet young, and the Church concentrated in a family or an individual, it would probably be by an immediate oral teaching; the Lord would speak with Adam; He would walk with Enoch; He would, in some pure ethereal garb, talk with Abraham, as friend to friend. And thereafter, as men grew, and worshippers were multiplied, He would give some favoured servant a commission to be His ambassador: He would say to an Ezekiel, "Go unto the house of Israel, and speak my words to them:" He would bid a Jeremiah "Take thee a roll of a book, and write therein all the words that I have spoken to thee:" He would give Daniel a deep vision, not to be interpreted for ages, "Shut up the words, and seal the book even to the time of the end:" He would make Moses grave His precepts in the rock, and Job record his trials with a pen of iron. For a family, the Beatic Vision was enough: for a congregated nation, as once at Sinai, oral proclamations: for one generation or two around the world, the zeal and eloquence of some great "multitude of preachers:" but, indubitably, if God willed to bless the universal race, and drop the honey of his words distilling down the hour-glass of Time from generation to generation even to the latter days, there was no plan more probable, none more feasible, than the pen of a ready writer.

Further: and which concerns our argument: what were likely to be the characteristic marks of such a revelation? Exclusively of a pervading holiness, and wisdom, and sublimity, which could not be dispensed with, and in some sort should be worthy of the God; there would be, it was probable, frequent evidences of man's infirmity, corrupting all he toucheth. The Almighty works no miracles for little cause: one miracle alone need be current throughout Scripture: to wit, that which preserves it clean and safe from every perilous error. But, in the succession of a thousand scribes each copying from the other, needs must that the tired hand and misty eye would occasionally misplace a letter: this was no nodus worthy of a God's descent to dissipate by miracle.

Again: the original prophets themselves were men of various characters and times and tribes. God addresses men through their reason; he bound not down a seer "with bit and bridle, like the horse that has no understanding"—but spoke as to a rational being—"What seest thou?" "Hear my words;"—"Give ear unto my speech." Was it not then likely that the previous mode of thought and providential education in each holy man of God should mingle irresistibly with his inspired teaching? Should not the herdsman of Tehoa plead in pastoral phrase, and the royal son of Amoz denounce with strong authority? Should not David whilst a shepherd praise God among his flocks, and when a king, cry "Give the King thy judgments?" The Bible is full of this human individuality; and nothing could be thought as humanly more probable: but we must, with this diversity, connect the other probability also, that which should show the work to be divine; which would prove (as is literally the case) that, in spite of all such natural variety, all such unbiassed freedom both of thought and speech, there pervades the whole mass a oneness, a marvellous consistency, which would be likely to have been designed by God, though little to have been dreamt by man.

Once more on this full topic. Difficulties in Scripture were expectable for many reasons; I can only touch a few. Man is rational as he is responsible: God speaks to his mind and moral powers: and the mind rejoices, and moralities grow strong in conquest of the difficult and search for the mysterious. The muscles of the spiritual athlete pant for such exertion; and without it, they would dwindle into trepid imbecility. Curious man, courageous man, enterprising, shrewd, and vigourous man, yet has a constant enemy to dread in his own indolence: now, a lion in the path will wake up Sloth himself: and the very difficulties of religion engender perseverance.

Additionally: I think there is somewhat in the consideration, that, if all revealed truth had been utterly simple and easy, it would have needed no human interpreter; no enlightened class of men, who, according to the spirit of their times, and the occasions of their teaching, might "in season and out of season preach the word, reprove, rebuke, exhort, with all long-suffering and doctrine." I think there existed an anterior probability that Scripture should be as it is, often-times difficult, obscure, and requiring the aid of many wise to its elucidation; because, without such characteristic, those many wise and good would never have been called for. Suppose all truth revealed as clearly and indisputably to the meanest intellect as a sum in addition is, where were the need or use of that noble Christian company who are every where man's almoners for charity, and God's ambassadors for peace?

A word or two more, and I have done. The Bible would, as it seems to me probable, be a sort of double book; for the righteous, and for the wicked: to one class, a decoy, baited to allure all sorts of generous dispositions: to the other, a trap, set to catch all kinds of evil inclinations In these two senses, it would address the whole family man: and every one should find in it something to his liking. Purity should there perceive green pastures and still waters, and a tender Shepherd for its innocent steps: and carnal appetite should here and there discover some darker spot, which the honesty of heaven had filled with memories of its chiefest servants' sins; some record of adultery or murder wherewith to feast his maw for condemnation. While the good man should find in it meat divine for every earthly need, the sneerer should proclaim it the very easiest manual for his jests and lewd profanities. The unlettered should not lack humble, nay vulgar, images and words, to keep himself in countenance: neither should the learned look in vain for reasonings; the poet for sublimities; the curious mind for mystery; nor the sorrowing heart for prayer. I do discern, in that great book, a wondrous adaptability to minds of every calibre: and it is just what might antecedently have been expected of a volume writ by many men at many different eras, yet all superintended by one master mind; of a volume meant for every age, and nation, and country, and tongue, and people; of a volume which, as a two-edged sword, wounds the good man's heart with deep conviction, and cuts down "the hoary head of him who goeth on still in his wickedness."

On the whole, respecting faults, or incongruities, or objectionable parts in Scripture, however to have been expected, we must recollect that the more they are viewed, the more the blemishes fade, and are altered into beauties.

A little child had picked up an old stone, defaced with time-stains: the child said the stone was dirty, covered with blotches and all colours: but his father brings a microscope, and shows to his astonished glance that what the child thought dirt, is a forest of beautiful lichens, fruited mosses, and strange lilliputian plants with shapely animalcules hiding in the leaves, and rejoicing in their tiny shadow. Every blemish, justly seen, had turned to be a beauty: and Nature's works are vindicated good, even as the Word of Grace is wise.

HEAVEN AND HELL.

Probably enough, the light which I expect to throw upon this important subject will, upon a cursory criticism, be judged fanciful, erroneous, and absurd; in parts, quite open to riducule, and in all liable to the objection of being wise, or foolish, beyond what is written. Nevertheless, and as it seems to me of no small consequence to reach something more definite on the subject than the Anywhere or Nowhere of common apprehensions, I judge it not amiss to put out a few thoughts, fancies, if you will, but not unreasonable fancies, on the localities and other characteristics of what we call heaven and hell: in fact, I wish to show their probable realities with somewhat approaching to distinctness. It is manifest that these places must be somewhere; for, more especially of the blest estate, whither did Enoch, and Elijah, and our risen Lord ascend to? what became of these glorified humanities when "the chariot of fire carried up Elijah by a whirlwind into heaven;" and when "He was taken up, and a cloud received him?" Those happy mortals did not waste away to intangible spiritualities, as they rose above the world; their bodies were not melted as they broke the bonds of gravitation, and pierced earth's swathing atmosphere: they went up somewhither; the question is where they went to. It is a question of great interest to us; however, among those matters which are rather curious than consequential; for in our own case, as we know, we that are redeemed are to be caught up, together with other blessed creatures, "in the clouds, to meet our coming Saviour in the air, and thereafter to be ever with the Lord." I wish to show this to be expected as in our case, and expectable previously to it.

We have, in the book of Job, a peep at some place of congregation: some one, as it is likely, of the mighty globes in space, set apart as God's especial temple. Why not? they all are worlds; and the likelihood being in favour of overbalancing good, rather than of preponderating evil from considerations that affect God's attributes and the happiness of his creatures, it is probable that the great majority of these worlds are unfallen mansions of the blessed. Perhaps each will be a kingdom for one of earth's redeemed, and if so, there will at last be found fulfilled that prevailing superstition of our race, that each man has his star: without insisting upon this, we may reflect that there is no one universal opinion which has not its foundation in truth. Tradition may well have dropped the thought from Adam downwards, that the stars may some day be our thrones. We know their several vastness, and can guess their glory: verily a mighty meed for miserable services on earth, to find a just ambition gladdened with the rule of spheres, to which Terra is a point; while that same ambition is sanctified and legalized by ruling as vicegerent of Jehovah.

Is this unlikely, or unworthy of our high vocation, our immortality, and nearness unto, nay communion with God? The idea is only suggested: let a man muse at midnight, and look up at the heavens hanging over all; let him see, with Rosse and Herschell, that, multiply power as you will, unexhausted still and inexhaustible appear the myriads of worlds unknown. Yea, there is space enow for infinite reward; yea, let every grain of sand on every shore be gathered, and more innumerable yet appear that galaxy of spheres. Let us think that night looks down upon us here, with the million eyes of heaven. And for some focus of them all, some spot where God himself enthroned receives the homage of all crowns, and the worship of all creature service, what is there unreasonable in suggesting for a place some such an one as is instanced below?

I have just cut the following paragraph out of a newspaper: Is this the ridiculous tripping up the sublime? I think otherwise: it is honest to use plain terms. I speak as unto wise men—judge ye what I say. With respect to the fact of information, it may or it may not be true; but even if untrue, the idea is substantially the same, and I cannot help supposing that with angels and archangels and the whole company of heaven, such bodily saints as Enoch is, (and similar to him all risen, holy men will be,) meet for happy sabbaths in some glorious orb akin or superior to the following:

"A CENTRAL SUN.—Dr. Madier, the Professor of Astronomy at Dorpat, has published the results of the researches pursued by him uninterruptedly during the last sixty years, upon the movements of the so-called fixed stars. These more particularly relate to the star Alcyone, (discovered by him,) the brightest of the seven bright stars of the group of the Pleiades. This star he states to be the central sun of all the systems of stars known to us. He gives its distance from the boundaries of our system at thirty-four million times the distance of the sun from our earth, a distance which it takes five hundred and thirty-seven years for light to traverse. Our sun takes one hundred and eighty-two million years to accomplish its course round this central body, whose mass is one hundred and seventeen million times larger than the sun."

One hundred and seventeen million times larger than the Sun! itself, for all its vastness, not more than half one million times bigger than this earth. To some such globe we may let our fancies float, and anchor there our yearnings after heaven. It is a glorious thought, such as imagination loves; and a probable thought, that commends itself to reason. Behold the great eye of all our guessed creation, the focus of its brightness, and the fountain of its peace.

A topic far less pleasant, but alike of interest to us poor men, is the probable home of evil; and here I may be laughed at—laugh, but listen, and if, listening, some reason meets thine ear, laugh at least no longer.

We know that, for spirit's misery as for spirit's happiness, there is no need of place: "no matter where, for I am still the same," said one most miserable being. More—in the case of mere spirits, there is no need for any apparatus of torments, or fires, or other fearful things. But, when spirit is married to matter, the case is altered; needs must a place to prison the matter, and a corporal punishment to vex it.

Nothing is unlikely here; excepting—will a man urge?—the dread duration of such hell. This is a parenthesis; but it shall not be avoided, for the import of that question is deep, and should be answered clearly. A man, a body and soul inmixt, body risen incorruptible, and soul rested from its deeds, must exist for ever. I touch not here the proofs—assume it. Now, if he lives for ever, and deliberately chooses evil, his will consenting as well as his infirmity, and conscience seared by persisted disobedience, what course can such a wilful, rational, responsible being pursue than one perpetually erratic? How should it not be that he gets worse and worse in morals, and more and more miserable in fact? and when to this we add, that such wretched creatures are to herd together, continually flying further away from the only source of Happiness and Good; and to this, that they have earned by sin, remorses and regrets, and positive inflictions; how probable seems a hell, the sinner's doom eternal. The apt mathematical analogy of lines thrown out of parallel, helps this for illustration: for ever and for ever they are stretching more remote, and infinity itself cannot rëunite their travel.

This, then, as a passing word; a sad one. Honest thinker, do not scorn it, for thine own soul's sake. "Now is the time of grace, now is the day of salvation." To return. A place of punishment exists; to what quarter shall we look for its anterior probability? I think there is a likelihood very near us. There may be one, possibly, beneath us, in the bowels of this fiery-bursting earth; whither went Korah and his company? This idea is not without its arguments, just analogies, and scriptural hints. But my judgment inclines towards another. This trial-world, we know, is to be purified and restored, and made a new earth: it was even to be expected that Redemption should do this, and I like not to imagine it the crust and case of hell, but rather, as thus: At the birth of this same world, there was struck off from its burning mass at a tangent, a mournful satellite, to be the home of its immortal evil; the convict shore for exiled sin and misery; a satellite of strange differences, as guessed by Virgil in his musings upon Tartarus, where half the orb is, from natural necessities, blistered up by constant heats, the other half frozen by perennial cold. A land of caverns, and volcanoes, miles deep, miles high; with no water, no perceptible air: imagine such a dreadful world, with neither air nor water! incapable of feeding life like ours, but competent to be a place where undying wretchedness may struggle for ever. A melancholy orb, the queen of night, chief nucleus of all the dark idolatries of earth; the Moon, Isis, Hecate, Ashtaroth, Diana of the Ephesians!

This expression of a thought by no means improbable, gives an easy chance to shallow punsters; but ridicule is no weapon against reason Why should not the case be so? Why should not Earth's own satellite, void, as yet, be on the resurrection of all flesh, the raft whereon to float away Earth's evil? Read of it astronomically; think of it as connected with idols; regard it as the ruler of earth's night; consider that the place of a Gehenna must be somewhere; and what is there in my fancy quite improbable? I do not dogmatize as that the fact is so, but only suggest a definite place at least as likely as any other hitherto suggested. Think how that awful, melancholy eye looks down on deeds of darknesss! how many midnight crimes, murders, thefts, adulteries, and witchcrafts, that would have shrunk into nonentity from open, honest day, have paled the conscious Moon! Add to all this, it is the only world, besides our own, whereof astronomers can tell us, It is fallen.

AN OFFER.

Nothing were easier than to have made this book a long one; but that was not the writer's object: as well because of the musty Greek proverb about long books; which in every time and country are sure never to be read through by one in a thousand; as because it is always wiser to suggest than to exhaust a topic; which may be as "a fruit-tree yielding fruit after its kind whose seed is in itself." The writer then intended only to touch upon a few salient points, and not to discuss every question, however they might crowd upon his mind: time and space alike with mental capabilities forbade an effort so gigantic: added to which, such a course seemed to be unnecessary, as the rule of probability, thus illustrated, might be applied by others in every similar instance. Still, as the errand of this book is usefulness, and its author's hope is, under Heaven, to do good, one personal hint shall here be thrown upon the highway. Without arrogating to myself the wisdom or the knowledge to solve one in twenty of the doubts possible to be propounded; without also designing even to attempt such solutions, unless well assured of the genuine anxiety of the doubter; and preliminarizing the consideration, that a fitting diffidence in the advocate's own powers is no reason why he should not make wide efforts in his holy cause; that, such reasonable essays to do good have no sort of brotherhood with a fanatical Spiritual Quixotism; and that, to my own apprehensions, the doubts of a rationalizing mind are in the nature of honourable foes, to be treated with delicacy, reverence, and kindness, rather than with a cold distance and an ill-concealed contempt; preliminarizing, lastly, the thought—"Who is sufficient for these things?"—I nevertheless thus offer, according to the grace and power given to me, my best but humble efforts so far to dissipate the doubts of some respecting any scriptural fact, as may lie within the province of showing or attempting to show its previous credibility. This is not a challenge to the curious casuist or the sneering infidel; but an invitation to the honest mind harassed by unanswered queries: no gauntlet thrown down, but a brother's hand stretched out. Such questions, if put to the writer, through his publisher by letter, may find their reply in a future edition: supposing, that is to say, that they deserve an answer, whether as regards their own merits or the temper of the mind who doubts; and supposing also that the writer has the power and means to answer them discreetly. It is only a fair rule of philanthropy (and that without arrogating any unusual "strength") to "bear the infirmities of the weak, and not to please ourselves:" and nothing would to me give greater happiness than to be able, as I am willing, to remove any difficulties lying in the track of Faith before a generous mind. I hang out no glistening holly-bush a-flame with its ostentatious berries as promising good wine; but rather over my portal is the humbler and hospitable mistletoe, assuring every wearied pilgrim in the way, that though scanty be the fare, he shall find a hearty welcome.

CONCLUSION.

I HAVE thus endeavoured (with solicited help of Heaven) to place before the world anew a few old truths: truths inestimably precious. Remember, they cannot have lost by any such advocacy as is contained in the idea of their being shown antecedently probable; for this idea affects not at all the fact of their existence; the thing is; whether probable or not; there is, in esse, an ornithorhyncus; its posse is drowned in esse: there exists no doubt of it: evidence, whether of senses physical, or of considerations moral, puts the circumstance beyond the sphere of disputation. But such truths as we have spoken of do, nevertheless, gain something as to—not their merits, these are all their own substantially; nor their positive proofs, these are adjectives properly attendant on them, but as to—their acceptability among the incredulous of men; they gain, I say, even by such poor pleading as mine, from being shown anteriorly probable. Take an illustration in the case of that strange and anomalous creature mentioned just above. Its habitat is in a land where plums grow with the stones outside, where aboriginal dogs have never been heard to bark, where birds are found covered with hair, and where mammals jump about like frogs! If these are shown to be literal facts, the mind is thereby well prepared for any animal monstrosity: and it staggers not in unbelief (on evidence of honest travellers) even when informed of a creature with a duck's bill and a beaver's body: it really amounted in Australia to an antecedent probability.

Carry this out to matters not a quarter so incredible, ye thinkers, ye free-thinkers; neither be abashed at being named as thinking freely: were not those Bereans more noble in that they searched to see? For my humble part, I do commend you for it: treacherous is the hand that roots up the inalienable right of private judgment; the foundation-stone of Protestantism, the great prerogative of reason, the key-note of conscience, the sole vindex of a man's responsibility: evil and false is the so-called reverential wisdom which lays down in place of the truth that each man's conscience is a law unto himself, the tyranny of other men's authority. Cheap and easy and perilled is the faith, which clings to the skirt of others; which leans upon the broken staff of priestcraft, until those poisoned splinters pierce the hand.

Prove all things; holding fast that which is good: good to thine own reasonable conscience, if unwarped by casuistries, and unblinded by licentiousness. Prove all things, if you can, "from the egg to the apple:" he is a poor builder of his creed, who takes one brick on credit. Be able, as you can be, (if only you are willing so far to be wisely inconsistent, as to bend the stubborn knee betimes, and though with feeble glance to look to heaven, and though with stammering tongue to pray for aid,) be able, as it is thy right, O man of God—to give a Reason for the faith that is in thee.

THE END.

www.ingramcontent.com/pod-product-compliance
Lightning Source LLC
LaVergne TN
LVHW021307110826
845150LV00003B/513

* 9 7 8 1 4 2 5 5 5 9 0 9 0 *